Discovering the Real America

Toward A More Perfect Union

Lewis W. Diuguid

Edited by Elsje M. Smit

Discovering the Real America
Toward A More Perfect Union

BrownWalker Press
Boca Raton, Florida
USA • 2007

ISBN: 1-59942-421-5 (paperback)
ISBN: 978-1-59942-421-7 (paperback)

ISBN: 1-59942-422-3 (ebook)
ISBN: 978-1-59942-422-4 (ebook)

BrownWalker.com

Photograph courtesy of *The Kansas City Star*

This book is dedicated to Dr. David Shapiro for the tireless energy he poured into eliminating bigotry and hate for more than 60 years before he died in 2005 at age 94.

We shall not cease for exploration
And the end of all our exploring
Will be to arrive where we started
And to know the place for the first time.
~T.S. Eliot

TABLE OF CONTENTS

Discovering the Real America: Toward a More Perfect Union

FOREWORD

On a recent visit to my eye doctor, I was told that, even though I am far-sighted, I have near-perfect vision. In other words, I have very little trouble bringing objects, words or people that are at a considerable distance into focus. I was also informed that the prescription for my reading glasses had not changed significantly. With my glasses on, everything about 1 foot away comes into focus beautifully. In my middle distance, however, everything is blurry. If I want to see today's date on my calendar on the wall above my desk, I need to either step up very close—to about 1 foot away—or step back about 5 feet. At any distance in between, all the numbers and words are illegible, blurred, uncomfortable.

This is the way most of us "see" people who are different from us. At a "safe" distance, they are in focus and "comfortable." We have some clarity about them—or at least we think we do. When they enter that blurry middle distance, however, we start to feel "uncomfortable," fearful, wary.

Legal gay marriage in Europe or Canada, for instance, does not in any way affect our heterosexual marriages in the U.S., but gay marriages "at home" are a potential threat (though I don't know why). Seeing Muslims in the Middle East on TV is easier, "safer," than seeing them in the grocery store around the corner. Keeping prisoners locked out of sight in penitentiaries with high walls and small windows is more palatable than hearing their choir sing at the church down the street.

When those different from us are at a distance, our relationship is clear. But when they move closer, they become more threatening because our focus is blurred. We don't know them. And we're not "close" enough to "see" them properly, to get to know them, to understand who they are, or to "see" their value.

Our first reaction when that middle distance is breached by something or someone unknown is often "Not In My Back Yard." We tend to move away because, after all, it's much safer than moving in for a closer look. A defensive mechanism kicks in, triggered by fear, and shutting down our natural curiosity. We quickly erect a barrier between us and them so that they won't get "too close for comfort."

This book takes us to those uncomfortable, fearful places, but it also admonishes us to allow our curiosity to conquer our fear, to put on our "reading glasses" and move in close. We must bring those who are different—be they gay, Muslim, inmates, black, white, Hispanic, old, young, disabled, homeless, or belonging to any other category we can dream up—into focus at a distance close enough to discover who they really are.

That takes courage and hard work. It takes stepping out of our comfort zones and talking to each other. It takes recognizing the value and richness of someone's differences.

I am a Third Culture Kid, or rather an Adult Third Culture Kid, or ATCK. That means I spent my formative years in parts of the world other than my home country. In my lifetime I have had to focus up close on different cultures, customs, norms and languages and try to make sense of them all. I've had to internalize, understand, or at least accept or cope with many, many "differences." That road to acknowledging and accepting diversity is not an easy one. Valuing the differences can be even more challenging.

In much of the United States, we don't need to venture far before we come face to face with diversity. And when we do, we should be prepared to overcome whatever fear we might have and value and learn from the experience.

This book can help us prepare.

The first 4 chapters point out the many kinds of bigotry that still exist in this country and what their effects are on all of us. They expose the pain felt by those who experience the needle of discrimination unexpectedly thrust deep into the soft flesh of their lives; the anger that grows when that needle pokes the same tender spot over and over again; the frustration at being told there is no needle, that the poking is "just your imagination." Those chapters can help us recognize and, if not understand, at least acknowledge the prejudice that we need to overcome in our diverse society.

The next section gives an explanation—admittedly incomplete—of where some of that discrimination comes from and how it has been bolstered. The section highlights bits of history that have conveniently been ignored in the process of "whitewashing" American society. It illustrates how the media have been a major force in downplaying the importance of—or even going so far as to ridicule or vilify—those who are not white or "mainstream." The last chapter in that section, "Hate: The Worm in the Apple Pie of America," illustrates the lengths to which people will go as they dig in for their long, lonely, fear-fueled and hate-filled battle against this country's diversity.

The hope expressed in this book is that they will stop fighting and emerge from their trenches—and that appeal is what the last and longest section of this book is about. Every day people are overcoming the discrimination, the fear, the hurt, the hate, and the divisions of this country. They are living its diversity by "putting on their reading glasses" and taking a closer look at those who are different from them. They are celebrating others' talents, talking with people for understanding and cooperation, and working for change. And they are doing all these things everywhere, in groups, alone, behind bars, on the street, in churches, in homes, through their art—in ways and places too numerous to list. The third section of this book is a celebration of those solutions, packed with information that gives us tools to act.

And act we must. No one has a monopoly on prejudice and no one is immune to it. We are all guilty of jabbing the needle—and bruised from being jabbed. Therefore we must find ways to use the information in these many pages and join the cause for diversity.

The many stories in this book must be used as fuel to light innumerable campfires of conversation everywhere. *Educators* at all levels can use the stories in their classrooms to generate discussions or projects that will help students understand and appreciate the richness of their diverse histories and lives. *Community, civic* and *faith-based groups* can broaden their diversity outreach using the stories and solutions as a foundation. *Government* and *businesses*—anyone in the work of diversity—can use the book to help their employees understand, accept, indeed *appreciate* the stories of those who are different. And *the media,* of course, must finally discover the importance of reflecting in their print, electronic, and other forms what the Real America is *really* like.

This book includes hundreds of voices—in columns, poetry, quotes from outside sources, personal stories, and readers' messages. As the book's editor, I suggested that we separate all the columns from the main text by indenting them slightly and using a smaller size of the main font. The title under which each column appeared in *The Kansas City Star* headlines the text. A complete list by chapter of the columns used can be found in Appendix A.

Readers' feedback contained in e-mails, voice mails, and letters is scattered throughout the book and uses a different font altogether to offset the messages from the rest of the material. Quotations from outside sources are formatted and referenced according to MLA style. A Works Cited page can be found at the end of the book. Two other appendices are also included: Appendix B, which contains a 62-point list of privileges whites enjoy, as identified by

Dr. Peggy McIntosh; and Appendix C, which contains very brief biographical portraits of the authors whose quotes grace the opening page of each chapter.

Some of the material in this book is painful and hard to stomach. In preparing the manuscript, as Lewis Diuguid and I struggled with how best to present the difficult material, poems started showing up in my e-mail box. After reading the first—very powerful—ones that Lewis wrote, I suggested he tax his own creativity ever further and write a poem for each chapter. Without realizing it, I had given Lewis the go-ahead to open the floodgates, and more and more poems popped up in my inbox. We sifted through the many pages of often-heartbreaking emotion and chose what we considered his best and most appropriate poems, which now jumpstart each chapter.

All of these bits and pieces combine into many voices that are meant to allow readers to learn and grow from the experiences described. It is important to take note of the value that each voice brings, in what it teaches as well as in the questions it allows others to ask and answer. As an Adult Third Culture Kid, I know firsthand how difficult such an exercise is, but I also have benefited from its many rewards. In "putting on our reading glasses" and becoming involved in diversity, we gain the ability to understand, to tolerate, to think on our feet, to empathize, to belong. We find out that we have missed so much and that there is much still to be found out. It is my sincere hope that this book will provide all who read it a way to discover for themselves those many undiscovered riches.

~Elsje M. Smit
Editor

INTRODUCTION

What's diversity got to do with it?

From Ruination

Does the sun set and never rise
Across these beautiful American skies?
It did more than 500 years ago
When great ships landed "discovering" these inhabited shores
Unloading whites calling themselves "explorers"
But actually they were "the exploiters" who came
Murdering, raping, stealing and enslaving in European kings' and God's name
Did the rains thereafter ever fall
Blessing some with life but never all
Potential withered in generations-long droughts
And darkness keeping minorities out
It's the color line these centuries kept in good repair
To showcase whites and keep others in despair
Never accepting the goodness that minorities bring
Pooh-poohing their stories with disgust and disdain
Yet the oppressed
Struggle nevertheless
Fueled by multicolors of hope they continue to profess
The truth so all one day will be forced to attest
And celebrate the irrepressible joys bubbling in their people's breasts.
It's America's real promise
Finally emerging like ghostly ships frozen in racism's pumice
Sailing one day soon from the long dark terrible nights
Into a dreamlike light
With luscious, life-giving rain that will kiss all
As it falls
In this undiscovered country
Calling us to a journey we must take
For the Real America's sake.

You know, Lewis, I had an excellent teacher at Paseo High School back in the '50s who told us we should be very grateful, proud and protective of our culture. Be particularly proud that we are Midwesterners, Protestants, white, and a load of other things that meant our Northern European cultural background. She told us to be proud of it and protective of it because there would be forces to try to dilute it and try to wipe it out in the future. You know, I have every right to protect the culture that I grew up with, which started this country basically, the Northern Europeans. It's well and good to talk about diversity and try to understand all of this. But I'm sorry. We're going to continue to protect what we have in our background. We have every right and responsibility to do it.

~Voice Mail, 2003

Bigotry and prejudice these days work their way to the surface in the most unusual manner. A Saturday, June 14, 1997, Father's Day column I wrote for *The Kansas City Star* was meant to be just a feel-good, multigenerational, extended-family piece featuring a man spending time with his children and grandchildren. It was a personal story about my dad, then 80 years old, who drove solo from St. Louis as he annually has to play golf with me and visit my sister, Renee, and our families.

Among the voice mail messages waiting for me the following Monday was one from a woman who left no return phone number. But I'll never forget what she said. The woman remarked in the kindest voice that she thought I was a good writer. She said the Father's Day piece was nice and well timed. Then she added, "Why did you have to ruin it by putting black people in it?"

I was dumbfounded. The line the woman objected to was this:

From "As always, gifts flow both ways"

> We met a friend the next morning for 18 sunny holes at Minor Park Golf Center. Another guy, whom we'd played with before, joined us in a foursome of African-American men.

That "nice" column was written to do a lot of heavy lifting. Like many columns that I write featuring my family, that piece had to counter the many, monstrous stereotypes about African Americans. It had to show that black men do care about families and travel miles to show it; black men are hard-working, taxpaying citizens; black men value education and want the best for their children; and black men aren't ashamed to be black and play golf at the same time. In fact, we value golf just as much as basketball, baseball and football.

But the caller, like many people who telephone and write to express their prejudices in an unabashed way, wasn't buying any of it. The things I described fit neatly in the perfect all-American world she envisioned for white people. For her, turning it into something that blacks also value was unimaginable. It so strongly offended her sensibility and sense of what was right, and she felt obligated to call to tell me.

The book will show hundreds of examples of such feedback. They are among thousands of responses I get every year, and they always make me wonder where that bigotry comes from. People like that just can't see the commonality that all of us share in this country. It is true that we are different in many ways, and it's empowering to learn from that diversity. But we all have deep feelings for our families, for motherhood, fatherhood and for our children. There is a reverence for older people, the history they have lived and the continuity and value those individuals add to all community relationships.

As people in America, we embrace the same ideals of hard work, discipline, patriotism, love, trust, honor, duty, friendship, ethics and morality. But a nuclear detonation occurred centuries ago on this North American continent, and continues to destroy identities and melt them all down into one that's white, Christian, heterosexual and middle or upper class. That fission obliterates and separates us. It guarantees a destructive future for us all. Its fallout assigns the best values to people who are white. Darker, baser qualities are seared into minorities.

Those qualities include the inclination to live a life of crime, poverty, sloth, always looking for a handout; incurable government dependence; welfare cheating; and an insatiable, maniacal appetite for sex. Individuals with these traits are viewed as the dregs of America. Sweet, white cream always floats to the top; bitter, dark coffee grounds always sink to the bottom. To link such people with the "sweet, white" characteristics as I had in that 1997 column was unconscionable.

But in the 21st century we now must ask: How did our country become so disunited? What will it take to erase 400 years of racism, bigotry, prejudices and discrimination? Will it require another 400 years to eradicate this multifaceted generational problem? Or is there a way to appeal to people's enlightened sense of self-interest to get them to embrace the racial, ethnic and other diversity that has always been part of the fabric of these United States?

This book will show the United States for what it is—a nation struggling to find its moral compass, questioning its will to explore and grappling for the courage to do so. *Discovering the Real America* will examine the history of racial, ethnic and other divisions in this country. It will show that we all lose from such separatism. It also will look at the history and media of America, show their faults and point to how the walls that divide us can be brought down. The book will point out that the bridge over the seemingly impassable chasm can and must be built by people sharing their stories with others of different races, faiths, ethnicities, sexual orientations, disabilities, ages, socio-economic backgrounds and neighborhoods. From such brave efforts it is possible to finally discover the Real America—that unexplored place which includes the long-overlooked contributions of the above groups and celebrates them.

But right now we don't really know each other. Following tradition, the schools help construct the walls that keep us apart, giving students inaccurate accounts of the triumphs and tragedies that people of all colors have been through in this country. The masons of the media follow. They have us think we know each other because of what they build for us to see and hear. However, television, radio, newspapers, movies, magazines, videos, DVDs and other media mostly reinforce existing stereotypes.

Truly knowing others takes more than relying on media images. Schools must offer multicultural curricula, textbooks and teaching. The media, at the same time, must change to reveal the truth about diversity in news reports, programs and advertising.

Newspapers like *The Kansas City Star* have ongoing diversity efforts to try to change the culture in the media to be more inclusive and more accurate, fair and balanced in its coverage. *The Star* now is viewed as one of the newspaper industry's leaders in diversity. But we had a rough go of it at first. My colleagues said, "We just want to do journalism. What does this diversity stuff have to do with it?" Well, the simple answer is *everything.*

One morning in December 1993 my youngest daughter, Leslie, was running outside to play when she stopped at the kitchen table where I was reading the newspaper. She pointed to a big picture on the cover of the features section of a little black girl with her hair in braids. Leslie said, and I'll never forget it, "That little girl looks like me."

Leslie was 6 years old then. The power of that statement is that I couldn't have said anything like that when I was 6 growing up in St. Louis, Mo. The *St. Louis Post-Dispatch* wouldn't have featured a little black boy like me—anywhere. *The Star* and *The Times* in Kansas City wouldn't have carried a photograph of a black child in 1961. Other blacks growing up elsewhere in the U.S. couldn't have said that looking through their local newspapers. But the devastating thing was that not even my oldest daughter, Adrianne, could have said that in 1989—almost 30 years later—when she was 6 years old growing up in Kansas City.

Very few people of color have had the benefit of seeing themselves in positive ways in the media. The book will examine that issue, too, and why the situation has been allowed to persist. We must keep insisting that people who are different show up in the media because they need to see themselves and people who look like them. But others who don't look like them need to see them as well. Diversity has *everything* to do with journalism. But the battle for inclusion is hard fought and painful.

Right now in much of the media, anything that doesn't fit in the well-maintained, traditional boxes of bigotry is to be doubted, cursed or dismissed as an exception to the rules. This book offers no easy answer, no magic potion or diversity flea dip for everyone suffering racism's effects. There is only hard work ahead. Dodging the task only prolongs the suffering of the victims and perpetrators. Racism in this country is an American problem, and it will require everyone's efforts to find solutions, so we can discover the Real America.

I found that out rather abruptly myself, and wrote about my own epiphany-of-sorts in this Nov. 18, 1993, column in *The Kansas City Star.*

From "Slaying the beasts in us all"

A gold-colored box of "silver bullets" sits on a file cabinet in my office.

New friends from newspapers nationwide fashioned the shells out of aluminum foil – partly for laughs and partly to send me home with what I had sought. Their gift represented the ammunition I wanted to combat stereotypes, biases and prejudices.

The firepower from the six-day Newspaper Association of America Diversity Facilitator Training Certification Pilot Program in Dallas was for the monsters that stalk our workplaces, terrorize our communities and show up in our schools and media. But I didn't realize before making the trip last month with two other editors at *The Kansas City Star* that I would use the first silver bullet on myself.

A call from a friend in Louisville, Ky., helped me see that I had been shot. She said it angered her when firms send African Americans to diversity training programs. Black people live the multicultural experience in America, she said, and understand too well why it's important.

The Dallas training was the sixth one I had been through both in writing articles on such sessions and in learning from them as co-chair of *The Star's* 11-month-old newsroom Diversity Committee. But more than the others, the Texas experience heightened my awareness.

You see, I flew to Dallas wearing what I thought was a pretty neat white baseball cap. It said "Atlanta Braves, National League Champions, 1991-1992."

The emblem included a baseball, an infield diamond and a tomahawk. I got it free with other giveaways at the National Association of Black Journalists July convention in Houston.

That conference hyped the Unity '94 convention, which will take place in Atlanta next summer. It will be the first joint ethnic membership gathering of the National Association of Black Journalists, the Asian American Journalists Association, the National Association of Hispanic Journalists and the Native American Journalists Association.

But I didn't see until after the Dallas training that the Braves cap was a racial insult to Native Americans – just as much as the Kansas City Chiefs name is and the chop and chants that fans do at every home game.

That white cap started to look pretty disgusting; especially as a gift given at a meeting of an association that prides itself on promoting diversity. The first silver bullet had found its mark, taken out a monster in me and created a new awareness.

Valuing diversity enhances our ability to respect differences in people, enables us to reach our productivity potential and boosts our communication skills. It doesn't diminish us or lower workplace, academic or community standards.

> Diversity troops are pushing into communities nationwide like the forces of the Civil Rights Movement did years ago. But instead of an enlightened few training folks on the streets to break forced segregation, the new effort is in boardrooms, workplaces, schools and communities, where harmony will be vital for everyone's future.
>
> But getting people to believe in diversity won't be easy. In Greater Kansas City, the areawide movement struggles against old ways.
>
> It also battles the Ku Klux Klan passing out despicable recruitment fliers, saying two white homicide victims were killed this year because of their race. The slayings were horrid but not race-related.
>
> The twisted army of prejudices that would make up such lies, however, will require a lot of silver bullets to knock down. But it's also important to save some shells for the subtle beasts in us all.

People often rile against diversity and affirmative action, thinking those two things are synonymous. They aren't. Alisa Lange, when she oversaw the University of Kansas Medical Center's diversity program in the 1990s, described the difference this way: Affirmative action is like having a car delivered to your driveway except nothing is assembled. In the driveway is just a pile of different parts and cans of the necessary fluids. Diversity is having that car delivered, but all of the parts are assembled in the proper working order. The fluids are all in the right place, and the vehicle runs like a top. Affirmative action then is having all of the right parts and fluids. Diversity is the proper engineering, collection, assembly and management of those unique parts and fluids so that the vehicle actually runs. That is what companies and other entities want to get out of affirmative action and diversity. Uniquely different people are needed in the workplace, schools, churches and throughout the community. Diversity is simply the management of that different talent so that the highest possible function is achieved. As merely a pile of parts, and containers of fluids, nothing works or goes forward.

This book will look at the real diversity in America and the challenges people face. It will examine how difficult their struggles to overcome the status quo remain for minorities and the majority. It will delve into the power of and investment made in maintaining the way things are. The book will go into the denial people of color face as well as the anguish and mental health issues of their being told that the racism they feel in this country is just their imagination.

Discovering the Real America is a coalescence of myriad puzzle pieces. They consist of textbook material clearly conveying the Real America—that which is disturbing and frightening, and that which offers hope to those who believe that this country and our world can be better. The book's puzzle pieces also include hundreds of columns spread over nearly 20 years that examine the problems of this country's many -isms and efforts toward solutions. The puzzle pieces include hundreds of e-mails, voice mail messages, letters and faxes filled with condemnation of efforts to expose the truth about diversity.

In this book, diversity includes myriad differences, not just race. In any large American city, the diversity of the population cannot be avoided or ignored. This book mirrors that reality. The text does not segregate different groups but is structured as we experience diversity in life. The only exceptions are the chapters on prisons and on homelessness. In *Discovering the Real America,* those conditions are mostly isolated because they are also kept out of our lives in this country.

So what is the goal of *Discovering the Real America?* People should be able to recognize themselves in the pages that follow. For some, what's reflected back will not be pretty. But this could be an opportunity for change. People will also see others in what follows. With new ideas they will be able to ask those different individuals informed questions and get to know them better. And the book should start people on their own journey toward valuing diversity and discovering the Real America.

The book mostly focuses on how Kansas City, the Heartland of America, has struggled to make this community more inclusive. Kansas City's work mirrors efforts going on all over the country to make the United States finally be that "more perfect Union" that the Preamble to the Constitution promises. Showcasing the work in the Heartland will help others in the struggle to save the spirit of America.

Lastly the book includes pieces of the puzzle that map out solutions. They show America as it needs to be and, like a treasure map, guide today's explorers along the way to discovering the Real America.

Dr. W.E.B. Du Bois, a founder of the Niagara Movement and the National Association for the Advancement of Colored People, wrote in his ground-breaking book *Souls of Black Folks* more than 100 years ago that the greatest challenge the United States faced in the 20th century was the barrier that the color line presented. That crippling wall has stayed intact in the America of the 21st century, and the garbage that has piled up on both sides continues to spread its rotting stench to all of us.

It won't go away unless people of all colors resolve to get to know each other, accept the humanity in us all and live and work in harmony. There is no hiding from it; there can be no slackers. People are starting to realize that our planet is too small and we need each other too much for there to be a divisive, unchallenged color line. We must all wield sledgehammers and together tear down the barrier. It is the only solution.

SECTION I

The Cutting Winds of Discrimination: The Situation Now

CHAPTER 1
Whiteness in Charge

21st Century Slave

They don't beat us no more
With the sting of the whip.
They don't chase us no more,
Shooting at us from the hip.
They don't sick the dogs on us
With sharp flesh cutting teeth.
They don't burn down our houses
Leaving us no place to eat or sleep.
They don't hunt us down like dogs
Or string us up like gutted hogs.
No. Things have radically changed.
But the bigotry – 21st century style – is all the same
Just more bloodless and now more corporate humane
The slurs are coded and so are the violence and the hunt
The prey's the same and so is imprisoning people for a blunt
The hunters' hearts are cold, beautifully cold
Righteously bold
Just like times long past
Enabling racism to forever last
Leaving us wondering as we're in flight
Why do whites think they're always right?

The greatest obstacle to discovery . . . is the illusion of knowledge.
~Daniel J. Boorstin

People think they know race. Nothing could be further from the truth, said John A. Powell.

From "Privilege feeds a system of racial division"

"Race is constructed by our social norms and practices, not by our biological makeup," said Powell, the Gregory Williams Chair on Civil Rights and Civil Liberties at the Ohio State University Law School.

Race is only 400 to 500 years old. It is not a black, Latino, Asian or American Indian thing. Powell said it's largely an Anglo-American phenomenon constructed "to keep poor blacks and poor whites apart."

"They wanted to create a divide, and out of that divide was created a concept of whiteness," said Powell, who is also executive director of the Kirin Institute for the Study of Race and Ethnicity in the Americas. "Everybody understood who was categorized as white.

"It had substantial consequences. It meant you could be a 'member of the community.'"

White people could own property, vote, hold public office and enjoy all constitutional liberties. Whiteness allowed those immigrants who qualified to become naturalized citizens. Laws and the courts blocked others.

"In all of these cases race measures something," Powell said. "It measures a set of privileges, benefits, status and assumptions that attach themselves to those categories or disabilities if you're not white.

"Privilege to white males causes missed opportunities for others in society," Powell added.

Such privilege causes minorities to subsidize the majority. How many Einsteins are in poor inner-city schools? Such students could develop the cure for AIDS, but that potential is smothered under a blanket of racism.

"Because we treat them a certain way, what we know about them becomes real," Powell said. "After the Civil War blacks couldn't join a union.

"If they couldn't join a union they couldn't work. Because they couldn't get work they were labeled lazy.

"So it's circular."

Since slavery, thousands of minorities with white skin and features have "passed" as whites to gain privilege. "Passing is normally in one direction," Powell said.

"People are passing from a lower status to a higher status," he said. "There are very few white people who will walk into work today and say, 'I look white, but I'm actually black.'"

Passing validates the system of inequality and lets it continue unchallenged. "It's strategic to just get along in life to avoid stereotypes and to avoid liabilities," Powell said.

> "Code switching" is another practice that enables minorities to fit in and function in mainstream America. They switch how they talk and act to gain acceptance, depending on whether they are among whites or minorities.
>
> "The question is: Why is there a need for this to go on?" Powell asked. "Privilege has to be called into question.
>
> "You can't address the racial hierarchy by passing into the higher race or ignoring the hierarchy itself."
>
> Powell said the good news is how we define race constantly changes. We see it in the census. "There has been no 10-year period where our racial categories have remained stable," Powell said. An example is how the census has changed its definition of Hispanics and multiracial people.
>
> "It's funny because we organize our whole life around race, but it's just a mess," Powell said. "It seems there is a common sense to race, but there is not.
>
> "Each generation sort of reconstructs race. The good news is we can influence that."
>
> And perhaps in applying that influence, the people of the Real America can collectively end racism.

What exactly is *white privilege?* Peggy McIntosh is associate director of the Wellesley College Center for Research on Women and has done groundbreaking work on white privilege. She calls it the "unearned assets" that whites possess but about which they are "meant to remain oblivious," the "invisible weightless knapsack of special provisions" that gives whites an edge over people of color from conception to grave (10). (See Appendix B.) Thandeka, who teaches at Meadville/Lombard Theological School in Chicago, offers another perspective in her book *Learning to Be White: Money, Race and God in America.* She describes the unearned advantage as a "wage of whiteness," which functions "as a kind of workers' 'compensation,'... a 'consolation prize' to persons who, although not wealthy, would not be counted as losers because they were, at least, white" (78). In her piece in *Multicultural Perspectives,* "My Class Didn't Trump My Race: Using Oppression to Face Privilege," Robin J. DiAngelo acknowledges the validity of that description:

> As I reflect back on the early messages I received about being poor and being White, I now realize that my grandmother and I *needed* people of color to cleanse and realign us with the dominant White culture that our poverty had separated us from. . . . Regardless of one's other locations [in social groups], White people know on some

> level that being White in this society is "better" than being a person of color, and this, along with the very real doors Whiteness opens, serves to mediate the oppression experienced in those other social locations. (52-53)

Thandeka adds that white people's "'race' was used to distract them from their shrinking value as wage earners. Diminished as workers, they felt shame.... Inflated as whites, they felt white supremacist pride" (78).

White privilege also blinds whites to the talent in others. It serves as a massive obstacle to all people discovering the history, the tragedies and triumphs of everyone except white people. There is no talk about others' contributions to America, leaving people to believe none occurred. Without talk creating a buzz that could lead to new discoveries there can be no change.

The effects of white privilege are most visible to members of multiracial families. The blending of the races is happening more now than in the past. It creates new realities in offspring, as well as new opportunities for people to better understand others and for whites to see their own position of privilege. The effects can be jarring and confusing, as some multiracial families explain:

From "True colors of white privilege"

> Cindy Taylor and Sarah Starnes gave me insight into a galaxy of white privilege that I'd otherwise never see.
>
> Taylor and Starnes possess the extrasensory perception of white women who are married to black men and are mothers of biracial children.
>
> "It's more than just a feeling," Cindy Taylor said. "When I'm alone, I'm not subjected to the same things."
>
> When Taylor is by herself, she isn't followed in stores, refused service or hassled. She's welcomed by white people.
>
> "The most amazing thing is even people of good will don't even appreciate how much they take that for granted," said Anthony Taylor, Cindy's husband.
>
> It's their exclusive *American express* to preferential treatment.
>
> Alisa Lange, a black woman, says some of that invisible privilege washes onto her when she's with her white husband. It's an ease and comfort in conversations and kindness that she's not afforded when she's alone or when she was married to her first husband, who was black.
>
> White privilege is the mother of all affirmative action. That preference supersedes today's endangered programs, which try to level the playing field for minorities.
>
> Taylor feels white privilege when she uses her checkbook or her husband's on purchases. "Nobody blinks," she said.

"When he writes a check they ask for two IDs," Taylor said. "It would be unthinkable for him to use my checkbook.

"He has to jump through hoops again and again."

At a Johnson County, Kansas, fitness center, Taylor has felt welcomed in a whirlpool with other white people. But she has noticed after she has left and her husband enters that the other white people suddenly get out of the hot water. "It's the same old thing, and it's endless," she said.

"You kind of develop a sixth sense, and so you avoid people and situations that are kind of uncomfortable or kind of unsatisfying," said Starnes, who prefers inclusive settings. "I value things about African-American culture. I feel like I've gained more than I'm sacrificing."

Yet, she's found some white people will assume when she's with her daughter, Amani, that they're not together or that Starnes adopted her. People of color, however, clearly see their likeness and their love.

"The assumption is that a respectable white woman would not have a biracial child," Starnes said. There also are the stares and rude questions that Amani in her emerging awareness of race finds unavoidable.

Sometimes the Taylors turn others' ignorance against them in sort of a mental martial arts exercise.

Cindy Taylor engages them and exposes the underworld of white privilege.

I wish more people did that. Then maybe America's invisible, white affirmative action would end and true equality could begin.

Whites are not often aware of their own privilege. Rather, they are practicing what Indigenous Peoples scholar Cornel Pewewardy recognizes as "dysconscious racism," whereby they "unconsciously [accept] dominant white norms and privileges" ("La Belle Sauvage"). As DiAngelo puts it, "White social power is so normalized that it is outside our conscious awareness" (55). One reason for this lack of awareness—isolation of the races—is pointed out by Jim Myers, author of *Afraid of the Dark: What Whites and Blacks Need to Know About Each Other*. Myers notes that isolation is more a problem for white people than black people.

<u>From "Obstacles abound in starting honest talks"</u>

"Most white Americans rarely encounter situations in which they are surrounded by black people," Myers wrote. "For the most part, whites avoid such situations. Black people have no such choice."

African-Americans represent about 13 percent of the population. They have to interact with white people. But it sometimes isn't good.

Myers described it as people who prefer chocolate living in a larger vanilla world:

"On occasion blacks might sense themselves as outsiders in a vanilla world, where the wishes and wants of a vanilla-loving majority consistently prevail.... [Blacks] are described as different and out of step, almost as if there is something wrong with them. Everyone, from entertainers to politicians, seems to talk exclusively about the love of vanilla. It's always vanilla, vanilla, vanilla.

"So it passes that majority tastes or concerns seem normal, sane and sensible, while minority tastes can seem abnormal, irrational or oddball."

The "mathematics of race" also is a problem, he notes.

"Across much of white America, there is a shortage of black people with whom whites might have the discussions," Myers said. "And in many black neighborhoods, there are too few whites to hold much of a discussion."

Peggy McIntosh, however, asserts that it's far more than a black/white thing. McIntosh leads discussions on white privilege across the country. In March of 2003 she visited the Kansas City area, where she and I co-facilitated sessions with people at the Minority Museum, where diversity regularly is discussed, and at Johnson County Community College.

From "Diluting the power of privilege"

She first asked people to get a partner, and for one minute, each was to tell the other the "hard or scary things about talking about privilege." She also asked each person to list the "good things about talking about privilege."

Later she had each person spend a minute telling personal stories of unearned disadvantage followed by a minute of recollections of unearned advantage. People also had to tell what it was like to hear the other person say such things.

"A minute can seem very long or very short," said McIntosh, a national expert on privilege.

African-Americans at the college said it was easier to speak of the disadvantage they've faced. Some whites said it was easier for them to identify their advantages but difficult to speak of their disadvantages to minorities.

"Any disadvantage I have is nothing compared to what he is feeling," one person said.

McIntosh said the exercise showed that everyone has unearned advantage and disadvantage.

"None of us is only a victim; none is only a villain," McIntosh said. "Our lives are nuanced.

"But I do see a hierarchy of oppression."

Women find the media, school curricula and history often exclude their challenges, triumphs, discoveries and contributions.

The same is true for African-Americans, Hispanics, Asian-Americans, American Indians, Muslims, people with disabilities, gays and lesbians. Instead they struggle against stereotypes, discrimination and exclusion.

People are left to believe that "men are knowers, and knowledge is male," said McIntosh, co-founder and co-director of the National Seeking Educational Equity and Diversity Project on Inclusive Curriculum. "Other people's knowledge is defective knowledge."

McIntosh said at least half of the people on the planet are women so half of the history, experiences and intellect of the world belongs to women. But that's not how it's recorded. "Men fill our half with their stuff," McIntosh said.

People who are right-handed discount their unearned advantage, too, she said. But left-handed people easily note their unearned disadvantages in a world dominated by right-handers.

McIntosh recalled black women arriving first at a restaurant, but a group of white women she was with was served ahead of them. She said the table of black women was served "too slow for justice." Conversely the table of white women was served "too fast for justice."

"It's the upside of discrimination," McIntosh said. "Racism as I experience it comes in the shape of white privilege, which confers dominance to my group from birth. I got it without approving of it."

That unearned privilege aids one group of people at others' expense. "Those benefiting from the privilege system are kept blinded to it to keep alive the myth of meritocracy," McIntosh said.

Those race blinders are not easily shed and awareness of white privilege does not come about without a struggle, even when meaningful discussions do take place. The inability to hear, see and comprehend what people of color are trying to convey adds to the invisibleness that Ralph Ellison wrote about nearly 60 years ago in his groundbreaking novel, *Invisible Man*. Whites in the U.S. can choose *when* and *when not* "to legitimize people of color's assertions of racism" because of their "social, economic, and political power within a White supremacist culture" (DiAngelo 55). The blinders stay on because recognizing differences in experience for different races is unnecessary for fitting into the dominant culture.

From "Blind to 'white privilege'"

Diane Kappen sent me a consoling e-mail after I had spent about three hours last week with her classes at the University of Kansas.

"The blind continue to maintain their blindness, it seems," said Kappen, who taught psychology on the Lawrence campus. "How can those who have never been disadvantaged ever comprehend the negative experiences that the disadvantaged consistently experience?"

Kappen had invited me to KU to show a diversity video to her students and to try to raise their understanding of the bigotry, prejudice and discrimination that people of color must regularly endure. A handful of black, Hispanic and white students in her classes said they could relate, and they shared their experiences.

But many other white students, particularly in the second class, said they couldn't accept the video's message or what I offered because neither fit their reality. I felt as if I had stepped back into the 1950s.

Those students said this nation's race relations problems, multicultural history and population were invisible in their white world.

They didn't know about the swastikas burned into a door and carpet at Oliver Hall, the "KKK" scrawled outside a student's room at Hashinger Hall or other hate crimes this year on their campus. What's worse is they didn't seem to care because none of those horrible acts was aimed at them.

I felt terrible for the minority students on campus. I've lived their pain.

They not only have to endure racism, but they also must contend with white students saying it's just their imagination. Many of Kappen's students also didn't seem to care about the nation's changing demographics.

By 2050 the minority population is expected to rise to 50 percent of the U.S. total. This is the students' future.

But many have elected to pull their white privilege cards instead of trying to equip themselves now to understand, better communicate and be productive in the more diverse America that lies on the horizon.

"There is always a home team," the Rev. Sam Mann said at the Civil Rights Consortium of Metropolitan Kansas City. "The white culture is the culture that is being integrated into."

Our Eurocentric history that has mostly excluded the struggles and accomplishments of minorities has given whites a grossly inaccurate view of others and themselves.

"White people wind up thinking more highly of themselves than they ought to think," said Mann, who is white and pastor of St. Mark's Church in Kansas City, Mo.

America needs to deconstruct its racist icons and its bigoted history, Mann said. The country then must repair centuries of damage

> caused by racism before it can progress into the 21st century.
>
> More and broader discussions on race will help. The happily ignorant behavior I encountered at KU will only serve to make things worse.

After my visit to her classroom and the ensuing column, Diane Kappen went on to build her doctorate in social psychology at the University of Kansas titled, "Acknowledgement of Racial Privilege, Endorsement of Equality and Feelings of Collective Guilt via Ingroup vs. Outgroup Influence," around the experience. In her dissertation and study, she added a surprising variable: One set of test subjects read a column I had written and saw me as I am—an African-American male—in the photo that accompanies my column. Another set read the column, but my photo was replaced with that of a white male.

From "Assessing white privilege"

> What Kappen found was fascinating.
>
> Her dissertation revealed that an audience can be influenced based on the race of the person presenting information. Kappen's study found that the white male test subjects accepted my "Blind to 'white privilege'" column when it appeared to have been written by a white male.
>
> However, the white female test subjects seemed to be more influenced by that column when they saw that it was written by a black man. "It shows the white guys are hard to influence," Kappen said.
>
> A second part of her study and dissertation also showed that white males have a hard time seeing and accepting that they are privileged. Gary R. Howard in his book, *We Can't Teach What We Don't Know,* called it an "invisibility" aspect of dominance.
>
> "Social positionality for whites in Western societies has afforded us a personal sense of invisibility related to the unfolding drama of dominance," Howard wrote.
>
> Howard's book and Kappen's dissertation show that invisibility also extends to white privilege.
>
> Kappen gave white male test subjects a "social logic" exam. They indirectly were told the test was biased toward white people.
>
> When quizzed afterward, the students acknowledged that test bias does exist. However, they attributed their high marks to their personal ability. "The low level of racial group identification observed in this study suggests that participants were distancing themselves from an unpleasant group membership rather than rallying in support of the group," Kappen wrote.
>
> What's also fascinating is that once unearned white privilege is

exposed, persons with this new vision should be compelled to act to help level the playing field for everyone.

"That our privileged dominance often threatens the physical and cultural well-being of other groups is a reality that whites, for the most part, have chosen to ignore," Howard, who's white, wrote. "The fact that we can choose to ignore such realities is perhaps our most insidious privilege."

But there is hope. Kappen found it in seeing white female test subjects influenced more by my column when they saw someone black wrote it.

"I strongly feel that women are more empathetic to the experiences of disadvantage," she said. "They've been there. It seemed to me in almost all cases women were more likely to acknowledge the privilege they have enjoyed because of their race."

That tells me that despite protests by some African-Americans, books such as *To Kill a Mockingbird* by Harper Lee should continue to be used in schools nationwide even though the authors are white.

They have an influence with white male readers beyond what black authors might enjoy.

The same is true for white educators and mothers in teaching racial understanding to white children. All voices need to be heard in the dialogue on racial healing.

White privilege deeply affects people's ability to accept information they receive about the continuing racial problem in America. This comes back to haunt me, for when I point out discrimination against minorities in my columns, I often receive messages like this one:

E-mail: Feb. 25, 2005

You Mr. Diuguid are a racist and bigot. Maybe you had a bad experience growing up but you obviously do not like white people. I have never read one of your columns when you say anything flattering about white people or where you expect African Americans to take responsibility for anything. Anything bad that happens to any black is always THE WHITE MAN'S FAULT. It gives a good excuse for failure. Think about this. I feel sorry for your sick look on life.

The State of Black America 1999: the Impact of Color-Consciousness in the United States helps illuminate the origin of the above, which is a new slur on race. Rhonda M. Williams writes that conservative commentator R. Emmett Tyrell, Jr. gave a caller "his present-day rule of thumb for dealing with race in the United States: in any discussion about politics, '...whoever mentions race first is the racist in the room.'" Williams continues:

Tyrell's response is important because his rule of thumb succinct-

> ly summarizes a core idea advocated by conservative intellectuals and politicians of this generation: not only is racism a thing of the past, but the very mention of race, at least in Tyrell's conservative circles, brands one a racist. His comments tell us that many white folks are just plain tired of race-talk. Recent polling data suggests the vast majority of U.S. whites agree with Tyrell: prejudice was bad, but now it's largely gone, and it's time for African Americans to carry on. Any remaining discriminatory behaviors that are personally or economically injurious should be handled via the enforcement of existing laws. Conservatives thus reject race-conscious policies, lambaste race-conscious sister-citizens and proclaim that we now live in a society that is color-blind; in other words, the foundation for racial economic justice is firmly established and here to stay. (137-138)

So quite clearly conservatives have turned the tables. But still people find themselves confronting the devalued nature of being black in America. Williams adds that "Many progressive African Americans, Latinos and Asian Americans (and some of our anti-racist white allies) do not share [Tyrell's] vision. Indeed, there are many among us who argue that deeply entrenched class, institutional and cultural legacies of white economic supremacy are still powerful determinants of African-American chances for economic survival and viability" (138). Thomas M. Shapiro puts a dollar figure on that supremacy. In the National Urban League's book, *The State of Black America 2005*, in a chapter titled "The Racial Wealth Gap," Shapiro writes that "the cost of being black amounts to $136,174. This is a measure of the accumulative disadvantage of being African American. Flipping the perspective, the accumulative advantage or the legacy of whiteness for the typical white family also is $136,174" (45). That difference is not lost to African-Americans particularly for those trying to be enterprising in mainstream America.

<u>From "Heritage is not something to hide"</u>

> ATLANTA - The questions in a city commonly known as the black mecca of the South seemed to come from a "Gone with the Wind" era of America.
>
> They were addressed to members of a panel discussion at a gathering of the National Association of Black Journalists. The man and woman in the packed room wanted to know whether in correspondence and phone calls they should conceal the fact that they are African-Americans from agents, publicists, publishers, the media and others to generate interest in their work.
>
> The questions brought back images of some black people from this country's darker past. They were the offspring of slaves and slave

owners. These mixed-race children had straight hair, fair skin and European features. Because they looked white, they could "pass."

"Passing" meant these black men and women had to disown their families, friends and all ties to African-Americans to be accepted as white.

The laws of this country said one drop of black blood labeled the person black - no matter how white the individual looked. As a black person, those fair-skinned individuals were not accorded the privileges associated with being white in America. They received the same racist, discriminatory treatment that all blacks did.

"Passing" enabled them to raise their status. They got the white privileges of freedom and opportunity that black people almost never received. Cradle-to-grave racial disparities in wealth, jobs, income, education, housing, health care, banking, public accommodations and entrepreneurship remain a legacy of slavery.

There is no way to know whether black authors are rejected by publishers, agents, publicists and the media because of their race. But it can't be discounted.

At the convention, journalists learned that African-Americans are disappearing from media jobs. The push for diversity has weakened in newsrooms across America.

Even former President Bill Clinton, who addressed the convention, said he noticed the trend. "I was always struck by the lack of diversity," Clinton said of the Washington press corps.

He said journalists of color ask "better questions" and provide "a different take" on local, national and world events. The return in information is better, too.

I explained to the questioners at the authors' forum that the same thing is true in book publishing. But I anchored the information in what my mother and father always told me: Never hide the fact that you are black; never hide who you really are.

Corporate executives in the 1940s had encouraged Dad to "pass" for white so his career would advance as a Cornell University doctoral graduate and scientist. But Dad refused, saying the cost of admission to white America was too high. He couldn't give up who he was and his family.

African-Americans need to understand that they provide empathy and depth of experiences to the news media and other industries. We possess the double consciousness that W.E.B. Du Bois so famously wrote about at the turn of the last century in which we see everything in this country both through the prism of being Americans and being Africans in America.

That stands out as an asset for all journalists of color, I explained to the questioners. There are some publishing companies, agents, publicists and media that realize it, which makes black authors more popular, attractive and bigger financial draws if everyone sheds the handcuffs of stereotypes about African-Americans. Too many people still wear them.

The inquiring man followed me outside with the same line of questions. The answer he accepted and noted was that if he were to hide his race, and others, thinking he was white, later discovered he wasn't, then he might risk being dropped and doom the work he had put into his book.

But if he were up front and accepted for the talent he possesses, then he would never have to worry about being outted by people who will never find comfort embracing him for who he really is.

Denial

A Monumental Barrier to Exploring the Real America

There is a perceived as well as real value to the quality that Thandeka calls whiteness. Many whites still deny the privilege they enjoy and the racism that privilege perpetuates. They often don't realize that they take that privilege for granted. David K. Shipler, in his book, *A Country of Strangers: Blacks and Whites in America,* describes what that looks like in real dollars to white people. Shipler writes:

> For any white who claims to have no negative reaction to dark skin, Andrew Hacker, a political science professor at Queens College, suggests an exercise. He presents white students with a parable: At midnight tonight, they are to become black. "And this will mean not simply a darker skin, but the bodily and facial features associated with African ancestry. However, inside you will be the person you always were. Your knowledge and ideas will remain intact. But outwardly you will not be recognizable." Each of them will live 50 more years as blacks. What compensation would they demand for such a change? "Most seemed to feel it would not be out of place to ask for $50 million or $1 million for each coming black year," Hacker writes. "And this calculation conveys as well as anything the value that white people place on their own skins." (236)

There is a deep dishonesty in denying that one has privilege because of one's skin color while at the same time valuing that color much, much more than others. As Robin J. DiAngelo writes, "We have to start being honest about the fact that we do notice race (when it isn't White) and then pay attention to what race means in our everyday lives. White people and people of color do not have the same racial experience, and this has profound and tangible consequences that need to be understood if we want to stop colluding with racism" (55).

No one likes to be told about racist things that are going on. My friend, Valerie Glauser, told me of a T-shirt she wore to her workplace in Philadelphia that helps illustrate why so many people react badly. The shirt said "Better Living Through Denial." If people of all colors deny that racism exists, that discrimination is something that people of color face because of it, then they also feel justified in denying that redress, court action or reparations of any kind are needed to correct the historic and ongoing wrongs. Consequently it's not necessary for them to feel remorse about the difference between their lives and others'.

Race relations problems tend to persist the most in the suburbs where whites dominate and few people of color live. Wealthy white suburban areas like Johnson County, Kansas, are where people fled to escape minorities. But they never want to be reminded of the motivation behind the move or what they left behind. They also realize after moving that there truly is no hiding place from the Real America. However, families of color face a real racial conundrum in moving to the suburbs, too. If they remain in urban areas, they pay the price in their children likely being enrolled in deficient schools. They pay higher insurance rates—if they can get insurance at all. Businesses and services as basic as pharmacies, grocery stores, shopping centers and day care are scarce. The value of their property is likely to remain stagnant at best. In the suburbs these same families of color will gain where they had lost in the inner city. However, where they are likely to suffer is in feeling less welcome, and in receiving consistently poor customer service in stores and other public accommodation venues. The schools might have better facilities and supplies, but their children may be treated as troublemakers, as being not as intellectually sharp as white students or as being incapable of learning. Again, it's all a matter of feelings, which many quickly deny. But racism in America historically has been described by minorities as being like the wind: you can't see it, but the victims certainly feel its presence:

From "Johnson County's race issue"

> A coward made a hangman's noose and then left it on the floor by Cedric A. Boyd's desk at Shawnee Mission East High School.
>
> It was a small thing, only about a foot long, fashioned from heavy duty string. But the consequences of the act against 15-year-old Cedric have been enormous.
>
> You see, Cedric, a junior honor roll student, is among only about 1 percent of the 2,000 students at the Johnson County school who are African-American. The perpetrator cloaked his identity in the

crush of white students entering and leaving the honors calculus class the morning of the incident. Cedric was the only black person in the room.

Sgt. Steve Hunter, with the Prairie Village police investigations division, said police and school officials had questioned students in Cedric's class and the one that preceded it to determine who left the noose and whether anyone knew anything about it. No one's talking.

The investigation is expected to be done by the end of this week.

Cedric said the incident would have a lasting effect on him. He sees it in the context of national events and things he has studied about Africans in America. That bigger picture isn't pretty.

"The noose symbolizes slavery and the Ku Klux Klan and black people being lynched," said Cedric, who plans to be an electrical engineer. "I hope people know the history of the noose.

"If they knew what it symbolized, they wouldn't play with it anymore. It has changed me."

Ironically, Cedric's older sister, Michelle Campbell, is a consultant with Johnson County school districts in efforts to get them to value diversity. She is dismayed by how Cedric has been treated.

Joel Zeddies, founder of Clergy and Church Against Race Violence, said the small noose was huge in the context of a cross being burned May 26, 1999, not far from the school at the home of a black family. In this hate crime, the white perpetrator was punished with a prison sentence.

Zeddies also cited problems African-Americans today face as victims of racial profiling in traffic stops and in stores where they get poor service, no service, are followed or are accused of shoplifting. "They'd better take this seriously because Johnson County has a real problem with racism," said Zeddies, who is white.

For Cedric and his mother, Joann Boyd, the incident unearthed numerous racial slurs and slights in which black students have received harsher discipline and fewer freedoms than their white peers. Boyd said Cedric also was denied admission into the National Honor Society even though he turned in his material on time and met all of the requirements.

"I contend that because of his race, he was not allowed in," Boyd said. School officials say they value diversity, she said, "but I know the way they treat our kids.

"I have a loss of trust."

Jack Prall, associate principal at Shawnee Mission East High School, said school officials were not permitted to say why students weren't accepted into the honor society. He said race wasn't a factor in how students are treated.

"We want every student to be given every opportunity to succeed and be involved at Shawnee Mission East High School," Prall said. "I am not aware of any students being treated unfairly here."

Boyd said she was fed up with officials continuing to minimize and discount black students' and parents' concerns. "There has always been a lot of racism, but not to this magnitude," said Boyd, who for 25 years has had children in Shawnee Mission schools.

Yvette Morton, president of the Johnson County Martin Luther King Jr. Holiday Committee, said the disparate treatment many black students face in Johnson County schools "says we still have to do battle, and the battle is a continuing battle in this country." She urged African-American parents and adults to become more involved in the schools so that black students will not be mistreated and their concerns will not be ignored.

Meanwhile, she said she and others would continue efforts to defuse the fear and racism with more events in the community. "It's a constant until Jesus Christ comes back and does his thing," Morton said.

Amen to that.

The reactions from readers that I received after that column were mostly negative and often racist, tasteless or nasty. The following letter came from a woman.

Feb. 2, 2000

Regarding the black boy in Johnson County School, Cedric Boyd, and the noose found by his desk – this will have to be overlooked as a "prank," which happens in many schools. Why make such an issue of it? He's in a "white" school, in a "white" neighborhood and the majority resents his being there. He moved into that area, did he not expect this? In other words, he is not wanted in that area and I would feel the same.

When a 'black' moves into an area – here comes his black friends and relatives, and then we whites are frightened from there on. Who commits 90 percent of the crime in Kansas City – blacks – and it's frightening to be around such. I believe in segregation and always have – you are not in my comfort zone and also you bring drugs, drive-by shootings, rape and killings into the community. Is there any wonder why we do not care for you people!!? True, not all whites are nice people, but I don't want to be around them either. Yes, I know a few nice, refined blacks, but I'd still rather be around those like me. I'm sick of February being ruined by 'Black History Month,' and I detest 'Martin Luther King' and the whole month of January being shoved down our throats – even our presidents never have such coverage on their birthdays. And this business about the 'Con-

> federate flag' flying on the state building in the South, if you don't like it, don't look at it!! That flag is their heritage and is their right. If you are all so up on African heritage, go there to live – we'd love to lose all of you – would mean less crime here! Over there, every 26 seconds, someone is dying of AIDS – would you want that? Look at the Kansas City school system – those schools (Southwest High) dropped to low after transporting all the blacks to white schools, instead of going to the schools in their area. This is what ruined the Kansas City schools. I am sorry sir, but this is how I feel, along with many people. Stay out of our areas and our schools, and we'll leave your kids alone.

Authorities eventually learned that an Asian student was responsible for the noose. It perhaps shows that racism isn't just a black-white thing. The Asian student denied any malice. But the victims of the incident remained skeptical.

From "A chance for understanding"

> Without question, generations of kids have tied nooses using string or rope.
>
> I did, too.
>
> But what's different in this case is the context. The noose was not shown to Cedric A. Boyd by a friend saying, Gee, look what I made.
>
> The noose appeared to have been left anonymously. Cedric, an honor roll student, picked it up in the context of racial slurs and slights that he and other black students have endured.
>
> Cedric and his mother, Joann Boyd, saw the noose in the context of slavery, the Ku Klux Klan, black people being lynched and centuries of oppression. The noose also surfaced in the context of the Boyds' filing a complaint in December with the U.S. Department of Education, contending Cedric was not admitted into the National Honor Society because he's black.
>
> That's also in the context of African-Americans saying school officials often minimize their concerns. Added to that is the Department of Education investigating a complaint by a former teacher alleging the district discriminates against students in its English as a Second Language program.
>
> People who've hammered me for writing about the noose said the media attention would damage the high school. But I've asked many of them what about Cedric and the black students at the school?
>
> What about the countless racial incidents they've endured? What about their perception and the damage done to their spirit and their sense of what's possible for them in America?
>
> Some folks responded that they're staunch segregationists, insisting that Kansas City schools are for blacks and Johnson County

> schools are for whites. But they live in a mythical America, not the real one where freedom and opportunity are supposed to reign for all.
>
> Prairie Village police and school officials investigated the noose, questioning students in Cedric's honors calculus class, where he is the only black person, and in the class before his to determine who left it. But it wasn't until late last week that an Asian-American student, 18, told police the noose happened to fall from his notebook by Cedric's desk.
>
> I'm happy that mystery is solved and that school district Superintendent Marjorie Kaplan has asked the U.S. Department of Justice to help gauge racial tension in the district. Students also are being notified of the district's zero-tolerance stance on racist behavior in classrooms.
>
> Those progressive steps will be great for the young people. But the foul feedback I've received makes me very concerned now about the community.

The denial over the noose issue quieted somewhat with the revelation that African-Americans throughout the city and the country were being victimized by this new form of racial hatred. Throughout the reporting and writing on this issue I felt as if the ghosts of thousands of night riders of the Ku Klux Klan were angrily screaming through the voices of individuals who don't like people of color and have segregated themselves into places where only the warped media images will expose them to African Americans. But I also felt a sense of haunting in the voices and words of the historically tortured spirit of black victims of lynchings, slavery and other atrocities of the world's worst holocaust, which some studies suggest could number as many as 300 million victims (Myers 181). They urged that the truth of the Real America finally be told:

From "Leaving a noose at work or school is no laughing matter"

> A lot of people want to dismiss or laugh off the many nooses that cowards keep leaving for African-Americans at work and in schools - except the FBI.
>
> Agents in the Kansas City area office are taking the growing number of cases seriously.
>
> "It seems to be the hate crime of choice right now," said Jeff Lanza, FBI spokesman. The FBI is investigating two noose cases.
>
> The issue surfaced after Cedric A. Boyd and his family took the first brave step with their public outcry about a noose someone left by his desk in January at Shawnee Mission East High School.
>
> Since then people have told me of 10 nooses metrowide and one in Omaha. Last week I testified before the Kansas and Missouri Advisory Committees to the U.S. Commission on Civil Rights on the

growth of this new kind of hate.

"We're seeing more and more of this activity," Lanza said. "Leaving a noose is an act of intimidation designed to deprive someone of their freedom."

A noose also enables a perpetrator who's caught to easily lie about his intent and say it was a joke, said Atkins W. Warren, then-regional director for the community relations service of the U.S. Department of Justice. His office has investigated noose cases, too.

"I'm sure some people are seeing them and are not making any comments at all," Warren said. "That's the disturbing part of it."

The FBI investigates noose cases as hate crimes. Convictions carry a penalty of up to 10 years in prison. No charges have been filed.

"There is a strong racial hatred behind the act," Lanza said. "They're trying to scare people. Anybody in his right mind is not going to do it as a joke."

More than the nooses, African-American victims in these cases have told me they've been hurt more when nothing was done, the perpetrators were promoted, blacks were forced into psychiatric treatment or workplace retaliation followed.

Larry D. Coleman, a civil rights lawyer, is representing two African-American noose victims. One is Marqueta Denise Charles, an Army Corps of Engineers employee in downtown Kansas City. She found a noose in her in-box in the summer of 1998.

Larry Crump, a Corps of Engineers spokesman, declined comment.

In Coleman's other case, Arthur Kyle filed suit in Jackson County Circuit Court against J.D. Franklin Corp. of Grandview, Mo., where he worked. The suit says a supervisor gave Kyle a noose in 1998, saying "Don't say I never gave you anything."

Kelley Sears, a lawyer for the company, said, "There was no intent involved to offend anyone."

Coleman said giving a noose to a black employee was like leaving a swastika for a Jewish worker or sex object for a female employee: "If the courts would do their part, you won't have these nooses. But why should people take them seriously if nothing is going to happen?"

A black Northland warehouse employee who found a noose made of rope at work understands. He reported it, but nothing was done.

"You can be the biggest Louis Farrakhan or Klansman in the world, but don't bring it to work," said the man, who still fears for his life. "I don't want to come to work in a place like that. I don't want to worry about whether a person is going to shoot me today or whether my tires will be flat."

Pastor Jason Branch of Life Changing International Ministries, who has counseled the man, said he was dissatisfied with the company's reaction: "The company said they always play like that. They always play racial jokes. I understand that we have racism in the world, but it should not be tolerated in the workplace."

A noose made of rope was found on a repair table in November 1999 at the Delphi Automotive Systems in Olathe, said Verna Brown, an operator, and John W. Hill Jr., a fork truck driver. The next day it was hanging from an overhead light. Brown and Hill said they complained to a company official.

"I grew up in Mississippi, the belly of racism," Hill said. "My momma's father in 1928 was lynched. That kind of stuff makes me angry."

But Personnel Director Andrew Kopac said he never saw the noose and said neither Hill nor Brown made a formal complaint.

"I think we have a very diverse work force, and they seem to be getting along quite well," Kopac said. He said he reissued the company policy on harassment but not in response to the noose.

Brown and Hill, however, said Delphi race relations were strained, and they were upset that nothing was done about the noose.

"We never saw any investigation or any person of authority asking questions," Brown said.

Madella "May" Henderson and Beverly Williams, longtime workers at the General Motors Fairfax assembly plant, said that since 1998 four nooses had been used to victimize African-Americans at the plant.

"That's just like burning a cross on someone's lawn," Henderson said.

Tara Condon-Tullier, plant spokeswoman, acknowledges one noose made of rubber stripping found two years ago: "It was determined there was no harmful intent involved."

Action was taken, including counseling, sensitivity training and a reinstatement of the company's zero tolerance harassment policy. U.S. Department of Justice officials also concluded company actions were appropriate, Condon-Tullier said.

In Kansas City, Kan., Marcus Moon, 15, found a noose made of rope and a threatening note near his locker in March at Pierson Junior High School. Moon, a ninth-grader, was shocked, and so was his grandmother, Bernice Brown, whose cousin was lynched years ago when she lived in the South.

No child should fear for his life because of his race, she said.

Pierson Principal JoAnn Stevens declined to comment.

Bob Wolfson, director of the Plains states region of the Anti-Defamation League, said because racists communicate on numerous Internet Web sites, minorities today face enemies with post-doctorate studies in hate.

> "People should be outraged at the suggestion that someone can put a noose in the workplace of an African-American and have it dismissed as a prank," said Wolfson, who told me of the noose case in Omaha in which the victim lost his job. "The message is you people don't belong here."
>
> My fear also is if this new form of hate goes unchecked, the symbolic lynchings will increase, and more people will be hurt by a resurrection of this country's racist past.

After that column ran, people told me of eight other nooses found at two other companies.

Four nooses were found at Steel & Pipe Supply Co. Inc. in New Century Industrial Park in Johnson County, Kansas. The FBI investigated the case as a possible hate crime, said Jeff Lanza, FBI spokesman.

From "Noose incidents reflect need for racial understanding in the Heartland"

> Phil Brokenicky, executive vice president with Steel & Pipe Supply, declined to comment, saying it's "an employee matter."
>
> African-American workers also found four nooses hanging from a break room ceiling at Consolidated Freightways of Kansas City.
>
> Robert Smith, group operations manager at the company, issued a memo saying the company had thoroughly investigated the incident and "concluded that it was intended as a joke between employees." However, his letter also said such activity might be construed as offensive.
>
> "Horseplay, jokes and other conduct, which is not related to our jobs, should be avoided in the workplace," Smith wrote.
>
> Police investigations of these incidents dead-end without charges.
>
> But neither excuse has curbed a Kansas City Human Relations Department investigation of the nooses at Consolidated Freightways. Mickey Dean, deputy director of the department, said noose incidents make African-American workers worry about retaliation.
>
> Mike Brown, director of corporate communications with Consolidated Freightways based in Menlo Park, Calif., said the company is taking the matter seriously.
>
> A noose should never be used as a "joke." Such humor is a weapon targeted like a smart bomb to hurt African-Americans and give the culprits a way to remove themselves from the conflagration. But the continuing damage and denial tied to hangmen's nooses in this community is immense.
>
> What befuddles me are the mostly venomous comments I've received.
>
> One woman caller said, "Well, as usual you've got your little racist column, and the Red Star don't know any better than to have someone like you."

> Another woman caller said: Come on, loosen up and quit being so paranoid. Kids will play pranks, and you'll have to get used to it.
>
> An e-mailer wrote: "I don't understand how nooses have come to be identified as a 'black hate' thing. It would seem to me like a noose would be an item of equal opportunity hatred and not necessarily a racial one."
>
> This person obviously hasn't studied black history or seen James Allen's new book *Without Sanctuary,* featuring black people and the white mobs that lynched them. Hangmen's nooses cause many African-Americans to recall that part of country's repulsive past.
>
> These new symbols of racial hatred are acts of domestic terrorism aimed at people of color.
>
> Yet many others don't see that. One e-mailer wrote, "With all the problems in our society, is this noose problem in the top 10 things for our FBI to pursue?"
>
> It's as if African-Americans don't pay taxes and merit the protection of federal, state and local authorities from criminal and civil rights violations.
>
> But another e-mailer explained: "Today blacks are their own worst enemy. You are not a victim of racism, you are a victim of your own actions! And the result is poverty and exclusion."
>
> The caustic feedback I get indicates some white people see themselves as victims when African-Americans are merely seeking their constitutional rights.

Seeing themselves as victims—whether real or imagined—is a part of white privilege and a much easier position for whites to be in than one in which they have to admit to racism. Robin J. DiAngelo states that "if racism is brought up and we become uncomfortable, then something is 'wrong' and we blame the person who triggered our discomfort (usually a person of color)" (54). To ease that emotional indigestion, America has as a defense turned Civil Rights icons like the Rev. Martin Luther King, Jr., Coretta Scott King, and Rosa Parks into what the Rev. Joseph Lowery called "cuddly" characters. Who couldn't love the warm, fuzzy, almost cartoonish figures they have become? But in accepting the softened images we forget the dangers these Civil Rights giants faced and the sacrifices they made on the pathway to a more egalitarian America. They took revolutionary stands for the downtrodden and the oppressed, most of whom were black, and posed an extreme threat to the establishment of the time. This new image softens the country's racist past and whitewashes its still racist present. The ensuing picture is more comfortable for the dominant culture, giving people the impression that the extreme problems of the past and present are just made up by people of color who have an exploitative agenda.

In the same way, Native American traditions are hijacked and mangled to fit an acceptable majority mold. Cornel Pewewardy writes about the customs that schools around the country have of using Indian logos, nicknames and gestures during sporting events. He states, "There's nothing in Indigenous cultures that I'm aware of that aspires to be a mascot, logo, or nickname for athletic teams" ("La Belle Sauvage"). He adds that

> [i]nvented media images prevent millions of Americans from understanding the past and current authentic human experience of First Nations People. My opposition to the use of Indian mascots for sports teams has always been because these trappings and seasonal insults offend the intelligence of thousands of Indigenous Peoples in this country. ("La Belle Sauvage")

Yet when confronted with the slur, "school officials state or say they are honoring Indigenous Peoples and insist their schools' sponsored activities aren't offensive, but rather a compliment." Pewewardy adds, "I would argue otherwise" ("La Belle Sauvage").

Many others share Pewewardy's viewpoint:

From "Inaccurate portrayals, symbols insulting to American Indians"

> Time and experience have left many deep rivulets of character throughout Rod Steiner's face.
>
> He wants young American Indians to have lives that are at least as long and full as his. But the 75-year-old Santee Sioux and retired roofer worries that negative images they'll face will affect their longevity and quality of life.
>
> What's worse is they may not even know what's happening. The mainstream press isn't telling the story. American Indian newspapers are. Steiner showed me.
>
> The American Psychological Association last fall called for an immediate end to American Indian personalities, images, symbols and mascots used by professional teams like the Kansas City Chiefs. It includes universities, colleges, schools and organizations.
>
> The action follows the NCAA last summer saying it would ban schools' use of American Indian nicknames and imagery at postseason tournaments starting in February because the symbols are racially and ethnically "hostile" and "abusive." It would prevent schools with American Indian mascots from being hosts of future NCAA postseason events. Band members and cheerleaders won't be able to have American Indians on their uniforms starting in 2008. It's long overdue.
>
> The psychological association's resolution also emerges from a growing number of social science studies showing that American In-

dian sports mascots have a harmful effect on the self-esteem and social identity development of young American Indians.

The association said racial stereotyping and inaccurate racial portrayals reinforce insulting and misleading images of American Indians. It affects the impressions of other people who have little contact with indigenous cultures and establishes an "unwelcome and often times hostile learning environment for American Indian students that affirms negative images/stereotypes that are promoted in mainstream society."

The association called the use of American Indian mascots and symbols "a form of discrimination against Indigenous Nations that can lead to negative relations between groups."

Steiner said at his Kansas City, Kan., home that at long last this concern was getting the attention it deserved. No one is supposed to wear the headdresses, feathers and other traditional native attire unless they've earned the right.

"They're very spiritual," Steiner said. That includes the feathers, face paint and drum. The stereotypes and abuse of the native culture leads to a diminished self-worth among American Indians, particularly young people. Steiner said he sees young American Indians with a low regard for themselves and others like them turn violently on each other.

Steiner highlighted another article he photocopied from the *Dakota Journal,* which described the effect as "lateral violence." It's a behavior among people traumatized by oppression.

Instead of turning to each other, their emotional injuries cause them to lash out at those closest to them.

Steiner pointed to a photograph that ran nearly three years ago in *The Kansas City Star* of a white man at a Chiefs tailgating party dressed in an Indian costume and drinking a beer. It's a compound insult because he shouldn't have been wearing American Indian clothing and feathers, and drinking a beer made it seem as if all Indians are alcoholics.

Steiner pointed to the picture, saying: "We couldn't lash out at this guy that's causing it. Why, you'd be arrested.

"They say we're honoring you. When I tell them you're offending me, they say no we're not. They come back with this viciousness. I don't understand that. I don't see how you can keep doing that with that attitude."

It sounds easy. Anyone could understand it, right? But the feedback from that column was overwhelmingly negative. The denial and the discrimination American Indians face will be with us according to what these people have to offer:

E-mail: Jan. 25, 2006

Sports teams liked the idea of Indian clothing and feathers because out of 500 different tribes in North America, around 400 were continually fighting one another for over 2000 years. The "Native Americans" had not progressed and remained in the Stone Age for centuries. I doubt that bows, arrows, and stones would have been much of a match for the German and Japanese war machines. Therefore, had it not been for the white man coming here and developing better weapons and bombs, you and I would likely be speaking German or Japanese today. Actually, I would think that sports teams today would be better off portraying themselves as all black since a high percentage of black males in our metro areas are much more violent than the Indians ever were.

E-mail: Jan. 26, 2006

Where does it all end with you liberals? I seem to recall a story I read several years ago in which American Indians for example believed that the name of Arrowhead Stadium was an honor to them. And do we hear Irish people complaining about Notre Dame? Where will it all end? Will we have to stop saying; Commander-in-chief? Chief of police? Fire Chief? Just how far will you liberals take this political correctness nonsense? I happened onto your paper and article by accident at work and it's no wonder I personally don't subscribe to it and won't be for a very long time. As long as there is an alleged "victim" you liberals will be right there on the bandwagon with your wet fingers in the air checking which way to sway with the wind. I have German ancestry and I demand that I be called German-American and I want some special privileges. And don't mention Hitler either because that offends me.

Voice mail: Jan. 25, 2006

I can't possibly see how you can come up with that viewpoint. It just really doesn't make sense of me.

Voice mail: Jan. 25, 2006

Your people, black people, are kind of in the forefront of this. Like the Washington Black Skins or the Washington Nigger Skins or all the teams that are primarily black in terms of percentage of athletes who know about stereotypes and say nothing, do nothing. Jews should know better. But they say nothing; do nothing. Kansas City Kites. It seems the liberals are the ones who are allowing it. It's the liberals who are afraid to do anything for or on behalf of American Indians – blacks, Jews, whites, whatever the case may be. So real distorted article. The fact is there's no one in the black community who points out the black hypocrisy in all of this. Of all groups of people who should know the best, know the most and say the most, it would be your people. The same

> with Jews. And who says anything? Who really says anything about black participation and supporting by saying nothing doing nothing more than black people? Your people. All the players, the majority [of the] Washington Red Skins – ought to be the Washington Black Skins or the Washington Nigger Skins. As a matter of fact that was on of the signs that one of the Indians had up during the last protest. That's how they really feel. Have a good day.

The attitude that Rod Steiner cannot understand of "we're honoring, not offending you" comes from the privileged feeling whites have that "we should be judged by our intentions rather than the effects of our behavior," says Robin J. DiAngelo. She continues:

> A common White reasoning is that as long as we didn't intend to perpetuate racism, then our actions don't count as racism. We focus on our intentions and discount the impact, thereby invalidating people of color's experiences and communicating that the effects of our behavior on them are unimportant. We then spend great energy explaining to people of color why our behavior is not racism at all. This invalidates their perspectives while enabling us to deny responsibility for making the effort to understand enough about racism to see our behavior's impact in both the immediate interaction and the broader, historical context. (55)

In other words, white privilege allows for a denial of racism which in turn allows for a denial of the discomfort that people of color feel when confronted with racist actions and of the racist history behind that discomfort. But people of color are repeatedly admonished to just "get over it":

> Voice mail: 2004
>
> Man, I am so sick of reading your racist drivel in the newspaper. I mean, everything. You can't get past a paragraph in your column without you whining about the African Americans. You were slaves hundreds of year ago. I mean, how long does it take to get over it? I mean, this is ridiculous. I mean, I pick up the paper and try to read it, and I try to be open-minded, but all you do is whine, whine, whine. We are so oppressed. We can't do anything because my great-great-great grandpa was a slave.

Because of white privilege it is easy for the caller to relegate history to a deep, shadowy, forgotten corner of the past. But for people of color it is jarring when our history is ignored or discounted. We constantly do the calculus, wondering whether every perceived racist incident is in fact our imagination or something dredged from this nation's horrid past. But what of the present? What of what we feel? And what now must we do in this all too Real America if the incident was verifiably racist?

From "Billboard ignores history"

> David K. Shipler, author of A *Country of Strangers,* wrote that it's a huge gulf separating blacks and whites: "To most of white America, slavery is an evil long gone, the segregation of Jim Crow is deeply buried and the Civil Rights Movement has wiped the slate clean.
>
> But "black America generally lives with a different memory, one that feels the reverberations of slavery, yearns for roots, searches for pride and reaches back to grasp at ancient uncertainties. Present events occur in the context, not in isolation, so they are interpreted according to what has gone before. Hence, in the eyes of many blacks, elements of the complex relationship of slavery are constantly being re-enacted... Slavery is a permanent metaphor."

Hope lies in e-mail like this: "I had thought things were getting better, that we had progressed beyond brute force intimidation of people and that, at most, [offensive] incidents were caused by insensitivity, not hatred. I am sorry to see that I was wrong." We need to admit that we have a problem in America and no one is immune; this has to happen before whiteness, its privileges and racism can be overcome. But the process is far from easy.

From "Step 1 Admit to racism"

> Fifi Wiedeman, a friend, and former Kansas City Board of Education member, said racism in America is like alcoholism. The first step involves getting people to admit to the problem. Then they must stop the centuries-old binge of being intoxicated about being white or feeling impaired if they're black, Hispanic or other people of color.
>
> Wiedeman's racism-alcoholism analogy won high marks at the National Council on Alcoholism and Drug Dependence, where motivational speaker Maurice Harper was leading an Opportunity to Succeed seminar.
>
> "I have a saying that America is so racist that it doesn't realize it's racist," Harper said. "We have a tendency in America to be in a state of denial."
>
> Minorities are in denial almost as much as whites are. It's the same as the effects of alcoholism on a family, said Preston L. Washington, program director for the alcoholism council. Victims of racism also play roles of enablers, heroes and scapegoats, which feeds the addiction.
>
> "They don't talk; they don't trust; they don't feel," Washington said. "People keep believing the lie until there is some intervention."
>
> Harry R. Davidson, a clinical and community psychologist, said that like alcoholism, he sees a cycle of dysfunction in racism.

That learned behavior is passed from generation to generation, giving one group a false sense of power and others a low sense of self-worth.

Nathan McCall, author of *Makes Me Wanna Holler: A Young Black Man in America,* called racism a dehumanizing social disease that people must confront. "It boils down to do we have the will," McCall said in a speech at the Housing Authority of Kansas City's Village Banquet.

People who do talk about race relations and begin to write what former Mayor Emanuel Cleaver called "the unfinished symphony" of race relations must do superhuman work to overcome the cunning, baffling and powerful community addiction to racism. Like alcoholism, people will have to destroy the enabling system to change racist behavior.

"That wall of denial will have to be broken," Washington said.

It won't be easy. "It's hard for thoughtful people to do something about it because the fringes of the different groups will tear at them," said Harles E. Cone, a psychologist.

That means that whites will try to prevent each other from confronting racism, and some minorities - especially those who have "made it" - will try to stop the dialogue, too.

The better way is for everyone to start talking, as Cleaver suggested, to develop a multistep RA, or Racism Anonymous, program. Then we can all say that we're recovering - never cured - of our addiction.

CHAPTER 2
Undeniable Discrimination

Where's Rosa Parks?

Where's Rosa Parks?
Have you seen her lately?
We've got trouble again
On America's bus
The 9-11 Pentagon and World Trade blasts
Blew people of color
Back to the past
To the back of the bus
That America rides
Into the future
Noting no black, Latino, Asian or Native strides
Prejudices and stereotypes dominate
In whites' quiet riot
Fueled by Nixon, Reagan, Bakke, the Bushes and O.J.
Inclusiveness now seems far, far away
Equality weakens; opportunity fades
Get to the back of the bus, nigger!
That's where you'll stay.
Has anybody seen Rosa Parks?

We who are clay blended by the Master Potter, come from the kiln of Creation in many hues. How can people say one skin is colored, when each has its own coloration? What should it matter that one bowl is dark and the other pale, if each is of good design and serves its purpose well.

~Polingaysi Qoyawayma

<u>*From "A sad case of hidden identity"*</u>

Rosana L. Bates admitted that she had succumbed to pressure to "white out" her family's race. She got down on her hands and knees to show what she'd hidden under the beds in her daughters' rooms.

Brittany's bed concealed a framed portrait of four black girls reading books and a large framed picture the 11-year-old had drawn of a black Raggedy Ann. The things spirited away in Courtney's room included a porcelain statue of a black girl in a graduation cap and gown, which the 16-year-old treasured.

Those and dozens of other items had to go if Rosana and Ricardo P. Bates wanted to sell their four-bedroom home in south Overland Park, Kansas.

For about two months she had resisted the advice of a visiting real estate agent who said: "You need to depersonalize your house by removing anything that denotes ethnicity. After all, you are in Johnson County."

For months the Bateses refused to hide their heritage when they listed their 5-year-old home after Ricardo Bates got a job in the Detroit area. They held out until just before his wife and girls joined him. Then black pride and identity had to yield to market forces for the former Hallmark Cards executive and Kansas City schoolteacher.

The prospect of two mortgage payments sent the family's heritage underground.

Family pictures were put away. *Essence* magazines got tucked behind white publications. Kwanzaa candles, African-American art and portraits of black leaders were stashed. Books by Bill Cosby and the Rev. Martin Luther King Jr. were hidden. Reginald Lewis' bestseller *Why Should White Guys Have All the Fun?* had to go.

The Bateses erased their African-American existence from the home, hoping to sell the property for $134,950.

"When you go into white homes, everything in it denotes who they are," Rosana Bates said. "Is that the only ethnicity that we accept?"

Unfortunately, it's something black people in one of the nation's wealthiest suburbs often face, said Yvette Morton, chairwoman of the Johnson County Martin Luther King Jr. Holiday Committee. She blames it on an unwritten code.

Johnson County has an image of offering "safety" and "good schools" to middle-class families. To many whites, that doesn't include black people.

"When blacks own a home, it taints a home for whites wanting to own it," Morton said. Fear and stereotypes are other factors. Whites may fear that the stigma of blacks owning a home before them will prevent its sale at a good price.

"If anybody thinks that racism is not ingrained in Johnson County, they've got another thing coming," Morton said. "It's here just like it's everywhere else." Historically the area's deed restrictions unabashedly excluded people of color.

The Bateses felt it when they first moved into the new subdivision. Someone put a "For Sale" sign in their yard, blocked their driveway with large, heavy stone pots, chained up their front door and egged their house.

"What's strange about it is they didn't want to let them in, now they don't want to let them out," said Vhanesse L. Rogers, Rosana Bates' mother.

The house is impeccably kept, well-priced and in a marketable area. It stood empty for months while it was for sale.

"It's really unusual," said Ninette Harrison, the family's real estate agent.

I worry about the Bates' children. The experience has saddened and angered Brittany.

"A white girl can keep out all of her white Barbies, and I can't," she said. "I think it's rude, and it's not fair."

No, Brittany, it's not fair.

The last six words of the Pledge of Allegiance, "with liberty and justice for all," are mocked time and time again by the reality of open discrimination found in many parts of U.S. society today. In this case, "fairness" was absent for the Bates family and others like them trying to sell their homes in mostly white suburban subdivisions.

<u>From "Racism taints some home sales"</u>

The house sold after the Bateses moved out, changed real estate agents and lowered the price.

The buyers and sellers didn't see or talk to each other. A good home exchanged hands. Neither couple knew the race of the other, Rosana Bates said Friday. Peggy McIntosh, noted for defining white privilege, would have called the sale "too slow for justice."

Calls, letters and e-mail I got after I wrote about the Bateses speak of other problems. Some sellers won't negotiate the price of suburban homes with black buyers. Some real estate agents won't put minorities' interests over those of the suburbs that people of color want to integrate.

Many black families also said they were told to white out their homes to sell them. The price they paid was the emotional toll of hiding their ethnicity.

They also suffered economically because their houses took longer to sell. They'd ended up reducing the price below comparable homes to make theirs OK to white buyers.

One e-mailer said he paid the higher suburban property taxes but didn't get the same value from his investment. Black families' net worth is negatively affected. They end up leaving less in inheritance for their kids than white people do. Those are hidden links in the chains of racism.

You must remember, a caller said, real estate remains the foundation of wealth. If black people pay more for property, pay as much in taxes and get less when they sell their homes, they're being held in an economic bondage.

It's a modern-day version of sharecropping, because some hard-earned wealth from black labor is covertly flowing into others' hands.

But many white people who contacted me said they don't see it that way. Some said they simply cried over the racism that's still part of America. Others, however, were vehement in their opposition to my column.

Here's an example:

Voice mail: 1997

You are a racist. You are against white people and every damn thing else like that. All you talk about is what the black people have gotten done to them and every thing else like that. You never say anything.... Even your articles on the schools and everything else like that, they just do not make sense when it comes to white people. You just are an outright racist. I challenge you to that. Thank you.

Crossing the color line to discover the Real America so that discrimination can be obliterated is not easy for anyone but is especially difficult for people like the man who left the voice message. They strongly resist making the journey. Is it any wonder? People of color exist outside of the barriers and razor wire of the well-guarded yet damaging America. Our stereotypes are well ingrained, even as they tend toward opposing poles, with the negative being more prevalent than the positive. Indigenous Peoples, for example, have been seen through "the mythic veil of mingled racism and romance" alternately as "sometimes terrifying and evil . . . less civilized and more barbaric," and "sometimes gentle and good," having an "exotic innocence," writes Cornel Pewewardy ("La Belle Savage"). In his book, *Orientals: Asian Americans in Popular Culture,* Robert G. Lee notes six different perceptions of Asians, ranging from the negative "pollutant" and "deviant" to the praiseworthy "model minority" (8). Linda A. Jackson's 1995 study, "Stereotypes, Emotions, Behavior, and Overall Attitudes Towards Hispanics by Anglos" found that the characteristics which Anglos attributed to Hispanics ranged from "more uneducated . . . dirty/smelly, noisy" and "less productive . . . [or] dependable" to "strong family, tradition-loving, religious, old-fashioned." Jim Myers, in *Afraid of the Dark,* notes the same kind of polarization:

> To many whites, graffiti-ridden walls, abandoned and trashed-out buildings, gaping windows, and rundown houses announce the presence of black people or the idea that "that's how they live." . . . Black neighborhoods are supposed to be more dangerous, too, but many Americans, white and black, somehow manage to imagine that black America is teeming with sound, life, and good times. On occasion, whites can seem a bit jealous. By comparison, white neighborhoods are supposed to be clean and peaceful but maybe too plastic to represent life lived to the fullest. (72-73)

And ne'er the different races shall truly meet. Myers writes that "the images we have of each other's worlds work to keep us apart" (71). So far apart, in fact, that the sting of discrimination is felt up and down the diversity spectrum.

The National Conference for Community and Justice's nationwide survey, "Taking America's Pulse II," showed that [sidelining prejudices is] not happening. The report follows a similar 1993 survey.

From "America's quickening pulse"

> The newer report showed that in just one month, 42 percent of African-Americans experienced at least one episode of discrimination; 12 percent had two or more episodes. Only 8 percent of Asians thought their race had to cope with great deal of discrimination. But 31 percent of Asians individually reported unfair treatment and discrimination.
>
> The survey showed that 16 percent of Hispanics and 13 percent of whites reported at least one occurrence of discrimination in the prior month.
>
> However, the report also showed that people are having more contact now with more diverse groups than in 1993. Interracial and interethnic encounters are up to 82 percent from 67 percent for blacks and 66 percent from 51 percent for Hispanics.
>
> But interracial/interethnic contact for whites hasn't climbed nearly as much. It is 87 percent now compared with 81 percent in 1993. For Asians it is 52 percent compared with 49 percent.
>
> Also, more than a third of the respondents said, "It's OK to have a country where the races are basically separate from one another as long as they have equal opportunity." This attitude exists despite the 1954 Brown vs. Topeka Board of Education ruling by the Supreme Court, which ended legal segregation.

There's no disputing, however, that separate is unequal. To illustrate this, specific examples of the discrimination and prejudice different minorities face as they try to live their lives in the Real America are featured in the rest of this chapter.

Profiling—Retail Racism

From "Paying a price for discrimination"

One infamous case of "shopping while black" involved Dillard's Inc., which operates department stores nationwide. An African-American family, the Hamptons from Overland Park, Kansas, faced discrimination at the Oak Park Mall store and went to court, as they said, to seek justice so that no one's children will have to endure the indignity of consumer racism. There is no greater cause.

The civil rights and legal odyssey began on Good Friday, 1996. Paula Hampton, her niece and four children went to Dillard's to buy a nephew an Easter outfit.

They made the purchase but were falsely accused of shoplifting and denied free cologne samples.

Testimony during the trial showed that Dillard's treated black shoppers as suspects, using "codes" to "track" them in the store. Oscar L. Hampton III, Paula Hampton's husband and the family spokesman, said the lawsuit's bedrock is as old as America: "This case is about segregation, black codes, and Jim Crow and nothing else."

The Hamptons' lawyer, Arthur Benson II, added: "This has moved the Civil Rights Act into the area of retail racism." Civil rights laws had been used mostly in employment and real estate.

The case hinged on whether old and new civil rights laws offer minorities protection from unfair treatment before and after money is exchanged for goods and services. "This case is about whether a commercial enterprise can say to its black shoppers that when you come to our store we can abuse you verbally, embarrass and humiliate you and do all those things because of your race," Oscar Hampton, a lawyer, said.

It's like bus companies in the 1950s allowing blacks to pay to ride but not to sit where they pleased. "This case is about whether we go back to the '40s and '50s," Hampton said.

In 1997 a U.S. District Court jury awarded Paula Hampton more than $1 million in her lawsuit against Dillard's Inc. The all-white jury found that the store had discriminated against Hampton because she is black.

Judge Kathryn Vratil upheld the jury verdict.

Dillard's asked the 10th U.S. Circuit Court of Appeals in Denver to overturn the case. The store's corporate spokesman declined to comment on the lawsuit. At the time, though, he did say that Dillard's had enjoyed good talks with a Kansas City civil rights committee.

Bill Clark, then president of the Urban League of Greater Kansas City, said the talks had yielded no new progress. The committee was appointed to resolve the retailer's treatment of minorities.

The Hamptons also were in limbo. They wouldn't get a cent of the jury award while the case was in appeals.

From "A just reward for injustice"

Oscar Hampton laughed when I asked in 2001 about people's assumptions of the more than $1 million federal court jury award his wife, Paula, had won four years earlier.

People had assumed the couple had been enjoying the money from the judgment in the suit.

Another incorrect assumption the media and many people made was that the Hamptons were black activists. Oscar Hampton said he and his wife were just good parents acting to protect their children from racism.

He said if they were a mother and father going after a drunken driver who had injured their child, they would be viewed as dutiful parents. It's no different with racial profiling because it results in African-Americans suffering humiliation and harm on the street, in stores and in other public places such as train stations and airports.

The Dillard's case had resurfaced in 2001 when the 10th U.S. Court of Appeals affirmed the 1997 award in a 2-1 decision.

Skip Rutherford, a communications consultant for Dillard's, said the company was encouraged by the split decision and had petitioned for a rehearing. It believed no discrimination took place.

The U.S. Supreme Court declined to review a U.S. District Court jury's award of more than $1 million to Hampton in December 1997.

From "Celebration muted in racial profiling decision"

One question remained unanswered after Paula Hampton learned in 2002 that she had finally won a hard fought victory over Dillard's Inc. in her "shopping while black" racial profiling case.

How does one celebrate?

So I asked the Hamptons and their lawyer, Arthur Benson II. They won, but they also showed that racism and discrimination persist then-34 years after the end of the Civil Rights Movement and at that time 48 years after the Supreme Court in Brown vs. Topeka Board of Education outlawed legal segregation.

"The win is good, but you don't celebrate," Oscar Hampton said. "Right now we feel very, very strongly that we made a wonderful contribution to all Americans in securing their civil rights regardless of their race."

Hampton said 90 percent of racial discrimination cases get dismissed. Less than 2 percent end favorably for plaintiffs. "Yet, people perceive it's like hitting the lottery," he said.

The Hamptons also didn't get much public support in the case. "There were people who, quite frankly, felt we were un-American for standing up for our rights," Hampton said.

He said if his family celebrates, it would be because "shopping while black" is less likely to happen today because of the court action.

Benson said: "It's a victory for civil rights laws and their enforcement. I think it's a small victory on the long road to racial equality."

Benson said everyone's faith in the judicial system should be renewed because it redressed "a pretty blatant case of racial discrimination, and it was achieved in Kansas before an all-white jury."

"Society at large may have a reluctance to understand that overt racism exists because they haven't experienced it," Benson said. "But once it's proven to exist, they're outraged.

"The average American wants to believe racist behavior was resolved with the Civil Rights Movement. It is a shock when they see how pervasive racism is in everyday life.

"It's difficult for whites to understand - including me - that even for upper-middle-class blacks, racist behavior by whites is something they experience all the time, often in small, subtle ways but also in not so subtle ways."

Such discriminatory behavior is costly to people of color who must endure the suspicion, the shakedowns, the humiliation and poor treatment. Companies pay, too, in lost business and sizable judgments. All consumers pick up the tab of society's racism in higher prices.

"You can't celebrate the fact that racism continues and that this brought that to light," Benson said. "We'd rather celebrate the end of it."

Hampton said maybe the court fight would help end the racial profiling their son and other minorities might face.

Authorities should stop people who break the law but never those whose skin color is all that's behind their being detained and treated as suspects.

As reasonable and as constitutionally American as that is, people weren't buying it. The only obstacle was the color of the victim's skin. What follows are examples of the feedback those columns generated:

Letter: Dec. 23, 1998

When in Rome, do as the Romans do. If you don't want to do as the Romans do then don't go to Rome. Don't try to make the Romans do as you like to do. Just don't go where you don't feel comfortable.

I once went to Gates barbecue and didn't get a free sample of barbecue sauce. Should I sue Ollie cause he discriminated against me or should I just not go back? What to do, what to do? Oh, the agony it is causing my family. It won't ever be the same....

Voice Mail: May 9, 2001

I was reading your article on Wednesday, May 9, I am a fellow who was in the retail business for over 25 years. I'm no longer in it. But I have to tell you that over 75-80 percent of all the shoplifting that went on in my retail business was done by blacks. And it's only normal and proper as a businessman when the blacks walked in, we watched them. We didn't accuse them. We didn't hassle them. We watched them. 'Cause it's my livelihood. It's my bread and butter. I don't care what you say, that's the way it is.

E-mail: March 1, 2002

Thank you for your columns, though I don't have much sympathy for the Hamptons in this particular matter, you do a great job of reminding us of the inequities and injustices that exist in this world.

Fortunately, not all whites turn a blind eye to racism when they witness such profiling. Some are brave enough to intervene on behalf of those discriminated against.

From "A just reward for injustice"

The Hamptons aren't alone in taking action against racial profiling. Vickie L. Riddle sent me an e-mail in March of 2001 expressing outrage over the racial profiling she witnessed and tried to stop at another Johnson County department store.

A clerk was helping her when another white store employee said in a normal voice so everyone in the area could hear: "Look up, over there, those black women ... you've got to watch them. They're going to steal those things .... You've got to watch them."

"I just couldn't be still," said Riddle, who's white. She told the clerks it was wrong and illegal to target people for suspicion because of their race. The offending store clerk argued that what she said was irrefutable.

Riddle went to the assistant store manager and then the manager. She only got a "lack of emotion or concern" from the assistant manager, and the manager responded as if he were "bored, indifferent and put out at my concern."

"My first concern was that their sales staff openly makes racist statements and, secondly, that the management staff showed no concern, no outrage over that fact," Riddle said. "They were absolutely unabashed in their belief that nothing wrong had happened."

Riddle wrote to me again just days before the decision against Dillard's.

She said a parent company official of the store she had visited contacted her and was "very concerned" about the situation that had outraged her. The problem prompted the company to immediately start diversity training for all employees at the Johnson County store.

The parent company official said the store manager failed "to understand how very serious this situation was."

"She was very contrite and said that they wanted me to be comfortable with the way the situation was handled at the management level," Riddle said.

I called Riddle a change-agent and one of my heroes. Riddle's actions exemplify the conviction expressed in the winning entry of the Midwest Center for Holocaust Education's White Rose Student Essay Contest, which I helped judge.

Daniel Sommerhauser, then a junior at Archbishop O'Hara High School, wrote: "Elie Wiesel, Nobel Peace Prize winner and survivor of a Nazi concentration camp, once said: 'Take sides. Neutrality helps the oppressor, never the victim. Silence encourages the tormentor, never the tormented.'"

Racism is always personal, even if others don't get it.

Voice Mail: 2001

I know where you are. You're over at a department store. Shoplifting. Well, affirmative action will continue, Lewis, because black people are muggers and robbers and stealers and murderers and rapists. So you'd better get used to it.

Profiling—The Discrimination Highway

From "Laws address discrimination, but biases must change first"

The Kansas Highway Patrol car zoomed out of nowhere and directed me to pull my van over.

No way was I speeding. The cruise control was set at the Interstate 35 speed limit on my trip from Kansas City to Emporia State University in Emporia, Kansas, to speak to the students and faculty about diversity. My lights were on, and my van was in tiptop working order.

The young trooper approached with his hand on his firearm. That was reassuring. "I'm stopping you for failure to yield to me," he said.

He had been parked on the shoulder of I-35 about three miles back. Normally I give anyone there a lot of room. But passing cars made that impossible.

I thought I'd get a warning. Instead I got nailed with a $240 ticket. An Emporia State University professor, who wondered why I was delayed, immediately said "driving while black" when I told her what had happened.

Since then I have watched dozens of white motorists fail to yield to officers in Missouri and Kansas with no one blocking the passing lane. None was chased by officers or pulled over.

When I got nailed, a racial profiling bill was pending in the Kansas Legislature, prohibiting law enforcement officers from stopping motorists only because of race or ethnicity. It's the law now.

Kansas Sen. David Haley, who introduced the bill, said at an "Understanding Racial Profiling" forum at Kansas City Kansas Community College that "the law was necessary to show that we value the diversity of our state." He added that motorists should not be "encumbered due to their race, county of origin or religion or mode of dress."

Missouri has had a law against racial profiling since 2000. The Kansas law requires data collection just as Missouri does so people can see whether there is a problem. In Missouri and other states that generate statistics, there is no doubt.

Missouri Attorney General Jay Nixon's 2004 racial profiling report released in May showed that black and Hispanic drivers were stopped at a disproportionately higher rate than their percentage in the population.

African-Americans were 38 percent more likely to be stopped than whites, and those who were stopped were 71 percent more likely to be searched than white drivers who were stopped. Hispanics were stopped at a rate about 7 percent more than their share of the population. They were nearly twice as likely to be searched as white drivers.

But on average, searches of African-Americans and Hispanics turned up contraband at a rate less than whites. Nixon, at a meeting with the Editorial Board of *The Kansas City Star*, said racial profiling remains a problem in the state and the nation.

But Missouri's fifth racial-profiling report also dispelled the myth that the law would "cause depolicing," Nixon said. Officers remain just as vigilant, but racial profiling has not gone away.

Haley knows that, too. "We're not free in an open society to move about, to drive about as we would like," he said.

At the forum, Danielle Dempsey-Swopes, executive director of the Kansas African-American Affairs Commission, said it was important for the state to tackle the problem.

"There is a lot of mistrust between law enforcement and our community," she said.

Then-Kansas City, Kan., Police Chief Ron Miller agreed that such feelings get in the way of citizens and police officers working well together to solve and prevent crimes. But he added that officers need to go further and erase biases in their minds against minorities, older people, younger people and women.

Wyandotte County Sheriff LeRoy Green Jr. said racial profiling "is happening all over, and we're trying to stop that."

"Right now the trust out there is a little shaky," he said. "We need to earn that trust back."

It didn't help, Green said, that he once had officers in his department who said they focused on stopping Cadillac drivers.

"Those individuals were terminated," said Green, who was a sergeant at that time. "I will not tolerate that."

Josephine Boone said she was pleased that the state was taking the issue seriously.

"A lot of things happen, and people don't know that it's happening to people of color," she said. "I hope the law will make more people aware of people's feelings and try to do right by everybody."

From "Pulled over unfairly"

What's clear is racial profiling is a toxin in America's stream of social consciousness. It shows people too often fear, devalue or treat minorities as suspects.

It causes whites as a group to advance while minorities get pulled over. Nixon wants law enforcement to recognize and eliminate the problem. Diversity training could help.

But everyone should worry that a way for police to achieve a racial balance is to stop and search more whites just because of the color of their skin. Knowing how that feels, I'd never want that to happen.

Many reactions I received denied there was any profiling going on:

E-mail: June 20, 2001

I disagree that blacks are pulled over unfairly. True, it is not fair that Hispanics are searched more. But it is often hard for police to be able to tell what race they are pulling over. I seriously doubt most could distinguish color if they came up behind a car. You say that treatment needs to be more equal, but if I was a police officer, I myself would search a black more often. Statistics show that African Americans commit much more violent crime than any other nationality in America. If racial balance needs to be established, maybe blacks should not distinguish themselves from whites in the form of African American clubs, radio stations, scholarships, etc.

Katheryn K. Russell notes in her book *The Color of Crime* that studies show that race does indeed matter when police engage the public.

> Police themselves have acknowledged that they practice racial targeting.... A variety of studies examine the prevalence of police/Black citizen encounters. In a 1994 study that looked at whether Blacks are more likely to be harassed by the police or to know someone who has been, researchers found a 'significant association' between being Black and being harassed by the police. Almost half the Blacks interviewed had experienced harassment, while only 10 percent of the Whites had. (37-38)

Russell says police use an "'out-of-place' doctrine" to justify legally "stopping and questioning Blacks at a disproportionate rate... The doctrine encourages police to view Black men as *de facto* guilty, without reference to legal indicators of criminal activity (e.g., reckless driving, speeding, making a drug sale)" (38).

In 2006 the Missouri Attorney General's office released its latest report on racial profiling of motorists statewide. The numbers continued to head in the wrong direction. Black motorists in Missouri "were 46 percent more likely to be stopped than either white or Hispanic drivers in 2005." Not only that, but "the disparity has widened since 2004, when blacks were 38 percent more likely than whites to be stopped." In addition, blacks who were stopped "were 78 percent more likely to be searched than whites—up from 71 percent in 2004." A confounding finding of the report was "contraband was found on black drivers at a lower rate—18.6 percent of searches compared with 23.6 [percent] of searches for whites" (Lieb).

Young People

Young people of color face a torrent of racism's fury. Such racial profiling extends beyond the reach of law enforcement and traffic stops and intrudes into life. It impedes their progress.

<u>From "American Indians face taunts"</u>

> Rod Steiner recalled the racism he encountered in the 1940s when he competed as a boxer.
>
> The epithets and taunts directed at the American Indian sear his memory.
>
> But it's even worse now - six decades later - because it's still happening. It's happening to young American Indians who compete in sports. Steiner, of Kansas City, Kan., keeps a copy of a *Corpus Christi Caller-Times* sports article from early 2002 when he was in Texas.
>
> The story was on racial slurs directed at college basketball star Chuck Archambault. Archambault is an American Indian.
>
> "Two generations have passed, and we're still getting stuff like this," said Steiner, a 71-year-old Santee Sioux. Like Archambault, Steiner was raised on a reservation; his is in Nebraska. Steiner said he was upset that the story didn't make national news. It was as if no one cared.
>
> Archambault is a 6-foot-2-inch shooting guard with the Texas A&M University Islanders. A Sioux, he wears a ponytail, grew up on a reservation in South Dakota and is the team's only American Indian.
>
> The racial epithets he encountered happened at a game the Islanders played in Nashville, Tenn., against the Lipscomb University Bisons. Archambault, a junior, told the *Caller-Times* newspaper that people yelled for him to go back to the reservation.

They shouted, "Where's your teepee?" and called him "Sitting Bull."

Archambault said the slurs were more intense than he had ever experienced.

Steiner recalled other incidents of racism directed at American Indians.

"Most of them say, 'So what? That's the way it's always been,'" Steiner said. "Where's the outrage?"

Racism still keeps young people of color from succeeding. That has to end.

Minorities have suffered more racial harassment since the Sept. 11, 2001, terrorist attacks. Too many white people's image of who's American now doesn't include American Indians or other minorities.

Racism damages people's spirit, Steiner said. He remembers how hatred drove many youths with great potential back to reservations.

Cornel Pewewardy, then-assistant professor in the School of Education at the University of Kansas, said people must understand the damage done by racism. It certainly has hurt young American Indians' self-esteem and impaired their academic and social performance.

Pewewardy, a Comanche and Kiowa, said he endured racial taunts when he played basketball in Oklahoma. Students at Haskell Indian Nations University in Lawrence, Kansas, still face that problem.

Pewewardy said his family helped him overcome the racism he encountered. But he worries about young American Indians today who may not have such support.

That's why he keeps working to get schools and professional teams to stop using American Indian names and related items as mascots. People may think they're honoring American Indians in this way, but they couldn't be more disrespectful.

Justin P. Orr, then-executive director of the Heart of America Indian Center Inc., said he used racist incidents at area schools as teachable moments.

"We do not show anger," said Orr, a Cowlitz. "We seize upon this as a chance to demonstrate, educate and show our culture."

Indian center officials go to all-school assemblies to dispel students' myths about American Indians.

Students of color who encounter racism as Archambault did also need to use these experiences as a catalyst for success.

Archambault scored 19 points, a career high, during the game in which he was called every name imaginable.

That makes him a superstar in my book.

Cornel Pewewardy notes that "the use of a suppressive language by society at large . . . has perpetuated the dehumanization of Indigenous

Peoples" ("La Belle Sauvage"). Jim Myers in his book *Afraid of the Dark* further explains that fear drives the arrogance in such behavior and language use.

From "Young people face harsh realities"

Turning 18 years old and getting to vote in 2006 had stood out as the biggest things in Jumoke Balogun's life.

But Balogun faced another major event. It occurred at a McDonald's restaurant in Cass County, Missouri. On Dec. 28 she and a friend went to McDonald's about 7 p.m. after shopping at a Target store. Her friend ordered a salad, and Balogun got a McChicken, fries and an apple pie.

A special at the restaurant ensured that she'd get two apple pies. The clerk behind the counter got her friend's order right, but she failed to give Balogun the second apple pie.

Balogun pointed that out to the clerk, who was white and in her late 30s. The woman disputed her claim. Balogun produced the receipt. The clerk got the other apple pie, "slammed it on the counter and slid it toward me."

"She said, 'Merry Christmas,'" Balogun said. Other people were waiting in line, and Balogun was the only African-American in the place. "I was very embarrassed.

"I was kind of mad after that, but I wasn't as mad as I was hurt," Balogun said. She and her friend talked, but her friend didn't understand what had just happened.

"I thought it was racially motivated," said Balogun. "She thought the lady was rude and overworked."

Balogun's friend said that if Balogun felt uncomfortable they should leave and eat their dinner in the car. "I wanted to cry," Balogun said.

"We were getting our food to leave," she said. "I didn't want to eat there at all. As we were leaving I heard a guy say the N-word.

"I know it was directed toward me. I looked down. I felt very, very bad.

"I didn't want the food anymore. We just left. I just wanted to get out of there as soon as possible. I was very, very uncomfortable.

"I felt really scared. I felt very small and alone. I still feel angry. That really never happened to me before."

She said she had never been followed in a shopping center because of racial profiling and never felt discriminated against. Only one other time when she was in fourth grade had a boy, who was white, used the N-word toward her, and that was at George Washington Carver Elementary School, Kansas City, Mo.

Balogun, who was a high school friend of my daughter's, shared her story at the All Souls Unitarian Universalist Church program on

"Dr. Martin L. King Jr.'s Legacy: Visions from a New Generation."

It's important to know Balogun's impressions because what she endured says a lot about this area's ongoing problems with race. I worry about millennials like her. They are African-Americans who are my children's age.

Many grow up now unschooled by Jim Crow. The best of America's bigotry was good at teaching preschool to college lessons in racism and discrimination to my generation and those before me.

The actions and words were undeniably clear. But our parents and other African-Americans worked diligently to steel us to take the onslaught and succeed despite it.

Many millennials have been spared both the brutality of racism at an early age as well as the black community's programming, deprogramming and reprogramming methods to help them cope.

Balogun, a student at the University of Missouri-Kansas City, and her high school friend unfortunately got a harsh lesson served with what were supposed to be happy meals.

She told the panel that much work needs to be done to make King's dream of equality and opportunity for African-Americans a reality. She said progress has been made, "but we're going back in time.

"Our rights are slowly being taken away from us," Balogun said. "We are on the wrong path.

"We have to get out there and not only protest but work toward change."

She said in an interview that it's not good that some people in their own country can't feel comfortable going out to eat with their friends just because they are African-American. "It was blatant racism," Balogun said.

Equally distressing was that her friend couldn't identify with what she had to endure. "It is a big, big, big, big problem," Balogun said.

I am glad she is aware of what she went through. Knowing that racism hasn't gone away is the first step needed toward vanquishing it once and for all.

Chapter 1 discussed the fact that any mention of episodes of racism makes people so uncomfortable that they deny the racism and blame the messenger and the victim because racism is no longer supposed to exist in their America. Such discomfort also leads people to make excuses that "explain" why racism was not a factor, as the following e-mail (and others like it) illustrates:

E-mail: Feb. 3, 2006

If Ms. Balogun thinks every time a fast food worker gets an order wrong is "racism", then I too, a white male in his 40s, have experienced racism a thousand times over. Come on, that is like blaming a red light for turning red on you because it is racist. (But it let all the white folks go on green, so it must be racism). Some times people are just mean and nasty, irregardless of your color.

By dumbing down racism, you are slowly watering down the true dangers of real racism. Ms. Balogun and others who think such acts are racist, will continue to hunt for "racism" in everything while missing the real reason for a person's actions. For example, if she doesn't get a job, must be racism. Doesn't get the mail on time, must be racism. Doesn't get the grades she wants, must be racism. Maybe, just maybe, it has nothing to do with racism but more to do with Ms. Balogun. In other words, if I fail, it is never my fault, it is racism.

To me the very nature of your article shows how little true racism there is in this area. If you have to attribute "racism" to who screwed up an order.....well, then we are much closer to Martin Luther King's dream than you realize.

Voice mail: Feb. 3, 2006

Whaaa! Whaaa! It's so sad to imagine an employee at McDonald's being rude to somebody. Oh and it's because they're black. You know I eat at McDonald's three to four times a week. They've all got bad service. But I don't sit there and whine and say oh they treated me bad because I'm white. I mean Jesus, man, that's all you niggers do is whine. Everything is because you're black. We're out of toilet paper. Oh, it's because I'm black. Speaking of that, why is toilet paper white? Why the hell can't we have black toilet paper in honor of Black History Month? Cause it's all shit.

Loud and Unmitigated Hatred

We find in this country, because of its past, that racism never rests. It is insistent and ruthlessly persistent. Such a dislike for others isn't limited to the color of one's skin. Homophobia, for example, roared to the surface and threatened to shut down a conference on white privilege that I helped facilitate at Johnson County Community College with Peggy McIntosh, associate director of the Center for Research on Women at Wellesley College. A woman in attendance was OK with diversity including women and people of color. But she balked loudly when confronted with sexual orientation also showing up under that big tent. Before she stormed out of the program, she condemned homosexuals as sinners, wielding her Bible and referring to a passage where gays are declared an abomination in the eyes of God. Others demonstrate their equally unwavering conviction and vehement intolerance in other public places.

From "Battling the cycle of hatred"

The "D" in "DIE" held its ground against 5,000 pounds per square inch of water pressure.

Hatred never yields easily. Any other day, rain-soaked and sun-baked Jerry Young and Bradford Williams would have been repairing bridges or roads for the Missouri Highway and Transportation Department.

But not this day. They had the dirty duty of removing gay epithets from a concrete barrier under a viaduct at eastbound Interstate 435 and southbound U.S. 71.

What a way to begin the first week of "Celebrate Community Diversity Month." They also had to blast a racial slur that an equal opportunity bigot painted under the Grandview Road viaduct on eastbound I-435.

Young, the crew leader, pointed to deep deer tracks made in the gray mud that gripped our shoes. He shouted about his find so I could hear him over the rain that slapped against the pavement and the whining vehicles that rushed anonymously by.

The hoof prints were the only evidence of beauty Young could find. Williams worked hard on the first, two-word gay epithet. The second, which started with "GOD" and "HATES," waited.

It was ugly work on a bad day, and unfortunately water blasting did not prevent passing motorists from seeing the slurs.

Young and Williams left and returned in their big yellow truck with paint and rollers. They simply whited out the obscenities, which had been up for at least two weeks.

Both said they thought a young vandal, too dense to accept equality, had written the filth.

"I call them love-to-hate groups," Young said. "The kid who wrote this probably should have been in school learning something."

Martin Hiraga sees such vandalism as part bad and part good. Headlines about gays and the need for Americans to embrace diverse cultures make minority groups targets for violence, said Hiraga, the director of the Anti-Violence Project with the National Gay and Lesbian Task Force in Washington, D.C.

But the push for civil rights also drives the issues out of the closet and forges bridges and positive accomplishments, he said. In an odd way the graffiti bring equality-minded folks together who realize after seeing billboard-sized gay and racial epithets that hatred remains a powerful enemy.

Hiraga, however, worries more about violence against gays, which has increased steadily nationwide since 1982, when the task force started keeping records.

The Rev. Jan Kross, minister of congregational care at the Metropolitan Community Church in Midtown, which has outreach to gays and lesbians, said gay bashing is increasing in Greater Kansas City, too. It's part of a cycle.

"When people feel threatened they strike out at the targets that they think are vulnerable," Kross said.

Donna Almai, then president of Harmony in Hickman Mills, said people who commit such acts really are saying they hate themselves.

"I do think it has to do with a person's self-esteem," said Almai, who took before- and after-pictures of the I-435 sites. "They're looking for a weaker group to take their hate out on. But I can't let them vent that hate on people I love."

Justifying that hatred in God's name is another act of a desperate person, said Carol Spring, then executive director of the National Conference of Christians & Jews.

What matters now is learning from the experience and growing more committed to taking action against it instead of just driving by and hoping someone else does the right thing to get it erased.

Jews, just as people of color do, feel the searing burn of overt racism, too.

From "Bigotry raises its ugly head"

A cigarette dripped from Robert Neff's hand in the blue crystal cold of the morning air.

The big man in work clothes had just finished a nasty job of covering someone's foul leavings, and he needed a smoke. The wet red paint on his brush closely matched the rust color of the building at 3000 Gillham Road, but the ugly stain of the white lettering it hid will be hard to erase from his mind.

Those words screamed anti-Semitic hatred from the north and south sides of the building to passing traffic. Of all days, I saw it on Thanksgiving.

Neff, the owner of Neff Management Co., said it wasn't there the day before. He painted over it on the first day of Hanukkah.

"We've had graffiti sprayed on things but never nothing racist like this," he said as a cleansing snow fell. "It's a heck of a thing to do on Thanksgiving, or any day, but I think that even compounds it."

Unfortunately, such graffiti is a sign of the times.

As a recession like that of 1991 squeezes the nation, separating people from jobs and factories from communities, hatred tightens its choke hold on ethnic and race relations. The David Dukes of the world spring from their sheets, and harmony gets mugged.

The writing on the Union Hill building was just one incident. Another erupted like a fiery blister at Missouri 291 and Interstate 70.

An 8-foot-tall swastika was set afire on a bluff overlooking traffic in Independence.

I. Robert Wolfson, regional director of the Anti-Defamation League, said data would be compiled in January. But from fielding reports, he says such public displays of hatred have increased over the last year as the recession drags on. Kansas City is simply a microcosm of the world, where love and understanding have taken a beating from bigotry.

"We as human beings tend to scapegoat - look for someone to blame for our problems," Wolfson said. "During hard times they tend to blame minorities.

"Unfortunately it happens to be an age-old human problem. We haven't quite figured out how to inoculate ourselves against this."

Wolfson called anonymous, anti-Semitic and racist acts "a quiet terrorism" in which the aggressor instills fear and discomfort in the community.

In Kansas City, the National Conference of Christians and Jews is combating the sludge with a year-old crusade. The organization periodically has public service billboards featuring a black boy hugging a white boy and both kids are smiling.

Underneath are the words: NOBODY'S BORN A BIGOT. And if you get even closer as I did when the sign was up at Blue Ridge Boulevard and Wornall Road you'll see the small print: Learning To Live Together: The Unfinished Task.

These troubled times make the billboards more necessary, said Carol V. Spring, then executive director of the Christians and Jews conference in Kansas City.

"I don't think people enjoy hating," she said. "It's a human response to people who have been hurt to hurt others."

People instead need good feelings reinforced.

"Not everybody is a David Duke," Spring said. "We're focusing on him as an inappropriate thing, a bad thing, a scary thing.

"A lot of people don't want to see a separation of the races."

We've come too far to turn back now.

Some of the children I got to know at the Islamic School were in college or working when the Sept. 11, 2001, attack hit. They felt the effects as adults. Many still do.

From "Intolerance scars Muslims in U.S."

On Sunday the cutest little girls dressed in costumes of many Muslim countries and shared sweet details of those nations at the 2004 Eid Celebration Dinner of the Crescent Peace Society.

It was clear from seeing them that kids of all faiths need to grow up in a peaceful world to have a productive future. But they're hurt by violence that adults create.

Muslim students discussed that at an "Exploring Islam" forum at Maple Woods Community College in Kansas City. Jessica Dumas, who teaches sociology and is a member of the Maple Woods Global Education Committee, said people need to know how world events affect Muslims at home.

Three students, Neda, Ashty and Hamad, said in our post-Sept. 11, 2001, world they've been scarred by others' bigotry. People equate Muslims with terrorism.

"Some people don't understand," said Neda, who is Palestinian, wears a head scarf, or hijab, and is studying to be a nurse. "I want to make them understand."

Hamad said that after the terrorist attacks, four men jumped and beat him in the small town where his mother grew up and where he had lived with his parents. His jaw was broken in four places.

Hamad also described how he and his father, who is from Libya, must arrive four hours before flights to pass security screenings made more intense for Muslims in America since Sept. 11.

Hamad, who's studying to be a physician, told of police handcuffing him after an automobile accident and threatening to deport him even though he's an American citizen.

He said his brother had to be taken to the hospital after a police officer at his high school kneed him in the back. Complaints the family raised were dropped when the police turned on them.

Hamad's experiences mirror the trauma other Muslims have faced in America. The Council on American-Islamic Relations reported that in 2003 Muslims filed 1,019 claims citing physical and verbal attacks, on-the-job discrimination and racial profiling by law enforcement. In 2002 the group received 602 complaints.

The jump was partly because of an increase in the number of regional offices that the Washington-based group has opened but also because Muslims have endured continuing physical, verbal and emotional assaults since the 2001 tragedy. The Patriot Act and other government attacks on civil liberties turn Muslims into targets, adding to their distress.

That also came up Sunday at the Eid dinner at the University of Missouri-Kansas City. One Muslim couple and their adult children confided their plans to leave the United States. What's tragic is that the couple came to America to give their kids a better, safer life.

Ashty, who is from Kurdistan and is studying to be a psychologist, explained how she accompanied her mother to an area hospital so her mother could be treated for an illness. But bigoted behavior by health-care professionals caused them to leave without getting the attention they sought.

"I won't ever forget it," Ashty said. "People aren't supposed to be that way."

The students said they have felt the pain and trauma of the Sept. 11, 2001, tragedy more than most people in this country because it's hitting them as Americans and as Muslims. Ashty said she has never seen her father so saddened.

"People are not supposed to hurt each other," she said. "I just hope nothing like that happens again."

The Muslim students said other young people give them hope that the racism, discrimination and bigotry they face can be overcome. Neda and Ashty said they depend on "a domino effect," believing more people will see the good in them and not think of Muslims as terrorists.

Neda also talked of the death of Palestinian leader Yasser Arafat and how it creates a new hope for peace between the Jews and Palestinians. She wants the occupation to end and for people of all faiths to live in peace.

"We have Sept. 11 in my country every day," Neda said. "It's God's land. I don't know why people would fight over God's land."

Individually the students said they try to show people that their faith has been hijacked by extremists. It's not right or accurate to equate Muslims with terrorists.

"My religion taught me to be nice to everyone," Neda said. Ashty and Hamad agreed.

The future has to offer great hope for children like those at the Eid dinner and students at Maple Woods. That's ensured only if everyone embraces all peace and diversity ideals and truly believes.

Pointing out how Muslims are being hounded these days is not the popular thing to do in the press. The feedback is always powerfully negative. What follows is an example:

Voice mail: Dec. 9, 2004

Lewis, this thing you wrote yesterday "Intolerance scars Muslims in U.S.," they deserve scarring, Lewis. We don't know how many sleeper cells are in this country. We don't know where they are living. You can have them living right next to you and they'll be there for 10 years. They don't step forward and tell what their people are doing. And here we have this organization right down here at Columbia, Mo. I can't understand where you are coming from in this article. These people deserve watching and watching closely. They can cry their eyes out, but that's too damn bad. These people that are in public office in

> this country have taken an oath to protect the citizens of this country. And being that this Muslim religion is like it is that they want their government ruling them through their religion that's what they want. They want the government, Muslim government, ruling them. Boy, this is a stinking rotten article, Lewis. Try again someday. I don't know. I'm wondering where you are if you aren't one of them. Thank you.

Racism as well as the ghosts of white supremacy continue to stalk this nation, and they result either in direct humiliation, injury, or death to people or we find ourselves indirectly affected. None of it is good, and all of it must end if we are to make progress and collectively prosper.

From "We must expose all racism"

> A police officer sent me a sad, disturbing e-mail about the racism he recently encountered.
>
> It involved a hate crime that he had investigated.
>
> "It never made the TV news or the papers," wrote the officer, who asked that his name not be used. "And although it did not involve a burning cross, it was the equivalent to Asian-Americans, in my opinion."
>
> An Asian-American man's car had been vandalized in a parking lot. "Raw eggs were thrown onto the front hood, and the front left fender bore the words 'Chink Go Home' printed in indelible marker ink," the officer wrote.
>
> "The victim stated he tried in vain to rub off the ink," the officer said. "He repeatedly asked why someone would do this, and how he was supposed to explain this to his family?
>
> "I did not have an answer for him."
>
> Neither did I. Yet I often get e-mail from whites who criticize African-Americans for railing against racism. Then my e-mailers point to Asian-Americans as the minority living the American dream with no complaints.
>
> The officer's e-mail revealed that Asian-Americans' experiences in their homeland aren't dissimilar from those of people who look like me. At a Unity convention of journalists of color in Seattle, I heard then-Vice President Al Gore say that shootings and killings in Illinois and Indiana showed that Asian-Americans were the targets of the most violent racism, too.
>
> "The local public rarely hears of hate crimes against Asians, and the Asian community often does not make waves," said the officer, who also is Asian-American. "Instead, we are portrayed as government spies, stealing precious nuclear secrets." (And in the case of Wen Ho Lee, that turned out to not be true and resulted in a large settlement to him from media organizations.)
>
> Such racism hurts Asian-Americans as much as other slurs injure people like me.

"I was appalled and dejected, embarrassed and angry," the officer said of confronting the Johnson County hate crime. "It stirred haunting memories of racial discrimination I endured while growing up in Oklahoma during the '60s and '70s.

"I tell my friends I fought Vietnam from Oklahoma. It did not matter that I am Chinese. My crime was just being Asian."

Yet the officer is patriotic.

"I was the All-American, baseball, hotdogs, apple pie, boy next door," he wrote. "Unfortunately, I did not look like 'him.'"

I sent my phone number by e-mail to the officer. He called and we talked. We also got to meet last week at a forum on race sponsored by *The Kansas City Star* and *The Kansas City Call.*

"There is no Asian Ad Hoc Group Against Crime," he said. "There is no spokesperson per se. There's no Alvin Brooks," a champion of African-American causes.

"There's a keep your head down. Go about your business. Suffer in silence."

Asian-Americans don't see themselves in the media, and their history goes untold. Like other minorities, they feel marginalized and invisible.

Racism, the officer said, isn't just a black, white, Hispanic and American Indian problem. It affects Asian-Americans, too. As their numbers grow, so could the bigotry they'll face unless the prejudice is exposed.

"I guess I was shocked that we still have to deal with the same old issues I dealt with in the '60s and '70s," the officer said. "It's disheartening."

Yesteryear's Civil Rights Movement has largely dissolved. Conservatism and commercialism now rule.

Some people think nothing of trampling minorities' rights.

And the beat goes on and on and on.

From "Racism is no longer undercover"

But the most frightening sign of our weird times was the slaying of James Byrd Jr. in Jasper, Texas.

Byrd, 49, was chained to the back of a pickup truck and dragged to his death June 7, 1998. It was a motorized lynching.

His murder occurred as President Clinton ended a year of trying to focus our attention on improving race relations. Clinton didn't try hard enough.

Each high point in the push for justice and equality always seems to have been followed by powerful explosions of lows.

Other incidents have been huge in racism's resurrection. An

internal memo from a national advertising firm in New York advised clients against placing too many ads on black and Hispanic radio stations.

The New York Daily News reported that the Katz Media Group memo explained that urban stations deliver listeners, but "advertisers should want prospects, not suspects."

That's part of an escalation of "consumer racism." Some stores now feel quite comfortable instructing guards and clerks to openly discriminate against people of color.

In Rushville, Mo., Dennis C. Pospisil was one of four men convicted for burning a cross in August 1997 on the lawn of a woman who they thought was dating a black man.

Pospisil got the longest prison sentence: 12 years. He told the judge he had gotten drunk and just expressed himself.

Excuse me, but there is no "Klan in a Can" beer. His hate is part of a rising national ailment.

It adds to the national rash of black churches being burned and several states entertaining proposals to join California in abolishing affirmative action. No, racism isn't nearly as covert in America as it used to be.

From: "New craters are blasted every day"

It has stepped from the shadows and into everyone's face.

And public displays of ignorance (or PDIs) unfortunately are everywhere.

I've encountered them at airports, where gift shops in the mid-1990s displayed big racks of *The Bell Curve*. That wrongheaded book erroneously said whites have higher IQs than black people do.

I also felt a PDI pelting in 1995 at Arlington National Cemetery on a family vacation to Washington. I was admiring heavyweight champion Joe Louis' grave site when a guy in a group of white people pointed at Louis' headstone and loudly said, "What's he doing here?"

It seemed inconceivable to him that Louis had enlisted in the Army in 1942. Louis lifted black America with his fists, holding the heavyweight title from 1937 to 1949. Also, many whites still don't realize that African-Americans fought for freedom abroad in World War II.

Jim Myers writes in *Afraid of the Dark*: "Whites still have difficulty treating black people as a normal part of the everyday scene. Whites are surprised when they encounter black people at the theater, opera, or symphony; or even on the ski slopes; or any other place where whites normally expect to be alone among other whites. And

> it shows. Some aspect of white demeanor—a gaping mouth or wide eyes—seems to ask, 'What are they doing here?'"
>
> A PDI also hit me during a daddy-daughter outing to go see the movie "Deep Impact" in 1998.
>
> A real-life jolt hit when Morgan Freeman, who starred as president of the United States, was talking in a live TV broadcast to the American people about the comet and a heroic space mission sent to destroy it.
>
> I was thrilled that Hollywood had cast the black actor as president. The disruptive theater-goers apparently weren't. Freeman's serious speech provoked a group of white males to laugh out loud.
>
> I disregarded it the first time, thinking they'd simply found the plot implausible. But the laughter erupted each time Freeman talked in the movie about the national emergency.
>
> These rude guys didn't laugh at anything else - only at Freeman as president. What seemed courageous and uplifting to me was ludicrous to them.
>
> This, after all, is America, where racism frequently crashes and burns its way into our lives.

There were some reactions, however, that did not share my viewpoint:

> Voice Mail: 1998
>
> Well Lewis, you've done it again. Only you could go to "Deep Impact" and make a racist situation out of white people laughing at something a black actor has to say. So I can only assume now that when we go to movies when black people laugh at something that white actors have to say that also is racist. We obviously won't get a column on that. I think you're pathetic. I think you are a total embarrassment to the paper and your race. Keep up the racism, pal.
>
> Voice Mail: 1998
>
> I think you need to relax a little bit. I just read your article in Saturday's paper. And I didn't even know that Joe Louis had fought in the war. Probably the man just assumed he was a fighter, and what was he doing in a military grave. I don't think it had anything to do with him being black. That would be my opinion. But you probably think I'm wrong. Relax, Lewis.

Notwithstanding such constant and vehement denials of discrimination, people of color continue to feel its sting. In 1992, on the eve of the 500th anniversary of the voyage of Christopher Columbus to the Americas, the tomahawk chop was being used by tens of thousands of fans at Kansas City Chiefs football games and other games around the country. It's just one of the things that are denigrating everything that American Indians hold sacred.

From "It's time to abolish the chop"

It's racism, blazing like a burning 20-foot Ku Klux Klan cross in a wind-whipped night sky. But few people in the majority culture recognize it.

That's because we grew up playing cowboys and Indians, conditioned to think that the Indians were always the bad guys. We watched Westerns on television and studied similarly biased history in school.

Now it's time to grow up.

American Indians want to help because they don't want their children to encounter the painful prejudice that they've had to live with. That's why they're protesting the chop, the chant and the name of our professional football team.

In a way, it's a continuation of 500 years of war. Many of the 2 million American Indians in the United States and 6,000 in the metropolitan area are fighting to regain their dignity, honor and respect.

Katrina M. Coker, a member of the Creek Nation, said it's American Indians' way to try to educate us to stop hurting them.

"People come up to me all the time and say, 'I'm really sorry about what my ancestors did,'" Coker said. "I say, 'What about what's going on right now?'"

Her voice rises as she recounts the centuries of murder, genocide, enslavement, poverty, unemployment, alcoholism and other problems facing American Indians.

Having sports teams' names mock or demean Indians is like having restaurants named Sambo's, said Michael Her Many Horses, executive director of the Oglala Sioux Tribe in Pine Ridge, S.D.

"The country reached the point where they said that's not very nice," he said. American Indians plan to fight for the same sensitivity.

The battlegrounds have included:

Berbiglia Wine & Spirits office at 1101 E. Bannister Road in south Kansas City, Mo. It was among sites nationwide of protests against the sale of the Original Crazy Horse Malt Liquor.

Oddly enough, it has ties to the chop.

Naming a malt liquor after the Oglala Sioux political, military and spiritual leader, who preached abstinence from alcohol, rubs salt into deep wounds. Crazy Horse led the Sioux and Cheyenne in the 1876 defeat of Gen. George Crook in the Battle of the Rosebud in Montana.

Eight days later, he led the Indian nations in the defeat of Lt. Col. George Armstrong Custer in the Battle of the Little Bighorn. The Sioux War had followed a U.S. Cavalry attack of an Indian village after the Sioux refused an 1875 U.S. government order to enter a reservation.

Work on a massive monument to Crazy Horse started in 1948

and continues today near Mount Rushmore in the Black Hills of South Dakota. Putting his name on a malt liquor defames him and the things American Indians hold dear.

"It's the same as if they had made a Martin Luther King Jr. malt liquor," said Coker, who protested at the liquor store. "It would be an affront to all black people and all people."

The malt liquor battle caught the attention of Congress, which passed legislation barring the Hornell Brewing Co. of Brooklyn from selling Crazy Horse malt liquor.

Mark H. Rodman, public affairs consultant for Hornell, called the action unconstitutional and the company fought it. In papers filed with House and Senate conferees, the company said banning the product "attempts to address issues that are clearly widespread and ingrained in today's commercial society."

It listed dozens of examples, including professional sports teams like the Chiefs.

Rodman insists that 200 distributors, 18,000 retail dealers including Berbiglia and 8 million Crazy Horse drinkers can't be wrong.

But they can. As Thomas Paine wrote, "A long habit of not thinking a thing wrong gives it the superficial appearance of being right." It hurts just as much as digging up the bones of American Indians' ancestors.

"There are more dead Indians in university museums than there are live Indians in universities," Coker said. "Grave robbery is a serious offense to any culture.

"If you went to a white cemetery and dug up anyone they would put you in jail so fast, but if you go to an Indian burial ground and dig up Indian ancestors they'll make you the head of an archaeology department of some university."

Schools also fail to tell the story of American Indians.

"History really was a history of white men in America," Coker said. "I take college level history courses that teach the same garbage."

Movies create more massive problems. American Indians find they must fight inaccuracies in this mass medium.

In 1992, producers flooded theaters and video rental store with movies about American Indians. They included "1492: Conquest of Paradise," "The Last of the Mohicans," "Christopher Columbus" and "Dances with Wolves."

Coker says each is filled with "romantic garbage" that promotes myths because the pictures display the dominant culture's point of view.

"They're pathetic," she said. "They don't tell our story the way it really was."

Her Many Horses, however, said that the movies are part of American Indians' being in vogue. It happens about every 20 years.

Turquoise jewelry becomes popular again and non-Indians brag about having a Cherokee grandmother.

"There are certain times in this country when Americans like us - for short times," he said.

Coker said it's when the "culture vultures" come out and pick at what's left of American Indians' religion and heritage.

So the battles continue. They include lawsuits and political fights with state officials over land, water and gaming rights.

The chop only adds to the problem.

"They're taking advantage of what is essentially our suffering," Coker said.

Bob Moore, then-director of public relations with the Chiefs, contended that the team cares, but it's just following what the fans want.

It's the same logic Hornell used: The majority of Americans can't be wrong even if what they want incenses many American Indians.

"Our humanity has been stripped from us," Coker said. "Once you dehumanize people you can do anything you want to them.

"The real problem is we have no dignity, no respect. It's been taken from us."

The low self-esteem breeds poverty, alcohol abuse and many other problems.

Coker sees conflicts with the Chiefs, Berbiglia, Hornell and others as continuing the 500-year culture war. Indians have suffered setbacks such as the Chiefs' reneging on the chop agreement and Hornell challenging the act of Congress.

But American Indians say that fits 500 years of broken treaties and promises. They also believe, however, that despite the setbacks they are winning in raising the public's awareness to the problems.

"Just the fact that they know we exist has been a major accomplishment," Coker said. "We're not going to let up until they stop using our people as a stereotypical negative image."

It's worse than awful when people with mental illness suffer the taunts and abuse of others who are supposed to be "normal." It must never be tolerated. Their struggles should never be theirs alone because others face similarly isolated bigotry.

From "Cruelty continues to fester"

Normally, when Jerry Armstrong and Sybil Noble call, we talk of progress the Ark of Friends of Kansas City has made for mental health consumers.

But not this time. This call was about taunting laughter, discrimination and intolerance that Noble, Armstrong and others in the Ark suffered and will never forget.

The incident happened in November 1992 at Arby's Roast Beef Restaurant, 3540 Main St., Kansas City. The couple and seven others followed a months-long tradition of going to Arby's for shakes after their Saturday Ark meeting at the Westminster Congregational Church.

It was supposed to be a treat for the mental health consumers. Instead, workers behind the counter laughed and pointed at the non-disruptive group.

Noble recalled that when she questioned them, they cursed her. Armstrong asked to speak to their supervisor, who came forward, cursed him and told the group to leave.

"I said we paid for our shakes; we'll sit here and eat them," said Armstrong, past president of the Missouri Mental Health Consumer Network. Despite feeling hurt, angry and frustrated, the group stayed.

Before leaving Armstrong got the supervisor's name, and Ark members later wrote to Arby's to complain.

I contacted Randy Scott, area director of operations for Arby's. He had not heard about the incident but was outraged that it happened. He said he planned to take action against the assistant manager but found that the employee had already been terminated.

Scott apologized to members of the Ark. "We can't have a situation like that take place in our restaurant – there's no way," he said.

"We do have some accidents and mistakes that happen like that," Scott said. "When we do find out about it, we take care of it.

"We want their business."

It should never matter that these patrons were disheveled or acted differently.

"These people were not there for a beauty contest," said Janice M. Kelly, then-director of the Mayor's Office on Disabilities.

Such incidents, however, are not uncommon.

"I've heard more about that kind of problem in the past few months than I have heard in the past several years," said Barbara Manning, then-executive director of the Mental Health Association of Kansas City.

It's happening as state hospitals release more people to live among us as out-patients.

"Society in general is going to have to tolerate the symptoms and behavior of people with mental illnesses," said John Dean, then-manager of the psychiatric rehabilitation program of Research Mental Health Services.

> Mental health agencies reported other incidents, including: mental health consumers not being served for two hours by pizza restaurant workers; others on the way to Blue Ridge Mall being laughed at by motorists passing their bus; and one consumer on an ATA bus from Bannister Mall being called a monkey. The most shocking thing was that the man began to act like a monkey to placate his abusers.
>
> "Consumers of mental health services are used to abuse," Armstrong said. "Some of them accept this as the normal way to be treated."
>
> But they don't need to.
>
> Fred Rich, a staff attorney with Legal Aid of Western Missouri contacted by Ark members about the Arby's incident, urges consumers to fight back for the sake of their self-esteem. "If you don't speak up and speak out, the same thing will happen again and again and again," he said.
>
> The Americans with Disabilities Act offers help. More consumers just have to become aware of their new rights, Kelly said, and use them.

Several people thought I was certain to get fired after I wrote that column because a key advertiser for *The Star* called the general manager of the newspaper to try to get the piece spiked before it could see print. But it ran. People at the newspaper valuing diversity could see the merit in the column. Diversity should matter to everyone and at all times. People with mental illness are members of our community, too.

Racially Biased Health Care

Health care is another area in which a staph infection of racism threatens to spread and debilitate people of color and even result in their death. Again, it comes down to an issue of communication. Discrimination and prejudices block health care professionals from providing the same services to people of color that they would to people who are white.

From "Unhealthy racism a la mode"

> I took an apple pie I'd made to a friend. It turned into an ironic gift when she shared her all-American story with me.
>
> The woman had been ill and felt fortunate to have visitors at her upscale home. She received the medical treatment she needed, but she paid an inhuman price because she's black.
>
> I shared that with students at an area nursing school in a talk about African-American health and economic issues. I also told them what I learned at a diversity session with another nursing college class.
>
> One student told me a patient shocked her when he used the N-word to describe someone. Another student was stunned when a white family used the same slur to insist that no black nurse treat their loved one.

That student changed the family's minds when she said some of the best nurses on staff were black. But such stories indicate that racism in health care is as American as apple pie.

Health care professionals must strive to communicate past racial barriers to treat all people as human beings. This didn't happen with my friend, whose respiratory trouble began the previous year.

A specialist wrote her off without a thorough exam, saying she qualified for disability and had three months to live. My friend was a regional office manager and asked that her name not be used.

She was distressed by the assumptions of many white health care workers she encountered. Her doctor assumed black people wanted a disability check and a way out of work.

She sought a second opinion. With the right tests, that doctor diagnosed and treated her chronic ailment. But more troubles followed.

In March my friend was admitted to an area hospital. Human error caused a nurse to give her five times the dose of a medication that her doctor had prescribed.

My friend's daughter realized something was wrong when her mother began to behave strangely. The daughter pointed out the overdose when she checked the chart showing what was prescribed compared with what was given.

The nurse apologized. "But that made me cautious when I went back in September," my friend said.

She was rushed by ambulance to the same hospital. Her daughter questioned all medication that was administered, prompting a nurse to say, "Well, you can just leave this hospital," my friend said. The nurse sent two security guards to my friend's room, saying the woman and her daughter might become violent. But they were just black women seeking good medical care.

The nurse had criminalized them for questioning her. My friend said other black women have told her similar stories. That's as American as apple pie, too.

My friend recalled less than respectful service on a second emergency trip to the hospital in September. She arrived at 8:30 a.m. and was treated but didn't get to a room until 3 p.m.

Then a hospital worker insisted on getting "welfare" details.

"When I realized what information she wanted, I said she didn't need that kind of information from me," my friend said. "I said I do not need that kind of service. She said, 'Yes, I have to have it.'"

My friend explained that she was employed and had health insurance. "She said, 'Well, if you say so, OK,'" my friend recalled.

Again, my friend had been victimized by racial profiling at the hospital. Her records showed she was well-covered. But the assumption was that because she was black, she was on welfare. Unfortunately, that's as American as apple pie, too.

"There was absolutely no reason for me to have that kind of visit and to be challenged on whether or not I am right," my friend said. "There is absolutely nothing wrong with a woman who happens to be on public assistance.

"But there is something wrong when people look at me and think, 'She's on public assistance.' You get that feeling that you're nobody, you're insignificant. It tells me that we certainly have to be advocates for ourselves, and sometimes we have to be aggressive advocates or we will be denied service we are entitled to.

"People are not yet willing to accept the diversity, whether it's the people they treat or the people we work with. It tells me you would be treated very badly as someone with no resources or no family."

My friend said people of color need to be vigilant when a loved one goes to the hospital. Ask questions and insist on second and third opinions.

It boils down to an apple-pie issue of trust. In health care, any lapse can have dire consequences.

The reaction? If you don't like the message, attack the messenger.

E-mail: Dec. 1, 2000

You continue to bleat on and on about racism. Can't you find a real subject to write about? You do your profession a disservice by failing to verify any of the "facts" your friend provided. Your statement of "she paid an inhuman price because she's black" is without merit! Where was the verification to the statement? You assume all people will accept your writing as being truthful. I don't!

Your apple pie theme is childish. You should write fiction for children's books.

Such viewpoints dominated the feedback. However, my friend's experience is anything but the exception to the rule.

<u>From "A death sentence for blacks" and "Treatment in need of treatment"</u>

A historical malignancy of racial disparities continues to infect health care.

Rodney G. Hood calls it a "slave health deficit." It's left an aggressive virus of "racism in medicine" that African-Americans are still trying to overcome.

"This is a very painful subject," said Hood, who spoke at the University of Missouri-Kansas City School of Medicine.

"There was a sense of the devaluation of humanity," said Hood, a physician, medical director/CEO of CareView Medical Group Inc. and assistant clinical professor at the University of California-San Diego. "I consider the issue that we're talking about to be like cancer."

It's serious and life-threatening, but few people want to talk about it or try to correct it.

The topic surfaced in Atlanta at the National Association of Black Journalists convention. Health-care professionals cited studies in which black patients were prescribed less advanced and aggressive treatment than white patients even though each used the same words and gestures to describe the same illness.

When African-Americans enter doctors' offices they are more likely to be misdiagnosed, said Altha J. Stewart, president of the American Psychiatric Foundation.

Former Surgeon General David Satcher wrote in a paper published in 2005 in the journal *Health Affairs* saying that middle-age black men compared with white men of similar age were dying at nearly twice the rate. He said one explanation for the disparity is that advances in access to health care have not included black men unless they were older and disabled.

Satcher wrote that the elimination of the racial gap in health care could prevent about 83,570 deaths annually.

The American College of Gastroenterology reported this year that African-Americans have earlier onset of colorectal cancer and a higher incidence and mortality than whites do. Cancer of the rectum or colon is the second most common type in black women and third most common in black men.

Pfizer Inc. and the National Medical Association reported that despite a decline in cancer deaths for Americans overall, black men were 36 percent more likely and black women were 17 percent more likely to die from cancer than whites were.

These are life-and-death issues. The racial disparities impair African-Americans' ability to lead normal, productive lives.

"When therapy suggests more is better, we get it less," Hood said.

In mental health, however, African-Americans often are forced into the system involuntarily by police, or medical and mental health professionals. Once in, black people get strapped into the most restrictive care.

They're often overmedicated and misdiagnosed, and disproportionate numbers land in jails and prisons because many hospitals that treat people with mental illness have closed. Blacks rarely get opportunities to enter "cutting edge" community programs, said William H. Kyles, president and chief executive officer of Comprehensive Mental Health Services in Independence, Mo. Kyles noted that in 1995 black people constituted 10.7 percent of Missouri's population but 25 percent of the clients in the mental health system.

Mark Miller, then-human resources development coordinator for the Missouri Department of Mental Health, said black people constituted 27 percent of the people in inpatient psychiatric care but only 15 percent of those in community-based services.

"Every study that I know shows that mental illness doesn't hit one race more than another," Kyles said. That's why the system must look at cultural biases in diagnosis and treatment.

Kyles added that minorities in treatment faced a double stigma of mental illness and being black.

Dianne Cleaver, then-mental health director with Swope Parkway Health Center, said the system had to be sensitive to their mental anguish. Blacks often must fight stereotypes to fit into society. But when they hit overload, black people don't voluntarily seek treatment because they either distrust the mental health system or their culture implores them to tough out problems. That can lead to substance abuse, anger and violence.

Cleaver also is concerned with how black children are treated. A disproportionate number land in Family Court compared with white kids who go into counseling or special treatment centers.

The difference is black people's behavior often is misinterpreted, because therapists overlook cultural differences. "People really misunderstand emotion and many times are quick to put a pathological interpretation on it," Kyles said. Sometimes a language barrier gets in the way, or therapists don't raise racial factors because they didn't learn it in school.

"That's why the therapists need treatment," Kyles said. "'One size fits all' never fit anybody."

Kyles founded the Minority Mental Health Foundation. Its goal is to have more minorities recruited into mental health professions, eliminate the double stigma, increase outreach and improve services to minorities. The foundation proposes to do that through scholarships, community grants, a speakers bureau, community investment, research and education.

In addition to being treated differently, blacks also are excluded from drug studies and therapies. "Clinical trials in America have always been race-based," said Winston Price, a physician and president of the National Medical Association. He said black doctors, researchers and colleges are not included in clinical investigations.

"We're not in the study group," Price said. "How can they determine new drugs for treatment if blacks are not in the study group?"

The same racial sickness infects stem-cell research.

"We are not at the table to a large degree in the development of stem-cell research," Price said. "There are very few minority researchers involved in that."

Yet when African-Americans are involved, the results are striking. An example was the Food and Drug Administration's approval of the cardiovascular drug BiDil. The first drug OK'd for a specific racial group was found to lower the death rate for patients by 43 percent, and the hospitalization rate was 33 percent lower.

"To reduce mortality by 43 percent, how can you not utilize the drug?" said B.J. Jones, vice president of marketing with NitroMed, the drug maker. "Clinical trials can be done with people of color and can be successful."

But schools of medicine and health-care professionals will have to shed backward notions about black people before racial disparities in research and treatment disappear. Doctors and other care providers will have to view black patients as people first and communicate with them as individuals before progress can be made.

In addition, said Kyles, "If we don't have African-Americans in administrative and clinical positions throughout the system, we're going to continually not have appropriate treatment." If dollars and cents matter, then misdiagnosis puts black people in the most expensive therapy.

"From a cost-effective point of view, attention to cultural diversity makes good economic sense," he said.

A lot is at stake.

When whites are placed in similar situations

Change will come only when people of all colors can identify with the oppression of minority groups.

From "Painful venturing outside one's own culture"

A white engineer at a monthly Diversity Coalition meeting described quite well how he felt when others excluded him from the mainstream in another culture.

The Rev. Martin Luther King Jr. would have been encouraged by the depth of the man's understanding. More people need his appreciation for minorities' challenges.

The man was a newcomer to the gatherings that David Shapiro convened until his death. Shapiro's friends continue the meeting at members' homes.

The gatherings offer folks with a curiosity about others an opportunity to enjoy the lost art of a polite, thoughtful, public dialogue.

It's where people of all colors discuss unthinkable things that keep us apart and learn from the insight.

We always part with a better understanding of the work ahead and the common ground we occupy. At the December meeting, the engineer spoke of his work in the Far East.

He often was the only American in a country of Asians. People on the street stared, whispered and used derogatory terms to refer to him. One was "long nose."

The man said it was like having an emery board constantly run across his skin. It didn't kill him or do a massive amount of damage. But it felt awful, took an emotional toll and left lasting scars.

I heard the same thing from a man last year at Johnson County Community College, where a conference was held for educators on white privilege. A white woman, who was incredulous about white people having privileges that others don't possess, encouraged the man to share his overseas experience.

He spoke of the ostracism he felt in an Asian nation. He explained how he was comfortable in America but didn't fit in overseas, and people let him know it.

He described feeling depressed and alone. He felt like not stepping outside, where he'd daily have to confront being different in a less-than-friendly environment.

It's how college students of color often feel on many Kansas City area campuses. Feeling isolated and the object of negative attention because of racial or ethnic difference can be debilitating.

The engineer at the Diversity Coalition meeting described the pain as the emery board's silent sawing. A woman said she felt a similar stress when people in an Asian nation constantly asked her to speak for all Americans.

I said the discussion brought the group closer to knowing what being black in America is like. People laughed when I said that instead of an emery board, the trauma that minorities feel is like having a belt sander chew on them. African-Americans face prenatal-to-grave disparities in health care, education, jobs, housing, income, wealth and opportunities.

Also, people fail to accept that the diversity among black people is as varied as it is among white people. It's ludicrous to ask any one person who is white to speak for that race just as it is for black people, Hispanics, Asian-Americans or American Indians to speak for theirs.

Accepting people as individuals with special talents that can benefit our society remains King's dream. It was never about being colorblind. It involves everyone being mindful of the beautiful differences in attributes and learning how they can enhance our community.

A black man at the meeting told the group that his father explained the essence of bigotry, prejudice and stereotypes imposed on minorities. His dad said he had to remain strong and focus on being successful.

He said he had a saying about people who stooped to racism and discrimination: "He who hates, hurts." It could be "she," too. The person hurts inside as much as the damage done to others.

The engineer said the resistance he encountered overseas melted when he showed pictures of his family to people with whom he wanted to do business. He also felt best about being away from the comfortable environment of the United States when he extended himself to fit in to the Asian country's culture.

Those lessons abroad need to be transplanted at home with everyone embracing the diversity in others and extending themselves into places well beyond their comfort zones. That would make King smile and further the dream he had for us all.

Racially Biased Justice

Unequal treatment, however, still happens far too often. In minorities' cases, the Lady Justice keeps peeking from behind her blindfold, and the balance of her Scales of Justice often weighs against people of color. In one case, justice was finally served, but only because of one man's persistence. Such diversity multipliers are essential to discovering the Real America.

From "Sykes takes rights seriously"

Alvin Sykes knelt and prayed in Buddhist chants on a baseball field at Penn Valley Park where assailants had beaten Steve Harvey to death.

That homicide has led Sykes to spend much of the last two decades searching for justice for victims of prejudice and hatred. But not once had Sykes visited the place of Harvey's death.

"There were times I started out to come here," Sykes said. "But I never made it. It was just a lot of pain."

Until I saw Sykes pray, I didn't understand what drove him to never give up his quest for justice for Harvey.

Harvey, 27, was a promising jazz musician who on Nov. 4, 1980, sought the solitude of the park to play his saxophone. That's where he was chased and beaten to death with a baseball bat.

Famed musician Herbie Hancock introduced Sykes to Buddhism more than 25 years ago at Union Station. It's what sustains Sykes, gives him clarity and devotion in seeking justice for others.

"I just know by my Buddhist faith if I stayed committed to it we would prevail," Sykes said. "All righteousness will be proven."

Harvey's death at 29th Street and Kessler Road west of the Liberty Memorial pulled Sykes out of the world of music and pushed him to become president of the Justice Campaign of America, a human-rights group. Sykes and I met under the clock at Union Station where we talked for about an hour about Harvey's case, his first. Then we took a long walk into the park to revisit the past.

Sykes said his faith kept him involved in the campaign after others had given up.

"They didn't understand and see the chance for it to be successful," Sykes said. "The sweet part is it deepened my faith."

A lot has changed since 1980. Back then people caught trains at Union Station, and no one then dreamed that construction cranes today would hover around the Liberty Memorial to refurbish it.

The restrooms at the park are gone, too, and instead of one ball field there now are two. We found the one where Harvey died.

Harvey was black. Raymond L. Bledsoe and two other men whom police arrested and charged were white. They had gone to the park to harass homosexuals.

Sykes, who was an associate of Harvey's and remains involved with the case, said a gay white man was attacked first, but he was let go. The attackers then chased and viciously beat Harvey, who was married, had two children and wasn't gay.

At an August 1981 trial, an all-white Jackson County jury found Bledsoe not guilty of first-degree murder. That was despite testimony from Bledsoe's two accomplices who said he had chased Harvey out of a park restroom and repeatedly beat him with a bat. The two who testified received probation.

After that trial, Sykes got involved. He went to the library with Harvey's widow to research law books in a quest for justice.

Sykes launched a dogged effort to get the Justice Department to seek a new trial under the federal charge that Harvey's civil rights were violated. That effort led a federal court jury in 1983 to convict Bledsoe of denying Harvey his rightful use of a public facility because of race.

Harvey's death was such a loss because when his saxophone caught the life in his breath it made people sing, dance and be happy.

"Steve's last words were: 'You can't do this to me. I'm a musician,'" Sykes recalled from the trials.

But getting justice for Harvey has cost Sykes a lot.

During the case, Sykes' father was stabbed to death in Los Angeles. Sykes, who's working on a book about the case, had to choose between staying with Harvey's case and pursuing justice for his father. He stayed with the case.

Since the 1980s, Sykes has been an advocate for several families seeking justice in the Kansas City area and elsewhere. But Sykes said he learned many lessons from Harvey's case.

"The case says violence can happen to anyone," said Sykes. "People can be victimized by hatred."

Harvey's case also shows that authorities sometimes don't pursue justice as hard as they should because of the race or sexual orientation of victims. "It sets up an atmosphere of vulnerability in what I consider a denial of equal protection under the law that allows these types of activities to occur," Sykes said.

Sykes remains active in justice-seeking and has reviewed hundreds of cases of injustices since Bledsoe's conviction. This year he helped block Bledsoe's parole. Sykes is now working to get Congress to pass federal hate crimes legislation to protect gays and lesbians.

The country needs more people like Sykes to intervene to make change possible. Racism wouldn't stand as a barrier then to people's discovery of the best in others who are different.

Institutionalized Racism

In a speech given at the first annual Unvarnished Truth Awards presented by Pacifica Radio on September 23, 2005, Dr. Michael Eric Dyson invited the audience to

> Come with me as we tour the inner city and the barrio and the Native indigenous people's reservation. Come with me through the post-industrial urban collapse of mothers who have long since surrendered the ability to exercise and leverage authority over the lives of their children, because the state has been in cahoots with an underground economy, expanding the possibility of a drug economy, while the above-ground economy takes the jobs away from their men and their mothers and their sisters. The state has conspired to do dastardly deeds and to do ultimate damage to vulnerable black and brown and yellow and red people. ("Professor" 3)

Dyson might have included the plight of another group: longtime rural black landowners—the heart and soul of America—who also suffer because of racism. They are African-American farmers whose ancestor's toil make up the foundation of the American agrarian economy. Yet these stalwart individuals continue to face institutional racism with the federal government's stamp of approval.

From "Tough times for black farmers"

George Hildebrandt bent over and scooped up the black earth in his big, beefy right hand.

This rich Leavenworth County, Kansas, river bottom land is what he lives for. His grandfather, George Augustus Hildebrandt, homesteaded the property by the Missouri River in the 1880s.

Hildebrandt's father, George B. Hildebrandt, farmed here, too. Hildebrandt took over in 1981. He grows soybeans and organic fruits and vegetables on 242 acres at the end of a county road that carries his family's name.

"I'm proud of it," Hildebrandt said. "My granddad and my dad struggled so hard to keep this place.

"I would like to leave a legacy for my kids. I would not want to be the one to lose the farm."

But that's a real concern. Hildebrandt, 61, was among the original plaintiffs in a 1997 class-action lawsuit against the government. The lawsuit charged that black farmers nationwide had been denied government loans and subsidies that white farmers received. A settlement was reached in 1999 to pay farmers like Hildebrandt a minimum of $50,000 each and forgive their federal farm loans as compensation for years of discrimination.

Officials estimate that $2.2 billion could be paid or forgiven because of the suit. According to the U.S. Department of Agriculture, more than 21,000 claims are being considered. The government approved 60 percent and has paid about $615 million.

Hildebrandt's claim was among those denied. That has forced him to appeal the decision and fight for his farm and his way of life.

For years and on several occasions he has joined more than 200 other black farmers at peaceful sit-ins and rallies at the Department of Agriculture facilities in different cities.

Black farmers have asked the Department of Agriculture's top officials to put a moratorium on farm foreclosures - especially on black farmers. The black farmers have never gotten a satisfactory response. It epitomizes what the Rev. Martin Luther King Jr. wrote in his "Letter from the Birmingham Jail": wait almost always means never.

Hildebrandt said the vigils and protests would keep the government from ignoring black farmers' concerns.

Alvin Sykes, president of the Justice Campaign of America, was among those at a protest in Tennessee and the meeting with the Department of Agriculture officials. Sykes, who is from Kansas City, said Hildebrandt had become a folk hero among black farmers for helping to champion their cause.

People forget that African-Americans have a rich history as farmers. As slaves they worked on the plantations of this country and continued to farm after emancipation in 1865.

Reparations never happened. Yet the majority of African-Americans continued to farm during and after Reconstruction.

In 1920 there were 925,000 black farmers. Poor economic conditions, racial terrorism by the Ku Klux Klan and other groups and nearly no government support pushed thousands of blacks to cities for jobs. Today about 15,000 black farmers are left.

The USDA has garnished Hildebrandt's income tax refund and crop subsidies amounting to $12,000 toward covering the $150,000 in loans that have not been forgiven.

The ordeal has been stressful, said Patricia Hildebrandt, his wife. "We live day to day, thinking we're going to go to the mailbox and see what it's going to say to us," she said.

"I don't know what we would do if we lost the farm," she added. "I don't know where we would go."

Hildebrandt said, "I feel like the good Lord is going to take care of it and fix it all one day."

I certainly hope so. But his activism also will help.

It may seem strange to some, but the feedback was largely negative—despite all the anguish and discrimination black farmers have endured. Here are some examples:

E-mail: Sept. 3, 2002

I read your article on black farmers and my comment is so what! Big deal. How many other farmers of other races were put off their land because they couldn't repay their loans? You mentioned that this particular individual has $150,000 of outstanding loans and couldn't repay them. Well, what are we to do, write the loans off the books because he is black?

You African Americans make me sick. All I hear from you is whining. My parents on both sides were born on poor, and I mean poor dirt farms in southern Missouri. The farms they grew up on would probably make the black farmer's farm you cite in your article look like paradise. They had no running water, no indoor toilet, no electricity and wood stoves for heat.

And they didn't own any slaves. All they did was work like slaves trying to keep body and soul together. And no, they didn't get any government loans. They lived through the Depression as young adults on those farms, and they didn't whine and complain because the government wouldn't help them out. And they didn't whine and complain because someone wouldn't let them cop out on their loans.

> Truth be told, many farmers and I would suppose many black farmers over expanded and in the 1980s when land was cheap, interest rates were low and crop prices were high they purchased additional land, livestock and machinery. Then the price fell out of crops and now when it comes time to pay the piper for the money they borrowed, they don't want to. How convenient for blacks to once again be able to use their race to leverage concessions.
>
> That seems to be the story for you African Americans in 2002 America. No matter what the transgressions, no matter what the ramifications of your actions you bring up old grievances like you are the only group ever to suffer. Who in the hell died and made you people the poster children for suffering.
>
> Bottom line for me I would say if this farmer had his claim denied by the government, there was probably a damn good reason why it was denied. He was probably trying to use his status as an aggrieved black to game the system. My suggestion, repay the loans or get off the land. That's what they told my parents. And by the way, their farms had been in the family longer than the black farmer you cited.

Activism is certainly a key element in fighting discrimination. Robin J. DiAngelo, of the University of Washington, maintains that "in practice [our] silence colludes with racism" (53). Therefore, we must search, explore and try to discover the Real America. As we do so, we will encounter savage attacks from those who refuse to have an open mind, to explore and to recognize the value of this country's diverse population. They represent the old Eurocentric ways, the "the majority's way is best" attitude that strives to maintain the status quo. They are part of the real, less progressive and damaging America. But they are not the enemy. They just must be convinced to join in the journey toward discovering the richness in diversity. Not seeing people's color or recognizing their difference is the biggest lie ever told in America. Minorities always are accused of pulling the "race card." But the people pointing the finger are the ones who do it the most in the exclusion, discrimination and prejudices they show toward people of color. It has a historically corrosive effect, and it must end.

CHAPTER 3
Undercover: Jim Crow, Esq.

By the Kitchen

A singer and two-piece band play
In the packed popular place.
A black/white couple enters
And with others wait.

But they get seated quickly,
And few heads turn.
Appetite's all set as bellies growl and churn
The all-white music drones to no applause
As a new preference for race hurries them without pause
To near the kitchen where they're served fast
and nearly unnoticed
Then hurried out but not at all crass.
Let it go, are the internal cautioning whispers
It's your imagination, are the others' internalized shouts
Time is a factor, just let us get out.
Progress made in Civil Rights
from the darkest of dark nights,
Where songs mournfully cried,
And no one was left with dry eyes.
Now We, too, sing America,
But a benign platitude that passes unnoticed from sight.
We're not "sent to eat in the kitchen" anymore
Just by the GODDAMN door!
Are they ashamed, Langston,
Or these 100 years hence is it just more of the same?

I am not quite America.

We know through painful experience that freedom is never voluntarily given by the oppressor; it must be demanded by the oppressed. Frankly, I have yet to engage in a direct action campaign that was "well-timed" in the view of those who have not suffered unduly from the disease of segregation. For years now I have heard the word "Wait!" It rings in the ear of every Negro with piercing familiarity. This "Wait" has almost always meant "Never." We must come to see, with one of our distinguished jurists, that "justice too long delayed is justice denied."

~Rev. Martin Luther King, Jr.
from "Letter from A Birmingham Jail," written April 16, 1963

People of all races sweat. But some are made to sweat more than others. Welcome to the subtle 21st century racism and discrimination that silently shuts out people of color from the "cool" mainstream.

At a Johnson County, Kan., NAACP Freedom Fund dinner a few years ago, people in the packed hotel banquet room were taking off neckties, jackets and other clothing. They wondered why it was so oppressively hot in the room while outside the hallways and the rest of the hotel were pleasantly cool.

At an awards banquet for an all-black young men's organization at a different Kansas City area hotel, the temperature inside the banquet hall was also uncomfortably hot compared to the rest of the hotel.

Public accommodation laws mandate that the facilities be open to African-Americans, but they don't necessarily have to have tiptop service. The difference in treatment taunts, teases and torments people of color who wonder, as they try to figure out the calculus of race, whether what they feel is their imagination or something that's still too shamefully real.

That needling sense of being treated differently is felt by many throughout society. It is impossible to prove, but it is very real to those who experience it. Subtle discrimination comes in many forms, but hurts everyone it touches in some way. Businesses are affected because they experience lower sales; individuals become suspicious or upset, lose their self-esteem or much-needed chances for success. But because it is hard to prove, it cannot always be fought. In many instances, the victims have to just "sweat it out."

In this chapter, various subtle forms of discrimination will be described. What kind of barriers do minority businesses face? What sudden and unexpected hurdles trip up individuals? And even though covert discrimination is a "feeling" rather than an irrefutable "fact," what action have victims taken to receive some redress for what they have endured. Whenever available, typical reactions from observers will also be examined to demonstrate how unprovable yet injurious this kind of discrimination truly is.

Minority Businesses

In November of 2005, the National Association for Multicultural Education (NAME) held its 14th Annual International Conference at the Hyatt Regency Crown Center Hotel in Kansas City, Mo. On the Friday evening of the conference week, attendees went to a reception at the Guadalupe Center to enjoy some of the community's Hispanic heritage. They had ridden special buses from the hotel to the Guadalupe Center. Problems arose when the educators, who had come from all over the country, wanted to return to the hotel or go to other spots for dinner.

Public transportation from this Latino tourist attraction in Kansas City was suddenly unavailable.

From "Marooned in KC by Subtle bias; Area needs equal accessibility to public transportation"

> More than a dozen people stood outside the Guadalupe Center as the reception inside wound down.
>
> In the retreating light of dusk the educators all had one hand raised to their faces, making it appear as if they'd stepped outside to smoke. But they actually were using cell phones to call cabs.
>
> It was a surreal and embarrassing Kansas City moment. This town's public transportation is deficient during business hours. But at night it's worse than abysmal.
>
> Some said dispatchers told them the cabdrivers were busy, and it would be a while before taxis would arrive. But when we got back to the hotel we found an armada of idle cabs.
>
> Conference attendees also said that when I met them for dinner earlier that week at Arthur Bryant's Barbeque at 1727 Brooklyn Ave. they had had similar difficulty getting a cab from that area of the black community. It took them an hour to finally get a ride back to their hotel.
>
> Such things show how underserved black and Hispanic businesses and other attractions are to tourists who depend on public transportation. That inaccessibility locks minority enterprises out of a lot of commerce.
>
> The educators learned a hard urban America lesson which is still a major embarrassment for Kansas City especially. It shows that public access to black and Hispanic tourist attractions remains terribly unequal.

Minority Customers

Minority businesses might not always have convenient public transportation access. However, people of color do have unrestricted access to dining and other business establishments. Even so, there are still many instances in which they sense that the service they receive is unequal. A negative image others have of minorities seems ever present. It haunts, it whispers, it hisses, it shames, it harasses, it embarrasses, it hurts and at the same time it constantly causes its victims to question whether it exists at all or is just their imagination.

From "Welcome mat is not in sight"

> A sunny day walk ended inside a dimly lighted bar and grill.
>
> I had arrived too early at Southwest High School, where I was to give a good-job speech at a student writing awards ceremony. So

I decided to spend a little shoe leather, see the neighborhood and be adventurous by having lunch someplace I had never been before.

I won't forget how the barroom crowd fell silent when the door closed behind me. I had on a suit and tie, but the all-white patrons only saw black.

I sat at the bar and ordered a hamburger, fries and a Diet Coke. The bartender then uttered the nicest words possible to let me know I wasn't welcome: "Is this to go?" he said.

It reminded me of an unforgettable experience 14 years earlier on a hot Sunday night at a Jackson, Miss., diner. My wife and I were touring the South in our old Volkswagen bus.

We pulled off the interstate tired and hungry and were directed from the Capitol to the only eatery open downtown. We stepped into the packed, brightly lighted restaurant.

It teemed with talk until the all-white patrons and waiters saw us. We sat at the counter.

From the kitchen pressed into the small window on the swing doors were the startled faces of the black cooks and busboys. Their looks told us we were out of place in their world.

We ordered and our waiter asked: "Is this to go?"

It's a reasonable question at a fast-food restaurant, but not at that eat-in Mississippi diner or at the Brookside bar. What stings is that we expected that treatment in Jackson, not in Kansas City.

I stayed at the bar, fetched my own condiments - which no one else had to do - ate lunch and realized that I should have not been surprised that such prejudices still exist.

A study by the Kansas City Human Relations Department released in 1989 showed that the area has a strong pattern of housing segregation because blacks encounter stubborn forms of racism. When we were looking for a house in the Southland that year, one couple refused to show us their home and told the agent that it was because we are black.

At another house for sale a racial slur, neatly framed and positioned, greeted us at the wet bar. No doubt its message was for people like us.

Add to that a Federal Reserve Board report released in October 1991 that said African Americans seeking home loans were nearly three times as likely as white borrowers to face rejection from lenders in the Kansas City area.

That may explain why we had such a tough time getting a mortgage in 1979 on our first house in Midtown.

No wonder young people are pessimistic about the state of race relations in America. According to a survey released in 1992 that was conducted for a civil rights group, 50 percent of the respondents said race relations in the United States were "generally bad."

So I walked back to the high school still intending to give that rah-rah speech to about 75 students and teachers. But something in me snapped as I looked into the young faces unbruised by the bare-knuckled environment just outside their school doors.

To them the world is a place of TV-like promise, and painful black experiences are largely bottled away in history books. So I unhinged, told them what had happened to me and read shock on their expressive faces.

Then I dovetailed it with the assigned topic of "Finding Your Personal Best," the need for racial harmony and told the students to never be afraid to explore in life even if it hurts.

And don't let anyone brush you aside by asking, "Is this to go?"

That column just happened to run on the day after many cities in America went up in flames following the April 29, 1992, not-guilty verdicts in the first trial of the Los Angeles police officers in the brutal beating of Rodney King. Now, more than 14 years have once again passed since I was made to feel unwelcome at that local eatery. But the trend continues relentlessly:

From "Ghosts of segregation; Decades after civil rights movement, businesses that discriminate deserve 21st century boycott"

Racism always has a cost.

What's surprising is how people continually are taxed by it but gain nothing from the degrading experience.

Reginald Davis helped bring that American-as-apple-pie fact to life. Davis, a black lawyer, was to meet a fellow attorney and that man's brother-in-law recently at an upscale restaurant near downtown Kansas City.

Davis arrived first. He and the other lawyer talked on their cell phones and agreed that Davis should hold a table at the restaurant until the others arrived. No one had made reservations.

Davis was told there would be a 20-minute wait before a spot was available. Davis, who was dressed in a suit, tie and trench coat, asked the restaurant owner about a table that was unoccupied but was told that it was reserved.

Davis went to the restroom and then took a seat at the bar to wait. When he looked up the other lawyer, who is white, was motioning to him to join him and the other guy at the table that Davis was told was reserved.

"Obviously it wasn't reserved," Davis said and he pointed out to the owner that what he had said was a lie. "His eyes got big as watermelons.

I said, 'You're trying to play me.'"

An argument ensued during which Davis pulled out cash to show he was a good customer. Yet, he had been mistreated because of the color of his skin.

The other attorney intervened to try to calm Davis down. He said he did not see the incident as being racially motivated.

"But when you're white, you try to explain away something like that," Davis said. The other lawyer said the owner probably was trying to keep the table open for his regular customers.

Davis still doesn't buy it. "I think they're in denial," he said.

"They've got an optimistic viewpoint of life in general," Davis said. "They don't want to admit there are racist acts that go on. They try to explain away things and lessen the tension. I still highly believe that was racially motivated."

A friend and I suffered a similar incident during breakfast at a Country Club Plaza restaurant. Some pastry she had ordered was stale. She asked the waiter for a replacement.

It never arrived during our hour-long meeting. We asked for the check, and it was never brought to us. We got the Hispanic man who was busing the tables to finally bring it to us.

Was it racism that prompted that poor service in that crowded restaurant? There was no way to know for sure. But it was something I couldn't discount.

That's one of the confounding things about discrimination. One rarely knows with certainty, yet there is always that deep sense people of color get when they have been visited by the all-too-American racist ghost of second-class citizenship.

Davis, 42, had no doubt.

"I was angry," he said of catching the restaurant owner in a lie meant to keep Davis from getting the table. "I don't know any other basis of how to explain it other than it was racially motivated. I just felt belittled and insulted."

Those emotions are some of the human costs of racism. The unfair tax gnaws at the souls of black folks.

But people who read of Davis' encounter had different impressions:

E-mail: Feb. 25, 2005

Perhaps that upscale restaurant owner is watching way too much local television news and is reading the KC Star metro section too often and therefore is seeing way too many factual reports covering black crime. A "lockup" today at Piper High...The police are profiling and picking on another black fugitive....Oh well. Like grandfather, like father, like son. No black father has ever been shot while doing the dishes!

White people have told me they've been victims of poor customer service. But often they can divorce poor service from race. Blacks don't possess that privilege.

E-mail: March 6, 2005

In the many years since I've been divorced, and have gone out to dine alone, I have often been overlooked when the host or hostess comes to seat patrons, from Denny's to the Olive Garden, to Steak and Shake and many others. I've felt invisible to the waiter or waitress at times. On several occasions a couple who came into the restaurant behind me, or a party of 3 or 4 that arrived after I had, has been seated before me.

Is it simply because it is expected that a single diner won't order as much, or leave as big a tip as a full table would? Or is because I'm a single, white, middle-aged male?

I can't even start to estimate the number of times I've been forgotten about once seated, once I ordered, asked for extra service, or asked for the check while dining alone.

This is 2005, not 1965. Discrimination lawsuits, hiring quotas, political correctness, Equal Rights, women's rights, rights for everyone. Well, almost everyone.

My skin is of the wrong color to complain. Who would listen? My gender is wrong. Who would care?

Like you, I ask myself is it racism? Is it reverse discrimination? Or is it simply that in this imperfect world we all have our own grievances?

Thanks for your time.

People of color many times also doubt that unequal service is because of race. But many get victimized a second time when whites in whom we might confide say we're paranoid, too sensitive or it's just our imagination. This feeds the doubt and adds to the mental trauma of being a person of color in America. Almost the only people who will believe us are minorities who often face such covert bigotry, too.

E-mail: Feb. 25, 2005

I cannot tell any difference in a Kansas City Country Club Plaza from the Delta country way down in Mississippi or South Georgia or South Alabama. There is no region that holds a title to racism today, and Racism with a capital R is alive and well in this land no matter where we travel.

In corporations from the top management all the way down to the lowest job level there is racism. Racism invaded all areas of our society, and as long as there is fear in the hearts of human beings, there will be racism. A person of integrity who has character and good morals has overthrown racism, bigotry, and major prejudices because that person is not afraid of anybody, anywhere, of any color, of any religion, or any political beliefs.

I think it is a crime when "so called" businesses of "class" employ such people who discriminate in the work place. That business on the

> Country Club Plaza is no better than the road house or juke joint on a dirt road in LA (Lower Alabama).

Individuals' stories of covert discrimination continue to abound, perhaps because, as Robin DiAngelo notes, whites want to believe in a colorblind society (55). They have stolen those very words, misappropriated them, from the Rev. Martin Luther King Jr.'s "I Have A Dream" speech during the 1963 March on Washington, D.C. Jim Myers writes in his book *Afraid of the Dark* that conservatives have discovered the value of those words for white Americans.

> These very same words became the means to free whites from the stigma of their past sins. And it worked like this: if whites were not judged by the color of their skin, then they could not be held accountable for the sins of white slaveowners, segregationists, and old-time racists. And if whites are not judged by the color of their skin, they need not be called upon to redress wrongs done by whites in other times and places. Perhaps whites need not even feel guilty about the evils of the past and instead could claim a clean slate on matters involving race, slavery, segregation, and discrimination, starting here and now.
>
> King's standard of character not skin color cast immediate doubt upon remedies undertaken in the name of righting past wrongs. Affirmative action would be wrong by this standard if it recognized people by the color of their skin. Instead, whites argued, it was time to put race behind us and be color-blind. . . .
>
> Many whites assumed that blacks who made such charges [of racism] were "playing the race card" or seeking to blame others for their own failings.... Blacks were no longer given great recognition as victims in the American experience. Whites had usurped that role for themselves. Once again the tribulations and struggles of white people were center stage. (141-142)

But, says DiAngelo, "if we pretend we don't notice race, we cannot notice racism. If we don't notice racism, we can't understand or interrupt it in ourselves or others" (55). Note the experiences of a Hispanic woman in 2003 when her family moved to Kansas City from west Texas:

From "We need a hospitality lesson"

> A real estate agent here "was quick to point out we would be more comfortable in the [traditionally Hispanic] Argentine area of Kansas City, Kansas." They settled in the Northland.
>
> "On registering our children at school, I was asked if my kids spoke English well enough or did they need English as a second language classes," she wrote. "I am embarrassed to say they do not speak much Spanish."

> When buying groceries she presented her debit card and was asked by the clerk what country the card was from. "Mazuma Credit Union was on the card," she wrote.
>
> "After a long day of unpacking, my kids and I ran to a nearby fast-food restaurant," she wrote. "In the parking lot was a police officer.
>
> "Not being very discreet, he followed us into the restaurant, back outside and then proceeded to follow us home."
>
> She said she and her family are still adjusting to encounters with ignorance and bigotry.

Another incident took place in Westport, a popular nightspot in Kansas City, Missouri, which offers bars, nightclubs, a movie theater, as well as shops and restaurants.

<u>From "Singing the Westport blues"</u>

> A weekend night out awakened Joi L. Preciphs and her friends to the blues African-Americans sometimes pick up in Westport.
>
> Preciphs and the other black women, ages 22 to 26, were celebrating a friend's return from Washington, D.C. The six started their Saturday night at an Overland Park, Kan., nightclub and then landed about 1:30 a.m. in Westport at Stanford's Comedy House.
>
> The place was packed, and each paid a $5 cover charge to enter, dance and socialize. Their problems began about 2:45 a.m. when Stanford's and other clubs closed, landing patrons on the street.
>
> That's when competing safety issues start to play out on warm weekends for customers, merchants, police and Westport security.
>
> Police, the Westport Merchants Association and black community leaders have met in the past to try to solve the issues. Preciphs and her friends, however, found that the same tired tunes for African-Americans were still playing.
>
> For safety's sake, police and security officers try to clear Westport as peacefully and efficiently as possible, said Kansas City Police Maj. Anthony G. Ell, Central Patrol Division commander. To ensure the process goes smoothly, Ell often joins about 32 police officers and about 12 Westport security guards.
>
> Ell said from April until two weeks after Labor Day, police arrive about 10 p.m. on Fridays and Saturdays and don't leave until about 3:30 a.m. when the job is done.
>
> But what happened to Preciphs and her friends seemed like a pedestrian version of racial profiling. Officers were dispersing the mostly black crowd leaving the bars in the mostly white area.
>
> It made Preciphs feel uncomfortable in her hometown. She said it felt like martial law in a police state.

Andrea Lessane, who was with Preciphs, said police dispersal efforts were splitting them up. This created competing safety concerns for them. "I feel safe being in a group with them and not just being by myself," she said.

But the women got back together and stopped to buy gyros from a Westport street vendor. Preciphs said they were the only African-Americans in line.

"Up and down the sidewalk area were crowds of young black men being told by security guards they couldn't stand and needed to keep moving," Preciphs said. It made her feel more uncomfortable.

The women who got their food first stood by the curb to eat out of the way of passing pedestrian traffic. A black police officer, believed to be Ell, told the women they could stand in the area as long as they weren't blocking the flow of people.

Moments later, a white officer insisted that the women leave. They did, but what they didn't like was seeing whites who weren't being ushered out as they were.

"It's very unfair," said Chariese Hudson, who was with Preciphs and Lessane.

Preciphs felt angry and hurt. The women were Westport customers who had spent about $100. Yet, they were treated as if they were trouble-makers. "I think it's debilitated my sense of trust," Preciphs said.

Lessane said: "I know it's not right. This isn't a police state. But I also know that because we're black, we're going to be singled out."

Ell, Greg Lever, executive director of the Westport Merchants Association, and Jim Nunn, executive director of Move-Up, said that was a perception they were trying to erase. Each knows that consistency in the 3 a.m. crowd control effort is essential.

Yet more blues play around a different safety issue. Allowing food vendors to remain open after the bars close foils the push for uniformity.

Lever said pizza, hot dog and gyros stands make the majority of their money from 2:45 to 3:15 a.m. "It's actually a good idea for people to get food in their stomachs," he said. That helps neutralize the effects of alcohol, enabling patrons to drive home sober.

Nunn said he could see how people would expect to be able to eat their food in Westport once they had purchased it.

Lever said, however, that after people buy their food, they were supposed to leave. "Uniformity is critical," he said.

The vendors' presence forces police to judge who's in line, who's waiting, who's eating and who's loitering. "It makes our job difficult over there to sort all of this out," Ell said.

The outcome often isn't right or fair.

People of color also are subjected to disparate treatment when they travel. Before the Civil Rights Movement, it was expected, which is why blacks often drove the highways at night and only stopped for gas or to use the bathroom along deserted roadsides. Families always packed the food they'd need because service would certainly exclude them. That changed after the Civil Rights Movement, or so people thought:

From "Racist arrows at Valentine's"

Racial discrimination lawsuits let people of color know that our experiences of unfair treatment aren't an imaginary thing.

A lawsuit against Adam's Mark was filed in December 1999. A federal investigation that began in July 1999 found that black hotel guests nationwide were forced to pay more than white patrons for comparable accommodations and were offered rooms in less desirable segregated areas.

Investigators also noted that black customers were kept out of hotel restaurants and lounges because the chain's corporate strategy said too high a percentage of blacks in those areas was bad for business.

HBE Corp., the parent company of Adam's Mark, denied the charges in the lawsuit filed in Orlando, Fla., under Title II of the 1964 Civil Rights Act.

Congress passed the civil-rights law so that African-Americans would not have to eat at segregated lunch counters or be victimized by "No Negroes" signs at motels and hotels.

Those are echoes from the deep, ugly parts of my childhood when second-class citizenship was all white America offered to people of color.

We're more than 30 years beyond the break-through Civil Rights Movement, which secured for African-Americans the constitutional freedoms that had been a whites-only privilege. But we seem to be going backward now.

Affirmative action has been reduced or eliminated. The Adam's Mark case also is just one of many in the 1990s.

Denny's restaurants and Texaco oil made headlines in multimillion-dollar settlements in racial discrimination cases involving African-Americans.

Such cases cause African-Americans like me to recount the many slights we may have dismissed as poor customer service. On my family's East Coast vacation in 1998, we were given a room that reeked of cigarette smoke even though we had reserved nonsmoking accommodations at the sold-out hotel.

When we complained we miraculously received a better room.

> That happened a couple of times in other hotels.
>
> The practice of discriminating against black people is being called "rational racism."
>
> Company personnel use business explanations to justify racist choices. An example was an ad-agency memo that warned against placing advertising on minority-serving stations because businesses wanted "prospects not suspects."
>
> In too many restaurants, bars and hotels, whites are given preference over black customers because some companies think the presence of too many minorities will offend white people.
>
> Combined with racial profiling and retail racism it's as if African-Americans are being told to stay home. This makes no economic sense in today's competitive marketplace. But neither does racism.
>
> Yet such covert things stand out for people of color as much as the cross that someone tried to burn at the Lansing, Kan., home of an interracial couple.

All of these (and many more) personal stories illustrate the cost of an unfair tax of prejudice, leaving people of color beaten and broken in spirit. Such incidents occur regularly. They are personal and wearying. One happened to me at a bank a few years ago. A certificate of deposit (CD) that contained enough money to pay my youngest daughter's tuition and room and board for her first two years of college came due. The rates for CDs weren't very good at the time, so I decided to reduce the term, keep the CD at the same bank and add funds to it, since my daughter then was several years shy of graduating from high school.

So on a Saturday morning I dressed casually and went to the bank in question with the necessary paperwork to take care of what needed to be done. The persons I needed to see had clients at their desks, and there was one other customer ahead of me. I was told by the attendant to take a seat, and she would see that I got my turn with the next available bank employee. I could make out that, at the far end of the bank, a male employee who could have helped me was having a nice conversation with an older customer. Closer to me a female bank employee was setting up accounts for a younger couple who knew friends of hers.

The male bank employee finished his business, stood up, shook the older gentleman's hand and that customer left. The person waiting ahead of me got his turn with the male bank employee. After about 15 minutes, he finished, too. The female bank employee was still with the couple. When I saw the male bank employee become free I started to walk toward him. But another guy suddenly walked in from outside ahead of me and took the chair at that bank employee's desk. I looked at the attendant, who was the gatekeeper, expecting her to intervene. She now said I had to wait until the female teller was available. I was the only African American in the bank, and I was furious.

I ended up waiting in that bank for nearly an hour before the female employee finally finished and was able to attend to me. By that time, though, I was out of patience and out of time. I was direct with the female bank employee. I had planned to add to the certificate of deposit that I had there, but now I just wanted a check for the amount and to never have to enter that bank again. She went over to the other employee, who happened to be her supervisor, and they tried to convince me not to withdraw the money. But my time was up, and I wanted out. They had no choice but to comply with my request. Unfortunately I have had to do that same thing at a number of banks, where I felt the service I received was different only because of the color of my skin.

I have no way of knowing whether I was treated differently because I'm black, but I can't rule it out either. That episode, however, should make clear the emotional cost of racism for people of color and the financial cost to institutions that discriminate through bad customer service.

Later, at a different bank, a manager who had immigrated from India made me aware of an unpromoted policy in which her bank bettered the CD rates advertised at other institutions. I had no idea such things occurred and neither did my dad, who has purchased CDs for more than 60 years. It's apparent that many people of color are kept ignorant of financial options that could enable them to grow wealth. Are there perhaps other investment opportunities that bank employees and fund managers who are white aren't letting people of color know about, while telling all to those who look like them? Could this be one of the benefits of white privilege, too?

I'm inclined to think so because of another banking experience I had. I am treasurer of the Kansas City Association of Black Journalists. I watch *The Kansas City Star* for any special rates on CDs. For instance, I saw an ad a few years ago offering about 7 percent interest for a CD. The ad ran only in what we call a neighborhood news section. Here is why that matters. At *The Star* I have access to all of the editions of the paper and its many neighborhood news sections. Periodically, some banks will run ads in the sections zoned only for Johnson County, one of the wealthiest and whitest parts of the Kansas City area. The cost for the ad is lower that way, but by segregating their message banks exclude a lot of people of color and others who don't live in Johnson County from taking advantage of that investment opportunity. It suppresses the wealth of people in urban areas while giving the ultimate advantage to those in the wealthier white suburbs. It reminds me of that old Billie Holiday song, "God Bless the Child":

Them that's got shall have
Them that's not shall lose
So the Bible said
And it still is news

Mama may have, Papa may have
But God bless the child
That's got his own
That's got his own

Some companies that advertise in newspapers choose to run their ads only in certain sections that are distributed within a limited radius of their business. They base their choice on marketing information they have and assumptions about which customers want to take advantage of their products and services. Newspapers would prefer ads to run in all editions because it's more profitable. The advertisers, however, have their own plans.

The decision cuts out people in the urban core based on assumptions that businesses make about who their clientele should be. Without a doubt in the 21st century, information indeed is power, and those with access advance, while those without fall further behind. But my advantage was that I saw the ad because of the special access I have to all sections of the paper. Call it privilege, but such an advantage must be shared, especially with those who are disadvantaged, so longstanding obstacles can be overcome.

I went to the bank in Overland Park, Kan., offering the higher rate that weekend and got a $10,000 certificate of deposit for the black journalists association. But in the process, the bank employee, seeing where I lived and what group I was with, asked incredulously how I learned about the special offer. I guess it was the tone in which she asked her question that bothered me. It was as if I was not supposed to know about the offer, which means I wasn't supposed to be able to take advantage of it. Again, I have no irrefutable evidence detailing that race was involved in this situation, but I can't factor it out.

The essence of these stories is the majority has the privilege of having access to such wealth-enhancing investments, whereas minorities often do not. The result is that minorities are squeezed out of opportunities. Exclusion, or the practice of selective silence, definitely hurts. The restriction of access to information may be the newest form of discrimination confronting people of color.

To take it a step further, minorities' losses because they aren't able to gain access to information and investment arenas result in their subsidizing the majority. Those with the least amount of wealth end up helping others with the greatest wealth make even more.

Unfortunately, even though "them that's got shall have [and] them that's not shall lose," in the end everyone in society loses when discrimination occurs—perhaps not in financial capital, but certainly in social and intellectual capital.

From "Diversity embraced in Taiwan"

> Imagine a young black Rhodes Scholar feeling welcomed in Taiwan but out of place in Overland Park.
>
> In the summer of 1994, a McDonald's restaurant in Johnson County became an institution of higher learning for Munro C. Richardson. The experience occurred during lunch breaks from his summer job at Black & Veatch, where he was praised as a model employee and a perfectionist in translating literature from English to Chinese.
>
> McDonald's was familiar, so that's where he often ate. But what bothered Richardson was what he didn't see: black people like him.
>
> The multicultural void surfaces at fast-food joints because they are modern-day streams, where people living and working nearby go to refresh themselves and socialize. But like reflections in water, fast-food crowds mirror the segregation of the areas the restaurants serve.
>
> Uncomfortable glances and silence at mostly white eateries make people like Richardson feel unwelcome. Conversely, he likes the McDonald's near his inner-city home because almost everyone is black.
>
> These aren't wild musings of a hypersensitive African-American man. Richardson, 23, has been in gifted and talented programs since fourth grade.
>
> He is a 1989 honors graduate of Lincoln Prep and a 1993 summa cum laude, Phi Beta Kappa graduate of the University of Kansas, where he earned his bachelor's degree in Chinese language and literature.
>
> "I knew he would go far and do a lot of different things," said his mother, Di Anna L. Richardson.
>
> "I think he's an amazingly curious, focused, determined young man," said Mary Klayder, honors program assistant director at the University

of Kansas. "He really looks for worthwhile experiences in life."

Richardson received a Mellon Fellowship for his master's degree work in East Asian studies at Harvard University. Harvard has offered him money to return for a doctorate.

In October, Richardson will travel to Oxford University on the Rhodes Scholarship. He has been overseas before.

In 1991 he went to Taiwan, where he taught English that summer. Then last summer he worked outside Taipei, the capital of Taiwan, doing translations for an American company and teaching English.

Richardson stuck out in Taiwan just as he did in Overland Park, but in Taiwan people were attracted to his uniqueness.

"Many people wanted to come up to me and talk to me," he said. "A young black man speaking Chinese is an oddity. I used my difference and the fact that I stood out to my advantage."

Richardson said America has many undiscovered black Rhodes Scholars. But few surface because not enough people believe in them. Low expectations and stereotypes cut the thin straps that such students need to rise above mediocrity.

"Many people have trouble equating intelligence with blacks or minorities," Richardson said. "I have no trouble because I've seen that my entire life."

He said college was more like Taiwan than Johnson County. As the only black man in many classes, everyone knew his name.

"The way of the world is, I am going to stick out," he said.

But McDonald's helped him see more clearly what being black in our racially divided metro area is like.

"It's been a learning experience to say the least," Richardson said. "It will prepare me for Europe and England."

I hope his two years at Oxford are more like Taiwan than the all-American meal he had to stomach in Overland Park.

Education

The situation is dire in public education at all levels, where the legacy of whiteness stalks and feeds, ensuring that people who are white get the best schools and others get what's left.

From "The lesson of education inequality"

Education has not budged from the 20th to the 21st century as a pivotal civil rights battleground for people of color.

Studies show that minority children in urban schools are gripped tightly today in a vise of segregation and poverty.

Whites have fled cities for schools in the suburbs and taken a wealth of resources with them. "The effects of 'checkbook segregation' 50 years after the Brown vs. Board decision seems almost as cruel as the explicit 'separate but equal' racial segregation of the past," Robert B. Aguirre wrote in a report "The Crisis in Hispanic Education: A Call to Latinos for a New Social Activism."

The report was among literature people received in October 2002 at the second annual Latino Civil Rights Summit at Kansas City Kansas Community College. Aguirre, chairman of the Hispanic Council for Reform and Educational Options, is an advocate of school choice. He wants Hispanic children and parents to have more options for a better education.

"What we have now is not meeting the needs of Latino children," Aguirre said. "What we have now is an educational state of crisis."

Aguirre showed that a smaller percentage of Hispanic students take college entrance exams than whites, and those that do on average score lower. His data also showed that a smaller percentage of Hispanics than whites also achieve basic competency levels on achievement tests in elementary, middle and high schools.

The schools are failing the children. "Today's system of public education is the most successful and most enduring racial segregation mechanism in the history of this country," Aguirre said.

"Where is the promise of America?" he asked. "Where is the opportunity? Where is the American dream?"

Those same concerns were voiced by Reginald Weaver in his speech at the 35th Annual Freedom Fund Dinner of the Kansas City Branch of the National Association for the Advancement of Colored People. The theme of the banquet was "Freedom Under Fire."

The government with little debate has spent billions of dollars to bail out the airline industry, build new prisons and beef up the military. But politicians argue endlessly without taking action to fully fund public education for all students, said Weaver, president of the National Education Association.

"Don't tell me there's not enough money," Weaver said. "This is just unacceptable."

Weaver said he was a strong advocate for public schools. Vouchers drain away resources to benefit a few at the expense of many students who are left behind.

That unfair system is pushed on urban kids. But parents in the suburbs have good public schools for their children without even a whisper of vouchers intruding.

"Public education is the great equalizer in our society," he said. It's unfortunate that public schools for minority children remain "the battleground in the struggle for civil rights."

It's an indication that racism endures. It keeps children of color from receiving the best education in urban public schools.

The disadvantage racism creates makes advancing to higher education tough and graduating more difficult. Yet, without college, the American dream of good jobs, better housing and more opportunities remains out of reach.

"We need to get angry and upset and beat the ugly face of racism," said John J. Mendez, then a member of the Unified Board of Commissioners of Wyandotte County and Kansas City, Kan., at the Latino Civil Rights Summit luncheon.

Urban minority students have a clear disadvantage when it comes to education, and challenging racism in the educational system isn't easy. But suburban minority students also have to deal with biases. Chapter 1 contains the story of Cedric Boyd, who found a noose made of string by his desk in his honors calculus class at Shawnee Mission East High School. Cedric and his mother, Joann Boyd, also filed a complaint with the U.S. Department of Education Office for Civil Rights, saying the school kept Cedric from being inducted into the National Honor Society because he's black. Other charges were that school officials retaliated against Cedric and failed to correct a hostile racial environment at the school. Even though the investigation into the noose incident concluded that there was no racial intent involved, Cedric said he would have raised the same concerns again.

From "Educators have much to learn"

"I just want them to get the whole picture that there is disparate treatment," Cedric said.

Most of his peers have been supportive. But some teachers and administrators have labeled him a troublemaker.

They need to read Gary R. Howard's book, *We Can't Teach What We Don't Know: White Teachers, Multiracial Schools.* "We tend to draw distinctions between in-groups and out-groups and quite naturally come to discriminate in favor of our own group," Howard wrote.

None of Cedric's problems would have occurred if Shawnee Mission East educators had studied Howard's book.

Cedric also isn't alone. I've talked with other African-Americans in the Shawnee Mission district who've felt mistreated because of their race. But the parents didn't file formal complaints, fearing retaliation against their children.

Joann Boyd is concerned about retaliation against Cedric, too.

Shawnee Mission Superintendent Marjorie Kaplan said many

parents who raise all kinds of issues fear retaliation by school officials. "The schools usually go to the other extreme to make sure they don't do that," she said.

Boyd said she planned to appeal the education department's ruling on the National Honor Society issue. Subjective evaluations kept Cedric from being inducted.

Kaplan said of the 136 who applied, 121 students were admitted to the National Honor Society at Shawnee Mission East. Five of the seven minority applicants were admitted.

Cedric was the only African-American who applied at the school, which is about 1 percent black.

Local standards and subjectivity are built into the selection based on scholarship, leadership, service and character, said David Cordts, associate director for student activities with the National Association for Secondary School Principals - the founder and sponsor of the 79-year-old National Honor Society. But the process is supposed to be fair.

Boyd said exclusion from such groups keeps blacks at a disadvantage for scholarships, college admissions and jobs.

What also troubles me is why Cedric would be excluded when he is just as qualified as my daughter, Adrianne, who was inducted into the National Honor Society that same year. The difference was her suburban high school is racially diverse, and the educators are more culturally aware.

"What it means is we still have a lot of work to do," Boyd said.

Kaplan agreed. Even though the education department ruling came out in Shawnee Mission's favor "this student did think there was discrimination."

"It heightened our awareness that we need to keep working in this area," she said. Kaplan said objectives would be set for diversity activities at schools. The district will continue to work with the U.S. Justice Department to improve race relations.

"I would never be one to say all of our problems are solved, but I think we're on the right track," Kaplan said. "It is important for every student to feel comfortable in the schools. I think if you feel comfortable, you'll be much more open to learning."

Creating that harmony for all students is everything. Allowing things to continue the way they are negatively affects children of color. Dr. Carter G. Woodson pointed that out in his book, *The Mis-Education of the Negro*. But families of color have to constantly contend with the vestiges of racism. Our kids get bombarded not only at school, but by the media, and in the community as well. Each situation sweetly tells them they are not as good as white people are and they don't deserve all the rights, equality, freedom and opportunities afforded the majority. This stuff hits them in the most insidious ways.

For parents of color, it becomes tiring to have to constantly program our children, deprogram them after they have encountered disparate treatment and then reprogram them so they can successfully navigate the experiences they face.

Since my daughters were born, they would see images of nicely dressed, well-groomed women flash across our television screen. Subconsciously, these people set standards for good looks, but unfortunately too few of them were black. White women with long, blonde hair become a beauty standard, which confuses young black girls. My daughters like all African Americans needed to be convinced that black is beautiful, too.

Barbie helped me build that understanding within them. The blonde, blue-eyed white doll has been adored by generations of girls since it landed on the market decades ago. When my daughters were little girls, commercials showed Barbie to be television's most beautiful doll, and my girls absorbed that standard as if it were sunrays. It was innocent enough, but the message didn't include the fact that beauty comes in more than just one form. So I added two black Barbie dolls and one that looked Hispanic to their collection. Even though my oldest insisted that the white Barbie was the prettiest, I told her that all of the dolls were pretty, but that I liked one of the black dolls the best.

Debbye Turner did a lot to help, too, by winning the Miss America pageant in 1989, chosen because she was prettier and more talented than all the other contestants in the competition. Turner is black, and it was important for my young daughters to see that she was enrolled at the University of Missouri-Columbia College of Veterinary Medicine.

Those are the tough kinds of self-esteem building exercises black parents must go through to help their children have a positive perception of themselves and people like them so the children can develop into emotionally, mentally and spiritually strong people. It is an ages-old concern for African-American parents. Kenneth B. Clark, a psychology professor at City College of New York, made this issue a central part of the Brown v. Topeka Board of Education case in the 1950s. A study he and his wife, Mamie Clark, conducted "placed identical dolls differing only in skin color in front of black children. The children preferred the white doll to the black doll, picking the black doll as looking 'bad'; more than half identified themselves with the 'bad' doll" (Ogletree 4). Thurgood Marshall, the lead attorney for the plaintiffs in the Brown case, had Clark testify

> as an expert witness to explain the psychological harm experienced by black children as a result of the racial caste system in the South. The doll test suggested to the Clarks that black children expressed positive identification with the white dolls and negative identification with the black dolls. Marshall's goal was to demonstrate forcefully, by means of empirical data, the harm that continued segregation had on children. (Ogletree 4-5)

Even though the 1954 Brown v. Topeka Board of Education Supreme Court decision ended legal segregation, the problem persists with children of color having a diminished image of people who look like them. The blame lies with the media and with schools not giving people an accurate or complete image of the Real America. Brown v. Board dismantled the law enforcing segregation but left the institutions behind it intact. The separation, therefore, was allowed to continue unchecked.

In schools, children find that people who look like them are not included in the history taught and recorded in this country. It just highlights Eurocentric accomplishments. People of color don't see themselves in textbooks, in the mosaic of this country's past, and consequently don't feel that the system of education includes them. It clouds their ability to grasp the relevance of the lessons. That leads them to think they are not invited to the table of this nation's present and certainly it looks as if they're excluded from its future. Every instruction becomes a turnoff. Losses are recorded in students of color suffering poor academic performance, becoming unproductive and disruptive in class. Their potential in school dies. The inculcation of non-inclusive education is like a "forced march" for African-Americans and other students of color not unlike what Native Americans experienced in this country's history as they were uprooted from their land and transplanted elsewhere. The casualties are in the losses, including prison for some students whom education woefully let down. Such human tragedies make today's education without a strong multicultural curriculum the nation's "21st Century Trail of Tears."

Missing in Action

From the perspective of a white woman who grew up poor, Robin J. DiAngelo writes that

> Growing up in segregated environments (schools, workplaces, neighborhoods, media images, historical perspectives, etc.), we are given the message that our experiences and perspectives are the only ones that

> matter. We receive this message day in and day out, and it is not limited to a single moment, it is a relentless experience. Virtually all our teachers, history books, role models, movie and book characters, are white like us.... Whiter environments ... are marked as the most socially and economically valuable. Reaching towards the most valuable places in society thus entails leaving people of color behind. (53-54)

Even, it seems, to the point of leaving them off our money:

From "A history ignored; American Indians deserve to be recognized"

> Change from a convenience store yielded a new quarter for my collection.
>
> It was the one for Kansas. New quarters out for 35 of the 50 states picture George Washington on the front with words, "United States of America," "Liberty," "In God We Trust" and "Quarter Dollar."
>
> Each state's quarter, however, also is unique in what it shows on the back. Kansas' quarter has a buffalo standing in some prairie grass. The bison is looking to its left. To its right is a bouquet of the state's signature sunflowers.
>
> I was happy to get the new quarter. But when I took the coin home and compared it with the others, I saw it was the only one that comes close to depicting this nation's American Indian heritage.
>
> The buffalo provided so much for many American Indians. A lot of tribes followed the great herds to hunt the animals. The bulls weighed 1,600 to 3,000 pounds. The females generally tipped the scales at only 900 pounds.
>
> The buffalo meat gave American Indians their food. The hides were treated so they provided clothing, shoes and skins for teepees. Other parts of the animal were used for ceremonial purposes for the Plains tribes.
>
> In 1850 the western plains were home to about 20 million bison. So large were some of the herds that trains had to stop to allow the animals to cross the tracks.
>
> Such impediments to "progress" didn't last long. White hunters slaughtered the animals, nearly wiping out a key source of food for many American Indians.
>
> By 1889, only about 500 bison could be found alive in the United States. Efforts began afterward to keep the buffalo from going extinct.
>
> But what fascinated me was none of the other quarters had any symbol of this country's American Indian origins. It's as if they didn't exist and have no importance now.
>
> Florida's quarter contains the space shuttle, palm trees, the Union entry date 1845 and an old ship with sails. But there's nothing about the American Indians who once populated Florida.

They were run out by whites who waged senseless wars against them often because they gave safe harbor to runaway slaves.

Virginia pictures three ocean-going vessels with sails, the Union entry date 1788 and Jamestown. But the quarter makes no mention of the American Indians who greeted Europeans who landed. It also says nothing of the Dutch ship that brought the first slaves from Africa.

School kids learn the history of Thanksgiving in the United States. American Indians' crops helped colonists survive. American Indians participated and provided a lot of the bounty for the first Thanksgiving in the 1600s in New England.

Yet none of the quarters for Connecticut, Maine, Massachusetts, New Hampshire, Rhode Island or Vermont contains any image of American Indians or any essence of their history, help or tradition. New Hampshire has the 1788 Union entry date, a rock with the words "Old Man of the Mountain" and the state motto, "Live Free or Die."

Maine has a lighthouse on a shore, a ship with sails in the background and the 1820 Union entry date. Vermont has its 1791 Union entry date, the words, "Freedom and Liberty," mountains in the background, a rail fence and a person with a coat, hat and scarf gathering sap in buckets from trees.

Massachusetts has its 1788 Union entry date, a Minuteman in period clothing with a long rifle, a picture of the state and the words, "The Bay State." Rhode Island has its 1790 Union entry date, a modern sailboat on the water with a suspension bridge in the background with the words, "The Ocean State."

Connecticut has its 1788 Union entry date, a great tree with no leaves and the words "The Charter Oak." The other new quarters I have speak to white, Eurocentric traditions and symbols.

Missouri has the Arch and explorers paddling in a canoe. Illinois shows Lincoln and Chicago's skyscrapers. Iowa has a one-room schoolhouse, the words "Foundation in Education" and white settlers.

But American Indians are missing, and so is much of the diversity in this great land. Fifteen quarters remain to be issued. That still leaves time for Alaska, Hawaii and some states in the Southwest, Northwest and Midwest and South to correct the unforgivable omission.

I'll keep counting the coins as they come out and will report whether the full 50 add up to anything close to America's real diversity. So far only Kansas comes close to the truth.

DiAngelo notes that "as White people, we are taught not to feel any loss about the absence of people of color in our lives" (53). The reactions to the column above demonstrate just how well that lesson has been learned.

E-mail: Jan. 13, 2006

Yes, Native Americans have played an important role in the development of America. However, America is by and large a nation of European immigrants. Why then is it a problem when the state quarters reflect this heritage? Yes, they may have Eurocentric themes, but that is indicative of the people who settled the area and their ancestors who remain in those areas today.

Why was it necessary to include the term "white" numerous times in this article? Examples:

White hunters slaughtered the animals, nearly wiping out a key source of food for many American Indians.

They were run out by whites who waged senseless wars against them often because they gave safe harbor to runaway slaves.

(Not all the Indian tribes were driven out of Florida. The Seminoles take great pride in being "unconquered.")

The other new quarters I have speak to white, Eurocentric traditions and symbols.

Why is it necessary to indict a whole race of people based on the actions of a few?

Diversity is not missing in this great nation as you claim. If you would become color blind for even a moment, you would notice that millions of people from different nations all around the world have come together to make America great. By claiming that there is a lack of diversity evident in the state quarter designs, you diminish the contributions of the many people who have forged this nation over the centuries.

E-mail: Jan. 13, 2006

What a terrible burden Mr. Diuguid must carry around on a daily basis as he constantly looks for examples of a lack of inclusion and "diversity" within American society. And what has his eagle eye now spotted to draw his contempt and cluck-clucking ire? Why, it's the fact that the commemorative set of state quarters don't include any reference to this nation's American Indian culture.

What an outrage! Never mind that there isn't much room on the back of the quarter to include all that he'd like to see, if what they do depict doesn't suit his version of a state's history, they are practically worthless! Whoever designed and approved each and every one of these coins is obviously an insensitive lout to have not taken Mr. Diuguid's tastes into account. Lewis (sorry, but I'm typing this thru tears of laughter), might I suggest that you give up on your numismatic hobby (that means coin collecting) and look elsewhere for fodder for your self-righteous columns?

ps;Thanks for the chuckle. That's about all your columns are good for, and I had a good one today.

DiAngelo continues that white people "are taught in our culture to see our experience as objective and representative of reality. The belief in objectivity, coupled with setting White people up as outside of culture and thus the norm for humanity, allows us to see ourselves as universal humans who can represent all of human experience. People of color can only represent their own racialized experience" (54). Is that perhaps why no dads of color were pictured in a book about fathers?

From "Book paints colorless picture of American fatherhood"

> Clinton Wynn called outraged over a "sweet" book he had picked up at a Hallmark store.
>
> It's titled *Dads: A Celebration of Fatherhood.* On the cover is a black-and-white picture of a man in a 1950s wide-rimmed hat, white shirt, suit and tie. He is running, holding hands with a boy in shorts and a girl in a dress. They're all smiling.
>
> The back of the book says: "Our earliest hero; our proudest supporter; our most devoted protector; Dad is the steadfast heart of the family. Celebrating the deep, enduring love he gives and the joy he brings, this charming book is a tribute to doting dads and the unbreakable bond of fatherhood."
>
> What's not to love about that? Wynn, whom I've known for years, persuaded me to buy a copy of the "cute little book."
>
> That's when I realized why he was so upset. The book is filled with touching black-and-white pictures from the 1920s through the 1980s. They are of children and their dads, including one from the TV series "Father Knows Best." The quotes are outstanding, too.
>
> One from Walt Whitman says: "I throw myself upon your breast, my father, I cling to you so that you cannot unloose me ... Kiss me, my father, Touch me with your lips, as I touch those I love, Breathe to me, while I hold you close."
>
> The accompanying 1955 photo is of a boy and girl in a park running into a man's outstretched arms. But noticeably missing in this wonderful little book are children and fathers of color.
>
> That's what upset Wynn. None of the people in this book compiled by Rose O'Kelly is African-American, Hispanic, Asian-American or American Indian.
>
> It's not as if people of color didn't exist in the 20th century. They helped build America, shouldering some of the heaviest, dirtiest and most dangerous loads.
>
> But minorities then and now often are invisible in the media, in books, in what our children learn in schools.

I liked what Cheryl Brown Henderson, president of the Brown Foundation, said at the fall National Association for Multicultural Education Conference in Kansas City: "'Leave It to Beaver' was not a documentary."

But many people view that hit '50s and '60s TV show as if it were. That was the image projected of America. It's tragic that the "Gift Book from Hallmark" does so, too.

It's also disappointing because it's a reversal of what Hallmark was doing in the mid-'90s, when it started a new line of cards aimed at the growing African-American, Hispanic and Jewish markets.

Gail Baker Woods, in her book, *Advertising and Marketing to the New Majority*, wrote that smart companies like Hallmark were reaching into the markets of racial and ethnic diversity. They see gold in directing products to long-ignored consumers of color, featuring people in ads and programming who looked like them.

"Ethnic markets can be lucrative sources of untapped consumer dollars," Woods wrote. "They are big and growing bigger."

But since the Sept. 11, 2001, terrorist attacks, people of color are disappearing from images that the media project. It's as if we don't exist at a time when the nation is becoming more ethnically and racially diverse.

Dads: A Celebration of Fatherhood just drives that painful point home even though African-American, Hispanic, Asian-American and American Indian men are fathers, too. We are workers, husbands and dads, and we deeply love our children and care about their health, safety, education, well-being and future. We want this country to live up to its ideals for them beyond what America has done for us, our fathers and their fathers.

Kristi Ernsting, Hallmark Cards Inc. spokeswoman, acknowledged that *Dads*, which Hallmark purchased from MQ Productions, lacks racial and ethnic diversity. "Based on your friend's comments, we realize we could do a better job in respect to dads," Ernsting said.

"We do really appreciate hearing from people," Ernsting said. "We want all of our products to reflect what people want and to reflect our entire consumer base."

She brought another Hallmark gift book to me that does. It's titled *Father Knows Best: Funny and True Tales of Fatherhood.*

Dads, however, also should include wonderful quotes and pictures of men of color and their beautiful children.

Men of color and their children in a nation that's open and honest about its diversity should never be left out of books like *Dads* again.

In the eyes of several readers commenting on the above column, dads of color are largely absent; therefore, not including them in the book is a reflection of that segregated "reality" which they choose to believe:

E-mail: March 2, 2005

Way to go Lewis. You have now written your most laughable column-even though horse manure is not really anything to laugh at. It's apparent you never speak with black women.

The typical black male is not steadfast in anything. Fathers of color are left out of books for good reason. The typical black male is not a father or a dad.

In fact, the black race has the highest number of non-fathers on the planet and deserve to be left out of books today-even more so than in the past. Take a survey among black women in America. The black male has nearly destroyed the well being of the black race.

It's time for you to be open and honest about this nation's diversity and the standing of the typical black male. Kristi Ernsting ought to put out a book about life in America's prisons and include lots of black and white pictures.

E-mail: March 2, 2005

Maybe if more fathers of color were around their children there would be more pictures of it.

Comments also showed people struggling with race:

Voice mail: March 2, 2005

You're constantly pushing this racial thing. Hey we want more black shown. You don't understand that back in the 1950s the white race, the northern Europeans were still in vogue and felt that they were America. That's the way that it was and still is much of the time. You can't change that. So they didn't want to look at the non-northern European people in ads or on television and radio and all of that. They didn't want that, and therefore the commercial people were not going to do it. And don't say that it's all changed now. You don't get around with the normal average white people and hear their comments. They don't want to look at stuff on TV with different races. You're just going to make things worse. Uh-oh, here's an incoming call. Probably from the Gestapo.

E-mail: March 3, 2005

For years you have boasted of the black organizations you belong to, sang the praises of Pete O'Neal, a fugitive criminal, ranted on and on about your father, including his foolhardy drive, at an advanced age, across the state in a car with no air-conditioning and told countless tales of your daughters wisdom, virtue and graciousness. Then you hit the ceiling because a book, Dads: A Celebration of Fatherhood, does not include blacks.

Just another instance where your racism and bigotry over rode common sense. You, sir, are a black version of the KKK.

Riane Eisler, in her book *The Chalice and the Blade*, discusses the "dominator model of human relations." Eisler gives examples of how the "rigid male dominance, and with it the dominance of 'masculine' values" works in Western democracies (166-167). In the racist version of this system, whatever is considered different—whether that is based on race, religion, or ethnic origin—is also considered inferior, needing to be "dominated." It is a model that sustains covert discrimination. Since the model imposes "'masculine' values" and considers "the return of women to their traditional subservient place [as] a top priority" (168, italics added), women continue to face the challenge of being sidelined and having their voices silenced.

From "Of women, silence and rage"

Cathy Stackpole had the full attention of her audience when she said many women lose their voices at age 8.

Stackpole, then-director of youth and family ministry for Unity Church of Overland Park, talked about that and related issues at the Starr Symposium.

She reviewed her lecture with me recently. What she shared is part of the unspoken history that women worldwide continue to endure. Researchers have found that girls do lose their voices as they and society defer more to boys.

Stackpole said the loss shows up years later, even when two women try to make plans for lunch. "One asks, 'Where do you want to go to lunch?' The other replies, 'I don't know, where do you want to go?'" Stackpole said.

"The idea is, women try to please the other person," she said. "It's always the sense of the other, so it's harder for girls and young women to say, 'What do I need?'"

Younger girls will speak their minds. But society too often mutes their voices as the girls age. That process starts at birth, said Rose Kemp, then-regional administrator of the Women's Bureau with the U.S. Department of Labor.

"People look at the girl child and say, 'Isn't she cute?'" Kemp said. "But they look at the boy child and say, 'Oh, he'll be president someday.' From that day on, they program the child."

The different treatment gets magnified in schools, robbing many girls of their confidence and self-esteem.

"They start to feel less OK about themselves at that early age," Stackpole said. "They become less likely to take chances. By taking risks, you grow, change and learn."

Kemp said the psychological shackles society puts on girls affects their education, college selection, career options, job performance, salary and promotional possibilities. Their talents go unrecognized, and "they are not equipped to make decisions for their future."

Girls internalize the pain. But their inability to even say a simple "no" may surface in substance abuse, depression, suicide attempts, teen pregnancy or dependence on an abusive relationship, Stackpole said.

When females do finally speak out, they may express the same rage that African-Americans express after stomaching racism too long. Others often don't understand, Kemp said.

Another issue Stackpole discussed focuses on male-centered pronouns. The power of our language came out in a class she taught at Webster University in which Stackpole replaced "he" and "him" with "she" and "her."

Women in the class enjoyed it. But the men became agitated and uncomfortable. One man said there's no way that he could be "she."

"We take for granted that we have to translate, and we don't even acknowledge the amount of energy it takes to see ourselves in those situations," Stackpole said. "It invalidates women's experience, women's place, and we do it a lot.

"I think, in particular, we do it to marginalize people. It's a subtle disregard for human life. The context is this person's life is not important."

Kemp said the language must change to become gender-neutral. Policeman should be police officer. Fireman should be firefighter, and staff should be used as a verb instead of "to man" a position.

"It gives you a different image," Kemp said. It's one that includes women and girls instead of excluding them.

Language in Action

Language is explosive. People identify themselves with a language group and will often refuse to acknowledge the legitimacy of the way others use language. Women encounter this attitude. People of color do, too. Some people will look at others and, by virtue of their appearance, assume they cannot speak English well. Minority journalists, for example, often are viewed as less capable than their white colleagues of using the English language well, even though it's not true. In addition, people of color are profiled and labeled when their language use is different from whites'. The perception, on the one hand, is based on the way a person looks and, on the other hand, on the way an individual sounds. Discrimination against minorities, youths, immigrants, and people from other regions, though often out in the open, also goes underground when it is hidden behind criticisms of how they speak.

Letter: Dec. 8, 2001

Please allow me to list the reasons as to why blacks are not popular with Caucasians:

1. Filthy language.
2. Much too violent. 90 percent of all crime is committed by blacks.
3. The way you all butcher grammar – "I be going" – "He going," "I be good," "It is they fault," and pronouncing the word "ask" as "ax," etc. How could an English teacher ever teach grammar to a black?
4. Loud and obnoxious – can't talk in a normal tone to the person beside them.
5. Always have that obnoxious loud racket (you call music) blasting to the hilt – even with headphones it's heard by all.
6. Lack of temper control.
7. Use your color as an excuse for not getting whatever you want.
8. Never want to work a full, five days per week.
9. Have too many babies by too many different men – ie Derrick Thomas!
10. An extremely homely race, huge nose, thick lips, big bubble butt and hideous hair.

Look these over and you'll see why Caucasians wish you would all return to Africa! True, our ancestors brought blacks to our country as servants, however, we had nothing to do with said transportation – and by their doing this – there's been trouble ever since.

No reflection on you, 10 percent of the blacks are OK – however, I prefer not to be around them.

Thanks for listening.

Sincerely,

Voice Mail: 1997

You're talking about the black youngsters and their English and everything. Well, I think most of them don't care anything about talking English. They have their own language and that's the way they want to speak. So I think that's just the way it is. Thank you sir.

Many people consider others' names a part of those individuals' identities. In some cultures, children are named only after distinctive character traits have emerged; in other cultures, a name might be passed on from generation to generation. Many naming traditions exist so it is hard to know why a person has a certain name; yet names are also used as a subliminal tool for discrimination.

From "What's in a name? Often, discrimination"

Parents invest a lot of love and care in naming their children.

However, a new study suggests that in spite of that devotion, some names may cause young people to be held back, while another set may help others advance.

Marianne Bertrand, of the University of Chicago Graduate School of Business, and Sendhil Mullaninathan, with the Massachusetts Institute of Technology, submitted 5,000 resumes they created to 1,300 help-wanted ads in *The Chicago Tribune* and *The Boston Globe*.

They picked one set of names, such as Aisha, Tamika, Tanisha, Latoya, Darnell, Hakim, Kareem and Rasheed, that are fairly common among African-Americans. The second set, more typical among white people, included Allison, Emily, Sarah, Brad, Greg, Matthew and Todd.

The researchers gave the black and white applicants they created the same education, skills and experience.

Their names were the only difference.

The results were not surprising. Resumes with white-sounding names received 50 percent more callbacks than black-sounding names. The study said, "This gap can only be attributed to the race-specific names, suggesting that employers discriminate (quite a bit) on the basis of race.

"Race also affects the reward to having a better resume," the study said. "Whites with higher-quality resumes receive 30 percent more callbacks than whites with lower-quality resumes, a statistically significant difference.

"On the other hand, having a higher-quality resume has a much smaller and statistically insignificant effect for African-American applicants. This lower reward for African-Americans suggests that, in the current state of the labor market, African-Americans do not have strong individual incentives to build a strong resume.

"Discrimination appears to bite twice, making it harder for African-Americans to find a job and to improve their employability."

The study also found that living in a wealthier, more educated and more white community increased the callback rate for white applicants. "But increasingly, African-Americans are not helped more than whites by neighborhood," the study said.

The report said, "Discrimination levels are the same across all the occupations and industries covered in the experiment."

The results are troubling. The love and care parents devote to naming their children isn't being equally embraced outside the home.

Black parents and their children still struggle against racism.

The study makes me wonder whether Hispanics and Muslims face the same name trauma. Hispanics now represent the nation's largest minority group and face similar harassment and discrimination that black people do.

Muslims since the Sept. 11, 2001, attacks have endured racial profiling, harassment and discrimination. It's not right. America as a land of mostly immigrants should treat all people of color as valued, taxpaying contributors to this country.

The name experiment shows why affirmative-action programs at universities and in workplaces are needed. How else would people of color get in the door to prove their worth?

However, the study shows the playing field is far from level. Companies are making choices on whom to invite to interview for jobs based on an assumption of race that names generate.

I have met and interviewed many people who are white who have some of the black-sounding names used in the study. I also know many African-Americans and other people of color with names used in the study that are typically thought to be white.

Our world is far too diverse for people in companies, schools, banks, civic organizations and housing to make assumptions based on a race and stereotypes they may assign to a name.

Businesses and people should accept individuals for who they are and embrace the differences. They also must at least respect the investment parents make in children's names.

In "Finding Words to Talk About Race," Maria Luisa Tucker points out that people with Hispanic names can face that same kind of racism. She writes:

I am the daughter of an Ecuadorian immigrant mother and a father from a Southern white ranching family. I was born in East Texas, in a town where people frequently called my mom "wetback" and "taco-bender" to her face. In an attempt to protect her children from this verbal brutality, my mother did not teach us to speak Spanish. She wanted us to quietly blend in, to be as unnoticeable as possible. . . .

My parents divorced long ago. My father remarried, to a woman who was both white and blonde. They wanted more children but were unable to conceive. Finally, two years ago, they adopted three Mexican-American siblings who had been in foster care. My left-leaning, hippie-esque father and I have never once had a conversation about race or ethnicity; the adoption of three little brown children didn't change that sad fact.

Secretly...I assumed we would share similar values and interests because we shared a Latin American heritage. [But] my father announced that, at the adoption ceremony, [the children's] names would be changed.

> Their "Mexican-sounding" names would be simplified into shorter, "white" names. Ostensibly, this was a protective measure to prevent the children from being teased. I wanted to scream at my dad; I felt this was a mistake worse than my mom abandoning Spanish. It was denying more than language -- it was denying their very identities. These three sweet-natured brown-eyed, brown-skinned children were being raised in a state that was about one-third Hispanic, yet their new parents' first lesson was that being Latino was strange and should be hidden. I couldn't understand why my father would do this. Two months ago, I got my answer.

At the funeral for her paternal grandmother, Tucker was approached by one of her uncles, whom she'd been warned to stay away from.

> "You know, your dad's problems started with those kids," [my uncle] said.
>
> I was silent.
>
> "Those Mexican kids, you know. I told him he needed to change their names. It's just a fact of life that old white guys like me will mess with them.... The world is full of old white guys like me."
>
> My uncle is right. There are a lot of old white guys like him. The world is full of people who unthinkingly buy into racism and prejudice.

Language can be used as an excuse to discriminate, no matter how subtly. But words are powerful tools that can themselves discriminate as effectively as any action. And despite what the popular adage says, words can and do hurt. In addition, advertisers and politicians have become adept at "framing" issues so that public opinion will be swayed in a direction that is favorable to them. However, when one is favored, false images are often created, and another can easily be hurt.

From "It's all in how you say it"

> Foul language has created some life-threatening consequences for clinics and doctors serving women and families.
>
> An anthrax hoax at Planned Parenthood in midtown Kansas City was just the latest tragedy. I think such domestic terrorism erupts when the media labels full-range health-care providers "abortion clinics" or "abortion doctors."
>
> Public reaction would be radically different if they were called "women's clinics" or "women's doctors," "family clinics" or "family doctors." The change would direct the news toward life and health instead of hate and death.
>
> How any issue is framed critically affects the public's response, Stanford University professors stressed at the conference of the Monroe Trotter Group of black columnists. Their lectures focused mostly on affirmative action.

The media shorthand for abortion is just as powerful. Such stereotypes create a new script for old rules of one gender controlling another.

Consider the following headlines: "Bomb at abortion clinic kills an off-duty officer"; "Abortion clinics vandalized with foul-smelling chemical"; and "Sniper kills abortion doctor."

The connotation and public reaction to the assaults would change if the headlines told the greater truth: "Bomb at women's clinic kills an off-duty officer," "Women's clinics vandalized with foul-smelling chemical" and "Sniper kills family doctor."

These acts then would be seen for what they are: cowardly domestic terrorism against women and families.

Jenell Clark, then-vice president of marketing for Planned Parenthood in Kansas City, said 86 percent of the services it provided to 42,104 persons in 1998 were for family planning.

About 28,000 patients visited Planned Parenthood for one of 10 birth-control options.

About 18,000 patients received pap smears, and 752 were identified as having precancerous or cancerous conditions. Clark said 1,757 patients went for HIV tests, 10,444 women for pregnancy tests and 1,452 males for reproductive health services.

"People don't see Planned Parenthood as being in the business of providing health care," Clark said. "When I talk about the range and number of patients we serve people are shocked because the 'antis' have done such a great job of positioning us as just abortion providers. We don't have the resources to out-market them."

The national attack language causes more lawmakers, courts and people to turn on places that offer full-range women and family health care. An appeals court in St. Paul, Minn., allowed Missouri to restrict Planned Parenthood from receiving state family planning money. The decision says groups cannot directly or indirectly use state family planning money to subsidize abortions.

Doctors and clinics also had been targeted in "wanted posters" on anti-abortion Web sites. Fortunately a federal jury in Portland, Ore., said that went too far.

But other language of death and hate is still there, and so is the gutless violence. Domestic terrorists have contaminated clinics with butyric acid. The colorless acid irritates the eyes, nose and throat and causes coughing and difficulty breathing. It's commonly found in rancid butter and perspiration.

People shouldn't fling such toxins at others. They wouldn't if they realized the attacks were on women and families.

Undocumented immigrants face the same verbal poison when the press labels them illegal aliens or just aliens. They are stripped of their humanity and susceptible to any abuse that others can inflict on them. It's wrong and it, too, must change.

Four small words in a nursery rhyme packed a powerful punch and were instrumental in starting a court case that made headlines nationwide but ended in heartache after passing through despair, denial, aggravation, and hatred. As mentioned in Chapter 1, the claim that racism was not intended does not mitigate the impact the words had on the women affected by them.

From "Nursery rhyme's racist roots; Airline case demonstrates why verse should become obsolete"

> The "Eenie, meenie, minie, moe" lawsuit against Southwest Airlines must have seemed like child's play to a federal jury.
>
> But the recent case actually is quite serious. It clearly shows how deeply divided this country remains on the issue of race.
>
> Southwest flight attendant Jennifer Cundiff, 25, on a crowded Las Vegas to Kansas City trip three years ago this month used a variation of the ages-old nursery rhyme. She said over the plane's loudspeaker, "Eenie, meenie, minie, moe; pick a seat, we gotta go."
>
> Louise Sawyer, 46, of Merriam, and Grace Fuller, 49, of Lenexa, who are siblings, contended that they were the only passengers in the aisle. Fuller said her epilepsy prevented her from responding immediately. She wrote to company officials later.
>
> They apologized but were dismissive. The rhyme "was meant to be humorous," one letter said. The lawsuit followed.
>
> Cundiff said the rhyme was meant for several passengers, not just the sisters. Sawyer and Fuller are black; Cundiff is white.
>
> The sisters' lawsuit said they were discriminated against and suffered physical and emotional distress because of what Cundiff said. Fuller testified that she suffered a small seizure on the flight and was bedridden for three days after having a grand mal seizure at home.
>
> Like many African-Americans, I felt Sawyer's and Fuller's pain. Many black people learn at an early age to loathe the original racist rhyme:
>
> Eenie, meenie, minie, moe; catch a n----- by the toe. If he hollers let him go. Eenie, meenie, minie, moe.
>
> But the eight-member federal jury in Kansas City, Kan., last month ruled in favor of the airline. Two things about the trial and verdict were telling: The jury was all white, and the panel deliberated less than an hour.
>
> The dirty little rhyme and its many variations still hit most African-Americans like an anvil. But that carried no weight with the white jury.

For me, "Eenie, meenie, minie, moe" resurrected my first brush with the N-word. I was about 3 years old, and my brother, David, was about 4.

A kid our age in the recently integrated southside St. Louis neighborhood had come to play at our home. The boy, who was white, started saying "Eenie, meenie, minie, moe..." to pick between my brother and me.

Our mother overheard it and chased the kid away. I had buried that racist incident as people of color usually do to cope in America. But it re-emerged in 1993 when a diversity facilitator brought that ugly memory out of me.

It was so vivid, and the pain was so fresh. The torrent of emotions included sadness, confusion, embarrassment, anger, frustration and helplessness.

Laughter usually accompanies the goofiness on Southwest flights. I can only imagine how that must have added to Fuller's and Sawyer's suffering.

I know why Fuller said, "There is no justice in America for blacks...." It's why African-Americans or other persons of color were needed for the sisters to truly have a jury of their peers.

Mary Frances Berry said it best in her book *The Pig Farmer's Daughter and Other Tales of American Justice*. The Civil Rights Movement elevated the stories of black people, sparking a "due process revolution" and "more civil liberties protection," said Berry, then-chairwoman of the U.S. Commission on Civil Rights.

However, because we live in increasingly segregated communities, the opportunities to share stories keep declining. "Eenie, meenie, minie, moe" remains rooted in the lexicon of America, and no redraft will erase its racist code.

That rhyme and racism in America actually are like a colorful grove of trees proudly planted more than 60 years ago near Zernikow, Germany, when Adolf Hitler was in power. Each fall the trees form a swastika visible from above. The embarrassed villagers repeatedly have cut down the trees, but the foliage stubbornly returns, reminding the world of the Nazis and the atrocities.

The flight attendant's age is no excuse for her not knowing how her words wounded her black customers. Yet, if there is any good that surfaced from the lawsuit maybe it will prevent others from using that rhyme again.

Hardly . . .

<u>From "History draws color line in U.S"</u>

Over the weekend, Louise Sawyer and Grace Fuller of Johnson County received hate mail because of their "Eenie, meenie, minie, moe" lawsuit against Southwest Airlines.

Race relations remain strained.

History intrudes here. The Oxford Dictionary of Nursery Rhymes traces the rhyme in America to the 1850s. Slavery still existed. Then the verse was "Eena, meena, mina, mo, Catch a nigger by his toe; If he squeals, let him go, Eena, meena, mina, moe."

The N-word was "an American corruption," the book said. By the mid-1970s it was "replaced by tigger, tiger, spider, beggar, etc."

White privilege may explain people's contempt for words that wound African-Americans because such things aren't aimed at hurting white people.

But Southwest Airlines' 34,000 employees in 58 cities should have known.

Charles Whitcomb, executive assistant to the provost at San Jose State University, testified at the trial that he had contacted Southwest in December 1996 after it put up more than 30 billboards in San Jose using that dirty little rhyme.

Whitcomb explained how the rhyme was "derogatory." He got a call in early 1997 from an apologetic official saying the billboards were coming down, and company employees would learn about the diversity issue. "It sent a real clear message that they were serious," Whitcomb told me.

But not really. A TV news story he saw in 2003 about the women's lawsuit revealed that the problem persisted.

Linda Rutherford, Southwest spokeswoman, said she doubted that other flight attendants would use the rhyme again. But, she said, the verdict was "appropriate."

Fuller appealed the case because the company needs meaningful diversity training, and it must hire more African-Americans. "I want my grandchild to be able to get on a plane and not be disrespected and belittled," she said.

Her cause and demands were just, even if the courts didn't agree.

Here are some of the people's comments the columns generated:

Voice mail: Feb. 4, 2004

I'm sorry eenie, meenie, minie, moe really bothers you. How do you feel when you hear gangsta rappers say he was going to murder faggots, bitches and niggers? I mean, my God, the poor lady would have a heart attack if eenie, meenie, minie, moe put her in bed for three days. You know, man, 50-Cent, my God, she'd be in intensive care. But that's OK. If I was a bleeding ass liberal my agenda would prevent me from telling the truth, too. But hey, good work if you can get it.

Voice mail: Feb. 4, 2004

Lewis, as far as I know, we still have the First Amendment in our Constitution here. It's called freedom of speech. And the word nigger is not outlawed. I mean there is not a law that says you can't call somebody a nigger. I've been known to call white trash niggers. The word nigger was originally started in this country for lazy white people, Lewis. Go back and check the history books, OK. It has nothing to do with blacks or anything else. It started out in this country and over in Europe referring to people of white descendants who were lazy and just wanted to set around on their butts and not do anything. And then that word was spread to blacks when they came into this country for whatever reason. So do a little research and stop fanning the flames of racism.

Let's just see. . . .

From "A linguistic weapon too risky for light banter"

Reference desks at the downtown library only pointed me to the place to get the book I needed.

When I called a store to have it reserved, a clerk kept thinking I said "Niagara" even though I spelled out the title. When I picked it up, another clerk asked, "Are you sure this is what you want?"

Randall Kennedy's 2002 book, *Nigger: The Strange Career of a Troublesome Word,* generates a lot of anxiety. I know now why a federal judge said he had someone else pick up the book for him.

Just asking for the book raises eyebrows. But I needed the book to provide food for thought for a forum at the Bruce R. Watkins Cultural Heritage Center in Kansas City, Mo., titled, "The N-Word: Have We Really Come That Far?"

The free community forum sponsored by the Kansas City Association of Black Journalists was to help educate the public on the history and continued problems associated with that awful word.

Kennedy quotes journalist and author Farai Chideya, who says the N-word is "the nuclear bomb of racial epithets."

Yet the N-word appears frequently in rap music, black comedians' routines and many movies as if it has lost its racially explosive meaning.

Nothing could be further from the truth. The Saturday forum explored the issue using video clips, a documentary, rap music, comic routines and the "Boondocks" cartoon. A panel discussion featuring a psychologist, economist and hip-hop artists also gave the audience a better understanding of the word and what the liberal use is actually doing.

"To be ignorant of its meanings and effects is to make oneself vulnerable to all manner of perils, including the loss of a job, a reputation, a friend, even one's life," Kennedy notes. He also shares with people the word's origin.

It comes from the Latin word for the color black, which is niger. Throughout its foul history, the word has been spelled and pronounced in different ways. Young people who think they're making it into a "nice" word by changing the traditional "er" ending to "ah" are deluding themselves.

"According to the *Random House Historical Dictionary of American Slang,* it did not originate as a slur but took on a derogatory connotation over time," Kennedy writes.

Stuart Berg Flexner said in his book, *I Hear America Talking,* that the N-word "originated as a northern England (and Irish) dialect pronunciation of Negro."

It was first recorded in 1587 in English as "neger," which is the Dutch word for Negro. "When the very first slaves were brought to the American colonies in 1619, John Rolfe of Jamestown, Va., wrote in his journal: 'A Dutch ship sold us twenty Negars. ...' This was the very first reference to blacks in the American colonies - and John Rolfe and others pronounced that word 'Negars.'..."

I know now why the federal judge wanted a copy of Kennedy's book. Kennedy cites many court cases involving the use of the word, how it has enraged blacks, resulted in the deaths of some whites and has been at the heart of civil lawsuits.

Kennedy notes that the N-word has a special place "in the lexicon of verbal abuse."

One ruling said, "Perhaps no single act can more quickly alter the conditions of employment and create an abusive working environment. ..."

But Kennedy said Presidents Harry S. Truman and Lyndon Johnson used the word in private conversations, "and yet both surprised observers by taking unprecedented steps to elevate the fortunes of Negro Americans."

Too many rappers, comedians and filmmakers think times have changed enough for the word to be tossed about as if it were as wholesome as apple pie. Among some African-Americans, the N-word is "a racial term with undertones of warmth and goodwill."

Writer Claude Brown said the word is "perhaps the most soulful word in the world."

Journalist Jarvis DeBerry said it is "beautiful in its multiplicity of functions."

"I am not aware of any other word capable of expressing so many contradictory emotions," DeBerry said.

Yet, neither the negative connotations nor its use today has vanished. I side with Bill Cosby, whom Kennedy quoted as saying that when the N-word pops out "all blacks are hurt."

Cosby fears that whites "will have negative impressions of African Americans reinforced when blacks laughingly bandy about the N-word."

The word will forever remain too serious to be used so lightly.

The Law in Action

Too often when people of color learn the rules of white society and play by them to advance, the rules conveniently change, leaving minorities locked out. It is a classic American story of disparate treatment because of skin color. It is as wrong today as it has ever been.

From: "Flaws were numerous in this dubious election"

They call it justice.

But there was no justification for how Jon R. Gray was prevented from becoming the first African-American presiding judge of the Jackson County Circuit Court.

The Kansas City branch of the National Association for the Advancement of Colored People justifiably voiced its concerns about the way Gray was kept from moving to the top seat on the court. In a prepared statement, the NAACP wrote, "We are extremely concerned about this abrupt and unannounced change in the selection process as Judge Gray is the most qualified to serve as the next presiding judge."

Presiding judges usually are picked in an informal manner that yields one nominee. Gray is second in tenure on the court behind Judge Edith Messina, who has served as Jackson County's first woman presiding judge. Gray was appointed in 1986 and retained in public elections in 1988, 1994 and 2000.

Yet Gray's tenure, including family court service, carried no weight. The NAACP charged that the normal practice "changed to selection by a secret ballot, which has not been done in many years."

Gray was nominated with Judge Peggy Stevens McGraw. In a closed ballot, the judges voted 16-10 for McGraw. Her two-year term as presiding judge starts Jan. 1, 2007.

Current Presiding Circuit Judge J.D. Williamson said in a prepared statement that the selection process in December followed the procedures established by law. He disputed the NAACP's charges and said tenure plays only a small role in who's picked.

McGraw was appointed associate circuit judge in 1995 and circuit judge in 2001.

But this is what's troubling: The action by the court is an example of the justice that African-Americans too often get on both sides of the bench. The presiding judge's decision raises serious questions about the system's fairness.

The court action gives the appearance of the rules conveniently changing when it seemed that the only African-American circuit judge would preside. Such occurrences always look like racism's markers.

This action is particularly onerous after the Kansas City Metropolitan Bar Association justifiably celebrated the 50th anniversary of its integration. In 1955 the all-white organization admitted African-Americans Harold L. Holliday Sr., Lewis Clymer and Carl R. Johnson, who had been elected Kansas City's first black municipal court judge.

Clymer eventually became the first black judge on the Jackson County Circuit Court. But legal backsliding seems to rule now.

A University of Dayton law school professor in an annual report found that the University of Missouri-Kansas City and the University of Missouri-Columbia in 2005 were among the whitest law schools in the nation. That's a retreat from 2004.

It's not good because the schools help provide lawyers for this area's legal system. The lack of inclusiveness makes the justice system look suspiciously tilted against African-Americans.

Gray should be presiding judge. His community work and actions to extend the justice system beyond the courts are unparalleled.

I've watched him speak to inmates at the Moberly Correctional Center and the Crossroads Correctional Center in Cameron. Gray always listens to the men - even those he had sentenced to prison. He maintains an open mind and treats the men as human beings.

Gray addresses them with respect and leaves them feeling good about themselves, their future and judges. I know of the help he has given to struggling law students and how he played a key role in bringing an exhibit here on black lawyers. Gray continues to help make the courts fair and just where neither is assured - especially for African-Americans.

That's why racial and ethnic diversity at all levels of law enforcement and the criminal justice system is so critically important. That's also why the Jackson County Circuit Court's judgment was flawed in bypassing Gray.

The bad decision needs to be overturned. If only there were an appeals process to make it so.

But the thought that an African-American judge had been dealt an unjust hand was not shared by people who reacted to what appeared in the newspaper:

E-mail: Jan. 27, 2006

Race had nothing to do with Jon Gray not being elected as Presiding Judge. Other issues were responsible for him not being elected. Contrary to what you believe, not everything is racial oriented.

Your article insulted a great many people of the highest integrity, you have offended the judicial system and make yourself look ridiculous. The process used was consistent with the law, there is nothing to overturn.

You will never be taken seriously as long as you continue to define every thing that doesn't go your way as racial. Quit acting like a victim. My ethnic background is Comanche Indian, we have been fighting terrorism and injustice since 1492 but unlike you, we are survivors, not victims.

Voice mail: 2006

How do we know the guy isn't incompetent? Has nothing to do with whether he's black or white. Maybe he's incompetent. But not you, Lewis, oh no. You want every incompetent black American male to be promoted because it's his right because he's black! And I have no rights because I'm white.

Many African Americans will protest mightily, but gay, lesbian, transgender and bisexual individuals face the same brutal discrimination and bigotry that impales blacks and other minorities. Recognizing that fact is part of the Real America that people must discover and work to change.

From "Politics with a conscience; Summon courage on gay marriage vote"

High emotions electrify the same-sex marriage issue.

The voltage likely will increase in the buildup to the Aug. 3 primary election when Missouri voters will decide the fate of a constitutional ban on gay marriage. The Missouri General Assembly in May voted to put it on the ballot.

It would restrict marriage, according to the state constitution, to being between one man and one woman. Last week, the Missouri Supreme Court set the election date for August instead of November. The judges were right to side with then-Gov. Bob Holden instead of then-Secretary of State Matt Blunt. The constitutional issue was destined to spark a large turnout, influencing other outcomes in the general election.

But Missourians must holster their emotions before deciding whether to restrict people's rights. They also must ignore President Bush's statement seeking a gay marriage ban in the U.S. Constitution.

Missourians must act on facts. More informed voters make better judgments.

Missouri voters should visit the Lesbian and Gay Community Center in Westport as I have. They should've gone to the 26th annual Kansas City Gay Pride Celebration at Liberty Memorial as I did with my family. At the very least they should go to mainstream services at places like Trinity United Methodist Church, which embraces gays and lesbians.

But to do all that and vote rationally, Missourians also will have to overcome their fears of gays and lesbians. Robert N. Minor wrote about that in his book, *Scared Straight: Why It's So Hard to Accept Gay*

> *People and Why It's So Hard to be Human.*
>
> "Like it or not, these roles of male, female, straight and gay were installed in us through cultural conditioning," said Minor, a professor of religious studies at the University of Kansas. Heterosexual or straight roles are rewarded and nonheterosexual roles are punished.
>
> "The institutions of our society profit from these coping mechanisms," Minor said. The system is reinforced in homes, schools, churches, work and in the media. "We ridicule and dismiss those who suggest any alternatives."
>
> The heterosexual role is also maintained through violence, threats, humiliation, isolation and rejection. "Conditioned heterosexuals, at a fundamental level, fear each other," Minor wrote.
>
> Ending the fear and rejecting the gay marriage ban will require courage from everyone.
>
> Minor wrote that "love should be honored wherever it is found and however ineloquently it might be expressed in order to counter the fear-based nature of society and its conditioning. The real issue should be love, not fear."

Sadly the voters resoundingly outlawed gay marriage as they did in states throughout the country. The Republicans skillfully rode the wedge issue into power. The dominant force is dead set against anything but the established heterosexual "norm." It handcuffs people into being something that is unnatural to them and prevents everyone from benefiting from talents they could unfold in their jobs, churches and community organizations.

Having to live with the emotional trauma and stomach the pain is the problem. Only pain surfaces for people who often face discrimination—however subtly. What people haven't realized in more than 500 years since Columbus landed is that the discrimination is endless, and justice is forever being denied. When people get angry about inequality, they often turn on one another instead of to one another committing what the *Dakota Journal* called "lateral violence" (see Chapter 1). People with real needs then become the problem, and they then need to be "fixed," not the injustice itself. Prison often is the catch basin for such "problem people." Yet somehow that anger must be channeled, not into self-destructive behavior, but into a passionate commitment to challenge the institutions and individuals behind the biases and forge change.

CHAPTER 4
Chained: Effects of Oppression

Tired of Being Black

In corporate America
We grin and smile

We colorize their many aisles

Call us token, affirmative action hires

We integrate despite
Eyes that burn with hate-filled fires

We may know the most and recite the best
But few listen or acknowledge and
wonder why we forgot the rest

Never to be accepted,
Never to fit in

Trying to represent the race
Feels like a sin.

In a country that has wiped out ALL my history,
stifled all my pride.
In a country that has placed a different weight of
indignity upon my age-old burdened back.
Inferiority is the new load . . .
The Indian has endured and still emerged the winner,
The Mestizo must yet overcome, and the Gachupin will just ignore.
I look at myself and see part of me who rejects my father and my mother
and dissolves into the melting pot to disappear in shame.
I sometimes sell my brother out and reclaim him
for my own when society, gives me token leadership
in society's own name.
I am Joaquin, who bleeds in many ways.
~Rodolfo "Corky" Gonzales, from "I am Joaquin"

Debilitating psychological and physical effects

People of color repeatedly hit the unforeseen obstacle of racism in the path of their lives. It can appear from nowhere, like a pole sticking up unexplained and unexpected in the pavement. It brings them crashing to a stop, bruised or broken from the encounter. Clearly racism remains an all too real fact of life for people of color. What many people don't realize is that it wounds minorities in body and spirit. It impairs their ability to be fully productive because the injury they have suffered diverts their attention. The scars that follow also have a lasting and often negative effect on individuals' ability to feel that they can fit in and be successful.

From "Browbeaten black and blue"

Arthur Robinson kept the receipts from his purchases at a Kansas City drugstore.

They verified that at 12:46 p.m. on Feb. 17, 2002, he spent $5.87 for cough drops and medicine for his mother, Mary H. Smith, and received $14.13 in change from a $20 bill. A second receipt showed he paid $3.12 for a greeting card and a 20-ounce bottle of Coke for himself and received $1.88 in change from a $5 bill.

But what's not listed is what motivated Robinson, 49, to keep those sales slips. That's the burden the longtime south Kansas City homeowner and hospital worker has been carrying these many months.

It's also clear in black and white.

I answered Robinson's letter and called so we could talk. It was the first positive response he'd received from the many letters he'd mailed to get someone to see what African-American men like him often face.

"This is the best I've felt since before the incident," Robinson said after we'd talked.

He explained that he'd been to the newer drugstore in a mostly white part of town dozens of times and frequented it because he liked its competitive prices. But on Feb. 17, something upsetting happened.

Robinson said the store manager, who was white, came up behind him and said, "Sir, I'm going to have to ask you to leave." When Robinson asked why, the manager explained that two persons said they had seen him shoplifting at the store on two different occasions.

Robinson said he was not a shoplifter and questioned why he wasn't arrested or asked to leave on those so-called earlier dates if he'd been seen stealing. The store manager responded that he would call the police and have Robinson arrested for trespassing.

Robinson insisted on finishing his shopping. The manager followed him through the aisles and to the register, where Robinson paid for his purchases and left.

But Robinson sat in his 1996 gray Chevy S10 pickup truck in the store parking lot for 15 minutes waiting for the police to arrive. He wanted to give his side of the story - how he had been misidentified and falsely accused of crimes he'd never committed. But no officers ever arrived.

"I was embarrassed, and I really was so shocked I couldn't get mad," said Robinson, who didn't get the manager's name. "For somebody to come up to you and say something like that to you out of the blue....

"It was out of the blue for me because it wasn't true."

I talked with a manager at the drugstore who said it's against company policy to accuse anyone unless a theft had just occurred and there was proof. That manager said he had no recollection of any incident like the one Robinson described.

What bothers me is Robinson has agonized over this from February to his attempts to get someone to listen to what he has endured. "If he can do it to me, he can do it to anybody," Robinson said.

It fits a too-familiar pattern of black men being lumped together as wrongdoers and not distinguished as hard-working, home-owning, taxpaying individuals.

"I've been carrying it for a long time," Robinson said of the anguish and frustration he's felt for months. "I was depressed about it.

"I really didn't get angry about it until an hour after I left the store."

Susan B. Wilson, a behavioral psychologist with the African-American Mental Health Task Force in Missouri, understands the emotional roller coaster black consumers feel from such false accusations. It's particularly troubling when there are no witnesses or evidence to back up the story.

"There are a lot of things that get kind of benignly neglected," Wilson said. "It's frustrating, and it's upsetting when you feel you've been harmed and nobody has been taking up your case.

"It helps to get over the case when the person feels heard and can take action."

That's when the anger, helplessness and hopelessness begin to dissolve. Unfortunately, Robinson is far from being alone in the false finger-pointing he's faced.

"Discrimination is real, and it has real aftereffects that are psychological on people," Wilson said. "The important part is for people to have some bona fide action they can take to overcome those psychological effects.

> "When you can't take action, when you can't get people to hear you, that's when it's psychologically handicapping."
>
> I'm glad that Robinson wrote to me and that his concerns were finally heard for his mental health and others' who often feel voiceless.

The importance of feeling heard cannot be overemphasized. In a speech titled, "Health and Poverty in the US," given on December 9, 2003, Stephen Bezruchka, MD, mentioned that Japan has the healthiest population in the world, even though "Japanese men smoke the most of all rich countries." The reason for their excellent health, he says, is that "Japan is a caring and sharing society that looks after everyone."

The United States, "measured by life expectancy…[was] one of the healthiest countries in the world" *fifty-eight years ago*. "Today," states Bezruchka, "there are some 25 countries that are healthier than we are. Think of it, all the other rich countries are healthier than we are, and a number of poor ones as well. It isn't just this one measure of health—life expectancy—in which we do poorly, but in every other measure, when we rank ourselves with other countries." He offers this explanation: "The difference now is that we live under more stressful conditions, a stress caused by the big gap between the rich and the rest of us…. The culture of poverty, the culture of inequality that surrounds us is what has the most significant effect on our health." He continues:

> Racism is [one] way that the gap operates to create worse health. Racism is all about difference and power. Minorities have always been put down, and feel the shame, even if they don't think about it. . . . An African American male in Harlem lives less long than a man in Bangladesh, one of the world's poorest countries. Or that a black man in Washington, DC lives less long than a man in Ghana, a country in West Africa.

To truly end racism, the truth has to be told. But the stress associated with the exposure to bigotry can be difficult for people of color to explain and damaging to their well-being. Many African Americans today feel "Rosa Parks tired" about race relations. Parks was the black seamstress who on Dec. 1, 1955, decided to break the law of the segregated South and not give up her seat on a public Montgomery, Ala., bus for a white man. Contrary to popular myth, Rosa Parks' feet weren't any more tired than normal after work. To quote Parks, "The only tired I was, was tired of giving in." There comes a point in the history of every oppressed people when one person loudly says no more and others stand behind the courageous act because they are "Rosa Parks tired," too. That's the way African Americans today feel about constantly being confronted with and having to discuss racial discrimination, never sure whether their experiences will be acknowledged by others. The emotional and physical tolls, however, pose serious dangers to people's health.

From "Victims of racial stress"

Stan N. Gerber invited me to the general psychology class he taught at Donnelly College to listen to his lecture on stress.

The emphasis Gerber put on the subject at the urban Kansas City, Kan., school is that the stress African-Americans, Hispanics, Asian Americans and American Indians suffer is more constant and intense than it is for whites. Gerber rattled off normal examples of stress.

They include waiting for someone who's late, being caught in traffic, waiting in line, waiting in a doctor's office, waiting for the government to act, waiting for a repair person, looking for a parking place and waiting for a plane to take off.

"You feel uptight," said Gerber, who holds doctorates in psychology and anthropology and has been an educator since 1969. "You feel nervous.

"You become discombobulated. Most people in the majority culture have periods of stress."

But for people of color, stress is unending. It's in the media, which often give the misimpression that dysfunctional families, drug use, dropouts, teen-pregnancies and crime are mostly the problems of minorities, Gerber said.

"It insults you so you're under stress," he said. When people of color leave home, the stress escalates.

I looked out the sixth-floor classroom window onto the city. For many people below, there's no escaping what Gerber described.

Black students face it in what has been called stereotype vulnerability in which they're deemed less capable of performing well in school and too often live down to that low expectation.

Many people of color also endure racial profiling in which authorities stop and question minorities at a disproportionately higher rate than they do whites. This stress is from being seen as suspects instead of taxpaying, productive citizens.

Yet some Kansas legislators considering a bill to study racial profiling thought the cost of examining the problem was too high. Historically the problems minorities daily face always seemed too expensive until they affect the majority, too.

Racial profiling puts young black males in an uncomfortable Catch

22 position, said Susan B. Wilson, behavioral psychologist. They ride together in groups for self-protection.

But then they're more vulnerable to car stops by police, Wilson said in an interview.

One other concern is retail racism in which people of color receive poor service, no service or are followed because they're suspected of shoplifting in stores. Then there's rational racism in which company personnel use business explanations to justify racist choices.

Also, there's the doubt in which many whites contend that racism is the imagination of people of color. This doubt can be debilitating.

"That's one of the most psychologically upsetting aspects of being African-Americans," said Wilson, who has a doctorate in clinical psychology. "You experience things every day that make you feel disrespected and discounted, and yet if you bring those things up to the majority race they will say you didn't experience what you experienced. You didn't see what you saw."

People's reactions underscore just how difficult it is for some to acknowledge the effects of discrimination or identify with the stress and trauma minorities must endure:

Voice Mail: Feb. 23, 2000

Well, I just read your article in Wednesday, Feb. 23 Star and see you're at your usual troublemaking procedure again. You just want to keep people stirred up. I don't know why you think that stress for a black person is worse than for a white person especially for a single white woman who raises her children alone. Well, I think in all fairness you ought to ask if they have an editor comparable to you who's white and let them publish a couple of articles a month about the stress that white people are under and all the problems they have.

Voice Mail: Feb. 23, 2000

Lewis, many people of all races are under constant stress in this society and people coming from other countries immediately feel that it's the way we live. I know blacks have a lot of stress. But I kept thinking, here we go again with no solutions. It wasn't until the very last paragraph, or the second to the last, that you said that the psychologist should work on helping blacks know how to cope with this. That's the only solution. You're not going to tell other people that they shouldn't have prejudice thoughts or thoughts of difference. It's natural. It's built in. You can't change it so work on the people your own people you're talking about being able to accept this in a different way to be able to see this in a different way

> so that it will help them. That is the only thing you can do. Don't expect whites to change ideas and feelings and natural leanings and urges and intuitions and blacks, too, that's nature.
>
> Voice Mail: Feb. 23, 2000
>
> I've got one comment for you. Whaaa! Why don't you cry, little baby? Maybe all this extra energy that you blacks have got because you're under stress all the time, maybe you ought to go out and try to find a job instead of running around pulling off drive-by shootings and stuff. By the way, when are you blacks going to come out and start writing about issues that affect every American in the United States, not just you African Americans? Why is it you folks only write about things that pertain to just minorities? What's the matter, aren't you intelligent enough?

Unfortunately this person doesn't realize that this is not just an African-American issue, but that it does in fact pertain to all Americans. Stephen Bezruchka states that "a bigger [wealth] gap society has worse health than an egalitarian society," and that it affects us all to some degree. It is undeniable, however, that racism has the potential to cause a deadly level of stress.

From "Victims of racial stress"

> Stan Gerber also said the many burning fires of race-fed stress have physiological consequences. The pressure triggers the body's fight or flight mechanisms.
>
> "The body is prepared to fight all of the time," he said. Stress activates the hypothalamus, the pituitary gland and the adrenal gland.
>
> The liver produces glycogen, which increases the amount of energy in the body. The heart races.
>
> "You are physically stronger to fight back," Gerber said. "The problem is the stuff destroys tissue.
>
> "It's not healthy."
>
> People's immune systems don't work as well, leaving them susceptible to colds and flus.
>
> "Most people don't function well if they are under stress all the time," Gerber said. "You're always ready to fight something."
>
> It is a costly health concern. Constant stress makes people prone to hypertension, heart disease, cancer, strokes, diabetes and other serious, costly ailments, Gerber said.
>
> Susan Wilson said some Africans who'd never experienced hypertension acquire it within months of coming to America.
>
> Gerber builds the stress lesson into his class hoping it will help his students cope with the problem. He wants them to also work to

> change the nation so everyone can have happier, healthier and more productive lives.

Discrimination causes stress; stress becomes chronic; chronic stress causes illness.

As Kai Wright starkly put it, "Dad died...from the side effects of racism."

Wright's father, a successful black surgeon, had adult-onset diabetes and died at the age of 57. In his article "Upward Mortality," Wright said:

> As you move up the economic ladder, black health drastically improves, but the disparities between blacks and whites do not.... What is [the explanation]?
>
> The answer, a growing number of researchers say, is that the vaunted black middle class ain't all it's cracked up to be. Black strivers have a much harder time turning their paychecks into the status, opportunity, and security that white yuppies take for granted.... The resulting dissonance – harder work and longer hours to reach success, stress from discrimination that you can neither mistake nor prove – eventually manifests itself in the bodies of people like my dad. They don't have time to take care of themselves, and even when they do, wellness is just not a priority. So as the white middle class has grown more healthy in recent decades, the tenuousness of black middle-class life has left many stumbling through a vicious cycle. It's harder for "bourgie" blacks to leverage the advantages of our nominal status, so we are more likely to be plagued by health problems associated with poverty, which in turn undermines our ability to sustain what class mobility we've eked out.

Another study on the health effects of discrimination that Wright cites was done by Nancy Krieger, a researcher with Harvard University:

> In 1994, she articulated a theory that posits we all "embody" the social and economic contexts we live in.... Krieger has found that women – of any class – who reported high levels of experience with racial discrimination were nearly five times as likely to deliver underweight babies as those who reported no experience with it. Low birth weights offer an ideal example of how embodiment works because they illustrate how health problems extend over a lifetime and pass from generation to generation: Underweight babies are more likely to develop heart disease, diabetes, hypertension, and respiratory disease later in life, and women who have these problems are in turn more likely to give birth to underweight babies.

And so the cycle of health problems perpetuates itself. The National

Urban League's *State of Black America 2005: Prescription for Change* reports that "in 2002, the three leading causes of death in both African Americans and whites were heart disease, cancer, and stroke.... [Yet] African Americans are 40-percent more likely to die from stroke and 30-percent more likely to die from heart disease and cancer than whites" (65-66). The report continues:

> The quality of mental health has a major impact on the development and severity of chronic diseases for all people. But its importance is even greater for African Americans because of African Americans' overall lower status in American society. The effect of being a part of a stigmatized group suffering from greater poverty, inferior access to healthcare and health insurance, and, to a greater degree, unfair working conditions, discrimination, and substandard housing significantly increases the likelihood of mental illness and chronic diseases. The death toll inflicted by these slow-moving illnesses continues to warn us that the efforts to prevent mental illnesses and chronic disease where possible and provide effective treatment when necessary must be focused and comprehensive. This will help stop the vicious cycle of disproportionate disability, disease, and death and maximize health status, well-being, and quality of life among African Americans and all Americans. (69)

According to *DiversityInc.'s* October 2005 issue, "[a]bout 50 million people in the United States have disabilities" (58). That's 16.6 percent of the total U.S. population, making people with disabilities the largest minority group in the country. The magazine calls mental illness the nation's "hidden disability" (69). It includes depression, affecting 20.4 million Americans age 18 and older; anxiety disorders hitting 20.4 million Americans ages 18 to 54; and schizophrenia, affecting 2.4 million Americans age 18 and older. Mental illness annually costs the nation $63 billion in lost productivity, $12 billion in mortality and $4 billion in incarceration (72). Mental illness is a huge concern for African-Americans because, like incarceration, a disproportionate share of black people are caught up in the system. For that reason it's critical that health care professionals provide culturally competent care to ensure the correct diagnosis and treatment for people who are different.

The Effects of Health Care

The need for good health care is evident. But there is also a great need for more African-Americans and other people of color in all aspects of the health care industry so that "culturally competent" care is more likely to be provided. Sadly, the number of minorities in health care is declining and so is the qualified medical treatment that people of color should receive.

From "Rx: More blacks in health care"

In 1996, Mid-City Discount Drugs closed as the last black-owned pharmacy in Jackson County, Mo.

Managed care changed the revenue stream, directing patients to large drugstore chains. Delia C. Young, a health-care consultant, has watched a similar silent rechanneling of dollars slowly strangle the private practices of black physicians, too.

"Managed care has devastated the entire provider spectrum of health care," said Young, president of Delia Young & Associates. "But anything that's a blow to the larger community is always going to be 10 times as tenacious to our fragile community."

African-American physicians had been the backbone of the black middle class. As business owners, each had a gross average taxable income of $400,000 and offices that provided health care and jobs, Young said.

Most black physicians 35 years ago were in private practice. Today, two-thirds of African-American doctors receive paychecks as employees, she said. Thirty years ago, 95 percent of the black population was treated by black physicians. Today, 67 percent go to white physicians.

The transition has been costly to the black community in the loss of businesses, jobs and doctors.

"The pylons that were undergirding our black community were doctors," Young said.

Now many of the physicians are gone or are near retirement, and there's little hope that they or the tax base they provided will be replaced, said Nevada Lee, a Senior Health Center physician.

Black corporate executives now occupy the top rungs but without the same clout or economic multiplier effect. Yet, they have more money, control of their work environment and free time.

Starks Johnson Williams, a physician at 2525 E. Meyer Blvd., Kansas City, Mo., said more black doctors were in Kansas City today. But that number has not kept up with the black population growth.

Williams and Frances Foster, an eye doctor at 21 N. 12th St. in Kansas City, Kan., said black doctors' practices were being excluded from managed-care lists of providers or their patient loads were being restricted.

"The patients come and say, 'I can't see you anymore,'" Foster said. "They've got to go wherever they are directed."

Williams added: "What's happening is, you are sort of systematically isolated. They say they made a business decision."

The coincidence is managed-care plans give contracts to large white doctors' groups. Black doctors' practices are smaller and aren't viewed as capable of offering cost efficiencies, Young said.

Sometimes the exclusion of black doctors is tied to the bias that they aren't as good in caring for patients or in generating revenue as white doctors are. Many of the chosen physicians' groups are in suburban areas, creating access problems for urban residents. Williams said managed care "creamed off" paying patients, leaving black doctors with the sicker clients who have fewer means to pay.

The silent assault on black physicians' practices also raises concerns of whether black patients get culturally competent care. A Johns Hopkins School of Public Health study in 1999 showed minorities had more difficulty getting appointments, waited longer for doctors and were less likely to be referred to specialists.

A study in the *Journal of the American Medical Association* showed black people, poor people and those in rural areas received deficient treatment for such things as regular mammograms for breast cancer survivors and annual vision tests for diabetics.

A Harvard Medical School study showed a racial gap in kidney transplants. Prejudice and communication breakdowns helped explain why white people were nearly twice as likely to get transplants or get on waiting lists.

In managed care, services get rationed, and because of racial biases, black patients may be excluded from treatment, Young said.

The system is strangling the black community, its physicians and residents. Managed care must be fixed if that chokehold is to end so true healing can begin.

The disparities in health care hit minorities on many levels—from availability of physicians who are sensitive to different ethnic health care needs to health insurance. In his "Race, Poverty, and Health Care Disparities" chapter in *The State of Black America 2006*, Brian D. Smedley notes that

> Americans spend nearly $2 trillion on healthcare annually, far more per capita than any other nation in the world. Still, the United States ranks 37th of 191 countries in a World Health Organization assessment of the world's health systems. The United States fares poorly in large measure because of its marked inequality. The number of

> Americans without health insurance reached an all-time high of 45.8 million in 2004, and more than 80 million Americans lacked health insurance for all or part of 2002 and 2003. (155)
>
> Sadly, the number of Americans without health insurance keeps climbing. Census data released in August 2006 showed that 46.6 million people in the United States had no health insurance, and 37 million were classified as poor (Bavley).

The Census Bureau in March of 2007 revised the number of Americans without health coverage down to 44.8 million people, or 15.3% of the population. A lack of insurance coverage is joined by negative stereotypes and subsequent discrimination. Smedley adds that "[f]our years ago, a report by the Institute of Medicine—*Unequal Treatment: Confronting Racial and Ethnic Disparities in Health Care*—disclosed that people of color receive lower quality of health care even compared to whites with the same income, age, health condition and insurance status. It noted the prevalence of bias and stereotyping among health care providers" (156).

President George W. Bush's much-touted health savings accounts (HSAs) "may exacerbate racial, ethnic and socioeconomic gaps," writes Smedley (159). He adds that "uninsured Americans [are] disproportionately people of color, immigrants, and the working poor [who] don't make enough money to pay taxes, so they would receive no benefit from the tax benefit of HSAs. [Also,] people with low incomes are less able to save enough, after taking into account housing, transportation, food, and other costs, to cover high deductibles typical of HSAs" (160). HSAs have the added punishing effect on the poor of making traditional health insurance "less affordable for those who need it most," because they would cream off healthier and wealthier individuals who keep existing policy rates low (161).

Effects on self-esteem

Besides the disparities in health and health care that are caused by discrimination, there is also the blow to a person's feeling of self-worth. Minorities are constantly confronted with "acceptable" images of people who look nothing like them. The implication is that their "difference" is unacceptable, and that therefore they are inferior compared to the "norm." They must conform if they are to be valued—except that conforming to become white is impossible. The stress comes from being expected to be something they can never be and striving to meet those expectations instead of being valued for who they are and the richness of their diverse talents.

From "Embracing diversity means accepting others and yourself"

All too frequently, well-meaning people compliment Shirley Chin on how well she speaks English or they ask whether she has journeyed back home lately.

I've told my longtime college friend that she should say the same things to people who make such insensitive remarks. For Chin, back home is New York, and she speaks better than most people because she has a journalism degree from the University of Missouri-Columbia.

Yet *Journalism Across Cultures* by Fritz Cropp, Cynthia Frisby and Dean Mills says people see Asian Americans as the "eternal foreigners."

Chin is teaching me such things about her journey to discover and love her special place in America's diversity. But the path hasn't been without tears. I handed Chin some Kleenex. My questions unearthed painful memories.

Chin called herself one of many "ABCs," or American-born Chinese. She is oldest of three daughters of Chinese immigrants. Her father, Denny Chin, joined the U.S. Navy after arriving in the early 1940s, and served in World War II.

He got married after the war. He and May Chin settled in New York where they opened a hand laundry, Laundromat and candy store.

"America was where you have a chance to make a better life for yourself, where the streets are lined with gold," Shirley Chin said. "It's like the gold mountain."

She remembered that as a girl in the 1960s she helped her parents study to become citizens. But other memories weren't as good.

The racial slurs and taunts she endured remain vivid and painful. Chin remembered trying to break up a dispute between younger kids. One turned on her saying, "What's it to you, you chink?"

Everything about Chin that makes her beautifully different was seen as a negative. She remembered that her grandmother used to pinch her broad nose to try to make it more pointy.

I shared with her that I had relatives who did similar things to my siblings and me. We laughed at how silly it was. But it wasn't funny for us growing up as excluded races in white America.

Chin said she hated her eyes, her skin, her hair, her nose, her lips and when her parents took her to play with another Chinese girl, she hated her, too.

"I hated the fact that I was Chinese because I was different," Chin said. "I just wanted to fit in with everyone else."

But from everyone else and the media she has been constantly barraged with the fact that she's different. It makes a lot of young people of color think they'll never measure up - never be accepted as Americans.

There could be no greater lie because this country has always been filled with a diversity of beautifully different people. Everyone in our nation needs to be accepting and supportive of the difference in others. Anything less is emotionally devastating and counterproductive.

Chin remembered that a journalism school professor always called her "the pearl of the Orient" or he'd say be "scrutable, Chin."

People still ask whether she's Hispanic, Mexican, Hawaiian or from the Philippines. She remembers always feeling angry in college and having a short fuse. But that changed by the time she became 30 years old.

"I really embraced the idea that I'm Asian; I'm Chinese, and it's great," Chin said. "I've come to accept more of who I am.

"I like who I am. There is no more fighting with myself because of who I am.

"As Martha Stewart would say, 'It's a good thing.' I don't have to expend my energy in a negative way. It's a positive thing."

Chin should never have had to take such an emotionally odious journey. Many Asian-American, African-American, Hispanic and American Indian children are being put through the same ordeals.

The outcome for some isn't nearly as pretty. "It can be a painful journey," Chin said.

No child should have to endure it. They should feel good about themselves as they are.

"If you love yourself, you can give of yourself to the universe," Chin said. "If you hate yourself, you withdraw and just want to curl up in a ball and be left alone."

Chin knows that self-love now.

"I have more to give to the world, to the universe when I love myself," she said. "I can act out of kindness."

Love is more productive than hate, and welcoming the diversity in others brings out the best. But that is still hard for some people to fathom.

E-mail: Aug. 12, 2005

Pass me the Kleenex, too!! That was a real tear jerker today! I can't believe that Shirley faced prejudice in the Bluest of Blue States- New York!! That's Hillary country!!

They say what doesn't kill you makes you stronger, it looks like Shirley has had the last laugh!! She should be laughing it up!! Those kids that made fun of her now probably work at Wal-Mart!!

I'm sure life isn't always a bed of roses. I worked with a Vietnamese guy once and he told me he felt discriminated against sometimes. He also owned a business on the side and drove a Jaguar!!! What a country!! You can have people making fun of you and still drive a Jag!!! He would be riding in a rickshaw or riding a bike in Vietnam!!

You should maybe look at the relationship between Orientals.

You would think they would all get along and see things the same. But they don't. There is a pecking order amongst Orientals and I have been told Chinese think they are at the top and it goes down to Filipinos at the bottom with others in between. Interesting isn't it??

Shirley Chin's feelings are widely held by many people of color. At a session for teachers on white privilege the day before the above column ran, a Chinese-American woman tearfully recounted the debilitating racial slurs people had used on her. "It still hurts," she said, "and I can't believe I am crying." That's a pervasive effect of racism. It damages the self-image and ability of people of color. It zaps their connection to others in the community and it scorches their drive to be competitive and productive. It is the deeply personal damage or what Claude Steele calls "stereotype vulnerability" or stereotype threat, which minorities suffer and many white people just don't get. Because they can't see it, they disavow racism and its effects even more.

<u>From "Challenge can defeat stereotypes"</u>

Claude M. Steele got me excited about our kids' future.

The Stanford University psychology professor did a study that may show why test scores of black students lag far behind those of whites.

Sure poverty, segregation, violence and teen pregnancies retard academic progress. But Steele thinks he has found a subliminal linchpin, which he calls "stereotype vulnerability."

It's a condition in which black students' academic achievements constantly are doubted.

He said schools often ignore or devalue the successes of black kids because they don't fit the stereotype of a race at risk. Also, he said educators tend to look only for black students' failures.

"Anything that fits the stereotype is going to be believed," Steele told the William Monroe Trotter Group, a think tank of black columnists. "It's like a choking phenomenon. That piece of psychology is disrupting our performance."

Steele, who is black, showed slides of test results of black and white students of equal academic standing. When told the exam was a test of their diagnostic ability, black students' scores were lower than white students'.

But when told that it was not a skills test, black students' scores pulled even with whites' because, he said, race as a subliminal element disappeared.

"A black student has stereotypes sitting on his shoulders," Steele said. With each problem comes a dread of confirming the stereotypes of failure.

"You just change the instruction of the test and the score goes way up," Steele said.

On a third test, white students' scores plunged when told beforehand that Asians outperform white males on the exam.

On a fourth written test, black students' scores topped whites' when both groups were told that it was not a test of their ability. But on the same exam, changed only to ask participants to note their race, black students' scores fell below whites'.

"Stereotypes are shaping our beliefs of what's plausible," Steele said. "This really has a concrete effect on test performance on students."

Stereotypes follow black students through college. The longer they stay in school the further they fall behind whites on test scores, Steele said.

In the Kansas City School District, minority students' scores in the lower grades are generally behind whites'. The gap widens in high school.

Many schools try to boost black students' performance through remedial programs. But Steele said toe-tagging black kids as "at risk" and baby-stepping them through school is a crutch that academically cripples them for life.

Affirmative action programs instead should put students in "challenge workshops" in which instructors value young people's abilities and push them beyond the normal course work.

Studies have shown that such efforts disarm stereotyped vulnerability and build black students' academic confidence, thus achievement scores rise, Steele said.

He calls it "wise schooling."

Effects on Education

Steele's work builds on W.E.B. Du Bois' double consciousness theory in which black people view life through the prism of being Americans and through their own unique vision as Africans in America. The same bonus ability is true for other minority groups and women as well. It's like individuals knowing a second language and being able to be better, more effective communicators with more people because of that diverse talent. For students of color, learning the ways of the majority in Eurocentric schools by no means dictates that they have to surrender their uniqueness. It just means schools have to enhance their curriculum with multicultural studies so that students can see beyond the stereotypes knowing that who they are matters and must at long last be valued by society at large.

This is not happening fast enough, unfortunately. On top of that, a May 2006 poll among black and Hispanic students showed that the schools these young people are attending are not providing them with safe environments that are conducive to learning. Students polled saw school as "a more rowdy, disrespectful and dangerous place than their white classmates. . . . Minority children in public middle and high schools are more likely than white children to describe profanity, truancy, fighting, weapons, and drug abuse as 'very serious' problems." The students largely create that environment for themselves in a self-fulfilling prophesy of living down to the stereotypes set for them. They also saw "more pervasive academic woes, such as lower standards, higher dropout rates, and students who advance even if they don't learn" ("Poll"). Schools with mostly students of color also are staffed with teachers with less than three years experience teaching (2005 *State* 28).

The inequities are many. Yet in 2002 the Urban League reported that

> According to the [*Washington Post*-Kaiser-Harvard] racial attitudes survey, half of all white Americans believe we have parity in education. In reality, there is a 10-percent gap in high school diplomas, an 11-percent gap in undergraduate degrees, and gaps in post-graduate degrees.
>
> If we had achieved this quest for equality in education, two million more African Americans would have their high school diplomas. Nearly two million more would have undergraduate degrees. Nearly a half million more would have master's degrees. And 180,000 more African Americans would have their doctorates—250 percent more than today. (17)

Students of color are clearly being left behind. This is especially true for young African American males:

From "Saturday's child works hard"

> Jeanene Dunn called to her son, John: "Hurry up so we can get you to school."
>
> The third-grader at Wendell Phillips Elementary School was among about 2,800 students whom Kansas City School District officials tapped in the spring of 2000 to attend Saturday classes. The goal was to get kids to make up and catch up on their reading, language and math skills.
>
> Helping them succeed academically was expected to enable the district to regain its state accreditation.
>
> But Saturday school means extra work for parents, too. The city was mostly still when we left the Dunns' house. Long shadows from tall buildings swept quiet streets as we drove to Primitivo Garcia Elementary School in Dunn's green Geo Metro.
>
> Garcia Principal Bob Wilcox greeted everyone at the door. We followed John to Kay Hall's classroom.

John, 9, was one of Hall's nine students. They listened closely as Hall read a book aloud and then had the children write essays. The low teacher-to-student ratio is a plus.

"There's an intense involvement of teachers," then-school Superintendent Benjamin Demps Jr. told me earlier.

Testing will determine whether the innovation at all levels has paid off.

Dunn said the extra instruction had helped John.

"I found that his comprehension skills have improved," said Dunn, who had taught second grade at Attucks Elementary School and then was a technical editor at Black & Veatch. "He's able to read a story and conduct a discussion afterward."

But she said the new skills he has picked up in Saturday school should have been provided in his weekday classes.

I agree. I went to Saturday school with Dunn because of what she'd told me earlier in the year after dropping John off for his first day of extra classes.

She was troubled because it seemed as if a disproportionately high number of black male children were in Saturday school. It wasn't her imagination.

Enrollment stood at about 532 boys and 372 girls at the Saturday elementary schools. Middle schools had 414 boys and 335 girls. High schools had 307 boys and 440 girls.

The gender imbalance in the majority black district makes me ask why so many African-American male children got left behind in the first place and who now have to do time on Saturdays?

"I think that school districts have not figured out how to provide a productive educational environment for males, particularly African-American males," said Susan B. Wilson, then-director of behavioral health with Model Cities Health Corp., and chairwoman of the Missouri Statewide Task Force on African American Mental Health.

"It's a national emergency of undereducating and miseducating African-American males," she said. "We're already paying the price by building more and more jails, which really don't solve the problem."

Educators who failed black male children jeopardized the district's accreditation, their own jobs and the kids' future. It's shortsighted and stupid to think of any child's failure as an acceptable loss.

Each eventually adds to an avalanche that can crush any system of education. That's why charter schools now are taking hundreds of students and millions of dollars in state financing from the district.

Saturday school, however, offers hope for the district and African-American males like John.

Wilson said boys need a visual and audio mix in education as well as action and context so they can see how subjects connect. Mutual respect has to be part of the equation, too. "Unless teachers convey a respect for individuals, no learning takes place," she said.

Hall, Wilcox and other educators showed a genuine respect for everyone. That's a plus. So is Saturday school in getting the district to make up the way it had failed so many students.

"It tells me that those young black males, whom most people seem to want to write off as lost, do have an interest in education, and they do want to improve their reading and math skills," Demps said.

Black parents and other adults must stay as engaged in regular school as they are in Saturday classes to ensure all students' academic success.

Effects on communities

Thorny race relations get in the way of people connecting not only in schools but also in their communities where they should be working together. The communications gaps disable understanding and stand in the way of progress. Lost are contributions that could benefit institutions, society and future generations. The past influences the present; the present in turn disables the future.

The National Urban League's *State of Black America 2006: The Opportunity Compact* reports that just as the Constitution only counted slaves as three-fifths of a person, the league's African-American Equality Index found that blacks register only 0.73 compared with whites as an index unit of one. That's up from 0.729 in the 2005 report. However *The State of Black America 2004* reported that the index was 0.76, so some slippage occurred between the two years (15). What's most disturbing, however, is that since the Constitution was adopted 218 years ago, there has been only a 0.13 point improvement in the status of African Americans (2006 report 13) Sadly, *The State of Black America 2007*'s index was only 0.733 (17) .

We've already seen that blacks lag behind whites in life expectancy, health and education. They also fare worse in earnings, jobs, housing, wealth and business ownership. Yet they disproportionately surpass whites in poverty and prison. "In fact, as a percentage of arrests, there are three times as many blacks that become prisoners," the 2005 Urban League book states (33). Many families live in poverty. "As a percentage of their population, over two times as many blacks live below the poverty line as whites," the report said (19).

Poverty

In 2002, the Urban League reported that "nearly one out of every two blacks earns less than $25,000. Only one in three whites earns that little. The median income of a black household is $27,000 compared to $42,000 for a white household" (16). Though the level and scope of the poverty is often ignored by the better-off majority in this country, one event brought the extent of the disparities and disgraceful situation into everyone's home and life: Hurricane Katrina in August of 2005.

From "Misconceptions, mistakes magnified a tragedy"

> African-Americans who were left behind in Mississippi and Louisiana were already suffering a hurricane of poverty before Katrina hit. She just knocked them down even more and peeled away the veil that hid the racism in America that decades earlier had left them stranded.
>
> But black and white people keep seeing different things in the news media's aftermath coverage of Hurricane Katrina.
>
> Some whites who've telephoned and e-mailed me in the last week have wondered why so many black people being rescued didn't leave when told to evacuate now-devastated Louisiana and Mississippi. These individuals' comments about the looting in New Orleans also were tinged with racism.
>
> One man wrote: "Also saw on television this morning long lines of handcuffed blacks who were arrested for looting in New Orleans. Same old story...taking advantage of a sorry situation to steal as much as they can carry off. Some things never change, do they?"
>
> Cable TV news channels did a wonderful job of creating the impression that all blacks loot and there was no desperation for essential items for survival. TV news stations repeatedly showed the same footage of the same black people in the flood-ravaged city carrying away goods from stores.
>
> One wire service photo on the Internet showed a white couple carrying goods through the floodwaters. The caption described them as "finding things." Another wire service picture of a black man carrying goods through the murky tide had a caption labeling him as "looting."
>
> Mary Kimbrough, president of the Bonner Springs NAACP branch, called to say the media coverage was "appalling." I couldn't agree more. It continues the ages-old, stereotypical image of black people as criminals who are to be feared and locked up regardless of their dire straits.
>
> Unlike whites, African-Americans after seeing many rescues and

black bodies floating in floodwaters wondered why so many black folks were left behind. These victims have an immediate need for housing, jobs and not to be herded from one domed stadium to another.

I blame incorrect assumptions by the authorities who ordered the evacuation and the media that put the word out to the public ahead of Hurricane Katrina. They assumed that everyone had access to a vehicle to transport families to safety.

Many African-Americans mired in a quicksand of poverty nationwide don't have cars. Either the bulk or a disproportionate share of public transit riders is black. That was true when I was a growing up just as it is now.

Those who do have automobiles may not have vehicles that could go any distance on the highway. That was an unfortunate reality when I was a kid, too. Poverty then as now has kept many black families and children from ever venturing outside of their community.

Money is an additional concern. Without it, families can't buy gasoline or pay for places to stay away from homes.

New census data released in 2005 showed that more Americans lived in poverty in 2004 compared with 2003. The poverty rate in 2004 was 12.7 percent, up from 12.5 percent. In real numbers, 37 million people were in poverty, which was up by 1.1 million over 2003.

The poverty rate was worse for African-Americans, holding at 24.7 percent compared with 10.8 percent for whites in 2004. Not surprisingly, the highest poverty rate was in the South, where the majority of African-Americans live.

The National Urban League's *State of Black America 2005* report said blacks and Hispanics "have shouldered the burden of tightening economic times in the Bush administration."

In her "State of Our Children" essay in *The State of Black America 2006* report, Marian Wright Edelman noted that black children were disproportionately hurt by Hurricane Katrina.

> One in every three children in New Orleans lived in a household that didn't own a vehicle and nearly all of those children were black. More than 98 percent of the children in car-less households lived in minority households and 96 percent of them lived in black households. Not surprisingly, families that didn't own vehicles also were likely to be poor.... Many of these families were also poor before the storm and are poorer still after the storm, having lost everything they had. Now that veil of neglect and inequality has been torn off showing the American empire was and still is unprepared to protect its children and families and vulnerable people from harm's way and to provide them with health and mental health and housing and other

> survival supports to go on with their lives, it is time to act. Not to know is bad. To know and to do nothing is inexcusable. (135-136)

What happened when Hurricane Katrina hit the Gulf Coast is indicative of the terrible storm that poor people, minorities and immigrants have faced all along in the United States but without the accompanying news coverage and public empathy. Edelman notes that their future is America's future. She quotes Dr. Bruce Perry, Senior Fellow at the Child Trauma Academy in Houston, Texas, who warned:

> The real crisis of Katrina is coming.... It will destroy a part of our country that is much more valuable than all of the buildings, pipelines, casinos, bridges and roads in all of the Gulf Coast. Over our lifetime, this crisis will cost our society billions upon billions of dollars. And the echoes of the coming crisis will haunt the next generation. This crisis is foreseeable. And, much of its destructive impact is preventable. Yet our society may not have the wisdom to see the real crisis of Katrina is the hundreds of thousands of ravaged, displaced and traumatized children. And our society may not have the will to prevent this crisis. We understand broken buildings; we do not understand broken children. (137)

Yet the feedback received admonished again and again to put a positive face on the tragedy. People don't want to feel guilty when confronted with the poverty from which our poorest and darkest citizens suffer; instead people prefer to be reminded only of the compassion, which thankfully emerged, so they can feel good. Unfortunately that compassion was decades too late to avert the deep loss and trauma wrought by the hurricane.

> Voice mail: Sept. 7, 2005
>
> I just read your article in the paper this morning about the Hurricane Katrina misconceptions. Thank God this is America where people are able to have differences of opinions and be able to express those differences. And after completing your article I would say to you I would be ashamed to write something like this. You have taken your position in this paper. You've used this opportunity to do nothing but to add further light on a situation that many people are calling racist instead of spending your words and your ink and time writing an article about how the people finally were helped, what's being done for them, the thousands and thousands of Americans that have donated and have opened their homes and their hearts to these people. Instead of dwelling on the positive you chose to do nothing but to continue to fester and to spread this racist thing. I think we all know as Americans there is this disparity. But we cannot get past this levy of racism if we don't start emphasizing the positive instead of where we've been and look at where we're going. Please do an article now on the good that's being done to overcome the heartache and the pain that these people black and white are suffering in New Or-

leans. Do a positive article. I really would enjoy reading that. Thank you.

Voice mail: Sept. 7, 2005

You ought to be ashamed of yourself. Everybody in this area and others are busting their buns trying to help people and you do nothing but get racist about it. If you want to blame somebody then blame the black mayor and the black governor of Louisiana. Neither one of them had any effectiveness at all in what they were doing. In fact, I am not sure they knew what they were doing. They were asked to evacuate before and they didn't do it. And they didn't prepare enough. And everybody in this area hasn't even looked at the color of people's skin. They have tried very hard to help with their money with their homes, with every other kind. What happened to all those buses sitting there that (New Orleans Mayor Ray) Nagin didn't use. There were school buses and city buses, 200 some odd of them who could have evacuated a lot of people. And those men who were looting everything should have been helping to carry out the old and the sick. And you should be ashamed for calling race on this. Everybody has tried their best to help. But you do nothing but,.... You're the worst racist I have ever seen.

Ownership and Worth

It might seem to an observer from another country that black America is actually subsidizing white America in resources for education, housing, societal amenities and jobs, to name a few. Minorities end up receiving less than their fair share in funding and opportunities for those necessities and a disproportionately large share of law enforcement, prison sentences and military service. In 2002, Frank D. Raines reported that "only 20 percent of blacks [held] professional or managerial jobs, while more than 30 percent of whites [did]. African Americans [were] also twice as likely to be unemployed" (*State* 15).

Yet the *National Urban League's State of Black America 2005: Prescriptions for Change* states that the black middle class remains undercounted. The report said in 1960 more than 750,000 black men and women worked in middle-class occupations. The number increased to more than 3 million by 1980 and to nearly 7 million by 1995 (42). But the racial wealth gap remains huge. In 1999, the net worth of an average white family was $81,000 compared with $8,000 for a typical African-American family (44).

"The typical black household makes 59 cents earned by the typical white household," the book notes (44). That helps account for black middle class households' being less likely to have sufficient rainy-day funds; yet they often have greater financial demands made on them by family members. Whereas whites can help their children or grandchildren with college tuition or home down payments, blacks don't have those funds available to them (Wright). Therefore inheritance in the form of financial help passed on from generation to generation is another factor making the playing field unequal. "Consequently, it is virtually impossible for people of color to earn their way to equal wealth through wages," the report notes; blacks "cannot out-earn the wealth gap" (43).

From "Unfair gap found in home value"

Homeownership is another area where the disparities are clear. The 2005 Urban League book states that "less than 50 percent of black families in America own homes. Conversely, over 70 percent of white families in America own homes" (21).

Unequal housing divided along the color line remains a serious problem. An October 2001 report from the Brookings Institution Center on Urban & Metropolitan Policy said unequal housing resulted in a "segregation tax" on black homeowners.

"This gap in home values, or 'segregation tax' imposed on black homeowners, primarily results from a high degree of racial segregation in neighborhoods," the report said. The study examined the top 100 most populated metropolitan areas in 1990.

It found that whites on average had an income of $54,015 and a house with an average value of $142,637. "Thus for every dollar of income, white homeowners as a group owned $2.64 worth of house," the report said.

African-Americans on average had an income of $38,293 and a house with an average value of $82,630. "For every dollar of income, black homeowners owned $2.16 worth of house," the report said.

"In short, for a dollar of income black homeowners received only 82 percent of the housing value that white homeowners received," the study said. "Nationally, black homeowners 'paid' an 18 percent 'segregation tax.'"

The report described the "segregation tax" as the "depressed value of homes and the reduced equity for homeowners in highly segregated neighborhoods." It reflects the burden black homeowners bear of past and present public policies.

The report said most African-Americans lived in neighborhoods that were at least 50 percent black. "Almost two-thirds of black residents would have to move in order for every neighborhood to be 13 percent black, which is the percentage of African-Americans in the U.S. population."

The isolation of black residents is part of the problem. White homebuyers avoid black neighborhoods, which negatively affects the

> demand for housing. Price competition is reduced, "home values are depressed and the 'segregation tax' continues," the report said.
>
> The black home value to income ratio was lower than whites' and lower than Hispanics', Asian-Americans' and American Indians'. Segregation among the other groups appeared to be lower, too.
>
> Floyd O. May, a deputy assistant secretary of the U.S. Department of Housing and Urban Development, said last year at an NAACP Civil Rights Town Hall Meeting that homeownership remains the key to wealth creation in America. But the segregation tax, predatory lending and unequal access to better housing kill the dream for African-Americans.
>
> These and other barriers must be eliminated. To end the segregation tax, the Brookings report recommended better zoning laws, rethinking school enrollment policies and vigorously enforcing fair housing and fair lending laws.
>
> Separate has never been equal in America, and every time segregation happens, African-Americans pay the highest toll.

Some of the feedback placed the blame for the inequities squarely (and solely) at the feet of the black population, making personal responsibility (or the lack thereof) the main solution (or the main problem). And then when black families do move to the suburbs, like the majority of America, they often encounter less than friendly circumstances. Recall the Bates family in Chapter 2, and whites not wanting a home even in the suburbs that had been owned by blacks. Race bedevils any attempt to lower the barriers that separate Americans.

> Voice Mail: 2003
>
> I just got back in town and read your article in this morning's Star, and it was an excellent article and you know one that I identify with. I've made some bad housing selections and not gained the appreciation that I've seen some other people do. There is no question that owning a home in the wrong part of town or the wrong home can affect your ability to accumulate wealth. The only thing I would say, however, and I wish you would have touched on (why) some people chose to live in a neighborhood because they can get more bang for their buck in a house. And I think you have a little of that in the black community. The second factor is statistically white married couples tend to stay together and raise their children in a higher percentage than black married couples. In fact a lot of black males don't marry their significant others. And two incomes buy more house than one. Second thing that you didn't touch on, geographically the worst parts of Kansas City are desirable, but they're just not safe. You know, as I read a lot of your articles they are

> relatively resistant to aggressively attacking crime in society. Crack cocaine has had just a devastating effect on the inner city and until the problems of the Crips and the Bloods are dealt with aggressively, until drive-by shootings are a thing of the past and until Kansas City is not one of the crime capitals of the United States, it's going to be troubling for a person to consider moving into some of the neighborhoods. Thank you for listening to me.
>
> Voice Mail: 2003
>
> If the black families can't keep their children in school and graduate out of high school, how do you expect them to go out and buy a home or any other equity type thing? I just turned on the TV just about an hour ago where General Motors and all the dealerships are trying to get young people in high school to go study how to be an auto mechanic. It pays anywhere from $100,000 to $150,000 a year. People can learn to be auto mechanics. They're begging for them. You've got to keep the people in school. There's the problem. You're so far out on your article it's unbelievable.

Jim Myers underscores these beliefs in *Afraid of the Dark,* noting that "millions of white Americans tend to consider themselves refugees, as if they were driven from cities by the coming of black hordes. Many white Americans grew up in neighborhoods that are now black; they look back upon idyllic youth, believing that black people were among the forces to expel them from Eden. Such tales are often insinuated: 'It was a nice neighborhood, full of decent people, until they moved in" (78).

Yet the statistics are so starkly in favor of discrimination being a major problem that taking personal responsibility cannot be held up as the ultimate solution. Thomas M. Shapiro in "The Racial Wealth Gap" chapter in the *State of America 2005* argues that the gaps between blacks and whites have worsened under the administration of Republican President George W. Bush. The recession and jobless recovery reversed the unprecedented growth seen in the 1990s during the Democratic administration of President Bill Clinton. Black and Hispanic families in the recession and jobless recovery

> lost over one-quarter of their wealth while the wealth of white families grew slowly. In 2002, a typical Hispanic family owned 11 cents of wealth for every dollar owned by a typical white family, and African-American families owned only 7 cents.... More than any other economic attribute, wealth represents the sedimentation of historical inequalities in the American experience, in a sense the accumulation of advantage and disadvantage for different racial, class and ethnic groups. In this way, it allows us a window to explore how our past influences realities today.... Closing the racial wealth gap needs to be

> at the forefront of the civil rights agenda moving into the twenty-first century. (46-47)

In her essay "Hurricane Katrina Exposed the Face of Poverty," in *The State of Black America 2006*, Maya Wiley concurs with Shapiro's position, writing that the labyrinth of disparity is

> almost impossible to escape for many people of color. We have eliminated legalized racial discrimination against people of color, but have left the structures it produced intact. This is structural racism. The structures produced racialized outcomes—disparate poverty and exclusion for people of color and opportunities for whites.... Across the nation the middle class is shrinking, quality educational opportunities are harder to find, jobs are less secure and we face a dwindling base to support our aging population.... Our ability to compete in a global economy, desperately and steadily reduce poverty, strengthen and expand the middle class and create healthy, sustainable communities is at risk. (144)

Parity and Disparity

The following statistics are from the National Urban League's *State of Black America 2002: Opportunity and Equality = One America* on the issue of jobs. It's from Franklin D. Raines' essay, "What Equality Would look Like: Reflections on the Past, Present and Future":

- "If blacks and whites had equal employment, 700,000 more African Americans would have jobs today. And nearly two million more African Americans would be promoted to higher paying and managerial jobs." (15-16)
- "If we had income equality in America [today,] the average black American household would get a 56-percent pay raise. Altogether, they would earn another $190 billion." (16)
- "If we had full equality, the wealth of black households would rise by $1 trillion. African Americans would have $200 million more in the stock market, $120 billion more in our pension plans, and $80 billion more in the bank. And we might have 31 African-American billionaires instead of one." (17)
- "If we were insured at the same rate, 2.5 million more African-Americans, including 620,000 children, would have health insurance." (17)
- "If the digital divide were closed, 3 million more black households would own computers and have Internet access." (18)
- "Equality would mean the automobile industry would sell 1.5 million more cars." (18)

- "The prison system would lose 700,000 African-American adults, and 33,000 fewer juveniles now in detention. This would save the country over $15 billion in the cost of incarceration." (18)
- "If you were to close the home equity gap, the wealth of African Americans would jump by $760 billion. And if you were to close the homeownership gap, there would be 3 million more African American homeowners." (20)

The above information can help people visualize the heavy compost mountain of inequity that has been piled on one group representing the real, largely undiscovered sector of America. Another example of the unacknowledged inequity is the mammoth myth about welfare. Black people for most of the existence of welfare were excluded from participating in it just as they were excluded by government sanctioned housing covenants from buying new homes in the suburbs. *The State of Black America 2002* reported:

> Maya Rockeymoore made the point that when the Aid to Dependent Children program was created during the 1930s New Deal, compromises with Southern Democrats led to the exclusion of African Americans from this vital part of the country's safety-net legislation. Those barriers were not removed until the Civil Rights Movement of the 1960s forced President Lyndon Johnson's War on Poverty to correct racial disparities. (39)

When African-American families finally were allowed to benefit from the federal aid program, welfare all of a sudden became a bad thing, a horrible thing, and the face of all welfare recipients became black. That's also when the recipient started getting the entitlement label. Along with that distortion came a sense that welfare was gotten unfairly or by criminal means. Mary Frances Berry, former chair of the U.S. Civil Rights Commission and professor of history and law at the University of Pennsylvania, notes in her book, *The Pig Farmer's Daughter and Other Tales of American Injustice*, that

> [t]he white public accepted the story that promiscuous, licentious black women who became pregnant out of wedlock caused the explosion in illegitimacy and raised welfare costs.... [B]lack women [were defined] as socially unproductive, undeserving persons who required punitive legal sanctions. White women [on the other hand] were socially productive: their babies, though conceived out of wedlock, could offer infertile couples their only chance to have families. (In contrast) blacks were referred to as living in "zoological tenements" that served as "breeding warrens," characterizations that might justify sterilization. White women, being

> deserving, could be rehabilitated and redeemed through casework, adoption, and return to the marriage marketplace. Public and private social service agencies facilitated adoption services for whites, [Aid to Dependent Children] for African-Americans. The different attitudes reflected and reinforced the story of black immorality and dependency. (172-173)

The Urban League 2002 book notes that the Welfare Reform law of the 1990s "was to put states back in control, and reopen the doors to discrimination in a program that had been an entitlement" all along for white people (39).

As flummoxing as racism and racial encounters are, they help individuals to be able to better contend with racial confrontations in the future. But the past still looms.

<u>From "New center a chance for a new start"</u>

> COLUMBIA–The wheels of my old one-speed bicycle spun through campus, chasing ghosts that still haunt me.
>
> Nearly 20 years had sped by since I'd pedaled my bike to classes at the University of Missouri-Columbia. Also, 21 years had passed since I'd broken a story as a Columbia *Missourian* reporter. Charles C. Schroeder, MU vice chancellor for student affairs, said the story is now part of campus legend. He retold the tale, unaware of my involvement.
>
> MU had allowed the old Black Culture House it owned at 511 Turner Ave. to deteriorate to a dangerous state. Yet the building still served about 700 black students on campus, offering tutoring, workshops, career guidance, seminars, lectures and a place to meet socially.
>
> I remember covering history-making speakers there in the '70s and going to the house to relax with friends. But by 1976 the place was falling apart. A black student was struck by a piece of wooden facing that had rotted away from the entrance.
>
> Schroeder chuckled, saying thank goodness those days are gone. But I still can't laugh.
>
> Embarrassing the university with the March 1976 story, which included racial bias issues, won me no friends at the journalism school.
>
> Times fortunately have changed. On my bike, I found that a multistory garage now stands where the Black Culture House had opened 25 years ago.
>
> Because of the furor I started, the facility moved in 1978 to a brick house at 823 Virginia Ave., where it became the Black Culture Center.
>
> But that house, which would take $250,000 to upgrade to today's building standards, was razed in 1998 after a new $2 million, 11,000-square-foot Black Culture Resource Center opened nearby. Black alums like me gathered at the Lincoln Building in Kansas City to toast

the construction and MU's commitment to diversity.

Because of the story about MU's neglect of the Black Culture House, my immediate professor told me I was a disaster as a journalist and was "taking up the space of a qualified student." At that time, *decoded,* he meant someone who was white. My grade was lowered and I was sent home for the summer with the clear message that it would be no use for me to come back. My dad got me a job with a black weekly newspaper for the summer. It paid nothing but gave me the opportunity to get many stories and pictures published and return to the journalism school unbowed. In 2004 I sent a note to a different professor at the University of Missouri-Columbia oddly thanking him for the adversity. I told that professor the prejudicial treatment actually added to my education, preparing me for what I would encounter in the newspaper industry.

In May 1977 when I started my newspaper career at *The Kansas City Star,* fewer than 4 percent of all newspaper jobs nationwide were held by journalists of color. We constantly had to work to overcome others' low expectations of us. We were thought to not know or be able to use the English language well enough to be journalists. Our skills often were doubted and we were not trusted.

Trust was a huge issue. Our editors and our colleagues were perpetually concerned about whether we would be blacks or journalists first. It's what black police officers faced with people wondering whether they would be "black" (as in their race) or "blue" (as in the color of their uniforms). Back then black journalists were mostly hired only to replace someone black who had left the newspaper staff. I was hired to replace a black reporter who was sent out on an assignment and didn't come back. Authorities found him the next day wandering the streets. He had suffered a nervous breakdown and didn't know who he was, where he was or how he got there. Suddenly, as someone who was seeking a job in journalism, I started to look pretty good to *The Kansas City Star/Times.* But I was told some time after I was hired as a reporter/ photographer that I was brought on to be a journalist and to "leave that black stuff outside." In other words, I was being asked to shoulder what R. Roosevelt Thomas, Jr., has called "the burden of cultural change," to "be melted down" (112) into the melting pot that was the business of journalism in those days, to leave the better part of me outside of the job. It was something I could never do.

What the majority fails to see is that people don't melt. They only get angry, possibly become disruptive, have a nervous breakdown (like my unfortunate predecessor did), or leave when pressure and heat are applied to try to force them to "melt." What's more is the media badly need journalists who represent the racial, ethnic and other diversity in our population so they can better and more accurately cover all of the community. The Kerner Commission report after the riots during the Civil Rights Movement urged the news media to hire journalists of color to address the explosive concerns in ghettoes nationwide. They were going unreported, which helped account for the conflagration that erupted. But the message journalists of color received in newsrooms was not one that encouraged those kinds of stories. On the contrary; we had to perpetuate the erroneous but nonetheless "traditional American image of diversity...: the melting pot, where ethnic and racial differences were sanitized and standardized into a kind of American puree"; we were being forced to "abandon most of [our] ethnic distinctions at the company door" (Thomas 112). When that happens, individuals' unique talents either become homogenized or get lost. And we are operating in a time in this country in which more and different talents are desperately needed. Like plant and animal life, the diversity of species ensures the survival of businesses, civic organizations, communities and nations. Also, it is from communities that have been long neglected, that have been excluded because of racism and discrimination and that have had to do without because of limited resources that some of the greatest innovations have emerged. That's the "What's in it for me?" aspect of diversity that people must recognize for self-improvement and survival.

To push newspapers to do the right thing in hiring and promoting journalists of color, the American Society of Newspaper Editors (ASNE) in 1978 set as a goal for the year 2000 to have the percentage of journalists of color in newsrooms throughout America equal the percentage of people of color in the population. But prior to 2000, the goal was pushed back to 2025. The 2007 ASNE Annual Report showed a drop from 13.87 percent in 2006 to 13.62 percent in 2007 in journalists of color in newsroom jobs, even though the percentage of people of color in the population increased from about 25 percent in the 1970s to more than 30 percent.

In *Bowling Alone*, Robert Putnam described newspapers as instruments which build social capital, that sense of community and sense of caring, that sense of hope, faith, togetherness and even reciprocity that grows from people getting together to talk and share ideas. He ties the demographic and social changes in our world partly to the dying off of a generation of people born before World War II. These folks also make up the core of faithful newspaper readers. Newspaper circulation peaked in 1947, and since then there has been a steady erosion in readership. That's because it is largely the dwindling pre-World War II generation which values newspapers and the information and analysis that publications such as *The Kansas City Star* offer. Putnam writes that reading newspapers correlates with high social capital, whereas watching TV does the opposite (218-220). Putnam also notes that TV viewing adversely affects social trust and group membership. Heavy television viewing tends to warp people into loners, thus making them less tolerant (242). Without journalists of color helping to change the racially stagnant culture in newsrooms and to tell the stories about the Real America, the stereotypes grow and so do the problems that result.

Stereotypes, benefit cuts and other life-threatening effects of discrimination

Without media change, the prevailing views about people of color will remain less than pretty. People do as the media do—normalize random events to verify long-held stereotypes.

> E-mail: Oct. 24, 2002
>
> At least two dark-skinned people who hate America were arrested at 3 a.m. this morning. 500,000 more and possibly we will have a country that is fit to live in once again.
>
> Was great to see the people of Hawaii out in a mass rally this week telling Muslim/Islamic people to leave the State and go back home to the Middle East. This will happen all over the globe in a few weeks–especially in Europe, in the Philippines and in Indonesia.
>
> The sniper shootings were hopefully the last straw for 85 percent of the civilized people in America.

From "Planting seeds that end hate"

> In October of 2002 more than 200 Muslims joined a choir of their children singing "America the Beautiful."
>
> The passion and love they have for this country made that part of the American Muslim Council Heartland Chapter annual dinner a Kodak moment. The theme was "Muslims: Part of America."
>
> This is their country, too. The 2 million to 6 million Muslims in the United States are trying to get others to accept that. It's a truth that the Sept. 11, 2001, terrorist attacks severely damaged.
>
> A man who's Muslim recently told me that until the tragedy he didn't give much credence to racial profiling of minorities. After the attack the country's suspicions shifted to people like him.
>
> The injustice of being perceived as a suspect instead of a tax-paying, productive citizen transformed the man. He has gotten involved in civil rights and other efforts to get people to accept individuals like him.
>
> M. Akhtar Chaudry has been engaged like that for years. He had

been chairman of the Urban League of Greater Kansas City and president of the American Muslim Council Heartland Chapter.

"We want our voices to be heard," Chaudry said at the council's dinner. "We want to move to the mainstream.

"We are Americans, and we are here to stay. Eventually we want to become a powerful political force that will represent our dreams and goals.

"We have a long way to go."

Despite President Bush's efforts to say it isn't so, the Sept. 11, 2001, tragedy also caused too many people to tie terrorism exclusively to Muslims.

Hate crimes followed as well as unwarranted questioning, detention, harassment and threats. Eric Erfan Vickers, executive director of the American Muslim Council in Washington, urged people at the dinner to become politically active, vote, run for office, form coalitions, join civil rights groups and show leadership and courage despite the intimidation.

Vickers encouraged people to help other Americans see that Muslims care about this country, too. "I think we have been too long in being shy about who we are and our place here," he said.

Mahnaz Shabbir is among American Muslims who haven't been shy. She tries to get people to see the injustices too many Muslims face when they're just trying to be Americans and live the American dream.

Shabbir, former vice president of strategic planning and business development at Carondelet Health, even offered her assistance to the chief executive of Larkin Community Hospital in Miami. Her appeal followed the unwarranted detention of three Muslim medical students in Florida as terrorism suspects.

Hostile e-mails to the hospital prompted the chief executive to tell the students they weren't welcome to continue their studies there. Shabbir's e-mail, however, was among many from the Muslim community countering others' hate.

I've watched Shabbir's recent presentations at Red Bridge Methodist Church and Grace United Methodist Church. She changes people's impressions of Muslims.

She and others keep planting the seeds to end the hate. People choke up and are moved to tears when she explains that it's because of her four sons and other Muslim children that she tries to give people a better understanding of the diversity of Muslims.

"We have a lot of good stories to tell in the American Muslim community," said Shabbir, who has two sons who are Boy Scouts. "We have good kids who are doing extraordinary things.

"Yet, all of a sudden we are being identified and singled out because we have a different religion from others. No parents would want that for their children."

Shabbir shares with her audiences a quote from Mohandas Gandhi to encourage them to be activists for change: "We are the change we wish to see in the world."

There is no greater truth.

However, people in the old, destructive America who exist inside the protective barriers of racism see things differently and aren't bashful about expressing their views.

E-mail: Oct. 9, 2002

The fact remains American Muslims face a monumental sales job persuading many, if not most, of their countrymen they don't have divided loyalties, or worse, malign intent. Seems like they should take every opportunity to reiterate their loyalty by allying themselves with America and against her enemies, especially in a venue discussing how they're being unfairly discriminated against, don't you think?

They do. But their statements don't get picked up by the news media.

Homeless people and those who are mentally ill represent another often invisible world of diversity in America. As the gap between the haves and have-nots grows, so does the negative attitude of the public for people who are less fortunate. This places the health of the entire population in jeopardy, as mentioned earlier.

From "Inject compassion into government"

Robert Tucker sat behind me on Easter Sunday at the Grand Avenue Temple.

The 91-year-old church at 205 E. Ninth St. was packed. But this flock is different from other churches'.

The temple is where people in suits and Easter dresses share pews with many worshippers who are homeless and mentally ill. Jerry Armstrong, president of the Ark of Friends of Greater Kansas City, and Sybil Noble, vice president and founder of the mental health advocacy group, invited me to the morning service.

Tucker said the church is an exceptional place. "We get solace here," he said.

"You come here, and you come as you are," said Tucker, who is homeless. "You have people here with many, many challenges. Society casts a lot of us out.

"But if Jesus were homeless, he'd be right here with us. Jesus would be where he felt he was needed."

I left Tucker when Noble and Armstrong arrived and sat with

them near the ornate windows. Noble gave me one of four photo collages she'd done of homeless parishioners who had died in the last few months.

She spoke about those untimely, tragic deaths at a midtown forum last month with state lawmakers titled "Impact of Proposed Budget Cuts on the Health of Our Community."

Missouri faces a $1 billion shortfall and a tax system that no longer produces enough money for services.

Health insurance for low-income residents, alcohol treatment and mental health programs are among services that would suffer multimillion-dollar funding cuts.

"People are dying," Noble said at the hearing. "People are falling through the cracks."

Then-Missouri Sen. Charles Wheeler, a Kansas City Democrat, said at the forum that the public must express its outrage. "I think you've got to march to Jefferson City and say this is intolerable," he said.

Larry Aaron, vice president and chair of the legislative committee with the National Alliance for the Mentally Ill-Kansas City, said this area has suffered a disproportionate share of state mental health cuts.

"Services are tough out there, and they're not going to get any better," he told the legislators. Badly needed training and rehabilitation programs have been cut as well as positions providing accountability. Others have been privatized.

But people with chronic mental illnesses are the hardest and most expensive to treat. "No one wants to serve them," Aaron said.

There's no profit for businesses taking over state services for the homeless, the poor and mentally ill. Companies out to make money won't do what churches like the Grand Avenue Temple have as their mission.

Government also has to own the responsibility of taking care of the less fortunate, then-Rep. Vicki Walker, a Kansas City Democrat, said at the hearing. "We cannot fund government exactly like a business if we are to be humanitarian, if we're to be fair," she said.

What Aaron fears is more people who are mentally ill will stop getting services, putting them and public safety at risk. "It's tough to have a loved one who has mental illness – probably the most horrible thing there is, and to not get services you need is the worst thing imaginable for people to go through," Aaron said.

It's unacceptable for people with mental illness to be treated in such an inhumane way.

"We're a statistic," Noble said. "We want to be treated like people."

On the wall at the church behind Tucker was a banner, saying, "Grand Avenue Temple, where everybody is somebody special, reaching out to unite all in God's love."

If only that compassion could be resurrected in national, state and local government, too.

Compassion, understanding and trust are all casualties of a history of discrimination that spills into the present. People who have shown prejudice against someone will have to make an effort to demonstrate compassion and understanding in order to regain the trust of those they discriminated against. Too many African-Americans remember the Tuskegee Study, for example, in which 28 black men died after going untreated in a federal syphilis experiment. From 1932 to the early 1970s, the government used 400 to 600 black men in Macon County, Ala., as if they were laboratory animals. That public health atrocity left deep scars. Once trust is lost, it is difficult to regain.

From "All blood is the same color–red"

Eager students at Southeast High School will roll up their sleeves Thursday and do something remarkable.

These kids at the mostly black school will donate blood to the Community Blood Center of Greater Kansas City. It's unusual because few black people today give blood.

African-Americans make up about 12 percent of the metro area's population but only 3 percent of the blood center's 56,000 donors. That's ironic, when people are learning that Charles Drew, a black physician, pioneered America's comprehensive blood-banking program.

Getting more African-Americans to donate blood is more than just a nice thing to do. It's a national concern.

The American Association of Blood Banks and other groups recently studied the issue because minority populations of some cities are now majorities. Unless they donate blood, shortages could develop and put health care at risk.

Already, problems are surfacing. "The need for increased minority donations has become acute," Joel M. Solomon, chief executive officer of the association, wrote in a newsletter.

He said that of the A, B, AB and O blood types, O and B are more common among blacks than whites. Because O is the universal donor type, it is used most frequently in emergency room cases.

The need for type O blood outstrips the supply. To meet the demand, blood centers must attract more black donors, Solomon said in an interview.

Compatibility is another issue. Sickle-cell anemia patients, who are usually black, often require matched blood that may be available only from donors of the same race.

Getting African-Americans to understand such concerns remains a challenge. The medical community also must build bridges to restore trust, said Jasper Fullard Jr., a physician and then-president of the Kansas City area Black Health Care Coalition.

Besides the history of experimentation on blacks, giving blood also carries a stigma of poverty, because some people sell their blood. And needles used to draw blood raise incorrect fears of hepatitis and AIDS, said Nevada Lee, a physician and Black Health Care Coalition member.

African-Americans also worry that their donations might be segregated for blacks only in this society where equality remains elusive.

That means blood banks must do a better job of explaining needs and reaching minorities in churches and schools with more culturally diverse appeals, Solomon said.

The workplace isn't good enough, especially when unemployment among black workers locally and nationally is twice that of whites.

The interest in giving has caught on at Southeast, where Dorothy B. Jones, interim curriculum coordinator, hopes more than 100 students will donate blood. They have toured the blood center and are aware of the need.

The students' donations would make Dr. Drew mighty proud.

SECTION 2

The History Leading to Today

CHAPTER 5
Removing the Whitewash

Pain

I've known pain
Like an avalanche
Breaking my spirit like bones
I've felt tearing hurricanes
Of sorrow destroying my home
Gusts blown in from an unstable world
Shaking what beauty hard work unfurls
Shattering health and crushing minds
Making survival and a future seem
Like sands blown capriciously in time
I've lived pain like an avalanche of hurricanes
Bracing, waiting; tomorrow's likely to be the same.

"We are caught in an escapable network of mutuality,
tied in a single garment of destiny.
Whatever affects one directly affects all indirectly."
~Rev. Martin Luther King, Jr.

In no way can this book offer a comprehensive examination of the history of all of America's peoples. Their contributions, their pain and suffering are more vast than the land itself. To chronicle it all would take volumes that would stretch from the Pacific Ocean to the Atlantic. Therefore, what follows is merely a beginning of the exploration that must be carried out if we are to be serious about discovering the Real America.

Whenever the subject of history comes up in conversation, people tend to swing from believing that "we've made a lot of progress" to lamenting that we can't go back to "the good old days." Neither of those positions is entirely accurate, since history is enticingly messy. For one thing, events in history are experienced differently by different "groups" of people. When President Lyndon B. Johnson signed the Civil Rights Act in 1964 and the Voting Rights Act in 1965, for example, those events were regarded as victories by blacks but as defeats by white Southern Democrats. The 1930s/1940s era that Archie and Edith Bunker sang about at the beginning of every episode of the old television sitcom "All in the Family" is not a time that minorities or women in the U.S. want to go back to:

> Boy, the way Glenn Miller played. Songs that made the hit parade.
> Guys like us, we had it made. Those were the days.
> Didn't need no welfare state. Everybody pulled his weight.
> Gee, our old LaSalle ran great. Those were the days.
> And you know who you were then. Girls were girls and men were men.
> Mister, we could use a man like Herbert Hoover again.
> People seemed to be content. Fifty dollars paid the rent.
> Freaks were in a circus tent. Those were the days.
> Take a little Sunday spin, go to watch the Dodgers win.
> Have yourself a dandy day that cost you under a fin.
> Hair was short and skirts were long. Kate Smith really sold a song.
> I don't know just what went wrong. Those Were The Days.[1]

Archie Bunker, of course, was depicted on the 1970s TV show as being someone who was deeply racist, bigoted, sexist, and homophobic, even though he also was shown as a loving family man and good provider. In a sense he epitomizes the unreal, media-fed view of American history that is widespread in this country: life past and present as seen through the eyes of a white male. He dismisses the inconvenient truths that not all history-makers are heroes, that they are human and imperfect, and that not all of them are white European men. History is diverse, interwoven and complicated, but that is not what people in the U.S. have been taught.

---

[1] "Those Were The Days," by Lee Adams and Charles Strouse.

This country's history has what should be seen as an undeniable richness in racial and ethnic diversity. The contributions and stories of *everyone* should be celebrated; instead those of America's minorities are too often cursed, dismissed, denied and damned. That is because the diversity of the history of this country is not known or acknowledged, giving rise to misperceptions and bigotry. To counter that, the United States' multicultural beauty has to be taught and appreciated in schools and in the media throughout everyone's life.

From "America's many faces tell its story"

Ronald Takaki opens people's eyes to the depth of the colors in our national mosaic.

His 508-page book, *A Different Mirror: A History of Multicultural America,* is a primary textbook for people teaching the lessons of America's many faces to college students. It helps them get the connections among people and discover the Real America, despite some resistance in these conservative times.

In person during a lecture at the University of Missouri-Kansas City and in print, Takaki unveiled America's history from the perspectives of its many indigenous and immigrant people.

"Multiculturalism forces us to reach for a more accurate vision of American society," said Takaki, a professor of ethnic studies at the University of California-Berkeley and a nationally recognized scholar in multicultural studies.

This is the history that all students should be taught in schools and that we should celebrate.

It's imperative. Takaki explained: Rioting occurred in U.S. cities in 1992 after the acquittal of Los Angeles police in the beating of Rodney King. King pleaded on TV afterward, "Can we get along?"

Takaki said: "How, unless we learn more about one another?"

His book peers at the roots of our colors. American Indians had great civilizations on these shores before whites arrived.

They farmed and lived in communities that were stolen, erased and replaced by U.S. cities. "What emerged to justify dispossessing them was the racialization of Indian 'savagery,'" Takaki wrote.

Racism also became the weapon that the landed aristocracy used to separate white indentured servants from blacks in the 1600s. Slavery made poor whites feel empowered, and it enabled the wealthy to exploit black labor to harvest untold riches from the new land.

"The 19th century was the crucible for the making of today's diversity," Takaki said. Economic conditions wrought in the rest of the world by the British Empire drove immigrants to America's shores.

The British forced Ireland from tillage farming to grazing for beef production. That left the Irish with no land, jobs or food. The Irish, who were oppressed in their homeland, headed to America, where many toiled in textile factories.

Russian Jews facing anti-Semitism at home hurried to these shores, where many suffered in garment industry sweatshops. The Opium Wars started by the British caused many Chinese men to come here for mining and railroad jobs. Fearing Western powers, Japan heavily taxed its people to build up its industrial and military forces. That drove many Japanese to America.

Mexico's territory in the Southwest included California and Texas. But wars with whites and the U.S. manifest destiny policy forced Mexicans out. The Mexican Revolution and U.S. jobs brought many Hispanics back, just like today.

Once here, each group endured exploitation, bigotry and hardships.

Some changed their names, shed their heritage and melted into white America. But people of color who helped build this country were excluded.

Only through unity in areas like labor and education did they gain economic and political clout. Otherwise each remained oppressed through the age-old American means of pitting one group against the other.

History teaches that unity must be sustained for us to thrive.

It is important, therefore, to note the overlapping and common histories of this country's minorities. Highlighting some of the unsung heroes of color also is important while taking a closer look at a different truth behind some of the "celebrated" white icons, starting with Columbus.

American Indians

What we were taught in school about Christopher Columbus was wrong. Obviously he didn't discover America, because there were millions of people already living here before he arrived. But he was also not the first to sail from the "Old" World to the Americas. James W. Loewen includes a table in *Lies My Teacher Told Me: Everything Your American History Textbook Got Wrong,* showing people sailed from Africa to Central America from 1000 B.C. to 300 A.D.; from Phoenicia and Celtic Britain to New England and perhaps elsewhere in 500 B.C.; and from Ireland via Iceland to Newfoundland and the West Indies in 600 A.D. Many explorers, in fact, from Indonesia, Japan, Siberia, China, Ireland, Iceland, Greenland, West Africa, Portugal and England made the journey to the "New" World before Columbus did (*Lies* 47). But, writes Loewen, "Columbus, like Christ, was so pivotal that historians use him to divide the past into epochs, making the Americas before

1492 'pre-Columbian'" (*Lies* 38). What the earlier explorers lacked were good public relations agents to spread the word that they were "first" to "discover" America. Loewen also wrote: "To grant too much human potential to pre-Columbian Africans might jar European American sensibilities" (*Lies* 51). At the same time, most history textbooks played down the plundering that Columbus did in this so-called New World. Loewen also writes that "typically after 'discovering' an island and encountering a tribe of Indians new to them, the Spaniards would read aloud (in Spanish) what came to be called 'the Requirement.'" It went something like this:

> I implore you to recognize the Church as a lady in the name of the Pope, take the King as lord of this land and obey his mandates. If you do not do it, I tell you that with the help of God I will enter powerfully against you all. I will make war everywhere and every way that I can. I will subject you to the yoke and obedience to the Church and to his majesty. I will take your women and children and make them slaves.... The deaths and injuries that you will receive from here on will be your own fault and not that of his majesty nor of the gentlemen that accompany me. (*Lies* 43)

Loewen continues:

> On his first voyage [to Hispaniola, now Haiti and the Dominican Republic], Columbus kidnapped some ten to twenty-five Indians and took them back with him to Spain.... Only seven to eight of the Indians arrived alive, but along with the parrots, gold trinkets and other exotica, they caused quite a stir in Seville. Ferdinand and Isabella provided Columbus with seventeen ships, 1,200 to 1,500 men, cannons, crossbows, guns, cavalry and attack dogs for a second voyage. (*Lies* 60-61)

Unfortunately for the indigenous people, the Spaniards followed through on their threats. Loewen explains:

> When Columbus and his men returned to Haiti in 1493, they demanded food, gold, spun cotton–whatever the Indians had that they wanted, including sex with their women. To ensure cooperation, Columbus used punishment by example. When an Indian committed even a minor offense, the Spanish cut off his ears or nose. Disfigured, the person was sent back to his village as living evidence of the brutality the Spaniards were capable of. (*Lies* 61)

The Arawak Indians of Haiti finally fought back. But the resistance gave Columbus an excuse to declare war on the Indians, whose "weapons" were no match for Spanish guns and armor. The Spanish prevailed and took the Arawak Indians as slaves and hunted others for sport and murdered them for dog food. On Haiti the conquerors also made the Indians mine gold for them in a forced system of labor. Some of the Indians chose suicide and even killed their families. Others who worked in mines saw their gardens go unattended. Malnutrition and disease claimed many of these Arawaks. Estimates were that there were 3 million Arawak Indians in 1496, but by 1516, because of "'sinister Indian slave trade and labor policies initiated by Columbus, only 12,000 remained'" (*Lies* 63).

A similar decimation of Native peoples took place on the North American mainland, where Columbus never set foot. An 1840 estimate put the pre-Columbian Native American population at 14 million people. By 1880 because of epidemics, warfare and deculturation the number of Native Americans had plummeted to 250,000, or a decline of 98 percent (*Lies* 83). The numbers may be even more dramatic. In "Fluff and Feathers: Treatment of American Indians in the Literature and the Classroom," Cornel Pewewardy writes: "[D.E.] Stannard [in his 1992 book *American holocaust: The conquest of the New World*] contends that close to 100,000,000 Indigenous peoples were exterminated.... [This] holocaust was, in a way, even more destructive than that of the Jews, since many American Indian tribes became extinct.... The white man's superior technology, hunger for land, and ethnocentrism seemingly knew no bounds."

Loewen draws on the science fiction story *War of the Worlds* by H.G. Wells to illustrate the terror and fear that Columbus—and other white "explorers"—brought with them.

> Wells intended his tale of earthlings' encounter with technologically advanced aliens as an allegory. His frightened British commoners (New Jerseyites in Orson Welles's radio adaptation) were analogous to the 'primitive' people of the Canaries or America, and his terrifying aliens represented the technologically advanced Europeans. As we identify with the helpless earthlings, Welles wanted us also to sympathize with the natives on Haiti in 1493, or on Australia in 1788, or in the upper Amazon jungle in the 1990s. (*Lies* 61)

As Gary R. Howard wrote in his book, *We Can't Teach What We Don't Know: White Teachers Multiracial Schools*, on continents worldwide hundreds of years ago indigenous people were terrorized by imperialist nations. It's as if the same playbook was used on every continent. Howard called it "the seven basics of western dominance." Those seven elements are bacteria (such as smallpox), bullets, beads, bureaucracy, books, booze and the Bible. (36)

Cornel Pewewardy writes about the "bacteria, bullets, and Bible" elements. He states that "Pilgrims, Puritans, and other colonists thought that Indians were heathens and savages, and according to some, the devil's disciples. Within 50 years of the "Thanksgiving Feast," thousands of Indians were dead at the hands of colonists and disease." But the early European colonists did not have a monopoly on racism. Pewewardy adds,

> The Declaration of Independence refers to indigenous people as "merciless savages." George Washington bought and sold Indian lands without tribes' permission, [and] fought and killed Indians without mercy.... In his [late 1880s] book, *The Winning of the West,* Theodore Roosevelt wrote that Indians are "filthy," "lecherous," and "faithless," in addition to living lives that "were but a few degrees less meaningless, squalid and ferocious than that of the wild beasts with whom they held joint ownership." ("Fluff")

The "books" element Howard mentions involves an imperial power imposing its history and way of life on others. Pewewardy notes that for North American Indians "[t]he final threat came in the form of schools; early American Indian education was truly an education for extinction" ("Fluff"). What consequently goes missing in the stories that are told about people of color are *their* history, *their* way of life, but especially *their* contributions, little of which make it into our mainstream history books. Those omissions are a cultural holocaust, genocide, or ethnic cleansing.

One example of what isn't being told is the profound influence Native Americans had on how the U.S. Constitution and government were shaped. Loewen writes that Native American ideals of

> liberty, fraternity, and equality found their way to Europe to influence social philosophers such as Thomas More, Locke, Montaigne, Montesquieu, and Rousseau. These European thinkers then influenced Americans such as Franklin, Jefferson, and Madison.... In recent years historians have debated whether Indian ideas may also have influenced our democracy more directly. Through 150 years of colonial contact, the Iroquois League stood before the colonies as an object lesson in how to govern a large domain democratically. (*Lies* 111)

Native Americans' good government practices and ideals "echo" in the United States Declaration of Independence—despite the slurs—and they're part of the mortar of the U.S. Constitution and the Bill of Rights. "Both the Continental Congress and the Constitutional Convention referred openly to Iroquois ideas and imagery," Loewen writes. He adds that "John Mohawk has argued that American Indians are directly or indirectly responsible for the public-meeting tradition, free speech, democracy, and 'all things which got attached to the Bill of Rights'" (*Lies* 111-112). Loewen repeats Mohawk's question: "Without the Native example, 'do you really believe that all those ideas would have found birth among a people who had spent a millennium butchering other people because of intolerance of questions of religion?'" (*Lies* 112). Yet we all know all too well who gets the credit for these admirable attributes of the American system…and it's not American Indians!

African Americans

We can give Christopher Columbus credit for setting the "New" World stage for another atrocity: slavery.

From "Teachable moments in history" and "Educational expeditions advance black history"

> Junius Rodriguez didn't want anyone in 2002 to overlook a significant anniversary in American and world history: The trans-Atlantic slave trade to the "New" World had begun 500 years earlier.
>
> Rodriguez is an associate professor of history at Eureka College in Illinois. He was the general editor of *The Historical Encyclopedia of World Slavery* and author of *Chronology of World Slavery.*
>
> He found that Spanish King Ferdinand on Sept. 3, 1501, signed documents for African captives to become slaves in colonies in the Americas. A Portuguese ship in April 1502 carried them to the Spanish colony on the island of Hispaniola. Slavery had existed "since the dawn of civilization," Rodriguez said. But this was uniquely based on race.
>
> Many people only want to remember that the United States outlawed the trans-Atlantic slave trade in the early 1800s, and the 13th Amendment to the Constitution ended U.S. slavery in 1865. But people need to see that in the history of slavery is the root of today's race relations and global problems. Rodriguez called the 500th anniversary of slavery "a perfect teachable moment for discussion and reflection."
>
> Such dialogues help people see the origins of today's racism, how it might be resolved and how humanity might finally heal itself from the festering wound that is more than 500 years old.
>
> "Coming to terms with the historical legacy is something that we as a society have not done a very good job of doing yet," Rodriguez said.
>
> The roots of slavery in North America trace back to August 1619 when a Dutch ship delivered about 20 Africans to an English colony of Virginia. Slavery also globalized trade. The Netherlands, Great Britain, Spain and France were among the participating Western nations.
>
> Slavery grew slowly until 1627, when Southern colonies began to export tobacco, indigo and rice to European markets. Multinational companies were involved in a triangular trade. Ships would carry 230 to 250 Africans often to "breaking plantations" in the Caribbean.

For about a year the slaves in these breaking plantations would be stripped of their names, culture, religion and dehumanized emotionally, psychologically and physically. They then would be sold to plantations in the Americas.

Renato Redentor Constantino, in "The Colors of Memory," writes about the ads that were placed for slaves at the time: "'Economic Section: Sales of Animals,' announces an ad in Havana, Cuba in 1839. For sale, for the sum of 500 pesos, 'a Creole negro woman, young, healthy, and without blemishes' along with 'a handsome horse of fine breeding, six spans and three inches.'

Constantino adds: "'Leeches – superior quality, just arrived from the peninsula,' goes a smaller advertisement – under the heading, 'Domestic goods for hire.' Preceding the announcement for segmented worms, another commodity is marketed: 'Negro women for service ...and for any work'"

Whites justified inhumane treatment of slaves, saying blacks had lower intelligence. Some whites even discounted early African-American scholars such as inventor and mathematician Benjamin Banneker and poet Phillis Wheatley.

Early Americans preferred the stereotypes of black people over the truth. That's largely unchanged.

The slave vessels would also pick up agricultural goods such as sugar in the Caribbean. They'd haul it to seaports in North America and pick up other cargo such as rum to take to European cities.

The ships would then pick up other goods to take to Africa to trade for more slaves. Slavery grew slowly but mushroomed as agriculture and other industries erupted, demanding more slaves.

"Within a very few years, the slave trade became an accepted and profitable part of European commerce," historian John Hope Franklin wrote in his book *From Slavery to Freedom*.

Western nations accumulated great wealth in this global marketplace. A slave might sell for $39,000 to $40,000 in today's currency. English North America had 25,000 slaves in 1700. That swelled to 250,000 by 1760. Colonies enacted laws to restrict slaves' movements, keep them from assembling, bearing arms and being taught to read and write.

The trans-Atlantic slave trade changed the world. Europe benefited; Africa suffered. Rodriguez said 11.7 million Africans were delivered alive from 1502 to the 1880s when all slave trade to the Americas was finally outlawed.

Millions of others were killed in fighting during their capture and in forced marches to seaports. They died in holding pens in West Africa and in the brutal Middle Passage. People forget that

> powerful kingdoms existed in Africa in the 14th century with cities and universities.
>
> "You found this civilization that was truly poised for greatness," Rodriguez said. The depopulation and brain drain of slavery "weakened Africa to the point of allowing imperialism and the takeover of land and resources."
>
> "We all share the burden of history," Rodriguez said. "How we understand it improves when we see the multiple angles of the story. I look forward to the day when everyone finds that their stories are being told."

One bit of history that rarely gets told is that hundreds of black soldiers fought in the Revolutionary War. There were also numerous slave revolts, as well as important abolitionists such as Frederick Douglass who spoke out against slavery and conductors on the Underground Railroad such as Harriet Tubman.

Native Americans and slaves also share a common history. Loewen notes that slaves often fled to Native American societies to escape bondage (*Lies* 109). That confounded southern slaveholders who had great amounts of wealth tied up in slaves. Loewen writes:

> Slaveholders dominated our foreign policy until the Civil War. They were always concerned about our Indian borders and made sure that treaties with Native nations stipulated that Indians surrender all African Americans and return any runaways....
>
> U.S. territorial expansion between 1787 and 1855 was due in large part to slavers' influence. The largest pressure group behind the War of 1812 was slaveholders who coveted Indian and Spanish land and wanted to drive Indian societies farther away from the slaveholding states to prevent slave escapes. Even though Spain played no real role in that war, in the aftermath we took Florida from Spain because slaveholders demanded we do so. Indeed, Andrew Jackson attacked a Seminole fort in Florida in 1816 precisely because it harbored hundreds of runaways slaves, thus initiating the First Seminole War....
>
> The Seminoles' refusal to surrender their African American members led to the First and Second Seminole Wars (1816-18, 1835-42). Whites attacked not because they wanted the Everglades, which had no economic value to the United States in the nineteenth century, but to eliminate a refuge for runaway slaves. The Second Seminole War was the longest and costliest war the United States ever fought against the Indians.....
>
> Slavery was also perhaps the key factor in the Texas War (1835-36). The freedom for which Davy Crockett, James Bowie, and the rest fought

> at the Alamo was the freedom to own slaves! As soon as Anglos set up the Republic of Texas, its legislature ordered all free black people out of the Republic....Our next major war, the Mexican War (1846-48), was again driven chiefly by Southern planters wanting to push the borders of the nearest free land farther from the slave states. (*Lies* 150-152)

And then, of course, there was the Civil War. About 186,000 black soldiers fought in that war; some 40,000 died. After the Civil War, writes Stanford L. Davis in "Buffalo Soldiers & Indian Wars,"

> Southerners and eastern populations did not want to see armed Negro soldiers near or in their communities. They were also afraid of the labor market being flooded with a new source of labor. General employment opportunities in these communities [were] not available to blacks, so many African-Americans took a long hard look at military service which offered shelter, education, steady pay, medical attention and a pension. Some decided it was much better than frequent civilian unemployment. Of course in some quarters, it was thought this [was a] good way of getting rid of two problems at the same time.

It is ironic that these black soldiers were stationed to fight the very Indian tribes who had harbored slaves during the centuries that slavery existed. At a 1997 Diversity Coalition meeting at the Minority Museum, the discussion focused on Native Americans and black people and how whites turned one minority group against the other. I shared what I had learned from Dorothy Arvizu with the Kansas Association for Native American Education.

<u>From "Matters we must talk about"</u>

> She said some former slaves joined the Army and eventually became Buffalo Soldiers. Their kill rate of Native Americans and the ferocity with which they carried out their orders was partly from a desire to prove themselves as courageous warriors against stereotypes that brand African-Americans as cowards.

Davis adds another dimension to this depiction of the Buffalo Soldiers:

> Black soldiers who fought in the Indian Wars, fought their opponents as they have done throughout this country's military history. They fought to win and to give their lives if necessary, for their personal beliefs. They wanted to gain the respect and equality they never saw as slaves and rarely received as freedmen. So, they continued on as soldiers. They were sadly mistaken in thinking they would gain these components of freedom, in a country built in-part by their enslavement and which still held deep racial and cultural prejudices.
>
> As soon as these soldiers were relocated into their hostile environ-

> ments, they were engaged in life and death struggles. They were under fire. Friends were killed and their oath to keep the peace, put to the test by Indians, settlers and those outside the law. Though they guarded railroads and telegraph lines, stagecoaches, arms shipments, towns, homesteads, whites and Indians, they never knew when they would be ambushed by foes or the very townspeople they were protecting! Not infrequently, just by entering a town or saloon, shoot-outs occurred. There was also the occasional sniper, waiting for a kill. Those that murdered troopers were never punished for their crimes, even when there were witnesses. The troopers always responded with a deadly intent of their own. When investigated by the military, those troopers found guilty were punished accordingly, but not always justly.

From "Educational expeditions advance black history"

> Freedom followed the Civil War with the 13th Amendment to the Constitution in 1865.
>
> States ratified the 14th Amendment in 1868, which provided equal protection under the laws to all citizens.
>
> Reconstruction and the Freedman's Bureau helped blacks make the transition to freedom. They valued the voting right and education, often devoting their life savings to sending their children to school.
>
> But when Reconstruction ended in 1877, Black Codes, the Ku Klux Klan and the Supreme Court made oppression, terrorism and segregation the laws of the land for African-Americans. Thousands of blacks were lynched.

Renato Redentor Constantino writes that "[f]rom 1899 to 1902, 'an estimated two thousand Black women, men, and children' die from racial attacks in America's deep South." In 1899 the U.S. annexed the Philippines, which was the first colonial war in the Far East in which African Americans were sent to fight. Constantino continues:

> From 1899 to 1901 – a mere three years after U.S. troops began firing on Filipino revolutionaries – an American general estimates the death toll of Filipinos at the hands of their U.S. liberators to number well over half a million.
>
> "To the colored American soldier," implored a public communiqué issued in the Philippines on November 17, 1899 and penned, some say, by the crippled, colored Filipino revolutionist himself, Apolinario Mabini: "It is without honor that you shed your precious blood. Your masters have thrown you in the most iniquitous fight with double purpose—to make you the instrument of their ambition, and also your hard work will make the extinction of your race."
>
> Fight for the flag! Under what colors? One African-American

> resolves his moral impasse. David Fagen, colored beacon, bless his soul —Fagen leads twenty other Blacks who desert the U.S. Army. Many join Fagen and enlist with the Filipino guerillas, an act "unprecedented in Black military history."
>
> "I fear that the future of the Filipino is that of the Negro in the South," commented U.S. Gunnery Sergeant John Galloway, a soldier-journalist who wrote in his journal the sentiments of Filipino civilians regarding independence and their relations with Black and white troops. A short period later, Galloway joins the ranks of the Filipino resistance.

The blood of American minorities has been shed in numerous wars, even as those same minorities were vilified or discriminated against in the very country they were fighting for. World War I was where African Americans in limited fashion were able to prove themselves on the battlefield. Many were awarded honor medals by such countries as France for their bravery. The bulk, however, were led by white, Southern officers and made to do menial labor. World War I did enable black soldiers to realize that overseas they were Americans and not second-class citizens. Many returning black veterans found America to be more brutal and hostile toward them. The Ku Klux Klan and other white supremacist groups went through a resurgence in the aftermath of World War I to greet the returning soldiers whose new ideas of liberty had to be squashed. Lynchings in America also soared and race riots involving whites violently targeting blacks spiked as well. Many towns in the East, Midwest and West completely evicted their black populations. The effects of these revolting actions linger to this day.

During World War II, the famous Navajo Code Talkers were used by the Marines from 1942-1945 in the Pacific to provide secure communications. "Were it not for the Navajos," said Major Howard Connor, a signal officer, "the Marines would never have taken Iwo Jima." Yet the Code Talkers' heroism was not officially recognized until 1992, ostensibly "because of the continued value of their language as a security classified code" ("Navy"). Howard Zinn, in *A People's History of the United States,* provides another example of society's hypocrisy:

> In the state of Washington, there was an old treaty taking land from the Indians but leaving them fishing rights. This became unpopular as the white population grew and wanted the fishing areas exclusively for themselves. When state courts closed river areas to Indian fishermen, in 1964, Indians had "fish-ins" on the Nisqually

> River, in defiance of the court orders....
>
> Some of the Indians involved in the fish-ins were veterans of the Vietnam war. One was Sid Mills, who was arrested in a fish-in at Frank's Landing on the Nisqually River in Washington on October 13, 1968. He made a statement:
>
> > I am a Yakima and Cherokee Indian, and a man. For two years and four months, I've been a soldier in the United States Army. I served in combat in Vietnam—until critically wounded....I hereby renounce further obligation in service or duty to the United States Army....
> >
> > My first obligation now lies with the Indian People fighting for the lawful Treaty to fish in usual and accustomed water of the Nisqually, Columbia and other rivers of the Pacific Northwest....
> >
> > My decision is influenced by the fact that we have already buried Indian fishermen returned dead from Vietnam, while Indian fishermen live here without protection and under steady attack. (526-527)

People of color have been allowed to die as whites do, but between conception and that final passing, minorities have had to struggle to be allowed to live like whites. The Rev. Martin Luther King, Jr., noted how whites and blacks were ordered to *fight* side by side in faraway Vietnam but weren't allowed to *sit* side by side at home. Black/white segregation was everywhere. Constantino writes:

> When America enters the Second World War, the great nation calls on its people to close ranks under the Star-Spangled Banner. The war accepts Blacks, writes Eduardo Galeano, "thousands and thousands of them, but not the Red Cross."...At first, the Red Cross and the military refuse the blood of Blacks in the [lifesaving] plasma banks, "so as to avoid the possibility that races might mix by transfusion." But later they relent—provided Negro blood is separated from Caucasian blood. Charles Drew resigns. Charles Drew is black.

Dr. Charles Richard Drew was the first director of the American Red Cross Blood Bank. He was also the scientist who discovered that blood plasma, unlike blood, did not need to be refrigerated and could be stored for months. This made it possible to ship lifesaving plasma to troops in Europe.

Another African American also offered lifesaving science to this country. George Washington Carver's life spanned from the era of slavery up to World War II. His many contributions—well beyond the peanuts that he is noted for—should be celebrated in our history books.

<u>From "Let's remember our heroes"</u>

> DIAMOND, Mo. - Sunlight sprinkled vivid colors along the shaded trail like paint thrown from the Creator's playful brush.
>
> Birds sang sweetly, and a creek babbled peacefully near a statue of

a slave boy. That kid was George Washington Carver. It's easy to see how this "laboratory" ignited his imagination and passion for agriculture and science.

Carver saved American agriculture. Carver triumphed despite slavery and racism.

In 1943 after Carver's death, then-Sen. Harry S. Truman was one of the key sponsors of a bill that Congress passed commemorating Carver's Missouri birthplace as the first national monument for an African-American. It also was the first national monument for an American educator; the first to an American for services in agriculture; the first in the four-state area of Missouri, Oklahoma, Arkansas or Kansas; the first for an American scientist; and the first memorial in recognition of world peace through interracial understanding.

Most school kids know Carver's story. He was born a slave during the Civil War. Missouri remained in the Union as a slave state.

Bushwhackers kidnapped Carver and his mother, Mary, from their Missouri owners to sell them in Arkansas. A Union scout returned Carver to his owner, but his mother was never found.

At the Carver memorial, people learn of the difficulty Carver had getting an education. Carver had to go to school in Neosho because those near his home weren't open to blacks. "This simply sharpened my appetite for more knowledge," Carver later wrote.

He continued school in Fort Scott, Kan., where he witnessed more Confederate history. "They lynched a colored man, drug him by our house and dashed his brains out onto the sidewalk. As young as I was the horror haunted me and does even now," Carver wrote.

He attended school in Olathe and Paola and finished high school in Minneapolis, Kan. Carver went to a Kansas City business college. In 1885 he was accepted at Highland College in Highland, Kan., but was rejected when officials realized he was black. A college in Olathe, Kan., also refused to admit him because of his race.

But he didn't give up. He enrolled in 1890 in Simpson College in Iowa to study art. "There they made me believe that I was a real human being," he said.

Carver's paintings in 1893 won honorable mention at the Chicago World's Fair. He transferred to the Iowa Agricultural College, where he was the first African-American to get a bachelor's degree, master's degree and be on the faculty.

That history is an all-American story of a remarkable man achieving despite incredible odds created by the foul history of slavery, which had him as someone who was less than human.

In 1896, the same year as the Plessey vs. Ferguson Supreme

Court ruling making segregation the law of the land, Carver accepted Booker T. Washington's invitation to be director of agriculture at the Tuskegee Institute in Alabama.

Marilyn Daniel, park guide at the memorial, said Carver found that cotton had depleted the soil.

In 1903 he began working with the peanut as a plant that would restore the earth's nutrients and free poor black and white farmers from the tyranny of "king cotton." Carver found that sweet potatoes and pecans also helped replenish the soil. He discovered more than 300 uses for peanuts and other restorative plants, creating new markets for farmers who planted the crops.

All Americans need to see this beautiful history involving a former slave – someone deemed less than nobody – saving America. It far surpasses supporting continuing elements of the bigotry and discrimination, which tear America down.

But as great as Carver's scientific accomplishments were, he also was revered for his philosophy on life. A speech in his own voice plays by a bust of him and his quotes fill the visitors' center.

People should spend a couple of hours at the memorial, reflecting on the quotes.

It apparently is very easy for some to brush aside the importance of a person of color, even though the value of his or her contributions is incontrovertible.

Voice mail: June 17, 2005

Lewis, a black man saving America? That's a little strong even for you.

E-mail: June 17, 2005

I wonder what Carver would have thought about young blacks today and their views on getting an education?? Most young blacks today probably think Carver was an Uncle Tom and a sell-out to the white man!! After all who did Carver think he was, a man who kept after what he wanted even though the white man was beating him down!! And I'll bet there were a lot more Confederate flags flying then!!

Why don't you do a column of Booker T. Washington? He doesn't get the recognition he should (he was a black Republican) but he may have been just as important as MLK Jr in his time. I think an article on Booker T just might have black Kansas Citians talking around the water cooler- and a few white ones, too!!

A Frederick Douglass quote says it best: "It is true that we are no longer slaves, but it is equally true that we are not yet quite free. We have been turned out of the house of bondage, but we have not yet been fully admitted to the glorious temple of American liberty. We are still in that transition state, and the future is shrouded in doubt and danger."

That's still depressingly true today. And, ironically, one reason might be the signing into law of equal rights for African Americans. Ekwueme Michael Thelwell, who was a field secretary of the Student Nonviolent Coordinating Committee (SNCC) during the Civil Rights era and is now a professor of Afro-American Studies at the University of Massachusetts, explained the history during an August 2005 interview on the radio news program *Democracy Now!*:

> [Forty years ago] the Democratic Party had a very hybrid and bastard characterization. For the one hand, its Southern arm really ran the country, because in the apartheid South, where 40% of the population, black people, were not allowed to vote, they were still counted in the census. So, the South got representation, as though the black population were in fact [full] citizens. And then only white people were allowed to vote. There was only one party, the Democratic Party, so that the Southern Democrats, the so-called Dixiecrats, had incredible longevity in the Congress, and they were totally overrepresented in the House of Representatives because the black vote was disfranchised.
>
> When L.B.J. signed the Voting Rights Act, he is said to have said, "I have just signed the destruction of the Democratic Party," which was something we cheered, because we thought that once black people in the South were able to vote, the progressive elements in the Democratic Party, the labor movement throughout the country, and progressives throughout would make an alliance with a more progressive liberal Democratic Party coming out of the South, and the Democratic Party would have a single characteristic. It wouldn't be divided anymore.
>
> To our distress, what happened was the Dixiecrats, the racists, the segregationists simply migrated wholesale into the Republican Party and since that time, there have only been two Democratic presidents, and both of them from the South. You know, so that the law of unintended consequences, we won a victory by which the whole country suffered, as a consequence of the taking over of the Republican Party by these really renegade, undemocratic, reactionary, backward elements from the Southern Dixiecrats. And they have run the Republican Party ever since....

...and have continued to attack affirmative action, diversity, integration, and immigration. They have also continued to try to drive a wedge between the different minorities, pitting one group against another.

But in his book, *A Different Mirror: A History of Multicultural America*, Ronald Takaki notes:

> On their voyage through history, Americans have found themselves

> bound to each other, especially as workers. Time and again, the paths of different ethnic groups have crisscrossed in this 'brave new world' – Bacon's Rebellion, the Market Revolution, westward expansion, the strike at North Adams, World War II. Below deck, they have found their lives and cultures swirling together in the settling and building of America from the first meeting of the Powhatans and English on the Virginia shore to the last arrival of boatpeople from war-torn Vietnam. (426)

Hispanics

Besides Native Americans, Hispanics were also interlopers in the perpetuation of slavery and as a result invited the wrath of whites. Loewen notes that "Mexico [w]as a standard bearer of freedom and a refuge for runaway slaves" (*Lies* 152).

From "Two groups share entwined history"

> History argues against any divisiveness between African-Americans and Hispanics.
>
> Both groups should celebrate with pride Hispanic Heritage Month in September and October, Black History Month in February and Cinco de Mayo in May. That was the lesson in Ron Wilkins' presentation at a national Brothers of the Academy Think Tank and Conference at the Kansas City Marriott Downtown.
>
> His community workshop was "Leadership and Coalition Building Across Cultures." Wilkins is a professor in the Department of Africana Studies at California State University-Dominguez Hills.
>
> His research shows that because of slavery, many Mexicans, other Hispanics and African-Americans have shared roots. They fought together for freedom and lived in harmony.
>
> Mexicans in the 1800s also helped blacks in the United States escape slavery. Wilkins wrote in the April 26, 2001, issue of *The Black Voice News*: "The large extent to which runaway slaves crossed the south Texas border into Mexico increased border tensions.
>
> "By 1853, the U.S. government stationed one-fifth of its standing national army along the border in a desperate attempt to stem the flow of runaways and intimidate the Mexican people." Wilkins quoted Rodolfo Acuna, author of *Occupied America - A History of Chicanos*, saying: "by 1855 some 4,000 fugitive slaves had run away to northern Mexico. Texas authorities valued the loss at $3.2 million and blamed Mexican authorities for encouraging slaves to escape."
>
> It's important to know this history as the census shows Hispanics continuing to outdistance African-Americans as the United States' largest minority group. This country has 36.7 million African-Ameri-

cans and 38.8 million Hispanics.

Blacks shouldn't be alarmed by the change.

"We've got good history," Wilkins said in his lecture. "All we need to do is talk about that history and build on it."

Unearthing ties between African-Americans and Hispanics helped the academy fulfill its purpose of black scholars generating new strategies to old problems. Wilkins showed slides of Mexicans with hair and features similar to African-Americans'.

"Those who teach history and have rewritten history don't want us to know these things," he said. "They want to keep us divided."

From 1521 to 1821 Spaniards brought 200,000 to 500,000 African slaves to colonial Mexico, or New Spain. They were put to work on the sugar plantations, in mines and elsewhere.

"Not generally taught in history textbooks is that Mexico was a key port of entry for slave ships and consequently had a large African population," Wilkins wrote in the fall 2000-2001 issue of *Turning Point* magazine. The blacks "took part in forging Mexico's great mestizo, or 'mixed' population, also comprised of Indian and Spanish influences."

Africans constituted the "third root" of Mexico's population, Wilkins said.

James W. Loewen in his book, *Lies My Teacher Told Me,* said a similar "triracial" mixture of "white, black and red" took place in the United States.

"Mexico's 'racial amnesia' and Eurocentric misconceptions persist, despite studies which show that by 1810, there were actually more Africans in 'New Spain' than there were Spaniards," one of Wilkins' handouts said.

"Black Mexico" refers to villages and towns with prominent African populations in coastal areas. Wilkins has taken students there to "Meetings of Black Villages," which are annual events affirming the people's African roots in Mexican soil, although after centuries of intermarriage there is no longer much of an African appearance.

"Our histories are very similar in the way we've been treated," Wilkins said. Knowledge of the shared past would help heal today's divisions.

"There is hardly a struggle anywhere in the world where we didn't have an ally someplace," Wilkins said.

Blacks and Hispanics still need each other to succeed.

The histories of Hispanics and blacks merged again at the turn of the last century when Hispanics were pulled into the United States as a cheap source of labor. The reasons for their arrivals are not much different from the reasons that bring today's Hispanic immigrants north, nor is the consternation each wave of Latino newcomers has created.

From "Culture must not be forgotten"

Valerie M. Mendoza gave me a wonderful gift.

It was a lesson on the origins of Latinos in this area. Mendoza, a native of Topeka, was hired as an assistant professor of history at the University of Kansas.

She received her doctorate from the University of California-Berkeley. Her 208-page dissertation capped a six-year study on Mexican immigration from 1900 to 1930 into Kansas and the Kansas City area.

"I didn't know any of this stuff before I started this project," Mendoza said. "This was very eye-opening."

Railroad companies sent agents to Mexico to recruit men for jobs. They provided the train transportation to Kansas and the Kansas City area and boxcars for housing.

The railroad jobs and the promise of prosperity pulled Mexican men from their homeland. The push was the Mexican Revolution, which had many farm laborers toiling like black sharecroppers in the post-Civil War South.

"Some would argue (the exodus from the revolution) is still going on today," Mendoza said.

She wrote in a 1994 *Kansas Quarterly* article titled "They Came to Kansas Searching For a Better Life" that 75 percent of all first-generation Mexican men worked as track laborers.

"As the railroad became more and more dependent upon immigrant labor, the number of Mexicans in the state grew from approximately 71 Mexicans in 1900 to 8,429 in 1910, and by 1920 the number escalated to 13,770," she wrote.

By 1910, Kansas had the fifth-largest Mexican population in the country. After area men became U.S. soldiers in World War I, Mexican immigrants also were hired in Kansas City's meatpacking plants.

"They did the hardest, most dangerous types of work and were paid the lowest wages," Mendoza told me. They intended to work only six months to two years and then return to their homeland. Few ever planned to remain in America.

"But it didn't work out that way," Mendoza said. "The situation in Mexico stayed bad."

About 1920, women and families began arriving in significant numbers and settling in the West Side and Argentine areas. That created new problems.

Mexican men felt exploited and oppressed at work and in the community. Churches and social service groups also infiltrated their homes to "Americanize" Mexican women.

"These social agencies unwittingly helped lessen male control over female family members through interaction between Mexican women and Americans," Mendoza wrote. It included American cooking, language, food and child care.

The American way also was patriarchal, but it made Mexican women feel more free. "It was so much more open in the United States," Mendoza said.

Social workers were trying to push the Mexican immigrants toward U.S. middle-class ideals, even though the newcomers could never attain good jobs, fair housing or equality back then.

The distance from Mexico, combined with the extreme Americanization pressures, forced the immigrants to surrender their language and much of their culture to try to assimilate in a land that would never fully accept their differences.

What was true then is less so now because of the Hispanic culture established in America in the decades since. Nevertheless, that history is important in understanding where we are today on issues of immigration. People need to see the connection with that history so they can appreciate the present and welcome the future.

From "Hispanics will help build future of U.S."

One clear message surfaced during the three-day Latino Civil Rights Summit 2004: This country mustn't ignore or suppress the needs or economic and political potential of Hispanics.

Jose Angel Gutierrez, a Dallas lawyer and author, said it best as the luncheon speaker: "We are the future of America. Unlike any prior generation, we now have a critical mass. We're going to Latinize this country."

People who were white, black, Asian American and Native American also attended the "Crossing the Bridge" summit to learn how the growing Hispanic population will affect the nation.

Gutierrez said people from Mexico, Central and South America are not immigrating to the United States. They are simply migrating because this land had been theirs. Spain had held it, and before that it had belonged to the indigenous people. Hispanics should never put up with others telling them to go back where they came from. "You don't have to apologize to anybody," Gutierrez said. But he urged Hispanics to develop a plan.

"We're talking about crossing the bridge, but is it to get across or is it to come back?" Gutierrez asked. "Is it a one-way bridge or a two-way bridge? You've got to have a plan."

On Saturday at the action planning session, Gutierrez pointed to Hispanic businesses on Central Avenue in Kansas City, Kan., as examples of America's future. "The potential is tremendous," he said.

"What we have at the moment is labor power and consumer power," he said. "We work and we buy. Political power will come later."

That's because half of the Hispanics in the United States are younger than 21. "We're spectators at the basketball game," Gutierrez said.

However, that also means that for every one Latino who dies, five white people will die because they are older. But that leaves five empty houses and five vacant businesses, Gutierrez said.

"The vacuum has got to be filled by somebody; otherwise all our economy and neighborhoods will collapse," he said. More people of color and minority businesses must fill the void for America to remain vibrant.

The third Latino Civil Rights Summit left Hispanics with a greater sense of empowerment than the previous ones. The numbers are in their favor.

In 2000, the nation had 35.6 million Hispanics, representing 12.6 percent of the U.S. population. Census projections show the Latino population will rise to 102.6 million people by 2050, amounting to 24.4 percent of the country's 419.9 million people.

In 2000, African-Americans made up 12.7 percent of the population. By 2050 that will increase to 14.6 percent. Audiences at the summit were told Hispanics and blacks must form more alliances to increase their economic and political strength.

Each must leverage the numbers to their advantage, Rogelio Lasso, a University of Missouri-Kansas City law professor, said at a forum on collaboration. "We are thinking 'Who is No. 1?' instead of thinking 'If we are 30 percent together, how are we going to get 30 percent of the pie?'" he said.

The summit included sessions on education and how the No Child Left Behind Act will negatively affect students of color. Resegregation also is occurring, stranding black and Hispanic children in poor schools, said Ruben Garza, an Austin, Texas, educator.

Patriot Acts I and II keep making life more difficult for immigrants. That's occurring as the nation is enjoying a record 33.5 million foreign-born residents. They are 11.7 percent of the population, Steve Camarota, director of research with the Center for Immigration Studies in Washington, said in a telephone interview.

The foreign born represented a record 14.8 percent of the U.S. population in 1890 and 14.7 percent in 1910. "It's very possible by the end of the decade we'll pass the all-time high," Camarota said.

But Lasso voiced concern about the rise in anti-immigration feelings since the Sept. 11 terrorist attacks.

"It feels like it's acceptable in this country to be anti-immigrant," he said. "I fear if we have another terrorist attack it will affect the immigrants first."

But our intertwined fates may be our salvation.

"The state of the Latino community cannot be separated from the state of America," said Elias L. Garcia, executive director of the Kansas Advisory Commission on Hispanic Affairs. "Our destinies are inextricably tied."

But that is not how a majority of people see it. They voiced a virulent anti-immigrant, anti-people-of-color sentiment:

E-mail: June 3, 2004

I hope they deport you and your racist friend Jose A. Gutierrez. Then you can see how great America will be when we become "Latinized," as the Mexican treason lobby so eloquently put it. It can be your own real life reality show.

E-mail: June 7, 2004

Are you suffering from some sort of weird and fucked, "guilty white man's syndrome?"

In your April 28 whine titled, "Hispanics will build the future of the U.S." you sure don't seem to have any trouble bending over and spreading your butt cheeks for the spics.

E-mail: April 28, 2004,

You are partially correct. Hispanics will indeed help build America. But blacks will not help build anything.

E-mail: May 7, 2004,

Are the Mexicans going to build a better America before or after they build a better Mexico?

Tell them to get back to me after they finish fixing up Mexico.

This is borderline hilarious.

E-mail: May 7, 2004,

How will we know when we have enough illegal aliens (criminals) in our country, and how will we stop them then.

E-mail: May 9, 2004

You're black, correct? If so, you are a traitor. Through massive unfettered immigration, Hispanics are colonizing this country. They are depressing wages of Americans and taking jobs away from Americans. This invasion affects blacks and the most at this point in time. You say we should build a "coalition" with Hispanics? What planet do you live on? Hispanics have a deep rooted hatred of blacks. Trust me. I see it every day. You should be outraged that this country allows an illegal flood to swarm past its borders, become the biggest minority and take away jobs from blacks. And you also have the nerve to equate the illegal invasion with civil rights? Your mind is rotting away from the leftist tripe you've allowed in. How dare you side with the same people who are undermining blacks. They're using you and you're too stupid to see it. Try defending your own people for a change instead of being in cahoots with the illegals that are destroying us.

Voice mail: April 28, 2004

You weren't quite the whiny guy that you normally are. But you're still the divisive guy that you normally are. There you go again, lines between blacks and Hispanics. I've got news for you, man. In about 10 to15 more years, two out of every five people in the United States will be Hispanic. Two out of every five will be white. One out of every five will be either black or Asian. So you are always trying to make alliances. I guess you just hate whitey. That's your deal. You just hate whitey. That's the way you always come across in your opinion or in your deal here. You're spouting off like we should just fold over because this land used to belong to the Hispanics? You know, what's hard for me to understand is it seems like you're always anti-European. But the Hispanics were European. What's a Hispanic to do? Does a Hispanic hold up the culture of the conqueror? Whose heritage do they hold up? The Aztec heritage? The Montezuma? Or Cortez? What's a Hispanic to do? The reason their population is getting as big as it is is because it's an illegal population that is getting big. They are growing four times the rate of any other ethnicity in this country and it's because of illegal immigration.

Voice mail: April 28, 2004

Hey, let's not beat around the bush about the Hispanic thing. Fuck the Hispanics.

Voice mail: April 28, 2004

I don't know if you're becoming a vile revolutionary or what is wrong with you and your thinking. Do you want to throw the European descendants out of this country that actually built this country? Take your message and take it someplace else. We built this country! These people from South America never owned any of this land in this country. The Spanish political part, they were not Spanish. Please. Pretty soon you'll be calling for armed revolution to take over this country.

It is clear that the people who wrote these reactions are existential victims of racism: they don't know the true history of the Real America because they've never received the complete picture and they jump to conclusions based on incomplete information. Ronald Takaki sets the record straight:

> In California, [the conquest of the Southwest] began in the small town of Sonoma. There, on June 6, 1846, General Mariano Vallejo was rudely wakened at his home by thirty armed Americans. They had arrived 'before it was quite light,' one of them recalled. 'We knocked on the front of his dwelling and one of his servants came out. We was standing all a-horseback....'
>
> So began the revolt to wrest California from Mexico and establish what would be called the 'Bear Flag Republic.' American westward expansion was reaching the Pacific, and the Americans were entering California. The rebels were mostly uncouth frontiersmen, viewed by the Mexicans as 'grimy adventurers' and 'exiles from civilization.' Some of them had crossed the border after the Mexican government had prohibited American immigration, and hence were *illegal aliens* [italics added]. Most of the intruders had been in California for less than a year, and now they were claiming the territory as theirs....
>
> Unlike his immigrant captors, Don Vallejo was a Californian by birth. As the commander of the Sonoma fort, he represented a long history of Spanish and Mexican efforts to secure the California territory against American and Russian expansion. (*Mirror* 166-167)

The Mexican-American War was viewed by people in the United States as a conflict "between a 'mongrel Spanish-Indian and negro race' on the one side and 'civilization and the Anglo-American race'" on the other (Mirror 174). However, in stark contrast to this belief, U.S. General Winfield Scott admitted that the American soldiers of that war—the ones who, according to the feedback above, helped to "build this country"—had

> "committed atrocities to make Heaven weep and every American of Christian morals blush for his country. Murder, robbery and rape of mothers and daughters in the presence of their tied-up males of the families have been common all along the Rio Grande." A Mexican newspaper denounced the outrages, describing the American invaders as "the horde of banditti, of drunkards, of fornicators...vandals vomited from hell, monsters who bid defiance to the laws of nature...shameless, daring, ignorant, ragged, bad-smelling, long-bearded men with hats turned up at the brim, thirsty with the desire to appropriate our riches and our beautiful damsels." (*Mirror* 175)

<u>From "California's Latino legacy"</u>

> In 1848 the war ended. The United States, in the Treaty of Guadalupe Hidalgo, acquired California, New Mexico, Nevada and parts of Colorado, Arizona and Utah. The total territory conceded was half

> of what had been Mexico. It fulfilled America's so-called "Manifest Destiny."
>
> The conquered Mexicans "did not understand the new language, English, which was now 'prevalent' on 'their native soil,'" writes Takaki.
>
> "They had become foreigners in their own land."
>
> It's not surprising, therefore, that Latinos today are talking about "coming back" instead of "getting across the border."
>
> The Gold Rush caused more problems, leading "to a massive migration into California; by 1849, the Anglo population had reached 100,000, compared with only 13,000 Mexicans.
>
> "Dominant in the state legislature, Anglos enacted laws aimed at Mexicans," Takaki wrote.
>
> It's not much different today with California passing anti-immigration and anti-affirmative action laws to make this once Hispanic land less hospitable.

Mexican Americans have been victims of discrimination for centuries, even though they have played a major role in U.S. history. During World War II, agricultural workers were imported in the so-called "bracero program." But what is perhaps less known is that, at the same time, some 500,000 Mexican Americans went to war for the United States. And even as the war was being fought overseas and Mexican-Americans were dying, they were being discriminated against, vilified and even beaten at home for the way they looked or the way they dressed. They were also forced to live in segregated communities (*Mirror* 394).

Takaki writes that

> One of the Chicano slogans of World War II was "Americans All." On his way to the European front, a Mexican-American soldier reflected on the possibility of dying and the meaning of such a sacrifice: "What if I were killed?... What would happen to my wife, my three children? My mother?... All the horrible thoughts imaginable would grip me, and before I could find the answers, other thoughts would begin to swirl in. I remembered about us, the Mexican-Americans...how the Anglo had pushed and held back our people in the Southwest.... Why fight for America when you have not been treated as an American?" But he was overwhelmed by "the feeling" he had for his "home" in America, the country where he had been born. "All we wanted," he decided, "was a chance to prove how loyal and American we were." (*Mirror* 393)

That loyalty remains visible today, in spite of the new version of an old slight that all Latinos—from Mexico as well as Central and South America—are facing in the United States. It is truly ironic that, during the era of slavery, troops were sent to the U.S. border with Mexico to keep slaves in; then during the Mexican-American War they were sent to drive Mexicans off their own land. In an odd turnabout now President George W. Bush has ordered thousands of National Guard troops to the border to keep Latinos from coming into the United States, where illegal immigrants are used as this nation's new exploited class.

From "U.S. needs a uniting solution, not a dividing wall"

Street vendors capitalized on the heavily attended Kansas City area immigrant rallies, selling everything from bottled water to hot dogs and U.S. flags made in China.

In this country, capitalism never sleeps. The dominant chant at the spring rallies, "Si, se puede," or "Yes, it can be done," could easily have been about opportunity here welcoming all who work for the American dream.

The rallies for immigrant rights have been pro-American, and that's a good thing. It's why President Bush's speech calling for 6,000 National Guard troops and other security measures on the U.S.-Mexican border made no sense. Bush should have gone to the rallies instead of responding to the loud and angry anti-immigrant screeds.

Many at the rallies wore T-shirts saying "Viva USA" and held signs whose messages included "Build Community Not Walls" and "We Are American, Too. Don't Turn Us Away." Most of the people in the crowds were Hispanic.

But Alicia Sanchez of Kansas City asked as she stood with others: "What is the true definition of America? It doesn't belong to one race or culture."

Brian McCrink of Bonner Springs explained the anti-immigrant hatred his Irish parents faced early in the last century.

"When my folks came to this country there were signs all over New York City that said 'No Irish need apply,' and they never let us forget that," McCrink said at the Liberty Memorial rally.

His wife, Kathy McCrink, said she was distressed by the scapegoating that Hispanics now face. "When people start feeling uncomfortable, they pick on these poor people," she said.

A House bill passed in December fueled the fervor. It would include a wall on much of the southern border, make it a felony to be in the United States illegally and crack down on people who hire undocumented workers. The Senate has struggled to craft legislation that would include a guest worker program and provide opportunities for 12 million undocumented immigrants to become U.S. citizens.

Bush and too many lawmakers seem to be responding to the negative forces. A Zogby poll of likely voters found that the majority of Americans favor the House bill.

The poll showed that Americans want less and not more immigration. People also had no confidence in the ability of the government to screen applications for increased immigration to separate out terrorists and criminals. The poll showed that 71 percent of the respondents thought that past enforcement efforts had been "grossly inadequate."

What distresses me is that the public and media focus on illegal immigration has been on Hispanics and the Mexican border when immigrants of all colors, ethnicities, religions and nations are in this country legally and illegally. Legislation to limit immigration also is not new. The Japanese, Chinese and Jews have been victimized by such actions in the past.

What people must see is that immigration lets in cheap labor, which has always been part of this nation's history dating back to colonial days. European criminals were among the immigrant workers. It was accepted then.

An immigrant friend is fond of saying the American Indians didn't build walls to keep Europeans out, insist that they speak only the native tongue of this land, surrender their culture altogether and completely assimilate. The exact opposite actually happened.

It is aggravating now to hear normally good people say such foul and nasty things about Hispanics when all Latinos want is to be American, too. Anyone who bothered to go to the immigration-rights rallies would have picked that up immediately.

Thousands of people sang the national anthem in English at the Liberty Memorial rally and the one last month at Ilus Davis Park. Melinda Lewis, director of policy, advisory and research with El Centro, registered dozens of eligible people to vote. She was enthused that the immigration issue has motivated more young people to become politically active.

Labor and black leaders spoke passionately to the crowds. Historical efforts to divide folks because of immigration status and race weren't working at the rallies.

Michelle Garcia, who was born and raised in Kansas City, held a sign that said "Immigrants are U.S." and "Fear and Hate Must Not Legislate."

I hope Congress and Bush are paying attention. The walls and armed guardsmen separating us have to vanish so everyone can live in peace and go for the opportunity to prosper as Americans.

But what's happening now to immigrants fits historical trends. For example, the immigration bill, which passed in the House in 2005, would criminalize illegal immigrants. It would also punish those who hire or harbor undocumented people and force police to get involved. It resembles the Fugitive Slave Law of 1850, in which authorities in the North had to abandon their practice of ignoring or helping runaway slaves to arrest anyone thought to be a fugitive slave based on even flimsy evidence ("Fugitive"). It was a third front in the Southerners' all-out battle to maintain slavery. They went after the Native Americans for harboring slaves; they did the same thing against the Mexicans. Northerners were the new target in the 1850s. Hispanics today feel similarly corralled—politically, physically, and in media-fed public opinion.

Asian Americans

Grouping all people of Asian heritage under the umbrella "Asian Americans" is similar to referring to all Indigenous Peoples as "Indians" and to all Central and South Americans as "Hispanics." We do it because it is less cumbersome, but it obscures their unique heritages and cultures. That can lead to dramatic problems. After the Sept. 11, 2001, attacks on the World Trade Center towers in New York City, a Sikh man was murdered because he was thought to be Muslim. In 1982, writes Angela Johnson Meadows in "To Be Asian in America,"

> 27-year-old Vincent Chin visited a suburban Detroit strip club to celebrate his impending nuptials. While there, Chin encountered a couple of disgruntled autoworkers, one of whom had recently been laid off. The autoworkers hurled insults at Chin and blamed him for the demise of Detroit's auto industry. After Chin left the club, the two men met up with Chin in front of a fast-food restaurant and beat him with a baseball bat. Chin, who was Chinese—not Japanese as his attackers had assumed—slipped into a coma and died five days later. (40)

Meadows adds that "Asian Americans represent nearly 25 countries and speak at least as many languages" (40). The largest Asian-American groups are Chinese Americans (2.4 million), Filipino Americans (1.9 million), Asian-Indian Americans (1.7 million), Vietnamese Americans (1.1 million), Korean Americans (1.0 million), and Japanese Americans (800,000) (Wu 20). But also included are people from Laos, Cambodia, Pakistan, Bangladesh, Sri Lanka, Myanmar, Thailand and other countries (47).

As of the 2000 census, there were more than 10 million people of Asian heritage in America constituting about 4 percent of the population.

Though small, the Asian-American population is one of the nation's fastest growing groups. Ronald Takaki writes in *Strangers from a Different Shore*, that "between 1970 and 1980 the Hispanic population increased by 38 percent, compared to 143 percent for the Asian population" (5). Frank H. Wu writes in *Yellow: Race in America Beyond Black and White:*

> The Asian American population has experienced staggering growth, driven by immigration. Between 1990 and 2000, the Asian American population nationwide grew by 48 percent, trailing only Latinos. The Asian American population in California grew by more than one-third to about 3.7 million (plus another half million of mixed descent that includes Asian), slightly ahead of Latinos. The Asian American population of New York City is half again as large as it was ten years ago, and Asian Americans make up one in ten residents, as the city itself continues a comeback based on Asian American and Latino immigration (the African American population stayed the same and the white population continued to decrease). . . . Geographically, Asian American populations are appearing outside cities that traditionally have had Asian American concentrations. The substantial Southeast Asian populations in Minnesota and Wisconsin, for example, are composed primarily of people who have arrived within the past twenty-five years; the Asian American population of Nevada tripled in a decade; and the number of Asian Indians in the Washington, D.C., metropolitan area doubled in a decade, making them the largest Asian ethnicity in the area. (20)

Historical trends have had an effect on where Asian Americans have settled. Wu writes

> In 1990, 60 percent of Asian Americans resided in [Hawaii, California and New York] (since then, Asian Americans have started to disperse). Furthermore, Asian Americans are much more urbanized than any other racial group, including white Americans. In 1990, 94 percent of Asian Americans lived within metropolitan areas. (54)

Because they tend to live in higher income areas, their average income as a group misrepresents reality, leading to the "model minority" myth that Asian Americans are all successful and well off. The truth is quite different. Wu notes that

> Asian American income is distributed unevenly. There are large numbers of Asian Americans at the top and at the bottom, rather than in the middle. Asian Americans have poverty rates higher than white Americans, 13 percent compared to 9 percent.
>
> The model minority myth also masks great disparities among

> Asian ethnic groups. Japanese Americans and Chinese Americans are closest to equality with whites, but Vietnamese Americans and other Southeast Asian refugees languish at the bottom of the economic pyramid, along with blacks. In the 1980 Census, for example, Vietnamese Americans were below African Americans on average. According to the 1990 Census, 25 percent of Vietnamese Americans and 45 percent of other Southeast Asians lived in poverty. Those poverty rates were higher than the rates for Africans (21 percent) and Hispanics (23 percent). (54)

Though Asian Americans came to this country to live and prosper, they were subjected to the same type of discrimination as other minority groups. The first Filipinos arrived aboard a Spanish ship in 1763, "jumped ship in New Orleans to avoid imprisonment and fled into the Louisiana bayou to establish the first recorded Filipino settlement in America" (Meadows 30). Almost 200 years later, when the U.S. entered World War II, Filipinos who were then U.S. nationals fought in the Philippines. After the war, however, their veterans' benefits were reduced by the passing of the Recision Act, and their role in the war was not recognized until 1990 (Meadows 43).

But all people of color, and not just Africans who were brought to these shores as slaves, have felt unwelcome. Takaki writes that "the Nationalization Law of 1790 had specified that naturalized citizenship was to be reserved for 'whites.' This law remained in effect until 1952." But other laws targeted Asian immigrants in additional ways. The most notorious was the Chinese Exclusion Act of 1882, which barred Chinese immigrants from entering the United States. Following that, the National Origins Act of 1924 banned Japanese immigration

> while permitting the annual entry of 17,853 [persons] from Ireland, 5,802 from Italy, and 6,524 from Poland. Furthermore, the 1924 law supported the formation of families in European-immigrant communities, allowing European-immigrant men to return to their homelands and bring wives back to the United States. Their wives were accorded nonquota status, that is, there were no limits to the number of European women who could come here as wives. The law had the very opposite effect on Asian-immigrant communities. Seeking to prevent the development of Asian families here, it barred the entry of women from China, Japan, Korea, and India. Even U.S. citizens could not bring Asian wives into the country, for the latter were classified as "aliens ineligible to citizenship" and hence inadmissible. (*Strangers* 14)

The nation was in a period of selectivity favoring whites and undeniable exclusion—often violent—of people of color. A famous example is the 1896 Plessy vs. Ferguson Supreme Court decision, which is cited as establishing segregation as the law of the land for African Americans. For Asian Americans, the Supreme Court ruling that stands out was in 1927. Frank H. Wu writes that Asians felt the cold isolation of segregation just as blacks did.

> On the only occasion when the Supreme Court considered whether Asian Americans were subject to the strictures of racial segregation, it reasoned in 1927 that if separate schools could be established for white pupils and black pupils, "we cannot think that the question is any different or that any different result can be reached...where the issue is as between white pupils and the pupils of the yellow races." Blacks and Asian Americans were equivalent and interchangeable; in legal parlance, they were "fungible." Yet now it is common to refer to an "Anglo-Asian" overclass in contrast to an African American-Hispanic underclass. (19)

Takaki notes that, although black and Asian workers were pitted against each other as cheap labor, they often were tarred with the same stereotypes. He adds

> Chinese migrants found that racial qualities previously assigned to blacks became "Chinese" characteristics....White workers referred to the Chinese as "nagurs," and a magazine cartoon depicted the Chinese as a blood-sucking vampire with slanted eyes, a pigtail, dark skin, and thick lips.... Chinese women were condemned as a "depraved class," and their depravity was associated with their physical appearance, which seemed to show "but a slight removal from the African race." (*Strangers* 101)

Yet Asian Americans' contributions to American society are undeniable. Many were brought to this country as agricultural laborers or to work on the construction of the transcontinental railroad. They came because of the promise of work and the promise of gold. During the mid-1800s, writes C. Stone Brown in "A History of Resilience," there were "two competing attitudes about the Chinese.... In the cities, their growing numbers evoked fear among whites.... However, capitalists viewed the Chinese as a vast source of cheap and exploitable labor, willing to do work that white men wouldn't" (56).

From "California's Latino legacy"

> On our sojourn in California, my family saw great beauty in the state's fruit trees, flowering plants and lush vegetation. Ronald Takaki wrote that was made possible by the open doors to Chinese immigration in the mid-1800s.
>
> "They helped to transform farming in California from wheat to fruit," he wrote. Takaki quotes historian Carey McWilliams writing, "Experienced farmers in the Pearl River Delta before coming to

> America, the Chinese shared their agricultural knowledge with their white employers, teaching them how to plant, cultivate and harvest orchard and garden crops.
>
> "Indeed, the Chinese built the agricultural industry of California."

Takaki credits "an early Chinese immigrant named Ah Bing" with the development of the Bing cherry (*Mirror* 12). However, another source says that in Salem, Oregon, "in 1875, [the planting of a cherry tree called] a Black Republican...produced a promising seedling that [Seth] Lewelling named 'Bing' after his faithful Chinese helper. The Bing cherry would be Seth Lewelling's crowning achievement" (Lucas). In the final reckoning, who is given the credit depends on whose history is accepted and whose is ignored. The contributions of Asian Americans, however, got lost as the public's perception of them shifted from positive to negative.

James W. Loewen, in *Sundown Towns: A Hidden Dimension of American Racism*, writes:

> Until about 1884, Chinese Americans lived in virtually every town in the West.... Between 1885 and about 1920, dozens of communities in the West, including towns and counties as far inland as Wyoming and Colorado and cities as large as Seattle and Tacoma, drove out their entire Chinese American populations—some briefly, some for decades....
>
> The retreat of Chinese Americans from Idaho was especially striking. In 1870, Chinese made up one-third of the population of Idaho. By 1910, almost none remained. In the 1880s, assaults and murder became common practice. In 1886, white Idahoans held an anti-Chinese convention in Boise, and a mass movement against the Chinese spread throughout the state, growing even worse after statehood....
>
> In May 1876, whites drove out Chinese from Antioch, California, one of the early expulsions, and in Rocklin the next year, they burned Chinatown to the ground. Explusions and anti-Chinese ordinances peaked in the 1880s but continued for decades. In the 1890s whites violently expelled Chinese people from the fishing industry in most parts of the state....
>
> The attacks on Chinese in the West grew so bad that Mark Twain famously said, "A Chinaman had no rights that any man was bound to respect," deliberately echoing Roger Taney's words in Dred Scott. (50-53)

Dred Scott was a slave whose lawsuit for his freedom went to the Supreme Court in 1857. Taney was the U.S. Supreme Court Chief Justice at the time, who wrote "African Americans 'had for more than a century been regarded as beings of an inferior order, and altogether unfit to associate with the white race, either in social or political revelations, and so far inferior, that they had no rights which the white man was bound to respect'" (*Sundown* 20). The expulsion of the Chinese bridges with the anti-black backlash that followed the end of Reconstruction. Loewen notes that many towns in the North, West and Midwest also evicted their black residents in what he called "the Great Retreat" (*Sundown* 47).

Journalism Across Cultures notes Asian mistreatment in America dating back to the 1800s. Chinese immigrants were seen as a threat first, followed by the Japanese. Each group was targeted for hate crimes and later exclusion. The contributions each made in industries such as the construction of the railroads and the improvement of American communities were routinely ignored (222-223). Internment camps for the Japanese-Americans became the ultimate humiliation.

As a group, Asian Americans throughout their history have had a difficult time assimilating in the United States. To prove that they indeed were "Americans," many Japanese-Americans enlisted in the U.S. military even though their family members were locked in internment camps after the Japanese government attacked Pearl Harbor. Wu writes

> Well before the war, numerous individuals within the Japanese American communities of the West Coast had assimilated as best as they could. Although many of them had earned degrees in professional disciplines such as engineering, pharmacy, law, or medicine, most of them were unable to find work in their fields due to racial restrictions and ended up returning to family farms or opening small businesses. But they took up baseball, tennis, bowling, and other American sports, forming their own clubs when they were prevented from joining white leagues and associations.
>
> The onset of war drove many of them closer to the United States rather than farther away from its ideals. (234)

War repeatedly has shown itself to draw long-excluded people of color into the mainstream. Obviously people of all colors have equal opportunity to kill or die fighting for their country. Imagine if industry, neighborhoods and schools were as welcoming on the home front.

Wu notes that the Japanese fought valiantly and fiercely to show they were "becoming 'better Americans in a greater America.'"

> A startling sight wherever they went, Asian faces in American fatigues, carrying tommy guns and speaking English, they suffered the losses of suicide missions.... The bravery of the Japanese American troops made for a novel story, which the press exploited in full. They were assimilated into their uniform with its regalia, under the command of white officers, even though their families remained behind barbed wire, within the sights of gun towers, and under the guard of fellow soldiers.... All Asian Americans appreciated the mortal sacrifices of

> the military veterans, which alleviated somewhat the enmity toward other Japanese Americans after the war and aided immensely the reparations movement much later. Some Asian Americans worry that the deserved exaltation of their magnificent deeds has the side effect of setting unfortunate expectations of deference rather than dissent, because of the implicit message that Asian Americans must be willing to march under a flag that does not fly for them. (235)

Even more fascinating was how different groups of Asian Americans tried to distance themselves from Japanese Americans after the Pearl Harbor bombing. Wu quotes Maya Angelou saying that the "Japanese disappeared, soundlessly and without protest" after President Franklin Delano Roosevelt's Executive Order 9066 (98). When they were sent to the internment camps, blacks escaping the bondage of the South took over some of the housing that the Japanese-Americans were forced to vacate, said Angelou. "It was as if they had never owned or lived in the houses we inhabited," she said. The sections of cities "became instant slums" (98). Wu also said that to distance themselves from Japanese Americans, "Chinese Americans wore buttons that said they were Chinese; Korean Americans wore ones that said, 'I Hate the Japs More Than You Do'" (98).

Journalism Across Cultures quotes H. Zia as writing:

> Ironically, near the end of the war in Europe, the Japanese-American GI's of the 442nd broke through the German defensive "Gothic Line" in northern Italy, and were among the first to liberate the Nazi concentration camp in Dachau, Germany. However, the U.S. military commanders decided it would be bad public relations if Jewish prisoners were freed by Japanese American soldiers whose families were imprisoned in American concentration camps (225).

◊◊◊◊◊

These stories and many more are often not told about people of color. From traditional history books we receive no clear picture of the interconnectedness of different cultural groups in America. Ronald Takaki offers us a look at just how much experiences have been shared across the groups:

> During the nineteenth century, for example, the Market Revolution employed Irish immigrant laborers in New England factories as it expanded cotton fields worked by enslaved blacks across Indian lands toward Mexico. Like blacks, the Irish newcomers were stereotyped as "savages," ruled by passions rather than "civilized" virtues such as self-control and hard work. The Irish saw themselves as "slaves" of British oppressors.... The United States annexation of California, while incorporating Mexicans, led to trade with Asia and the migration of

> "strangers" from Pacific shores. In 1870, Chinese immigrant laborers were transported to Massachusetts as scabs to break an Irish immigrant strike; in response, the Irish recognized the need for interethnic working-class solidarity and tried to organize a Chinese lodge of the Knights of St. Crispin. After the Civil War, Mississippi planters recruited Chinese immigrants to discipline newly freed blacks....
>
> In 1903, Mexican and Japanese farm laborers went on strike together in California:...strike meetings were conducted in Japanese and Spanish... Speaking in impassioned Yiddish during the 1909 "uprising of twenty thousand" strikers in New York, the charismatic Clara Lemlich compared the abuse of Jewish female garment workers to the experience of blacks [during slavery].... During the 1920s, elite universities like Harvard worried about the increasing numbers of Jewish students, and new admissions criteria were instituted to curb their enrollment. Jewish students were scorned for their studiousness and criticized for their "clannishness." Recently, Asian-American students have been the targets of similar complaints: they have been called "nerds" and told there are "too many" of them on campus. (*Mirror* 10-11)

The history of Native Americans, African Americans, Asian Americans, Hispanics and other groups that make up the diverse fabric of America shows that each group is closely linked in how it has suffered but prevailed in America. But it's undeniable that the value of the diversity of cultures has always been evident in this country and its history even if it has forever been discounted. Takaki notes that we have to unlearn "much of what we have been told about America's past and [substitute] a more inclusive and accurate history of all the peoples of America.... [For all people to] become visible is to see ourselves and each other in a different mirror of history" (*Mirror* 426).

CHAPTER 6
The Media: Continuing the Indoctrination

A Long Journey

Walk with me
Beyond low expectations
Turn away from the TV
Noise in this troubled nation
That sweetly says you're nothing
With no dispute and not a bit of fussing
Stand strong like proud African-American girls and boys
Who hear the adults' voices of pride and joy
Trumpeting their heritage rooted in important things
Teaching the handed down hopes of slaves and kings
So that freedom will some day ring
From the mountaintops to the lowest valleys and all across the plains
But it starts with following these first few steps
Tracked in blood and ancestors' pain
Who had high expectations that you would be as free
As the birds, the bees and the giant redwood trees
But the journey only comes about
When the sweet racist noise is tuned out.

You may write me down in history
With your bitter twisted lies,
You may trod us in the very dirt
But still, like the dust, I'll rise.
~Maya Angelou
from "Still I Rise"

Americans get mostly distorted images of people of color from the media. They come into our homes in surround sound and on little and big screen color, black and white, high-definition or plasma televisions. At best, the minorities on the flickering TV sets are the ones who entertain us, make us forget our troubles and make us laugh. At worst, the images we see are of the troublemakers, the ne'er-do-wells, the nefarious. In short, we are seduced into accepting the ones who are to be dismissed, discounted and avoided.

This is not just a recent creation. It's historical. Clint C. Wilson II and Félix Gutiérrez write in their book *Minorities and Media: Diversity and the End of Mass Communications:*

> Much of the post-Civil War literature paints a negative image of Blacks designed to reinforce institutional and social racism. Many of the accusations against Black integrity that emerged during Reconstruction are now too familiar: laziness, slow-wittedness, loose standards of morality, fondness for alcoholic beverages, and so on. (71)

Latinos show up differently albeit it equally badly in the American media. Wilson and Gutiérrez point out that "[w]hen Mexicans were not being portrayed in Anglo literature as lazy and indolent, they were assailed for uncleanliness." In one story written by Albert Pike in 1934, "the women of Santa Fe are described as 'scudding hither and thither, with their black hair flying, and their naked feet shaming the ground by their superior filth'" (72). In an April 15, 2005, Democracy Now! broadcast, columnist Robert Rodriguez told show host Amy Goodman that every day Chicanos are "mischaracterized . . . censored . . . and on a good day . . . we're misrepresented. . . . Whenever we go anywhere, that's probably the number one complaint that the media [are] misrepresenting us. They're forcing an identity upon us. They're commercializing us" ("Chicano").

In the colonial literature, Native Americans were depicted as "noble savages." However, the colonists realized the futility of getting the American Indians to conform to their ways and "easily rationalized that the natives had to be removed as a barrier to the 'civilization' of the continent" (Wilson *Minorities* 68).

Asian Americans at first were welcomed as a cheap source of labor in America's Industrial Revolution boom in the 19th century. But later they were viewed as a threat, and branded as a "yellow peril." Laws were passed in the late 1800s and early 1920s to stop Asian immigration to the United States. The Chinese Exclusion Act of 1882, which prevented the Chinese from immigrating and wasn't repealed until 1943, was a direct outgrowth of the "yellow peril." The Immigration Act of 1924 banned the entry of all foreigners not eligible for citizenship, "although the legislation was clearly targeted for the Japanese." The media again were at the forefront of disseminating the hysteria, ensuring that "Chinese and Japanese persons were viewed as devious and vicious. Popular literature warned of the dangers of intermarriage with Asians and charged openly that Asian men purposefully sought White women" (Wilson *Minorities* 74). Henry George, a journalist, even wrote in 1869 that Chinese immigrants were "utter heathens, treacherous, sensual, cowardly and cruel."

These and many other concerns permeated the media. The stereotypes about people of color made the truth unbelievable. Wilson and Gutiérrez write:

> The technique developed by the mass media in dealing with racial minorities and others outside the mainstream involved symbols and stereotypes. The mass media, because they dealt with a wide audience, came to rely on symbols and stereotypes as shorthand ways of communicating through headlines, characters, and pictures. Dramatic portrayals such as those of rich bankers, heroic cowboys, or old spinsters were used so audiences would understand the character the first time he or she appeared on the screen or in the short story. (*Minorities* 41)

The portrayals were of complex characters whittled down to much simpler versions, so that they became stereotypes in the minds of the audience. These stereotypes showed a clear, defined set of characteristics that the audience recognized. The same stereotypical characters were repeated again and again, to cement the character traits in the public's mind. No alternatives were offered in the mass media, so that to the audience the stereotypes became reality. And whereas whites were portrayed as both "the good guys" and "the bad guys," Blacks (and Latinos, Native Americans and Asians) were locked in denigrating, one-dimensional prisons of prejudices (Wilson *Minorities* 41-42).

Who can forget little Shirley Temple, barely out of diapers, giving orders ever so wisely to the wide-eyed black man three times her size who bowed and nodded and smiled rather inanely as he accepted her wise counsel and authority? Or the unkempt Latino banditos and the vicious Indian "savages" that preyed on innocent white folk in Westerns? Or the shifty-eyed Chinaman of Fu Manchu fame lurking in the dark alleys of Chinatown? These unfair and incomplete characters were never counterbalanced by more true-to-life portrayals, as the white characters were.

Why did this happen? Wilson and Gutiérrez write that because almost everyone in the United States was white, "Blacks, Latinos, Native Americans, Asians, and other people of color were treated as fringe audiences, not important enough in numbers to dictate the content that would be directed to the mass audience" (*Minorities* 39). And since the mass media was meant to appeal to the masses (i.e. the majority), it had to "look for commonalities among members of the audience—common themes, ideas, and interest areas that would attract and not offend the mass audience" (*Minorities* 39-40).

People inside this target audience felt a sense of belonging, of trust, of togetherness, of community, a feeling that was passed down to each successive generation. It was a legacy; an inheritance. Among whites it created a cohesion. It is the sense of community that Robert Putnam writes about in his book *Bowling Alone*. The social capital and reciprocity generated is selfishly retained by people who are white. But it meant the exclusion of people of color who were set apart as not being like them. People of color who were excluded also helped those in the target audience bond more firmly because they at least were not minorities lying outside the norms or the media's chief aim, which is white society. That remains a problem today. Ray Suarez describes it as the "melanin-free zones" that the media offer to people who are white. In his book, *The Old Neighborhood: What We Lost in the Great Suburban Migration: 1966-1999*, Suarez writes how popular television shows in the 1990s excluded people of color altogether, or at best misrepresented them:

> The writers and casts of *Seinfeld, Mad About You, Friends, Ellen, Caroline in the City*, and other popular television programs extol the excitement, sophistication, variety, and sheer with-it-ness of urban life. But these shows seem to exist in urban environments unrecognizable to millions of their nonfictional neighbors. Most Latinos in the United States live in large urban areas. Most blacks in the United States live in large urban areas. The networks beam their vision of white urbanity and cozy consumption into the homes of millions of white suburbanites without having to recognize or apologize for the real black-and-brown world that exists just beyond the camera frame occupied by Jerry, George, and Kramer.
>
> The dramatic urban landscape is another matter entirely. Unlike the melanin-free zone of Caucasian sit-comedy, the urban jungles of *Homicide, The Commish, NYPD Blue*, and other programs feature brown and black characters galore. They are cops, secretaries, victims, and most notably, suspects. The membrane between late prime-time and your local news grows thinner with each ratings period, as the clenched jawed realism of black-and-brown urban pathology segues easily into the mayhem of local news. It must be a comfort to an increasingly suburbanized reportorial staff, management, and audience that the "alleged" wild men in their

center city are far, far, [sic] away. (127)

In her book *Learning to Be White: Money, Race and God in America,* Thandeka notes the sense of togetherness such media misinformation creates in mainstream white America. She adds that racist images from minstrel shows in the 19th century to stereotypical media programs featuring African-Americans in the 21st century help reinforce whiteness by putting down blacks. "White superiority was established through negation: the ceaseless and pervasive degradation of the black," the author writes (71).

In "Watermelon Man," Larry Gabriel writes

> Minstrel troupes were the first popular entertainment in the United States. The troupes first appeared as a formatted style of blackface entertainment in the 1840s. White actors blackened their faces with burnt cork in order to portray blacks as buffoonish, ignorant characters. There were other caricatures—Chinese, backwoodsmen, Irish—in the popular idiom, but it was the blackface actors, dancers, musicians and comedians who captured the fancy of a white America torn apart by the issue of slavery. The minstrel originators, however, were hardly familiar with blacks; most of the songs about longing for the good old South were written out of the fantasies of white Northerners who'd had little contact with blacks or plantation life. These minstrels, who marketed themselves as depicting the true culture of Negroes, created a narrow and demeaning set of character types that still live with us today.

The truth about people of color isn't getting picked up and disseminated by the media to the same degree that the stereotypes are being reinforced. The conundrum that African Americans and other minorities face is that any successes are seen as exceptions, as unlike the rest, while the group as a whole is seen as failing. Failures have the damnable effect of verifying the stereotypes of people of color, and successes go mostly unnoticed or unreported. For whites the opposite is true. They may fail individually, but their success is generally measured as part of their racial group.

Muslims also find themselves in the same trap with minorities, especially since the Sept. 11, 2001, tragedy. They now are racially profiled and often viewed as suspects who must be closely watched. Many mainline Muslim organizations have repeatedly denounced the violence from extremist groups, yet few media outlets have reported it, so their condemnations go unnoticed by the public. Many people then insist that the silence of "the good Muslims" shows they consent with the atrocities:

> Voice mail: Dec. 8, 2004
>
> Maybe it would help Muslims in this country if they would actually come out and speak against the terrorist acts and speak against what happened

> on 9-11, but we don't see that going on in this country, do we? They're just not speaking out. They're just really kind of quiet on the whole thing. Maybe they should come out and say we don't like what these terrorists did to the United States. Let's hear it from those people.
>
> E-mail: March 29, 2006
>
> Why not a column about Muslim leaders who have not openly opposed world wide terrorism by Muslims and insurrection by Muslims in Iraq? I will be among the first to stand up for Muslims, as much as I do for Christians, Jews, and other faiths but only after Muslims publicly denounce terror and insurrection by Muslims. Until that happens, all Muslim leaders can kiss my ass.
>
> E-mail: Oct. 8, 2002
>
> If American Muslims want to rise above suspicion and be accepted by their fellow citizens, the quickest and best solution is to condemn terrorism and repudiate maniacal fundamentalism. None of the Muslims in your column was quoted as doing so, as have few others elsewhere.

Nothing could be further from the truth.

Muslims felt that same vilification after the bombing on April 19, 1995, of the Alfred P. Murrah Federal Building in Oklahoma City. After the media reported the terrorist attack, authorities and people in the press immediately assumed that Muslims were responsible. It turned out, however, to be a home-grown, traditional white supremacist case of terrorism.

The Kansas City Star, like many news media covering that big story, sent a team of white reporters and photographers to Oklahoma City. An immediate criticism among minority staffers was that the newspaper missed an opportunity to include journalists of color on the assignment. *The Star* had totally disregarded what had been learned during months of diversity training. The white staffers sent back stories and pictures to white editors. What ran in the newspaper the first few days featured only those victims and rescuers who were white even though many of the individuals who had been working in the heavily damaged federal building were people of color. The newsroom diversity committee, which *The Star* had had in place since 1993, pointed out the inaccuracy and the regression to the traditional, autopilot, non-diverse coverage. As a result, a corrected coverage followed. But what about the news media that didn't have that fail-safe? What about the print and broadcast press that didn't have diversity committees critically evaluating their coverage?

That historical cycle of outright silencing continues to make existential victims of us all, because we are being forced to form judgments and make choices based on largely misleading or severely restricted information. Most of us have no way of knowing that the track has been laid for us to make bad choices based on biased information. A perfect example was when the executive staff of *The Kansas City Star* in the mid-1990s was going through a diversity exercise. Two high-ranking, white corporate officials were given an assessment of diversity awareness at *The Star* by Maggie Finefrock. She told the executive staff that one black newspaper employee related a story of how her manager, in a complimentary fashion, said she was as cute as a pickaninny doll he used to have as a child. The one top newspaper official turned to his second-in-command and asked quite sincerely, "What's a pickaninny?" The other man responded, "I think it's a dog," confusing the slur with a Pekingese.

These two executives were unfamiliar with the word because they had not had the life experiences that most black people have. White privilege nursed them, sheltered them and kept them from needing to know the bigotry that people of color cannot escape. They themselves were victims of their own ignorance, but they also made others victims of that lack of information. The limits of their experience—as two top executives at a major newspaper—caused the company as a whole to suffer the same deficit. Because they could not fathom what minorities must endure, they were not able to ensure that diversity was practiced inside the newspaper and then projected to the outside. Furthermore, their privilege as white men made it unnecessary for them to be aware of what they and everyone else who was white were missing. They were able to escape existential victimization only when Cheryl Thompson, then a reporter and diversity co-chair at *The Star*, and I—the only African Americans in the room—enlarged their knowledge. We took them beyond racism's cuddly cradle of limitations. Such bridgings have to occur to help more people discover the Real America.

This was one instance at one newspaper. But imagine such a diversity knowledge deficit occurring repeatedly at companies and in communities around the country. It makes the unchecked existential victimization affecting everyone seem insurmountable.

All persons in the news media should practice culturally competent journalism. They need to get to know other people and cultures that are different from their own. But that's not the way things are now.

Mary Frances Berry helps explain the effects of that truth-failure in her book, *The Pig Farmer's Daughter and Other Tales of American Justice: Episodes of Racism and Sexism in the Courts from 1865 to the Present.* The book points out that it is only when people of color's stories of their triumphs and tragedies are shown to be part of the landscape that helped shape America that those groups can expect equal treatment, equal opportunities and justice in day-to-day disputes and conflicts—especially from law enforcement authorities and the courts. If their stories are negated, if they are not seen as valuable contributors to the country that they have helped to build, then they will be discounted in everyday situations, too. Berry writes:

> Whose story counts in legal decisions rests heavily on who controls political and economic power, in a process that is circular and progressive. The stories of the powerful are the only ones that count, and the counting further enhances the power of the tellers in the economic and political arena. The exclusion of their stories reflects the historical silencing of African Americans. (4)

That silencing includes the full spectrum of stories of Asian Americans, Hispanics, Native Americans, people with disabilities, the lesbian, gay, bisexual, transgender community, youths, older people, and many more. These excluded people are troubled by the silence in the media because the stories of their triumphs and tragedies are not being told. It's in the silence that the stereotypes flourish, and these often criminalize and marginalize those who are left out, so they are viewed only as troublemakers in our country:

E-mail: April 1, 2006

> Can Muslims be Good Americans?
>
> Can a devout Muslim be an American patriot and a loyal citizen? Consider this:
>
> Theologically, no. Because his allegiance is to Allah, the moon god of Arabia.
>
> Scripturally, no. Because his allegiance is to the five pillars of Islam and the Qur'an (Koran).
>
> Geographically, no. Because his allegiance is to Mecca, to which he turns in prayer five times a day.
>
> Socially, no. Because his allegiance to Islam forbids him to make friends with Christians or Jews.
>
> Politically, no. Because he must submit to the mullah (spiritual leaders), who teach annihilation of Israel and destruction of America, the great Satan.
>
> Domestically, no, because he is instructed to marry four women and beat and scourge his wife when she disobeys him.
>
> Religiously, no. Because no other religion is accepted by his Allah except Islam.
>
> Intellectually, no, because he cannot accept the American Constitution since it is based on Biblical principles and he believes the Bible to be corrupt.
>
> Philosophically, no, because Islam, Muhammad, and the Qur'an do not allow freedom of religion and expression.

> Democracy and Islam cannot co-exist. Every Muslim government is either dictatorial or autocratic.
>
> Spiritually, no, because when we declare "one nation under God," the Christian's God is loving and kind, while Allah is NEVER referred to as our heavenly father, nor is he ever called love in the Qur'an's 99 excellent names.
>
> Therefore after much study and deliberation....perhaps we should be very suspicious of ALL MUSLIMS in this country. They obviously cannot be both good Muslims and good Americans. Call it what you wish...it's still the truth. If you find yourself intellectually in agreement with the above, perhaps you will share this with your friends. The more who understand this, the better it will be for our country.
>
> Pass it on. The war is bigger than we know.

All of the above are widespread and media-fed notions.

Wilson and Gutiérrez in *Race, Multiculturalism, and the Media* write that historically "racial minorities were consigned to economic second-class standing and members of those groups were either ignored in the mass media attracting the majority society or portrayed in a way that made them palatable to the majority" (40). One such example involved campaign videos that a major charitable organization used to solicit funds benefiting antipoverty, not-for-profit, civic and community-based organizations. An official told me that the agencies under its funding umbrella serve people of all colors and people of different income groups. YMCAs are great examples, and they are in urban and suburban communities. Yet that official said the promotional and fund-raising videos often focus on African-American, Hispanic and elderly aid recipients. Like those in other agencies, the officials found, she said, that people are more inclined to give when the faces of those on the receiving end are people of color, the elderly or children rather than an accurate representation of everyone in the community who actually benefits from charitable giving. The funding recipients are mostly white and mainstream—just like in the Real America. But the image often projected in the campaign is the stereotypical poor person, playing on people's sympathies. In an odd twist, the prejudices about people who lie outside of white middle-America get turned into cash, which largely benefits white middle-America.

Still the exclusion locks many people of color out from full acceptance in the United States. Wilson and Gutiérrez add that racial minorities, identifiable by their facial features or skin color were often placed outside the melting pot, unable to blend over generations because of physical characteristics. Blacks, Native Americans, Asians, and Latinos were groups whose physical appearance permanently identified them as different from the European Whites who had come from different countries and 'melted' into the society of the United States.... When they were treated, it was often in stereotypic roles, such as a Black Mammy, an Indian Maiden, a Latin Lover, or a sinister Asian Warlord. (*Race* 42)

That sounds so much like many of the wildly popular Disney cartoons, which inculcate young audiences with these incredibly potent and constantly perpetuated preconceived notions. Jannette L. Dates and Edward C. Pease take a more classical approach to the topic in their essay, "Warping the World: Media's Mangled Images of Race," in the *Summer 1994 Media Studies Journal: Race—America's Rawest Nerve*. They quote an icon of American journalism:

> Walter Lippmann, recognizing the importance of cultural forces in society, once noted that "the subtlest and most pervasive of influences are those which create and maintain the repertory of stereotypes. We are told about the world before we see it. We imagine most things before we experience them. And those preconceptions, unless education has made us acutely aware, govern deeply the whole process of perception."... [As a result, we] view people as types locked into certain stereotypical, inalterable (and inaccurate) modes. Puerto Ricans are oily and drive Chevies with loud stereos. Black women are single mothers on welfare; black men are violent. Asians (any variety) are inscrutable (and good at math). Mexicans are in this country illegally and have large families to support. White men are successful, happy and drive BMWs. And so on. The media project images of each of these groups and others that create, reinforce and perpetuate popular "knowledge" of them that rarely is grounded in reality, "knowledge" on which members of those groups themselves as well as others in society form judgments and act. It is a dangerous, divisive and wasteful world that the media create. (91-93)

Cornel Pewewardy reminds us that "[s]tereotypes sell. To this day, consumers recognize the stylized Indian chief on cans of Calumet Baking Powder and the kneeling Indian maiden on packages of Land O' Lakes butter. The athletic fortunes of the Braves, Indians, Chiefs, Redskins, and Black Hawks are followed by professional sports fans across the country" ("Fluff"). Those stereotypes are then elevated to marketing tools that help generate profit that businesses crave, regardless of what the stereotyped minorities think.

From "Are 'Homies' the right images of Hispanics?"

> A girl inserted two quarters into a giant gum-ball machine at a Northland grocery store and out popped her prize neatly encased in a plastic bubble.
>
> "They're cute," the preteen said of the 1 1/2-inch tall gift she planned to give it to her aunt who collects them.

But "cute" is hardly how Fred J. Sanchez would describe the gumball gang called "Homies." Sanchez, an anesthetist at St. Luke's Northland Hospital and former Jackson County legislator, said the Homies plastic figurines were stereotypical images of young Hispanics.

Many of the more than 100 male and female figures look like gang members. Some have tattoos, baggy clothes, dark glasses, pool sticks and skull caps. Some stores in other states have pulled the figures, saying they glamorize gang life.

But area grocery store managers I spoke with say Homies are simply hot collectibles. They're like Beanie Babies were in the '90s, except with an attitude.

Carl DiGerlamo, general manager with Roca Vending Inc., stocks Homies in machines in stores, restaurants and laundries metrowide and in Missouri, Kansas and Nebraska. They began selling in 2000.

"For some reason they have a lot of appeal," DiGerlamo said. Children, teens and adults buy them. He wouldn't say who his supplier is.

A machine at a midtown store listed a Web site of www.homies.tv. It said Homies were created by David Gonzales and shipped from the West Coast. No telephone number was listed, and Gonzales did not respond to an e-mail I sent to him.

Sanchez learned about Homies when one of his preteen daughters brought four home. Sanchez went out and got several more "just to see if what I was seeing was correct."

I understood why they bothered Sanchez. It was the negative image that "Homies Hoodrats" conveyed of Hispanics to everyone investing 50 cents on each of the figurines.

Sanchez wasn't overreacting, although he said some people in the Hispanic community told him he was. He said he remembered the days of fighting segregation, discrimination and unfair treatment of Latinos.

A lot of work and suffering went into building up the image of Hispanics. "Now it seems we're going backward in two ways," Sanchez said.

"It's tolerated within our own community," he said. "And what we're not seeing are Hispanics in lab coats, with stethoscopes, Hispanics as teachers, astronauts, police officers, lawyers, firemen, nurses and reporters.

"Instead we have gang members."

Homies don't represent a wholesome image for Hispanic children. It sets up a self-fulfilling prophesy if they see their future as being like Homies and if that's what other people think of Hispanics, too.

Sanchez said the dropout rate of Hispanic teens already is far too high.

According to the census, the number of Hispanics who dropped out or never attended high school rose by more than 50 percent in the

1990s. In 2000 about 1.56 million people in the United States age 16 to 19 were not high school graduates and not enrolled in school. Of that number, nearly 34 percent, or 528,000, were Hispanic.

"We need positive images," Sanchez said. "We don't need images that encourage those kinds of statistics."

The Hispanic culture Sanchez knew and that he and his wife, Linda, work to pass on to their daughters, Morganne, 11, and Tedi, 9, is one of positive attributes. That includes strong families, an emphasis on education, respect for society, discipline, responsibility, and a commitment to their church and this community.

"It's certainly not to be a drag on this community," Sanchez said. "It was to be an asset."

Homie figurines with names like "Gangsta Hoopa" don't convey positive images to anyone.

The reactions showed that, oddly, many Latinos accept the "Homies" stereotype while others stereotype Latinos. Sanchez's concerns were even more valid than anyone could have imagined.

E-mail: Feb. 3, 2003

I'm a 33-year-old social worker with a master's degree, and I collect Homies. I collect them because they're cute, and because they're funny because I am a therapist and sometimes use them to role play with my clients. But mostly I collect them because they testify to my existence. They validate the American Latino culture for me in a way that nothing in the popular media ever has. I grew up in Albuquerque, New Mexico, and The Homies remind me of home. There are some of The Homies that bear very close resemblances to people I know; the kid that grew up down the street, the bass player in my brother's band, a girl I had a crush on when I was in the ninth grade (Sad Girl is her Homie name). These are the people with whom I went to high school, my neighbors, aunts and uncles. This is a culture that is Mexican in roots, but uniquely American in reality. These figurines go far beyond stereotypes, they are actually people from an actual neighborhood, most of them look to me like they have jobs, families, friends and dreams; they have humanity.

I have a collection of about 40 of the Homies. Some of them look like thugs, but most of them look like people. In fact, on my shelf I have a professor, a cop, a graduate and a political activist, all Homies. To say that the gangster looking Homies are the wrong role models is also to say that the professor and the graduate are the right ones. The cop, well, he's a stereotype, depicted eating doughnuts; and the ones with the clown makeup seem a bit of a departure from reality, but those seem to be exceptions in the group. And let's face it, if your child is walking around dressed like a cholo wearing pantomime makeup, a discussion about his role models is probably overdue anyway.

Voice Mail: Jan. 31, 2003

I collect Homies. The first time I saw them was when I went to Honey Mom's restaurant. And they had one little one in the salt and one in the pepper. They were really great. One was a little police officer. The other was just a really sharp dressed looking guy. He looked kind of like just a sharp guy in a zoot suit. Anyway, I love them. I give them away as gifts. And, you know, I don't think that anyone who would look at them as a negative or use any image as a negative against another culture. I think that's kind of racist. I think that's kind of low. I love the Homies, and I am proud of them. I think they're cool. Some of them remind me of my cousins. Some of them remind me of friends, and some of them remind me of people I've seen in other cities that are more diverse and more interesting like Chicago, Detroit or New York. And there is a downtown, and you see people walking around and hanging out. Anyway, I love them and I'm Latino and I don't see anything wrong with them.

Ronald Takaki writes, however, that "[i]n 1943, antagonism against Mexicans exploded in the Los Angeles 'Zoot-Suit' riots when hundreds of Anglo servicemen went on a rampage, beating up scores of young Mexican Americans who were despised for their sharp dress and stereotyped as gang members" (394). Now it seems that all Hispanics are being tarred with the same anti-immigrant brush. Nevertheless, the support for "Homies" remains strong among some while the bigotry against Hispanics is disturbing in others.

Letter: Feb. 5, 2003

What gives you the right to label these tiny, 1 ½-inch, plastic figurines, anything more than a toy? Come on people, let's think. Do Barbie dolls represent all blond women? Do action figures like wrestlers, or super heroes represent the majority of men? Of course not. They are just toys, right? Well that's what the "Homies" are, just toys.

I am an 18-year-old senior on the verge of graduation in May, and also a Hispanic woman. I'm sorry Mr. Sanchez if you think the culture is being represented in any way but for the best. My grandmother who was born in Monterey, Mexico taught me well, Mr. Sanchez, and that is why I don't base my beliefs and life on the parts of my culture or my beliefs around that same 1 ½-inch doll that you find so offensive. I base my beliefs and life on the parts of my culture that she has successfully passed down to me. Cinco' De Mayo', family supers, and most importantly my religion, this is what my Hispanic culture has been to me all my life. This is what a Hispanic/Latino home is to me.

"Homies" are not the enemy; they do not create a stereotype. It is narrow-minded people with nothing better to do than to criticize a doll. This could be what is holding back the Hispanic communities, and dear Mr. Sanchez if you cared to bother, they do make educated

"Homies." I have been collecting the figurines for the past two years, and sitting in front of me is a police officer Homie, a graduate holding a 2002 diploma Homie, a speaker in front of a podium Homie and the one that I hold most dear to me, my wheelchair Homie. This is the Homie that shows you what could happen to you in a gang life or if you make the wrong decisions in life, hardly, a self-fulfilling prophesy.

Do you know these "Homies," Mr. Sanchez? Are these not good messages to send to young Hispanic teens: a police officer, a teacher, a graduate? I think somebody owes Mr. David Gonzales an apology. He is not living the gang life, or selling drugs to kids. He is making an honest living by crafting tiny figures of our culture and making honest profits. Who are we to stop him here in America? Is that not a good enough image for you, the entrepreneur way, the American way? Mr. Gonzales is just a marketing genius who found his niche in our culture, by means of a tiny doll.

Thank you Mr. David Gonzales.

Voice Mail: Jan. 31, 2003

I was reading your article this morning, "Are Homies the right images of Hispanics?" Have you been outside, Mr. Lewis? Yes they are, man. Matter of fact, you need to write this about them. You know what white people call Mexicans now? They call them the new niggers. I'm going to educate you to what's going on out here on the streets. Oh, I don't live in the ghetto. I live in the suburbs. They call them the new niggers. So yes, you have them depicted right on those little bobble-head figures or whatever they are. I'll tell you what you really need to be writing about, Mr. Lewis, about these Mexicans. Number 1, there are more of them in the country now than there are of blacks. And when they come over here, they just don't come to work. They bring marijuana over here. They bring all the cocaine in here. They're not just bringing themselves and their 13 family members, sir. They're bringing drugs over here and at an alarming rate. That's what you need to write about Mr. Lewis W. Diuguid or whatever your name is. I'm not mad at you. I'm keeping it real with you. You guys sit up in them offices all day. You don't know what's going on out here on the streets. Yes, Homies is the appropriate image. They dress like black guys just like the little white kids do, man. Do you see the little white kids with baggy pants and goatees and baseball caps turned around backward? Everybody is on that hip-hop stuff, man. But the story you need to write about these Mexicans is what they're bringing into this country as they flood this country. Man, don't you know Mexico supplies the United States with 70 percent of its marijuana? Yes! Seventy percent, man. You need to come out of that office and get on the street. And they bring guns in and they bring crime with them. So you've got a race over here that's almost double the black Americans now and they're not just coming

> by themselves now. They're bringing baggage with them. That's what you need to let the American people know and how do so many of them keep getting in here. Do you see that Mexican man raping those little girls in California? They are bringing crime with them. They're not just bringing cheap labor work, man. And the cheap labor work goes back to Mexico, and they live better than we do over here. And another thing. Have you ever watched Mexican movies where people go to Mexico? We get treated like shit, man.

Certainly "making honest profits," "the entrepreneur way" and being "a marketing genius" are considered the American way. But if it is done by promoting stereotypes at the expense of minority groups, then it's unethical, immoral, illicit and wrong.

From "Fog blocks the truth"

> ORLANDO, Fla. - A thick, lazy fog blurred any hope of seeing the off-road ground on my pre-dawn cab rides to the National Association of Black Journalists' convention at a Disney World hotel.
>
> I asked one cabdriver during the four-day convention how he liked this central Florida community. He made a wavering motion with his right hand. "Too much Disney," he said. "Everywhere you go it's Mickey Mouse, Mickey Mouse."
>
> But he wasn't sure whether that marketing fog covering everything here was because Disney and Mickey Mouse are what people demand or whether they're part of the genius of making people believe they can't live without them. Disney World is a more than 30-year-old factory of fantasy and fun, and the fog of good times it produces only dissipates for individuals when the money they feed into the production runs out.
>
> A friend who lives in the area drove me through a new Disney community called Celebration. It's the perfect suburban town mixed with the colonial quaintness of New England with 1,000, $194,000-to-$2.6-million homes, shops and a downtown.
>
> "Can you think of anything more vanilla?" my friend asked. "It's the land of signature T-shirts and designer jeans."
>
> Walt Disney, who got his start creating cartoon characters in Kansas City, is responsible.
>
> The fog also was pointed out at the convention in speeches by entertainer and human-rights activist Harry Belafonte and former newspaper publisher Jay T. Harris. Each questioned whether the public is getting the information it needs from the media to make decisions or if fogs of marketing, lies, greed and a lust for profits are threatening this nation's democracy.
>
> "I am loathe to suggest a conspiracy," Belafonte said. "But our people in America as a nation know so little about the world in which they live.

"In the community of black America, how little they know of themselves and know of their history."

Without countering voices telling the truth, media stereotypes of minorities prevail, Belafonte said.

Belafonte said people were unaware of the civil rights and freedom struggles after World War II in this country and all over the world. People of color like him fought the Nazis and then battled to free their homelands of racism and oppression. Many of them paid with their lives for the promise of a future they wanted everyone to have.

But the Disneyfication of history and the news creates a happy fog that keeps many from knowing the efforts of yesteryear's heroes. The school groups that Belafonte addresses, so as to raise concerns, ask him no questions and offer no analyses or answers.

"They know none of this," he said. "They do not know where to inquire or where to go. We have miserably failed because so little is known."

The happy fog keeps the truth covered. People don't know or care that this nation locks up massive numbers of its citizens. A disproportionate percentage are black and Hispanic people.

Little comment follows the growing disparity of wealth, the lack of health care for all, the global AIDS crisis, the disenfranchisement of African-American voters in Florida and Ohio, which resulted in George W. Bush being president, and this country's decision to bypass the U.N. World Conference Against Racism.

"This country cannot walk away from the conference on racism," said Belafonte, who planned to go to it in Durban, South Africa. "Our world is being devoured by it.

"Our children are being murdered by it. How can we not go?"

Public apathy also disturbs Belafonte.

"We seem to be indifferent, and we do nothing about it," said Belafonte, who also chastised the black journalists' group for meeting in Disney World. "Where have we missed the boat?"

Harris told the convention that the depth and diversity of ideas and concerns, which the press provides, are being reduced in today's corporate quest for profits. Harris resigned as publisher of the *San Jose Mercury News*, citing parent company Knight Ridder's cost-cutting plans. Knight Ridder also owned *The Star*.

Severe cuts industrywide affect quality journalism. "Readers and citizens have the greatest stake," Harris said.

Without in-depth coverage, the fog of lies hurting the public spreads. Americans depend on the free press to deliver the truth so people can correct society's problems.

> Burning away the fog will help ensure that truth in our democracy stands a fighting chance over conformity, apathy and greed.

As mentioned in Chapter 5, the truth about history, the real stories about minorities in the United States have been distorted, tarnished, if not omitted for centuries. In addition, the popular media have done little to create accurate pictures of minorities. Instead, the images that prevail broadly include the stupid but benign, the romanticized and mysterious, the subservient and humble, the lazy, dirty and drunk, the bumbling and scatterbrained, the vicious and cruel. Rarely were minorities given leading roles, more often than not portraying a sidekick or helper. The language they spoke was often broken or heavily accented, so that it's clear they should never be allowed in mainstream white America as a group.

Native Americans, for example, were all lumped together in "the myth of the monolithic 'Indian' without regard for the distinctions of more than 2,000 different cultures, languages, and value systems the concept represented. The literary stereotype began as part of the western frontier writing formula developed after the Civil War. . . ." Writers such as Mark Twain and Bret Harte "wrote of the picturesque scenery and romantic lifestyles of the frontier in contrast to the 'savages' who occupied the land. . . . Literature during the Indian wars is rife with tales of Indians burning, looting, raping and scalping the pioneers who were fulfilling the fervor of 'manifest destiny.' Elimination or subjugation of the Native American was seen as merely an evolutionary step in the development of industrial America" (Wilson *Minorities* 69).

Little changed when entertainment progressed to movies and TV. Popular westerns, for example, contained the stereotypical images of frontier strife. Tonto of Lone Ranger fame was played by Jay Silverheels, a Mohawk, but his heritage was of no consequence. More importantly, he was easily recognizable as "Indian" because of his stereotypical dress, pinto pony and halting English. His role as the Lone Ranger's "faithful" companion was also stereotypical; the white Lone Ranger was always the center of attention and emerged at the end of each episode as the only real hero. In addition, Wilson and Gutiérrez note that in many television programs that included Native Americans, they often were played by white actors (*Minorities* 96).

Lately, Native Americans have been portrayed as more benevolent, noble, and wise. Pocahontas has been "Disneyfied," and romanticized, becoming older in the process, because she was probably only about 10 or 12 years old when she first encountered white men, including John Smith. Historical American Indian women such as Pocahontas have been "elevated to royalty status like princesses and queens. To suggest that indigenous females were princess [sic] and queens is contrary to many tribal beliefs. It's a European concept," writes Cornel Pewewardy ("Fluff"). Is this perhaps another stereotype that helped to make "Indians" more palatable?

Journalism Across Cultures notes how poorly the news media cover American Indians. Journalists don't understand the history, the people or their culture. Few bother to learn of the sovereignty issues, the "unique legal status that their 550 federally recognized tribes hold: tribal sovereignty. This grants tribes powers of self-government as 'domestic, dependent nations' and exempts them, with some exceptions, from the laws and regulations of states in which their reservations or communities are located," *Journalism Across Cultures* notes (133). As a result the media often report stories from the perspective of white people with grievances about differing tribal and federal laws. Even President George W. Bush stumbled badly on the sovereignty question at the August 2004 UNITY: Journalists of Color Convention in Washington, D.C.

From: "Too many discount the minority vote"

> He seemed clueless about sovereignty for American Indians and how to resolve conflicts between tribes, federal and state governments.
>
> "Tribal sovereignty means that, sovereignty," Bush said to audience snickers. "You've been given sovereignty and you're viewed as a sovereign entity. Therefore the relationship between the federal government and tribes is one between sovereign entities."

Journalism Across Cultures adds that the mainstream news media fail to chronicle Native American issues well because the coverage often falls into three categories of "Indian stories: (1) treating Indians only as problem people; (2) consigning them to history (or the 'trash heap of history,' in the words of a former president . . .) and (3) not taking Indians seriously" (139). Native Americans and alcoholism stories often run in the media. However, American Indians were the only group of Americans whose number of alcoholics declined each census (143). "The only way you can inform your readers is to become more informed than they are," the book advises. If you don't, the ignorance, prejudices and biases that infect the news media don't just taint them alone. They are disseminated and contaminate the population as a whole. And because media images are among America's biggest exports, those U.S.-grown stereotypes then get shared with the world.

Like Native American depictions, early portrayals of African Americans in the minstrel shows were also provided by white actors. Larry Gabriel writes, "When in the late 1800s and early 1900s black minstrel troupes became dominant, the format and characters were so set it was nearly impossible for black entertainers to break the mold. These black minstrel shows were advertised as presenting 'real coons.' Yet, ironically, even real coons had to don burnt cork to represent themselves." The parts were demeaning and comic and set the stage for future African-American performers. Al Jolson, for example, "[refined] minstrel show affections to indelibly stereotype an ethnic group in American entertainment" (Wilson *Minorities* 77). In literature the situation was similar. After the Civil War, portraits of blacks were painted with the scathing brush of racism. They were depicted as being stupid, licentious, lazy, and drunk, among other things (*Minorities* 71).

That trend continued into the age of television. Blacks have not been portrayed with the diversity that reflects reality. In 1950, three network shows featured African Americans. They were *Beulah, The Jack Benny Show* and *The Stu Erwin Show*. In each blacks were pandering servants. "The Beulah character was a maid and mammy figure in a white household," who had a scatterbrained girlfriend and a shiftless boyfriend. Jack Benny's valet Rochester "played imitative Stepin Fetchit roles" (Wilson *Minorities* 96-97). Sadly, television has not advanced far from such scenes. Add criminal, belligerent characters or those with foul attitudes and "little intellectual capacity" and that just about covers the waterfront (Wilson *Minorities* 98).

The stereotype of minorities was reinforced with Hattie McDaniel's being the first black person to receive an Oscar award on February 29, 1940, for her part as Scarlet O'Hara's mammie in *Gone With the Wind*. Nearly 50 years later, Denzel Washington won an Oscar for playing a rogue cop in *Training Day*, and, on the same awards night, Halle Berry won for her role as a promiscuous black woman in *Monster's Ball*—all stereotypical roles for blacks. McDaniel's role now seems to be legitimized by a stamp produced by the U.S. Postal Service, honoring her contribution to film as a mammie. Jadakiss f and Anthony Hamilton ask, in "Why," their rap song, why those actors were given awards for those specific roles:

> Why Halle have to let a white man pop her to get a Oscar
> Why Denzel have to be crooked before he took it . . . .

Those are legitimate concerns, but perhaps once again a reflection of what is stereotypically acceptable. In 2007, the trend continued. Oscars went to Forest Whitaker for best actor playing villainous dictator Idi Amin in the *Last King of Scotland* and to Jennifer Hudson for best supporting actress for her role as a black Motown-like singer in *Dreamgirls*.

Cruelty describes the white portrayal of Mexicans largely because of the wars that were fought over their land. But that's not all.

> American naval Lieutenant H.A. Wise wrote that Mexicans were "beyond comparison the laziest and most ignorant set of vagabonds the

> world produces." George Wilkins Kendall penned: "Give them but tortillas, frijoles, and chile colorado to supply their animal wants for the day and seven-tenths of the Mexicans are satisfied; and so they will continue to be until the race becomes extinct or amalgamated with Anglo-Saxon stock." (Wilson *Minorities* 72)

Apparently Hispanics' very survival depends on their becoming white! History is the problem. The media and popular culture continue to demean Hispanics, their language and heritage. Wilson and Gutiérrez continue:

> When the Mexicans were not being portrayed in Anglo literature as lazy and indolent, they were assailed for uncleanliness. Texas romance writer Jeremiah Clemens gave his version of the origin of the term "greaser" and why he felt it was appropriate: "The people look greasy, their clothes are greasy, their dogs are greasy – everywhere grease and filth hold divided dominion, and the singular appropriateness of the name bestowed by western settlers soon caused it to be universally adopted by the American army." (*Minorities* 72)

By 1900, the stereotype of the Hispanic was firmly in place. *The Cisco Kid,* which ran from 1950 to 1956, was the Latino's inroad into television. "Cisco was a bandito-type character who preyed on the rich to help the poor, a la Robin Hood" write Wilson and Gutiérrez. He "was vintage 'Latin lover,' except he never got romantically involved with the love-stricken ladies" because the show was watched mostly by children. His sidekick, Pancho, was a fat, outgoing character, who spoke with a heavy accent and provided comedic relief. Other shows that included Hispanic characters were *The Real McCoys, The High Chaparral, Chico and the Man, CHIPS, Fantasy Island* and, of course, *I Love Lucy.* Ricky Ricardo, Lucy's on-screen husband, was a stereotypical hot-tempered Latin who "exploded into a torrent of Spanish when Lucy's ill-fated activities were revealed." Again, the characters were either comedic, Latin-lover types or they played the straight role to the humorous, white characters (*Minorities* 99).

Even though people of Asian heritage have had a significant presence in the United States for only a little over a century, their stereotypes are also well established. Most immigrants from Asia arrived on the West Coast. Initially the Chinese came to work on the railroad, but that work ended in 1869 when the western and eastern lines were joined in Utah. By 1870 more than 60,000 Chinese had settled in California, working on farms, in mines, factories and homes. They initially enjoyed about 20 years as a "welcome source of cheap labor" and earned a "reputation for industry, honesty, thrift and peaceful disposition," write Wilson and Gutiérrez (*Minorities* 73). But that ended when whites couldn't find work. The Chinese had jobs and were targeted as the cause of white unemployment. They were viewed as "debased, clannish and deceitful," were disliked and disrespected, and became the victims of violence. In 1882 the Chinese Exclusion Act was passed, virtually halting Chinese immigration. But farms began to suffer because of the shortage of labor, so Japanese immigrants were brought in to fill the gap. Their fate was no better than the Chinese, however, because they, too, were seen to be "driving Whites out of the job market" (*Minorities* 74). This became known as the "Yellow Peril." In 1924 the Immigration Act in turn stopped the Japanese from coming to the United States.

And so after being feared and scorned, Asians in America faded into the background. Movie-goers, however, were treated to images of China, in which "the American audience was given the impression that Chinese people are prone to violence, anarchy, corruption, vice, and prostitution" (Wilson *Minorities* 86-87). The focus returned to the Japanese, however, after the attack on Pearl Harbor during World War II. Wilson and Gutiérrez write that

> In films produced between 1942 and 1945 Hollywood dusted off the old images of Japanese duplicity, inhumanity, and lust for White women. Unlike the Germans, who were portrayed as a respectable but misguided people under the influence of the Nazi regime, the Japanese were seen in American theaters strafing Red Cross ships, bayoneting children, and delighting in applying torture techniques handed down from centuries of malevolent practice. (*Minorities* 88)

In 1949, "Asian portrayals came to television . . . in an ABC crime show called 'Mysteries of Chinatown.'" Stereotypes prevailed, with the lead character owning an herb and curio shop in San Francisco's Chinatown. As the title shows, the program reinforced the perception of the "'mysterious' Asian," even though "[t]he regular supporting cast was all white" (*Minorities* 101). Other "Asian" TV programs also featured all-white casts. In the 1956 Charlie Chan series, a white actor played Chan, and Asian actors portrayed his bumbling sons. Martial arts series followed, including *The Green Hornet* in which Bruce Lee played Kato, the sidekick of the main character again played by a white actor. "Interestingly, *The Green Hornet* was the creation of George Trendle, who also developed *The Lone Ranger*," write Wilson and Gutiérrez. "In both concepts, the hero is supported by a trusty ethnic minority sidekick, perhaps for the purpose of adding fantasy appeal for the mass audience." *Kung Fu* followed, with a white actor again playing the main Asian character. Asian actors also played "houseboy" characters as was the case in *Bonanza* and *The Courtship of Eddie's Father*. *In Hawaii Five-O* Asian portrayals were more "varied and diverse, although definite stereotypes were projected. The show's vulnerability to stereotypical criticism was its portrayal of white superiority and leadership in a predominantly Asian environment" (*Minorities* 101-102).

Not much has changed over the years. In most mainstream productions, Asian Americans are still "subservient" to white characters. *Journalism Across Cultures* quotes the Asian American Journalism Association, saying the press Asian Americans receive falls into five categories: "eternal foreigners," the "model minority," "honorary whites," people who are "from nowhere in particular" or simply "invisible" (232).

The media definitely contribute to the problem of denigrating some groups while maintaining whiteness and racism—and have for centuries. Jane Elliott, a former third grade teacher in Iowa, in 1968 after the assassination of the Rev. Martin Luther King Jr., exposed her students to her now famous "brown-eyes, blue-eyes" experiment to get them to know what it felt like to be discriminated against. She said in her visit in the 1990s to Kansas City that the best way to raise a racist, sexist, homophobic, elitist child was to put that kid in front of a turned-on television set and walk away. The same is true for a lot of popular music.

From "Gangsta rap feeds into the media's image of urban despair" and "Gangsta rap's sharp, deep wedge"

> Pop culture heroes, no matter how vulgar, never seem to die.
>
> I learned that at a panel discussion on the late Tupac Shakur at Paseo Academy in Kansas City, Mo. Some young people think Tupac is not dead. The 25-year-old gangsta rap artist and movie star simply faked his death Sept. 13, 1996.
>
> Sure their hero suffered gunshot wounds in a drive-by shooting Sept. 7, 1996, in Las Vegas after the Mike Tyson - Bruce Seldon boxing match. But instead of dying, Shakur simply went underground to heal until it was safe to surface as an even bigger star.
>
> I laughed because in my mind I kept seeing Shakur and an overweight, aging Elvis Presley lying low together.
>
> Shakur was bleeding, and Elvis was eating. They partied on beer and gin and juice in some undisclosed safe haven, where no one would rat them out.
>
> But unlike the king of rock 'n' roll, Shakur's remains were cremated in a private service. So there's no earth to turn and no body to exhume to disprove the urban legend that Tupac is not dead.
>
> But what's tragic is that young people at the forum worship rap music's violent, vulgar and venomous lyrics, saying it's just a reflection of hopeless conditions in our community. One girl even said that the sun doesn't shine in her neighborhood.

What's sad is she and too many others have bought the media reality of total urban despair put out by the rapping pimps of platinum profits. The truth, I told her, is that the sun did rise, the grass grew and everyday black people went to work as always to make things better today and tomorrow.

She had just become too caught up in the distressing prose for profits to know that there has always been a reality of hope in our urban community.

But the media through music like Shakur's, radio, television, cable, movies and videos have created "a big bang" negative view of life.

Young people thrive on such large and loud media things for stimulation. But they ignore small everyday wonders such as the seasons changing, dew cracking in the morning grass and each glorious sunrise.

The amplified and angry voices turn off kids' curiosity to learning and life and herd them toward man-made profanities.

Some overdose on it.

Yet young people at the forum organized by Nimrod Shabazz, a critic of the anti-gangsta rap movement, said all gangsta rap isn't bad.

One after another testified as if they were at a U.S. Senate hearing, saying that negative rap music had not damaged their lives.

Gangsta rap was about someone else's hopelessness, not theirs.

Four years earlier most of the 14 students at Bishop Hogan High School discussing the music agreed. Gangsta rap simply defines in colorful terms the feelings, frustrations and realism of urban life.

Their music, like our beloved rock 'n' roll, is private and personal. They said that when older people attack it they're assaulting the younger generation.

Sound familiar?

It's also big business.

Kids aged 10 to 17 bought 56.4 percent of rap recordings. White people purchased more than half of it, data show.

And that's a problem in our segregated society if the only image white kids have of African-Americans is what they pick up in gangsta rap.

But the students said we're just not listening.

We hear unprintable language. They hear street poetry chronicling problems that need to be solved, said Chudney Manning, 17.

We hear the promotion of violence. They hear angry black artists trumpeting ways to improve city life, said Ed Greer, 16.

We hear songs of lost lives, dead ends and despair. They hear sirens warning against pursuing destructive lifestyles, said Andre McKinney, 18.

The music is simply entertainment and a way to make money, said

> Janet Hendrix, 18. But it has become a scapegoat for one generation to blame another for drugs, violence, teen pregnancy and dropouts.
>
> Alvin Brooks, then-president of the Ad Hoc Group Against Crime, said at the Paseo Academy forum: "The majority of us are strong, but the weak will pull you down. This community of ours is a lot more beautiful than drug dealers, pimps and prostitutes." Negative rappers, too.
>
> Brooks added that it's OK for gangsta rap to follow black music history and sing of the trials and tribulations of African-Americans just as old spirituals, the blues and jazz do. But the difference is that the other music offers people hope. Rap often doesn't.
>
> I think everyone needs lyrics of hope - especially young people - if we're to have a prayer of singing tomorrow.

In addition, Steven F. Gray notes in "Recognizing Stereotypical Images of African Americans in Television and Movies," that gangsta rap feeds stereotypes of urban youths. He says "the group being stereotyped begins to internalize the negative images and actually mimic some of the behavior and attitudes portrayed in the negative imagery."

From "What kind of heroes are these?"

> A man-child stepped from the darkness over the neon-lighted threshold, turning a mundane wait for chicken to go into an eye-opening experience.
>
> Inside were the cardboard masses served assembly-line smiles at the fast-food restaurant: A working mom tried to quiet hungry children; high school guys came to pick up a teen-age date finishing her shift; and a woman tired of wasting gas at the drive-up window stood with men like me sent for the family meal.
>
> But the man-child in his expensive athletic shoes and starter jacket was different from us.
>
> The young workers understood the code and reacted to him as if he was a superstar among faceless people.
>
> Under his jacket he wore faded bib overalls with the left shoulder strap dripping at his side. Attached to it swinging perilously close to the floor was a black beeper.
>
> His were the fashions of gang members, and the beeper was the way his crowd, as well as drug dealers, communicates.
>
> No one said anything that night to the man-child whose face and angular frame lacked time-and-labor-worn badges of whiskers, bulk and calluses. But the behind-the-counter body language spoke volumes.
>
> The young workers' steps carried an extra hop, hand movements were stylishly exaggerated and the teenage employees' eyes darted to

their VIP with "please-notice-me" glances. The man-child waited in line and played to his audience with a cool defiance that comes from belonging to a young, dark underworld.

It's where school has no meaning, and dropouts contributing to today's low graduation rate are kings. Drugs, crime, sex and violence for them are initiation rites and rewards.

The man-child suddenly stepped out of line and into the men's room while the young workers' anticipation of waiting on him grew. But after a few minutes he exited the rest room and the restaurant.

The bathroom was what he wanted all along, but embarrassment, youth-gang arrogance or misplaced pride in his public image forced him through the charade.

The impressionable workers unfortunately bought the act because the man-child in these confusing times is someone they and too many youths wrongly revere.

Fortunately some young people are making a career out of fighting stereotypes in the media.

<u>From "Young woman speaks out to change minority stereotypes"</u>

Sometimes our children do things that make us burst with pride.

Gwen Richards felt that way about a letter her daughter, Rickeena Richards, wrote recently. It was to the newspaper at St. Louis University, where the younger Richards has been studying.

Gwen Richards e-mailed the letter to me, and I swelled with pride, too.

Rickeena Richards' letter to her college newspaper responded to an ad that had run in the *University News* encouraging members of the urban university to get involved in "Make a Difference Day."

But the ad featured white St. Louis University students holding black children, and everyone was smiling. Richards points out that the ad furthers "frequent depictions of African-Americans (and minority groups in general) in subordinate, submissive and negative roles within the media."

The newspaper "failed (as we all do) to recognize stereotypic messages that infest our media. After all, these messages influence everyone including the media.

"Take a second look at the picture through a different lens: Who is 'making a difference,' and who is dependent on the difference being made?

"I've acknowledged that, as some may argue, I could just be overanalyzing. In my defense, I'm currently pursuing a communication degree and an African-American studies certificate from St. Louis University. I have been well-trained to do so.

"By no means do I consider myself a radical nor am I set out to start any kind of revolution (I plan to get a master's degree before even considering this). I just hope that in the future, the publication I've admired for its efforts to call attention to issues at SLU will be more careful to not contribute to them."

Richards was one of 13 students to graduate in the summer of 2005 from the Urban Student Journalism Academy run by the Kansas City Association of Black Journalists at Penn Valley Community College.

On Saturday, she also became the sixth recipient of the Laura R. Hockaday/KCABJ Scholarship. The annual award is named after Hockaday, who until she retired in 2000 was *The Kansas City Star's* society editor. Hockaday received many awards for making her columns and stories inclusive of the racial, ethnic, gender and other diversity in the Kansas City area.

Richards continues to prove that she has the same sensitivity. I first wrote about that in a July 19, 2002, column after I heard her tell audiences that we each have the power to "break down the barriers that prejudices build."

The St. Teresa's Academy graduate and Northeast Johnson County NAACP Youth Council member is a powerful speaker. But she also is an exceptional student and a quick learner.

Richards demonstrated that in the two-week program at the journalism academy. She was one of the better students and asked good questions when students had to interview newsmakers such as Kansas City Police Chief Jim Corwin and Gwen Grant, president and CEO of the Urban League of Greater Kansas City. Richards turned in her many in-class and enterprise stories on time and did the required rewrites.

We push young people because schools rarely do. The students keep up with current events, become critical thinkers and pick up what David Shipler in his book, *The Working Poor,* calls the "softer skills" of life.

That includes making eye contact with people, giving everyone a firm handshake and knowing the importance of punctuality, diligence, discipline and possessing a can-do attitude.

But we also instill in the students the importance of diversity - particularly in the media because such stories, pictures, art and ads affect how people of color will be treated in society.

Accurate images of minorities in the media help dispel the stereotypes and dissolve racism, discrimination, bigotry and prejudices.

In her letter, Richards positively pointed out the problem. The ad should have included St. Louis University students of all colors as well as a racial and ethnic mix of children who were the recipients of Make a Difference Day.

But people's reactions showed that their prejudices overshadowed any hope that they, too, might empathize and share the pride.

E-mail: Nov 16, 2005

I hope your swelling goes down soon or you will need to seek medical help. A check-up from the neck-up is what I'm talking about. Black children being held by white students displayed in a photo in a school newspaper should not cause such dismay. Rickeena is a sweet girl being trained to race bait by Black Journalists....I wish she had chosen law.

Now Lewis, look on page B-6 of *The Kansas City Star.* A photo of a white woman appearing to be a medical worker is checking the carotid artery for blockage in a black man. She no doubt is trying to prevent the possibility of a stroke. He looks so subordinate and submissive. How insensitive is that picture? Often Rickeena and your messages do more harm to your cause than help. You both are picking nits, and most people are not fond of nit pickers.

P.S. How diverse in the name Rickeena? It's not her fault....I just hope her middle name is Leslie.

Voice mail: Nov. 16, 2005

Practically everything you say pushes separation rather than integration. I don't understand how you all have come to that mindset. You have to help yourself. Nevertheless you have to join the society at large so to speak to even each other out.

It is obvious from these comments that race serves to confuse people, preventing them from accepting information because of who may be delivering it. Diane Kappen's study, mentioned in Chapter 1, clearly showed how important the messenger is to whether or not the message is palatable. Black journalists are affected by the same problem. We are educated to value those things that are news about white people and white males in particular. Journalism schools teach us to value the quotes, clipped succinct phrases and pointed statements of whites. The stories, parables and seemingly rambling discourse from blacks, Native Americans and Hispanics in particular rarely fit the tidy framework of "good journalism," so such comments and their points get excluded. *Journalism Across Cultures* advises that short responses deemed "good quotes" in the profession don't work when covering Native Americans. Lessons "to rein in an interviewee" who wanders off the subject is a no-no not only with American Indians but many other minority groups. "A response to a seemingly simple question may come back in the form of a long story. These stories or anecdotes illustrate a point and are meant as an answer to your question," the book notes (145). All journalists also pick up the biases in the media about people of color, which tends to perpetuate the problem of inaccurate, unfair, imbalanced coverage of minorities.

From "Reminders of battles fought for civil rights"

An old bus in the Civil Rights Museum in Memphis, Tenn., helps give visitors a feel for what Rosa Parks endured on Dec. 1, 1955, when she refused to give up her seat in Montgomery, Ala.

The driver's voice berates Parks to move or be arrested. It's one way to keep Parks' historic act of defiance from dying with her.

Parks, 92, died Oct. 24, 2005, in Detroit. She joined presidents and war heroes as the first woman to lie in honor in the circular room under the Capitol dome.

Parks is being revered today as the bold mechanic who fixed America's frozen constitutional machinery. But she was either ignored or reviled half a century ago by the mainstream media.

Newspaper articles that appeared in the white press at the time are displayed at the Memphis Civil Rights Museum, which opened in 1991. These also seem to depict blacks' great gains as setbacks to America's established order. Part of the established order once was the institution of slavery. Black codes and Jim Crow laws were accepted, and so were broken Reconstruction promises.

Activist Supreme Court justices in the 1896 Plessy v. Ferguson ruling made segregation the law of the land. The National Association for the Advancement of Colored People challenged it, resulting in the high court's 1954 Brown decision outlawing legal segregation.

As an NAACP member, Parks helped get the wheels of true justice in America to finally turn. Other victories followed, including the Civil Rights Act and the Voting Rights Act.

That history must never be forgotten especially now as segregation grows, the courts become more conservative and civil-rights gains are being threatened.

No one should forget what Parks did and the times in which it occurred – lest America slip back into the unjust era that predated her historic bravery.

But her courageous act was not immediately reported by the mainstream press. In fact, the first article about it didn't run in *The Kansas City Times* until Feb. 22, 1956. The perspective was telling:

A grand jury today indicted 115 persons involved in Montgomery's Negro bus boycott.

The grand jury gave warning that violence is inevitable unless race relations improve.

The boycott has been under way 11 weeks in protest against segregated seating on buses, required under Alabama law.

The grand jury report said the boycott is a violation of Alabama law, which prohibits boycotting without "a just cause or legal excuse."

The jury said the boycott originated with 18 members of what it called the interdenominational alliance composed mostly of Negro ministers. Those 18 members created the Montgomery Improvement Association, which has financed the boycott to the extent of some $18,000, the report continued.

The state law enacted in 1921 and originally aimed at labor disputes makes an organized boycott unlawful without "a just cause or legal excuse." Violations are punishable by a $1,000 fine and six months in jail.

The boycott began Dec. 3 in protest against the arrest of a Negro woman who had refused to move to the Negro section of the bus. The defendant, Mrs. Rosa Parks, was fined $14.

Negroes overwhelmingly rejected a compromise settlement last night. The boycott has brought some violence but no injuries. Dynamite bombs were exploded at the homes of two of the leading figures in the Negro protest movement, the Rev. Martin Luther King Jr. and E.D. Nixon.

King is pastor of the Dexter Avenue Baptist Church and one of the most outspoken boycott leaders. Nixon is a former state president of the National Association for the Advancement of Colored People.

Isn't it amazing that the violence the press reported and that authorities feared was not by black people but against them? Historically, whites have committed acts of violence against blacks. But crime and violence since the end of the Civil Rights Movement have been colorized as black through the media.

"Millions identify crime with black men," writes Jim Myers in *Afraid of the Dark* (305). But the fear is media fed and largely unfounded. Myers adds:

> The largest single category of robberies in the United States, slightly more than a third of all robberies, involves black robbers and white victims. Next comes robberies in which robber and victim are white. . . .
>
> Meanwhile, more serious crimes like murder and rape have their own stark pattern of racial segregation. Whites are seven times more likely to be killed by a white murderer than a black one. Murders in which a black person kills a white person are only 6 percent of all homicides. White women are seven times more likely to be raped by a white rapist. Rapes in which the assailant is black and the victim white account for only 9 percent of all rapes.
>
> In fact, the most serious criminal threats to white people come

> from other white people—and whites should, perhaps, be warned about this. Robberies, however, appear to be skewing white attitudes. Enough robberies—and carjackings, assaults, rapes, and murders, too—occur in which the perpetrators are black and the victims white to fuel white fears about black people. Indeed, this fear of being victimized by black criminals might be considered a national white obsession were it not considered indelicate to mention it. (56-57)

The media, however, do a good job of saying what others find too "indelicate to mention" showing mostly black and brown suspects in newscasts and newspapers when the statistics give a different picture. The effect, however, shows up in the feedback from whites who swallow hook, line and sinker the picture of crime they are fed.

> E-mail: Feb. 4, 2005
>
> The small number (4%) of black males in this country ages sixteen to forty are committing 70% of the crime. Is this due to racism or drugs?
>
> Of course black folks-such as Nat King Cole, Earl Garner, and Sarah Vaughn who I hung out with in the mid-50's at the Blue Note, Chez Peree, and Mr. Kelly's on Rush Street in Chicago probably never rubbed shoulders with the sort of black thugs we have on the streets in Kansas City and other metro areas today who kill innocent men, women, and children.
>
> Voice Mail: 1998
>
> I wish you would quit whining and stop making excuses for African American crime amongst other things. Stop committing the crimes – the burglaries, rapes, robberies, murders – and you're going to get respect.

The bias of the media also affects what is reported and how. Even journalists of color inadvertently pick up the biases, too. An example is one in which a black reporter was sent to cover the funeral of a prominent African American. I also was there. People of all colors spoke eulogizing the man. I sat several rows behind and to the right of the reporter and watched as he took notes. I realized from where I sat several seats away that he was only taking notes of what the white speakers said. He did not write down anything that the black speakers said. The newsroom diversity committee has focused on omissions and inaccuracies in the coverage of people of color. That heightened awareness caused the reporter to call me after the event, realizing he had that diversity gap in his notes. Together, we reconstructed the themes of what some of the black speakers had conveyed so that the reporter's story had the needed accuracy and diversity balance.

But that example points out that journalists of all colors are trained to value more what white people say and perhaps more importantly, how they say it. The black speakers at the funeral talked in rambling stories that had a point, but none of it represented what we view in journalism as highly valued brevity or as "good quotes." What the white speakers said, on the other hand, did represent "good quotes." Since they are more acceptable, they generally are what get copied down in journalists' notes, used in stories, and survive in the editing process for publication. It is a self-perpetuating, all-American concern that skews the images that the media conveys to the public.

In their book, *Race, Multiculturalism, and the Media: From Mass Media to Class Communication*, Clint C. Wilson II and Félix Gutiérrez offer ways to gauge how stereotypes invade the media. They point out that the media in the United States boil down to five basic functions:

1. *Surveillance*, the sentinel or lookout role of the media watching the society and horizon for threats to the established order and information on people or places of public interest;
2. *Correlation*, interpretation and linking function of the media, which helps the audience understand, interpret, and comprehend the different things that are happening in and out of the society and how they affect each other, as well as stay in touch with others in the society;
3. *Transmission*, the socialization function of the media, which defines the society, its norms, and values, to the audience and through their portrayals and coverage assists members of the society in adopting, using and acting on those values;
4. *Entertainment*, the function of the media for diversion and enjoyment, which provides stories, features, music, and films that are designed to make the audience laugh, cry, relax, or reflect, rather than gain information; and
5. *Economic Service*, the role of the media within the economic system of the society, which in the United States means most media function as corporations serving the needs of their shareholders and other corporations by attracting audiences that will pay for the media product and/or serve as the target for advertising messages. (37-38)

Gail Baker Woods in her book *Advertising and Marketing to the New Majority* offers some instruction on how to examine the effects of the five media functions on minority groups (78). Woods notes that the media's effects and effectiveness can be seen more clearly when demographic audiences are examined individually instead of as a whole. So we need to ask how and where people of color show up in representative demographic numbers in the five media functions. African Americans, for example make up 13 percent of the U.S. population of 300 million Americans. But where do African Americans have parity in the media? Black people stand out big in surveillance with the media checking out what African Americans are doing wrong in this country. Black people also show up larger than life in entertainment as they dribble a ball, throw a ball and catch a ball, act buffoonish or sing and dance to entertain the rest of America. But African Americans are mostly invisible in the other three media functions of transmission, correlation and economics.

Hispanics represent at least 14 percent of the population and now are the nation's largest minority group. Yet they show up prominently in surveillance because of intense focus on illegal immigration, crime, and the change they cause in American language and culture. But they are invisible in the other four functions of the media. Asian Americans, who make up 4 percent of the U.S. population, and Native Americans, who are 1 percent to 2 percent of the total, don't have media parity at all. They are the invisible people. Gays and lesbians show up only in surveillance largely because of the same-sex marriage issue. Before the Sept. 11, 2001, terrorist attacks, Muslims, who represent about 6 percent of the population, were largely invisible, too. But in this post-Sept. 11, 2001, world in which we live, Muslims now show up in surveillance. People who are Muslim have said they were quite happy when they were invisible compared to how they have to live with media surveillance now. By the way, more than a third of the Muslims in the United States are African Americans. To the government and the media, they have become a super-class of those Muslims suffering undue surveillance.

What's interesting is how women fare in the five media functions. They represent about 52 percent of the population but show up in representative numbers only in the surveillance function because they are so dainty and helpless they must be watched. Women show up in representative numbers in entertainment as they play mostly second fiddle to men. They surface large in economic service because women control 80 percent of the purchases in all households in this country, amounting to trillions of dollars. Advertising, which is part of the economic function, includes not only the products and services valued in the community, but often also images of the people who are the ideal consumers of those products and services.

The negative or deficient depictions of minorities burden them with negative and deficient outcomes throughout their lives. They always have to prove stereotypes wrong. The majority doesn't carry that burden.

For the sake of thoroughness in examining segments of our population, it's important to ask where white males show up in the five media functions. They represent only about one third of the U.S. population. But they dominate and remain the majority populating the media. They control the images. It is no secret that they show up in all five of the media functions in numbers that are representative of their percentage of the population. And that's great. That's how it should be. White males give themselves and everyone else an accurate depiction of people in their group. They have problems as surveillance notes, but correlation and transmission also reveal that there are also many problem-solvers among them and people whom we want our children and others in the community to emulate. Entertainment tells us that they are active in sports, comedy, dramas, singing, movies, theater and dancing. But entertainment is only one aspect of who they are. The economic function tells us they are among the producers, manufacturers, service providers and consumers that we are to revere. All of that is good. But the completeness of the image that white males give of themselves should be the same for everyone else, too.

An example of white male dominance in the media showed up in a National Urban League study titled "Sunday Morning Apartheid: A Diversity Study of the Sunday Morning Talk Shows" (in *State 2006*, pages 189-228). The 2005 report covering 18 months of programming showed that only 8 percent of the guests on major Sunday morning talk shows were African American. The study found that more than 60 percent of the programs had no black guests. The shows the study covered were: NBC's *Meet the Press*, ABC's *This Week*, CBS's *Face the Nation*, Fox television's *Fox News Sunday*, and CNN's *Late Edition*. *Meet the Press*, the talk show with the largest number of viewers, had no black guests on 86 percent of its broadcasts, the study found. The Urban League noted that the Sunday talk shows are important because they help people digest political issues, domestic concerns, and international conflicts such as the Iraq war. Because few African Americans are included, their views overall go largely unheard.

Deficiencies in the depictions of people of color in the five media functions should be viewed as opportunities to enlarge those coverage areas. I call that The Peculiar Rule: when I was the bureau chief of a suburban office, my reporters were responsible for covering a small, white, Missouri town called Peculiar. The reporters didn't do stories often about people who lived there, but we knew we could not ignore them. They had to be in the pages of *The Kansas City Star* for news about that city and its residents. So on a regular basis, I had the reporters write about Peculiar, so the people of that community would see themselves and others would see them. The same thing must apply for people of color, so they appear in all five media functions in numbers relative to the percentage of their population.

What's fascinating is the public's perception of people of color would change dramatically if minorities were to show up only in the economic, correlation and transmission areas of the five media functions. They would rocket from being society's problem people who as a group are to be suspected, doubted, mistrusted and avoided, to individuals who are highly sought, for they can benefit everyone because of their merit and their mettle.

Yet that's not what the media images portray. Katheryn K. Russell wrote in her book, *The Color of Crime: Racial Hoaxes, White Fear, Black Protectionism, Police Harassment and Other Macroaggressions* that the overpowering, consistent and persistent negative images of "Black deviance" have been "seared into our collective consciousness.... Images of everyday Black life are overridden by images of Black deviance" (3). She added:

> The public's perception's [sic] that crime is violent, Black, and male have converged to create the *criminalblackman*. By itself, this mythical criminal Black figure is scary enough. However, the figure has become ominous because we do not have anything to compare it with. There is no *criminalwhiteman*. There is every reason to believe that if more images of White criminals and White criminality were put in the media spotlight, the public image of crime would change. The damage of this Black stereotype, however, cannot be undone simply by highlighting White crime. The media and the academic community will also have to expose the *criminalblackman* stereotype as a misrepresentation. (114)

Steven F. Gray adds Hispanics to the color of crime. He says "we accept as norm . . . whites being mugged by blacks and Hispanics." *Journalism Across Cultures* notes that the media contribute to that image and continue to stumble when it comes to showing Latinos in America. The book notes that a 1995 study by the National Association of Hispanic Journalists found that only 1 percent of the 12,000 stories aired on television the previous year focused on Latinos or Latino issues: "Of these, 35 percent covered crime; 22 percent, affirmative action; and 22 percent immigration. The next most frequent category was welfare. In other words, more than 75 percent of the news about Latinos focused on problems consistently evoking negative images" (53).

Nationwide rallies in 2006 for immigrant rights attracted millions of mostly Hispanic people. The media covered them largely as anti-American screeds in response to a December 2005 House bill that would have criminalized illegal immigrants and those who hire or help them. National Public Radio directly stated in some broadcasts that those at the rallies were immigrants. Nothing could be further from the truth. People at the rallies displayed pro-American feelings in the flags they waved, the Statue of Liberty crowns they wore, and the speeches they made. Even their protest signs were pro-American. They want to fit in and be counted, not criminalized.

The rising percentage of Hispanics in many cities throughout America creates many opportunities and challenges.

<u>From "The rising voice of Hispanics"</u>

> For one, economic exploitation continues to follow the Hispanic population gains, said Juan Jose Gutierrez, a Los Angeles immigration lawyer, at a Latino Civil Rights Summit in 2001.
>
> "Politicians want the labor to be here," he said. "They just don't want the labor to have any rights."
>
> U.S.-based multinational corporations profit from America's borders being opened in our global village. "But why should we have a situation where businesses don't have borders but people do?" Gutierrez said.
>
> That double standard is twisted into racist rhetoric seen recently in anti-Mexican immigration ads that ran in *The Kansas City Star* and on television. A group called the Coalition for the Future American Worker paid for the ads.
>
> I also saw it in a Fox television newscast and in *The Charlotte (N.C.) Post* stories I read about black people using ugly language to describe Hispanics. That is unconscionable, and it has to end. African-Americans can't afford to victimize other minorities the way blacks have been victimized.
>
> "On this whole issue of immigration, the peddlers of evil are trying to divide us again," Gutierrez said. "Today we have all these undocumented workers - the modern-day slaves – that's what they are."
>
> Gutierrez said the U.S. Border Patrol arrests and deports 1.5 million people a year. He said thousands of people have been killed crossing from Mexico. Hispanics pay U.S. taxes yet they're fearful and don't speak up for their rights.
>
> African-Americans point to Rodney King, James Byrd Jr. and Amadou Diallo as blacks who were beaten or killed in white America. Hispanics have Esequiel Hernandez Jr., 18, who was herding goats on May 20, 1997, when he was shot to death by a Marine patrolling the U.S.-Mexican border for drug traffickers, Gutierrez said.
>
> Michael Rodriguez, with the Mexican American Legal Defense and Educational Fund, said deportation divided families. Hispanics also are illegally being denied public education and are required to show identification that no one else is asked to produce.
>
> "We're entitled to keeping our families together," he said. "We are entitled to justice."

But some people have a different view of justice and don't think Hispanics or African Americans deserve such equal rights:

E-mail: May 4, 2001

The title says it all. What rights do criminally present persons deserve?

The Hispanics' work ethic has displaced many blacks in the job market, hence the ugly language used by some blacks to describe them.

Some of the problems they have stem from their reluctance to learn and use the English language and to adapt to the social mores of the country they chose to enter. The blacks share the latter problem in not adapting to the mores of the society in which they live and at least claim to want to share.

The reason blacks and Hispanics are increasing in numbers is irresponsible breeding, which in the Hispanic community is partially explained by their dominant religion. Irresponsible breeding aggravates most continued poverty throughout the world and even in Kansas City.

I think the Hispanics will do well if they refuse to adopt the "poor little picked on me" attitude espoused by the current black leaders.

Justice will be served when everyone gets the real picture of Hispanics, and all Americans make them feel welcome. People should help Latinos plug in their best talents so they, too, can feel good about working to keep this country strong. And people must recognize that for Hispanics to be productive they must be accorded all of the constitutional guarantees that everyone else should enjoy.

The media also do women a disservice in depicting them inaccurately. Women show up in representative numbers in only three of the five media functions, and then their portrayals are often dramatically distorted.

From "Media bear responsibility for dysfunctional views of women"

Media images of males and females have changed in response to women's growing power and influence in today's society.

But the changes haven't necessarily been accurate or good, Jackson Katz told hundreds of people at the University of Missouri-Kansas City. As a matter of fact, the media's reflection of males and females in society has been cartoonish.

Katz, founder of the Mentors in Violence Prevention Program at Northeastern University, used slides showing that women often appear in the media as thin and waifish. He contends that those images deflate women's importance in the world. But men are shown as well-tapered and bulging with muscles. That exaggerates their dominance, power and control, Katz said.

Women are seen as less threatening, compared with men, who often are pictured as more violent. Other slides showed that as men have been pictured as more imposing and formidable in the last 50 years in the media, they also have brandished bigger guns with more killing power.

The images Katz showed went from Humphrey Bogart with a .38-caliber revolver; to James Bond with a long-barreled automatic; to Clint Eastwood as Dirty Harry with a Magnum; to Sylvester Stallone as Rambo with a machine gun; to Arnold Schwarzenegger as the Terminator with a massive weapon.

"His whole body is a killing machine," Katz said. Katz's 2005 Starr Symposium lecture was titled "Pump It Up! Men and Masculinity: The Media's Impact on Relationships and Families."

The changes in men's and women's media images affect outcomes for each in society.

"The media is such an unbelievably important institution in our culture," Katz said. "The great pedagogical force in our time is the media."

The media speak to people more than anything or anyone else. They influence children and families and inculcate everyone with the standards of our highly commercialized culture.

Katz played misogynistic rap video clips of scantily clad, rump-shaking women. Men threw money into some females' gyrating pelvis areas. In one clip, a rapper ran his credit card down a thong-wearing woman's backside.

Such media images mute women's voices and commodify females as sex objects that can be bought and sold. It's a 21st-century slave culture, Katz said.

"All the things that influence me influence my parenting of my son," Katz said. "The media is much more overarching. It profoundly affects all of us."

The media help normalize male dominance and sanction the use of force. "Boys and men act violently because part of being a man is acting violently and maintaining control," Katz told the audience of mostly women.

In the last decade that I've attended Starr Symposium lectures sponsored by the UMKC Women's Center and Women's Council, I've always wished more men would be in the audience. Katz said men hear the word "gender" and automatically figure it's not about them.

It's no different from some white people hearing the word "race" and assuming it's a discussion meant only for minorities. But white people and men need to be part of such dialogues, too.

Some gender concerns involve issues of rape, sexual assault, molestations, domestic violence and stalking. Katz said more than 99 percent of the perpetrators are men. "But it's a women's issue?" he asked. The numbers show men must be part of gender discussions. Right now, girls and women are taught how to avoid being assault victims.

"This is not prevention," Katz said. "This is risk reduction."

Some girls and women will still suffer sexual assaults.

"These are people issues," Katz said. "Domestic violence is not just a women's problem. It's everyone's problem."

Change will happen when men speak up. "It could be transformative," Katz said.

But some men speak up and make matters worse:

From "Taunts can't mask lack of leadership"

Arnold Schwarzenegger's "girlie man" label recently landed on me.

I was not surprised. California's Republican governor used the slur on lawmakers in his state because of budget delays, and he never apologized for the remark.

Schwarzenegger spat the insult again at the 2004 Republican National Convention in New York saying, "To those critics who are so pessimistic about our economy, I say, 'Don't be economic girlie men.'"

Callers and letter writers put the label on me after columns I wrote criticizing President Bush for limiting stem-cell research and for getting America to turn corners leading to economic, political and international trouble.

The girlie man insults show how national media buzz phrases get picked up and regurgitated by everyday people as if they were original thoughts.

Combined with the gay marriage wedge issue, the masculinity question has been a Republican weapon of mass destruction against the Democrats. Meanwhile, GOP spin doctors keep injecting Bush's image with megadoses of testosterone and steroids, showing him on battleships, in flight gear and with U.S. troops.

Robert N. Minor in his book, *Scared Straight*, explains why: "In our national culture, 'masculine' traits define our ideal of leadership. 'Masculinity' is in charge of our public life. Our institutions, from the military, to government, to corporate board-rooms, are identified with conditioned masculinity."

Boys and men who are chastised for "not being man enough" must respond to disprove the accuser. "To recover from the shame of the initial threat to his manhood, [male victims of accusations of feminine behavior feel] it is necessary to display an even more 'manly' reaction than the one that threatened him," Minor wrote.

But that also shows how the girlie man label is a propaganda tool pushing people to accept Republican domination.

Media corporations like Fox and conservative talk shows have been more effective than Pravda in skillfully manipulating the public to play along.

Bob McChesney, author of *The Problem of the Media,* said in the video *Outfoxed:* "The first rule of being a great propaganda system and why our system is vastly superior to anything in the old Soviet Union is to not let people think they are being subjected to propaganda. If people don't think that, they aren't looking for that, they're much easier to propagandize.

"And that's the genius of our media system. It's a system of ideology, of control compared to an authoritarian system."

The media messages aren't just in the news. In programming they come at us strongest in advertising. Tony Ramos, a world-renowned artist who lives in France, said at a 2006 forum in Kansas City, Mo., that advertising recruits, trains, and employs the best artists, photographers, writers, psychologists, sociologists and anthropologists to craft irresistible messages for products and services. Consumers are mostly unaware of the whispering high art that gets in their head and influences their judgment.

From "Harmful reflections; Some ads create pictures of perfection that are unattainable for women"

Advertising also continues to promote unhealthy images of girls and women.

The audience of hundreds of people gasped in the darkness at the University of Missouri-Kansas City when Jean Kilbourne showed slides of advertisements featuring women and girls.

One ad had a caption saying, "Put Some Weight On." It featured a desperately thin woman with a watch band that easily fit around her right arm near her shoulder. The ad was selling the watch, but it promoted a sick, ghostly image of women.

Another ad for jeans showed three men attacking a woman. It suggested that women have to be assaulted to feel irresistible to men.

A third ad with a casually dressed woman said, "Score high on nonverbal skills," suggesting that women are most alluring when they wear the right clothes and are quiet.

"Girls, seeing these images of women, are encouraged to be silent, mysterious, not to talk too much or too loudly," Kilbourne wrote in her book, *Can't Buy My Love: How Advertising Changes the Way We Think and Feel.*

The dozens of slides she presented were part of her lecture titled, "The Naked Truth: Advertising's Image of Women."

Her assignment at the Starr Symposium was to make people more aware of the media's effects so they'll know how to counter them. The toxic environment "sacrifices our health and our kids' health for corporate profits," said Kilbourne, an internationally recognized author, lecturer and filmmaker on women's image in the media.

Yet people think they can simply tune out the ads without the messages having any effect. Kilbourne said that's not possible. Only 8 percent of any advertising message is received by the conscious mind. The rest works its way into the recesses of individuals' psyches.

Ads cleverly affect people's decisions as consumers. Advertising dictates that the most important thing for women is how they look. But the ads present picture-perfect images of women that few individuals can achieve.

"Failure is inevitable," Kilbourne said. Then she showed a slide of an ad with a woman in it. "She has no scars or blemishes. Indeed, she has no pores!"

The audience laughed. Cosmetics and airbrushing remake people into perfection.

Technology now allows an ad to feature the head of one woman, the hands of another and the legs and breasts from other women. "No one can achieve this ideal standard of beauty and of worth," Kilbourne said.

Yet people try because advertising has made that our societal norm. "You can't opt out of being judged against this standard," she said.

Kilbourne showed slides of ads featuring little girls heavily made up, wearing tight clothes and positioned in sexy poses and women dressed and posed to look like little girls. The ads tell girls to grow up fast and women to remain girls. They send mixed and destructive messages to girls, women, boys and men.

Some advertising trivializes sex, causes social isolation, affects people's ability to have relationships and to be truly intimate. "We end up being half or less than we otherwise might be," Kilbourne said.

Many ads sexualize products and objectify women. That creates a climate for widespread violence against women, she said.

"It's part of a climate in which women are seen as a thing," Kilbourne said. "It's very difficult to abuse a human being. But when a person is dehumanized and seen as less than human then violence becomes inevitable."

Men and women might recognize the absurdity of advertising objectifying women if jock straps and men's underwear were marketed like Wonder Bras, Kilbourne said.

Meanwhile, America must join other developed nations, ensuring that people become more media literate so they'll be aware of the messages embedded in advertising. It's a public health concern, Kilbourne said.

What's at stake is people's ability to have absolute authority over their lives.

One minority group that now is trying to harness the power of the media to their own potential benefit is the Muslim community.

<u>From "Unmasking myths is taxing for Muslims"</u>

In the years following the Sept. 11, 2001, tragedy, the American Muslims created their own media, Bridges TV, to undo misconceptions people have of them. It's one of many actions they're taking to help show people who they really are.

Too many people since the Sept. 11, 2001, tragedy have instantly assumed that Muslims are terrorists.

To help counter that stereotype, the Council on American-Islamic Relations also had a yearlong advertising campaign called "We're All Americans." The first ad ran in *The New York Times.*

The ad had images of an Asian man, a white man and an African-American girl and asks, "Which one of us is a Muslim?" The answer: "We all are ... we're American Muslims."

Such messages help promote greater understanding and counter anti-Muslim sentiment.

The State of Black Kansas City 2002 calls such extra efforts a "cultural tax." White people are exempt, but minorities pay this toll in extra time, resources and money to combat stereotypes.

The cultural tax includes serving on diversity committees, mentoring young people and being the group's representative or spokesperson. Like African Americans and Hispanics, American Muslims have been paying a heavy cultural tax, too.

"Muslims themselves saw they needed to come out and be part of society," said Javid Talib, then-president of the Crescent Peace Society.

American Muslims like Mahnaz Shabbir have given speeches on their culture, convened community prayers for peace and participated in such events as the Central Zone Conference of the Islamic Society of North America. It's where Jamal Badawi, founder of the Islamic Information Foundation, told a banquet audience in Overland Park that Islam embraces kindness, justice, love, respect and the plurality of society.

"A Muslim should busy himself or herself first with the love of humanity," he said. The Qur'an teaches that they should be about "peace, not war; love, not hate; human brotherhood, not conflict."

Yet, American Muslims nationwide have had to contend with negative media labels, disparaging statements by some Christian leaders, racial profiling, hate crimes, discrimination and having their names on government watch lists.

Such indignities cause embarrassment, shame and anger. Many American Muslims like African Americans and Hispanics respond by paying the higher cultural tax. They spend more time away from

> home and work to get people to see the truth about them.
>
> The cultural tax is not fair or just, but for now, it is the only way Muslims and people of color can hope to gain acceptance and feel welcome in this diverse country that is their home.

The media remain a huge sentry valiantly helping to maintain the color line. The words in the television programming and news serve to maintain the established order regardless of how much the right wing and its farther right cousins denounce the press for being liberal.

How do we overcome this? People must first realize that this ongoing status quo, non-inclusive encampment exists, and that it is at the heart of inaccurate and deficient coverage of people of color by the entire journalism industry. One solution is for all journalists to expand their résumé of personal and professional experiences, so they can better empathize with all people they must cover.

Another solution was proposed in 1978 by the American Society of Newspaper Editors (ASNE). Its goal was to have the percentage of journalists of color equal the percentage of minorities in the U.S. population. Newspapers, however, have fallen far short. The 2006 ASNE report found that only 13.87 percent of the newsroom jobs were held by journalists of color. It dropped in 2007 to 13.62 percent, marking only the second time since 1978 that the percentage actually dipped. The first decline was in 2001. The news media slippage happened despite minorities comprising more than a third of the U.S. population. The 2006 report also noted that only 37.7 percent of jobs were held by women journalists even though women make up 52 percent of the U.S. population. The number of women in newsroom jobs dropped to 37.5 percent in 2007. News industry experts know that it's not just a newspaper employment problem. Newspapers with no or few journalists of color are less likely to cover stories accurately or at all. Stories about issues involving people of color in the communities they serve are less likely to be considered stories. Unaddressed, the problems fester and the public's misinformed views and biases are allowed to grow. The goal remains important and must never be abandoned to ensure that the stereotypes are countered with the truth.

There is an additional, mechanical essence of race about the media. In photography light must be measured to obtain the correct exposure. Better cameras are equipped with light meters that read the amount of light needed for images to show up in the right density on the film. Many cameras today are automatic so the user merely has to point and shoot. However, the right shutter speed and aperture of the lens is determined measuring the light on what Charles Swedlund's book, *Photography: A Handbook of History, Materials, and Processes,* calls the Kodak Gray Scale (87). The light is divided into a value scale of 10 zones, moving from white at zero to gray in the middle range to black at 10. A "gray test card" is used to assist the light meter in getting the best reading of what is to be photographed. It is the middle gray. Barbara Upton and John Upton note in their book, *Photography*:

> You can often find an object with a similar tone and in similar light nearby that can be metered instead.
>
> One object always with you that can be metered is the palm of your hand. Average light-toned skin is about one stop brighter than the middle-gray brightness for which meters calibrate an exposure, so if your skin is light, give one stop more exposure than the meter indicates. If your skin is dark, use the indicated exposure. Metering your palm is a good technique when you are photographing in a fast-moving crowd situation. (130)

The medium is designed to photograph white skin, which is why people of color often appear unnaturally dark in photographs. So even the very film that journalists use isn't inclusive. Good photographers know that they must make adjustments to allow for longer exposures and more light so that the skin tones of African Americans, Native Americans, Hispanics and Asian Americans turn out the way that they should.

But people in other aspects of the media must also make adjustments when interviewing, taking notes, writing, editing and displaying stories, pictures and art about people of color for publication so that what runs is void of appearing as if it's being projected from a male, Eurocentric perspective. The first step is to recognize the need to do so. Anything less is deficient.

◊◊◊◊◊

The blanket of silence the media maintains covers Native Americans, Asian Americans, Hispanics, the homeless, people who are poor, people with disabilities, young people, older people, gays and lesbians. Yet each adds to the richness of America. Each also is more than any of the enduring stereotypes and because of the history and heritage embodied in their stories, each is more than just a color or what people see on the surface.

The good news is many media companies are training their staffs to value diversity and to appreciate the richness of America's multicultural population. *The Kansas City Star* is among the leaders in the newspaper industry. These media businesses are trying to include the full range of stories of people of color in the mainstream press. It makes good business sense. The stories, because they have never been told, represent news. Because they are different, they add to the knowledge that people in the mainstream have of their neighbors with whom they live and work. The "news" would also be fascinating because it would be different from the same traditional, boring fare, which would further encourage people to pay attention to the new information. The media must value and project the truth about diversity, offering it as "*news*" now. As noted in *The Annals of the American Academy of Political and Social Science: The African American Male in American Life and Thought:*

> The aim is to tell the truth and give the public a fuller and more accurate picture of all the people of this nation. Perhaps more important is more print and broadcast media are training, recruiting, hiring and promoting more African Americans and other people of color. This will enable the media to do a better job of telling the stories of African Americans from the historical perspective of being black in America. Dr. Carter G. Woodson, wrote years ago [in his book, *The Mis-Education of the Negro*], (p.180) "As an English abolitionist said more than a century ago, 'The portrait of the Negro has seldom been drawn but by the pencil of his oppressor, and the Negro has sat for it in the distorted attitude of slavery.'" (124)

Farai Chideya wrote in *Don't Believe the Hype: Fighting Cultural Misinformation about African Americans:*

> Pointing out times that the media has misrepresented the African-American community can only make the media better. Pointing out issues and problems facing the African-American community, no matter how painful, can only make the community better. The media belongs to all of us. If we want it to work, we have to work. (11)

This book, and the columns that comprise it are intended to push the truth in front of Americans to help end their existential victimization. Think of this as a 21st century payment in the reparations owed to all people of color. Randall Robinson described it in his book, *The Debt: What America Owes to Blacks:*

> Once and for all, America must face its past, open itself to a fair telling of all its peoples' histories, and accept full responsibility for the hardships it has occasioned for so many. It must come to grips with the increasingly indisputable reality that this is not a white nation. Therefore it must dramatically reconfigure its symbolized picture of itself, to itself. Its national parks, museums, monuments, statues, artworks must be recast in a way to include all Americans—Native Americans, Hispanic Americans, Asian Americans, African Americans as well as European Americans. White people do not own the idea of America, and should they continue to deny others a place in the idea's iconograph, those others, who fifty years from now will form the majority of America's citizens, will be inspired to punish them for it. (173-174)

CHAPTER 7

Hate: The Worm in the Apple Pie of America

Enduring

A hero in my eyes, one of diversity's longtime champs
Felt suddenly, terribly wounded because she had been unjustifiably stamped
A racist over something misinterpreted
In a place where she had worked
By a black newcomer who felt she was an insensitive jerk
A discussion ensued days later with friends trying to explain
It sort of settled things,
Sort of, but the pain
For my Latina friend remained.
And she said something profound as she often does
"I have to find a place to put this" so she could go on just because
And that's how I view the spitting hate from those who always mean well
They've just been "carefully taught" differently from all that I can tell
To embrace stereotypes, share prejudices and act with discrimination
To exclude people who aren't white in this always diverse nation
And bark in a "how dare you" voice when someone challenges such foul notions
As being far from the truth but a paralyzing and wounding, damaging potion
For people of color, for lesbians and gays
For people with disabilities, the poor, the homeless and others who stray
From the mainstream of what schools and media tell us is just and right
All of the wholesome goodness of America is always pictured as white
So I've been "finding a place to put this" terrible pain
Remaining open to feeling what these "good" folks call sane
And not avoiding diverse topics or developing thick skin
For I need to know how the damaging America feels to try to make it end
So like my Latina friend I continue to champion
Diversity's cause. Wash away the blood, the muck and the spit and go on.

Not Ready To Make Nice
Taking The Long Way (2005)
The Dixie Chicks
It's a sad sad story when a mother will teach her
Daughter that she ought to hate a perfect stranger.
And how in the world can the words that I said
Send somebody so over the edge
That they'd write me a letter
Sayin' that I better shut up and sing
Or my life will be over . . . .

Juan M. Rangel Jr., then-executive director of the National Conference for Community and Justice, once explained to me that a quarter of the population is progressive and truly is working for racism to end. But at the other extreme, a quarter of the population is dead set on maintaining the status quo, doggedly reinforcing racism. In the middle of the continuum are people whom Rangel called "bystanders." They are perched to go either way. The danger in these retro times is that more are moving toward a less inclusive, more hateful America and feel that that is justified and good.

For more than 30 years people upset with the gains of the Civil Rights Movement have been chipping away at efforts to end school segregation, improve inner-city public education and continue affirmative action and programs left over from the Great Society that were meant to eradicate poverty. They have stolen the playbook from the Civil Rights Movement, capturing the media's attention and anchoring their efforts in fundamentalist churches. The conservative media create the buzz and win converts; the churches create a sense of righteousness beyond mere earthly pursuits. It makes the Conservative Juggernaut seem impossible to refute. They have also taken over the AM, or what I call the "angry man" radio band and filled it with conservative talk shows that continue the dictate against people of color, but in a coded fashion. The hosts and their followers yearn for the "good old days" in America of exclusiveness, stereotypes and widely accepted prejudices. They continue the epic, historical fight against diversity—against the Real America.

The voices of anger and hate are like the ghosts from the worst times in this country. The physical lynchings of 4,742 black men and women between 1882 and 1968 have been replaced by the 21st century verbal lynchings that take place every day and are directed at those who dare to tell of the Real America. The parallels are many and stark. In *Without Sanctuary: Lynching Photography in America,* Leon F. Litwack writes about the perpetrators of lynchings, quoting a leading Atlanta newspaper: These people are "orderly and conservative, the descendants of ancestors who have been trained in America for 150 years. They are a people intensely religious, homeloving and just. There is among them no foreign or lawless element" (10). Litwack goes on to describe them as "ordinary and respectful people, few of whom had any difficulty justifying their atrocities in the name of maintaining the social and racial order and the purity of the Anglo-Saxon race" (19). A Meridian, Miss., newspaper noted, "The men who do the lynchings . . . are not men who flout law but men who sincerely believe they have the best interest of their fellow men and women at heart" (20). Their efforts were directed at maintaining "white supremacy, [while] some also perceived and expressed alarm over the destabilization of the social order and the descent of their region into anarchy and barbarism" (22).

The same is true of people now whose verbal violence wounds, disables and kills the spirit of people of color. Those who express today's hateful views aren't backward bumpkins but law-abiding and upright citizens. Many are articulate, thoughtful caring people who have taken the time to write or phone. These individuals see themselves as being part of the core of middle America, and they are. And they regularly express alarm about what they believe to be the violent and immoral nature of those who are "not like them." They base their beliefs on what they see in the media. They don't dare venture outside of their mostly segregated communities to discover the truth. The media cause them to place the blame for minorities' transgressions, crime, poverty, and a host of other problems almost invariably at the feet of the minorities themselves, and they wonder out loud, without a hint of irony, why those people have not been able to become more mainstream, to toe the (mainstream) line. Although they are sometimes sympathetic to the problems, their sense of superiority is unmistakable, as *Without Sanctuary* notes of a more brutal period of American history.

Using blacks as an example, racism and the viewpoint that African Americans are "inferior" have long, hungry roots. *Without Sanctuary* notes: "The Negro as beast became a fundamental part of the white South's racial imagery, taking its place alongside the venerated and faithful Sambo retainer, and whites were perfectly capable of drawing on both to sustain their self-image. Blacks, after all, possessed a dual nature: they were docile and amiable when enslaved or severely repressed, but savage, lustful, and capable of murder and mayhem when free and uncontrolled—like the blacks who had grown up since the Civil War" (23). *Without Sanctuary* also points out what got black people lynched in the 19th and 20th centuries:

> Many of the transgressions by blacks would have been regarded as relatively trivial if committed by whites and were not grounds anywhere else for capital punishment: using disrespectful, insulting, slanderous, boastful, threatening, or "*incendiary*" language; insubordination, impertinence, or improper demeanor (a sarcastic grin, laughing at the wrong time, a prolonged silence); refusing to take off one's hat to a white person or to give the right-of-way (to step aside) when encountering a white on the sidewalk; resisting assault by whites; "*being troublesome generally*"; disorderly conduct, petty theft, or drunkenness; writing an improper ("insulting") letter to a white person; paying un-

> due or improper attention to a white female; accusing a white man of writing love letters to a black woman; or living or keeping company with a white woman; turning or refusing to turn state's evidence; testifying or bringing suit against a white person; being related to a person accused of a crime and already lynched; political activities; union organizing; conjuring; discussing a lynching; gambling; operating a "*house of ill fame*"; a personal debt; refusing to accept an employment offer, "*jumping*" a labor contract; vagrancy; refusing to give up one's farm; conspicuously displaying one's wealth or property; and (in the eyes of whites) trying to act like a white man. (24-25)

Taken metaphorically or literally, many if not all of these actions by blacks are similar to what draws fire in negative electronic feedback directed at journalists of color who write on issues of diversity.

Today, letters, e-mail and voice mail serve the function that cameras used to when they "memorialize[d] lynchings," capturing and delivering the crowds' fearsome message to "independent-minded black men and women who had not yet learned the rituals of deference and submission" (Litwack 10-12). "The idea, after all, as one black observer noted, was to make an example, '*knowing full well that one Negro swinging from a tree will serve as well as another to terrorize the community*'" (16)—intimidation writ large—and the distasteful feedback that many journalists of color writing about diversity in the mainstream press get today is similar in its intent to silence.

The people who send negative letters, e-mail, faxes and voice mail have let me know that they thoroughly enjoy it when I use some of their responses in follow-up columns. It makes them seem like the smiling people pictured in *Without Sanctuary*, who proudly dressed up and posed for camera shots around the bodies of the black men and women that they had brutally lynched. Both those pictures from about a century ago of "fine upstanding citizens" and the feedback that I too often get from a similar crowd are foul and ignoble.

This country has a "propensity to define race and the underclass through hateful language, and hateful acts," Hilton Als writes in *Without Sanctuary* (38, 39). The "hateful language and hateful acts" are fueled by fear and resentment, just as similar feelings today compel people to rail against the truth that America's diversity enhances all of us. Their purpose is to silence those who write about the diversity of the many degraded groups. The owners of the hateful feedback strive to keep the truth forever concealed and the barriers to discovering the Real America in good repair. In fact they partially succeed. The messages are so startling and jarring that few who are hammered by such hatred will speak of it to others.

Journalists of all colors often don't know what to do with the barrage of negative feedback they receive. An attorney specializing in sexual harassment said at a forum in the 1990s that companies are responsible for shielding their workers from such abuse both in the office and in the field. Such action is required to eliminate a hostile work environment, and companies that don't follow harassment policies are open to lawsuits. But journalists don't have that same luxury as people in other professions. Journalists have to remain open to receiving all information, including gender and racial harassment. Protection from it mutes a journalist's effectiveness. It also closes the door to trust, which must exist between editors and reporters so that the editors will hire reporters of color and then be assured that they will do well in any situation—even one that is electric with racism. One other benefit is such openness creates the opportunity for a dialogue if both parties are willing.

So how do journalists contend with encounters with racism, prejudice, discrimination and bigotry of the most subtle and obnoxious kind? Some laugh it off. Some throw it into "file 13." Some steer clear of doing stories that might cause them to get such reactions from the public. Others say they harden themselves to the inevitable onslaught. None of these reactions is beneficial.

The ugly responses are no laughing matter. The feedback leaves my soul at times feeling as if it has been lynched and left hanging from a poplar tree like those black men and women captured in the still shots that fill *Without Sanctuary* and like the mournful music Billie Holiday made famous when she sang "Strange Fruit." The angry voices, which are also part of the Real America forbidding the exploration of the wilderness of this nation's diversity, terrorize the spirit. They embody an angry mob like the one that kidnapped Emmett Till in 1955 from the safety and comfort of the black community, brutalized him, killed him and tossed his body away like trash. Yet I respond to each of their hateful calls, letters and e-mail when their authors give me that option. I have gone to breakfast, lunch and dinner with those who have wanted to talk more. I have met with them for coffee, tea and soft drinks. And I continue to do it regularly. For they must never be laughed off, pushed off or belittled as being ignorant or stupid. They have to be understood if there is to be any hope to counter the things they have learned and the heavy investment they have in the continuation of racism in America.

Throwing such terrible verbal assaults away won't make the words, the people who utter them, or the racism behind them disappear. Not doing stories about people of color isn't a good solution either and is terribly debilitating because then minorities are institutionally silenced. Laughing off or throwing away the feedback, or hardening oneself to the barrage eventually causes journalists to lose their sense and sensibility. They then don't recognize stories because of the shell they have built to protect themselves. Without the ability to listen and care, the reporters, editors and photographers will continue to neglect the stories about people who are different.

What must be done is to bring the negative barrage into the open so people can truly see how the sentries of the status quo manipulate reality. People must see the efforts that continue to turn back the clock, maintain the public and institutional investments in racism and ensure the continuation of the barriers to real progress. I tell people that I have to put myself in the shoes of a termite exterminator who tears up boards, pokes into narrow caverns and pounds hard on wood to search for signs of the damaging pests. When they scurry into view, the exterminator knows he has exposed the perpetrators. I feel the same way when negative feedback pours in showing that what I have written exposes the often hidden perpetrators of racism, discrimination, prejudice and bigotry in our society. Hidden from view, they make life intolerable for people who find themselves outside of the mainstream and whom the media define in a shorthand of stereotypes.

Plato said that as mere mortals we perceive reality as being like shadows projected on the wall inside of a cave. Only deities can perceive reality as it truly exists in its many dimensions and colors. Humans can't. We are left only with the shadows of what's truly real. Journalists and the media, however, perform a vital role in adding definition to the shadows. They describe the images from different angles, heights, distances and perspectives so that people viewing or reading what the media describe come away with a better impression of what reality must truly be like. That's when the media function at their best. However, conservatives pressure the media; the media limit the information disseminated to the public; and the people are existentially victimized. Therefore most people don't learn reality; misinformation and fear seem justified, causing angry voices to grow, and the dominance of whiteness and stereotypes is reinforced.

Throughout the book is an abundance of negative feedback inspired by the columns I have written on diversity. What follows is a bundling of the negative voices recorded in literally thousands of letters, e-mail messages, faxes and voice mail that I have saved over nearly 10 years of feedback. Delivering this compacted collection in one place irrefutably reveals the power and clarity of the voices against diversity. I have used much of this feedback in numerous diversity talks, and it speaks more convincingly of the need to discover the Real America than I ever could. None of what follows is repeated elsewhere in this book. The responses come equally from women and men. They are from older people and younger people. They are from affluent sections of town as well as poor communities. They also are from minorities themselves. Because of the wire services and the Internet, they also come from throughout the country in cities where other newspapers have run my columns. Many are far too foul to be printed in any mainstream newspaper. Of the small minority of responses that were positive, only a very few are included in this book.

If the voices of hate are allowed to go unexposed, unchecked, if they are allowed to continue to chew at the foundation of our society, then they will have won and the stereotypes and prejudices that have dogged this "New World" will continue to afflict each generation hereafter. It is important to be able to "hear" what these folks really are saying. It is important to deconstruct the messages, the emotions and reconstruct them into something that is intelligible. Often hidden in the anger and hatred is a question or a message pleading for the truth to be measured against the stereotypes these folks have always known. The truth is so much more important. It is the Real America that people must discover.

~~~~~~

You've Got To Be Carefully Taught
South Pacific (1958)
Rodgers and Hammerstein II

You've got to be taught to hate and fear
You've got to be taught from year to year
It's got to be drummed in your dear little ear
You've got to be carefully taught.

You've got to be taught to be afraid
Of people whose eyes are oddly made,
And people whose skin is a diff'rent shade
You've got to be carefully taught

You've got to be taught before it's too late
Before you are six or seven or eight,
To hate all the people your relatives hate,
You've got to be carefully taught!
~~~~~~

Editor's Note: Some of what follows has been edited for grammar, spelling and brevity. The editing was done with care, so as not to change the meaning of the message or the writers' passion or intent.

E-mail: April 2, 2004

Being a champion of diversity, you have lost your way. Your columns have zero diversity and are so predictable and one sided that they are irrelevant. One doesn't even have to read your columns to get your message. All a person has to do is skim through it and look for these catch words:

White person – racist
Minority person – repressed
White liberal – enlightened
Minority conservative – racist
Democrat – good
Republican – racist
Socialist – good
Capitalist – greedy
Poor – good
Upper middle class – bad
Private sector businesses – greedy
Union workers – good
Business owners – greedy
People on welfare – good
Depending on the government – good
Depending on yourself – bad
Public schools that fail – good
School vouchers – anti-union
Military – bad
United Nations – good

You could run the same column every week and no one would notice because they all have the same theme.

Shameless Racial Slurs

Voice mail: 1999

You don't have to go to St. Louis to find one of those destroyed 62-acre plots that was destroyed by cave people. We've got one here called Wayne Miner Court. We had the same experiences here where the city ran out of money and didn't have enough money to clean up the trash. And you people want integration? Good luck, nigger.

Voice mail: 2000

Is this Amos of Amos and Andy? Yeah, you've got it right kiddo. You spooks are puking at windmills. Thanks for another racist column.

Voice mail: Sept. 12, 2001

I was reading your article in the morning paper and the reason you don't understand is because you're a dumb liberal nigger. Thank you.

Voice mail: Oct. 19, 2001

Regarding your personal view that we need to pursue peace given what's happened, I think you're completely wrong. We have a situation that requires action. We're dealing with animals, not people. And the only way we are going to have peace is if we rid ourselves of the problem, and that means just going in and killing them. It's a sad state of affairs that we find ourselves in. But I think that's just the reality of the situation. I don't see that there's any other way to do it. You have your views, but I think you're wrong. We're doing the right thing.

E-mail: Dec. 10, 2001

Yet another realistic equation: Fried chicken plus sweet potato pie plus malt liquor equals one satisfied negro.

E-mail: Feb. 15, 2002

After the U.S. military cleanses the very backward stone-age Middle East of murdering terrorists who kill their own people and kill Americans, our plan may be to move on to Africa and free up another stone-age part of the world from warlords who have killed millions without Diuguid having expressed in writing any concern whatsoever!

After all, it was necessary for the U.S. military to do the same thing here in America 150 years ago where approximately 400 Indian "stone-age tribes" had been continually at war with one another. Warring people who held nightly blood sacrifices on hilltops. People who lived here for thousands of years and had not progressed or developed anything except arrows, clay pots, and basket weaving yet believing there were "spirits" in alcohol.

These backward native people certainly would not have been a match for the attacking Japanese or German war machines in 1941 – or would they?

Perhaps smoke signals, praying and negotiations would have scared the Japs away from Pearl Harbor and kept the German army from taking over Europe and Russia!

With The Diuguid flawed thought process, and with his very serious naïve fundamentalist, we think he would fit in very well living in backward times in the Middle East or in Africa.

It's funny that Lewis should write about the peace prize nomination for Bush and Blair. Diuguid's President Bill Clinton should have been given the piece prize. After all, who has had more "pieces" than former governor and President Clinton – who has now become the laughing stock of the free world.

E-mail: March 29, 2002

It's been a long while since one of you spear chuckers have incited me. You monkeys never learn do you? One hundred one of 114 counties passed concealed carry in the state of Missouri three years ago. You can go check that out if you're literate enough to research it. It was the 10 inner-city counties where your brethren were led by their nose rings where it failed. Even outer lying districts in Kansas City and St. Louis passed it.

It's going to be a long, long seven more years, Lewis, with President Bush in control and the NRA sitting there by his side. Hehehe. You juju's haven't thought through what's coming have you? The NRA and all us white honkies fully expect Holden to veto the upcoming bill. Then we will slide through our conceal carry with ease, and it won't matter a whit what you apes out in the trees think! Just think, Lewis! There's about 5.5 million citizens in the state, and you have what support in the Kansas City and St. Louis areas? Maybe a million of that? You apes are going to get out voted next time around, Lewis, and there's not a damned thing you can do about it. You should stick to scratching yourself and eating bananas.

I can see it now! Yard signs down in nigger town saying Chittlin Chewers Unite! We must strike down the great evil Satan, the NRA. Lewis, you must know it's a lost cause. The NRA is a well organized machine run by white men with computers and guns and at the right hand of the president of the United States! What can a bunch of monkeys down from the trees hope to accomplish against such great odds? Now go have some more ribs and watermelon and don't trouble yourself further. America is now in saner hands than the Clintonistas. You spear chuckers are back out in the cold on gun control. Please feel free to write many more columns on the subject at hand. You're a laugh a minute now just as Rush Limbaugh predicted. It's gonna be a painful seven years for you, Lewis, but the NRA is gonna enjoy every minute of it.

By the way, did you know Sarah Brady is getting ready to give up the ghost! It's a new day dawnin', Lewis, and you ain't gonna like any of it.

E-mail: Sept. 17, 2002

I have excellent news, Lewis. I know how you negroes can receive the reparations that you claim you deserve. All you need to do is move back to your filthy motherland. Page A-9 of Tuesday's *Star* states that the U.S. is giving $5 billion "assistance" every year to your aids-ridden motherland to "extricate Africa out of her long night of misery." To put that in terms that you people can understand, Lewis, $5 billion represents 416,666,667 slabs of ribs a year!! Boy, Lewis, after five years, that's 2,083,333,335 slabs of ribs!! I submit that 2,083,333,335 slabs of ribs would extricate a lot misery out of a lot of negroes.

E-mail: Oct. 30, 2002

Haitians. The news is reporting another 200 of the brothers arriving on the beach in Miami. Just what Florida needs... 200 more ignorant AIDS infested niggers!

E-mail: Feb. 26, 2003

I see you are back to quoting your ever credible sources as "Looney Lani Guinier and Angela Davis." What is this limp-wristed hack's claim to fame, an affirmative action degree from Bumfuck University? Your ignorance is only exceeded by your cowardice.

E-mail: July 15, 2003

Cadillac dealers nationwide laugh when they tell how black people will take a new or used caddy for a "test drive" and are gone for three hours showing their friends they finally have made it "big time" then they bring the car back to the dealers littered with Kentucky Fried Chicken boxes and bones. Same old story – all glitz!

Bottom line Lewis: The problem is not racism and it's not skin color – it's the culture of the black race. No success in America or even Africa.

E-mail: June 22, 2004

I see not only are you a nigger lover, you're also a faggot lover. Do you teach your children to be gay? Never mind. You and I could never get along. You don't have a love for the Confederate Army of America. I as a descendent of the South find the flag as a great source of pride and respect. You somehow find it offensive, however, if I was black (thank God I'm not) I would be very thankful that I didn't live in Africa. So please explain to me why you would rather be a loin cloth wearing native with some type of sexual disease than the journalist that you are? After all, since I have four daughters and no black friends they ask a lot of tough questions that I can't always answer. One is why would anyone want to be black? Not only in America but especially in Africa? Hope you can give me a reasonable answer to some very real questions!!!

Letter: Oct. 20, 2004

Four thoughts:

1. "A vote for (Democratic presidential candidate Sen. John) Kerry is a vote for evil."
2. What do you call something that's dark, obnoxious, weighs 275 pounds and is a bitch? Answer: Oprah!
3. What do you call something that's loud, dark and is just plain sickening? Answer: Jesse Jackson!
4. They found weapons of mass destruction: Al Sharpton's mouth.
5. Have a good day, Lew!

E-mail: May 27, 2005

Your denial leaves me sniggering, Lewis. I am not surprised that you do not wish to reveal your tribal origin. I don't blame you for being ashamed of your filthy jungle heritage. I understand your embarrassment. It must be so awful to be a negro. I feel your inner pain. It's so obvious that you wish you were white. Poor Lewis.

Letter: July 14, 2005

The unemployment figure of 26 percent for blacks tells the world something you will never understand. Niggers are essentially unemployable except for sports clowns and movie clowns, tire changers. Look at your heritage, Africa ha ha ha ha world class welfare basket case.

E-mail: Oct. 3, 2005

I think we should have picked our own cotton!

It appears our African friends have found something else to be pissed about. A black congresswoman reputedly complained that the names of hurricanes are all Caucasian (that would be white, as in European-Americans)- sounding names. She would prefer some names that reflect African -American culture such as Chamiqua, Moeisha, and Jamal. I can hear it now: A black weatherman in, say, Houston intoning, "Word up, Muthas! Hehr-i-cane Chamiqua be headin' fo' Galveston like Leroy on a crotch rocket! Bitch be a category fo'! So, turn off dem chitlins, grab yo' chirren, and head fo' de nearest welfare office."

Non Sequiturs: God, Gays and Race

Letter: April 7, 2004

The next time you take a stroll down the avenue with your Muslim friends, think about the true teachings from the Koran that motivates Islamic peoples. They are instructed to kill you because you are not a Muslim.

Go ahead. Have a peace talk with them.

Listen to God's word – The Bible.

Get some wisdom.

E-mail: Oct. 22, 2004

I am deeply saddened and hurt by your open animosity towards Christians. I respect that there are different schools of thought, but I would never openly attack folks that do not support my views. I find it ironic that you were at the soup kitchen to serve and while you were having this political conversation you were "interrupted by a man getting one of the free meals." Was that not your purpose for being there?

I get the distinct impression after reading your column that day that you have little use for people who have placed their faith in Jesus Christ as Lord and Savior. I am not sure if that is the message you wanted to promulgate, but that is certainly the way the article read.

I was especially shocked by your comment that read: "The wedge issues include prayer in school and the irrational demand for the Ten

Commandments to be on government property. Never mind the constitutional separation of church and state." You should research that separation of church and state.

Voice mail: Feb. 18, 2005

Confederate flag - Lewis, you really are a thin skin little baby boy.

Voice mail: April 23, 2004

I was seriously thinking about voting third party this year because I have really not been happy with a lot of things that Bush has done. But thanks to your article or in response to your article, I'm going to vote for Bush because I didn't realize what he did, you don't realize something until you take all things together and see a history, and I applaud President Bush for his protection of the unborn child from letting women kill their children. And so, I'm going to vote for him. As far as the AIDS issue is concerned, if a person would not let another male stick their penis up their anus they wouldn't get AIDS. It's impossible to get AIDS from normal heterosexual sex of a penis being inserted into the vagina. Impossible. The only way you can get it is from a penis being inserted up your anus. As far as contraception goes, if today's women would learn how to keep their legs closed they wouldn't need contraception. Anyway, Lewis, thanks for taking my comments. Bye.

Voice mail: June 11, 2004

Having read your entire editorial, I wonder why did you leave out the Bible and God? God the creator of everything says that homosexual sex is wrong. So apparently you can't blame it on culture or anything else if God said it was wrong, it's wrong. End of discussion.

Voice mail: June 11, 2004

I would just like to know have you considered the biblical connotations with lesbians and gays as they say? As a person as a heterosexual who is not scared of them I would mention that the purpose of marriage is for childbearing. I don't think two gays and lesbians can have children. OK, but that is just from the biblical standpoint and so I would like to know how you feel about that because from your column, I think maybe you just kind of went off on the deep end. Thank you.

Voice mail: March 16, 2005

It's not about hate. It's about same sex marriage, which is definitely a sin regardless of how you want to put it. These are Christian people. I'm just a little bit shocked that you believe in tolerance of sin. This is so sickening. Did you not realize that 13 other states ban same sex, and there are going to be more. It's a sin. Are you for children or are you against children? Who wants to raise children up in this horrible society when anything goes and there is no sense of right and wrong? Parents have a horrible, horrible, horrible job on their hands trying to get their children to do the right thing when it's so easy for them to have homosexual sex. It's just about sex.

Letter: July 22, 2005

While your article was published with good intentions I find you to be just as gullible as the rest of society when it comes to women and their claims of being victimized and abused.

Yes, I'm sure women are abused, but we must remember that man was created first and then a woman. It wasn't Adam that was deceived, it was Eve, and therefore women brought sin into the world. Women are deceptive and manipulative creatures who in most cases have learned to use their sex to control things or get what they want. But then when tables turn on them they are the first to run screaming "abuse," and with child or children in tow – everybody seems to feel sorry for them. "Hope House."

This happened to me a few times, and I assure you I was the victim. In the judicial system, men are considered nothing more than sperm donors, and (that's) why we get hit so hard with child support. Guys are even still made to pay when it is discovered the child isn't even theirs. We are just sperm donors and money coffers until some men do go over the edge from being done so unjustly by the judicial system.

I'll almost bet anything that most of the women in those Hope Houses come from immoral situations to begin with. Have illegitimate children – low education and/or trade skills and on some kind of welfare program? But yet it's all the man's fault.

E-mail: Sept. 21, 2005

It now appears that the hurricane is now heading toward Houston. Could God be following the black people who were bused from New Orleans to Houston or is the media and white people causing this?

Voice mail: November 2005

Racial Profiling: I guess you think you're above the law.

Voice mail: March 2006

You're not recognizing the fact that Islam is insensitive to Western culture also. You're just giving a one sided story here, sir. It's time you started giving both sides of certain issues that you take upon yourself especially important ones like this.

Voice mail: March 29, 2006

I just want to remind you that all of the people that attacked us on Sept. 11, 2001, were Muslims. I just want to remind you that there are Christians in the world, and our tax money was used to pay for an artist to urinate in a bottle and stick a cross in it and entitle his artwork, "Piss on Christ," our tax dollars were spent to send that exhibit all over America. But you did not see Christians rioting, burning, looting and killing. No, we didn't do that. No. But let a caricature of Muhammad be drawn and Muslims go around killing people. That is the difference. That's why Americans are suspect of the Muslim religion. They are so violent.

E-mail: March 29, 2006

Do your friends have comments about the "death to Christians" chants being shouted in the demonstrations going on now? I mean the demonstrations protesting the release of the Afghan citizen who faced a possible death penalty for the crime of converting to Christianity. There are clerics in the streets insisting that in Muslim law, the penalty for apostasy is death, and it must be enforced.

This kind of event tends to bolster the credibility of what the old world history textbooks I studied in high school said. That in Christian countries which were conquered by Muslim peoples, the choice was often "Koran tribute or the sword." Then again, maybe the holocaust and the Children's Crusade didn't happen either.

E-mail: May 24, 2006

I have read your articles over the last year and have come to the conclusion that you live in a land of dreams.

Today you crossed in to the land of "Laws are made to be broken." We have law that states that a person who enters this country without permission has broken the law and should be deported. We also have a law that any employer who hires a person who is not legally here is subject to fines per person per day. The problem is that our government has not enforced these laws and it is common knowledge to the world.

Had these laws been enforced we would not have 12 million illegal aliens in our country.

These aliens are taking the jobs the poor citizens would love to have at a decent wage. A wage that would have to be paid if the employers could not go down and pick up a truck load of aliens for less that normal wages. By the way these employers do not withhold taxes they pay in cash daily. This way there is no record for the IRS.

Please check some facts about these aliens before you embrace them. They fill schools for part of every year then take the children and families back to Mexico. You can check the facts by going to Armourdale and checking out the school there and talk with the people that live there.

They use our hospitals for free while here. They entered by sneaking across our border.

The Majority of Irish, Italians, and Jews all entered this country thru the legal way they immigrated and were called immigrants.

You do not understand why this country grew to be so great. All the immigrants before wanted a new life and a new chance for freedom. They left behind the old country and knew that to succeed in this new land they must become United States citizens and embrace its language and become Americans not Irish-Americans, not Polish-Americans, not English-Americans just Americans.

E-mail: June 28, 2006

You have a few good points. As usual though, everything is NOT ABOUT RACE or RACISM. I wish people would stop feeling that their own actions are not relevant to how they are viewed. If you are doing something illegal, it is not about race! We do not have to patrol the Canadian border better because Canadians aren't flocking to our country illegally! DUH! You made the point that we have two totally different bills that are being bandied about. Where is the middle ground? People like me (middle class, taxpaying) are tired of the far right and the far left, but that's all we get from our government and our newspapers. Most of us use something called common sense to make decisions. Why can't our politicians see that most Americans want that so-called middle ground, i.e. common sense.

I have friends who are of Mexican descent, some quite recently from Mexico. They feel the same way I do. If you are here illegally, you are breaking the law. Our ancestors had to go through customs, fill out paperwork so that they could be counted and LEARN THE LANGUAGE. We are the melting pot. But our pot is overflowing. We have thousands of people with no health insurance, people with no jobs and people with jobs living below the poverty level. Our jails are so full we are forced to build more jails! Our schools have so many kids with "special needs," including non-English speaking children that they cannot keep up with it all. Our hospitals are caring for people with no funds to pay for their care. All of these issues are increased by people who are here illegally.

As a taxpayer and one who pays my bills, I feel overwhelmed. Is it too much to ask that as an American citizen, our borders be closed to illegal crossing? That we find these criminals and deport them? Not put them in our already crowded jails! That when their children come to our schools, we ask for papers? We cannot be everything to every country and we need to stop trying, at least until we help our own citizens!

Thanks for letting me vent!

Voice mail: June 28, 2006

You had to pull out that infamous race card, didn't you? "The racial tinge to the anti-immigration noise also is disturbing. It's why a fence is being proposed and troops are on the border with Mexico and not Canada." Well Lewis, the last time I checked we don't have a bunch of Canadians crossing the border into America at least I haven't seen anything or heard anything about it lately. Maybe you have, and I'm not aware of it. These people are coming across in hoards, and you know it, down along the Mexican border, and you know that, so it was kind of absurd to say that.

You mention after that: "Another number is 41.3 million. That's a census estimate for the Hispanic population" in this country and they far exceed the number of over 65 Social Security recipients. Well, first of all those 41.3 million Hispanics here in America, a lot of them are children and they are not able to vote, OK. But these numbers that you cited these 35.2 million people on Social Security, they're all capable of voting. Plus that, plus the fact that out of these 41.3 million Hispanics, there's also a lot of Hispanics here illegally and can't vote in the first place, which brings me to the end of your column where you advocate that people who can vote must use the power to get rid of lawmakers.

Thoughtful Rants and Uninformed Assumptions

Voice mail: March 20, 1999

I am a white, lower-class woman. Yeah, I live in Johnson County, but not the one you're thinking of. Not the one you're familiar with. I live in Johnson County, Mo. I'm a single mother, college student. I think I claimed about $18,000 on my taxes last year so I guess the gold nugget of being white didn't work for me, yet. You know it's so discouraging every time you get an opportunity to play the color game you take full advantage of it. Well on my end of it I feel like there is enough affirmative action in the world that black people get pretty much things they don't always deserve. And I think there are a lot of white people pushed aside for that.

Voice mail: 2001

You should keep Christian anything and Jesse Jackson's name completely separate. You might as well take the reverend away from his name because to me a reverend is somebody who seeks to bring peace and goodwill to all men. And all that Jesse Jackson seems to do is incite ill-will among men. I truly believe Martin Luther King wanted to do what was best for African-Americans. No, I'm not an African American. But I did at least respect him. But I have none for Jesse Jackson. And it's about time that you guys realize that this man is trouble and quit putting him up on a type of pedestal.

E-mail: May 21, 2001

The next time you write about racism please think about the white doctors and nurses traveling to Africa year after year to help the African children because their African leaders refuse to do anything for them. As I write this, there are several teams working to get African babies inoculated against many diseases. You should acknowledge this fact. And you should mention they are white.

Many disfigured African children are adopted by the white nurses and doctors treating them. They're brought over here because they have a better chance at survival. When African leaders remove the hands of children, as we have seen on TV, we bring them to the United States, when we can get them out of the country. Yet, I have yet to hear the most vocal civil rights activists rant and rage regarding this carnage going on in Africa. It should be done on a daily basis, but there isn't too much money to be made as a result of this action. It's more popular to trash whites.

Perhaps if you would acknowledge the fact that there are good, decent whites out there, and don't be afraid to say they're white, there would not be a feeling of hopelessness among many young black adults.

There is a lot of good communication going on out here. Just because a person doesn't agree with you, or any other black on a particular subject, does not make the white a racist.

Voice mail: 2002

Lewis, I hope you can realize there is a natural tendency and desire among people to be with their own kind racially and culturally. They feel most comfortable that way. And this doesn't mean they hate anyone else. And they may look around now and then. But they want to be in their social relationships that are comfortable. And so this is going to continue. This is free America. Always remember that. Free America. Freedom of association. Freedom to chose those you wish to be around – not because you hate anyone, but because those of your own kind and culture racially, culturally and everything else, background-wise, those are the people you feel comfortable around when you have a little time to socialize. So please don't in any way ever indicate that this is wrong. This is natural, of nature, will always be the case and let people have what makes them comfortable, Lewis. This is free America. Free, free, free.

Voice mail: 2003

Lewis, you're not doing any good. Your opinion on two groups share entwined history is silly, man. What is this? The first premise is you're relying on someone from California State University. Isn't that the same university that gave us Ron Karanga, the guy who made up Kwanzaa? So how can we rely on any history from any professor from California State University? And the ending really says it all: "There's hardly any struggle anywhere in the world where we didn't have an ally," so in other words, blacks are looking for an ally in a struggle? Why not come together? Why not bring everybody together? The whites, the blacks, the Hispanics and let's all be friends. Let's build a nation instead of dividing the nation.

Voice mail: 2003

I'm tired of your articles about how the poor minorities are all so poor about everything. You know we all deserve universal health care. I'm a good citizen, paid my taxes, worked hard and I'm still paying back student loans. But I went back to school at the age of 45 to finish my college degree. It wasn't easy. I had three kids in school and I did it on my own. But I am getting really tired of this oh poor us. You know we work really hard around here. We're good citizens. It's time to quit saying one group doesn't get what the other one doesn't get and start working together and to truly be a good American instead of saying poor you because you're a different color than I am.

Voice mail: 2003

Is white flight due to the repugnance of my black skin or is it because our bodacious behavior is intimidating? It appears to me that our black leaders will not even examine the issue. I certainly would like for you to think about it, and thanks for listening.

Voice mail: 2003

I read your articles and so many times I notice that you write negative things basically about whites. And unfortunately I always think how come there's never anything ever written basically pointing the finger at blacks instead of whites. For example that terrible shooting over the weekend at that dance where that teenage girl got killed. You're terrible. It shows such a difference, the number of young blacks that are armed, armed with weapons ready to shoot at any moment and give no thought to it. That's one difference between blacks and whites as a whole and generally it is not likely to ever happen – not like that – at a white dance. That isn't to say that they are better. But why are these blacks so armed?

Voice mail: 2004

As a black American, I don't say African American because I have never been to Africa. I have African in me, but I have a lot of other stuff, too. I tell you what, I just think black people as a whole, we need to stop. We can't call names. We think we're going to get away with it. And then when the white man calls names, and then we jump on them. It doesn't work that way. It's got to be equalization for both sides. And I've said this for a long time. I was in a club, a prestigious club here in Kansas City, and we wouldn't let a white woman in. She adopted twin black girls. This one woman teaches at Shawnee Mission schools did not want her in. She said I hate white people. I'm shocked. I said how could you say that when you teach these children every day and you don't want the wife and husband to be in our club because they adopted two black children? And you say you teach them every day and you hate them? Now what if that had been taped? This is the thing that comes to mind. Now if a white person had said that, I hate black people, I don't want them in there, everybody would have gone off, the NAACP would have had their flags up going around with little banners up. We have to stop this. It doesn't work that way. I am 50 years old. It doesn't work that way. We need to stop it. We cannot call names and think we're going to get away with it. And when they call a name, we're out marching and carrying on. I'm for fairness.

Voice mail: Feb. 18, 2005

I think we're all in trouble when we look at all people of a particular color or shade of skin in one myopic way. All people of one skin color are not all the same way.

Voice mail: Feb. 18, 2005

It's a part of our tradition our culture to exhibit the Confederate flag whenever we choose to do so in a peaceful demonstration if we so choose. I am very proud of Missouri's southern heritage. We were the 12th star in the Confederate flag, and I'm very, very proud.

E-mail: March 17, 2005

1. Move out of your south Kansas City neighborhood and into a midtown home where people of all colors get along just fine. You need a reality check.
2. Visit an elementary school classroom in the district that you currently live in. You will notice that the children there do not view and judge the world through the color of each others' skin but the content of each others' character.
3. Stop attending on a regular basis the idealistic symposiums, lectures and get togethers of those who are more intellectually refined than the rest of us.
4. Get over the obsessed and maligned view that nothing has changed in race relations during the last 40 years. You will be happier. Here is a happy thought for you, I think, I probably hug at least 20 children of color every day. They thank me for caring about them and at times tell me they love me through their wonderful voices and pictures they draw. It is better now. And it is getting better all the time. It is never going back to what it was! Myself and many caring people who happen to be white (as if that matters) won't let it. Children of color hold many promises. They are succeeding. They are smart articulate individuals that have so much to offer this world. You will not have to wait much longer. They are on their way to make our world a better place. They are truly beautiful inside and out.
5. I am not sure if you are for real or not. If you are just trying to yank people's chains, shame on you. If you are actually sincere, then I do feel sorry for you. There is so much love in this community between all colors of people. You are missing out on it.

E-mail: Aug. 14, 2005

In your column this week about diversity you tell the story about a young American woman of Asian descent and how she was browbeaten until she "accepted" that she was NOT and American but rather an Asian-American.

This young lady was born in the United States. She was raised in the United States speaking English. She was never told that she was Chinese by her parents. She faced prejudice borne of lack of knowledge and the concept of division based on heritage. Her grandmother had issues with her looking too Chinese but I think that an objective person can see that as a misguided, dare I say ignorant (borne of a lack of understanding not of stupidity) attempt to help her granddaughter fit in. It sounds like even grandma wanted her to be an American. Miss Chin was not raised to be an Asian-American. So, why did she finally "embrac(e) the idea that (she is) Asian"? I think that it is because of all of the "enlightened" liberals who kept harping on her "heritage." Those who kept asking her whether she had "journeyed back home lately." Those who kept focusing on her Asian features and appearance and ancestry. Those who wondered how an "Asian" could speak English so well. Those who insist on grouping people based on appearance and ancestry and keeping those groups separate.

I doubt that those people were conservatives. I say that as a conservative who wonders why diversity seems to always mean the division of people into groups. I tell people with pride that I am an American mutt of European descent. Many of my ancestors would have never met and certainly would not have married if they had stayed in Europe because of the "diversity" that exists over there. Cross-cultural marriage is still discouraged in many European countries. My children have the wonderful honor of being able to trace their roots to two and maybe three continents. Do I need to tell them that they are Native American-European-African(?)-Americans (or is it African(?)-Native American-European-Americans or ... well you know what I mean.) I tell them that they are, and raise them to be, Americans because that is who they are. They are shining examples of the success of the melting pot that has made this country so great and such a destination to so many people around the world. Their ancestry - their heritage is how they became the people they are. Not who they are.

Why have so many people given up on the concept of the melting pot? Is it because they do not love this country and the strength it gains from that melting? Why can we not be Americans first and Irish or Latino or Chinese or Korean or Japanese or African or whatever second. And why can't we celebrate the diversity of our heritage as we unite in our America ness (sorry I know that is not a word)?

Martin Luther King Jr. prayed for the day when people would be judged by their character and what was in their hearts and not by the color of their skin (their appearance). I pray for that day too.

E-mail: Aug. 26, 2005

Since you insist that racial bigotry directed by skin color is a main factor in the failure of blacks to be allowed to achieve, why in the world would you suggest that a black light enough to "pass" shout out his racial background. It appears that you would rather have him fail due to bigotry than to succeed as a pale skinned person. Shame on your desire to fill a self-serving prophesy.

It is a type of backward and self defeating thinking that you champion. It has slowed advancement of all blacks, regardless of degree of pigmentation.

Diversity doesn't refer to varying skin color,...it refers to varying thought processes and views.

E-mail: Sept. 5, 2005

I'm beyond mad – I'm angry! The subject is the welfare City of New Orleans, the State of Louisiana, the federal government, and the media. I am sick and fucking tired of hearing all the bitching and griping on the major media about the response to Katrina and the levee breaks in New Orleans.

To say that nothing was done in advance is completely bullshit! The liberal biased press in this country never ceases to amaze me. None of the media except Fox even bothered to cover any of the advanced planning and effort that really took place. And even as I write this, Fox is backtracking on some of its harsh words used over the past few days. More importantly - folks need to fully understand that the Mayor of New Orleans is first in the line of responsibility and authority. He had not done shit to get the city ready for an emergency of any size – let alone one of the magnitude of Katrina. He did unleash the prisoners of the city jails on the local population AFTER the hurricane struck and parked the hundreds of city school buses that could have been used to evacuate these prisoners and local residents who had no transportation. All one needs to do is go back and play the tapes of New York City Mayor Rudy Gulianni on and after 9/11 - then compare them with the tapes of this dipshit mayor of New Orleans and you can clearly see the picture. One is a lean forward man of action - firmly in command and producing outstanding results. The other - a bitching, crying, laid back lackluster waiting for others to do his job and blaming his failures on others. He had plenty of time - years - to make ready evacuation routes, plan and arrange for transportation (the school buses) of those of his people who don't have vehicles of their own, and on and on and on. But what did he do? Not a goddammed thing! Finally the Black community got a chance to show what it could do under Black leadership in a city that was demographically Black. The results of this unfortunate example are a bad "dust cloud on the horizon." Look around the US at many of the cities that are now run by minorities - unfortunately you will observe the same damned thing - and I saw much of it first hand traveling with the Homeland Defense folks to work initial coordination planning efforts. So many are more interested in maximizing their intake of welfare program dollars than they are in planning for emergencies.

Next in the line of responsibility and authority is the Governor of LA. She too had accomplished nothing to prepare the state resources to be ready to respond.

Next, what kind of Americans do this to each other? I'll give you a clue! Demographically, New Orleans is 67% Black, and led by a Black mayor and a Black administration. We all saw what was being done by those residents of New Orleans - looting, raping, murdering each other. What does that really tell you about the moral fabric of that part of our society, a society raised on a welfare system that encouraged handouts in place of work? And, that insane welfare giveaway system was put in place by the liberals of the nation - and no one else!

There is always room to improve and rest assured there are many lessons to be learned from the disaster and recovery of Katrina. Many of these lessons involve our liberal (can you say "Guns & Butter" by LBJ) social programs that are designed to make a segment of our population dependent on the state and federal government who then in turn receive ballot box affirmation in exchange for those welfare programs. These programs have got to change by requiring those folks to WORK and be at least somewhat responsible for those moneys received through the government from those of us who do the work and pay the taxes.

Too many folks are paying way too much attention to the liberal biased press and media whose mindset is to do anything and everything that will make a Republican administration look bad.

E-mail: June 29, 2006

As Hispanic, I find your column somewhat disturbing. Most of those here illegally are not here as the victims of luck, fate or some other injustice carried out by our government. They are here because they made the conscious choice of breaking our immigration laws.

People of Color: Ne'er-Do-Wells

Voice mail: 2000

Why do you have to put on rags in order to be avoided? Your color is enough. Check the front pages of your paper. Who robs, who rapes, who kills and who sets fires, and who shoots up school? The blacks. Get a life. You're flogging a dead nigger.

E-mail: Feb. 25, 2001

Did you happen to catch Channel 9 news at 10:00 Saturday evening, Lewis? They reported that police were searching for three negro suspects in connection with a robbery-based shooting at an apartment complex in North Kansas City. Witnesses said that one of the negroes had a "gold front tooth"… not surprising. Witnesses also reported that one of the other negroes had a "gold front tooth with a diamond in it…." That's right, a gold front tooth with a diamond! Epic. That's pretty negro-ish even by your standards, eh Lewis? Do you think he obtained the diamond-studded gold tooth to celebrate brown history month?

A thieving negro sporting a diamond-studded gold tooth.... And you wonder why whites stereotype? Monumental.

E-mail: Jan. 4, 2002

I guess I'll just come right out and say it. People don't want to shop at Bannister Mall because it is perceived as the "black" shopping center in Kansas City. Truth or fiction, perception is reality. Put 60 whites in a room with 40 blacks and the whites' perception will be that there are more blacks than whites in the room. Given the choice of shopping as a minority (even if a perceived one) whites will gravitate to a place where they are the majority (or feel they are one). So the whites leave a mall. The whites then have not avoided contact with the blacks, but they have effectively reduced them to a minority again. Sad? Of course. But true.

If is an old story. People have always felt that if they moved further out from the city they could get away from the problems of the city. Unfortunately, people bring their problems with them because the city is not the problem; the people are.

E-mail: April 4, 2003

You know when I read your column today I couldn't help thinking about Chris Rock's joke about how in every major city there is a Martin Luther King Jr. Blvd. He said, "You're more likely to be shot on MLK Blvd. than any other street in America." That's a funny joke, but sad, too. Isn't it ironic that it is dangerous to walk down a street named for a man of "peace"???

I think MLK is less relevant than ever today. Most people under 45 have no relevance to him at all. Queen Latifa is more relevant!!

It's time you realized the '60s are over and time has marched on, but you have not. The 1960s were liberals' last hurrah and they have been adrift ever since because most of their ideas crashed and burned long ago. However, I don't want you and your friends to become extinct. I think we still need a liberal dinosaur to remind of that they once roamed the nation.

Voice mail: May 16, 2003

I must be psychic. Lewis, on page 2 they've got that crackhead Rodney King in today's paper on May 16 on Friday on page 2 doing 100 miles per hour again high on PCP crashed into a power pole and got locked up. I'm psychic. I knew this guy was no good. The police deserved to beat him up. I hope he got another beating. You just can't let these people run lose on dope. I don't care what race you are. If a person puts a crack pipe up to their mouth ....

Voice mail: 2004

Black males have a greater chance of dying from homicide than they do from a number of diseases that kill black males. I know you know that. They're getting killed by other black males. Of course black males commit crimes at a higher percentage. It's transparent. That one statistic is incontrovertible. Black males kill black males. And the more black male thugs, I'm not talking about black males. I'm talking about criminals who happen to be black that we put in prison, the further the crime statistics drop. If you turn them lose on society they'd go out and kill each other and innocent people and most of the people they kill would be black. They wouldn't be out killing white folks, generally. I really wish you'd take a step back and take a look at what I said. Black folks are victims of crime. You can't have it both ways. You just can't. You can't be the victim and feel soft for the criminal. Anyway, thank you for listening.

E-mail: Nov. 10, 2004

Will you never quit crying about how the poor black men that commit rape, robbery, burglary, murder, assault and whatever that can come to mind are picked on? They only do hard time because they do hard crimes. The "Three strikes" law only applies to people that commit three crimes, and if it looks as if you are going to continue this lifestyle then you should be locked up, white or black. Your comparison of 6 percent white and 1 out of 3 blacks will spend time in jail, doesn't that openly say they commit more crimes. You should work the streets trying to change their lifestyle instead of training them to be leaders in society. All they are learning is how to be a better pimp or how to sell drugs and not get caught. Bill Cosby had the right idea, but unfortunately, the black community didn't like what he said. Good luck in your endeavor to change some lives.

Voice mail: Feb. 25, 2005

On the attorney having trouble getting waited on in a restaurant, that's the least of your problems.... If you want white people to love black people, you've got to wait about another 1,000 years.... They don't want your business. If you've got five black people on a used car lot buying a car, and two little old white ladies are out shopping for a car and they see these black people on the lot they're not going to stop. Well, the black criminal is your problem. Until you get rid of the black criminal, white people are going to be scared. Is this guy a dope dealer, going to rape me, going to rob me? Your black attorney should have called for reservations and announced himself as an attorney and he would have gotten served. There are a lot of rich wealthy black people out there, a lot of rich, wealthy honest, hard working black people. If they are going to go out to eat what they need to do is to get to know the owner before they get there. They don't know who you are. You get to know the owner, you tell him who you are and the white guy he'll respect you. But with these black criminals running lose, wanting to kill you at the drop of a hat.... Just like you. You don't even know all of the facts. You're a little hostile yourself.

E-mail: March 3, 2005

Right on Lewis.

Just what I need at age 70...To move to Northeast Jackson County or KCK and sit up all night in those "nice neighborhoods" holding a 9mm in one hand and a 357 magnum in the other! Ha ha ha.

Well, Maybe the Aryan Nations will clean up this metro area and then move on to East St Louis and Gary!

E-mail: March 9, 2005

The safe thing about walking around dressed like a bum is that your black brothers will not rob or kill you.

Dress like someone with money, park a nice vehicle downtown - or in the northeast sector, or in KCK, and it's highly likely you will get much attention from black thugs within two nights.

Do the same in Jackson, Mississippi, the per-capita murder capital of the nation, and you would probably not last one night.

Voice mail: March 16, 2005

How many times have you written about the killings in the Negroid American neighborhoods. They're down there killing each other. That's got to be hate crimes against each other. How many times have you written about that? I don't think you have. As a matter of fact, the Negroid American ministers have come out many times against same sex marriage, but you don't. But you must hate your own people. I just don't understand why you wouldn't write about it. Why you wouldn't be concerned about all those killings and so forth. That after all is hate. It's hate right in your own community.

E-mail: May 10, 2005

Another typical week so far in eastern Jackson County.

Three dark-skinned individuals shoot and kill a fourteen-year-old boy over a lawn mower incident and also fire shots into the house hitting a twelve year old and an eighteen year old.

Dark-skinned man douses his girlfriend with lighter fluid and sets her on fire.

Perhaps Emanuel Cleaver (the local property tax dodging deadbeat in Congress who does not pay his local taxes) can do something about black violence in America and Africa and also convince Congress to bail out Detroit, East St Louis, Benton Harbor, Baltimore, and Gary?

E-mail: Aug. 30, 2005

The "Rev" Al Sharpton was "profiled" this week by county officers when his vehicle was pulled over for doing 110 miles an hour not far from Crawford, Texas while he was visiting goofy Cindy Sheehan and her crowd.

Also saw on television this morning long lines of hand-cuffed blacks who were arrested for looting in New Orleans. Same old story...taking advantage of a sorry situation to steal as much as they can carry off. Some things never change do they?

Voice mail: Sept. 30, 2005

I'm calling about your stupid article you had in the paper today, "Racist bias cries out in what isn't being said." Come on now. Listen. I'm black. Every night, we're killing each other. We're raping people. We shoot, we're mugging, just sin, sin, sin. That's the biggest problem with black folks. There's churches around every corner. But apparently somebody is not doing their jobs. The ministers, the mommas and poppas. When you get married. Wake up. Stop putting the solutions in there. In the '50s when I came up, we did not have these kind of problems. Of course black folks, had mommas and poppas. We were poor. And the ministers were preaching the word of God, not politics. But it's turned political now, and that's why people are killing each other every night. I can't take much more of this garbage.

E-mail: Oct. 1, 2005

A number of things aren't being said. Does black crime rate ring a bell? Or more specifically, the homicide rate of black on black? As of yesterday, there had been 94 mostly black homicides in KCMO, with three more months yet to go for the yearly records.

Sir, until the black community can end this terrible string of senseless killings (and injuries to innocent bystanders), you will not find many white people at the Blue Room of an evening. It's not a matter of racial bias as much as a matter of personal safety.

Can I tell black people to stop shooting each other? No. But you can.

Do you ever go to Arthur Bryant's for lunch? Whites sometimes outnumber blacks there. Does the lure of good barbecue transcend fears of violence, or is the restaurant considered to be in a relatively safe area? I don't know, but in my annual visits there, I'm never totally at ease. But I do go there at high noon, if not very often. Hey, I'm no Bill Bennett and nowhere near those of his ilk. Every civilization since the beginning of time has had its share of bad apples. Isn't it about time that you, et al, stop complaining, holding vigils and preaching to the choir, and start working on your own internal problems?

Only when the violence subsides and black areas are perceived to be safe will all kinds of businesses begin to prosper and race relations improve for all. I think it's that simple.

E-mail: Nov. 27, 2005

I have a novel solution to the problem of racial profiling by the police. How about having minorities NOT COMMIT A DISPROPORTIONATE NUMBER OF CRIMES? If there weren't so many minorities breaking the law, the police wouldn't have to spend more time "watching" them. It's not rocket science.

Blacks make up roughly 13% of the overall population; but anybody who watches the news or sees a prison roster can see that they commit a lot more than 1 in every 8 crimes. Who would you keep an eye on if you were the police? And the sentiment that if the police treated minorities with more respect, then they would act more respectful is a cop-out (no pun intended). The onus to obey the law rests with the individual. You can dismiss this opinion as the diatribe of an "unenlightened" or "ignorant" individual. But you shouldn't. This sentiment is shared by a large number of white folks, who in this age of political correctness would never voice it to a minority (except maybe an Asian; why are they so often exempted from these types of issues? Could it be because they keep the family unit together, study hard in school, and generally don't commit many crimes?)

Speak of Race and Get Labeled a Racist

Voice mail: 1998

Lewis, with your typical weekly racist column, why doesn't it surprise me that racists like you think that blacks should be put in jail according to quotas? It always amazes me how blacks don't believe facts, or truth, or honesty. The bottom line is this: there are more blacks in jail because more blacks are committing crime. And if you don't believe the facts or statistics go to countries that have fewer or little blacks and see what their crime rate is. Basically it's zero. Does it bother you that although that there's only 13 percent of the population that's black that 85 percent of the NBA is black. Does that quota bother you? I doubt it. Grow up. Quit being a race baiter.

Voice mail: 2000

Well today, Lewis, you start out with environment and ecology but right away you get into racism. You draw a line. You know this is pretty sad. You do more to polarize racism here in this area than anything imaginable. Don't you realize that? You don't have a clue do you? I challenge you right now to write a column that doesn't have racism in it. Try.

Voice mail: Jan. 2000

I happen to think you are the most racist person I have ever come across. You harp on this all the time. I want you to know that many of us do not believe like you believe. I have white friends who take care of a neighbor child. A little black boy while his brother goes to school. She thinks as much of him as if he were her own grandchild. I was the first one to welcome a black family across the street. I went across and visited with them. I went to their house blessing. Most of us don't feel like you do. We don't look at someone and think that they're black or they're white or they're purple or they're green. We think they're human beings and should be treated as such, and we will treat them with respect as long as they treat us with respect.

Voice mail: Nov. 15, 2000

I always get a kick out of reading your editorials just to see what kind of racism you're spreading in the city. It's very interesting to see how you fan those flames by your little quotes and out of context quotes and the "clan of segregation." I like that. You know, it's absolutely incredible how you do more divisive writing than any kind of positive writing.

Voice mail: Nov. 15, 2000

Sir, you must be a complete racist. I can't imagine anybody having an opinion so strong racially except Jesse Jackson. There has been a lot of good done by both sides for all minorities – not just blacks, not just Asians. But, sir, you're way off base. You are acting like a racist whether you admit to it or not. Good evening.

Voice mail: Nov. 15, 2000

Lewis, you should have someone pre-read your stuff a little bit because you came off sounding like a real racist in your Wednesday, Nov. 15 writing. I know you really can't be that far off.

Voice mail: 2001

I forgot to call in last week congratulating you on your column where you mention racism, and in the very same column you were at a black journalists convention. Isn't that kind of racist? And then also, about diversity on TV, what about the Black Entertainment Channel? How many white boys are on that? It must be nice to be able to be in a position of vice president and yet whine and cry about racism. You have no credibility. You're two-faced. Would me or a white, or an Asian or Hispanic be welcomed at the black journalists convention? Think about it. Have a great day, Lewie. Bye.

E-mail: June 11, 2001

There you go again – spouting off your mouth! You are so incredibly racist that you can't see the forest for the trees (original, isn't it?) From 1861-1865 we fought a little Civil War – it cost us the lives of hundreds of thousands of young men. In the 1960s we almost tore this country apart during the civil rights movement (might not be such a bad idea again – tearing the country apart, I mean). Now we are saddled with an affirmative action program that is divisive, polarizing and makes a mockery of the equal protection clause of the Constitution. We have spent literally billions of dollars and wasted the lives of countless numbers of young men trying to pull blacks into the mainstream of this society. Enough of this! I say with conviction. No! to reparations! Yes! To repatriation! Blacks should be given the opportunity to go back to the great paradise in South Africa. Blacks did not ask to be brought here. Give them the opportunity to go back.

I will fight reparations with all my effort. Hopefully, it will be a peaceful fight.

Voice mail: Sept. 12, 2001

I think you're a coward. You won't even answer your phone. You're a racist. After that column today I really don't know what you are. You're just an asshole.

E-mail: July 11, 2003

There you go again.... You would find a racial slight in a new born child of Martian decent. I choose my movies as much by ones that

I don't think a bunch of loud teenagers will be present almost as much as whether I'll enjoy the subject or featured actors/actresses. In St. Joseph we don't have much of a racial issue, and the black teenagers are really no different. So, I'm not influenced. Somehow you can't seem to allow that adults in Kansas City might have similar preferences and are looking for an adult atmosphere with no racial influences whatsoever.

Lewis, your glass isn't half empty.... It's bone dry.

Voice mail: Sept. 26, 2003

Every time I read one of your columns my blood pressure goes up at least 50 points. You're the biggest racist at any newspaper that I read. I can't imagine why *The Kansas City Star* leaves you on the payroll. You're a disgrace to the paper. You are so completely biased.

Voice mail: 2004

I feel sorry for you. You're so bigoted. It's just a shame that you can't open your mind to realize that all white people are not evil. I would like to see you write a column someday that is generally a nice column. But you are so bigoted that I feel sorry for you.

Voice mail: 2004

The undertones of racism that you write into your columns is very sad especially for a man with your education. Unfortunately, you have a column that you can write this information down in. But believe me you're just as bad of a racist as these guys out here wearing the white sheets and putting white hats on. Thank you.

E-mail: March 2, 2004

As I suspected, your mind is closed. You are forever, as a matter of personal choice, a whiner and a promoter of racism. If it wasn't for rednecks and racist idiots, what would you have to write about???

I am truly sorry you don't want to learn, that you don't want exchange of ideas, that you don't want to be an individual (as opposed to being a groupie in your fabricated world of self-pity). Nor do you want anyone else of color to be successful, to be standouts as individuals.

You obviously wish to promote racial division and promote the acceptability of being a member of the downtrodden masses and make excuses for failure.

Sorry, old man. You just don't get it.

Voice mail: Feb. 18, 2005

Actually, you know what I think? I think you're a reverse racist. I think you're a racist against whites. That's my opinion.

Voice mail, Feb. 25, 2005

I just wonder if you ever write about anything besides segregation and racism, sir?

E-mail: March 5, 2004

Short and to the point. Pity for the stupid.

I really do feel sorry for you. You are nothing but a moronic racist pig.

Voice mail: March 16, 2005

When you are writing your articles just remember you are the biggest bigot and racist of them all.

Voice mail: Aug. 24, 2005

Once again this shows how racist you are. You pick only the black issues. On the black issues, you defend it to death even if it's wrong. Your statement, going slower and respecting the people who live in the east Kansas City neighborhood should be the rule. Why don't you just be honest. What that really says is as you drive through our community we want you to genuflect to recognize our contributions.

E-mail: Sept. 8, 2005

I usually try to not read your articles, already knowing how racist YOU are. However, I could not help myself when this article seemed like it would be about the gulf tragedy and not particularly about politics or race. But, you again managed to spin your weary story of the poor, disadvantaged blacks left behind, suffering, etc., etc. Do you not realize, man, that there were MANY white individuals affected by this tragedy, also. Watch the news carefully and you will see that it was not only a disaster of black Americans, but white Americans, also. And so much of your article is simply not correct!

E-mail: Sept. 9, 2005

About the rantings of an UNFAIR NEGRO RACIST: I'm convinced you're the most intolerant, unfair, intellectually Dishonest NEGRO.... You use the printed word to condemn, criticize, and make wild, unfounded conjectures......and of course you are a careless Negro apologist for even the most guilty...... Why don't you undertake to correct the moral decay that has beset the Negro community....no, you are so stupidly zeroed in on lambasting any and all things "Republican" you are oblivious to what could be a constructive movement that would benefit the Negro community.....but being "positive" obviously is not in your warped make-up.... It seems you are dedicated to being "divisive" and nothing suits your intentions any better than painting a target on President Bush....

As a practitioner of "hate the white establishment," you swallowed every half-truth some of your fellow critics had to say about the ego-driven Cindy Sheehan...............saying she is an irresistible force that can't be diminished or discounted...hogwash!! And to flatter yourselves by saying we're not in the mainstream.............wake up!! Smell the coffee!!

E-mail: Feb. 15, 2006

Your continued focus on "people of color" is both biased itself and divisive.

Voice mail: April 2006

I would like to commend you. You do more to keep the races apart than anybody I know.

Voice mail: June 28, 2006

Man you are one of the biggest black racists I have ever met in my life. What we used to call when I rode with the Vultures, which was a black motorcycle gang and a half-white motorcycle gang, you are a redneck. You are a racist, and you shouldn't write this crap that you continually write about these illegal immigrants destroying the black community. That's what you should be talking about how they are destroying the black community and the poor white community. But man, you're a redneck, black racist, and I'm sick of your lousy comments. Quit your business and start doing something else man because you're a racist pig.

The Blame Game

Voice mail: 1997

If you continue to want to use the term African-American for black people I think you ought to also use the term European American for white people. And secondly, if you point out that whites vote along color lines if you don't think that blacks also are just as guilty of polarizing along color lines when they vote that's being naïve.

Voice mail: 1997

As far as affirmative action, in my opinion, it should have been done away with a long time ago. It is completely ridiculous. I think the black people should be given the opportunity to succeed, and they shouldn't be just put into positions.

E-mail: Sept. 14, 2000

Lewis, haven't you ever noticed that when you black writers bring up eliminating "racism" that you are always meaning whites have to change or modify their behavior? What about the racism by blacks against whites that I see and read about every day? Many blacks are rude to whites, and it is obvious that it is a racist act. And many blacks commit crimes against whites, and it often seems to be partly because of race. If we are all to get along, it would help greatly if first we "liked" each other. That will not happen until blacks learn to be more polite, and not be so loud (in public, in private they can be as loud as they like) and learn to speak the kind of English you expect to hear from a radio/television announcer or over a public address system. If you actually want the support of more whites, try being more balanced and fair to all sides, not just the black side.

E-mail: Dec. 8, 2000

Your article in today's paper seems to imply that, as usual, blacks are a victim of the devil white people. This time, blacks are being forced to accept degrading roles in television sitcoms reminiscent of minstrel shows from the 1800s. If I understand you correctly, and that's what you are saying, then I would suggest to you that these same degrading sitcoms are produced by black producers. Nobody is forcing them to produce these shows and nobody is forcing the black actors to take the roles. I guess maybe there is some big white conspiracy forcing these poor victims to take these degrading roles, but I haven't seen proof of this. But I'm sure it's in no way the black actors' fault for accepting the roles and I know the black producers bear no responsibility in making these modern day minstrel shows. Doesn't it get old crying all the time about being a victim?

E-mail: June 8, 2001

You are so lucky blacks are "innocent of everything" and whites, in your mind, are "guilty of everything." Do you ever give any credit at all to our society for the success of blacks, such as yourself? Or do you just always blame whites for any and all problems and failures of blacks? And when encountering black success, such as yours, have you noticed you give all credit for that success to the black and none to white society? I am pleased you have recently become somewhat of an extremist, in my eyes and that of others because you are finally starting to reveal yourself to be the black propaganda minister you have been all along.

E-mail: June 13, 2001

As I have been aware of you over the years, I have never observed that you have found any black problems that you don't try to blame on whites.

E-mail: Oct. 25, 2002

Ninety percent or more of "people of color" have voted for one party for as long as they have been able to vote and you still declare "victim" status. What does that tell you about your voting?

In as many of your columns you lament over the loss of civil rights and in today's article you are against "whites" fleeing the inner city. Are you opposed to "whites" living wherever they choose?

Do not blame the "system" for people of color making poor grades in math, science, history, English/Spanish, P.E., home economics, driver's education, business education and I could go on. "You people" who bitch and moan in a continuous manner will never achieve your potential until YOU take responsibility for what happens to you. Stop playing the race card and blaming the "whites" for your perceived problems.

Voice mail: 2004

You're constantly blaming the white community for the problems of the blacks. You ought to read your own newspaper. We've got one black thug killing innocent white people one after another never stops.

It continues because the black leaders in this community will never do anything to stop it – including yourself.

Voice mail: 2004

I don't understand why you're putting the guilt trip on the white people. They're the cause of all the problems that the blacks have. I mean they're different cultures, they're different. It's not racial discrimination that's causing all these problems. And your articles are so one sided it's unbelievable. You're doing nothing but driving a wedge between the white people and the black people in this community.

Voice mail: 2004

Once again you alienate me as a white person. You talk about how we should work together, but you write an article today talking about how Hispanics and blacks should buckle up. You couldn't care less about whites. Once again you misuse statistics to try and prove that you're only interested in the good of people. No you're not, Lewis. All you're interested in is black people. Always. Only in black people. I don't know why they keep you on staff because you don't represent the community. You only represent black people.

Voice mail: 2004

I am a white male who lives in Overland Park and also a subscriber to *The Kansas City Star*, and I was wondering do you hate me because I'm white and live in Johnson County, Kan.? Because basically the way I perceive your articles, you hate all white males who live in affluent neighborhoods who have money. You assume that we don't like you. You have in your most recent article related voting for George Bush in the South to promoting slavery. I want to know how are you helping black people? All you do is preach hate. You're turning blacks against whites. You're not helping anybody but yourself. I'm going to cancel my subscription to *The Star.* I'm going to urge others to do the same. I'm going to clip your article out of every paper you write. I'm going to send it to Bill O'Reilly at Fox News, who I'm sure you hate because he's an even-tempered guy, he sees both sides and he's going to see that you're not and he's going to embarrass you publicly. I'm going to make it happen because you do nothing good for society, the United States, nobody but yourself. Thank you and goodbye.

E-mail: March 1, 2005

Well your favorite month has finally ended. As usual, you had several columns with your favorite theme...racism. Now tell me...when is White History Month going to start?

Voice mail: March 23, 2005

Your piece in today's *Star* equating what's going on in Iraq with the Civil Rights Movement and you being a victim, which you're always a victim no matter what you write, you're the victim. You're the victim, victim, victim. The world is out to get you. It is just amazing that you can write this drivel. How can you say that liberating all these Iraqi people was a bad thing? You are a staunch supporter of Saddam Hussein, and I hope you sleep well at night.

E-mail: July 20, 2005

Gee, I thought slavery was abolished in 1865 or thereabouts. Personal responsibility, choices, hard work are the criteria now. Get your head out. You, the blacks, are the ones who have over 50 percent out-of-wedlock births that dump the cost on responsible citizens. Quit blaming others. Quit watching BET on TV, which never talks about morality or anything intellectual – just jive talk music that will not prepare you for the future. Good golly.

E-mail: Jan. 25, 2006

In your world, does every white person in the country live in a big house on a hill?

E-mail: Feb. 3, 2006

Have you ever been a white person and walked into an all-black McDonald's? You ought to try it sometime.

Voice mail: Feb. 17, 2006

I don't think I can take any more of the black thing. You've got to give it a frickin' break, man. It's so old. I can't take it anymore. You've got one less subscriber. I think you've done a good job. I hope it works for you. I don't think it has. But keep blaming whitey. I think it has done well for you. I don't think it has done well for the rest of you guys. But it has done well for you. Keep it up. Let's try for another 200 years.

Voice mail: Feb. 17, 2006

It became apparent to me that you're really not interested in a white man's ideas. But at any rate I continue to think that you overdo it. I just think that a man who has a nice life like you shouldn't be complaining about conditions so much that are not being inflicted upon you by white people.

E-mail: Feb. 17, 2006

Your glass is always half full....not surprising for a professional victim during Black History Month.

E-mail: Feb. 17, 2006

If you ever wrote an uplifting article about anything, I think I'd drop dead.

"Lew's credo" blame white guys for everything. Avoid personal responsibility at all cost and when you can, spread all the lies possible by using my column. Your constant harping on your list of "social ills" is tiresome, at best. The only person in this world who gives a damn about you succeeding is the guy looking at you in the mirror and the helping hand you are always wishing you had is located at the end of your shirt sleeve.

E-mail: Feb. 20, 2006

You fell off your bike. Period. End of sentence. No race stuff. No silly stuff. No white/black stuff. You fell off your bike. Give it a rest and write about something else. You are supposed to be community resources. WHY is the only community you ever write about the black one.

I feel discriminated against.

E-mail: March 29, 2006

Yessiree those good old Muslims are a real friendly bunch unless; you dislike having your head cut off on the Internet, or decide Christianity might be for you and then POW you are issued a death sentence. Now if you like the slightest provocation to riot, burn down cities, wound and maim innocent folks and just generally act totally uncivilized then Islam might be for you! Kinda reminds you of home don't it? Just like Watts, KC, etc.

Experts on Blame

Voice mail: July 25, 1998

I do not abide by any sort of racism. But at the very end of your column, how in the heck can you equate racism with states entertaining the proposal to join in abolishing affirmative action? How does racism and affirmative action coincide? Can you please address this issue? I'd be interested to know. Thank you.

Letter: Dec. 18, 1998

Since you missed most of the course in Race 101 let me fill you in....

1. NBA... in the '50s basketball was all white. It was a great game. Now it's all black and a mess. There is no defense. The black players just run-a-gun-slam-a-jam. The blacks let each other score so they can roll up the score and help themselves at contract time. Scores of 140 to 135 are not rare. Bill Russell said he saw racism come full circle. In the '50s black players were not invited to team parties... and by the '70s... white players were not invited to the team parties. Black players tell us they can't live on $2 million a year so the whole league is shut down. Greedy black players have wrecked the whole thing. The public is fed up paying $40 a seat to see all-black teams play. The end is near.
2. Mike Espy. Mike admitted he took money from companies and that it was wrong and a dumb thing to do. But he was acquitted at trial because the jury was all black. Very few papers reported the makeup of the jury.
3. Tom Bradley, mayor of Los Angeles. They raved about Bradley and how he brought Los Angeles together. But Tom actually sold black people out making deals with whites and Mexicans to run the city. The Mexicans took most of the jobs needed in the black communities. Bradley let 3 million illegal Mexicans invade Los

Angeles and never said a word. When the spark came, the riot of 1992 erupted and much of the city was burned down. After the mess was cleaned up and the bodies located, a strange thing happened....Over 50 percent of the looters were found to be Mexican. They had risked their lives to go into a burning, black area to loot stores. So much for the wonderful Mexicans who were supposed to be such great workers. After the Miami riots, a black man said it all...."We been here all our lives and we got nuttin'.... But them damn Cubans just got off the boat and they give them everything...." Right on, my man, get the big picture.

4. Africa. The whole continent is one big mess. Every country is in civil war or chaos. You told the whites to get out and with unlimited natural resources, it should be booming. Mandela's South Africa is just as bad....Crime is out of control. What's the deal here?
5. Oprah, Michael Jordan and Bill Cosby make over $180 million a year. That's enough to get every deserving black student into college. How much is actually spent on helping black kids??? My guess is most goes into buying big homes and fancy stuff. Very little goes to helping black kids. Over $100 million should have been donated each year by those three alone.
6. Michael Jackson is a known child molester. He just paid off some kid $20 million to keep quiet. But blacks don't care. They buy his records, and he is a hero. If he was white, they would run him out of town. Phillips, the star running back at Nebraska, beat up his gal-pal and threw her down a flight of steps. But blacks don't care....They don't want to see his career derailed. Black music has gunfire in the background, and women are called whores and bitches....Then you wonder why there is so much crime in black areas. You do it to your own people. Speak out against that horrible rap music. It's killing black kids!!! Boxer Archie Moore was a real role model not that crook Mike Tyson.
7. Bill Cosby's wife wrote a letter to *USA Today* and said all us white people were racist and caused the death of her kid. The facts showed the guy who shot her son was an immigrant from Russia who should have never been allowed in the country. He was allowed in because of the liberal policies of Maxine Waters and Carol Mosley Braun. Your own stupid liberal policies killed their son. If you had joined us against immigration, her kid might still be alive. I suggest to Mrs. Cosby that she join me on a tour of Civil War cemeteries. At the Antietam and Shiloh and dozens of other places are the graves of 500,000 Union troops who died to make black people free. Most were farm kids from Michigan, Indiana, Kansas and Ohio who never even saw a black person but gladly went for the cause. I have been to those cemeteries and I

walked past every grave. Many black people need that tour so they could get the big picture.

You were right about the inner-city Marshall Plan. Let's stop foreign aid and close our southern border. Let's fix all America first and let the Third World twist in the wind.

E-mail: Nov. 2, 2000

Get off the government plantation. When are you and other African American leaders going to realize that the government is not going to give you anything? Government mandates are no substitute for excellence. Don't even talk about a level playing field. There is no such field. Build African American excellence, and "they will come."

E-mail: Nov. 13, 2000

A recent report released by the surgeon general stated that although breast milk is considered "babies' perfect food," the rate of breast feeding among black women is "alarmingly low."

Perhaps that is why you people grow up and have such disgusting eating habits, resulting in obesity, diabetes and general poor health. One would think black women could at least breast feed correctly. After all, it is free.

Voice mail: Nov. 15, 2000

Why is it that you think that qualified women and qualified minorities should get jobs over other qualified people – just because they happen to be a woman or a minority? I don't understand that. Maybe you can enlighten me. I don't understand why. It should just all be an equal playground. Just because you're a minority or a woman or whatever, you should not have a better chance at getting whatever job. That's ridiculous. I don't know why people believe that. And I'm even a woman.

Voice mail: Aug. 2001

The most important reason we've had such an increase in Latinos in this country since the last census count is due directly to illegal immigration – people coming across the border into Texas, California, Arizona, etc. And I think you would agree with that. As far as watching Hispanics roof a house across the street from you, I've seen this happen myself, and personally I can't think of a harder working crew out there. It would certainly put any all African-American team to shame that I have ever seen. I can guarantee you that. But having said that, you Democrats better be getting busy because it's my understanding that the Latino population and the so-called African-American population don't exactly get along too well. The blacks are so eager to get a handout from the liberals and the federal government that they of course have sewed up their vote. The Hispanics have a little bit of family values to their lives and stuff and they don't believe in all that crap. So you people better get busy out there or you're going to have a hard time in politics. Other than that, Lewis, you have a great day. Keep on writing. Bye.

Letter: Nov. 20, 2001

I thought after 9-11 the black community would have the good sense and judgment to become "American" … no longer hyphenated. No longer suggesting primary allegiance to something other than America. No longer suggesting split allegiance. It's time everyone got on the same page.

You can't have your cake and eat it, too. I believe most racial problems today are the result of the black community failing to step up to the plate. Much was done, and much has happened but the more given… the more asked. You can't have two standards … one that says blacks can play by one set of rules and whites by another. And, it will get worse, if it doesn't get better.

Lewis, the next time you find (as you always do) a racial implication… read that problem … in almost anything that happens in the community … stand in front of the mirror … take a long look … you have finally clearly come face to face with the problem.

Voice mail: May 22, 2002

I like your article on May 22. Real good article. At least you got off of that idea of trying to tell white people how to treat people of color. You know it should be the other way around. You should be telling people of color how to treat white people. Then we wouldn't have a problem. But people of color are causing the problems. Otherwise there wouldn't be so much racism. Let's find out what the people of color are doing wrong and see if we can get them to change their ways a little bit. Like talking too loud is one problem I have with these people. Why do they have to talk so loud and disturb other people? Why don't we get into that. Discrimination on the job and all that, I'm with you on that. But these people, you know, they need to tone down their voices a little bit. I don't disrespect people with loud talking and hollering.

E-mail: Oct. 30, 2002

Leadership is the key in business, politics, journalism and the church. Blacks in America never make any progress because any possible leader who is black is also a person who has the victim mentality. This mentality leads to the failure of any movement. Enjoy.

Voice mail: 2003

Hey, you already got reparations It's called welfare, AFDC, food stamps, Section 8, subsidized lunches, breakfast at school, free health care at Swope Parkway, Truman Medical Center, Samuel Rodgers, the Ewing Kauffman Foundation, Red Cross, Salvation Army. You already got it. We're already supporting all of your relatives.

Voice mail: 2004

Before you take on the world's problems you should stop all the violence in the black community. You criticize white flight when they want to escape the crime. But you live in a safe neighborhood yourself. My family was the victim of black crime because we stayed in the south-east area too long. A black minister had to tell us to move before we were killed. Many of our neighbors were also victims of black crimes.

E-mail: Feb. 13, 2004

Please consider this point of view: Stop the whining and finger pointing. Although there is plenty to whine and finger point about, it just comes across as passive and powerless. Start taking at least some responsibility for the state of today's African-American family.

Where are the fathers of 48 percent of the children living with a single mother? By their absence are they not accountable for the "feminization of poverty"? Are fatherless children not at greater risk for poverty, drugs, etc?

Just maybe full equality would be attainable if we all first looked inward for strength and solutions.

E-mail: Oct. 20, 2004

If black women and their kids (who have an atrocious life thanks to the typical black male) actually had the black father living with them, and working for a living, the black household net worth would increase greatly. On the other hand, if 75 percent of the black males in America (age 18 to 40) went back to Africa, every metro area police department in the nation could reduce its manpower by 50 percent.

E-mail: March 18, 2005

In Prison Because They Could Not Obtain Living Wage? What a laugh! So you are still blaming the problems of the black race on schools. Please don't give us more of the poor school cop out Lewis. You must think Star readers are ignorant. It is not having fathers that hamper black kids future. Apparently there is simply no end to the excuses black people can come up with for their wide-spread failure.

Voice mail: Sept. 17, 2005

This is about joblessness, helplessness breed anxiety and violence. Gee, maybe if we didn't have as many illegals coming into this country there might be more jobs. But guess what? I do recall you had some opinion some time ago saying you needed to band with the Hispanics, you needed to band with the other minorities. Well, go ahead and band with them. Go ahead and band with all the illegals because guess what? They're taking up the jobs. Well hey man, joblessness and helplessness breed anxiety and violence, and so do a bunch of illegal immigrants. Why don't you get on that issue.

Voice mail: Sept. 30, 2005

Man, you continually strive to find racism in every facet of life. And every shortfall for blacks is always a product of the system of bias? You cite all these low graduation rates and college. What about the high number of dropouts among blacks during a free education? What about the incredible number of black fathers who don't stick around to help raise their kids? I know, I know. Somehow it's the system or white people forcing these decisions.

Voice mail: February 2006

Black people will sit up there and get up on a crutch and get support. You know what the big joke is now? Martin Luther King Day is where everybody gets something free that day. Welfare day is what they call it. Have a nice day. You celebrate black month? How about white month?

E mail: Feb. 17, 2006

I think you give too much power to the forces of racism and too little attention to personal responsibility. There is no doubt that racism exists but it's a copout to blame the problems facing minorites solely on racism. You imply that black folks have no power to better their lot in life and I think this sends the wrong message. A better message would be proclaiming that regardless of racism the power to achieve is in the hands of the people and that even though it's a hard road, it is possible to overcome. Starting at the point that you don't control your own destiny by proclaiming that others hold the power to determine how your life turns out is not a recipe for change, it's a recipe for howling at the moon.

Prejudice: Totally Imagined

Voice mail: 1998

I'm offended by the fact that you think that racism is so pervasive in this society when we in Kansas City, Mo., have a two-term black mayor in a city that is three-quarters white. It's offensive, and it's stupid.

Voice mail: 1998

My colleagues, many of whom are black, and I read your article yesterday. We felt it was so ridiculous and laughable and it borders on the absurd and the insane. It's almost to the point where we feel sorry for you. You're such an extremist and have really perverted the language unfortunately and it's to the detriment of everyone. And it's just extremely unfortunate. You're so far in the liberal extreme you're in outer space. It's so perverted it's laughable and sad at the same time. Our condolences to you. The creator was certainly niggardly in giving you intelligence.

E-mail: May 26, 2000

If I find a cracker on my desk should I call the FBI? I think you might be putting ideas in people's heads by continually focusing on the subject (of nooses). I still think it could be other blacks doing this after finding out another black co-worker was a Republican! You never know!!

Voice mail: Nov. 24, 2000

In your articles, you constantly bring us numerous so called examples of how the poor blacks are disenfranchised and intimidated and discriminated against. That must happen all around us, I guess. The funny thing is myself and other white people, we don't see it happening. So are we blind or stupid or racist? Why don't you check with your white friends and see if they notice all this terrible, terrible treatment of the black people and this terrible discrimination going on. If they don't see it ask yourself why.

Voice mail: 2003

If diversity in and of itself is good then the staff of *The New York Times* and the staff of *The Kansas City Star* needs to have pedophiles on it. They need to have convicted murderers on them because they could more accurately write about murder trials, murder arrests, about murder investigations. You see, I think the idea you're promoting is nonsense. Besides that, this skin color thing, you and I go over this again and again. There is only one race, the human race. There is no black race and white race. There is a human race. But there are pedophiles and murders in the human race, and I don't want them on the staff of my newspaper.

Voice mail: 2004

Hi, Mr. Diuguid. I do wish you would start writing more about your bicycle and cookbook because I am going to stroke out when you keep writing these peacenik articles. You need to watch more O'Reilly and read less MoveOn.org. If there weren't wars, where would you be? You would be in an oven somewhere. If there weren't wars, what would any of us do? We have to retain them over there so they don't come over here. There indeed were weapons found of mass destruction. There were also incidents of cruelty to prisoners. But that was just a few. It isn't our doing as a whole. Also, you appear to be racist. You're the one. I mean, I live around a lot of black people. Nobody plays the race card. Do you know why there are a lot of black people where I live? Because they like to be together. The Spanish, all these people like to be together with their own people. It's not a race thing. Watch O'Reilly more. Write about your bike. You do such a great job with that. I just don't know. I'm going to stroke out if I keep reading your column. I get so heated up. Have a nice one. Bye.

Voice mail: 2004

I don't read your column very often because it's always racial. I mean, it's like everybody is bad to the blacks. You know, I am Mexican American, and I get a lot that goes on in my life, too. But I don't run and cry about it. It just makes my skin thick. It just gives me alligator skin. You know, you're going to run into this year in and year out, year after year. But you know what, it makes you a better and a stronger person. It makes you do good. It makes you, it just makes you a better stronger person. You know, I just get tired of reading your columns about that all the time.

Voice mail: June 25, 2004

Hey, Diuguid, I'm going to give you some advice. As Ronald Reagan would once say, there you go again. Your garbage that you put out in this rag of a paper is nothing but cheap, crappy tripe. And if I was like you, I would make a statement saying that the only thing wrong with this country is we have minorities in it and they cause all the problems. That's the sequel or just the opposite of what you're saying in this paper. You say the same crap and the same old bullshit. You're like a black Michael Moore. Why don't you, how is it you even have a job. Go read a book called *Out of Africa* by another minority that has a perspective because pal, you don't have a perspective. Get a life.

Voice mail: 2006

I guess you think you're above the law. White people, black people, Hispanics, everyone breaks the law. But it's a shame you guys think you should never be stopped. You should be treated just like white people or Hispanics or Asians or anybody else. No one should ever racial profile. But you guys do more harm to yourselves by always writing this crap in your paper and stuff. It's a shame that you guys do this. We try to fight and fight to prevent it. But if you didn't move over, you obviously saw the patrol car with its lights on. At night time I am sure the patrolman knew you were black if you were going by driving a van. Whether you got a ticket or not, yeah, maybe he should have given you a warning. But you got a ticket, and I am sure it had nothing to do with you being black while he wrote you a citation. I am sure he didn't have his hand on his gun, but if he did, it's only for his protection. It's not to intimidate you at all. That's the sad thing of it. The sad thing of it is you can write whatever you want. It's your right.

E-mail: April 1, 2006

Abdalla Idris Ali, needs to get his head out of the sand. The truth is Islam is not a peaceful religion. Islam cannot be a peaceful religion when it allows the beheadings of people who do not agree with them. Islam issues death warrants for people who turn away from the Prophet Muhammad. Tell me why, if you can, are Muslims killing each other in Iraq? Don't repeat that far left rhetoric, about the fact that the Americans are there. Most Iraq Citizens welcome the Americans, they are better off now than when Saddam was in power. If the Muslims would stop killing their own and destroying the schools, power plants, water supply installations, and let a new Government form, who knows perhaps peace might come to a small part of that world. How tolerant is a religion that gets angry when a cartoon depicts what a large percentage of the free world believes? Then the followers of this "peaceful" religion go out and destroy buildings and put out a death warrant to the person who depicted what he felt is the truth in the form of a drawing.

America: Love It "As Is" or Leave It

Voice mail: 1999

Yes, you're at it again. You'd think you'd get your brain working. All you know is cut down anybody who wants to be a patriot who cares about their country and all you care about is your race. Well, let me tell you your race is going nowhere but down.

Voice mail: Feb. 18, 2000

Hey Lewis, if you don't like being black in America, move.

Voice mail: Nov. 24, 2000

You guys need to get over this race baiting thing. Your column today is freaking joke. Why don't you and Jesse Jackson go jump off of something really, really tall.

Voice mail: 2001

As usual, Mr. Diuguid, you show your ignorance and hatred for anything morally straight, upright, heterosexual and white. I read your hate in the paper several times a week and as the Bible says, pull the log from your own eyes as you seek to cast the splinter from mine, or words to that effect. You should examine your heart for the hatred and racism that you have. Thank you.

Voice mail: Sept. 12, 2001

You're a fucking traitor, man. Why don't you go back to Africa.

Voice mail: Sept. 12, 2001

The real tragedy of Sept. 11 is that you weren't present in the buildings of the World Trade Center.

Voice mail: Oct. 19, 2001

Mr. Diuguid you would do us great pleasure by going to live with your Muslim friends since you are so excited about comparisons, which is apples and oranges. It's a shame that *The Star* kept you on. You're their little token boy, it's obvious. You can't write a decent article. Your themes are absolutely absurd. The editorial page, the opinion page is more worthy of something of value. So why don't you catch the next airplane over there with your Muslim buddies. The terrorist attacks were against the American people. Period. You want to talk to them Ha ha. Go over there and do your talking.

E-mail: Oct. 30, 2002

Here's hoping if any shooting takes place it will be you shooting yourself. That would be sweet music to rational people of all colors. You are one sick son of a bitch!

Voice mail: 2003

Hey, you know, one thing about you that's really consistent: you're a racist. You know you are always bemoaning the fact that you're being mistreated because you're black and all that crap. People get tired of hearing that. Cause you're a racist. Face it you're a racist and a bigot. And secondly, I don't think there is a terrorist that you have ever not loved. You love Saddam. You love the Palestinians. You know it's too bad that one of these thugs – Palestinian thugs or Iraqi thugs – hasn't walked up to your house. I suppose if they walked up to your house and blew themselves up I'm sure you might think differently. Or probably you'd embrace them. But like I say, when it comes to evil you acquiesce to it. And as far as I'm concerned you're an accomplice.

Voice mail: 2004

I'll tell you if you don't like this country I don't know why you just don't leave. I don't know where you get all of this hate and confusion you've got. I think it must be from your childhood. But if you don't realize about the 3,000 people – Americans – that were killed in, you know the twin towers, you have to go after terrorists. We don't want to be fighting them right here. Certainly not around *The Kansas City Star*. It might stop you from having a good lunch up there if some terrorist were to shoot the cook or something like that. You wouldn't be able to get your lunch. Wouldn't that be a shame? Terrible the bunch of hardships you have in this country. But I'd pay your ticket if you'd go to some other country. I really would if I had to pick up aluminum cans to buy your ticket, I would. But those twin towers if we had anything like that around *The Star* and they fell there and killed about 3,000 people, I'd think the way you want to do it is call the police and give them a ticket and maybe have them go to traffic court, right? That's your level of mentality. Boy, I'll tell you, you're something else.

Voice mail: 2004

I just want to convey to you that I think you are intensely dangerous to this country and to this area. You are so opinionated. I sure hope *The Star* cleans your ass and gets rid of you.

Letter: May 28, 2004

If you hate America so much why do you stay? Maybe you would be happier in an African country. I'm sure you don't like living here in the U.S.A. I'll pay for a one-way ticket if you're interested. I hope that your hatred is just racial (instead of) really hating the country that gave you freedom to be able to criticize untruths and be able to be around the next day. Many places in the world are much more difficult.

E-mail: July 21, 2004

You must be miserable living here. Maybe you should think about moving to Holland.

E-mail: Oct. 30, 2004

Why don't you try to contribute something to America instead of hate?

Voice mail: Dec. 8, 2004

If they don't like it here why don't they go back where they came from? They will never assimilate into our society. They are what they are. I don't see any of them ever speaking up in favor of our nation or supporting our country or joining the military. They don't like us. They never will. And if it was up to me I'd send all 7 million of them back – a one-way ticket. Maybe they'll figure that out someday. Any religion that believes in doing what they do doesn't have any business in this country. But I am glad you wrote the article to give me a chance to express myself. There are a lot of others just like me, and we're winning, and we're going to win some more. Bye-bye.

E-mail: March 25, 2005

In view of the fact a very high percentage of Africans (like yourself) express continual hate towards America we are bewildered as to why most Africans here don't go back to Africa?

The answer to this question is simple. There are no free handouts in African nations-only killing and rapes by African warlords, and by UN forces.

Voice mail: April 2005

I know what side of the American flag you're on – none since it doesn't have any black in it. America is made up of all kinds of people. If you'd get off your backside and start taking care of your kids like you're supposed to you wouldn't have to worry about the schools. Thank you.

E-mail: June 12, 2005

It was nice to read your recent closing comment with respect to "Old Glory." Apparently all black people do not hate America.

Voice mail: July 6, 2005

OK, Lewis. Here's your grade for the July 6 article: You get two grades today. One's a T; one's an I. The T stands for traitor. The I stands for ignorant. Congratulations.

Voice mail: Sept. 7, 2005

Mr. Diuguid: Die and go to hell.

Voice mail: October 2005

Yeah, listen you poor abortion jerk, why don't you go and join the rest of the baby killers and stick your head in the sand or maybe go and jump in Lake Michigan. One of these days you're going to stand before almighty God and you're going to give an answer if you don't repent, and you're going to burn in the lake along with the rest of these abortionists. Don't you forget it.

Voice mail: Feb. 17, 2006

Almost every one of your articles is about race. Have you thought about moving to Africa so you can just be around black people? I'm Jewish. So every time I see a German person should they give me some money or something? What about the Armenians? Every time they see a Turk should the Turks give them some reparations? I could go on and on and on. How about the Mexicans? Should the Spanish give them reparations? Same with the Filipinos? Your topics are so off base. You ought to be more concerned about class and economic measures than about race.

Go to Appalachia. There are plenty of poor white people there. Go to Independence. There is nothing but white trash there. You are nothing but a race baiter. My thing for you is why don't you move to Africa? That way you don't have to be around white people. Move to Chad or Nigeria. How about in Africa where the Arabs are slaughtering the black people. Why don't you say something about that?

Voice mail: June 28, 2006

Did you read your article yourself? One of the things you wrote in there is you said illegal. Now what part of illegal don't you understand? What part of the law can I break? Why don't you go move on the east side of town, where you don't want to live? Hey, you're a hypocrite. And you call it bigotry cause we don't want illegal immigrants? Give me a break. Again, that's one of your cop outs. You're a cop out, sir. You always bring on race. Everything is race. Oh God, poor little immigrants. They're a minority. They're a different color.

Outraged by Diversity

Letter: Feb. 2, 2000

In my next life, I will return as a black person. When I am old enough to work, I will obtain a job from the white establishment. Will work long enough to establish that the firm has "dissed" me; will "jive on down" to the courts and sue "whitey." Then I will live the good life on my settlement. I will buy me a hundred acres; build a sumptuous home in the middle of these hundred acres, draw my money and never have to be "dissed" again. In fact, I may purchase a country in Africa – and never be "dissed" again.

Letter: May 2, 2001

You blacks just don't get it. You are so naive to think that others dislike you just because of the color of your skin. That is irrelevant! There are far more other legitimate reasons for civilizations to shun you. I hope you will take the time to consider these thoughts, as they are simple observations meant to help you understand your predicament.

1. Too many blacks demand respect, demand jobs, demand money and benefits. The list of demands goes on. You just don't get it! None of these things are given by demand, they are earned through hard work, discipline, responsibility, motivation and ambition. Here is the number one secret for blacks to truly become a part of America's opportunities: master these character traits, and you will blend in with open arms. Take Hispanics for example. Their numbers are increasing greatly, but it is common knowledge that they are hard working and expect to receive only what they earn. They are ruling the construction industries as prized, responsible and hard working men. No one says that about black workers, in fact it is exactly the opposite. Do not worry about them crowding

you out of your coveted down-trodden minority status, they will quickly pass you with their self-reliant attitudes and efforts.

2. White people do not have to do anything to hold back blacks. We don't need to. You are doing an excellent job yourself. Disintegrated families, constant drug use, rejection of education, absence of motivation -- these are your problems, and they are not imposed upon you by whites. Also, by nurturing an entitlement mentality you keep yourselves in the role of slaves, always being provided for by someone else's guaranteed handouts for slackers. Do like everyone else that came to this country, reach down and grab your bootstraps, then pull them as high as you can.
3. Education comes hard for the black race and is considered suspect by many blacks. Look at any number of studies and reports for proof. *The Kansas City Star* annually publishes school standings by race, and blacks consistently make up the lowest, essentially illiterate ranks. Education is a fundamental building block for participating in civilization.
4. It's sad to say, but I am not surprised to hear blacks asking for yet another handout in the form or reparations, in their ongoing self-pity victimization routine. Would a people with any self-respect ask for, let alone accept, unearned money for something that never happened to them? The black race seems to have quite a history of accepting unearned money and benefits. One of your colleagues, Mr. Leonard Pitts suggested a figure of $50,000 for every black. That is over $1.5 trillion! Where in the world do you think that money would come from? Beggars don't know or care where federal government money comes from. The only form of reparations that blacks could justify is free transportation to the original country of origin. Please pick up on this suggestion, return in masses to the cherished motherland and build it up into the free homeland you have always dreamed of. Show the world what you can do! Anyway, I secretly support your calls for this blatant extortion attempt of reparations, because you will finally waken the sleeping giant of white outrage, and it will expose your race to be what your enemies have said all along. Even my most liberal give-em everything friends are expressing disbelief and outrage. Keep it up!
5. Your insistence on being referred to as African Americans is an embarrassing secret joke that you just don't get. What people in their right mind would ever declare allegiance to the most backward, poverty and disease stricken, primitive, world-class welfare continent on earth? Ha ha! You really don't get it! American citizenship is the envy of civilization yet you degrade even that by your insistence on claiming African heritage ahead of

American. Modern African conditions are a perfect example of what happens when the black race is in charge. For a closer example, refer to Washington, D.C., and the results of the Marion Barry administration. Ha ha!

I normally sign all correspondence but choose not to in this case. You have been successful in one thing, that is, the slandering and name calling of anyone that questions or disagrees with your motives. With the above comments, you and your kind will label me with your most cherished slander, racist. Well, most of the actions of your race, easily justify racist sentiments. So be it, racist is not a dirty word.

E-mail: Feb. 13, 2002

I enjoyed your article today, until I got to the "blacks overrepresented" part!!! It shows how consumed by race you are!! Are blacks overrepresented in the NBA, the Oscar nominations? At Gates BBQ?? Probably, but who cares!!! Do you take a calculator and figure out injustice of a black represents 13.1 percent??

The military is an honorable profession, and you should be proud of them!!! It is also voluntary!!! No one forces them in!!! Why do you have to keep score?? Let's face it, the vast majority of people who have died for America at Pearl Harbor, Iwo Jima, Normandy, Korea and Vietnam and other places were overwhelmingly white, but it would not be P.C. to say that!!! I doubt the 16 percent of blacks overseas are as concerned about that as you are.

As for black police, is there a "keep out" sign at City Hall?? I don't think so!! But really, how many black kids growing up in the hood want to be cops? Can you imagine the grief a black kid would get if he told his buddies he wanted to be a cop?? He might as well go all the way and say he wants to be a Republican, too!!! If there is one thing blacks in the "hood" hate worse than a white cop, it's a black one!!

E-mail: Jan. 22, 2003

I don't know how you ever were appointed to *The Star's* Editorial Board when you can write such outrageous things as you did today. I have to wonder if your lofty position isn't, in fact, a perfect example of affirmative action gone astray, and proof of the folly in awards based on race. For you to liken Bush's pronouncement on the Michigan issue to the placing of a 20-foot burning cross on the White House lawn is so absurd I can hardly believe *The Star* accepts your rantings as thoughtful journalism. It's guys like you who are a millstone to the whole process of moving ahead with race issues.

Come on, Lewis, there's enough hatred and ignorance in the world without you adding to it. More than ever, the black community and the black culture need intelligent leadership and inspirational thought. In fact, I daresay that we all yearn for that! We had that from Dr. King. But you certainly aren't emulating his example.

E-mail: June 27, 2003

Reparations!!! What in the name of Strom Thurmond are you talking about!!!? You know we are in a fight against terror, and the economic slow down, and you want what??? Give it up. What do you think affirmative action, Aid to Families with Dependent Children, Head Start, welfare are?? If we gave out reparations the money would wind up back in the hands of the white man anyway. If blacks want more money why don't they stop eating at McDonald's all the time, going to movies and buying rap albums, and stay in school so they can earn more!! Not having kids out of wedlock might keep a few more bucks in their pockets!! The destructive family lifestyle many black engage in holds them back. Reparations just make them look like they are begging for more money. Enough is enough!!

But I am not without compassion. I would be willing to pay reparations, let's say a one-time payment of $50,000 if you're black, ($25,000 if your half black or light skinned) in return for an end to affirmative action, welfare, Head Start, Aid to Families with Dependent Children. How about that?? Or how about if you can get the illegitimate birth rate down from 70 percent to let's say 30 percent? You know, use a little incentive!! What do you say?? White people are not going to dig deep without something in return!

It's time for blacks to take off the training wheels and have white libs let go of the bike.!! I think blacks could do quite well if they stopped the group think and started to think as individuals.

E-mail: Oct. 20, 2004

You know, I read your opinions largely to get myself irritated. I just thought this time I would respond … not that you'll actually read this or care. Your views are consistently ridiculous. Everything has to be a "black thing." When you wake up and realize that all you do by espousing the old and tired "white man keeping the black man down" routine is further the entitlement culture of black society and in fact further the racism in American society. How long do you want white people to pity black people for ills perpetrated in the past? I suggest you look at the cultural history of the Chinese or possibly the Irish… both of which have become viable power blocks in American society.

Respectfully, (but just barely)

E-mail: Nov. 12, 2004

It's been a few weeks since I bothered you. My doctor would probably recommend that I quit reading your columns based on the effect your opinions have on my blood pressure. I'm pretty sure that today's dose of Accupril went for naught.

I keep reading liberal columnists making the statement that the

Republicans and Bush are "driving a wedge" in America. I hear about "two Americas." I only hear that from Democrats and liberals. I am not aware of any Republican strategy to exclude anyone from the party. However, I fear that when you write a column only from the perspective of black journalists, it divides people. I have no more control over my being white than you have over being black.

I believe that your quote of Mr. Bositis, "I can't believe the rest of the country is finally going to concede the Civil War to the South," is inflammatory and divisive. I don't hear any of my Republican friends advocating a return of the institution of slavery. I don't believe that you could find a majority of white Republicans who would advocate a return of slavery. I was born in the Deep South in 1949. I lived through the Jim Crow days. I can tell you that people who denied blacks the opportunity to vote were overwhelmingly Democrats.

The Democratic Party has, in my lifetime, been a coalition of affected groups: blacks, gays, women. Now there is a division or wedge. And it is in the Democratic Party. Two of those groups are at odds with each other over the issue of gay marriage. That does not bode well for the Democratic Party in future elections.

My hope is that the Republican Party will reach out to blacks as never before with its message of self-reliance, smaller government, and, yes, values.

Thank you for your time.

E-mail: March 5, 2005

Oh my gosh Louie! If I were such a cynic with an incredible knack of picking out all things racist, I would never be able to leave the house. For attempting to be a "man of the people," your constant rallying cries to incite the masses is actually doing the black community a disservice.

Would it hurt you to write a positive column? Maybe something about the city's housing program spending $1.1 million to "refurbish" two homes in the ghetto? You know, how several minority contractors over billed the city on superfluous sub jobs. That would be an excellent story. You'd win a Pulitzer.

Keep up the meaningful work you do, Louie. If nothing else, you make me laugh.

Liberalism: Give It A Rest!

Voice mail: 2000

The real cause of problems, and the biggest enemy blacks have in this country is the NAACP and the Democratic Party. The biggest enemy the United States has is liberalism. Now I know you don't agree with me. What's going to happen is the economy of the United States is going to completely collapse. We're going to go into a worse depression than 1929. The only way to save this nation from destruction is a total economic collapse and a Christian revival and that is exactly what's going to happen. If you want to know how I know the economic collapse is coming, get out your old King James Bible and turn to Amos 3:7. If you call me after the economic collapse I will tell you how to survive it. If you call me now you won't believe me in the first place. In the second place I am moving to Indiana. But when the economy collapses I will tell you how to survive it. The reason I'm doing this is because I really like you. I don't agree with you all the time. But I do have respect for you. So give me a call after the economy collapses because until it does, you won't listen. Have a nice day.

Voice mail: 2003

Lewis, are you trying to stir up a racial war. This would be the final thorn or whatever you want to call it that would do just that. Reparations. That will never happen. Representatives would not even be allowed to even introduce … well they'd be laughed out if they tried to introduce such a bill. It's not going to happen. But look what is going to be stirred up by it. All right. You're going to cause whites and blacks to have to decide what side they're on. You're going to stir up a racial war. Get off this thing. Anybody can come up and say things that they want money for. The American Indians have just as much or more reason than blacks do. We're not going to do it, but you're going to stir up a racial war. Get off of this now. Don't go any further. Who are you going to expect, how are you going to expect people to decide which side they're on on this thing? It will be on race, and you'll have a racial war on your hands. Now quit it, please. You're going to stir up something you'll never be able to undo. It won't happen so why even try to stir this thing up. There are so many reasons why it's wrong. Get off it please before it's too late.

E-mail: Jan. 29, 2003

Why is it that pacifist cowards like you are the first to bleat your whinny liberal causes but also the first in line to benefit from the efforts and fortitude of others?

Voice mail: Sept. 26, 2003

Lewis, you're talking about President Bush inspiring division. You inspire division in race and gender every day that you write. I think you need to go look in the mirror because you are definitely confused. Have a good day.

Voice mail: 2004

As per usual your column is so far out in left it's almost laughable to read. You ought to get some facts and quit writing from a black bias at all times.

Voice mail: 2004

Just the hypocrisy and then the whining about Fox news is just mind boggling to me. It's a proven known fact that most of the national media is extremely slanted. Even anybody would say it's a little slanted. And one station, one channel, Fox News, which may slant the other way, and you hear no end to screaming and hollering and moaning and groaning about and your Republican domination. That's ridiculous. One channel out of CNN, MSNBC, NBC, CBS, ABC, all of them slant to the left. One channel, and it's just ridiculous. What a bunch of hypocrisy. I read and try to keep an open mind, but it's just ridiculous. And that "OutFoxed" movie, it was proven, it was a hack job. Just give me a break. If you can't take one channel that gives another point of view without whining. We have put up with it for years.

Voice mail: 2004

I'm surprised you haven't blamed George Bush for the hurricanes in Florida. You're nothing but a girlie man journalist.

Voice mail: 2004

Why don't you speak out against the hate speak against black Republicans like Clarence Thomas and Condoleezza Rice? The day that that happens I'll have respect for you, and I'll start reading your column.

E-mail: Aug. 13, 2004

Same sex marriage bad debate goes on?? Nooo, it doesn't. When 71 percent of voters are against gay marriage, there is no debate left worth mentioning. Perhaps you and the 29 percent who are for it need a bigger box of Kleenex to dry your eyes and wipe your oh so "tolerant" noses with. You and your ilk disgust me. Whenever I come across another one of your smarmy little articles, with your smug face plastered over it, I have to resist the urge to retch all over my morning paper. Isn't there some liberal rag in San Francisco that you could be writing for rather than polluting the pages of *The Kansas City Star* with insipid drivel?

I've been reading this paper for 40 years. Heck, I used to deliver them when I was a kid. You are an affront and an embarrassment to the tradition of a great metropolitan newspaper. Your writing skills stink. The only logical rationale that I can arrive at for you having a job there is that "diversity in the newsroom" charade you constantly espouse. I hope they pay you what you are worth, which is far less than the $34 that I just mailed off for my two-month subscription renewal.

E-mail: Sept. 10, 2004

I must say that after reading what you wrote in the 9/9/04 issue of *The Kansas City Star* paper, I can't believe you'd write such nonsense… affirmative action…. Listen, you should be thankful you are black. There are more scholarships available to blacks. You pander to the media about how people of color are so mistreated, etc. You are basically saying outright lies, and I can't believe a paper would print your bullshit!!!!

I am not a big fan of President George W. Bush, but remember it is Sen. John Kerry who wants to fight a kinder gentler war, yeah right. I'd rather fight it in their back yards than mine.

Again, on the economic front you are ignorant. Bush can do nothing about jobs going overseas, or the ending of jobs. It is about money, and he (President Bush) can't just stand up and say...."Hey, I demand that you keep the jobs in America, or companies YOU HAVE TO create more jobs...." It just doesn't work that way in a capitalist society.

One last thing, I am canceling my subscription to the paper because I am so tired of reading crap that you write. Granted you have your opinion, and I have mine, but your liberal stances are the ones that are destroying the country from within.

E-mail: Nov. 12, 2004

It's rather amazing, Lewis, how you manage to maintain the consistently negative attitude reflected in many of your columns. Such distorts even your better ideas or suggestions.

E-mail: April 8, 2005

What a liberal elitist you are!! I'm glad you were able to psycho-analyze the voters!! Everyone else is wrong, but you're right!!

You know many Christians do feel they will be judged at the end, and they don't want support for abortion and gay rights on their resume!! Eternity is forever and much more important than a liberal government program they might benefit from for a few years!! Jesus said goats (hell bound liberals) will go to the left, and sheep (righteous born-again Christians) will go to the right!! Even Jesus talked about left and right!! I think Jesus is archiving your columns, he will use them against you when you stand before him!! Only a cruel God would allow you into heaven!! You clearly don't want to be around a bunch of born-again Christians!! That would make you miserable! Heaven would be a bummer for you!!

I think you need to get your nose out of these left wing books and wake up and find out which way the wind is blowing!!

E-mail: Feb. 23, 2006

What color is the sky in your world? Louis you need to stop reading all these silly books and going to diversity conferences. I wonder if you could write every column about race if you were white. I wonder if you would be a Vice President of *The Star* if you were white. If you don't get that rather large chip of your shoulder I fear back problems for you in the future, sir.

E-mail: Wednesday, June 28, 2006

This has to be the stupidest article ever from the piece of trash *Kansas City Star* what a joke, the backlash is coming and the illegal criminals will be leaving soon and all you liberal jerks can leave, too.

E-mail: June 28, 2006

I am sympathetic with the immigrants, but 12 to 20 million is an invasion.

They should swoop down on the people actually working, take their fingerprints and issue a card they can use to come and go with, but amnesty only encourages more to come to our already overburdened system and cheats the people who are in line to come here legally.

Insanity and Profanity

Voice mail: 1997

Hey Diuguid, I didn't realize you were such a goddamn expert on politics. Now you write a column today that says the whole thing against (President) Clinton was just a charade. You know that's what really goes against the whole deal. I realize the people down there at *The Star* have to have a few burrheads like you around. That's just part of the program. But you know, that's what ruins the whole goddamn thing. They get an uppity nigger like you – a decent foreign boy who can write something and he thinks he's a fucking expert. Why don't you go back down there in the goddamn ghetto with all your dope smoking, welfare recipients, fucking buddies and shove some paper up your fucking black nigger ass. How about it there? You Goddamn stupid son of a bitch, you and that big fat fucker who writes about football. Boy the pair of you, hell I'll bet you're down there sucking old Clinton's dick either that or looking for another handout, you nigger motherfucker.

Voice mail: 1997

I haven't even read your article this morning. But due to the fact of the way you write about race and things and everything like that, you know, when I was picking up Sunday morning's paper and read about the equality of the queers and every damn thing like that, and then right below that there was an article in there about the World War II veterans. I'm sure that my dad, my two brothers and my brother-in-law did not fight for the equality for those fucking queers. Excuse my language.

Voice mail: March 20, 1999

Lewis, I'm sorry, but you are completely nuts.

Letter: Sept. 27, 2001

After reading your racist, African slanted bullshit for a year I finally had to write.

What kind of an American (if you really are one) are you? You left wing liberal Jesse Jackson assholes make me sick. If you don't like living in Kansas City or the United States get the fuck out and stay out. As taxpayers we have doled out (free of charge) 5 trillion dollars of welfare and other goodies to you people, for what reason I'll never figure out. I would put you in the same sewer with Louis Farrakhan, Jesse Jackson, Barbara Lee, Al Sharpton who all make a living of hating white people. You should be ashamed of yourself and your anti-government, anti-American attitude. I'm sure if it weren't for affirmative action (basic race discrimination) you would not be where you are today. So it's no wonder you are on the left, Democratic and socialist.

Wake up and if you don't like it in America, get the fuck out. This in America is home of the brave, not a society full of cowards and victims. Now that we have a real president (Bush) your side is not looking so good. Move in with the only "Negro President" in history – Clinton. Come to Grain Valley, Mo., come try to spew your rhetoric bullshit. See what happens.

Letter: Oct. 19, 2001

Prick Diuguid:

Reading your shit smelling columns I was in a rage!!

My Dad said, "You've got to consider the source. He is a stupid fucking nigger! He is a draft-dodging asshole. It is too bad that the pile of shit was not in the twin towers. But it is hard to kill some vermin. Hope you break your back. You are a cowardly son-of-a-bitch. You bad mouth the government that got you your job through black "quota." With luck you will be shot in your kinky head. I would be glad to furnish the gun and ammo. You think you are "cool man." But when you wake up in the morning, you are still a motherfucking nigger! The lowest form of puke on earth.

E-mail: Dec. 5, 2001

Boo Hoo Hoo!! You poor little liberal nappy-headed asshole. Have your feelings been hurt by some reasonable and patriotic people who dislike your continual grind of anti-government bullshit? Listen dumb ass, 90 percent of the people disagree with your pacifist position. We don't like the idea of people killing thousands of our innocent citizens in the name of some bass ackwards religious beliefs. You must make your family feel like crawling into a hole. Imagine your poor daughter trying to explain to her fellow college students why her father is such an asshole and writes such bullshit. You are such a dick.

E-mail: Dec. 7, 2001

"Diversity Multiplier".... What profound bullshit. Your subject matter has always been very narrow and thin in content, but is this something you dreamt up lately? I will think of your "diversity multiplier" the next time I drive through the city and one of your unemployed (by choice) beer drinking, dope dealing brothers gives me the one finger salute in an attempt to start a confrontation! Instead of trying to convert the masses to your biased lines of thought, why don't you instruct your "bros" on common decency.

Letter: Dec. 22, 2001

Jesus loves you. The rest of us think you're an asshole.

E-mail: Nov. 20, 2002

You are a complete idiot! I never read your pro-government liberal horseshit, but much to my regret, I did today and was compelled to waste more of my limited, precious time sending this e-mail.

You are just such a typical knee-jerk liberal. You should have stopped writing a long time ago and let people just think you were stupid instead of proving and confirming it with columns like the one today.

Get a clue, you moron. As a professional, you really need to do a better job (of) thinking before writing.

E-mail: Nov. 27, 2002

When will you ever free yourself from that opium pipe and live in the world of reality? The views you continually express including today's "we must embrace our Iraqi brothers" are so pathetically naïve. Your views on race relations are just as devoid of real-world mainstream opinions. Idealism is generally a good thing, but you must learn to temper it with reality, if you ever expect white Americans to do more than reject and ignore your naïve "we're all brothers" world view.

Voice mail: 2003

Reparations would help America shed the chains of oppression instead of continuing to drag them? Shit, Lewis. The only guy who's dragging them this morning is you. Get real.

Voice mail: 2003

I just canceled the paper today and one reason is your column in the Friday paper. I hope I never have to see a column again with your picture ever again as long as I live.

Voice mail: 2003

You know without hate or race baiting, you'd be nothing but a sophomoric clerk at *The Kansas City Star*. You couldn't find a job if you didn't have race to stir up all the time.

Voice mail: 2003

Maybe you're just trying to lash on to a fast growing minority because your minority group isn't cutting it just number-wise. But actually I think you should concentrate on what's necessary, the cohesiveness of the nation, and that's a common language, a shared history and a common regard for the law—meaning the Constitution. This business about black history, Hispanic Heritage Month, blah, blah, blah, blah, if we celebrated the traits of every group that contributed to this country, there aren't enough months in the year to celebrate even one trait from every group that's contributed to this country. I think your opinion is divisive. I think multiculturalism is divisive, and, man, if you want to catch the coattails of the Hispanics, man, go ahead. But I think you look foolish, man. Good luck to you. Bye.

E-mail: June 27, 2003

Your column is worthy of but one word: BULLSHIT.

E-mail: June 27, 2003

If you really think we are going to pay reparations to a bunch of lazy-ass deadbeats who hang out on nearly every corner in the city you must still be smoking that silly weed from your college days.

Considering: Affirmative action, Head Start, earned income tax credit, food stamps, AFDC, Pell Grants, et. al. I think we have more than compensated you for the plight of a few hundred slaves. None of which you nor 1 percent of your brothers can lay claim to be descendents of same.

This is one honky that will not participate in direct payment for some idiocy cause. I guess if society is so dumb as to continue giving you folks everything it probably isn't unreasonable for you to continue asking for handouts! You should pray that all the feel-good liberals continue to dominate our government.

Voice mail: 2004

Lewis, do you really think those sons of bitches over there are going to sit down at a conference table and work their problems out? You've got to be dreaming. This has been going on over there for thousands of years, and the only way to get their attention is to rattle their goddamn cage. Thank you.

Voice mail: 2004

I wish to Christ I did not have to see your face or your writings in *The Star*. You're slanted. You're a bigot. I hope *The Star* fires your ass. Or better yet. Do us a favor and quit.

Voice mail: 2004

Between you and Madeleine Albright, I think the only way I could sum that up would be dumb and dumber, or maybe much dumber. You being the much dumber.

Voice mail: 2004

After reading your article this morning in *The Kansas City Star,* I really think probably you should take some time off and get some rest. I hope you have a real good day.

Voice mail: 2004

Jeez Lewis, I don't know after today's article, I think you ought to resign. You're getting so paranoid it's terrible. I think black people really are responsible for the crimes that are committed. It's not the white people causing them to do it.

Letter: April 16, 2004

Well I knew it wouldn't be long before you wrote something totally repugnant to my moral sense. I accuse you of ignorance and moral anesthesia. The only thing you know in your head and feel in your heart is black suffering.

E-mail: April 25, 2004

When you grow a pussy, maybe you will have the insight to speak about women and their birth control choices. Abortion benefits men who get women they do not love and respect – the women they knocked up – more than it protects women. Why don't you, as a man, advocate responsible sex rather than killing little babies you and your dick pals create but don't want to support? Don't speak for "women" as if you know what you are talking about. The baby killing "choice" is not all it's cracked up to be for the woman who has to live with the reality that she murdered her first baby because she had unprotected sex with a loser.

E-mail: June 3, 2004 (Reaction to a column on the Hispanic Civil Rights Summit)

You are an absolute disgrace for putting a happy face on this racist, imperialist asshole's hopes for this country's future.

E-mail: Oct. 21, 2004

I call you what you are, and the shit you write says a lot about you. Look at your fucking party. You left wing socialist traitor. Remember, terrorists will not spare you just because you are a pussy, nor would they spare a real patriot (which you are not, pussy).

E-mail: Oct. 21, 2004

What a bunch of shit. Only an ignorant dumb ass like you would type such stupidity. I hope the next terrorist attack gets you and the likes of you. The nation and the world would be a better place. Man.

Voice mail: Oct. 27, 2004

Every time you write you prove what a lame moron you are. Bye.

E-mail: Nov. 12, 2004

Keep the comedy coming! Do you actually believe everything you write, or do you laugh as much as I do when you invent much of it?

Voice mail: Dec. 9, 2004

You're still there? I'd have thought *The Star* would have fired you months ago.

Voice mail: December 2004

I just want to disagree with you again. I always find it amazing that those who implore us to be tolerant are sure intolerant of those who you don't want to be tolerant of. If we don't accept gays and can't embrace their lifestyle, we're intolerant, but you can't tolerate the fact that we're not accepting them as gays. I feel sorry for you. I pray for you all the time. I feel you're so lost. I mean if it snows it's because you're black. I've never heard or seen anyone so sad to be black. You know you should really be proud of the color you are. You shouldn't blame everything on the color of your skin. And when someone tells you they don't see color that's really what they mean. They treat people like a white sheet of paper. And that doesn't mean they don't see you as a black man. That just means they see you as a black man, but they're not judging you as a black man when they say we're not seeing color. They don't mean, oh we don't actually see color, well of course we see color. But what we mean is, hey, I see the color of your skin is black. It means nothing to me except that you know, maybe there are some cultural things behind that. It doesn't mean anything about what kind of person you are. That's what someone means when they say that. So don't try to excoriate someone for that. Anyway, Merry Christmas.

Voice mail: 2005

You put Jesus Christ and Martin Luther King in the same sentence? You must be nuttier than I thought.

E-mail: March 9, 2005

Once again you have demonstrated your inability to learn. If I look at you, I'm "glaring"; if I don't look at you, I'm "avoiding." Doesn't it ever occur to you that most people are actively doing something and don't have the time to be bothered by what you're wearing. Neither do they desire to start a conversation with you, regardless of what you're wearing. You would find, as I've written before, you would be treated, in a like manner if you wore a tux.

Voice mail: March 18, 2005

Lewis, you're not going to enjoy this little message because you're still the most intolerant, bigoted, prejudice idiot you've always been, and you'll never learn what the real world is like. You're just blind. I feel so sorry for you.

Voice mail: March 23, 2005

What pictures do you have to have your job? You're a joke. Do you understand that people laugh at you and joke about you and what a joke you are? Get a life, give me a break and why don't you do everybody a favor and quit *The Star*, you moron.

Voice mail: March 23, 2005

I don't know why in your picture you're smiling because man it seems like you are very unhappy. Everything you write about comes down to a racial issue and you know that's pretty laughable. Let's just go back to the Civil War. Let's just say it never happened. Where would you be today? Would you still be a slave? Would the South still exist and maybe there would be a Mason Dixon line. There'd be a North and a South and maybe there'd still be slaves. For everything to come down to a racial issue in this world, it's just ridiculous, man. Can you write about anything else? I don't think you can. I don't think you know anything else. Obviously there's just not much up there in your brain to write about. It's amazing. Maybe you're just at *The Star* to be a racist, to throw the racial card down to see how it plays. Man, you've written some stuff before that's been fairly good, but I just don't get where you're coming from. Yeah, I do. You have a one track mind.

Voice mail: April 8, 2005

After reading years of your articles, I have determined that you are a mentally deranged individual and possibly retarded. So please relieve yourself and relieve the public from writing any more articles. You stink.

Voice mail: July 6, 2005

I am inclined to think that you need to be replaced or seriously observed. Your article is meaningless of intelligence. You're a bigot. I hope you find another job.

Voice mail: Sept. 30, 2005

You are so paranoid. For crying out loud, quit your whining.

E-mail: Nov. 18, 2005

Why can't you EVER discuss something that doesn't have something to do with race. ENOUGH ALREADY !!

E-mail: April 1, 2006

Attention wetbacks: You fuck with this gringo you get shot. Know what? Let these monkeys start shit. I'm in with some good ole, militia boys that not only love to shoot but shoot good. You are poor and can't afford the kind of toys we have.... We'll just start mowing you down like the roaches you are.... They infest and breed like roaches.... Good ole can of Raid known as automatic weapons should do the trick plain and simple.

You want war? You got it. But you're a dumb breed of people not smart enough to know strategy. We'll fight a war with ya. But you know what? When we're done killing all of you we're going to march on Mexico City! That's after we bomb it! Fuck with the gringo; meet the Grim Reaper!

E-mail: July 12, 2006

You have played the race card so much that if it were the Queen, her tits would be rubbed off!

SECTION 3

Discovering the Real America

CHAPTER 8
The Undiscovered Country: Taking Arms Against a Sea of Troubles

Discovering the Real America

Where's the cane to tap out a way to see
Through the darkness and all the misery
Beyond America's blindly racist,
Sexist, homophobic, elitist, disabling past
Beyond the brutal Manifest Destiny
To a better life, where good people
Discover peace, hope and solace at last
A place to breathe deep, sit tall
And not be slumped and bowed
By the wearying weight
Of generations' morass handed to present
And threatening tomorrow's path?
This new exciting undiscovered country
In us all is where people with disabilities
Are embraced with those who shared the shun
Of yesterday's disgrace.
It's not about ships or bullets, bacteria or beads
But questions we ask and answers we receive
That chase away the darkness and turn on the light
Illuminating the vast wonders in others
That racism and exploitation hid from our sight.
Now parade their multi-talents, enjoy, learn
And grow rich from the wealth of a new light.
Both women and men of all the world's colors
Seeing new lands of possibilities as sisters and brothers
Harvesting unimaginable gold in ideas for better tomorrows
For a world of peace, no wars and no sorrows.
They give us hope for a new day
When we can see clearly and
Discover the Real America
This 21st century in all the right ways.

"Life is either a daring adventure or nothing."
~Helen Keller

Daniel Wildcat said something profound in the 1990s when he was on a panel about diversity in front of hundreds of federal workers at a Unity conference in downtown Kansas City. Wildcat, a long-time professor of American Indian Studies at Haskell Indian Nations University in Lawrence, told the audience, "We're still trying to discover the real America." It has been unreachable for centuries because of thickets of stereotypes, bogs of bigotry, deserts of hatred, treacherous cliffs of intolerance, mountains of biases and forests of racism (not to malign nature!).

People doing diversity training for companies, civic, community and church groups often speak of the business case that must be made to sell diversity. But frequently they neglect to explain the business benefits that racism generates. For businesses, low wages are the biggest bonus of racism. If poorly paid white workers think people of color will make less for the same job, they are less likely to complain about their income. In return workers get low standards of living with white privilege yielding just a smidgen above the rest for those who qualify. Racism suppresses unity and depresses social capital by pitting workers against each other. The nation is seeing that worker conflict blossom once more now with the large influx of Hispanic immigrants into the United States. People at the bottom are fighting over the scraps they're tossed as jobs. Often that pits blacks and Latinos against each other.

Those benefits of racism have kept it in a self-regenerating mode throughout history. It can be tracked from Colonialism, through the Revolutionary War, past the signing of the Constitution, throughout the antebellum period of American history, into and beyond the Civil War. The trail continues through Reconstruction, the violent eviction of blacks and Asians from towns throughout the United States, the turn of the last century, the rise of white supremacist hate groups, through different waves of immigration, past World War I, the Great Migration of African Americans from the impoverished, agrarian South to the promise of equality and factory jobs in the North, past the Great Depression and World War II. Follow it through the hope forged by the Civil Rights Movement, the Women's Movement, the American-Indian Movement, the Chicano Movement and the despair in the re-segregation and the economic, racial and social regression of the 1980s, 1990s and into the 21st century. Thandeka offers some insight into the history of the economic power of racism in her book, *Learning to Be White: Money, Race and God in America:*

> As the slave population began to increase significantly, [the] colonial tobacco planters, landed gentry, and English-appointed governors, [had] to generate

race laws to create animosity for the African slaves among the white servile and working classes. To this end, they legislated white race privileges for a class of persons they both despised and feared: ex-bondsmen.

> To understand the fear, we must note that until 1660, the majority of workers on the Virginia tobacco plantations were indentured servants who were kept in separate servant quarters, supervised by overseers and whipped as a means of "correction." Like their eighteenth-century slave counterparts, they were often underfed and underclothed. (45)

The history of many Europeans in America is not vastly different from blacks'. Thandeka quotes Jim Goad's 1997 book, *The Redneck Manifesto: America's Scapegoats: How We Got That Way and Why We're Not Going to Take It Anymore*, writing that

> '[H]alf and possibly as many as two-thirds ... of ALL white colonial immigrants arrived in chains."...
>
> "In Virginia and Maryland during the 1600s, the white-servant quotient was even higher. A study of Virginia from 1623 to 1637 showed that white servants outnumbered white freemen by three to one." The ratio was six to one in Maryland at one point during the 1600s....
>
> "According to accounts from both Virginia and the West Indies during the 1600s, roughly EIGHTY PERCENT of white slaves/servants died within the first twelve months after arrival."...
>
> These indentured servants, which Goad calls "white temp-slaves," could not vote, sit on juries, or marry without their master's permission. Their "[s]o-called 'privileged' white skin was brutally ripped open on plantation after plantation."...
>
> "An indentured servant was legally 'the property of his Master' as paraphrased by West Florida's Governor Johnstone in 1766.... White servants were listed as property on tax returns alongside livestock, the chattel next to the cattle," which meant that they "were bought, sold, traded, and inherited like any other disposable goods."...
>
> "As with Africans, white families were frequently broken apart and sold to different bidders. At auctions, white servants were often purchased in bunches by men known as 'soul drivers,' who chained groups of newly arrived white slaves together and herded them on foot through rural areas, selling them at a profit."...
>
> "During a 1659 parliamentary debate on the white-servant trade to the colonies, legislators used the word 'slaves' rather than 'servants.'" Goad notes that "[a] Virginia law of 1705 mentions the 'care of all Christian slaves,' Christian being a contemporary euphemism for European." In 1751, a writer for *London Magazine* noted that "a British convict shipped overseas became a 'slave in America.' Not surprisingly, 'White indentured servants frequently referred to themselves as slaves.'"... (131-132)

So the great majority of Europeans in America saw their fates linked with Africans as exploited beasts of burden. The man-made creation of "whiteness" established a unique and false sense of superiority as a new identity for Europeans and forever cemented the race problem in America for blacks, Hispanics, Asians and Native Americans. Laws were enacted as early as 1661 in Maryland, firmly barring miscegenation. By the 19th century, nearly every state had such laws (Takaki *Strangers* 101). Government therefore came down hard against racial mixing, strictly maintaining whiteness. After all, it was this nation's benefit to those who qualified. It was as if every white person in America had been given the gift worth his weight in gold. Each new wave of European immigrants to America is made to give up its history, traditions and its past in order to accept this "gift" of being "white" in America. Thandeka writes:

> The process of forgetting their prewhited selves began to empty the workers' core sense of self and of values that transcended the workplace and its behavior-modification requirements. The premodern and its desires had to be thought of as loathsome, and thus had to be suppressed. These strangulated desires are where the premodern Euro-American and immigrant met the "black," who was permanently locked out of modern America as a thing to be despised. The hateful met the hated. (69)

The ruling class manufactured the psychological figment that enabled low-income white people to truly believe they were in at least one respect in league with the wealthy, landed aristocracy. From the 1600s until now that pseudo-bond enabled indentured servants and the Europeans who followed to look down on Africans and their offspring as slaves, and therefore inferior; Native Americans as savages; and Hispanics and Asians as unworthy eternal newcomers. That elevation of one race in this diverse nation is the self-generating business case for racism, discrimination, prejudice and bigotry. The majority of Americans are heavily invested in it. The faux-reality is at the heart of white privilege. It fuels flight from urban cores; it creates unequal schooling, housing, job opportunities, health care and life expectancy for minorities. It permeates every aspect of how people live, their goals, expectations and their dreams along the many divides in America. And the walls that isolate whites from everyone else are heavily patrolled, and who gets the white privilege goodies is strictly enforced by police, the courts, the military, businesses, civic and faith groups, and self-appointed, heavily armed vigilantes.

"This entire racialization process makes persons with white identities initially aware of the fact that the racial advantages they have been given can be lost," writes Thandeka (86). Thandeka labels this as a form of "racial abuse" against white people by their own, beginning as child abuse and continuing through adulthood and to the grave (40). It leaves white people confused, bewildered, ashamed, fearful and strictly controlled. Thandeka says it has resulted in a "fear of dropping down." That fear is powerful. It and "white shame" create a "'psychological hook' that links poorer 'whites' to the interests and lifestyles of the rich" (101).

We often see that pseudo-bond in politics in which poorer whites vote against their economic self-interests because they feel a connection to whites who are rich. People in so-called red states elevated George W. Bush to the presidency in 2004 even though his tax cuts in his first term heavily benefited the wealthy and he cut funding for many social programs that would have helped low-income families. Thandeka quotes Donald R. Kinder and Lynn M. Sanders in their 1996 book, *Divided by Color: Racial Politics and Democratic Ideals*:

> This pervasive system of white racial resentment, Kinder and Sanders conclude, has "racially encoded" white political thinking. Whites vote for their perceived race interest rather than for the immediate economic and social well-being of themselves and their own families. . . . Clearly, their objectively groundless fears make these voters prime targets for manipulation by political and economic interests all too willing to use race-baiting tactics to achieve their own ends. (91)

This confounding yet powerful emotional force has withstood the ravages of war and time. What's even worse is the United States' "race problem" has been shed by whites as a concern only of people of color. Instead it has been a rich white system of exploitation of whites and everyone else all along. Thandeka writes: "These low-paid wage earners were not held in high esteem by their white bosses, who exploited their labor while consoling them as whites. The workers were, in effect, exploited twice: both as workers and as 'whites.'" (78)

The system leaves them open to lifelong exploitation by schools, colleges and universities, politicians, law enforcement, judicial, community, civic, religious, media and corporate authorities. The business case for maintaining the status quo is that the majority in America are heavily invested in continuing the system of whiteness. Thandeka writes: "The nonwhite zone must be vigilantly patrolled, then, for along its border lies the terrain of race-mixing" (26). What also lies there is an even greater threat: unity, and a real elevation of all groups who for generations have been oppressed and exploited.

Throughout time we have faced insurmountable obstacles in race relations, gender conflicts, strife among generations, immigrant vs. native-born, ability vs. disabilities, straight vs. gay and lesbian, and the list goes on and on. We can't seem to learn from the mistakes of the past. We keep falling on the swords that impaled our parents, their parents and their parents' parents because of the long-established business, civic and community case for maintaining whiteness.

It's also why Daniel Wildcat correctly says, "We're still trying to discover the real America," and why so many barriers keep getting erected blocking the journey.

I call this same expansive notion "Our Undiscovered Country." I pulled this concept from William Shakespeare's play, *Hamlet,* in an old Shakespeare textbook that I've kept since my college days. It is in Hamlet's well-known soliloquy:

> To be, or not to be: that is the question:
> Whether 'tis nobler in the mind to suffer
> The slings and arrows of outrageous fortune,
> Or to take arms against a sea of troubles,
> And by opposing, end them? To die: to sleep . . .
> To sleep: perchance to dream . . . .

In that famous scene, Hamlet talks of ". . . The undiscover'd country from whose bourn/ No traveller returns . . . ." Hamlet is speaking of death and the place to which people go from this earth after they have passed on.

My redefinition of the "undiscovered country," however, is that this brave new domain is here on our planet. Men and women have spent centuries journeying across our globe, discovering new frontiers in science, medicine, industry, transportation and communications. Those discoveries have enabled us to physically extend our reach to the depths of the ocean floor, the peaks of the tallest mountains, the tangled centers of the rain forests and the coldest most frozen regions of the Arctic and Antarctic. We are even moving further in exploring outer space. But as the kids used to say, "Been there; done that." What's next?

What lies ahead, what remains is that undiscovered country for all of us. It is the domain that people have to venture into without fear, to explore and learn about the richness that lies in the humanity of others. It is the missed opportunity that is more than 500 years overdue. Christopher Columbus and his men took the human race down the wrong path by violently imposing European standards on people who had their own language, culture, religion, government, housing, economy and system of education. By not valuing those differences but eradicating the majority of them and the Indigenous people, Columbus left the vital domain undiscovered. Imperialism ruled then and its foundation upon which much of our civilization is built today remains an impediment to people's learning, truly embracing diversity and growing from that diversity and from what others can teach.

The Manifest Destiny that propelled the 19th century westward expansion in the United States must be transformed into an even more powerful force driving the exploration of the undiscovered country. The destiny of the 21st century must be one in which people explore, discover and settle new communities of understanding, generating harmony without imposing dominance, exploiting others or destroying the richness that individuals have to offer. The undiscovered country contains the gold that will enrich us all with new social, intellectual, scientific, financial and human capital, enabling humanity to be competitive in the global marketplace by producing new intellectual products.

Whiteness, which Thandeka correctly describes, has to be exposed for the brutal system of abuse and exploitation that it has been for centuries. It has victimized white people and people of color. Whiteness has kept Americans and America from reaching their potential. Therefore the undiscovered country has to be explored. It is the long, hard, treacherous journey that each of us must take in finding new ways for all of us to get along. It will not be conflict-free. But it is through the difficulty of conflict that new ideas, understanding and alliances can be forged.

This great exploration goes far beyond tolerance. Tolerance is just looking across the borders that continue to separate us. No, the exploration is about embracing diversity, recognizing that we have nothing to fear and everything to gain from it. It's about raising standards far above the Eurocentric teachings that most schools, government, church, civic and community groups, people and media have dumbed us down to. We have to venture into the infinite wilderness of the undiscovered country and find and establish new ways to get along. That will enable us to benefit from each other's experiences and create a wealth of new intellectual products from our collective, diverse and invaluable intellectual capital. Venturing into the undiscovered country is what I call humanity's "21st Century Destiny." In sharing our hopes and dreams and absorbing the aspirations of others, we will grow as individuals and as a people. That will take us all further into charting new courses in the undiscovered country along paths of understanding and cooperation, so that we can work together to better appreciate and profit from our diversity as human beings.

Doing nothing and allowing whiteness and the racial and other anti-diversity problems it has perpetuated to continue will be extremely detrimental to the United States' ability to compete in the global economy. *Project 2020*, a report by the National Intelligence Council released in January 2005, says that in 2020, "Asia is likely to be the main engine of the global economy [and] India and China will be major powers.... The United States will remain 'the single most important country across all dimensions of power,' but will wield less authority because of the greater influence of India, China, and possibly other nations such as Brazil and Indonesia" ("2020 foresight").

This bleak look into the future from our own soil can be changed if the richness in diversity is harnessed in America to help this country maintain its competitive advantage. Living on a one-sided view of the past is never sustainable. Allowing things to continue the way they are negatively affects everyone but especially children. In order for us to progress as humanity, conserve the environment, stretch the world's precious resources, save all species of the world from endangerment and ensure that there will be a better world for our children and our children's children, we must change course.

We have to examine the unique histories of all people in this country, appreciate others' struggles and know that they, too, must have a hand in maintaining this country's competitive advantage. Everyone must see people of color, gays, lesbians, people with disabilities and other discounted groups as the truly valued contributors to this society that they really are. Everyone has to accept us – all of us – and go beyond tolerance and not dismiss our history, our heritage and our contributions to America. Change will occur and the demonization will disappear only if all of our history, our literature and our stories are included in the books, teachings and media of America.

Each group—using the boot of the dominant, oppressive culture—keeps its foot on the necks of the other groups, preventing everyone from progressing.

An expanded resource of ideas from more and different people will allow for a greater selection to occur letting the best of the solutions surface and be at our disposal. That happened with the Navajo Code Talkers saving the Allies during World War II. The code used their native language, which was part of their history and heritage. The irony is that it survived even though Europeans who came to this country did everything they could to eradicate the language, culture and even the Navajo themselves from the North American continent. But it's a good example of just how important it is to appreciate, train, prepare and enlarge the diversity that we have and the problem-solving skills those individuals possess: they have the potential with their special talents to save us in the future from horrible fates that might befall us and which we have no way of predicting. In the United States, because of marketing and capitalism, everyone instinctively wants to know, "What's in it for me?" It is a selfish pursuit; nevertheless the question must be answered to get people to abandon racism and value diversity. But that would take knowing the truth about people of color instead of the stereotypes. One truth, in addition to the Navajo Code Talkers, is that George Washington Carver—a former slave, less than nobody, who stubbornly held to his desire to get an education—saved American agriculture at the turn of the last century (see Chapter 5). We are living at a time when we have to expand humanity's gene pool of ideas so we can successfully overcome the most recessive aspects of the global marketplace.

Gary R. Howard's book, *We Can't Teach What We Don't Know: White Teachers, Multiracial Schools* calls exploring the undiscovered country "Our Unfinished Work." Howard wrote:

> There is the old country of oppression and racism from which we are attempting to emigrate, and the new country of hope, transformation, and healing that we are only beginning to explore and inhabit. We have of necessity been border travelers, attempting to map a new route toward positive White identity, while at the same time being inextricably tied to the weight of former images. . . . There is a feeling of adventure and discovery in growing toward a greater awareness. There is a personal renewal and hope to be found in the possibility of change and the opportunity to believe and act in new ways. There is a positive and healing privilege gained through our connection and collaboration with colleagues and students from other racial and cultural groups. And there is a joy in knowing that we have chosen to be in this struggle, that we are part of a movement to dismantle the foundation of our own past and present dominance. (115-116)

Chapter Nine

CHAPTER 9
Diversity Formula One—Indestructible Talent

Whales

Sometimes the best things
Emerge from the world's worst horrors.
Who'd imagine the nauseating,
Ocean-covering vomit from whales
Would make the world's most fragrant perfume, big sales.
Who knew a century ago that insignificant mold
Could produce penicillin and be sold
Curing death-sentence diseases
It's more than sniffles and sneezes.
Or that God's creature, an insignificant mink,
When laced together, though dead, link
To warm bodies with the most beautiful wraps
Racism has the same effect
Awful in its most ugly splendor
Yet forces the indomitable spirits never to surrender
Pushing on to more glorious things
Their souls soar on powerful wings
From the worst piles of manure men historically still produce
Some of the prettiest most brilliant flowers that seduce
Showing God's hand
Despite the worst ugliness from the theater of man.

I could not at any age be content to take my place in a corner by the fireside and simply look on.

~Eleanor Roosevelt

The business case for racism, discrimination, prejudice and bigotry are firmly entrenched, as Chapter 8 helped illustrate. That makes it difficult to get people to surrender such historically reinforced practices from which many may continue to gain. The benefits of white flight, for instance, are banked outside of the nation's many urban centers, where people of color mostly don't live. The bonuses are counted in higher housing values, better schools, accessible and lower insurance rates, plentiful and low mortgages, and convenient health care, shopping and other amenities. An added privilege in these places where people run to is the warm embrace of hospitality. All of those things could be available in inner cities throughout America if people didn't buy into racism and flee to the ever-expanding suburbs. The off-the-books costs of such actions are logged in family-absorbed expenses for each move, declining property values in the spreading ghost towns of homes and businesses that white flight abandons in urban cores nationwide and the hidden price of relocating children to different neighborhoods and schools. Also uncounted is the effect that such upheaval has on people of color who watch with dismay as block busting sets in and neighborhoods, schools, businesses and faith communities seem to change overnight.

The flight is fueled by people firmly believing the worst about people of color: that they are prone to crime, bring about urban decay and are inherently inferior. The business case for racism would disappear, however, if everyone saw the value that people of color add to life in America.

Diversity trainers teach that there are two ways to try to change people. The first is called the "missionary method." Missionaries in the colonial era of the world assumed that people who were being conquered and colonized were uncivilized. They then imposed on those people the religion, laws, housing, food, schools, government and economics of the occupying force. Often this method met with fierce resistance because the missionaries falsely assumed that the people with whom they were unfamiliar didn't have their own workable institutions—or that, even if the conquered people did, the Western ways were far superior.

A second method is the marketing approach. Applied to discovering the Real America, it allows people to keep their own customs and traditions because no one wants to be conquered, colonized and held to the missionary method. The marketing approach sells people on new enhancements that compel them to abandon the business case for racism so they can see the value of embracing diversity while cleansing themselves of bigotry and discrimination. That can be done if we recognize that everyone possesses real talent. That realization will compel people to appreciate the "what's in it for me" aspect about diversity, which is mostly missing when people talk about the subject as being a nice thing and a good thing for others. Often we fail to sell diversity as something that will benefit each of us as individuals just trying to do our jobs better. In this capitalistic country, "what's in it for me" permeates everything. And as selfish as that might sound, "what's in it for me" is the way the business case for diversity must be presented to counter the business case for racism, bigotry, prejudice and discrimination. The value of being fully invested in diversity far exceeds the benefits of continuing the oppression of the past, and it has to be sold that way so the journey into the undiscovered country can be successful for everyone.

Talent x Diversity = Productivity

Simple algebraic formulas for diversity developed from scores of training sessions and lectures on the subject can help people see the true talent, value and merit of minorities without history's blurred lens of intolerance and oppression. Formula I is ***Talent x Diversity = Productivity,*** which assumes that talent, like the standard definition of matter in physics, can be neither created nor destroyed. That talent is in everyone. It often is different and simply must be enabled by others to really flower.

That is where diversity comes in. Diversity in the formula is the multiplier. That factor should be a positive and high number. If the diversity multiplier is zero or a negative number then productivity—whether in schools, communities, churches, businesses or civic organizations—will come out zero or result in negative outcomes. That talent, which is in all people, will then seek other paths, and often it will not be as productive. In fact, such situations encourage that talent to become counterproductive or simply leave. Each of us, therefore, must be a positive diversity multiplier for others so that we enable them to be successful. And we must seek positive diversity multipliers for ourselves so that we prosper as individuals as well.

Schools are where the formula best illustrates how valuing diversity works. Teachers are from mostly middle-class, white America, yet an increasing number of students in schools are children of color. The U.S. census reported in May 2006 that 45 percent of the children in the United States younger than age 5 are minorities. And "one in three Americans is now a member of a minority group.... Projections show that by 2050 the minority population and the current majority of non-Hispanic whites would each make up about half the total population" (Cohn). Teachers, therefore, cannot continue to treat all children the same with a one-size-fits-all form of instruction in the classroom. Educators have to be at the forefront of discovering the Real America, learning all they can about the multicultural groups from which their students hail. That will enable them to better communicate and recognize the talents in each child and not discount anyone's diverse backgrounds. They must be positive and high diversity multipliers for each student so every one of them can achieve the highest productivity in grades, homework and class participation.

Teachers also should encourage students to function as diversity multipliers for each other so that, combined, they enhance the productivity of the class, causing academic achievement to soar. Students must reciprocate by functioning as high and positive diversity multipliers for all educators as well. In addition, teachers must seek the same diversity boost for themselves and for their students from other teachers, administrators, support staff, school board members, parents, people in the community, businesses, and civic and faith organizations. That way their ability and the students' desire to learn are encouraged and enhanced. When all of this diversity boosterism occurs recognizing the talents of individuals then the academic achievement and critical thinking skills in the class expand exponentially. When it involves all students regardless of race or background then persistent achievement gaps will disappear.

Former Kansas City, Mo., school board member Fifi Wiedeman said in a conversation over coffee that people should want to function as positive and high diversity multipliers as she does out of her love for all of our children of many beautiful colors. But when we diagrammed that thought positioning her love against America's hate for black schools and black children we saw a stark contrast. What became apparent was the bitterness from the block busting that followed the integration of neighborhoods throughout America. White flight resulted from black families moving into areas that had finally become available to them thanks to integration. Whites lost bundles of money as they sold out and moved to the suburbs. But they also lost memories and physical property of their old homes, neighborhoods, schools and sense of community that became the property of people they hated. So the hate grew from the change, which added to the "not us" feeling that many white people harbor toward African Americans. The only way to convert the hate to love is to help people understand how to eliminate the "not" so that all that's left is "us." That can only happen if diversity—whether in schools, the community, businesses, civic organizations or faith groups—is sold to people from the standpoint of "what's in it for me?" The only way to break through the ice of hate is through talking with others. In journalism I call that a "currency of conversations." From conversations journalists develop stories that then are invaluable intellectual capital, which feeds into published reports, also known as intellectual products. It is through our "currency of conversations" that we can see value and richness in all people's stories and in getting to know others who are different. The "currency" we exchange includes stories, ideas, problem-identifying and problem-solving skills.

Each individual grows from such exchanges, becoming stronger, smarter, more knowledgeable and more marketable to companies and communities desperate for new ideas in our global marketplace where competition daily becomes more intense. It is what helps us transition from hate to love. Education continues to be a way to break down barriers. Those who do the teaching are diversity multipliers of the highest order. Schools can do a lot to teach students to value diversity.

From "Schools add AIDS to curriculum"

Children used to play schoolyard tag and yell: "You're it! You've got cooties!"

But the game has changed. Now they say, "You've got AIDS!"

It happened in the Center School District in south Kansas City, and that bothered Lea R. Murphy.

The new twist to the old game showed that children in Center and other districts didn't know about acquired immune deficiency syndrome, the virus that causes it and that there is no cure for the fatal disease.

Couple that with the increasingly lower age at which kids have sex, and it's easy to see that Kansas City has a problem. In our town, about 13 percent of all seventh-graders are sexually active, about 40 percent by eighth grade and 75 percent in high school.

Yet parents refuse to believe their saintly sons or darling daughters have crossed virginity's threshold.

Murphy, an Avon representative, wasn't excited about her daughters picking up playground lessons about AIDS or sex. That's when she came calling at Center.

She helped the district quietly set up an AIDS education program, which debuted Dec. 1, 1992, on World AIDS Day. It began with sixth-graders at Red Bridge Elementary School, her kids' school, and then moved to Center Middle and Center High schools.

Young people with AIDS visited students, dispelled myths and told how the disease changes lives and destroys dreams. "They told the kids over and over that 10 minutes of fun isn't worth dying for," Murphy said.

Students quizzed them on pregnancy, condoms, abortion, the incubation period for AIDS, treatment for the disease and whether a cure would ever be found. The sessions showed how misinformed the kids were, which troubled Murphy.

"We need to be responsible and give our kids the correct information," she said.

The program started in the lower grades to drive home the message before those kids begin dangerous experiments with sex. Between

> September and December 1992, parents became aware of the PTA program and the need for it.
>
> Murphy, who is part of Parent and Family Life Education with the Council of PTAs, said 95 percent of the parents in the district supported the project.
>
> The program is non-offensive and deals with children's health, said Harold B. Frye, then-Center's assistant superintendent of curriculum and public relations. It has avoided the problems and criticisms that have befallen other districts because parents pushed this project.
>
> "It's hard to say no when parents are saying this is something that we need," Frye said. A $5,000 grant helped finance the initiative.
>
> Kathleen Cooper, then-executive director of the Good Samaritan Project, which offers programs for people who are HIV-positive, applauded Center's work.
>
> "Children need to understand not only for their protection but also so that they treat people with the disease with the dignity and respect that they deserve," she said.

When students are exposed to others—including their teachers—who have benefited from high diversity multipliers, they become aware that our different talents should be accepted and celebrated, not dismissed outright for their "difference." One such person is a teacher, whose talents are lauded.

From "Teacher's Specialty: Inspiration"

> Colorful inspirational posters cover the chalkboards and help make Darcell D. Luke's classroom different at C.A. Burke Elementary School in South Kansas City.
>
> Luke, then the school's speech therapist, laughed about that.
>
> "Since I'm not able to use the chalkboards, I choose to use them as bulletin boards," said Luke, who has taught at the school since August 1975. "I like lots of bright cheerful things.
>
> "It makes me feel good."
>
> Luke carries that boost into the school each day and infects her students and other teachers with her cheer and optimism. That feeling follows her as she rolls through the halls and in her classroom in her electric wheelchair.
>
> She has used a wheelchair since she was injured in a car accident in February 1987. Her spinal cord was damaged when her neck was broken in two places.
>
> Luke was off from school recovering from her injuries for 1 1/2 years. She returned to Burke Elementary School for half days in 1988-89 and has worked full time since 1989-90.
>
> She went back to Burke because she loves to teach.

"It's through the Lord's grace that I'm still here, that I'm still able to function," said Luke, who is married and has a 19-year-old daughter.

"I enjoy working with the children, and I hope that through working with them that I can motivate them to be the best they can be. I like to share love with them - lots of hugs and lots of praising.

"I think it helps."

Burke Elementary School is built all on one level with ramps and easy-to-open doors. Wide halls and doorways also accommodate Luke's wheelchair.

She shares a classroom with Barbara Hulett, the learning-disabilities teacher. Each teacher operates independently on her side of the room.

Luke helps students at Burke with language, articulation, voice, speech and fluency. They stream into her room and immediately go to her for hugs.

Herman Campbell, 8; Kelvin Harrell, 9; and Bianca Brown, 8, are among them. They finished their participatory lesson with Luke at a table shaped like a half-moon. Afterward the students were rewarded with more hugs and low-fat, low-sugar animal cookies.

"I enjoy this age group. For the most part they are still smaller than I am," Luke said, laughing.

After the lesson, she rolled down the hall to join counselor Nancy Lovegreen and special-education teacher Jean Hilgedick in a conference with Daisy Young about her grandson, Taylor Hoskin, 8. There was straight talk but also a lot of praise for Taylor and promise for what he'll be able to accomplish.

Lovegreen said Luke was admired for what she did in supplementing the work of classroom teachers. The additional practice, small-group instruction and Luke's special talents are a godsend for the Hickman Mills District school.

Luke inspires the children, Hulett said. Her compassion, strength and courage motivate them to not let obstacles impede their development.

Luke also heightens students' awareness of people in wheelchairs. They know she's different. But she's more than capable of doing her job.

"It's challenging," Luke said. "A lot of things come up that I have to make work best for me."

Luke has a lot of students who want to help her. "Sometimes I have more helpers than I know what to do with," she said.

They include Justin Brown, 11, and Josh Gunning, 12. They said it makes them feel good as Boy Scouts to help Luke.

Helping others fits the principles that Luke lives by.

"If you approach life with a positive attitude, the fact that you can see the brighter side of things, hopefully people will want to be around you and have a better outlook themselves," she said. "I don't think folks would want to be around people who do a lot of complaining."

That's a wonderful gift that Luke plans to keep sharing with young people for years to come.

People with disabilities and their families, too, are as sensitive to positive or negative diversity multipliers as other minorities are. Their productivity—indeed their lives—is greatly enhanced when others realize that their disability doesn't preclude a valuable talent. The disability is often visible whereas the talent only becomes visible when it is recognized and enabled. But in order for that to happen, many obstacles must come down.

From "Barriers call them to action"

Their children turned Linda McDonough and Lillian J. Keyes into activists for people with disabilities.

The women met at a workshop on diversity. They were there because of their jobs.

But what mattered were McDonough's son, Tim, and Keyes' daughter, Patricia.

McDonough told Keyes that Tim has Duchenne muscular dystrophy and is in a wheelchair. She talked about the life they enjoyed, the places they've been and how she wrote letters, congratulating businesses with good accommodations for people with disabilities and criticizing others that are inaccessible.

Keyes lit up. Her daughter had to use a wheelchair. She had cerebral palsy and was 10 years old when she died in 1971.

Keyes praised McDonough's advocacy, saying it helped stretch the small world for people with disabilities into new frontiers. It complements the Americans with Disabilities Act, which outlawed discrimination against people with disabilities in public places and mandated that businesses become more accessible.

But when Patricia was a child, neither businesses nor churches nor schools had designated parking spots, ramps, specially designed doors, bathrooms or other necessities for people with disabilities. The barriers clearly said that people who were different weren't welcome.

Keyes bore the frustrations but insisted that no one deny her daughter access to public places. Often it meant carrying the 80-pound girl and wrestling the wheelchair up and down stairs, into restrooms that were too small and through doors that refused to cooperate.

Keyes got her hands and clothes dirty, but she never surrendered. "I wasn't going to hide her in the house," she said.

Keyes also educated people along the way. Don't stare at Patricia because that made her uncomfortable; don't pity her because it does no one any good. Patricia was a smart, personable girl who knew she was different, but Keyes made sure that she never faced discrimination alone.

That enriched Keyes, who told McDonough: "Only special parents are given children with disabilities. Everybody can't handle it.

"I don't feel sorry for myself. I feel very special because God chose to give her to me."

McDonough feels blessed, too, and works to pry open the world for people with disabilities.

She sent a McDonald's restaurant in Independence a laudatory letter because it had tables made to accommodate wheelchairs, spacious restrooms and parking spaces for people with disabilities.

She criticized a nearby restaurant for its poor access and small facilities. A workout club and a Johnson County shopping center got demerits for being inaccessible, and a video store frustrates her because non-disabled customers park in spots designated for people who are disabled.

McDonough writes for her son and others with disabilities. "You can't assume that people are going to show up on two legs," she said.

She and Keyes are role models for our children, and they spur everyone to do the right thing, said Deborah D. Herr, then-executive director of Whole Person Inc., an advocate for people with disabilities.

We all profit from that.

People who are different benefit by teaching ways in which they have overcome obstacles. Their talent, however, needs to be heard, appreciated and magnified by diversity multipliers so it can lead to productive ends for them and others.

From "Keep the 'able' in disabled"

"My clients have faced death, and they're turned on by life," Clayborn Jones said to about 20 persons with area businesses, colleges, agencies and churches at a Greater Kansas City Diversity Councils Roundtable.

The topic was "Workplace Issues of the Disabled."

Jones, then-employment coordinator of the Disabled Persons Rehabilitation Employment and Mobilization (DREAM) Job Network with the Good Samaritan Project, helps people with HIV/AIDS find supportive employment. New medication has given many people with HIV/AIDS a second chance to live, and they want to make the most of this gift. Being productive at work is one outlet.

The law shields people with HIV/AIDS from discrimination, allowing them to be employed.

That's all people with other disabilities want, too. They seek the opportunity to prove how good they are and to push workplace competition to a new level.

The Americans with Disabilities Act and civil-rights legislation have a close kinship in promoting equality.

Despite the law, a lot of barriers remain. The biggest problem is attitudinal, activists for people with disabilities told the roundtable.

Those advocates included Jones, Mark Ohrenberg, research associate for the University of Missouri-Kansas City Institute for Human Development; Patrick Palmer, senior disabilities rights advocate for Whole Person Inc.; Richard Baillif, a drafting technician for Burns & McDonnell; and Randy Fisher, ADA information specialist with the Kansas Commission on Disability Concerns.

The men also answered questions and buried many myths during the safe haven that the roundtable provided. One person with a company of more than 40,000 workers nationwide said he'd never seen anyone in his workplace with a disability.

But many disabilities such as mental illness or HIV/AIDS aren't visible. A lot of times people hide them because despite the law, discrimination occurs, and it prevents people from getting and keeping jobs.

Once a disability is discovered, some employers have terminated workers, said Fisher, who uses a wheelchair. "The fear is they will be discriminated against," he said.

A Harris poll commissioned by the National Organization on Disability found that people with disabilities are more likely to live in poverty with household incomes of less than $15,000. Although 81 percent of working-age people without disabilities held part- or full-time jobs, only 32 percent of the disabled people did.

That's down from 1986 when 34 percent of people with disabilities said they had jobs.

People with disabilities also don't want pity. They know their rights, and they're unwilling to accept excuses.

At the roundtable, a person mentioned that frequent travel for jobs at her company might be an obstacle for persons with disabilities.

But Palmer, who's blind and whose guide dog, Campbell, was with him, said work-related travel was something people with disabilities could do. "Sometimes we have to come in early and stay longer to get the job done," he said.

People just want the opportunity to show what they can do, he said.

Baillif, who uses a wheelchair, agreed.

"Employers don't think people in a chair can do the job," he said. "We're eager. Give us a chance, and we can do it."

He had hoped the roundtable would delve deeper into issues people with disabilities face daily. This included how co-workers can be more supportive.

Ohrenberg, who has muscular dystrophy and uses a walker, said he would like the topic discussed more so people would develop a comfort and ease in learning from the conversations. "I still sensed that people were scared to talk about this subject," he said.

That discomfort often stalls progress in tearing down the barriers that keep us from prospering from the diversity among us. We've got to get past the way things have always been and work to make opportunities for more people to enjoy the American dream.

Some agencies specialize in ensuring that people whose sight is impaired are able to earn a living as valued workers. They offer employers "gold" in a motivated staff. If only more companies could see that through Diversity Formula I *(Talent x Diversity = Productivity)*. These individuals expand the "what's in it for me" aspect of diversity.

From "Avenue of Hope: Alphapointe Association for the Blind fits into revitalization of Prospect"

Before he died of a gunshot wound in 1979, Bernard Powell envisioned what few others could see: Kansas City has no ghettos – just gold mines waiting for the right entrepreneurs.

Imagine that it took a place whose workers are mostly blind or vision impaired to see the same thing Powell imagined for the economic development of Prospect Avenue in Kansas City's urban core. Alphapointe Association for the Blind in 2002 moved from 18th Street and Broadway to the new 120,000-square-foot, $14 million headquarters it built at 7501 Prospect Ave.

Alphapointe was started in 1911 by Catherine Hale as Allied Blind Workers of Kansas City. Five years later it was incorporated as the Kansas City Association for the Blind.

Everything about the one-story building is modern except the large photographs of Fairyland Park on the walls. That longtime Kansas City attraction was on the same property until the late 1970s when it was closed. But for most of its operation it was segregated, refusing to admit blacks. Alphapointe isn't like that—thank goodness.

The large Alphapointe complex also is accessible for people with disabilities.

Ken Roberson, chairman of the board of Alphapointe, said the floor is designed with two textures so workers who use canes can tell where they are.

Alphapointe is near U.S. 71 and is on a major bus line, making it accessible to people whose impaired vision causes them to rely on the Metro bus service for transportation. More than 70 percent of Alphapointe's work force is blind or has multiple disabilities.

Counter to the stereotype of people with disabilities, these individuals work for a living, producing pens for government agencies and businesses. Some of the black, red, blue and yellow pens have familiar labels such as AlphaGrip and Skilcraft.

Others have company names and logos on them such as Capri Casinos. Tom Healy, president and chief executive of Alphapointe, said workers make 11 million pens a year at the plant.

"They have a place to come for employment," Roberson said. But Alphapointe also provides people with disabilities a place to socialize. "This gives them a sense of self-worth."

The association, however, cited a drop in government business for the layoffs of 15 blind workers. But production continues.

Lucinda Kincaid showed me how she put pens together. She said she enjoyed her job and the location.

"This place is nice, real nice," she said.

Alphapointe also manufactures plastic pharmaceutical bottles. Many of them are used by the military, some in Iraq. About 30 million bottles a year are produced by Alphapointe workers.

They are specially designed and patented by Alphapointe to prevent leakage and to withstand the harmful effects of sunlight as well extreme heat and cold.

The pen and bottle manufacturing operations combined generate about $7 million in revenue a year. The organization also relies on grants because of what it does for people in the community.

The community tie is important because 10 million people in the United States – 3.4 million older than 40 – are blind or visually impaired. In Missouri, 76,000 people are blind, and in Kansas there are 39,200. Alphapointe officials estimate that 52,100 of them live in the Kansas City area.

But nearly 60 percent are employed. That's why Alphapointe also offered a number of services for people who are visually impaired.

They include programs for health and wellness, elderly low vision services, the work adjustment center and the adaptive technology center.

Clay Berry, assistant director of education and rehabilitation, explained that the programs help ensure that people who were born blind or recently lost their sight can still maintain their quality of life.

"The most simple things become complicated when your vision becomes compromised," he said, explaining how a mock kitchen helps people realize they can learn to make it on their own.

Specially adapted exercise equipment is there for people who are blind, and so is help for diabetics who need assistance monitoring their blood sugar levels. Social workers and occupational therapist also work with young people. Some computers offer large print. Other computers respond to voice commands.

People no longer need to sit at home in the darkness. The gold mine at Alphapointe is where they can learn to live safe and independent lives.

It's a new prospect on Prospect Avenue.

Perhaps the most electric issue in diversity in the 21st century involves sexual orientation. Americans often fail to recognize the talent in gays, lesbians, bisexual and transgender people. Homophobia blocks their vision. Robert N. Minor correctly identifies it as "the fear of getting close to one's own sex" (51). He explains that in his book, *Scared Straight: Why It's So Hard to Accept Gay People And Why It's So Hard to Be Human.* He writes that homophobia supports our market economy with products and services that reinforce established norms for masculinity and femininity. He adds that "oppression, prejudice, and discrimination directed toward gay people are in reality the means for installing, maintaining, enforcing, and valuing gender roles, which are our conditioned definitions of what a 'real' man or woman is in our society" (53).

Mary Frances Berry, in her book *The Pig Farmer's Daughter,* adds that race and sexual orientation collide in what Minor described as individuals' own sexual identity fears. Berry writes:

> Despite the changing climate [for homosexuals], racial stories continued [in the 1970s] to have a major influence when black gays were prosecuted. At a time when adult consensual sex was punished lightly if at all, courts upheld convictions of African Americans for consensual homosexual sex and gave them comparatively heavier sentences. As recipients of anal intercourse or participants in oral sex with another man, gay African Americans defied both gender and racial mores. They challenged the white male's deep ingrained notions of black male sexuality, which remained psychologically necessary to his own definition. (67)

Berry continues her historical perspective:

<u>From "Politics with a conscience; Summon courage on gay marriage vote"</u>

> "Before the mid-19th century, when their story was closeted - those who engaged in same-sex sex neither sought public acceptability nor threatened the values of marriage and family - their behavior evoked no sustained public attention and few attendant demands for legal intervention.
>
> Homosexual conduct was practically invisible in the courts before the 1880s."
>
> But the laws and court decisions changed. Around that same time period, coincidentally perhaps, Reconstruction ended, Indian wars intensified and anti-immigration laws aimed particularly at the Chinese

were passed. The country was in a state of massive political and social regression. Then, "in 1953, the Eisenhower administration barred gays and lesbians from all federal jobs," Berry wrote. Police actions against gays and lesbians were "reminiscent of the Red scare" with intelligence investigations against unmarried men and women.

Change started to occur in 1974 when the American Psychiatric Association determined that homosexuality "does not constitute a psychiatric disorder" and "implies no impairment in judgment, stability, reliability or general social or vocational capabilities." That resulted in the U.S. Civil Service Commission ending its ban on hiring gays and lesbians.

"Coming out became increasingly popular, but a vocal, well-organized resistance continued," Berry wrote. Gays and lesbians publicly insisted "that their relationships receive endorsement."

"In doing so, they disputed the assumption that heterosexual marriage and family were the only acceptable lifestyles," Berry said. "Their position went well beyond hidden homosexuality, which most people tolerated or ignored."

As long as homosexuality was hidden, everything was fine. A historical "don't ask, don't tell" attitude, a policy later popularized for the military when Bill Clinton was president in the 1990s, made homosexuality more comfortable for heterosexuals. But once homosexuality became visible, that feeling of comfort began to erode. The fear people nationwide now have of their own sexuality being threatened helps explain why so many states have passed constitutional amendments banning same sex marriage. The backward effort to limit individuals' rights means that people who are lesbian, gay, bisexual or transgender (LGBT) are confronted by a majority of others who are negative and high diversity multipliers. It's causing those in the LGBT community to not feel welcome and not have their talents, which benefit our society, reach their full potential.

Yet, positive diversity multipliers continue to work against the stream of well-established oppression. They show us—as Formula I demonstrates—how enabling others to succeed can be done, if more of us would simply have the courage to try. Their efforts bring out the best in everyone and show how people who have suffered because of bigotry in America continue to strive to overcome backward behavior.

If people bothered to open their eyes, they would see gay, lesbian, bisexual and transgender people throughout our community. What gays in the closet face is similar to what black people who are "passing" contend with.

From "Don't 'pass' on pride"

It wasn't too many generations ago that many black people would have been overjoyed to have been born with an accommodating complexion, features and hair texture that would have enabled them to "pass" from black to white.

Through the centuries-old practice of miscegenation, thousands did.

"It's a crucial aspect of black history, but it's one that hasn't been developed or explained to people," said F. James Davis, author of the book *Who is Black? One Nation's Definition*, which was published in 1991.

"It's been so neglected and so put down and not talked about among the black and white communities. But it needs to be much better explained or understood in order to put the whole aspect of our race relations history into proper perspective."

Passing has taken place as long as there have been black people in America. For centuries, it was a phantom car on the underground railroad offering a ticket to freedom to fair-skinned children of slaves who had mated with white masters.

After the Civil War, however, passing increased steadily from 1880 to the turn of the century, Davis said in a telephone interview. It peaked from 1900 to 1910, when 12,000 people annually passed from black to white, said Davis, quoting estimates made by Walter White, who headed the National Association for the Advancement of Colored People from 1931 until his death in 1955.

Many people passed to escape discrimination, Jim Crow laws enforcing segregation and terrorism campaigns by such groups as the Ku Klux Klan. Lynchings and race riots were condoned white-on-black crimes.

Such hostile conditions at the turn of the century, especially around World War I, pulled thousands of African Americans who could pass away from their families, churches and communities, said Davis, who finished his book after he retired in 1985 as a sociology professor at Illinois State University in Normal.

People, like phantoms, ceased to exist in their birth race simply by reappearing as whites after moving to distant towns and states where no one knew their past. Bleached out in the process were family ties and the rich history of their ancestors' accomplishments despite slavery and other adversity.

"The individuals, once they crossed over, they would never reveal it," said Edward Beasley, a retired professor of African-American culture at Penn Valley Community College.

At the same time that Jim Crow laws and hate organizations compelled people to pull up their roots, family members were pushing those African Americans who could to pass as whites. There was a great sympathy in the black community to help those who could escape the bonds of racism in America, Davis said.

Beasley added that black people also assisted because they enjoyed knowing that white people - who were so hung up about race - were getting bamboozled by African Americans who suddenly were walking, eating, socializing, marrying and having children with the privileged class.

"There were many people who considered passing an advantage to them and, of course, it was an advantage," said Walter C. Daniel, a retired University of Missouri-Columbia English professor emeritus, under whom I studied black history and black literature decades ago.

People who slipped through the cracks in the color barrier would shed all of the disadvantages, discrimination, segregation, prejudices and stereotypes of being black. They could ride in the best seats public transportation offered and not have to give up their spot if someone white happened to get on a crowded train, trolley or bus.

They could shop anywhere and pay a fair price, live in better neighborhoods, drink from "whites only" water fountains, get served at any lunch counter, go to clubs and restaurants without restrictions, attend better public schools, go to college, get better jobs and hope to be an equal shareholder in the American dream.

The separate and unequal condition that black people faced was as old as slavery in America. Beasley referred to statements of W.E.B. Du Bois, educator, historian, author and a founder of the NAACP: "The problem of the 20th century would be the problem of the color line, and it's still there."

Part of the frustration was over the "one drop rule," Davis said. Anyone who had one drop of black blood or one black ancestor was considered black.

That definition, he said, dates to the 1640s. "I think Americans don't realize that our way of defining blacks is unique to the world," he said.

Other countries such as South Africa, Brazil and Haiti view African Americans differently because each of us is a multicultural blend of many races.

Davis laughed when I asked about his race.

"I'm white, and I guess I should say, 'as far as I know,'" he said. "But who knows?"

Because of the number of people who have passed, experts contend that as many as one in 20 to one in 10 whites actually are black people by the "one drop" American standard, Davis said.

As long as people don't know, their bigotry isn't triggered; but once they know, all of the biases and hatred kick in, and they feel threatened.

The fact is people who are different pose no real threat. Homosexuals, for example, are only trying to make a living just as others are, but must do so while hiding, dodging and contending with many negative diversity multipliers. In essence they are "passing" for straight in much the same way as some fair-skinned blacks "passed" for white decades ago, as the above column shows. It makes no sense that gays are OK when viewed as if they were anyone else but are untouchable when they are found to be homosexual. They are no different in their talent, but the biases against them suddenly become barriers to their success and acceptance.

From "Stories of gay community have found a voice"

> My daughter, Leslie, unearthed something I wrote more than a quarter century ago that adds insight into the same-sex marriage issue.
>
> What Leslie found were stories I wrote in 1978, which I buried after being unable to get them published in the Kansas City newspapers or national magazines.
>
> The stories were provocative, but the timing was all wrong. They were about Lea Hopkins, her partner, her 4-year-old son, Jason, and Kansas City's growing gay community. They also told how Hopkins had been "out of the closet" since 1969 as a gay, black woman and former Playboy bunny.
>
> The story died because people weren't ready to hear about a gay couple's love, their family and their activism. However, I was glad to see it re-emerge under other *Kansas City Star* writers' bylines in 1994 with a big front-page Sunday photograph.
>
> That aspect of the diversity in our community won't stay in the closet any longer. Gays, lesbians and other now enlightened Missourians also are unwilling to comply with any effort to restrict the rights of same-sex couples.
>
> "I will never understand how gay marriage undermines the institution of heterosexual marriage," Hopkins, said in a recent interview. "It doesn't degrade marriage.
>
> "It's about doing what's fair and doing what's right. If you are to be a responsible voter, you need to know the truth. Gay couples are just like any other unit in our society. We want the same things."
>
> Reporting in the 1970s on the emerging strength of the gay community in Kansas City showed me what was as close as gays could get then to being married.
>
> Hopkins, who is an advisory board member of the Lesbian and Gay Community Center in Westport, called it a "holy union." Same-

sex couples who filled the church were just as joyous as heterosexual couples are at weddings.

"They're just as beautiful and just as meaningful," Hopkins said. In such ceremonies, the person officiating asks people "to nurture and not hinder the relationship." The change to the Missouri Constitution violates that beautiful directive.

Like me, Hopkins opposed the amendment to the Missouri Constitution. People must come to grips with gays, lesbians, bisexuals and transgender people living in our community.

"We are your neighbors; we are your friends," Hopkins said. "People come in contact with gay people every day. People just don't know."

They're our co-workers, people who provide services for us in stores, restaurants and in government agencies.

"But as long as we're invisible, everything is fine," Hopkins said.

However, society's desire to keep them invisible continues to fade.

In the 1978 articles, Hopkins told me Anita Bryant's much-publicized gay bashing was a catalyst making many homosexuals and lesbians more vocal advocates for gay rights. The outrageous opposition to gay marriage is having the same unintended effect.

For proponents of the amendment, it's part of a culture war that they insist on winning. For opponents it's a struggle akin to the Civil Rights Movement, which they can't afford to lose.

"But whether this passes or fails, we are not going away," Hopkins said. "It's not about threatening anyone's marriage, anyone's family or getting involved with your children. It is the fair and equitable thing to do in terms of treating all taxpaying citizens equally."

Defeating the amendment would have helped to end the fear that many gays, lesbians, bisexual and transgender people face. It also might have dampen the unfounded fear that many heterosexuals have of others whose sexual orientation is different from their own.

Hopkins knows that fear. It was on people's faces, in their voices and the laws of this great land for her as an African-American before the Civil Rights Movement, the Civil Rights Act that was passed more than 40 years ago and other legislation that tried to emancipate the nation of such backwardness.

"This is just my second fight," Hopkins said. "As an African-American woman, I understand that all too clearly."

It's a worthwhile fight for talent that this country needs. People must become positive diversity multipliers in order to draw out the best that others have to offer so that everyone gains. But we are asking people who aren't "straight" to conceal a large part of who they are on their jobs, in public, in churches, synagogues and temples and in the community. We need to see the beauty that they can share and give them the opportunity to share it.

From "'Until everyone has those rights'- New office welcomes students of all sexual orientations to UMKC"

Two comfortable couches, blond furniture and computers hardly tell the significance of this new office at the University of Missouri-Kansas City.

When classes start, the doors of this welcoming space opened for lesbian, gay, bisexual and transgender students. It's called the LGBT Initiative, and it's part of the UMKC Women's Center.

African-American, international, Hispanic and other student groups have office space. The facility for lesbian, gay, bisexual and transgender students springs from an ongoing effort at the university to better serve its diverse student body.

"It's an amazing first step in the history of this institution," said Jane M. Wood, then-director of the Women's Center. "A value of the university is inclusiveness."

The LGBT Initiative also occurred at a pivotal time in the nation's history. The Episcopal Church's House of Bishops approved New Hampshire priest V. Gene Robinson as its first openly gay bishop.

The country's first public high school for gay, bisexual and transgender students opened in New York. It is named after Harvey Milk, San Francisco's first openly gay city supervisor. He was assassinated in 1978.

Also, the U.S. Supreme Court ruled against a Texas law that banned private consensual sodomy among homosexuals. In addition, TV networks are shedding their apprehensiveness about airing shows about people who are gay. These new programs are quite popular.

"We're in a state of evolution," said Tobi Leuthardt, program coordinator of the LGBT Initiative/Women's Center.

"These bits and pieces in the news make me more excited for the future," said Stephanie Mountain, a communications major at the university and work study intern who was planning to use the office space. "It's great for us to be this age and experiencing it.

"It creates a very optimistic feeling. This is part of a more hopeful time. Not everything in the news is Matthew Shepard. Not everything in the news is about hate crimes."

Mountain said colleges in other states have similar initiatives.

UMKC has just joined some progressive universities. The LGBT Initiative makes a strong statement about the university valuing diversity.

"My hope is that in the long run it will mean that our LGBT students are successful at UMKC," said Deb Lewis, assistant vice chancellor for student affairs at the university. It will help students know they are welcome so they can learn and develop to their potential.

The space is where lesbian, gay, bisexual, transgender and other students can study, network, put together fliers and work on Web sites, Leuthardt said. The office generates programming and resources to raise awareness and address such concerns as homophobia, racism and sexism.

A campus group, Queers & Allies, is expected to use the office. "This is a safe space where they can hang out and not worry about any form of discrimination or harassment," Leuthardt said.

People at freshman orientations have received information on the LGBT Initiative. Kansas City's gay, lesbian, bisexual and transgender community also has embraced the initiative and was planning a benefit for scholarships.

"LGBT people are standing up more and being assertive," Leuthardt said.

Lewis said the university has not gotten negative feedback about devoting space to lesbian, gay, bisexual and transgender students. In addition to education, integrity, innovation and accountability, three other core values at UMKC are respect, inclusiveness and diversity.

"We cannot achieve those things until everyone has those rights," Leuthardt said. "We basically want to show LGBT is a viable part of the campus.

"We all have to work together."

The best education happens when all students are learning and growing because everyone is fully engaged, welcomed and involved.

Feedback, however, showed that there remain a lot of negative diversity multipliers among us on the issue of accepting gays, lesbians, bisexual and transgender people.

Voice Mail: 2003

I can only tell you how shocked I am that you believe in homosexuality. I am just in shock. I have no words. Goodbye.

Voice Mail: 2004

Stories of gay community have found a voice. They've had a voice for a long time. They've had a lot of voices. The voices are getting louder, however. Unfortunately, they're not getting any more logical. But they are getting louder, and you're part of that group. Something you wrote more than a quarter century ago that adds insight into the same sex marriage issue. You flatter yourself, sir. In your arrogance, you assume you have added understanding or insight into the matter. And you've done nothing but stir up the same old rhetoric that was always there. When you say people must come to grips with gays and lesbians, OK, does come to grips mean you take something

> you know is intrinsically wrong and you say it's right? Is that what you mean by come to grips? Perhaps you can explain that to me. You talk about the unfounded fear that many heterosexuals have of others. I don't know that heterosexuals have a fear of homosexuals. I don't. There is a difference between having a fear of something and viewing something as being wrong.
>
> Voice Mail: 2004
>
> One thing you need to consider is many of your readers are Christians. And as Christians, we need to answer for what we do. If you are a secularist, or an atheist or whatever you are exactly you're not going to give that a thought. We can't go along with something that the Bible really states that we can't do and aren't supposed to do anymore than we could sanction murder, robbery or anything else that is considered to be immoral. It's clear as a bell to Christians that you're obviously going to have to answer to it later.
>
> Voice Mail: 2003
>
> Well, well, well. So along with all your racism, you're the biggest racist I know next to Jesse Jackson. Now you're also dick-see lecturer as I always suspected. Yes, I'm sure you're gay after reading that article today. I hope you're proud of yourself.

People who can speak out and be the positive diversity multipliers required in Formula I for homosexuals and lesbians should not be afraid to do so. They gain far more than they might risk losing.

The bigotry and stigma attached to exclusion also affects people with mental illness. It limits their ability to feel welcome in the population and even worse, to recover and plug back into society as productive individuals. Often they must be their own best advocates and serve as diversity multipliers for each other. Two such champions, Sybil Noble and Jerry Armstrong, repeatedly over the years have shared stories of people like them who have mental illness. Their work, chronicled in the following columns, has helped destigmatize mental illness and expand people's ability to see the talents in others that biases and bigotry have hidden.

From "New ideas on illness are needed"

> Their Kansas City Northland experience made Sybil Noble and Virginia Kitterman's setup at the Ward Parkway Center in south Kansas City seem like heaven.
>
> The display at the Antioch Shopping Center up north was nice enough, but the people didn't know how to respond to information about mental illness handed out by the Ark of Friends of Kansas City.
>
> Noble laughed while Kitterman demonstrated: Kitterman peeked from behind a large plant before starting sheepishly toward the table of the mental health consumers group. She reached for handouts but looked off in the distance as if she really weren't picking up the information.

Then she scurried away quickly so that no one would notice that she, of all people, had stopped. That was the norm for the eight persons who ventured by the Ark's display - except for one man.

The man told Jerry Armstrong, then-Ark vice president, that if everyone with mental illness had a 10-foot boa constrictor and touched it regularly it would cure their problems. Those Northland experiences reinforced the need for people with the Ark to get the word out on mental illness.

Stigma and misinformation have run unchecked for too long. The public must be educated, said Noble, then-Ark president.

Cody Burnett and David Gates handed out literature at the Broadway-Valentine Shopping Center in central Kansas City, but Noble and Kitterman had the best experience at Ward Parkway. People were more receptive.

"We've had such a good response here," Noble said. "I know we will do it again."

At Ward Parkway, sun rays tumbled from skylights, a nearby waterfall rustled soothingly and rhythmically with piped-in Muzak, and many people cruising in heavy traffic on the white marble floors stopped by the Ark's peach- and white-colored tables.

Signs, featuring spring-like colors and flowers made by Kitterman, called out: "People with Mental Illness Enrich our Lives." Names on the signs included Winston Churchill, Abraham Lincoln, Patty Duke, Ernest Hemingway, Ludwig van Beethoven, Vivian Leigh, Michelangelo and Vincent van Gogh.

"Those celebrities are obviously bright people who happen to have mental illness," said Kitterman, who with her husband, Gill, do volunteer work for the Ark. "We were really impressed with what they are trying to do.

"It really gives us a neat perspective."

More than 100 people picked up fliers about support groups, suicide, sexual abuse, schizophrenia, manic depression, eating disorders, emotional problems and stress.

They also got magnets and buttons featuring a paintbrush splashing a rainbow of colors and a caption that said, "Paint a Different Picture of Mental Illness." Many even signed up for a raffle of a T-shirt with the same design.

"Just think of how we would have felt if we had stopped after going up North," Gill Kitterman said. "This is uplifting."

People who stopped asked questions, took some of the fliers and thanked people in the Ark for the information.

"Topics like this shouldn't be whispered about," said Mark Fischer, who works at a bank and is a volunteer with the Good Samaritan Project. "They should be out in the open, and people should not be ashamed."

> Thomas Gaston III, a mental and medical health care worker, added: "It's just like the button says. There's a wrong perception of what mental illness is."
>
> Suzaye Junod said the Ark's thoroughness impressed her.
>
> "I'm glad they had it," she said. "Probably a lot of people have mental illness that may not know where to go.
>
> "This will help."

We, as a society, should be judged by how well we treat others who are less fortunate. Such progressive action enables them to get stronger and brings out the best in us. Again, people with mental disabilities often have to be their own best champions. But they need diversity multipliers to help them be all that they can be. It enables them to be better, more open talent enhancers for others, too.

An often overlooked, though growing, aspect of diversity is the portion of the U.S. population that is incarcerated. The United States, with 2.3 million people in prison, locks up more people than any country on the planet. And even though only 13 percent of the entire U.S. population is black, nearly 50 percent of the people in U.S. prisons are African American. That disproportionate reality shows how black people are encountering an inordinate number of diversity multipliers in schools, communities, law enforcement and the courts that are negative and high. Those negative multipliers are destroying any hope of African Americans' having productive lives, and are existentially turning too many toward negative outcomes. Add in racial profiling as an institutional high and negative diversity multiplier, and it's easy to see how incarceration is an all-too-easy outcome for many black people. But it wouldn't be that way, if more people in the community would work to help youths get a good education, direct them toward positive outcomes and away from crime. Even if they land in prison, the need for positive diversity multipliers is imperative to getting ex-offenders on the right path. Positive and high diversity multipliers inspire ex-offenders and give them hope.

From "Prisoners get another turn at bat"

> Buck O'Neil earnestly glad-handed and backslapped every one of the 104 men who stepped on stage with him. His distinctive voice also carried to the back of the chapel at the Lansing Correctional Facility in Kansas.
>
> "Frankie, God bless you!" O'Neil said. "Keep it up, James!
>
> "Clarence, all right! Chavez, congratulations!"
>
> I had seen O'Neil give speeches before, but this one was among his best, and it was delivered to a pretty tough audience. These men were in prison for every imaginable offense.

They could only dream of the gateways to fame that O'Neil stepped through. Most of the men also weren't even born in O'Neil's heyday.

From 1937 to 1955, he was first baseman and manager for the Kansas City Monarchs, a Negro Leagues Baseball team. He became the first black coach in the white major leagues in 1962 with the Chicago Cubs.

O'Neil, then-chairman of the Negro Leagues Baseball Museum, wore a Monarchs jacket, jersey and ball cap to the men's graduation. The uniform was a source of pride to him, just as the caps, gowns, high school equivalency, vocational education and other diplomas were to the inmates who received them.

O'Neil, then 86, got the usual respect when he said he'd shaken hands with Presidents Harry S. Truman and Bill Clinton. The audience also laughed when he said he'd hugged Hillary Clinton.

Then he swung home-run hard, aiming to inspire the inmates, their families and others in the most unreachable seats.

He said he once was one of the two top contenders for general manager of the Cubs. He knew the system and players and was ready to be baseball's first black general manager.

But he didn't get the job. The other guy had college degrees and was working on another.

"Had I had that piece of paper. Had I had this, man … ," O'Neil said, picking up one of the diplomas. "That's what you're going to get.

"This is the inroad to everything in the United States. You've got an opportunity here that I didn't have."

O'Neil also told the men about his baseball career, how he'd hit home runs, stolen bases and played with Satchel Paige, Babe Ruth, Jackie Robinson, Dizzy Dean and other baseball legends. He said he was blessed with caring parents and people who helped him succeed.

Honorable people and hustlers got him to finish high school and two years of college. "(Rapper) L.L. Cool J said education is one of the most important things you can do for yourself," O'Neil said as he swept the air with his big hands.

"It's remarkable," he said. "It's like a garden growing in your life.

"It actually continues to grow. But to keep the garden growing, you've got to water it."

O'Neil told the men he faced problems, racism and hatred. But he overcame the obstacles and became a better man.

"But I never learned how to hate," he said. "I hate cancer. I hate AIDS. I hate what the Klan and what skinheads will do.

"But I can't hate the man. That's God's creature."

In his speech, baseball also was a metaphor for life. The game is filled with responsibility, rules and success.

"I don't care how high you go, you need to abide by the rules," he said. "Someone is going to be the boss over you. But this is America. It is the greatest country on earth.

"There are some things in this country that need changing, and that's why I need you out there to help change things."

The legendary coach got a standing ovation. Then he shook hands and helped award diplomas. From where I sat, he had succeeded in inspiring new recruits to fulfill their great potential.

Good diversity multipliers take away the obstacles that would befall others so their talent can reach productive ends, as Formula I demonstrates. Once ex-offenders get out of prison, they continue to need those positive forces to propel them along the road to a more productive and uplifting life.

From "Dismas snub hurts ex-offenders"

Dismas House's literature explains what it has tried to do for 30 years as a Kansas City halfway house for ex-offenders.

It reads, "'Dismas' represents the 'good thief' on the cross (with Jesus) who in his dying hour asked to be remembered in paradise. The concept was simple: it's never too late to reform if an individual chooses."

The Rev. Everett Thornton and the Rev. James H. Flanagan started Dismas House in 1972. It has always been faith-based, using compassion to help rehabilitate ex-offenders.

But all that would soon be history. A corporate for-profit corrections company won a five-year, $10 million federal contract over Dismas House.

The bid to the Federal Bureau of Prisons from Dismas House was for $59.98 per resident per day. It would enable ex-offenders to live and work in the community as they re-enter society to be productive citizens.

But Correctional Systems Inc. of San Diego got the contract with a low bid of $44.98 per resident per day. It eventually opened a facility in a converted Leavenworth warehouse.

Dismas House, at 3124 Forest Ave., Kansas City, Mo., had been a longtime recipient of federal and local contracts.

Russ Millin, a former U.S. attorney in Kansas City and a Dismas House board member, has gotten area elected and other officials to write letters to help get Dismas House's contract reinstated.

What matters more than the numbers is the history and compassionate service Dismas House provided. It's in two apartment buildings with large front porches across from the Kansas City police Central Patrol Division. It employed more than 35 persons and served more than 100 clients.

About 80 percent of the residents are from the Kansas City area, and 98 percent hold jobs nearby. Public transportation let them independently get to work and visit family.

But Correctional Systems' facility in Leavenworth would be about 50 miles away. Sven Jones, with the Federal Bureau of Prisons, said Correctional Systems will drive clients to and from Leavenworth.

But can that match being here in the city's heart?

Correctional Systems is a publicly traded corporation that contracts with government agencies in different states to operate jails, community correctional centers and halfway houses. Correctional Systems' literature says it has a "corporate commitment to providing safe, secure and humane correctional services."

It sees that structure as "perhaps their (the ex-offenders') first and best opportunity, to make positive changes in their lives."

Correctional Systems operation is based on a "framework of rules, guidelines and sanctions for infractions." Progress comes from accepting responsibility for one's behavior.

Dismas House has a history of rehabilitating people whom others had given up on. Thornton, executive director of Dismas House, said those served included Cubans from the Mariel boat lift in 1980.

Dismas House connects ex-offenders with the community, their families and their faith. Thornton said the spiritual and compassionate approach works. He said his employees know they have to love the people they serve.

That's not a corporate approach, said the Rev. Ladell Flowers, director of programs at Dismas House.

"It's really, really a sad thing," Thornton said of Dismas House's fate. "But I'll tell you something.

"We rest on God. We know that there is a purpose. We walk on faith. We began on the word of God. We know he cannot fail."

The corporate interests overruled compassion, and Dismas House got nailed to the cross, losing its contract and closing its doors.

Being a positive and high diversity multiplier for the many underappreciated groups in our society goes hand-in-hand with compassion and love. But it also goes against the business case for racism. Overcoming that bias requires helping others to see the benefits of enabling the talents in individuals who are often overlooked. Being positive and high diversity multipliers magnifies others' productivity. Here's how: Try the following diversity exercise with any group to discover the importance of Formula I: Ask individuals to take out a piece of paper. Have them use a pen or pencil to draw a large circle. Then instruct them to use three lines to divide the circle into eight parts. (Some clues you might give if people ask are: a) The lines do not have to be straight.

b) The lines do not have to remain in the circle. And c) the parts do not have to be of equal dimensions.) Invariably you will get different "solutions" to this problem from your group of problem-solvers. Ask them to show their work.

The learning experience from that exercise is that a diversity of people will come up with different solutions to any problem. Therefore, more people need to be given the opportunity to be problem-solvers. Business and industry need the variety of solutions from which to choose as they confront a variety of problems today and in the future. They desperately need to have those diverse choices to remain competitive in today's global marketplace. But problem-identifiers and -solvers must be cultivated constantly by positive and high diversity multipliers, so they will emerge with new solutions now and in the future.

In the same way, more minority businesses must be enabled so that they can thrive. Anything less works against us all.

From "A minority of minority businesses"

> A lot should have happened to boost financing and networking opportunities for African-American and Hispanic business owners.
>
> But little has occurred to address the findings in a May 1999 report showing that the Kansas City area falls below other places nationally in minority business ownership. The study was done by Rhonda Holman, a former downtown bank manager and later vice president of public sector and community entrepreneurship at the Ewing Marion Kauffman Foundation.
>
> Our area's sorry situation stands out. Holman's study noted that one in 28 African-Americans in Seattle owned a business compared with one in 51 in Kansas City. One in 13 Hispanics in Atlanta owned a business compared with one in 37 in Kansas City.
>
> "There is still so much work to be done," Holman told me. Her report showed that blacks in Kansas City owned businesses at a fourth of the rate that whites did.
>
> Revenues for black-owned firms nationally averaged \$52,000, compared with \$43,000 for Kansas City area African-American businesses and \$193,000 for all U.S. firms. Hispanic businesses fared better with average revenues of \$94,000 nationally and \$97,000 in the Kansas City area.
>
> Corporations are discovering that the Hispanic market is pretty cool, and they want to do business with Latino entrepreneurs, said Michael Barrera, president of the Hispanic Chamber of Commerce of Greater Kansas City.
>
> The study tells A. Marie Young, executive director of the Black Chamber of Commerce of Greater Kansas City, how far behind Kan-

sas City area African-American entrepreneurs are.

Young has sent the report to more than 250 company executives and the media to try to get the problem corrected.

"We thought that once the report was made public there might be some dialogue that we could do something that the other cities were able to accomplish," Young said. "But Kansas City has not embraced diversity like everywhere else has. They don't bring it into the formula for success."

Young rattled off a list of longstanding black companies that have folded in the last year. "I feel like I've been going to a funeral once a month with another business biting the dust," she said.

Yet a Small Business Administration report showed the number of minority-owned businesses was up 68 percent between 1992 and 1997 and sales soared 144 percent.

Hispanics owned 1.4 million companies compared with 881,646 for African Americans.

Holman's report based on 1992 data said nine of 10 black and Hispanic entrepreneurs were in startup businesses. Most are isolated from circles where capital, technical assistance and network opportunities are.

They never arrive at a safe, established period with ample financing to meet growth opportunities and technological and market changes. Many aren't in areas with quality schools that can supply well-trained workers.

They struggle for opportunities to connect with corporations and government agencies for contracts.

"It's not that we can't do the job," said John Ross, owner of Brass/Ross Vending. "Often it's that they won't let us have the opportunity to do the job."

Getting that exposure will be harder now because Kansas City has fewer corporate headquarters where purchasing decisions are made, said Gregory D. Baker, founder and former executive director of the Minority Supplier Council.

Jeffrey Comment, then-chairman and CEO of Helzberg Diamond, agreed.

"It's not a black/white thing," Comment said. "It's a citywide, metrowide problem."

Business leaders must resolve it for the sake of all businesses and nonprofit groups. Minority firms also must be pulled more into the mainstream, he said.

Holman said territorial barriers needed to fall for minority entrepreneurs to advance.

"The alternative is too disheartening a legacy to leave for future generations," her report said. "African-Americans and Hispanics must not be condemned to a permanent working-class status any more than

> white Americans should have to carry a disproportionate share of the responsibility for the nation's well-being."
>
> Jim Abbott, Minority Supplier Council president, said the solution lies in leadership and collaborative efforts.
>
> Holman said the Kauffman Foundation will help spur more opportunities for minority business growth.
>
> I hope everyone does more so minority businesses thrive, jobs are created and this community grows in more diverse ways.

We are at a time in this country when everyone must contribute, and we all need to look positively at the potential of others. Imagine what communities in America would be like if that diversity formula were plugged in everywhere and people valued the talent of others, worked as diversity multipliers to channel that energy into more productive uses, and sought positive and high diversity multipliers for themselves as well. That, as Daniel Wildcat said in Chapter 8, would help us discover the Real America, which has been hidden for centuries by the many obstacles erected by racism.

Race is America's electrified fence. People often are afraid to touch it, fearing that it will disintegrate them. Yet, controlling it and harnessing its power are how they can feel the current of diversity and transform it for the community's well-being.

CHAPTER 10

Diversity Formula Two—Talk is Priceless

The Real America

Talk with me, tell me what I don't know
About your people's pain and problems
That try their very souls
And I'll share with you mine
So we'll eternally grow
Beyond the struggles for crumbs
That aren't worth fighting over and grabbing
Toward something that's rich and the envy of having
Then we'll share our newly found knowledge
So others can enhance it and dance with glee
They'll be fulfilled like you and me
And our understanding will flower
And our wealth will grow with our new power
And knowledge forged from unity
From talking in our shared community.

They didn't know who I really was.
They didn't know how much the smallest amount of recognition would have meant to me and how the smallest amount of criticism could undo me.
~Amy Tan

Nothing improves the opportunity for people to discover the Real America more than simple, old-fashioned talking. The discovery is in the difference they find in others. I noted earlier that journalists trade in what I call a "currency of conversations." Those conversations provide journalists with intellectual capital, which then gets converted into the intellectual products that consumers readily buy. That means everyone's stories have value. That's what valuing diversity is. However, sometimes people have a difficult time picking up what others might be saying because of the bias filters listeners possess. That creates some Odysseus-like challenges to discovering the Real America.

Here's an example: in a diversity workshop I helped facilitate among journalists in the 1990s, one veteran reporter said during an exercise that he only takes down in his notes what he himself would have said if he were the person being interviewed. That might sound as if it is the mark of a bad reporter, but he actually was sharing something that was quite important. All of us are a compilation of our experiences growing up. We get our value system from everything we have picked up in our past. We were socialized based on those occurrences and encounters with others. The things that we find noteworthy today were established by what mattered most to us in our many yesterdays. Another veteran journalist in that same diversity workshop added that suddenly something that a friend of his had said years ago made sense. His friend had interviewed Gen. Douglas MacArthur and said afterward that it was as if he were having a conversation with himself, and MacArthur just happened to be in the room. That's because everything that MacArthur said reflected the things the journalist conducting the interview also valued and strongly believed.

Again, all of the things that any of us might hear and remember at any time are based on experiences that were noteworthy to us in the past. Journalists then do indeed record what resonates or connects with those things they value from their own experiences. If a journalist's experiences have been limited, if that person's past has not included friendships with people of different races, education levels, ages, incomes, disabilities, ethnicities, genders, sexual orientations and other aspects of diversity, then his or her reports will be incomplete. Without contact with and exposure to people who are different, what the journalist notes; what he or she writes; how he or she structures his or her stories; what quotes, pictures, artwork and commentary will be used and which ones will be discarded will reveal a quiet bias. Where the story runs, if it runs at all will be determined by the experiences of that individual as well as those diverse experiences of other people in decision-making positions in the media. Journalism students therefore need to have broad-based lives outside of their chosen profession because as journalists they will only be as good as the depth and breadth of their experiences in life. Their résumés then must include a vast exposure to multiculturalism and diversity. If not, we can expect the stories they'll turn in to project the biases of the dominant, non-inclusive white society. That corresponds with the mostly segregated communities in which most of America lives. We don't know each other, and that ignorance continues to be perpetuated in the media, in schools and in literature. The second diversity formula can help eliminate the ignorance.

Talk x Diversity = Social Capital

That equation is ***Talk x Diversity = Social Capital.*** Diversity again is the multiplier. The greater that factor is, the more social capital one receives. Social capital is what grows when people talk. Diversity is the listener, the encourager, the cheerleader, the enhancer. Robert D. Putnam's book *Bowling Alone: The Collapse and Revival of American Community,* explains that social capital "refers to the connections among individuals—social networks and the norms of reciprocity and trustworthiness that arise from them" (19). Putnam quotes L.J. Hanifan, who wrote that social capital referred to

> those tangible substances [that] count for most in the daily lives of people: namely good will, fellowship, sympathy, and social intercourse among the individuals and families who make up a social unit....The individual is helpless socially, if left to himself....If he comes into contact with his neighbor, and they with other neighbors, there will be an accumulation of social capital, which may immediately satisfy his social needs and which may bear a social potentiality sufficient to the substantial improvement of living conditions in the whole community. The community as a whole will benefit by the cooperation of all its parts, while the individual will find in his associations the advantages of the help, the sympathy, and the fellowship of his neighbors. (19)

The positive outcomes are many. People feel a greater sense of community when they talk. Putnam notes that "[a] society characterized by generalized reciprocity is more efficient than a distrustful society.... Trustworthiness lubricates social life" (21). There is a greater sense of togetherness and shared purpose, too. In addition, new ideas are hatched when people talk. Those shared concepts serve as the incubators for intellectual capital, which leads to new intellectual products. This enhances not only individuals but our entire society because businesses, government and our community pay handsomely for such innovations that can be marketed as products that consumers will buy.

But that sharing often doesn't extend to all quarters in the full range of diversity that makes up the Real America. White privilege limits the sharing, the expansion of resources and prevents people from exploring the unknown. These mostly uncharted places are where we must go to discover the Real America and bring out the richness in talent and new ideas that will make this nation more competitive in the future. Those who are diversity multipliers must be able to hear what folks who are different from them are saying. Each party in the conversation will have to ask questions and grow from the new knowledge that the inquiries yield.

Talking in ways that racism and bigotry have prevented in the (so-called) New World's first 500 years will provide great yields in understanding how best everyone can be productive. But to benefit to the fullest extent from the exploration into the Real America, people will have to abandon the tried and true Golden Rule. Many know that the Golden Rule says do unto others as we would want them to do unto us. But it is flawed because it assumes that everyone is the same and therefore would accept being treated the same way. In diversity circles we are impressed to instead rely on the Platinum Rule. It says do unto others as they would prefer you to do unto them. That means we have to get to know other people in the way that they want us to know them and ensure that they get to know us as individuals, too. It means that we have to talk, ask questions, get answers, and from such conversations our understanding of others—and theirs of us—will grow.

When people of diverse backgrounds get together to talk, a lucrative form of social capital emerges called social bridging. Individuals engaged in such rich conversations are exploring the Real America embedded in each other. Social bridging exposes them to new ideas, mannerisms, styles, cuisines, customs, and the list goes on. Like explorers, they benefit from others whose skills are different. Chapter 13 explores that concept in greater depth. Social bonding, on the other hand, is what takes place in "gated communities" where "[o]ne might expect the numbing homogeneity of these new suburban enclaves to encourage a certain social connectedness, if only of the 'bonding,' not 'bridging,' sort" (Putnam 210). Bonding is also present on the Internet in what Putnam describes as a "cyberbalkanization" of people sharing common interests. Putnam writes, "Real world interactions often force us to deal with diversity, whereas the virtual world may be more homogeneous, not in demographic terms, but in terms of interest and outlook. Place-based communities may be supplanted by interest-based communities" (178).

"'Birds of a feather flock together' is a folk adage that reminds us that tendencies toward community homogeneity long predate the Internet,"

Putnam adds (178). Yet bridging yields more richness, less isolation and less animosity. Communication is the key. The *Star Trek* series offers a good analogy:

From "Dance to the Music"

> The original TV shows started in the 1960s and have lived on in reruns, in spin-off programs and in the movies. In them, massive starships served both as scientific exploration vessels and as warships.
>
> But what was clear was that when the starships were on "red alert" with their weapons ready to fire and their protective shields at maximum strength, they couldn't "beam," or transport, anyone or anything aboard the spacecraft or continue to explore the galaxy. What was obvious was that whoever provoked such combat-ready tactics also could "sense" the red alert status of the opposing vessel.
>
> The other ship then became armed for a fight, too. It's never productive both in the fantasy of science fiction of our times or real life for people to have their shields up and their weapons ready.
>
> Then everyone is thinking the worst of others. We all should strive every day to move out of our comfort zones and be approachable, especially to people who happen to be different.
>
> It would enable us to explore a galaxy of diverse cultures and harvest the richness in experiences that others offer.

It's from talking that we can learn of the tragedies that others have had to endure and the triumphs they have celebrated. They tell the story of, and add depth, dimension, texture and spice to the individuals who make up the Real America.

Examples of Formula II

1. *Talking across racial lines*

Walk any street or shopping mall in America and this nation's richness in race, ethnicity, age, ability, faiths, gender and sexual orientation will be ever present. People just have to have an awareness of the multiculturalism that is America and be willing to open their eyes to enjoy it. The diversity that lives and works in this country is nothing to fear.

However, that's not the perpetual drone of what people are taught in schools and told in the media about people of color. Minorities often state that the media are biased against them, that the reporting of the news is slanted to paint them in an unfavorable light. (See Chapter 6.) Certainly that was the case with the infamous June 1994 *Time* magazine cover featuring O.J. Simpson after the former football star and actor's arrest in the bludgeoning deaths of Nicole Brown Simpson and Ronald Goldman. *Time* darkened the photograph to make Simpson appear more sinister. *Newsweek* ran the same picture unaltered. David K. Shipler in his book, *A Country of Strangers*, quotes Toni Morrison's *Beloved*, saying

> "White people believed that whatever the manners, under every dark skin was a jungle. Swift unnavigable waters, swinging screaming baboons, sleeping snakes, red gums ready for their sweet white blood."
>
> When the old notions surrounding blackness are combined with America's racial history, they produce a chemistry of emotions that many whites fail to recognize even in themselves. (236)

Katheryn K. Russell in her book, *The Color of Crime*, writes: "Blacks are the repository for the American fear of crime. Ask anyone, of any race, to picture a criminal, and the image will be a black face" (xiii).

The great experiment to end segregation provided opportunities for people who had been separated to vanquish that fear and finally talk.

From "Time to Relive the Experiment"

> The many earlier reunions got away from me.
>
> But this year I plan to attend my 25th high school reunion in St. Louis. My classmates, now middle-aged, took part in the national experiment called integration in the '60s and '70s.
>
> I was one of about 25 black students among more than 600 teens in the Southwest High School Class of 1973. My friend Terry told me about the reunion. Rosemary had told him.
>
> The three of us had graduated from a mostly black grade school. For the next four years, we struggled to learn the cultural, language and social differences on the other side of segregation's fire wall. Often we found that we walked without the asbestos shields that our families provided. But so did the white kids.
>
> In addition to classwork, white kids gave us an education in their food, hair care, language, suntanning, history, music and dances. We also exposed them to ours.
>
> Some kids were cool in that post-civil rights era of "black is beautiful," big hair and Afro combs. Others weren't.
>
> Their facade crumbled when they hung out with other whites. The baby-boom-era high school of thousands of kids then was way too small.
>
> I remember rounding a corner in a crowded hallway and hearing a so-called friend, whose neighborhood I helped integrate, profess his disdain for black people. I can still see the laughing faces as he said: "You don't understand. You don't have to live with them."
>
> I was one of "them." Going back for reunions of the school, which

closed in the 1980s, could unearth long-buried pain. But there were also truly cool people like my friend Kimberley.

We became buddies in a sophomore history class. We gossiped and traded stories of our parents, friends and different crushes. She and I shared a curiosity for each other's culture.

Kimberley also surprised me with something that I thought was absolutely wonderful. She told me one day that she wished she was black, too.

I asked why. She said she thought the language, culture, music, art, dance, emotional openness and expressiveness that she found among black people were incredibly cool.

She and her other true friends could dig forever on the triumphs of the Civil Rights Movement and how people like me went from being Negroes and colored folks to Afro-Americans and then proud black people. They loved the unity forged in the struggle and the color-coded badge of honor that went with being the few Afro-wearing Davids in an America of Goliaths.

They embraced being black because of the history, pride, ethnic heritage and generations-long rebellion against the establishment that accompanied the race. They loved the emergence of blacks on television, radio and movies—even in all-white neighborhoods where they lived.

It was a cause when so many young people in this country desperately needed to put their arms around something that was real and substantive. Kimberley's revelation also became a wonderful moment of joy about being black for me.

She's encouraged me to help find the disproportionately high number of African-Americans on the reunion's "unable to locate" list. Another grade-school friend, Deidre, and her parents have helped.

Kimberley and I have remained in touch since high school, exchanging Christmas cards, meeting each other's spouses and sharing pictures of our kids. We've giggled like teen-agers again in long-distance anticipation about the reunion.

My friendship with Kimberley Casey, now a New Hampshire legislator, became the focus of a cable TV program about the 1998 reunion of our newly integrated high school. The reactions of some of the viewers demonstrated just how important Formula II is for breaking down the false barriers we have erected around ourselves and rejoicing in our diversity:

From "After years, friendship lingers on"

From Canada: "Your marvelous friendship is to me all the more remarkable given the era in which your friendship was forged. Throw into the mix girl/boy and black/white along with cities burning and wars raging and it is not to me a recipe for success."

From Texas: "Also, revealing the friendship between a man and a woman was so enjoyable! A friendship between a black and a white, that was such a real friendship—nothing sexual or racial—just friendship!"

The experiment remains unfinished. In fact, some connections made in high school didn't take until years later. But the shared environment, social changes and common friends made talking possible so that a new social bridge could be forged, even after many years had passed.

From "Talking about race relations breaks the ice"

The things that kept Kris Acquistapace and me apart more than 30 years ago dominated our recent lunchtime conversation in Lee's Summit, Mo.

We were freshmen in 1969 at Southwest High School in St. Louis and graduated in the Class of 1973.

That was before there was a Black History Month. It also was at a time when we were thrown into the great American experiment called integration.

Kris is white. I'm black. Until we talked, neither Kris nor I realized how similar our roots are, how they had shaped our values and how much we have in common.

She lives in California with her husband, David, and daughter, Holly.

We got together when she recently visited Missouri relatives.

Getting together was a treat. Race relations became our icebreaker.

White and black students in our mostly white high school didn't mix much.

Even at our recent outing in Lee's Summit, Kris and I were the only interracial pair at the restaurant.

Kris, an assistant professor of English and art history at Crafton Hills College, said what's odd here is commonplace in California. "It's kind of a global community there," she said.

"I can't think of any place in California where you can depend on seeing mostly white people in a group," Kris said. Hispanics, Asian-Americans, African-Americans and American Indians are the majority. It feels natural and good, she said.

California sets trends for the rest of the nation. In our lifetime, minorities are expected to become the majority.

Kris said many of her students laugh when they fill out enrollment forms that ask them to select one race.

"Their ancestry is so varied," she said. "They usually select 'other' or leave it blank.

"They are amused by that - to try to think of themselves as a category because they can't be reduced to one thing."

My assumptions about Kris were wrong, too. Her roots trace to

Czechoslovakia, Ireland, England and Switzerland. She equates Ireland and Czechoslovakia with struggles. She wasn't "uniformly white," as people often assume. White people have a heritage and a history that is just as rich as any. Gary Howard explains in *We Can't Teach What We Don't Know* that whites had to know their background. Thandeka says in *Learning to Be White* that many had to surrender that ethnicity to be accepted in America.

Kris grew up near a St. Louis steel mill in a working-class, hardscrabble community. It caused her to feel just as unwelcome in other circles as I did as an African-American.

Kris's sense of never quite fitting in, feeling accepted or being viewed as just as good as anyone else, drove her to exceed others' low expectations of her. Similar sentiments became the engine behind the success of many women and minorities in those changing times.

The pressure of conformity couldn't define or confine Kris. She graduated from high school and was the first woman in her family to do so.

She also was the first in her family to graduate from college. She graduated in December 1976 from Washington University with three bachelor's degrees in English, education and art history.

"I never knew anyone with a college degree growing up," Kris said.

Although she and I escaped the confining boxes in which people had put us, Kris and I realized that we value society's better rules of good manners, responsibility, hard work, courage, resourcefulness and friendship.

Kris enjoyed reconnecting with those Midwest mainstays compared with California, where just about anything goes.

Somewhere there's a happy medium. Perhaps one day we'll find it, just as Kris and I found a new friendship in our past.

Integration continues to be interrupted by those who fear that its outcome will be successful. But the truth is that the more time we spend with people who are different, the richer our lives become. There is no such thing as too much of this type of good thing. A good time for people to talk is on a walk through places where one normally doesn't venture. It helps us scale that well-maintained wall which separates us and keeps us from going deeper into the Real America.

<u>From "Walking together is one step closer to racial understanding"</u>

Gene Fox and I traded e-mail and then phone calls before we finally got together for a long walk toward understanding.

First he and I shared thoughts in cyberspace, got connected by phone and then took our walk before summer faded to fall.

I never would have gone to the Ward Parkway's genteel neighborhood of beautiful homes except at Gene's invitation. But his curiosity helped me to see the area in a better light and get to know him as one of its residents.

As we walked we bounced dozens of questions off each other and listened to our many responses. People normally don't talk about race in mixed groups, partly because they're afraid of offending others.

But ages-old stereotypes breed in the darkness of silence, where the cleansing light of conversation fails to shine. Segregation, fear and hatred also grow when bigotry festers. We walked where too many others won't go.

Cars whizzed by as we talked about our differences – Gene's white, and I'm black - and the things we have in common. We're both runners and we're married and have kids, although his are older than mine are.

We talked about *The Kansas City Star* and broadcast journalism, where he'd worked for years in sports, and about his current job with the Missouri Department of Conservation.

Gene combines his work in the department with his love for gardening. We talked about a black woman who jogged past us and how her presence raised questions about whether she lived in the area, unlike white joggers and walkers who people assume are part of the neighborhood.

Troost Avenue isn't the impenetrable barrier that it once was in keeping black and white people from living and working together.

There's no escaping the multiculturalism of our metropolitan area, and that's a good thing. We got to 63rd Street and then headed back toward Gregory Boulevard.

Somewhere along the way back Gene asked how people of color, who sometimes are the object of scorn, ill treatment, discrimination and hate, contain their rage and desire to strike back. Some can't keep it bottled up, I said.

But fighting hate with hate doesn't pave a path toward understanding. Walking and talking with others who are different does.

We got back to Gene's house, had some pop and looked at pictures before I left. We agreed to get together to walk again. Next time, Gene said as I stepped to my van, he'd try to get me to do the distance a little slower.

That'll be hard, I said. We've got so much ground to cover and so precious little time.

Getting past prejudice often means walking in others' shoes. We need to take more walks with people who are not like us. The insights we gain applying Formula II *(Talk x Diversity = Social Capital)* on such journeys with others help us discover the Real America.

From "Celebrating a culture step by step"

A new moon glowed large over downtown's skyline.

Alfredo Parra was right. West Side residents own a million-dollar view of Kansas City.

I saw that and more when Parra, Rita Valenciano and her daughter, Gloria, took me on a three-hour sidewalk tour of Kansas City's historic Mexican-American community.

Our walk took place as the nation celebrated Hispanic Heritage Month. It's as significant as Black History Month is in February, especially as the United States' Latino population continues to rise.

The number of Hispanics in the U.S. now eclipses the projected black population. Latinos are the nation's largest minority group.

Hostile immigration laws and attacks on affirmative action in other states added to the 38.8 percent growth in the area's Hispanic population from 1990 to 1997. The growth for the black population was 13.7 percent, and it was 5.9 percent for whites.

Census data also show that in Johnson, Platte, Cass and Clay counties - this area's fastest- growing communities - Hispanics already are the largest minority. By 2050, the white population won't be the country's majority.

The walk on the West Side, where this area's Hispanic community grew up, was a fascinating look into the past, present and future.

Annual Hispanic events like the Fiesta Hispana and the National Convention and International Expo of the U.S. Hispanic Chamber of Commerce "showcase Hispanic culture, [and] speak to the importance and centrality of the Hispanic community in Kansas City," said Valerie Mendoza, then-assistant professor of history at the University of Kansas.

Parra and the Valenciano showed me the big picture.

We walked more than a mile to a street overlooking the city skyline and Interstate 35. The highway gutted this community of hundreds of homes and residents when it was built. We went as far north as 16th Street, where we saw airplanes flying into Downtown Airport.

We walked as far south as 29th Street, as far west as Jarboe and traversed all the avenues in between. Parra and Valenciano showed me the parks, schools, churches, civic and other community centerpieces.

We walked through La Colonia, at 24th and Belleview. "This was supposed to be the birthplace - like 18th and Vine for African Americans," Parra said.

Rita Valenciano pointed to the old railroad viaduct.

"They called this the depot from Mexico," she said. "People would come on the trains and get off on the boulevard."

> Mexicans settled here. The area grew from the immigration that supplied turn-of-the-century labor for railroads and meat-packing companies.
>
> Points of pride include all the new housing, thriving businesses, streets, schools and places named after Chicanos. Areas of need are more housing, businesses and home repairs.
>
> This walk was rich with dialogue. Parra and Rita Valenciano shared their families' past, spoke of the brown berets they wore at the height of the Chicano Movement of their youth, and greeted people on the front porches and the street.
>
> This is Kansas City's global village, where newcomers, immigrants and old-timers are working to feel at home. It's where whites and blacks also live, visit and embrace the Mexican-American culture.
>
> That's worth celebrating every month with more walks on the West Side by everyone.

The growth in the Hispanic community does not diminish any part of the Real America. It only makes all sectors stronger and better. But those qualities can't be attained unless people take the time to talk across the cultural and racial divide.

<u>From "Hispanics are on the move"</u>

> Max Cerda and I got together to walk the streets of Kansas City, Kan., where he grew up.
>
> We met at La Unica, 618 Kansas Ave., which Cerda called the anchor of the Kansas Avenue community. It's a business that enjoys a lot of customers.
>
> But it and other Hispanic businesses are surrounded by vacant lots, broken and uneven sidewalks, weeds and other signs of longstanding neglect. "It's kind of a forgotten part of the tax base," Cerda said.
>
> We went to Art's Mexican Products, 615 Kansas Ave, where Bob Gutierrez is president. He and Cerda reminisced about the old Hispanic neighborhood that used to be south of Gutierrez's longstanding business.
>
> Seventh Street was this community's Troost Avenue. Cerda said Hispanics were mostly segregated to the east. Whites lived on the west.
>
> Industrial property lies behind Gutierrez's store now.
>
> "It was the death of the neighborhood," Cerda said. "What I would like to see is an area like this become developed, cleaned up and landscaped."
>
> People who grew up in this community still shop here and have a strong sense of ownership and pride. City officials should do more to promote Hispanic businesses so that Kemper Arena crowds could also eat and shop on Kansas and Central avenues.

"Unless someone brings you down here, you don't know, but it's gradually growing," Cerda said.

He added that unlike the past he now saw many people who looked like him; that affirmed his heritage and culture.

"I feel as comfortable walking down here as I do on the Plaza," he said of the upscale and popular white shopping district. "It's all home to me."

It's also good for business. In La Unica, people can exchange foreign currency for dollars, buy music, magazines, clothing, religious items and other things that families used to only find in Mexico.

Cerda pointed to posters of musicians. "These are superstars in our culture," he said.

The Hispanic population boom has caused businesses to stock goods that serve the new market. We entered Reyna's Mexican Bakery, 727 Kansas Ave. Cerda showed me soft drinks imported from Mexico.

We went to Reyna's Food Mart, 939 Central Ave. Manuel Reyna, owner of Reyna's Enterprises, said the Hispanic growth had caused stores and restaurants to offer more authentic Mexican food. People who were used to toned-down fare may have to adjust.

At a nearby supermarket, customers spoke Spanish. Many mainstream businesses now must employ bilingual workers. Goods in this store's aisles also cater to the Hispanic market.

"They're ready to buy," Cerda said. "To turn them away is just plain foolish."

But Cerda and I also worried about exploitation. Signs of that are on the street, too, in pawn shops, payday loan places and pay telephones, which take costly phone cards.

We also worried whether new residents felt welcome. The rapid growth raises cultural tensions between Hispanics and whites and also between Hispanics themselves. There is tension between established Hispanics and recent immigrants.

Differences in language, class, education, dress, behavior, urban vs. rural roots and culture remind me of the 20th century tension in the black community when thousands of African-Americans migrated from farms in the South to cities in the North for jobs.

"It will take some work on both sides for them to understand each other," said Cerda who grew up in a migrant farm family. "The remedies attempted can be very insulting and very cruel. What may be acceptable in small-town communities may not go over well here."

The newcomers like everyone else are here to improve their lives. We must be patient and understanding.

Cerda and I went to Laura's Restaurant at 13th Street and Central. Laura Martinez, who owns the business with her husband, expanded recently to a former fast-food restaurant to keep up with customer demand.

That trend will only continue as this Hispanic community keeps growing.

Many people, particularly those of different races, prefer not to discuss issues of race. It is either too painful, or people get too upset. But the only way to discover what we are missing in America is to talk about race and other differences. The intimidation will pass. So will the fear if people trust in others and seek opportunities to use Formula II at each available chance.

From "Matters we must talk about"

David's friends finished watching the last part of the video "A Color Adjustment" at the Minority Museum.

I had shown the documentary to many other groups since I'd videotaped the show in 1992 when it aired on KCPT-TV, Channel 19. But I was fascinated that it took the coalition of blacks and Jews three months to get through the two-hour program, which probed the history of television and how poorly it has portrayed African Americans.

The group, which David Shapiro, founder of the museum, assembled isn't slow by any means. The video just delivered such a wealth of material and spurred so much discussion that we stopped the tape several times so that people could share long-buried joys, pains and concerns at the Minority Museum.

The museum is a haven that David opened for about 10 years to his friends to continue the dialogue toward harmony that then-Kansas City Mayor Emanuel Cleaver started in April 1996 with the release of the Mayor's Task Force on Race Relations. It followed then-President Clinton's National Dialogue on Race.

The last part of the video included clips of "Good Times" and described how that 1970s TV program featured a nuclear black family living in the projects. It had great potential in delivering social, economic and racial realism to American viewers.

But "Good Times" didn't live up to black people's expectations because it used humor through the minstrel-like character J.J. to deflate each meaningful moment.

Bernice Powell Jackson, executive director of the United Church of Christ Commission for Racial Justice, told people at the Country Club Congregational United Church of Christ how a real-life drama let her down. When the burning of black churches appeared on national TV, Powell said, she thought it would spur people to talk about race.

Instead the media minimized the church burnings, and the public drifted to other concerns.

Yet, race remains a problem.

"I think we've got to talk about race in America if we're going to deal with it, if we are to survive as a nation," Powell said.

"A Color Adjustment" also contained clips of "Roots," which opened America's eyes to what black people had endured.

The 1970s miniseries was critically acclaimed for showing a black family's epic journey from slavery to freedom. But it also was criticized for being "packaged" to make the people and their suffering palatable for TV viewers.

I stopped the tape because Cynthia, a black woman, said she still couldn't watch "Roots." Willie, a black man, offered that it perhaps was because of the pain the show resurrected.

From a book he brought, he shared that the slave trade to North, South and Central America over more than 200 years had resulted in the deaths of more than 60 million Africans. It was a global holocaust whose victims were fed into the New World's economic and social cravings for free labor.

Discussion then shifted to self hate among minorities and how one of the dynamics of oppression is the oppressed adopting the biases of their oppressors.

That keeps people from studying or promoting their history and using such events as Black History Month as an opportunity to learn more about their own and other cultures. The Jewish people at the museum said denial was a problem in their minority group, too.

We closed by talking about skin color among blacks, Hispanics, Asian-Americans, Native Americans and Jews. Hue plays a role in whether members embrace or reject those in each group.

We've learned a lot from each other.

More of such gatherings are desperately needed along with more open and rich conversations. They expose the pain of the past, but that's the only way a genuine healing can take place.

<u>From "On permanent probation"</u>

Betsy and I frequently encounter each other at community gatherings. We first met when I stepped as a stranger into her one-story Kansas City, Kan., home. But I'll never forget its warmth or the meal and conversation I shared with her, Tess, Wanda and Mary.

They're part of a group of women of different races, religions, ethnicities and professions who get together to have supper and fulfill their desire to discover an understanding of other women of difference. The hosts change.

So do the meals, with each person bringing something different. But the sharing keeps growing.

Wanda told me about the group earlier this year and the rich returns the women get in the safe havens of their homes. They ask questions about normally untouchable topics of race and ethnicity and are rewarded with honest answers.

I asked Wanda whether I could attend one of the meetings to watch and note the interactions. She got back to me with a condition: I had to participate in the dialogue, too.

I arrived a little before the 6:30 p.m. start. Betsy welcomed me into her home, and we talked as the sun made its daily journey below the western horizon.

Seeing daylight eclipse into shadows in her living room felt so familiar and natural. The conversations that evening went the same way.

Betsy and I found that although we were different – she's a woman and white; I'm a man and black - we also have a lot in common: children, a parent who had Alzheimer's disease, a love for older homes, an eclectic taste in furnishings and a mountaintop of hope for the future.

Mary, Tess and Wanda arrived, bringing dishes that added to the stew Betsy had made and served from a pumpkin gourd. We looked at pictures Betsy had of her trip to Alaska with her grown son.

Dinner was a culinary delight with the stew, an Oriental salad, wine, Jewish pastry, and sliced apples and honey.

Mary blessed the meal with a Jewish prayer. This was different from the diversity coalition discussions that Minority Museum founder David Shapiro holds each month.

But this was more familial. The conversation flowed freely.

We talked about marriage, spouses, wedding anniversaries and divorce. We focused on our unique identities - two African-Americans, one Asian American, one Jewish woman and one woman who was white.

We shared experiences of how difficult it was for minorities to get others to recognize how our race plays a big part in who we are. We found that it always hurts when whites say, "I don't see color," or "I look at you as being just like me."

We shared the often silent pain we feel when others erase that part of who we are to make us marginally acceptable to them. That reminded me of what a friend once said: Being a minority in America is like being on permanent probation. You never know when your privileges of being "one of the good ones" will be revoked.

We devoted a lot of time and discussion to our children. Minorities learn at an early age what the score is in America.

> We shared our frustrations as parents in getting our now older children to see the beauty in African-Americans, Asian Americans, Hispanics and American Indians as people - in their heritage and their toys. As early and voracious media consumers, our kids have swallowed the images of beauty that are white.
>
> Schools back up that "education" with mostly Eurocentric lessons. Parents of color have to "home school" their children and set them on a course of independent study to discover the diversity of history and contributions of all this nation's people.
>
> That "home schooling" includes how to survive encounters with authorities. We learned that racial profiling is as big a problem for Hispanics, Asians and American Indians as it is for black people.
>
> Shopping also is a shared concern. The better malls, stores and bargains are in far-flung, mostly white suburban communities.
>
> The likelihood of ill-treatment toward minorities increases in those areas, too. But shopping only in urban stores boosts the chance that consumers will pay more and the selection and quality probably won't be as good.
>
> People of color often have to calculate on different days which price - social or financial - is too high. These were among the otherwise invisible things we touched.
>
> Without such discussions, we'd all continue blind, unaware of the barriers people of color face or the privilege that many whites can't see that they possess.

2. *Talking across lines drawn by faith*

The scapegoating and fear mentioned earlier are also present today in how Muslims in America are being treated. But that kind of treatment is not new. Loewen points out "none of the [history] textbooks credits the Muslims with preserving Greek wisdom, enhancing it with ideas from China, India, and Africa, and then passing on the resulting knowledge to Europe via Spain" (*Lies* 45). The Sept. 11, 2001, tragedy just gave license to continue the scapegoating and fear while ignoring many Muslim contributions to society.

From "Fear could stop the peace train"

> Abuse has been widespread with thousands of people being subjected to questioning, searches and detention in the so-called war against terrorism. Muslims face profiling not unlike what African-Americans and other minorities suffer. Such things should be outlawed.

But when people talk and share their thoughts and impressions of events, we all learn and grow from the knowledge that's exchanged. No one leaves the same; nobody!

From "Filmmaker gives glimpse of the road from terrorism to peace"

Lessons on the futility of violence hit the big screen at the recent showing of "My Terrorist."

The documentary at the Glenwood Arts Theatre was part of the Halfway to Hollywood Film Festival. Dotty Hamilton, a board member of the series and instructor at Avila University, had Sheila Sonnenschein, who's Jewish; Mahnaz Shabbir, who's Muslim; and me field questions after the show.

"My Terrorist" examines events in the Arab-Israel conflict through the experiences of Yulie Cohen Gerstel. In August 1978, Gerstel was part of an El Al Israeli airline flight crew.

She had boarded a bus in London with co-workers. She recalled seeing Fahad Mihyi.

She remembered the hate in his eyes. Mihyi, a member of the Popular Front for the Liberation of Palestine, opened fire on the bus, killing a flight attendant and wounding Gerstel and others.

Gerstel was a witness at Mihyi's trial, where he received life sentences. That started her on a journey toward becoming a peace advocate.

No doubt, 27 reserve pilots in the Israeli air force who signed a petition saying they would not take part in "illegal and immoral" strikes in Palestinian areas have embarked on similar, personal treks toward peace. The film also made me think of Albert Einstein. Fred Jerome in his book, *The Einstein File,* wrote that in the 1930s, the famous scientist and social activist said a lasting peace among the Arabs and Jews would happen only through mutual respect, "honest cooperation" and power sharing.

Jerome wrote that Einstein said a few years later: "The most important aspect of our (Israel's) policy must be our ever-present, manifest desire to institute complete equality for the Arab citizens living in our midst....The attitude we adopt toward the Arab minority will provide the real test of our moral standards as a people."

Gerstel's "My Terrorist" examines her awakening to the futility of violence and bloodshed on both sides and the need for reconciliation. Gerstel traces her family back more than 150 years to the land that is now Israel.

She was a proud captain in the Israeli air force, saying: "We are the best. We are the strongest, and we'll go all the way around the world to free our brothers."

The film showed footage of major events, including the 1967 Six-Day War, the 1973 Yom Kippur War, the 1978 Camp David Accords and the 1993 Oslo Accord.

But Gerstel was the focus. She wrote to Mihyi and went to visit him in prison more than 20 years after his attack and eventually agreed to help him obtain his release.

His eyes no longer burned with hate. He apologized for what he had done.

People in the audience told Shabbir and Sonnenschein they wanted to know more about what motivated him to be a terrorist. He said he was young and had been manipulated.

The audience identified with Gerstel. The film showed her children, her fear for them and her anguish over surviving the attack.

She was confronted by an angry and tearful mother whose daughter died in the attack. Gerstel faced men who condemned her peace efforts as aiding enemies of Israel.

That sounded like Bush administration rhetoric since the Sept. 11, 2001, terrorist attacks.

The film showed the poverty and oppression of the Palestinians.

"'This is how terrorists are created,' I thought to myself," Gerstel said.

That also should be a lesson for America in its wars in Afghanistan and Iraq.

Gerstel said vengeance-fed killings on both sides fuel a "vicious circle."

"They kill us; we kill them," she said. "Hurting them is hurting us."

Gerstel's commitment wavered after the Sept. 11, 2001, tragedy. A friend helped her recover.

"Fear leads to hate," she said. "Instead of being afraid we hate. It is fear that breaks you."

But for peace, Gerstel said people embroiled in conflicts *need to talk*. "We owe this to the children of the future," she said.

Shabbir said, "On the other side of fear is freedom."

That's where we all need to be.

Accepting other faiths and beliefs without fear is among the things that enrich life. Yet too few people have that openness in mind when they encounter someone who believes differently. They miss out on an affirming and enriching moment when they can question others without being judgmental and grow from each new engagement. All of the stereotypes people harbor and that Hollywood promotes must be vanquished for the diversity of the moment to yield its bounty.

From "Absolutely nothing to be afraid of"

Jana had five magic words to offer when I asked whether I could visit her Cass County, Mo., home:

"Come with an open mind," she said on the phone.

That was important advice on a rainy day. It seemed to echo on the long drive south past cities and towns - out where livestock grazed and recent harvests have left the countryside's rolling hills quiet and subdued with fall's Monet-like colors.

Her one-story home with a TV antenna on the roof and two-car garage seemed like others off the highway. But look again and notice a tall May pole in back near a 25-foot in diameter stone circle with a rock altar.

A five-pointed, multicolored star and Thor's hammer adorned the blue front door. The hinges yielded, and the daylight tumbled inside, making Jana's red hair and blue eyes shine.

The self-professed witch dressed in blue jeans, sneakers and a gray sweatshirt extended a handshake and a warm welcome. The Wicca priestess' home is the coven's place of worship.

People shouldn't fear or hate witches, the 32-year-old married homemaker said.

Halloween is a good time to dispel some myths, said Kenny Klein, a Wicca priest. "We're real people; we don't wear pointy black hats and have warts on our noses," he said.

To Wiccans, Halloween is Samhain, and in their multithousand-year-old worship it's their Memorial Day. It's when they honor their ancestors and it's the start of their new year, said Rhiannon, a nurse and Midtown resident.

Jana sat at her desk. Behind her on shelves reaching to the ceiling sat squat jars of incenses, oils and herbs. Two charms hung in the room and another altar rested on the floor.

Jana had found many of the things on it at garage sales, at the Renaissance Festival or on hikes. Folks need to understand that Wicca is a religion and its followers include blue-collar and professional people.

Witches don't worship Satan, kill babies or make sacrifices. That's poppycock and Hollywood babble.

Jana explained that Wiccans believe that all life and nature is sacred. Everyone must be responsible for their actions.

"Wiccans do not preach or proselytize or try to convert," said Jana, who wore a pentagram necklace. "We respect other people's religions."

It's worship based on nature and full of respect for living things and the environment. The philosophy is do what thou will but harm none, Rhiannon said.

"We're a happy people, a life-oriented people," said Rhiannon, a Wicca minister, president of the Heartland Spiritual Alliance and the Kansas City Interfaith Council Wicca or pagan member.

It is among 13 faiths on the council, said the Rev. Vern Barnet, minister in residence with the World Faiths Center for Religious Experience and Study and convener of the interfaith group, which meets in Midtown.

"Paganism is concerned with the focus of nature," he said. "There's no concept of a separate and distinct evil.

"Our culture, which is so environmentally destructive, needs very much to encounter the spirituality that respects nature, which is Wicca."

But instead people harass Wiccans and persecute folks like Jana and Rhiannon. Raven E. Ambrosius said that Halloween was among the worst times of year for her and many Wiccans.

It's when she has to skip taking part in the Wiccan celebrations and stay home to guard her Northeast area house from vandals. Teens and young adults are a problem.

Children aren't. On Halloween they just want goodies.

They have the open mind that everyone needs.

3. *Talking across gender lines*

Every year the University of Missouri at Kansas City (UMKC) holds the Starr Symposium to discuss issues that are of concern to women and families. The symposium, the first of which was held in 1993, was named after Martha Jane Starr, who established an endowment from which the event is funded. Nationally acclaimed experts on women's issues speak in Kansas City to address areas that are critical to women's lives. These conversations using Formula II (*Talk x Diversity = Social Capital*) offer insight into the challenges that women today face in our society and into their mostly unheralded triumphs.

From "Both sexes must resist the wreckage that dooms partnering"

A new resolve seemed to emerge from the recent Starr Symposium on "Women and Men Creating the Future Together."

A follow-up session made me think of how the symposium at the University of Missouri-Kansas City ended with eager participants brainstorming at round tables.

It was as if we were in lifeboats, rowing across a sea of changing relationships between men and women to a new world of partnerships.

Chairs and marker-scarred easels that we'd used were strewn about like debris from a shipwreck. Charting a new course isn't neat or easy.

But the initiative will benefit communities, families, religion, government, schools and businesses. That's because power-sharing partnerships are far superior to continuing traditional fear and violence-driven roles of one gender dominating another.

More meetings are set to develop the partnership plan. But the journey faces many challenges, including a threat from Republicans and conservatives dominating Congress, pushing old family ways.

Voters said they wanted the winds of change stopped and reversed because the new progressive direction scares them. Symposium leaders Isabella Conti and Alfonso Montuori, authors of *From Power to Partnership: Creating the Future of Love, Work and Community*, said it's natural for people to swim back to their wreckage instead of going into an uncharted future.

Some people are falling back to traditional roles of male domination, and some are moving forward with partnerships. The confused and worried majority is stuck in the middle, Conti said.

"We're seeing families fall apart," Montuori said. "People are saying we should go back to the old ways. But the reason families fell apart in the first place was because the old ways weren't working anymore."

Symposium organizers hope to identify successful partnerships and promote them as role models.

Men and women working together can do more creative problem-solving than men can dictating policy alone. But persuading men to share won't be easy when men have been trained to fight for power and never let go.

Guys can be convinced, though, that we gain from partnerships with women, particularly when women have job or cognitive skills that we don't possess.

Women's ideas and methods create new resources for production, and cooperation replaces violence and fear in relationships. A new world of untapped human potential opens up, giving all of us an advantage in our competitive global economy.

But people at the symposium and follow-up session said that for partnerships to work women will have to be assured that they can exert their special influence without fear of retaliation or ridicule from men.

In addition, symposium participants said committed folks must push the movie, music, television, news and other media to scrap gender stereotypes and shift to images of strong women and strong men in power-sharing partnerships.

The symposium is just the start of the change, Conti said. The journey toward greater productivity will happen if we keep talking about it, have patience, stay informed and avoid quick fixes.

"Part of the problem is we have a tendency to measure everything in human years," Conti said. "When you are transforming a community or an organization, the time involved is much, much longer."

The rich promised land of partnerships among men and women lies ahead, maybe not for us, but for our children and our children's children.

4. *Talking within one's group*

Another group whose diverse contributions are often overlooked is teens. Through talking amongst themselves and with adults, though, they can build their status, accomplish community-creating goals, form new ideas and create new social capital that no one can ignore.

From "Teens are Friends, indeed"

A group called Friends has broken some chains that bind our youth by making an elbow-grease investment in the community.

Friends established a foothold in the Southland this fall and, with the right encouragement, should spread across the metropolitan area. The group is unique because it was founded and is run exclusively by teens who want to contribute something positive to the community.

No one holds a gun to their heads, and they're not working for badges, praise or pay. They're just bursting inside with the impulse to do something good for others.

A few months after members first met, they were already busy assisting reading specialist Barbara Ham in her after-school Santa Fe Reading Club.

Friends helped Santa Fe Elementary School students become better readers and, in the process, became their role models. "I think it's a wonderful thing that they do," Ham said.

Friends helped Harmony in Hickman Mills, a diversity-promoting organization, with an exhibit during the Ruskin Homecoming Parade.

"They're not picky or choosy about who they help," Harmony President Donna Almai said. "They just want to help in their community."

Friends have volunteered at Harvesters-the Community Food Network, 1811 N. Topping Ave., and at the Lord's Table Soup Kitchen at Westminster Congregational Church, 3600 Walnut Ave.

Pam Cutelli, secretary treasurer of outreach at the church, said it was the first time a youth group had offered to help without prodding.

"They keep asking what else can we do," Cutelli said. "Everything we've offered has been received so joyfully."

Friends have held food and clothing drives at Ruskin High School for the Lord's Table, Harvesters and the Community Assistance Council. Some donations were distributed Saturday.

For Christmas, Friends will have a book and magazine drive for Westminster, said Kristi Attwood, Friends vice president.

Because of the high Friends get from helping others, their membership has climbed from about 12 to 30 teens and expanded from Ruskin to Hickman Mills and Southwest high schools.

Ruskin Principal W.L. Elliott said the group's actions were educational. Teens learn they can make a difference in their community, and adults find that our youths are good people.

It's an alternative to gangs in which service overpowers death, drugs and destruction, and beaming smiles with bouquets of thanks kill the fear that has stalked our streets.

"They're saying 'I know my community is in trouble. What part can I play to help?'" Elliott said.

In addition to service, Friends President Mahlon Cathey said another goal was to get all students - black, white, jocks, scholars, social butterflies and wallflowers - to participate and become better friends.

"We learned that it is kind of hard to bring people together, but it can be done," said Mahlon, 15.

For Marquita Miller, 14, Friends is a chance to get involved instead of sitting around the house.

For Rochelle Strother, 16, Friends is better than talking aimlessly on the phone or spending her Mom's money at the malls.

"Friends gives me a sense of accomplishment," she said. "It makes me feel a lot better about myself because I helped somebody."

James Travis, 15, said working with Friends erased the stress of school, put his mind at ease and allowed him to think more clearly. "It's a pretty good experience," he said.

Everyone in Greater Kansas City needs Friends like this.

5. *Talking across corporate lines*

During a Kansas City Harmony/National Conference for Community and Justice Diversity Council Roundtable discussion at Ameristar Casino, the importance of Formula II for the corporate world was emphasized. The topic of the roundtable was "Acquisitions, Mergers and Joint Ventures: How is Diversity Addressed?"

Tammy Edwards, director of inclusion and diversity with Sprint Nextel, was among the presenters. She said the two telephone giants, which completed their corporate merger in 2005, benefited greatly from discussions involving people from each company who worked in similar areas. Talking was the critical element that dissolved barriers of differences in the competitive corporate cultures of each company.

I had not realized that diversity plays a role in corporate mergers until Jane Elliott pointed that out in a visit to Kansas City in the 1990s. Elliott is the third-grade teacher in Iowa who rose to fame in the documentary, "A Class Divided," featuring her brown eyes/blue eyes experiment. She helped her all-white, third-grade students after the assassination of the Rev. Martin Luther King Jr. in 1968 understand what it means to be different. She praised blue-eyed students and demeaned brown-eyed students one day and then reversed the situation the next day. Elliott pointed out that merging corporations need the same diversity eye-opening experiences so the different cultures can better understand each other. It is why talking is an integral part of diversity Formula II in building social capital among different groups.

Edwards told the gathering that when an executive at her company was asked to quantify the value of diversity and how it could be measured, he equated diversity to "integrity." It is a value for which there are no metrics; however, it, like diversity, is needed for a corporation to operate efficiently. Sprint Nextel was ranked no. 28 in *DiversityInc* magazine's 2007 list of the top 50 companies for diversity.

Paulette Markel, director of workplace diversity solutions with Harmony/NCCJ, recounted her experiences in a corporate merger. She noted that without talking efforts to join operations will breakdown. If groups do not allow for forgiveness of errors and missteps, if they do not respect differences, the situation will devolve into miscommunication, misunderstandings, mistrust, misdirection, difficulties, barriers, personnel and market-share losses, finger-pointing, scapegoating, and hatred.

6. *Talking across international boundaries*

Strangers from faraway places can see us in ways that would be invisible otherwise. Talking and sharing with others reveal and expose new ideas and generate social capital.

From "U.S.S.R. was never like this"

> The Republic of Kyrgyzstan has nothing like Bannister Mall or Wal-Mart's Hypermart USA, which once thrived in south Kansas City.
>
> The community's great shrines to capitalism dazzled Julia Orlova, 26, and Sultan Raev, 36. The shopping centers were among the places I took the visiting journalists from the new republic in the old Soviet Union.
>
> "Where do you find enough people to eat this stuff?" Orlova said as we walked through Hypermart's food section.
>
> "I think that in America there are more things than people need," Orlova concluded, half-joking, after we strolled through Bannister Mall.
>
> She and Raev, a newspaper editor in chief, explained that through the National Forum Foundation they'd left behind spouses and children to come study the U.S. press, government and people. They felt compelled to touch, see, hear, smell, taste and analyze America so that as journalists they could recount the experience for the people back home.
>
> Home, Orlova explained, is "near fun places like China and Afghanistan."
>
> Their work, she and Raev said, will help their country make the transition toward democracy.
>
> "It is very important for us to learn how a democratic society works - to see some of the problems that exist in a democracy so that we would not repeat some of the mistakes," Orlova said through interpreter Yelena Nisenzon, 25, of Washington, D.C.
>
> From the eyes of strangers it's possible for Americans to learn, too.

The tour included the luxury homes of Hallbrook and Loch Lloyd, middle-class neighborhoods and lunch at the Hillcrest Country Club with the South Kansas City Chamber of Commerce. Then-Jackson County Prosecutor Claire McCaskill spoke about crime and drug-fighting efforts. That struck a chord with Orlova.

"When I looked at those wealthy homes, and what I heard with the crack and the drugs, it looked like there are two different ways of living in America and that the wealthy people and the poor people never meet each other," said Orlova, a reporter who covers human rights issues. "It's almost as if you have two separate countries.

"Unfortunately when they do happen to meet it can have unfortunate and dire consequences."

We drove down Main Street in Belton and peeped into the building that houses the horse-drawn hearse that took Carry Nation to her grave in 1911. Russia had its temperance movement, too.

But it never took hold, said Orlova, who sometimes must prove her journalistic mettle by outdrinking sources.

Richards-Gebaur Air Force Base was another stop. When the Cold War ended between our countries, so did the future of the south Kansas City installation and some jobs.

The same thing happened in Kyrgyzstan and other republics in the old Soviet Union, where many people lost work.

We cruised through trailer courts, where Raev and Orlova noted that despite the poverty they still saw new cars and pickup trucks parked outside. Then we headed north, eventually landing on Prospect Avenue, but we had to detour around police barricades at a shooting scene.

The Kyrgyzstan visitors noted the city's segregation, the sights, sounds and the stench of poverty and a lot more. "The place looks like people have lost hope to get out of here," Orlova said, pointing to the absence of well-kept lawns and newer vehicles.

We went over to Troost Avenue and then north to Truman Medical Center before I turned south and dropped them off at their hotel near the Plaza.

America, what a country!

They learned a lot that day, and so did I.

Even in The Heartland, America can present challenges as well as learning opportunities for visitors from other countries, as long as they reach out, compare and share.

From "U.S. through another lens"

The Alfred Friendly Press Fellowship took Jianxiang Yang and his 11 classmates through a course months ago that attempted to prepare them for the culture shock of America.

The fellowship placed Yang and the other journalists from countries worldwide in U.S. newspaper jobs. He was my deskmate at *The Kansas City Star* from the spring to the fall when he returned home to his wife, Song Xiaomin, and his job as a feature writer for the Xinhua News Agency in Beijing. As a newspaperman, he's a trained observer, and some things about our culture have intrigued him.

First there's housing. Many Kansas Citians live in houses, compared to the densely packed apartment complexes in Beijing. Kansas City and Beijing seem to be about the same size in land. However, Beijing has many more people.

"You have a deserted downtown area but prosperous suburbs," said Yang, who studied English as a second language. "People living in the suburbs, it's very beautiful."

The spaciousness, the well-manicured lawns and cleanliness have been incredible treats.

"It seems like a park," Yang said. "In Beijing there are only a limited number of places where you can go and have this environment.

"I really appreciate the clean air here and blue skies. We don't see blue skies often."

Then there's transportation. Beijing has a good public transit system that moves the masses efficiently. In Kansas City, Yang had to learn to drive, take the tests to get his license and then rent a car to get around.

He found our food to be a bit much. Colleagues treated him to the best of our barbecue restaurants. "Big is too big," he said of the portions served.

What we eat is good. But Yang said he preferred Chinese food.

He liked the people. "Most of them are very nice, very friendly," he said. "Western people are more outgoing.

"Even if you are a total stranger, you say hello and greet each other. We do not do that in Beijing."

But Yang was befuddled by a column I wrote about racism in America in which the words "Chink Go Home" were printed on the front fender of an Asian-American man's car. Yang didn't know what the racial slur meant until I explained it to him.

Yet, he is convinced that diversity is this country's strength.

"There will be some conflicts, but inevitably the U.S. system is good," Yang said. "It incorporates the best parts of different cultures."

Our many styles in art, architecture and other things in this land of mostly immigrants seem to be imported from elsewhere.

"I also wonder if there will be a time when things go together so well you'll unify or create a unique taste," he said. "But presently I think no style might be the style."

This nation also has made my Beijing colleague more wary and watchful. America is a more violent place than his home.

Since Yang has been here, mass shootings and killings have occurred on the streets in Illinois and Indiana, at stock trading offices in Atlanta, at a Jewish community center in the Los Angeles area, at a church in Fort Worth, Texas, at a Xerox Corp. building in Hawaii, and a shipyard in Seattle.

Yang said Americans seem to kill without purpose. "I think the most important reason is you have a free policy on guns," he said.

"I understand why you have guns," Yang said. "The purpose is to defend yourself. But, unfortunately, the guns are used to kill other people."

Yang asked about gun buyback programs. I explained some of their problems. Some people take in old guns that don't work. Yet they collect money for them.

I always wonder whether that money will be used to help pay for new guns. Compared to China, most of us are still cowboys in an untame, uncivilized land.

Yang pointed out some of our other problems. "People seem to lack sufficient communications," he said.

We're independent here. But we don't really communicate much, valuing instead to live far apart as if we were on an open range.

Paranoia, disrespect, contempt for others, our community, government and our leaders breed in that isolation. "In China there are so many people you cannot avoid communicating with people," Yang said.

He joked that before he returns home his fellowship will take him through a "reverse culture shock" course to prepare him for re-entry. I hope that helps him take the best of what he has found here with him and leave the worst with us on these bloody shores.

African journalists are foreigners in our land, yet because of racism they get treated in an all-too-familiar way. They find that discrimination in America isn't pleasant.

From "A few things are worth taking home"

A six-month fellowship - and what I've called the Americanization of Doyin Adedeji - ends this week.

She will return to Nigeria as an assistant editor for foreign news at the *Nigerian Tribune*. She'd been at *The Star* in the Alfred Friendly Press Fellowship.

Adedeji was among 15 journalists in developing nations that the fellowship placed in U.S. newspaper jobs. The good impressions she's picked up of America have included our free press and our computerized, efficiently run society.

She's been pleased with the ethical behavior of our public servants, our good health care and our efficient elections. "I ask myself, 'How much of this can I use at home?'" she said.

I've also ribbed Adedeji about her own Americanization. She got her license to drive here.

Mass transit and walking worked fine in the big city she calls home. She's seen how we eat and is mystified by how much Americans consume and how much we waste.

She's dumbfounded by how little Americans know of the world's other places. "Americans like to export their culture to other countries, but they hardly know us - other people's cultures," Adedeji said.

American cable TV also has kept her up late many nights. Nigeria has only a few stations, compared with dozens available in Kansas City alone. Her homeland's stations are on just a few hours daily, compared with 24-hour programming in America.

"Here you can switch on the telly and watch and switch from one station to the other," Adedeji said. "I'd bet at any given time there must be an interesting program somewhere."

She's been fascinated with old movies, musicals and music on cable TV. She said our TV commercials are irresistible.

"It is the visuals," Adedeji said. "You see really glamorous commercials.

"The other day I saw a chicken moving like a human being and dancing to a beat. I said, 'How did they do this?' It was very, very funny."

But she also endured things that weren't so funny. They've added to the Americanization of Adedeji, too. She promised herself before coming here that she wouldn't get tangled in America's race problem.

But racism in America was unavoidable. She found herself treated poorly or ignored by many white people. When she'd ask them for directions she'd get none, or they'd move away out of fear or loathing.

"It is very, very painful," said Adedeji, who'd never had such encounters in Europe or in Africa. She also found that she'd unwittingly humble herself in white people's presence.

"I'd get so nervous," Adedeji said. "I feel, 'How will they react to me?' I've studied apartheid in South Africa, and I told myself, 'My God! I am becoming a South African!' I hate that."

But Adedeji found comfort in our churches, in Mayor Emanuel Cleaver's office, where she was made an honorary Kansas Citian, and among area residents who look like her.

"I've discovered that those who really care are African-Americans," Adedeji said. "If I am lost, some African-American will stop and say, 'Sister, is everything all right?'

"Here it makes me feel that here are my people. We have different cultures and different accents, but basically we (black people) are the same."

She'll take all of these truly American things back to her homeland. I hope the good things take root and the bad things die in Africa's fertile soil.

Bigotry blinds good people and conceals the truth. Getting past this centuries-old debility will make the journey into the Real America difficult, painful and problematic. However, Formula II *(Talk x Diversity = Social Capital)* offers some solace.

7. *Talking across the generations*

One large, often-overlooked universe of diversity is age. Older people see life differently and they communicate the things they value through the lens of their experiences in a history that is their own. They can provide a wealth of ideas that reflect the histories of the nation and the world. People with that kind of knowledge can offer so much if people who are younger will just pause to learn.

From "Mother Newman's wit and words are always worth a smile"

Sometimes the news boils with bad goings-on, forcing me to seek a friendly refuge.

I found it not long ago at an East Side house and returned there in the spring to help two daughters like my own celebrate their mom's birthday. Mom in this case is Ora E. Newman, known affectionately as Mother Newman to her friends.

Her "girls" are Alta Wilburn, 83, and Ernestine Stuteley, 78. How old is Mother Newman? She's 105 and counting.

I took her and her "girls" sweet candy flowers from Bitterman Family Confections. They were lemon yellow, vanilla white and strawberry red.

The gifts inspired Mother Newman to offer something sweet of her own—poetry, which she said she had recited since she was "knee high to a duck."

Mother Newman laughed, and everyone else did, too. Then she recited the first poem, which became a precious gift to me:

If you give me a rosebud now,
It can be yellow, pink or red.
I would rather have just one today,
Than a hundred when I'm dead.

"I thought it was a million," Wilburn said.

"Either way," Mother Newman replied.

Between poems Mother Newman offered advice: "Don't get old, honey. Stay young. You know when you get to be my age everything doesn't work like it did when you're young."

I told her I respected that advice, but I didn't like the alternative to growing old.

Mother Newman smiled.

Then I asked her for her secret to youth. Helping others is one way, reciting poetry is another. That led to her second poem, which Ma Bell would love:

Why don't you have a telephone,
You would find it just the thing
You would telephone to the grocer man
And tell him what to bring
To the butcher or the baker
Perhaps you would rather call
You could order a whole dinner
And never leave the hall.
If your baby had the measles
And you thought it was quite sick
You could telephone to the doctor
And he would be there twice as quick.
There is one thing I am certain
That would make your home just right
It's an ever ready telephone
To use both day and night.

Mother Newman's third poem was whimsical and fun for all ages. I think about all three when the days are long and the news is blue. They help me get through:

Where could a man buy a cap for his knee
Or a key to the lock of his hair?
Could his eyes be called an academy
Because there are pupils there?
Could the crook of his elbow be sent to jail,
If so what could it do?
How do you sharpen your shoulder blade?
Oh, I don't know, do you?
In the crown of the head, what gems are found?
Can you cross the bridge of your nose?
Can you use, while shingling the roof of your house,
The nails that grow on your toes?

> *Can you sit in the shade of the palm of your hand?*
> *Can you beat on the drum of your ear?*
> *Can the calf of your leg*
> *Eat the corn on your toes?*
> *Then why grow corn on the ear?*
>
> Thanks, Mother Newman, for sharing and making us all smile.

Soon, many people among the 76 million strong baby boom generation will join the ranks of older Americans. *Journalism Across Cultures* notes that the first baby boomers will turn 65 in 2011. "In 1995 there were about 24 million people over the age of 70. By 2030, when the baby boom generation is fully retired, this figure will have nearly doubled to 47.8 million. . . ." *Journalism Across Cultures* notes (119). Here is the bottom line: older people will need younger people.

> In 1965 when Medicare began, 5.5 workers were paying into the system for every beneficiary. By 1995 that ratio had fallen to 3.8 workers per enrollee, and by 2030 it is projected that there will only be 2.2 workers per enrollee. . . . Today, approximately 38 million people are enrolled in Medicare. By 2010, this will grow to 47 million, and by 2030 over 75 million people will be enrolled in Medicare. In 1996, Medicare spending as a percentage of gross domestic product (GDP) was 2.7 percent. By 2010, the Congressional Budget Office projects that this will grow to 4.4 percent, and to 7.4 percent by 2030, under current policies. . . . (119)

For people to benefit from having insurance and Social Security in their retirement, everyone must realize that we all need to work together because we each truly need and must support one another. For that reason, we all can learn from what people who are over 65 have experienced and are enduring. When they talk, we must listen, so our social capital grows.

If learning from older people yields benefits once, more time with them will generate more results. They share with others their reverence for the things that matter. They socialize us just as they were socialized by others, face to face, in three-dimensional color and with voice and body language, with humor and concern. They help teach us and our children the values that they picked up from adults of even earlier generations. Instead of socialization-by-television, sharing, listening and learning among real people should be the basis of socialization of children.

Just because people have grown old doesn't mean they are ready to park themselves out of the mainstream. Even though their bodies may slow, older people mostly view themselves as vital, vibrant contributors in this country.

<u>*From "A century of life has been filled with the spirit of Christmas"*</u>

Far from the Plaza Lights and just beyond rolling hills untouched by time, Christmas in its purest form lives in the heart of Mary Lucille Bundy.

But Mrs. Bundy laughs because she once missed the biggest holiday of the year. That was Dec. 25, 1889, three days before she was born as the oldest child of Sydnor and Laura Lee Dale of Freeman, Mo.

Since then, however, Mrs. Bundy and her family have celebrated her birthday on Christmas Day. This year will be the 100th time she has enjoyed both.

She expects to be surrounded Monday by her family at the home of her oldest daughter, 78-year-old Mildred Branaman of Harrisonville.

Last week, in her one-story, gray house where she lives by herself, Mrs. Bundy talked about Christmas and its meaning. Listening to her was a pleasure.

She sat in her favorite chair mounted on wheels and rolled from her dining room to the living room to talk. A ceiling fan spun overhead as she explained what she had learned from a long stay in the circle of life.

She drew close with a kind of my dearest-friend nearness, where feet without embarrassment touched and she could make her point with the warmest of a reassuring hand. She smiled with each question and seasoned every answer with 100 years of wisdom.

You see, when Mrs. Bundy was growing up, the holiday was centered around the church. That was before automobiles, electric lights, television and commercial hype.

"Christmas was a thrilling time for a child," Mrs. Bundy said. "We didn't have a Christmas tree at home."

"Churches had the Christmas tree that went almost to the ceiling, decorated with popcorn and cranberries. We didn't have a lot of gifts.

"All children were treated very much the same."

She then pulled out one of her many journals, which line the walls of her living and dining rooms. She rested it on her knees and mine and opened the pages to one of her favorite poems, which she had copied by hand.

Because I've seen the flowers,
I know what color is;
What fragrance is; what beauty is;
Because I've seen the springtime's divine awakening,
I know what hope is;
What faith is; what joy is;
Because I've listened to the birds at daybreak,
I know what gladness is;

Because I have seen the seeds reveal their wonders in radiant life,
I know what mystery is;
Because I have looked upon the mountains, the oceans and the trees,
I know what majesty is; what grandeur is; what poise is;
Because I have seen the sun, the moon and the stars and their ponderous courses,
I know what power is.
Contemplation of these revelations mounts faith almost to understanding.

The anonymous verse symbolizes how simple things shaped her understanding of Christmas beginning in her childhood in the late 1800s.

Those were times when during warmer months she and girlfriends would play in fields of bluebells and run giggling back into town after decorating themselves with the bell-shaped flowers.

"I've thought of that several times," Mrs. Bundy said.

It was when she would ride trains to Kansas City to visit relatives. She remembered walking from the edge of the big city through the woods to a house her aunt had built at 42nd and Harrison streets.

Back then, 31st Street and Troost Avenue was the end of the cable car line. Her uncle had an ice cream parlor nearby, and she often marveled at firefighters practicing harnessing horses to the firewagon at the station across the street.

Her memories are as clear as if the events happened yesterday and are reinforced by her notes in books in what she calls her house/library/museum. Her journals contain poems, newspaper clippings, pictures and genealogy charts tracing her family to relatives who fought in the Civil War, the Revolutionary War and on back to the 1600s.

She talked about teaching school from 1908-1910 and giving it up to marry T.C. Bundy in 1910. She moved to his farm halfway between Freeman and Drexel, where she gave birth to T.C. Junior, Mildred, Dorothy and Lois. "Moving to the farm, I thought I was going to the end of the world because one thing you had to do was stay at home," said Mrs. Bundy, who is president of her Cass County Extension Homemakers Club.

"I never did learn to milk a cow," she said of the farm where her husband raised cattle and hogs. "I didn't do any sort of farm work that farm women sometimes do.

"I did raise chickens, and I loved to do gardening. After an adjustment I liked the farm, and it was a great place to raise the children."

She taught them the basics before they began formal schooling. Hers also were Golden-Rule-type lessons she held on to as the world developed.

Mrs. Bundy saw gravel roads with horses and buggies change to paved highways and motor cars. Her first big trip was in 1921 when her family drove east to visit relatives in Virginia.

She also noted the switch from oil lamps to electricity. Drexel got power in 1918, she said, but most farms without generators had to wait until 1947.

In 1945, the Bundys moved from the farm to a house in Drexel, which celebrates its centennial in July. Her husband died in 1955, and she moved again in 1958 to her current home.

Since then she has traveled, written extensively in her journals, regularly attends church, gone to college in nine states at Elderhostels with her youngest daughter, 73-year-old Lois Patterson, and enjoyed life. Another hobby is hand-sewing pillows – 713 of them so far – made from scrap materials, stuffed with used plastic bags and given as gifts to people throughout the region and the world. She said it was her part in the recycling effort.

Mrs. Bundy has quite a family. She is the only survivor among her three brothers and two sisters. Her son died at age 55, but her three daughters, six grandchildren and seven great-grandchildren live in the two-state area.

Mrs. Bundy has taken her share of falls but has never broken a bone, and her rosy complexion and her own teeth are just two signs of her good health.

Despite having osteoarthritis, every day to her is like a wonderful Christmas gift. She said she never expected to live so long.

"I can hardly believe it myself," Mrs. Bundy said. "I don't feel old."

That's what makes her so inspiring.

"I do admire her very much for her attitude on life and for her desire to want to do things," Patterson said.

Carolyn Moody, adviser to the Missouri Extension Homemaking Association, also thinks the world of Mrs. Bundy, who has been an extension member for 55 years. "She handles any problem that she has with cheerfulness and a smile," Moody said.

Mrs. Bundy, who prepares her own meals, credits the homemakers group with her good diet. Her advice is don't eat too many calories, too much fat or too much sugar.

Her view of Christmas is as clean and simple. She described it in six words:

Praise. It comes from the blessings that we receive day by day.

Love. No person lives alone, and because of our relationships with others that makes love an important part of Christmas.

Happiness. Mrs. Bundy smiled. "We are created to be happy," she said.

Faith. It's the unseen, yet profound, justification for life. "We all need to believe in something," she said.

Thanksgiving. It's for life and to be thankful for the things we receive.

Hope. "Hope is the assurance that we have for eternal life," Mrs. Bundy said.

Her feelings are rooted in her deep, faith in God and her belief that Jesus was born on Christmas day.

The First Baptist Church of Drexel, where she has been a member since 1916, had a special service this month that Mrs. Bundy believes captured the true spirit of Christmas.

The Rev. Dana L. Burris, pastor of the church, called it the Hanging of the Greens during which the church was decorated and people talked about the symbols of Christmas. They include:

- Evergreen trees, which stand for God's grace and eternal life.
- The advent candles, representing the gifts of hope, joy, peace and love from the Holy Spirit, with the center candle being Christ.
- Tree lights, which represent stars.
- The star atop the tree, symbolizing the Bethlehem Star, which led the three wise men to Christ.
- The Wreathe, which represents the world and reminds us of the fellowship of believers coming to celebrate and share the knowledge of Christ.

Mrs. Bundy knows.

"Through the years she's really understood what the true meaning of Christmas really is – that Christ was the savior of the world," Burris said. "I think the world probably would be a better place, and Christmas would be more meaningful if we all had Mrs. Bundy's perspective."

Older people add insight and context to their families and everyone whose lives they touch. They serve as our direct link to our heritage as it lives and breathes. They bring us joy, hope and inspiration for what we might become and help us strive to be better people and citizens. And sometimes the old and the young find unexpectedly that they have something in common. For one thing, they relish their freedom.

From "He's back on the road to freedom"

A moped has resuscitated freedom for Harry C. Coleman.

The two-wheeler is a life-support machine for teenagers needing parent-free, economical transportation. But Coleman's no kid.

He's 80 years old. The Kansas City, Mo., resident is simply in a life-cycle that has him sharing the road with youths.

As a kid, Coleman used to ride a Harley motorcycle and afterward always drove barge-sized American cars. But diabetes damaged the World War II veteran's eyes.

The former security guard and Bendix plant supervisor no longer could see distant objects, and a few close calls prompted him to give up driving his Ford LTD three years ago.

"I didn't want to have the responsibility of wheeling a car down the road knowing that my vision is handicapped," Coleman said.

He apparently has a lot of uncooperative company. A study by the Missouri Drivers Bureau showed that the elderly lose their driving privileges more than any other age group, said Diane Gaines, state bureau administrator.

The report found that 16 persons ages 16 to 30 in 1989 surrendered their licenses, had them revoked or canceled. The number rose to 38 for people ages 31 to 50; 37 for ages 51 to 60; 74 for ages 61 to 70; 145 for ages 71 to 80; 194 for ages 81 to 90; and 15 for ages 91 to 100.

"The older folks like to hang on to their driver's licenses," said Chief Examiner Fount Foushee, who heads the driver examination program for the Missouri Highway Patrol troop in Lee's Summit. "They just hate to give that up."

Coleman found out why. He suffered loneliness, boredom and the loss of mobility.

"Those are the three things that make life hell for old people," said Coleman, whose wife, Betty, died in 1973. "You don't know how rough it is to get old and lose mobility and lose the constant association with people.

"You have no freedom. You're just hunkered down in one place."

That changed about a year ago when he bought a 1980 Sears moped. He has put 2,400 miles on it and six months ago purchased a 1980 Sachs moped, which he has driven 200 miles.

Coleman said he rides defensively at a top speed of 30 mph and has never had a near miss. He goes to parks, stores and places where he can meet people.

"It gives me back freedom, independence and a sense that I manage my own affairs and that I'm not just a pawn on a checkerboard but a player," said Coleman, who lives on Social Security.

That didn't surprise John Whitesitt, general manager of Freedom Honda Kawasaki in Grandview. Scooters and mopeds traditionally are popular among teenagers and college kids, but Whitesitt said people over 50 now buy 25 percent of the vehicles.

Most older people strap them to the back of campers and use them in Florida, Arizona and New Mexico. But rising gas prices and the 50- to 100-mpg fuel economy of mopeds and scooters have more older people on fixed incomes considering them for everyday use, Whitesitt said.

Coleman said mopeds helped him adapt and learn just how much older people have in common with youths. For example, both groups crave mobility and must be where people and things are happening.

Also, nobody understands teenagers. Older people suffer the same fate, Coleman said.

Then there's money. "Young people don't have the money to do the things they want to do, and neither do most old people," he said.

Get used to it. Coleman's cycle may soon be our own.

The bridges that older people establish with people from other generations creates that greater sense of community described in Robert D. Putnam's book *Bowling Alone*. The social capital generated is what the rest of society needs. Strength comes from it.

From "Trusting union from days past"

Bill Lippert pushed a picture across the table to me at Charlies Lodge Restaurant & Bar.

He was among the kids on the steps of St. James Church in the St. James Grade School's 1930 graduation photograph. So were Barbara Meitner, Jack Nestor and the spouses of Helen Kirk, Dorothy Shannon, Marjorie Lippert and Dorothy Nestor.

They're among students in the 41-member grade-school class who get together regularly with their spouses to reminisce and enjoy each others' company. The gatherings stem from their unusual 50th reunion in 1980.

It's odd because most people attend their high school reunions. Grade school gatherings seem unthinkable.

But most folks just haven't thought it through like the seven persons at the recent St. James school luncheon. They'd shared the same classrooms for eight years unlike four scattered years of different classes and even different high schools.

They played and worked in the same midtown neighborhood unlike kids who funneled into high schools from miles around. They shared the same history, upbringing, religion and virtues, which have steeled them against adversity and made them almost inseparable.

Keeping up with the 70- and 80-year-olds was tough. They're so close that often they finished each other's sentences.

Meitner explained that some of them had taken trips together to Europe without advanced plans. "We'd just buy a ticket, and then we'd start out," she said.

They drew their courage and taste for adventure from the love of their past and each other's company. Their friendships have grown stronger with time, too.

I adored listening to them.

"We aren't in competition," Meitner said. "What you see is what you get, and we all like each other."

Marjorie Lippert said one of the neatest things they'd done was to revisit the area where the now-closed school was at 3941 Tracy Ave., the Catholic church at 3901 Harrison St., where Jack Nester and Bill Lippert were alter boys, and the neighborhood where they lived.

"I thought that was fascinating," Helen Kirk said. "Would you believe my house was torn down? There's a beautiful park there now."

They spoke of how the good education they'd received and the values the nuns drilled into them enabled them to go to college, enjoy good careers and raise strong families. That was despite graduating from grade school in the heart of the Great Depression and becoming adults in the vortex of World War II.

Each survived the hardships and the battles. They share and cradle memories of this century's simpler times. Horses and buggies roamed Kansas City's streets when they grew up. The avenues were lighted by gas lamps.

The boys worked as soda jerks at drugstores or delivered packages by bicycle. Everyone went to the Troost Avenue movie theaters and rode the trolleys to get around. "Back then your recreation and practically everything was neighborhood-oriented," Marjorie Lippert said.

Manor bread trucks made door-to-door deliveries along with the iceman, the milkman and the occasional "huckster" selling vegetables. "Nobody locked their door," Bill Lippert said.

Often doors were left open so deliveries could be made when no one was at home. "How trustworthy we were," Helen Kirk said.

Trust remains their bond.

Yet that same trust doesn't get extended to all cultures and people in the Real America. If it did, conversations would blossom and social capital would grow.

Vernon Jarrett, a dear friend, columnist and fellow member of the William Monroe Trotter Group of Black Voices in Commentary, often used to ask when referring to bigoted whites, "What are they so afraid of?" I think it is the double consciousness that Dr. W.E.B. Du Bois described more than 100 years ago in his groundbreaking book, *The Souls of Black Folk.*

From "Our fates are linked together"

We have a shared fate on this fragile planet and must work together for a better future.

That was the message in Lani Guinier's Black History Month lecture Saturday to the Association for the Study of African Life &

History: Lorenzo J. Greene Branch.

Guinier, a civil-rights advocate and the first black woman to be a tenured law professor at Harvard University, told about 500 people at the Nelson-Atkins Museum of Art that racism, bigotry, prejudice and discrimination have no place in the world she envisions.

"People need to be challenged to critique and rethink common assumptions," said Guinier, who was asked by President Clinton in 1993 to lead the U.S. Justice Department's civil rights division before her nomination was withdrawn. "We need to be innovative in our ability to problem-solve.

"It's important to value multiple perspectives."

Guinier reminded the audience of one of the first black Harvard doctoral graduates, W.E.B. Du Bois. The noted historian, sociologist, educator and author wrote several books, including *The Souls of Black Folk* in 1903.

Du Bois, who helped found the Niagara Movement and the NAACP, wrote 100 years ago that African-Americans were viewed as the nation's problem people, Guinier said. He also said the color line would be the problem of the 20th century.

It's remarkable how little has changed.

But Guinier said everyone should view African-Americans as Du Bois did - as people "gifted with a second sight," possessing a "double consciousness" that elevates them from being problems to "the stature of seers."

African-Americans see the world through the twin lenses of being Americans and Africans in America, making them "sources of energy and inspiration," Guinier said.

But racism causes blacks to struggle "behind the veil" of bigotry, she said. People must learn that we have a shared fate.

The trauma African-Americans face affects others. Guinier said people should view blacks as canaries in the mine, alerting everyone to dangers ahead.

"The canary becomes enormously important to help us to see what is happening to all of us and then to fix the atmosphere in the mine and not just to fix the canary," Guinier said.

The threats include the suffering of working- and middle-class Americans in the poor U.S. economy. African-Americans feel it more, having twice the jobless rate of whites and less access to wealth, Guinier said.

Government spending on prisons is another problem. It has grown faster than financing for education, making incarceration America's answer to social ills, Guinier said.

Prisons pull money from higher education, causing universities to raise prices for students at a time when companies cry for more college-educated people. Guinier said entrance exams create a "testocracy," which allocates education as a scarce resource.

But such tests don't give people time to think, and often they work against minorities and women.

Lawsuits against affirmative action cite exam scores. The suits "focus on the canary" when they should target the underfunding of education, Guinier said.

Also, high entrance exam scores are a poor measure of who will graduate to be community leaders and better workers, Guinier said. Good test takers often have a sense of entitlement and privilege compared with affirmative action graduates who are compelled to give back to the community.

Guinier urged people to critique how races are pitted against each other, resist that abomination and develop a vision for the way things should be. "We have to link our fate one with the other," she said.

It's the only way we'll overcome and make the nation better now and in the future.

The double consciousness described by Du Bois and Guinier gives people of color the added ability to see life both as Americans and as people from their own unique groups. Minorities possess a mostly undiscovered ability to be problem identifiers and problem-solvers. Talking and being heard lets such special talents surface. Diversity multipliers help create bridges to new understanding and opportunities for being productive, building social capital and promoting positive change that all of us will benefit from. It's the what's in it for me aspect of diversity. And it's why the Real America must be discovered through many conversations across the lines of race, ethnicity, age, gender, sexual orientation, disabilities, income and others that separate us.

CHAPTER 11

Diversity Formula Three—Act for Change

Beyond Prayers

Prayer vigils follow each
human tragedy
With the faithfuls' heads bowed and clasping hands
Hard work must trail after that and forever demand
That the community found inseparably
to work for justice and peace
Each person has a role to play change comes when no one sleeps
Staying unattached, uninvolved, out of harm's way
Waiting for someone else to be a King or hero to save the day
But there's no safety or hiding place to the problems of today
Only need, desperate need, that insists
on everyone's commitment
Without it we'll all slip into a desperate abyss
Dragged down by finger-pointing and resentment.

. . . yesterday, the same man-made forms of law declared it a crime punishable with $1,000 fine and six months' imprisonment to give a cup of water, a crust of bread or a night's shelter to a panting fugitive tracking his way to Canada; and every man or woman in whose veins coursed a drop of human sympathy violated that wicked law, reckless of consequences, and was justified in doing so. As then the slaves who got their freedom had to take it over or under or through the unjust forms of law, precisely so now must women take it to get right to a voice in this government; and I have taken mine, and mean to take it at every opportunity. . . . And I shall earnestly and persistently continue to urge all women to the practical recognition of the old Revolutionary maxim, "Resistance to tyranny is obedience to God."

~Susan B. Anthony
(June 19, 1873)

Chapters 8 and 9 explain the business case for racism. Such oppression has an ugly, profitable history in the Americas, dating back to the 1400s when Christopher Columbus first set foot on these shores. Religion figured into the conquest, subjugation and racism inflicted on the indigenous peoples. So did greed. Gold was discovered in the Americas; what followed was the enslavement of the Indians and later the Africans to extract the riches in order to fatten the treasuries of European nations. But there was also food. James W. Loewen writes in *Lies My Teacher Told Me*:

> The Americas affected more than the mind. African and Eurasian stomachs were also affected. Almost half of all major crops now grown throughout the world originally came from the Americas. According to Alfred Crosby, adding corn to African diets caused the population to grow, which helped fuel the African slave trade to the Americas. Adding potatoes to European diets caused the population to explode in the 16th and 17th centuries, which in turn helped fuel the European emigration to the Americas and Australia. Crops from America also played a key role in the ascendancy of Britain, Germany, and finally Russia; the rise of these northern nations shifted the power base of Europe away from the Mediterranean. (68)

In addition, "more than two hundred drugs derive from plants whose pharmacological uses were discovered by American Indians" (68). But Loewen writes that such information often is left out of the history books that students use in school. When that happens it diminishes the contributions of those whom imperialism brutalized and it cleanses the Europeans of the global crimes of murder, kidnapping, enslavement and theft. Loewen states that:

> the west-to-east flow of ideas and wealth goes unnoticed. Eurocentrism blinds textbook authors to contributions to Europe, whether from Arab astronomers, African navigators, or American Indian social structure. By accepting this limited viewpoint, our history textbooks never invite us to think about what happened to reduce mainland Indian societies, whose wealth and cities awed the Spanish, to the impoverished peasantry they are today. They also rob us of the chance to appreciate how important America has been in the formation of the modern world.
>
> This theft impoverishes us, keeps us ignorant of what has caused the world to develop as it has. (69)

That ignorance causes a biased view of the New World as "savage," or at the very least lacking "civilization," that is wholly unjustified. Howard Zinn writes in his book, *A People's History of the United States: 1492-Present,* that

> Columbus and his successors were not coming into an empty wilderness, but into a world which in some places was as densely populated as

> Europe itself, where the culture was complex, where human relations were more egalitarian than in Europe, and where the relations among men, women, children, and nature were more beautifully worked out than perhaps any place in the world. (21)

In spite of these positive qualities, Native Americans had to be painted as savage, heathens and lazy with "inborn group traits that rendered them naturally incapable of civilization," writes Ronald Takaki in *A Different Mirror*. Colonists had to dehumanize Indians and associate them with the devil. He writes that "[t]his social construction of race occurred within the economic context of competition over land." (38-39) The need intensified with the cultivation of tobacco as a new cash crop in the Americas. (35)

This is the time-honored system of the conquerors reshaping the image of those who possess resources so that those usurpers will feel justified in taking what they believe should rightfully be theirs. Such deliberate re-crafting of history perpetuates the massively profitable business of racism, discrimination, prejudice and bigotry through today.

Often people of conscience mistakenly chalk up such bad behavior to ignorance and stupidity. Instead what must be done is to recognize the intelligent design of racism, how it perpetuates itself like a virus, how it benefits the majority while disabling minorities and how easily people pick it up through disinformation and continue to spread the damaging social infection. Once racism is appreciated for its skill and power to mutate and survive, it can be isolated, attacked with antibodies of truth and, in time, eradicated.

That change, however, will require a *better business practice* through diversity. People are less likely to let go of a system they are fully invested in unless they can be convinced that something else will benefit them more. Discovering the Real America has to start with explorers of America's diversity offering a bolder way of thinking. To them multiculturalism must embody the wealth of the nation in people and ideas. These folks will have to think expansively and sell the riches of inclusiveness to others. Diversity explorers will have to be intrepid risk takers, pushing past the resistance of established norms. They will have to be adventurous thinkers, getting more people to explore the undiscovered country that is the United States of America.

Alfonso Montuori and Isabella Conti write of a new paradigm in their book, *From Power to Partnership: Creating the Future of Love, Work, and Community*. The model of domination, motivated by fear, is falling apart. A partnership model has to emerge in its place. "Creativity must become an ongoing process of participation and co-creation with the world, rather than something which occasionally strikes us on the head and spends the rest of its time hiding behind some mental clouds," Conti and Montuori note (23). "For the first time, we may collectively be coming up with quite a different vision of what it means to be human," they write (11).

(Hope/Prayer + Work) x Diversity = Change

But having a vision is only the first step. Often people turn to hope and prayer when they face seemingly insurmountable odds. Racism, prejudice, bigotry and discrimination in America pose that kind of challenge. Although hoping for conditions to improve and praying for it is good, such coping mechanisms often fall short. Prayer and hope alone lead to inaction. Such faith must be coupled with hard and sometimes fearful work against a firmly entrenched status quo. For diversity to work, the following formula must be applied: ***(Hope/Prayer + Work) x Diversity = Change.*** Prayer and Hope must be coupled with the hard, gritty, nasty Work of venturing into the wilderness to find the hidden truth. What people will discover are the contributions made, the horrors endured and the triumphs celebrated by the often-discredited people who populate the Real America. As in Formulas I and II, the diversity multiplier applies. It is the ally that everyone must enlist to serve as a positive and high multiplier so that efforts to push past the obstacles that historically have enforced separation and stagnation will succeed.

A good illustration of Formula III is what became known as the Precious Doe homicide. Precious Doe was the little girl whose decapitated body was found on April 28, 2001, in an overgrown area on the East Side of Kansas City, Mo. The community held numerous prayer vigils to bring attention to the case. People hoped that the little girl's identity would be discovered and that her killers would be brought to justice. Police worked hard on the case, doing composite drawings and building sculptures in what they thought was her likeness. People in the community brought her case to the attention of national television hoping someone would step forward to identify the girl so that authorities could find her killers. But nothing happened. It wasn't until the spring of 2005 that community activist, Alonzo Washington, got *The Call* (a black weekly newspaper) to run an ad about Precious Doe around the fourth anniversary of her death. He convinced General Mills to pay for the ad. And then *The Call* was distributed in the Kansas City metro area, but it also went to Oklahoma, where a family there saw it. A man telephoned Washington with a tip. Washington then contacted the news media and the Kansas City Police Department. The Oklahoma man had been trying for years to interest the police in his tip but was ignored. Washington, as the diversity multiplier, made things happen. He brought together the man with the tip, the police, the press and the work, the prayers and hopes of the community. They combined to reveal that Precious Doe actually was 3-year-old Erica Green. Charges were filed against the girl's mother and the mother's husband. Without Washington as the diversity multiplier, none of the breakthroughs in the case would have been possible. Each individual, just as in the previous diversity formulas, must function as a diversity multiplier for others and seek diversity multipliers for him- or herself so progress can occur.

This third formula combined with the one on talent and productivity in Chapter 9 and the one on talking generating social capital in Chapter 10 can indeed help reshape America and the world. They can encourage people to abandon the old business-as-usual paradigm of the past and venture into discovering the Real America because of the wealth that lies ahead. The truth, a great beauty, real idealism, new ideas, better trust and a greater sense of community encompassing everyone rest in each new phase of discovering the Real America. But as in any exploration, the most adventurous among us will have to lead and overcome the population's urges to maintain things just as they are.

The following columns will highlight Formula III in action featuring the efforts of different groups that as diversity multipliers are combating prejudice to push for change.

From "A hard shell to crack"

> About 150 people stood in the cold Friday beneath murals of the Rev. Martin Luther King Jr., where they expressed their love and commitment for diversity.
>
> The gathering of people of many colors and faiths at Linwood Boulevard and Troost Avenue, Kansas City, Mo., was in response to nearly 20 black churches and two businesses receiving racist hate mail during Black History Month.
>
> Speeches were made, signatures were collected, 10,000 letters of love were promised and follow-up sessions were planned.
>
> The rally followed fund-raisers for diversity groups and a full-page ad in *The Kansas City Star*, which carried the names of about 1,500 people and groups denouncing the hate mail.
>
> The Rev. Ralph J. Crabbe, pastor of St. Paul AME Church in Independence and president of the Concerned Clergy Coalition Inc., received some of the hate mail postmarked Feb. 12, 2001. He said rallies help raise public awareness, but he has opposed efforts by many to hold a prayer vigil at his church in response.
>
> "One of the things I've been resistant to is having another 'Kum Ba Yah' party," Crabbe said. He's also surprised that people were shocked that black churches were hate-mail targets.

"Every church I've pastored in this city I've received some form of hate mail," he said. "This isn't the first piece of hate mail I've received as a pastor, and it probably won't be the last."

In 1994, a swastika was painted on his south Kansas City church. In the 1990s, several African-American churches in other states were burned.

"It's emotional terrorism," Crabbe said of the hate mail. But he also said it was "senseless and empty."

"This type of tactic may have worked 100 years ago, but it's not working today," he said. "Unfortunately it has confirmed for some African-Americans the mind-set in the majority community."

The ad in *The Star*, the rally and the letter-writing campaign should offset those feelings. "I think love will always conquer hate, but love's got to speak up to do it," David Nelson with the Human Agenda told me at the rally.

"Today is the beginning of an expression of togetherness," former Mayor Emanuel Cleaver told the crowd.

"I am very confident that a high percentage of the people in the metro area are like the people standing here today," former Mayor Richard L. Berkley told the gathering.

But more than rallies and prayer vigils, Crabbe wants the community to get serious about ending racism.

"We need to involve citizens in talking of inclusiveness and how to function as a society and instill zero tolerance," he said. "I want to see something that's sustained."

Joel Zeddies, then-chairman of Clergy and Church Against Race Violence, said the hate mail was a racial threat just as vicious as the many area cross burnings his group had protested. Such acts should offend everyone.

That reminded me of Martin Luther King III's speech at Penn Valley Community College. King, then-president of the Southern Christian Leadership Conference, said if his father were alive he'd be proud of African-Americans' accomplishments. But the Civil Rights Movement leader also would be disappointed that racism stubbornly persists.

"We're racially profiled in every aspect of our life - in malls, in airports, in communities with redlining in lending and at work," King said.

But such acts shouldn't be tolerated.

"If anyone does anything that's visible to stir up hate then some reaction has to occur that's bigger and bolder," said Ed Chasteen, founder of Hatebusters. "We're playing for our community's life and character. We're going to have the last word."

The hate mail sent to black churches indicates that a lot of work remains before the last words are spoken and the community can genuinely be healed.

> "It points us to the fact that we have not done comprehensive sustained community building," Crabbe said. We still suffer hate borne of fear. We're not profiting from our diversity and embracing our shared humanity.
>
> "We still have that work to do as citizens," Crabbe said. "I'm not taking any of it personally. But the societal manifestation shows positive activity needs to take place."
>
> The positive actions mark a new start at "cracking the hard shell of racism," Zeddies said.
>
> Crabbe said he'd like to see more white people help build the bridge racism keeps torching.

Too often the construction of the bridge is seen as minorities' problem and responsibility, which keeps change years behind and embarrassingly underfunded:

> Voice Mail: March 14, 2001
>
> What I noticed about your article today was you started out trying to be even and fair handed. But it ended up like so many black articles it blames white people and you want the white people to bridge the gap while the blacks sit there and wait. We sure get sick of that.

It is evident that explorers of the Real America have to constantly be vigilant, bold and tireless as diversity multipliers.

From "Hope springs eternal"

> Joel Zeddies sent me e-mails and faxes showing how three communities keep wrestling with race.
>
> Zeddies was coordinator of Clergy and Church Against Race Violence, based in Kansas City, Kan. He wrote that the group helped organize a rally in Springfield, Mo., in the summer of 2001.
>
> The rally followed the stabbing June 17 of Maurice Wilson at a restaurant by assailants whom witnesses described as skinheads.
>
> Wilson, who's black, was with his girlfriend, who's white. Springfield was ranked among the top 10 whitest cities in the country with populations of 100,000 or more.
>
> No state charges were filed. Jeff Lanza, spokesman and special agent with the FBI, said the agency opened a federal civil-rights investigation in the case.
>
> Another flare-up was in Noel, Mo. Lanza said the FBI was reviewing a July incident at a food-processing plant in which "KKK" and racially intimidating statements targeting Hispanic workers were written on a wall.
>
> Those racial choke holds contrast with the "Messages of Hope" display I saw at Pine Ridge Presbyterian Church in the Northland area

of Kansas City, Mo. They're some of the thousands of cards and letters people sent to black churches and businesses after these establishments received hate mail attributed to the Ku Klux Klan.

Pine Ridge parishioners contributed 170 letters. "It's inspiring to me and inspiring to all of us that our voices were added to others throughout the community," said the Rev. James Gordon, church pastor who's with the antiracial violence group.

Some of the responses were placed on Time Warner Cable's Road Runner home page. Carol Rothwell, then-vice president of public affairs with Time Warner Cable, said the "Kansas City Coming Together" site has attracted 36,000 unduplicated visitors. It features two fists - one tattooed with the word "love"; the other marked "hate."

The hate site shows some of the racist letters the African-American churches received. The love site gives responses.

This is from Josh: "I'm sorry that people are mean to you. I'm 7 years old, and I know better than that. I'll pray for you. Keep on preaching."

Cheryl wrote: "I know as a child of God and a citizen of the United States that none of us is safe unless all of us are safe. If you are hurt, I am hurt. I may not be able to prevent the voices of hate from speaking, but I certainly can become a voice of love whenever possible and hold you and your situation before God in prayer. Minority group status is something I am familiar with, as I have used a wheelchair for 50 years because of childhood polio, yet I have never experienced this kind of hatred."

This letter came from a rabbi: "While we constantly hear about the growing religiosity of America and deeply held beliefs in God, we also experience acts which deny these fundamental truths. The most basic of them all is what is written in Genesis 1 - that all people have been created in the image of God. The senders of hate mail of any kind obviously do not know this fact. While they may never learn it or believe it, we will continue to stress it and counter those who hate with words of love and support."

George wrote, "May the scoundrels fade! Keep the faith!"

Rothwell said the feature was unusual because normally the content is lighthearted. But the response has been positive. "It's a worthwhile use of the Web site," she said.

The feature will remain accessible through its archives.

Zeddies and Gordon said the letters would renew people's commitment against race violence.

"It says I was really part of something big," Zeddies said. "It's to get them back in touch with that deep concern they had."

People who wrote cards and letters will receive suggestions in the fall of how they and their congregations can continue to work against racism.

"The bottom line is people with that kind of deep concern must continue in some way to involve themselves in the fight against racism and racial violence," Zeddies said.

Robert Putnam notes in *Bowling Alone* that churches generate high amounts of social capital. The Civil Rights Movement was anchored in the churches. Is it any wonder that they play a key role in the discovery of the Real America and Formula III?

From "All are diminished when one person is demeaned"

Joel Zeddies, who's white, has always impressed me with his ability to empathize with minorities.

On Feb. 1, 2002, Zeddies stepped down as coordinator of Clergy and Church Against Race Violence to finish an autobiography and devote more time to his safety education business. The Rev. Greg Suttington, executive board chairman of the group, will succeed Zeddies as spokesman. Suttington, at a recent gathering condemning race violence, said, "We are all one people trying to live on one world in peace and harmony."

If it were only that easy.

During the Clergy and Church Against Race Violence rally at Donnelly College, Suttington and more than a dozen clergy, community leaders and elected officials decried another public display of hatred in Kansas City, Kan.

Maurice and Marisa Gray in January found backward swastikas and a racist epithet spray-painted on a shed behind their home. In December 2001, David Coleman Jr., who lives near the Grays, discovered a backward swastika spray-painted on his car.

Police investigated the cases, but no arrests had been made.

Whether drawn accurately or not, the swastikas sent a clear message. These are racist symbols of hate.

During the Donnelly College rally, Maurice Gray asked the more than 120 adults and students present: How do black parents explain such slurs to their children? Are such epithets merely pranks or are they threats? Gray said such public displays of racial hatred made him relive long suppressed painful feelings.

Coleman expressed similar sentiments. He said that the racial epithets made time and civil-rights progress seem to retreat nearly 70 years, when segregation was the law of the land and many whites terrorized minorities without fear of prosecution.

Instances of such bigotry make African-Americans feel unwelcome in their own country, Zeddies said.

Despite hateful sentiments, what Coleman said at the rally rings true. "There are more good people in the world than bad," he said.

> The "good people" are those like Zeddies and others in Clergy and Church Against Race Violence.
>
> Other rally speakers offered these insights: Whenever one human being is demeaned, we all are diminished, the Rev. Tom Tank said.
>
> The Rev. D. Thomas Ford Jr. urged the perpetrators of the crimes to surrender their hatred and "come into the community of peace, love and harmony."
>
> The Rev. Lynn Lamberty said, "We all have a challenge to live better lives every day - lives in which everyone is affirmed."

The columns below will showcase some individuals and actions as positive diversity multipliers making a difference in a variety of ways. Such efforts have helped often oppressed, maligned or conveniently forgotten segments of our society.

Investing in the community

The Million Man March was probably the single best thing that could have happened to African-Americans toward the end of the 20th century. It occurred in 1995, 27 years after the assassination of the Rev. Martin Luther King, Jr. Black men walked together in peace promoting responsibility and reconciliation. It was a hopeful moment in our time amid so much that gives us pause. Men marched in Washington, D.C., but they also marched in smaller processions in places like Kansas City, and they even marched in their own fashion in prisons across America.

Yet the forces at work to undo progress remain busy. Jim Myers notes in his book, *Afraid of the Dark: What Whites and Blacks Need to Know About Each Other,* that even President Clinton, often praised by blacks, left town for Texas to give a speech about race when the black men assembled for the march:

> But the president wasn't the only white person who skipped town. The Million Man March was seen by many, whites in particular, as part of the tearing apart of America that the president mentioned. Elsewhere in downtown D.C., the streets on October 16 [1995] were curiously—*strangely*—deserted. Estimates were that at least 40% of the federal workers in D.C. stayed home, but only 9% were black men who might have gone to the march. Most of the absentees were white. *The Washington Post* reported that commuter traffic from D.C. suburbs was down 70%—70%! Suffice it to say that many whites in the D.C. area were uneasy about the Million Man March, some believing it would unleash violence and destruction in the city, because many whites still believe that is what large gatherings of black people are likely to do. (19-20)

That fear was reflected in the more extensive way the Million Man March was covered versus the way the media covered the later marches.

Because violence was expected during the first march, it got over-the-top attention. The other events were seen as passive, benign, non-threatening and received back-story treatment.

Nevertheless, the inspiration that the marches brought was moving.

From "From hope to growth and beyond"

> ST. PETERSBURG, Fla. - Short-term success puts long-term gains at risk.
>
> That was one thought about the Million Man March which was discussed at the Monroe Trotter Group conference of black columnists. Many of us gathered at the Poynter Institute for Media Studies and watched some of the historic event on television and then quizzed colleagues who arrived a day late because they attended the massive gathering in Washington.
>
> The march made some of the toughest, most cynical people I've ever met cry with tears of awe, pride and happiness. They eagerly talked of the crowd's politeness, men hugging each other, sharing addresses and praising the heavens that stereotypes about them were dissolving in the face of such great truth.
>
> Never before had so many African-American men gathered to share peace, promises of reconciliation and a resolve to unite to improve themselves, their families and communities. The Trotter Group pondered and pontificated afterward with no clear answers on whether the short-term success of the march would result in long-term gains.
>
> It wasn't until I returned to Kansas City that the big picture of the Million Man March came into focus. I spoke of it in a speech at the 132nd Anniversary Banquet of the Second Baptist Church, where the theme was "Honoring the Past, Faithful in the Present, Investing in the Future."
>
> I told the audience that the march was the cornerstone of a new Black Renaissance building in America, partly because never before have so many African-Americans been so educated.
>
> Census data show that only 214,049 black people had attended college by 1940. The number had grown to 381,080 by 1950, 649,448 in 1960, 1.06 million in 1970, 2.89 million by 1980 and 5.89 million by 1990.
>
> That growth made me see why *The Atlantic Monthly* in a cover story had pegged this nation's "new intellectuals" as an impressive group of black writers and thinkers. In overcoming racism and oppression they had emerged from the political upheaval of the 1950s and 1960s as America's new public brain trust today.
>
> They include Toni Morrison, Shelby Steele, Cornel West, Ellis Cose, Thomas Sowell and June Jordan. These people and many others,

the magazine said, have redirected attention from "race-based identity politics to the importance of American citizenship for race relations."

"The significance of this approach is simply that it considers race to be a manifestation of a larger American project; it conceives of the problems of African-Americans as inseparable from the problems of America," the article says. Race and citizenship are "twin points on their moral compass," and the new intellectual elite dissect the ills of this great nation from both perspectives.

The new Black Renaissance emerging from the Million Man March only seems natural from such intellectual growth. Add to that the thought that buses and cars that carried the men to and from Washington were more than just transportation.

To me, they were think tanks or minicolleges, where committed, thoughtful people shared a wealth of ideas to take home and implement from seeds of hope sown at the march. The breakthroughs they could create in science, literature, economics, art, business, medicine, citizenship, mechanics and music would add to the decades of gains that grew from the Harlem Renaissance of the 1920s.

The difference is that this new fruit will spring from Everywhere, U.S.A.

Women put together their own marches. But what was disturbing was they did not get the media coverage that the Million Man March got. The light interest in the women's march stemmed largely from no or little concern in the media with issues that matter to women. The poor media coverage may have resulted in the light turnout, too.

From "Marching in pursuit of happiness"

Planning for the Million Woman March kept Sahj Kaya's phone ringing.

She answered: "Hello, sister. How are you? I'm blessed, sister, I really am."

Kaya, Missouri coordinator of the march, rarely sat. "I don't like to sit unless I have to, because I was in a wheelchair for 10 years," she said.

Kaya also was national chairwoman of the physically challenged for the march. She was among the black women who boarded buses for the journey to the Oct. 25, 1997, Million Woman March in Philadelphia.

To me, Kaya embodied the unabridged will of black women in the march for reflection, repentance, redemption and resurrection. Kaya was 6 years old when her mother died of Hodgkin's disease. Two years later, doctors said Kaya had muscular dystrophy and only six months to live.

Kaya said she was on her deathbed when she dreamed her mother came for her. But Kaya responded: "Mom, I can't go with you now. There is something I have to do."

Kaya recovered and returned to school. Surgery enabled her to walk with braces. She got married and graduated from college in 1981. But an auto accident killed her husband, Reginald Gibson, in 1982 and nearly claimed her life, too.

Doctors said she wouldn't live or certainly wouldn't walk. But Kaya recovered. She is able to walk better than before.

The "something" she had to do is help get black women to the march. "This march is to bring out those people who are ready to change our environment," she said.

"We realize in 1995 that the brothers atoned," Asia Coney, march co-chairwoman, said of the Million Man March on Oct. 16, 1995, in Washington. "As sisters there is a lot we need to do to pull ourselves together."

Unlike the Million Man March, no one person claimed credit for the Million Woman March. A grass-roots network of women decided to do it.

In 1 1/2 years of planning, women developed a 12-plank, 21st century platform. It included strengthening bonds with young people, aiding women leaving prison, creating educational opportunities, combating homelessness and supporting black businesswomen, politicians and professionals.

The irony of the location fascinated me. Philadelphia is one of the birthplaces of liberty, yet black people were excluded from the promise in the Declaration of Independence and the Constitution. Change is past due.

The Million Woman March, like the Million Man March, was expected to reveal the compassion, strength and commitment that grow from so many black women coming together. That was long overdue, too.

A National Center for Health Statistics study found black women to be America's unhappiest people. White, middle-aged, suburban males were the happiest.

Black women were most likely to respond yes when asked whether they were depressed, restless, bored, upset, lonely or anxious in the previous two weeks. It's not surprising when education, race, gender, age and place of residence are factors in one's psychological well-being.

Possessing fewer opportunities, black women suffer more even though they have nurtured America for generations. That's another odd irony.

Yet like Kaya, African-American women have an unstoppable spirit. They marched, and others like me cheered their progress. Undoubtedly a new happiness for them one day will emerge.

From "The next positive step comes today"

An incident at Bea's Liquor and Grocery gave me hope for the new future that the Million Woman March was to create.

Delia C. Young was standing in line one night at the crowded store at 4455 Prospect Ave., Kansas City, Mo., to buy a copy of *The Call*, a weekly black newspaper, cat food and pop when a man who had been drinking entered. He wanted more liquor and started cursing when he saw the line.

Young said she normally would have kept quiet so the man wouldn't turn his anger on her. But not this time. Not after the Million Man March.

"I said, 'I thought the brothers weren't supposed to be doing that anymore,'" Young said, recalling the nationally televised event. "'I thought after the Million Man March that was over.'"

Other customers in the store chimed in, reminding the man of the African-American men's march for atonement, responsibility and reconciliation. The unruly man apologized and quieted down.

"It was such a profound moment," Young said.

Her experience was among the many incidents of change that continue to ripple from the Oct. 16, 1995, Million Man March in Washington, D.C. Those ongoing waves were amplified when African-American women throughout the country gathered in Philadelphia for the Million Woman March.

Kansas City women at planning meetings for the march have quoted civil rights leader Malcolm X. He said that if a force for good improves the life of a man, then mostly one person benefits. But if the same power is focused on a woman, then it uplifts a family because women are the primary caregivers for children.

Black women and children in some fashion experienced the same awakening and boosted self-image and purpose as black men did.

Some took that back to their communities, which were in some ways transformed, said Ron McMillan, a Kansas City community activist who went to the Million Man March.

He credited the march with the continuing drop in crime. The Justice Department reported that the rate of violent teen crime dropped 9.2 percent from 1995 to 1996 on top of a 2.9 percent decline the previous year.

The number of children and teen-agers killed with guns also dropped for the first time in more than 10 years, falling 9.4 percent from 1994 to 1995. The number of young black males killed by guns dropped 20 percent from 1994 to 1995, National Center for Health Statistics data showed.

> In addition, FBI statistics showed that violent crime in general fell 6 percent in 1996 from 1995 and property crimes were down 2 percent. Murder dropped 9 percent; rape, 2 percent; robbery, 7 percent; and aggravated assault, 6 percent.
>
> Crime in Kansas City has followed those downward trends. Serious crime dropped the most in the largest cities, with a slight rise in the suburbs and an increase of 1.8 percent in rural areas. Authorities credit community policing, stiffer sentences, get-tough juvenile justice laws and more prisons.
>
> But McMillan credited the gang summits in Kansas City, the truces that followed and the march. It gave African-Americans an unparalleled positive sense of what they could accomplish through unity.

Overlooked in all of these marches is the often-discounted diversity in people and their concerns. African-American men marched to bring themselves together around a common cause that few besides them can recognize or address. Black women marched for solidarity, which is ignored when white women's concerns overshadow all others. And black youths marched to address concerns that are specific to them and that lie outside the mainstream focus for young people. The negative feedback, however, strongly states mainstream racist viewpoints.

> E-mail: Sept. 4, 1998
>
> Subject: Million Jig March
>
> I urge all white racialists in the New York/New Jersey area to head over to good ole New York City for the Sept. 5th "Million Nigger Youth March." Could you ask for a better time to recruit whites? It will be a great time to actually get our point across to a lot of people who refused to see it before, after all, the evidence will be right in front of them.... Indisputable concrete evidence of our racial superiority.

Even though the media gave the build-up to the march and the actual event modest coverage, the demonstration was closely monitored by hate groups on the Internet. What follows is a single example of hundreds of e-mails forwarded to me through the hate groups.

> E-mail: Sept. 28, 1998
>
> Subject: Million Nigger March
>
> (888) MYM-2084....This is the number to call for general information on the Million Nigger March. I couldn't find the time it was starting at any sites I looked at, but for whoever wanted to know about the time.... I hope this number helps. I unfortunately live in New York (thankfully not in New York City). So if I find out any more information, I will keep you posted.
>
> Racial Regards,

In spite of the solidarity marches, the historical trends hold: unity and cohesiveness have remained elusive qualities in minority communities. Deliberate division has always been successful in destroying the social capital that is supposed to knit people together in any community. African Americans have been victims of that social capital destruction since the first slave ship landed in Virginia in 1619. The forced generational divisiveness eats away at the black community like a computer virus that constantly mutates and adapts to re-infect people and families. It is therefore necessary for folks to constantly work to eradicate the contagion using Diversity Formula III ***(Hope/Prayer + Work) x Diversity = Change.***

From "Economic freedom could end income inequity"

George Fraser spoke intimately and frankly in offering sage advice for 21st century advancement to a small group of African-Americans.

Fraser, author of *Success Runs in Our Race*, said at the Red Vine Restaurant that black people struggled nearly 250 years in America to be free of slavery.

From 1619 to 1865, Africans in America united around freedom, said Fraser of Cleveland, who travels nationwide giving more than 100 motivational talks a year.

From 1865 to 1964, black people shared a goal of getting long-withheld constitutional rights and civil liberties.

"It gave us a sense of purpose," Fraser said. He said the 21st century struggle for African-Americans must be closing the income and wealth gaps that separate black and white America.

"The only color that matters is green," Fraser said. "This is evolutionary, not revolutionary."

But achieving that goal means that black people will have to increase their economic literacy and leverage to create wealth, jobs and a new sense of freedom - one based on financial independence.

With financial freedom, people can choose where to live, where to send their children to school, how to invest and what to do with their time.

"Wealth is the ultimate and highest form of freedom," Fraser said. "That's driven by money."

Fraser urged black people in the Kansas City area to leverage their resources - to connect the dots. He said African-Americans have $670 billion in buying power, $5 trillion in intellectual capital, $500 billion in formal education and an untold wealth in managerial experience.

"We have a lot of Ph.D.s," Fraser said. "We now need some PhDoers."

He encouraged African-Americans to promote "best practices"

examples among businesses so others could learn from those highlighted successes. Fraser said black people must support black businesses if they want others to patronize them, too.

Kansas City Harmony is doing that, promoting diversity initiatives that work.

"It's not about me; it's about we," Fraser said, using buzz phrases to underscore his message. "It takes team work to make the dream work.

"The essence of networking is serving. We've got to get together to get ahead."

Fraser said other successful groups of people make such things their focus. They also celebrate successful business people the way others make heroes of athletes and entertainers.

Fraser said he is working on a new book titled *Connecting the Dots: A Black Agenda for the 21st Century*. He shared 10 things that the black community nationwide must do to close the income gap with white America. They included African-Americans changing their conversation topics.

Discussions must be focused on business, wealth and job creation instead of on reality TV and sports.

Support those who back black businesses. Fraser cited a civil rights era sign used by blacks that said "Don't buy where you can't work."

He said successful business people must be held up as heroes in the black community. That would help build an entrepreneurial culture and mind-set.

Fraser encouraged blacks to become politically active. It's more than just registering and voting. He said African-Americans should make financial donations to candidates who support their agenda.

African-Americans must create alliances and collaborate with others to add value to their efforts. He encouraged blacks to increase their personal investment in education and training.

Fraser said African-Americans must spend more than the current 1 percent of their income on personal development and training. Blacks also must get involved in the education of their children.

More than 85 percent of America's teachers "don't look like our children," he said. Too many have little or no expectation for black children's success. African-American adults must frequent the schools and remain involved in the education of children to ensure that kids get a good education.

Fraser encouraged African-Americans to think small and long-term. Too often people fall short when they think beyond their reach and resources.

None of what Fraser shared is new. However, it needs to be repeated constantly. African-Americans' success depends on the steady drumbeat of such wisdom.

Raising awareness

Illuminating the problems many face as a result of discrimination is part of the gritty work that Diversity Formula III requires of everyone. It's important to do whatever it takes to get the message across that people have nothing to fear from the racial, ethnic, cultural, religious, sexual orientation and other differences of individuals in America. Greatness comes from accepting those who are different and being enhanced by the variety. All individuals should adopt a bumblebee approach to appreciating others—sampling the nectar of ideas, innovations, problem-identifying and problem-solving capabilities that all of the many beautiful human "flowers" among us produce. Losses in potential greatness result when people feel excluded from being welcomed or from fitting in. Conversely, a forced fit into a group causes people to experience a loss of individuality and results in others who aren't included feeling even more like misfits. One way to help people understand diversity is to put them in the shoes of others who feel the bite of discrimination.

From "Color this board game frustrating"

> Fun doesn't describe the new board game, "Life As A Black Man." Tense and frustrating does.
>
> Its creator, Chuck Sawyer, did a good job of incorporating into the game real race-related obstacles that African-Americans often face.
>
> One can buy "Life as a Black Man" for $36.95 from Underground Games Inc. When I bought it, I found few people eager to play it except for some people at Kansas City Harmony. It's Harmony's mission to help people value diversity.
>
> My fellow players were Diane Hershberger, then-executive director of Harmony; Darryck Dean, then-associate director; and Jessica Dumas, then a community builder. Hershberger and Dumas are white; Dean and I are black.
>
> The realism in Sawyer's game includes racial profiling. It's a relevant topic. A recent report from the Missouri attorney general's office revealed that black motorists are disproportionately more likely to be stopped by police than whites and are more likely to be searched.
>
> African-Americans also contend with housing problems, another issue in the game.
>
> There are also disparities in health care based on race and income.
>
> The game "Life As A Black Man" underscored those disturbing trends and more.

> As we played, we began at different starting points: Dumas was an athlete in the entertainment industry. Hershberger was an intellectual at a black university. I was an intellectual in the military, and Dean was an intellectual in the ghetto. Each of us was to play as an 18-year-old black man.
>
> The winner, through rolls of the dice, is the first person to land at the top of the board in "Freedom." As players land on different spaces on the board, they choose cards from among 12 piles. We learned that those decks often were stacked against us.
>
> The paths Dumas and I took led to trouble with the law. Hershberger encountered fewer problems as an intellectual in college.
>
> Dean became frustrated as an intellectual in the ghetto. He missed turns and landed on spaces that let him pull career cards. But he couldn't keep the jobs because he hadn't gone to college.
>
> Crime cards were optional. Dean pulled them despite warnings from Dumas and me. He said he had nothing to lose.
>
> Hershberger noticed the tension the game caused.
>
> "It didn't feel good to play the game," Dumas said. "I think it's almost too real."
>
> We also played differently. Dean and I took more risks.
>
> As black men, we've lived this game. Dumas was cautious, she said, because some of these challenges were new to her.
>
> "I had more to lose," she said. "I was playing it a lot more safe."
>
> Hershberger concentrated, advancing from the black university into corporate America, gaining money, a car and a spouse with a career.
>
> Hershberger made it to "Freedom," winning the game.
>
> "You talk about who won, who got there first," Dumas said. "But what do you have when you win?"
>
> Hershberger said: "Freedom is not defined. You get there, but you lose different things."
>
> I donated the game to Harmony, so the staff can use it to raise people's awareness. Maybe playing "Life As A Black Man" will help end people's refusal to accept that real obstacles exist for African-Americans. Life isn't a game.
>
> Perhaps the experience of playing the game will encourage more people to work with Harmony and change things from what they have always been.

Resistance, however, remains ever-present. Many people in power stubbornly cling to what they were taught in their own life's game in which they benefit from white privilege. Not knowing about others' troubles is to their advantage.

Voice Mail: June 12, 2002

Lewis, Lewis, Lewis. Now racism is a game, and we're going to play a game with this stuff? Man, you need a vacation. By the way the other day we published stories about 10 who came back and committed crimes when they got out of jail. Eight of them were black. Do something about that.

Voice Mail: June 12, 2002

First of all I find it appalling and almost racist that they have created a game Life as a Black Man. Now surely to God if somebody had created a game called just the opposite, Life as a White Man, you people would be raising holy hell and you know it. So there's a double standard there, and I am really sick and tired of it. Also, there you go with your statistics again on racial profiling. But yet, you don't mention the statistics and the numbers when it comes to the crime rate around this area and why so many of those blacks get pulled over in the first place. Again, go back and check on the homicide rate for the last several decades and find out who's been committing most the heinous crimes around here, Mr. Diuguid. Also you mentioned housing is a situation that black Americans face. Well is it because they have higher defaults on their home loans with lending institutions than any other race. Maybe that's part of it. Then you talk about health care. Well sir, I've never heard you mention anything about the explosion of the AIDS epidemic in the black community. Now there's something that people can do something about. They can either stop their homosexual acts or stop shooting IV drugs into their arms that's illegal with a dirty needle. These are things that can be prevented, sir. Why don't you write about that instead of keep telling how we are supposed to accept your race the way it is? Why don't you people police yourself and try to straighten your own people up first before you bitch about us, all right? Have a nice day!

Denying that racism exists won't make it go away. In fact, denying racism very successfully covers it up for those who are not its targets. Those who are targets of racism, however, are powerfully aware that it exists. Long before racial profiling became a buzz phrase, African-Americans and Latinos mostly knew of its existence. Racism halts their progress and belittles and embarrasses. For many young people of color, racism's energy and effects do not emerge until their world experiences expand. They must be forewarned by diversity multipliers striving to forge change.

From "Time hasn't yet erased U.S. racism"

The music stopped on KPRS-FM, and then the disc jockey on Kansas City's No. 1 radio station introduced Alvin Brooks.

Brooks, then-Ad Hoc Group Against Crime president, had a message aimed at young African-American males. He lectured them on how they should react and the IDs they must show if stopped by police.

I hadn't heard anyone say such things in 25 years. That was when my parents and other adults drilled safety lessons into me about growing up black in white America.

Times have changed, but not enough to eliminate the need for the message.

Brooks' instructions to young black men ring many of the old self-preservation bells. He asked them to follow officers' instructions, keep their hands in sight, avoid running, carry no weapons or illegal substances and show the appropriate paperwork.

Many cry it's not fair, but being stopped is a reality many young minorities still face.

Brooks' on-air message is still needed, partly because of crime, fear, zero tolerance and stereotypes. Parents and police praise Brooks for his lectures.

They hope young people will listen so that traffic stops won't escalate into major problems. Brooks sees the need because he is an instructor at the Kansas City Police Academy, a former police officer and someone who hears complaints from young black males.

"The best thing you can do is to follow instructions," Brooks said. If harassment or racism are factors, then victims should file complaints after the initial encounter has ended peacefully.

That could help ease tensions between African-Americans and police. I wish such radio advice wasn't necessary. But until inequity is in our rear-view mirror, Brooks' message from the past fits our bizarre times.

Fortunately, there are some people who understand and deeply care that conditions in our society are far less than just.

Voice Mail: 2003

Subject: Racial profiling

A few minutes ago I was on the Plaza coming home from Barnes and Noble, my place of employment, for lunch. I was waiting for the 39th Street bus at FAO Schwartz. A man, elderly, African American man in his late 50s was waiting for the bus with me also. He sat down on the sidewalk to wait for the bus. Well, the Highwoods Property people, their little security people came along and they harassed him. They ran his I.D., but they didn't ask for my I.D. But they didn't ask me if I was waiting on the bus. It was blatant what they were doing to him because of him being an African American man waiting on the bus. And it just really, really upset me. I just wanted somebody who I know who cares to be aware of that. (Starts to cry) It really upset me. Thank you for listening, and I am so sorry that we still live in a time when people are judged by the color of their skin. The man was not doing anything wrong and they really shook him up. So, OK. Thanks for listening. Bye, Bye.

Diversity multipliers face constant challenges from those who benefit from maintaining the status quo. The latter create a Sisyphean task that confounds diversity multipliers.

<u>From "Becoming attuned to the sensitivities of Islam"</u>

The Danish cartoons of the Prophet Muhammad turned a Saturday open house at the Islamic Center of Greater Kansas City into an opportunity for area residents to learn the truth about him and Islam.

From news stories, people think Islam is a violent religion spread by the sword, said Bhaa Elashkar, an organizer of the event.

Abdalla Idris Ali, director of the Center for Islamic Education in Kansas City, cited a *Washington Post*-ABC News poll that said 46 percent of Americans had a negative view of Islam. That is 7 percentage points higher than after the Sept. 11, 2001, terrorist attacks, when Muslims often were singled out for scorn and violence.

The Post said the tension was fed by the wars in Afghanistan and Iraq, the uproar over a plan for an Arab company to manage U.S. ports, and Muslims' violent protests over the Danish caricatures.

"The atmosphere is so explosive," Ali said. "We want this to disappear."

But it won't go away unless efforts are made to better understand Islam.

"The truth is, it is a peaceful religion about doing good," Elashkar said.

One example: The Muslim Students Association raised $60,000 for victims of the Pakistan earthquake and the drought in Africa with a dinner March 11 at Longview Community College.

At the fundraising dinner some speakers provided badly needed clarity to the intense responses worldwide to the Danish cartoons. The speakers showed links to the reactions and historical events involving American blacks.

Imam Johari Abdul-Malik, Muslim chaplain of Howard University, compared the Muslims who have protested to African-Americans after the Rev. Martin Luther King Jr. was assassinated in 1968. Cities, including Kansas City, exploded, with black people rioting and dying.

The Prophet Muhammad symbolizes hope to Muslims just as King did for African-Americans, said Abdul-Malik, an African-American who grew up in Brooklyn and converted to Islam in the early 1980s.

"Blacks felt a hopelessness when the symbol of their hope was attacked," he said.

Some Muslims responded violently because of the character assassination that the Prophet Muhammad sustained, Abdul-Malik said. People acted out of a sense of desperation and hopelessness because of concern that the next attack could be on them.

Protests have taken place this year in Libya, Pakistan, Turkey, Indonesia, Iran, Syria, Lebanon, Afghanistan, India and Nigeria. Abdul-Malik said the low literacy rates of 15 percent to 20 percent in some of these countries contributed to the violence.

"Everybody can understand a picture," Abdul-Malik said. Even a negative picture "is worth a thousand words."

Ali, who is from Sudan, also spoke at the fundraiser.

"Our religion is not just a faith," he said. "It is a practice."

Muslims pray five times a day.

"The prophet is alive in people," Ali said.

The first thing Muslims learn is to honor the Prophet Muhammad.

"I just want you to imagine the intensity of the relationship between the people and the prophet," Ali said. "It's one thing to be critical. It's another to slander. The cartoons were considered slander, because of the way people put it."

Neither King nor Muhammad would have endorsed the rioting, Abdul-Malik said. Ali said it was OK for Muslims to express their anger, but not with violence.

The U.S. and worldwide media must respect how Muslims feel about the Prophet Muhammad. The press must hire and promote more Muslim journalists to expand news beyond Western standards and sensibilities.

The press must borrow pages from the civil rights era in which the news media hired more journalists of color to make their coverage more accurate and inclusive. Doing the same thing for Muslims would lessen Americans' negative view of Islam and prevent stereotypical material from flowing into print again.

Pointing out the truth resulted in a downpour of negative feedback. What follows are a few fierce examples.

E-mail: March 29, 2006

To use Martin Luther King name in the same sentence with a disciple of the devil is WRONG.

King was a man of peace. He would never have said that if a person decides to change their religion they should be killed.

All Muslims hate non Muslims.

All Muslims are EVIL and should not be allowed in the USA.

E-mail: March 29, 2006

We non-Muslims don't need to learn more about Muslims, they need to understand that while they are free to believe whatever they wish, the rest of us have the same privilege. It's interesting that they are compared to the blacks. I've long thought that the unproductive "mob" behavior of each was quite similar and attempts to justify it had no real truth, ... explain, maybe, but that is not justification.

As long as you equate "explanation" and "justification" there will be no solution for Muslims or blacks and "whining" will persist. Both groups need to "grow up".

Voice mail: March 29, 2006

I strongly disagree with your article. I think you should resign because you're unqualified. You should learn not to quote people. I know it's a struggle for you to write a whole article without quoting people. Because I've noticed you fill your article full of quotes. I could tell it's a struggle for you. In other words, you're an imbecile. It's a peaceful religion. Yeah, yeah, and you print that. Maybe in your next article you could put a location of maybe a class I could take to become more sensitive to Islam. Gosh, I know it's very important. I want to become more attuned to the sensitivities of Islam. I want to learn how to cut somebody's head off if they don't agree with their religion. I know they are very sensitive about that. If you know where I can take a class like that you can give me a call. Lord knows we need to be real sensitive to them. I'm not a hate monger or nothing like that, but I can't believe your article. Unbelievable. How you got your job I'll never know cause you are very unqualified. I don't get it. There is not one race that is any more perfect than any other. I don't get it. Over some cartoons? They get that upset? Yeah, I'd probably be upset myself. But I don't understand it, and I don't understand your article either.

Teachers are diversity multipliers and must work hard for an inclusiveness and change, as outlined in Formula III. Schools have a responsibility to raise kids' awareness about others who are or aren't like them. They help people in their adventures to discover the Real America.

From "An education for everyone: Schools need multicultural effort"

Schools can do a lot to promote racial healing if they teach multicultural education.

But that rarely happens.

Education overall lacks an inclusive curriculum. Defining that problem is the first step, said Fred Rodriguez, associate professor of curriculum and instruction at the University of Kansas and the education association's regional director.

Nettie Collins-Hart, Lawrence Public Schools curriculum director, helped me see just how big the multicultural education void is. She did it by getting people in her workshop to share what we knew about the Supreme Court's 1954 Brown vs. Board of Education of Topeka decision.

We recalled that the case was the culmination of other decisions that led to the overturning of legal segregation in America.

Thurgood Marshall, who later became the first black Supreme Court justice, argued the case for the plaintiffs. Key concerns were issues of safety and equality for black schoolchildren.

We also knew that women, people with disabilities and special education students benefited from the decision. Collins-Hart then handed us history books used in schools today and told us to look up the Brown case.

We found that we knew more about the ruling that pushed America toward equality than what the books teach our children. Some textbooks never even said that the plaintiffs were black.

It's no wonder that students think desegregation and busing were inflicted on them by the federal government and not sought by African-American school patrons to correct centuries of injustices. Collins-Hart said history also failed to note that many black educators were laid off after the court ruling because whites didn't want blacks to teach their kids.

"There are multiple perspectives, and there are many ways of looking at the same event," said Dorothy Arvizu with the Kansas Association for Native American Education. Students will be more interested in education if it is more inclusive. The truth also may lessen their feelings of anger and powerlessness.

What we have now nationwide is mostly a white male, Eurocentric education system, said Peggy McIntosh, associate director at Wellesley College Center for Research on Women. She said at the conference that schools must push past exclusion to the futuristic phase of multicultural education.

It has the potential to lessen conflict among people, because they would have developed at school an appreciation for the diversity in everyone.

"It's trying to make a better society for everybody," Rodriguez said. "We're changing gradually in this country, but we are changing profoundly."

Problems, however, exist. Many educators told how they must deprogram their own children who suffer the damaging effects of stereotypes at school. Others said a fear of change or of being fired kept them from injecting more multicultural lessons into the curriculum.

But they've got to get past that fear and develop new teaching strategies, including bringing in more outside speakers and having students do multicultural research and report their findings to the class. Everyone would gain a respect and appreciation for diversity, Rodriguez said.

Education is the key to the exciting frontier of understanding.

Breaching walls that divide

Another source for expanding the search for the Real America can be found in our criminal justice system. Many folks just want to lock up offenders and throw away the key. However, a lot would be lost to the greater community if that were to happen. No one should have to go to prison. But those who are there confront the huge contradiction of suddenly being "free" of the distractions that invade our lives outside the razor wire. Incarcerated men and women must immediately contend with seemingly limitless time for introspection. They must bore deep within themselves to find the never-discovered essence of who they are, what motivates them and what is left in their lives that can give them joy beyond the sorrow of solitude. The rebirth gives them the gift of an indomitable spirit, a quest for knowledge, a stronger link to their faith and a commitment to others. Fortunately, some diversity multipliers see the beauty in what the incarcerated people have to share. These folks on both sides of the razor wire encourage change in communities so others don't end up in prison.

From "From behind bars, men reach out to help Kansas City; charter school receives boost from inmates in NAACP branch"

> CAMERON, Mo. - Diana Swezy's chest heaved with a deep sigh in the Western Missouri Correctional Center parking lot.
>
> She'd had a long day as then-principal of Gordon Parks Elementary School in Kansas City, Mo. Yet between daylight and darkness she'd gone into the prison.
>
> It's where most people wouldn't think to go. But Swezy braved the journey for her kids and for herself.
>
> Prison was where the Dream Builders NAACP Branch 4095 had its Second Annual Black History Month Program. Swezy's fourth-graders won the NAACP's essay contest.
>
> Charles M. Johnson, president of the National Association for the Advancement of Colored People branch, gave Swezy $200 for the school.
>
> "We're trying to give back what we've taken," Johnson said. "Us being incarcerated, we've taken a lot."
>
> The men are in prison for myriad offenses. Yet acting on the wishes of their past NAACP president, Eric L. Wesson, they adopted the kindergarten through fourth-grade Kansas City charter school to help its 157 children in ways they were never helped.
>
> "Me being a father and a grandfather, I understand the importance of education," Johnson said. He said that despite being incarcerated, the men feel they're also part of the village responsible for raising this community's children.
>
> The men raised the $200 for the 4-year-old school by selling chicken dinners, which deeply moved Swezy and other guests at the program. Johnson said such fund-raisers for Gordon Parks will be ongoing.

"What they need and we're able to provide, we're digging into our pockets," he told inmates and guests, which included ministers and choir members from Palestine Missionary Baptist Church in Kansas City who spoke and performed. "They are our future doctors and lawyers and teachers."

Swezy said, "The gift is incredibly generous."

Johnson added: "Our children are our responsibility. Education is a must. Some of us are in the situation we are in today due to a lack of education.

"They say we're bad people. We've done some bad things. But we're not bad people."

In the parking lot before our drive back, Swezy reflected on everything Johnson said, on other speeches and the music. Many of the men's beginnings were not unlike the children's at her school.

They grew up in poverty in inner city communities in black families that struggled to make it. Swezy said it was "statistically reasonable" that some of her pupils could share the men's fate.

But she has seen how well her children can think and academically perform. Swezy hopes Gordon Parks inspires them to be lifelong learners.

However, the prison visit and gift from the NAACP strengthened her resolve to do everything humanly possible to keep incarceration from being in her pupils' future. She shook the hands of more than 50 inmates that night thanking them for the gift.

"I am truly honored to be in the room this evening," Swezy told them after Johnson gave her the check. "There is such a remarkable power in all of you in this room."

But visiting the prison also left her more than a little sad. Gordon Parks school adds $2,100 per child to the state and federal funding it receives to boost the school's per pupil cost to $10,000.

Tim Kniest, then-public information officer with the Missouri Department of Corrections, said the state spends an average of $35.52 a day, or $12,964.80 a year, on each of more than 30,000 inmates in its more than 20 correctional facilities. That's low compared with what other states spend to incarcerate people.

Yet it's such a waste. Society would be so much better off if people and the government invested more in the education of all of the community's children to prevent them from making wrong choices that land them in poverty, prison or the grave.

Swezy, Johnson and the NAACP members want the children to become productive, tax-paying citizens. The gift from the least of us was inspiring, and I pray it helps the children stay on the right path.

Giving to those less fortunate is something that has caught on with men in the NAACP prison branches as they function as diversity multipliers behind bars directing the hopes, prayers and work of others toward change using

Formula III. Following up on their generosity revealed the crushing needs that exist in rural America and just how far a little help can go.

From "Living on generosity; Tough times are tightening the 'poverty belt'"

JEFFERSON CITY - Marylyn Geraghty DeFeo stood before the men at the 11th Annual Hilltop NAACP Freedom Fund Banquet and expressed her gratitude.

"It's a beautiful thing," she said of the $1,000 check the inmates at the Algoa Correctional Center gave her from fund-raisers at the prison. The money was for the Samaritan Center in Jefferson City.

"God wants us there," DeFeo, the center's volunteer executive director, said. "Miracles happen every day."

I've seen men in Missouri prisons give gifts to community groups. I've seen prison officials like Superintendent Michael J. Murphy and Hilltop NAACP President Melvin Hayes praise them for their efforts. But I hadn't seen the Samaritan Center, so I returned the next month to check it out.

People start lining up an hour before the 9:30 a.m. opening. They come from the city's "poverty belt," and mid-Missouri seeking food; government commodities; clothing; toiletries; disposable diapers; infant formula; utility, rent and day care assistance; free dental and medical care; and free legal advice.

About 645 volunteers each week serve them. DeFeo stopped in the kitchen. Bread, rolls and garden fresh vegetables waited to be handed to clients.

The ecumenical Samaritan Center has depended on people's generosity since it opened in 1987. The volunteers formed a circle and held hands, for the blessing.

Mostly women and children filled the waiting area.

"I come here pretty much about every month," said a 22-year-old woman, who was with her sister, 18, and 1 1/2-year-old daughter. "It really helps until I get paid."

She works at a nursing home; her sister works at McDonald's. They fit the profile of the 850 to 900 families the Samaritan Center serves. They work but don't make enough to live. The center served 1,057 families in June.

The center has seen a rising tide of people needing help since the 1993 Missouri flood. The area never really recovered, DeFeo said.

"The towns are dying for one thing," she said. "Jefferson City is the lifeblood for all the towns around."

But state retirements and layoffs have affected donations. "I know the economy is moving on, but my people are not in jobs where they are going to get raises," DeFeo said.

Their hours also are kept low so employers don't have to provide them with benefits such as health insurance and sick leave.

"That's unjust in America," DeFeo said. "Everyone's entitled to support themselves and make a just salary and not have to worry about their families."

These folks travel to the Samaritan Center from the Lake of the Ozarks and throughout the region. Some are family members of people in prison. Others are newly released inmates.

Most are individuals who never dreamed the suffocating poverty in this bucolic community would victimize them.

"You can see the terror in people's eyes," DeFeo said.

Many travel from other counties because they're frightened and ashamed to ask for help in places where they're well-known. I saw that fear and shame in their eyes and heard it in their voices.

"It's amazing there's not more mental illness, there's not more crime," DeFeo said. She called her clients "the silent people," individuals whom politicians ignore.

Yet President George W. Bush's message of family values resonates with them. Instead, they should have listened to Democratic vice-presidential challenger John Edwards talk of two Americas - one that's profanely wealthy and the other that's poor like them.

Men in Jefferson City's two prisons understand. The center received a total of $1,500 from inmates at the Missouri State Penitentiary. Men at Algoa also have made toys and furniture for the children. If they can do that, then elected officials need to do more.

I asked DeFeo about the more recent gift of $1,000 from Algoa. "Long gone," she said.

"They may think $1,000 isn't much, but $1,000 buys 1,000 pounds of hamburger," she said. "That means 1,000 families had spaghetti dinner because those men thought about reaching out to help somebody."

She takes in thousands of pounds of canned and dry goods from Boy Scouts and postal workers and $600,000 in cash donations a year. In June, $12,000 went for utility assistance. Soon families will come for school supplies.

"I really, really worry about the children," DeFeo said. "If we can't stand up and do good for them then we're in a very sad state in America."

As inmates reach out, others reach in and endeavor to make a difference. One organization that should be noted for its efforts to make prisoners' lives more fulfilling is the Arts in Prison Inc. program. It taps the men's undiscovered positive, creative talents. These volunteer diversity multipliers help those both outside and inside of the prison system see that change is possible.

From "Unlocking the voices of inmates"

Prison yard noises wafted into the chapel at the Lansing Correctional Facility.

They tumbled in the open windows, bumped against the backs of the pews and fell to the floor with the long shadows from the setting sun. In exchange, the chapel in the minimum-security unit gave back joyous music from the East Hill Singers and their conductor, Elvera Voth.

She's chorus master at the Lyric Opera and the Utah Festival Opera. Before retiring in 1994 and returning to her native Kansas, Voth founded the Anchorage Opera, the Anchorage Boys Choir and the Alaska Chamber Singers.

Voth created the department of music at the University of Alaska-Anchorage. Now she has injected a pioneering spirit and music into the prison.

"Singing, I think, promotes responsibility to a group," Voth said. "If you sing in a group and sing one wrong note, the whole group looks bad. I really believe a choral group is a terrific rehabilitation tool."

The East Hill Singers perform annually outside of prison with members of the Rainbow Mennonite Church in Kansas City, Kan. Their concerts include a variety of musical styles, such as Gregorian chants and classical, spiritual and folk music.

Rappers, rockers and toneless inmates dropped out when they saw that their music wasn't Voth's.

"She put a challenge to them, and they're really interested in learning a new craft," Byron Alexander, Lansing activities specialist, said of the chosen few. "I think what they get out of it is striving to be successful.

"They come up here, and they forget all the problems they had outside these doors."

During practice, Voth sits at the piano. Inmates whose prison ID numbers are taped to their jeans and shirts surround her.

The singers are behind bars for crimes that include car theft, drugs, burglary and murder. Yet, in the chapel, they're eager-to-please saints making music.

"One, two, ready, sing," Voth said.

"Ma-ri-a. They call the wind Ma-ri-a ... ," the men sing.

Voth interrupts. "Don't even think about going down there."

She said later: "Once I'm in a rehearsal, everything goes from my mind but trying to make the music right. I don't know why anyone is in there or for how long. I'm there to judge them by their commitment to the group, how hard they work and how good they sound."

The men try again and get it right.

"She's great," inmate Billy Blackman said. "She never quits on us, and I don't plan to quit on her."

Kate Walker, with the Alaska Chamber Singers, said Voth infects people with her energy. Walker said Voth was named an Alaska Woman of Achievement.

"A big reason for that is she doesn't know how to stop," Walker said. "She rallies support, and her vision goes beyond what most people can accomplish."

Voth said the inmates saved her from the cold shock of retirement. They inspire her to give in her Mennonite tradition of social service to others.

In doing so, Voth opens a huge door of what could work at other prisons to inspire inmates to be better people.

"It's like a dream come true for me," inmate Dennis Edwards said.

I wish others would join Voth in this compassion revival so more inmates might envision what they could become with the right direction.

Art of another kind helps to inspire and change inmates in prison to be better people. Such rehabilitation by committed diversity multipliers is how recidivism is reduced, and ex-offenders, when released, become productive.

From "Artists in residence"

Weights from heavy lifting clanged over the voices of men working out at the east wing of the Lansing Correctional Facility.

But inside a building a short walk away was the silence of other inmates creating pictures in the Arts in Prison Inc. program. I loved the contrast of such beauty springing from a place as harsh as prison.

Johnny Ingram was drawing a tomato. Frank Escobedo was working on a portrait of his mom who lives in California.

Gene Wiens was drawing his daughter, Shelley. Farmon Williams was redrawing a portrait of actress of Lucy Liu, and Clint Grier was working on a picture of an American Indian.

Grier said he spent eight hours on the image. His mind is on home when he's concentrating on his art.

"It takes me away from being here," Grier said.

Wiens said art makes him feel better about himself. "It's the only way we can really express ourselves in here."

"I get peace of mind," Escobedo said. "It gives me a place to escape."

The Arts in Prison program is a nonprofit, privately financed initiative based in Kansas City, Kan. Its goal is to use art as a rehabilitative medium to enhance the social and creative skills of inmates. It's an expansion of Elvera Voth's effort in 1995 that started the East Hill Singers at the Lansing prison.

The program now includes the painting and drawing class; jazz, blues, classical, country and rock guitar lessons; gardening; storytelling, studying and preparing for on-site drama performances; and poetry, fiction, nonfiction, journaling and other forms of writing.

The men's works are displayed during the public concerts of the East Hill Singers.

"People don't expect that from inmates," said Christopher Kurtz, coordinator of operations for Arts in Prison. "The mindset is prison is a big bad place full of big, bad people."

Kurtz's office walls at the Rainbow Mennonite Church are covered with copies of beautiful water colors and drawings that the men have produced. There are colorful birds and detailed landscapes of farm scenes and lighthouses and a striking portrait of Jesus on the cross wearing a crown of thorns.

The artist captured Christ's pain and disappointment in humankind. The inmates tap the root of their own agony and build that emotional depth into their art. Their paintings, writings and music have a powerful and moving effect on people who attend their concerts, Kurtz said.

"What inmates want people to know is, 'We made mistakes. We want to learn from our mistakes. We're just like everybody else,'" Kurtz said.

Herman Gerber, drawing and painting instructor for Arts in Prison, retired in 1997 from the Kansas City, Kan., School District, where he had been director of art education and taught art at Harmon High School. For nearly three years he has regularly gone to the Lansing prison to help the men develop their artistic talent.

"I believe if we're going to incarcerate people that there must be something of value to them," he said. Developing that talent is their best hope for the future.

"I think their art takes them to a place that's nonthreatening," Gerber said. "You see the good side of who they are. I call it the goodness of heart. I don't know the mistakes they've made."

Gerber focuses on the men's interests, the art they produce and how he can help them become better than they are. "These guys are so eager to learn," he said.

High school classes move more quickly, but the inmates are more attentive and more focused. "As far as the men go, it's one of the best classes I've ever had," he said.

Williams said Gerber helped him broaden his skills. That enhancement will help him when he's released from prison.

The men like working with Gerber because he treats them as students instead of inmates. "It's kind of a breath of fresh air," Wiens said.

The men I spoke with on a recent visit all said they send what they've created home to their mothers and other family members.

Tim Gloston, activity specialist at the prison, said he was grateful for the Arts in Prison volunteers. "It keeps the guys happy, keeps them out of trouble and it helps them enhance their creative niche," Gloston said.

My only regret is there aren't more programs like it getting young people to create beautiful things that keep them out of trouble that would land them in prisons like Lansing.

Empowering women

Diversity multipliers have to connect people pushing for change on a micro-local level with those working on a global-macro scale. These connecting multipliers are the ones who will help us all fly to new heights.

From "Symposium helps better opportunities for women take flight"

Ruth L. Margolin laughed when I asked about the three doves she helped release at the end of the 1995 Starr Symposium.

The birds symbolized peace, development and equality for women at the "Thinking Globally, Acting Locally" conference in November at the University of Missouri-Kansas City. The meeting brought to town the same spirit and goals that were to take flight after the United Nations Fourth World Conference on Women in Beijing.

Margolin, then-Women's Center director at UMKC, laughed about the birds because two came back.

Symbolically, the dove of equality has been the only one to fly. More women are breaking the glass ceiling, entering board rooms and starting businesses.

Peace and development haven't taken off yet.

Violence against women has grounded the dove of peace, and the bird of development can't fly, because women still represent 70 percent of the 1.3 billion people in poverty worldwide.

But those birds are being energized for flight as the spirit of the Beijing conference and the Starr Symposium continues to grow. Meetings in Kansas City reviewed the commitments and pledges of governments, agencies and businesses to promote women's rights.

Starr Symposium leaders reported the progress to President Clinton's Inter-Agency Council on Women. Clinton created the group to implement the action platform adopted in Beijing. Much work remains undone.

U.S. commitments include pumping $1.6 billion over six years into fighting domestic violence, stopping threats to women's health and security, improving working conditions, boosting access to financing, promoting women's political involvement and legal rights, establishing a White House Council on Women and removing barriers to the education of women and girls.

Kansas City already stands out in bringing the Beijing spirit home, said Teresa Loar, the Inter-Agency Council's representative in the State Department.

Marjorie Margolies Mezvinsky, director of the U.S. Beijing delegation, said: "They had the vision immediately, and they knew exactly what they had to do."

That includes the creation of the video "Voices of Women: Thinking Globally, Acting Locally," a gift from women and children's advocate Martha Jane Starr. It chronicled the Beijing conference and its participants. Carol Tally Davis, then-Women's Council executive director, said more than 400 copies of the tape were mailed nationwide from UMKC.

Margolin said: "It has been the thread that has kept women connected all over the country. It brings out that we are all women and have so much in common."

The Starr-UMKC video on Beijing has inspired women and kept the momentum going, said Rose Kemp, then-regional administrator of the Labor Department's Women's Bureau and chairwoman for the 1995 Starr Symposium. Women are receiving more scholarships for training, and a "Working Women Count" honor roll has been created for employers who pledge to improve working women's lives.

"Some of it would have occurred without the Beijing conference, but it would have been more limited and more self-contained," Kemp said. "What I see is people are beginning to recognize that something is wrong, and we've got to set it right."

Attacks on affirmative action and retro-politics challenge the momentum. But I think that adversity will inspire more women to vote, and eventually everyone will see that women's rights are simply human rights.

The spirit of Beijing will grow stronger so that development and peace take off and equality soars.

Dr. Martin Luther King Jr. famously said that "True peace is not merely the absence of tension, it is the presence of justice." Right now America and the world enjoy neither. Until diversity multipliers help others work toward the change King wanted, conflict and bloodshed will prevail.

It only takes a few committed people to start a tidal wave of change. They give direction to others yearning for positive action to overcome what seem like insurmountable situations.

From "To effect change, we must unite"

Sharon Cheers has worn a special armband and helped to keep the peace among peace-keepers during anti-war protests near the Plaza.

Donald Scott has been active at the peace rallies, too. Ester L. Holzendorf has spoken at the gatherings and been a facilitator at monthly meetings of a new group the anti-war protests have spawned called Movement for a Just Future. Loretta C. Rogers is a regular at those meetings, too.

Kimberly Baskett McEnany had served as executive director of Kansas City Interfaith Peace Alliance. What these individuals share is they are among African-Americans who've joined with people of other races to protest against violence and the wars in Afghanistan and Iraq.

Like the Rev. Martin Luther King Jr. more than a generation ago, they're proponents of peaceful solutions to local and global conflicts.

"It represents everything I was fighting for," Cheers said. Spending billions of dollars on the wars makes no sense when millions of Americans are without health care and close to 40 million live in poverty.

But Cheers, McEnany, Scott, Holzendorf and Rogers often stand out at peace gatherings like the one Sunday near the Country Club Plaza because few black people attend.

McEnany said some African-Americans may see the efforts as being beyond their ability to make a difference. She said she's involved because of the children she plans to have. "I don't want people to ask the question, 'Where was Kimberly Baskett McEnany, and why didn't she do something?'" she said.

Holzendorf's adult children motivate her. Her sons, Caleb and Quentin, are in the military. They enlisted believing President Bush: They'd make America safe from weapons of mass destruction.

"It's very difficult to say to your child, 'That may not be true,'" she said. "They're playing games with our kids, and I don't like it."

Holzendorf said the peace movement is connected to other struggles for justice that black Americans face.

A disproportionately high number of African-Americans are in prisons, a disproportionately low number are in college and a disproportionately high number are unemployed, live without health insurance and subsist in poverty. A disproportionately high number of African-Americans enlist in the military, seeing it as one of a few opportunities for a better way of life.

But in the military they're often used against the world's other oppressed people of color, Scott said. "It shows the United States is using its poor citizens to fight against the poorer people of the world and poorer people of color," he said.

Holzendorf said, "Poor people and people of color fight many battles for this thing called peace, and so far we haven't found it."

Scott said so few black people attend the peace rallies because "so many have been beaten down so much, and they are so discouraged."

Rogers remembered the excitement African-Americans felt when they were involved in Great Society programs. Disappointment followed as the advancements were rolled back.

"When they got dismantled, African-Americans just lost faith in all community-based organizations," Rogers said. "They took the trust the people had that they could work together and see the results.

"So much has been taken from the community. African-Americans are concerned about practical things now like making a living and getting a job or feeding their families."

But African-Americans need to see as Scott does how systems of oppression keep people down at home and abroad. "As African-American men, I think it's important because we have to show the kids the correlation between globalization and racism in this country," he said.

The peace rallies help to enlighten people.

McEnany said the movement is bigger than any one race.

Scott added, "I really believe we need to come together with other races and let each other know what we have in common."

Rogers said, "I haven't given up because I know change happens when people work together."

Unity is our only hope.

Yet feedback showed that the public sentiment worked largely against what the diversity multipliers hoped to accomplish.

E-mail: Oct. 5, 2003

Way to go, Lewis. Your most recent column is very possibly the most laughable of all the columns which you have written. But don't get me wrong. Like many of your other columns, it's also a "master stroke" in that you include the names of naive peace whackos which creates a small group of individuals who love to see their name in print and will then write to "letters" telling readers how much on target you are! Actually, most of everything you put in print is symbolism over substance – especially the Great Society programs, which were a total waste of our tax dollars. Even more so than what Bush is spending in the Middle East in his futile attempt to create democratic governments

> and civilize people of dark skin. Apparently the few white peaceniks who do hang with you don't really understand that a very high percentage of black males are a drag on every metro area in America. They don't give a squat about anyone or anything – especially your laughable "peace gatherings." Black females are not nearly the drag on society. They simply get so overweight that society eventually needs to take care of them when they have finished being the sole head of over 70 percent of black households. Donald Scott needs to be placed in a home for the mentally ill. If he should some day become mentally sane, he needs to be informed that the black race will make up more than 50 excuses for the situation they find themselves in all over the globe. I think you need to become a realist like Michelle Malkin, Lewis. Fortunately your Jewish boss generally places (Malkin's) column on the same page as yours so that creates some sense of balance!

Balance is one of those tricky words used by those whose goal is to thwart positive change. The status quo reinforcing the America as is, with all its flaws, is the only thing that matters. So many profit from it. Yet the benefits of diversity could enlarge the pie of prosperity for all. Diversity multipliers just need the opportunity to make such a change possible.

CHAPTER 12
Community Solutions: Doing More

Deeper Than Skin

Face to face
The beauty of the human race
Shows in wonderful colors and noses
Flat, wide, pointy or flaring like a lovely bouquet of roses
And lips that range from thin to thick
Yet each offers kisses, though different but quite rich.
Some have hair long, blond, brown, gray or black
Growing far down their back
Or tightly curled
Defying all "beautifying" efforts to unfurl
So natural and cool in its beauty
Not like the others' - each unique - and that suits me
As an explorer, for fortunes in those heads behind the noses, different lips and hair
Are yet to be discovered for those who dare
To venture past the stereotypes tied to the features and skin
To harness the beauty that lies within.

When the Nazis came for the communists, I remained silent; I was not a communist.
When they locked up the social democrats, I remained silent; I was not a social democrat.
When they came for the trade unionists, I did not speak out; I was not a trade unionist.
When they came for the Jews, I did not speak out; I was not a Jew.
When they came for me
there was no one left to speak out.
~Pastor Martin Niemöller

In September of 2002 I received an important thought in an e-mail:

From: "Protecting everyone's civil rights"

"The idea is for everyone to touch base with their immediate neighbors," the sender wrote.

"Visit them and offer to help them at anytime. Become close to one's neighbors like we did in generations past.

"If just half the people would do this, what a better place this could be."

The writer is right. But I would extend that community fellowship more broadly over the walls that separate the races, religions, classes, generations, ethnic groups, men and women, gays and straights, and countries.

Yet to some people diversity is almost a four-letter word, and valuing or practicing it is foul:

E-mail: January 22, 2003

Nowhere in the Constitution does it say anything about ensuring diversity. This is a buzzed-up PC phrase that is used as an excuse to trample all over fundamental rights of all, led by pin-headed liberals such as yourself.

Almost 10 years earlier, I had written about how inspiring diversity is when given a chance to flourish. Businesses have had to become wave makers because diversity now is vital to their survival.

From "Diversity is a wave of future"

To Frederick A. Miller, diversity will take hold by pick-axing its way into America's workplaces. Miller, then-president of the Kaleel Jamison Consulting Group Inc. of Albany, N.Y., saw diversity as undiscovered gold at our feet.

We just have to pick it up.

Its currency is in everyone recognizing the uniqueness of others. The new awareness will buy companies better management, problem-solving, communication, learning and productivity from all workers.

In tag-team fashion, Miller; Kent D. Linder and Marjane Jensen, both Kaleel Jamison consultants at that time, drove the point home at a Harmony in a World of Difference seminar at the Hyatt Regency Crown Center hotel in Kansas City.

They want people to see diversity as an open window of opportunity. But the window won't stay open forever, Miller said.

"You cannot serve a diverse cultural base from a monocultural base," Linder said. "There's a business reason to understand and be aware: Business that you lose a lot of times you never get back."

People of color are underserved because for years companies treated them as "darker-skinned white people," Miller said.

As a result, advertising never completely reached these unique groups. Businesses now realize, however, that these folks represent rich markets for companies offering culturally sensitive sales messages.

It's a brave new world lying largely undiscovered here at home, which some companies are starting to explore.

For example, Ford Motor Co. has women engineers help design new cars. Because of their input, cars accommodate women's driving demands such as foot pedals that are easy to operate for women in high heels and skirts, door handles that won't break fingernails and seat adjustments that are made for the way women are built.

It's long overdue, considering that women purchase about half of all cars and provide input into about 80 percent of all auto purchases, Linder said.

Market research also has prompted the Pillsbury Co. to get into the act. The firm is trying to spice up some of its products and has made its trademark Doughboy more lively.

He now even wears his hat cocked to the side and occasionally says a Spanish word, Miller said. It's the company's attempt to tap into more markets.

That kind of bottom-line pressure is driving diversity into new territory.

Even feeder industries that don't serve the public directly will have to change as the good ol' boy business network they depend upon for their sales, goods and services begins to include more women and minorities.

They must adapt to the new "like-us" corporate culture to survive.

Linder is counting on the "ripple effect" to carry diversity into education, churches and the community.

Businesses just happen to be the wave makers.

In the workplace, diversity isn't just a way to make more money. It's also a safety issue no different from requiring employees on some sites to wear protective shoes, clothing and eyewear.

Harassment because of race, sex, age, disabilities or sexual orientation is an on-the-job hazard, Miller said.

It cuts down on efficiency, increases absenteeism, turnover and training costs, and robs workers of their value. Apply pressure and heat on people to conform to the majority culture and problems develop.

That's reason enough to discard the image of America as a great melting pot because people don't melt when exposed to the fires of assimilation. They just get frustrated and angry.

> When companies don't welcome and accept individuals for their abilities and who they truly are in our great mixing bowl society, then businesses suffer wasted talent, potential and profits, Jensen said. Also, diverse people who are hired don't advance.
>
> "We spend a lot of time talking about the glass ceiling but not enough time talking about the sticky floor," Miller said. Only a token few get to rise to where the glass ceiling is an obstacle.
>
> "The sticky floor has multitudes of people stuck to the bottom rung, and they can't get off that," he said.
>
> Companies must welcome different people and ideas that will help them navigate and survive in the changing marketplace. It's not enough for newcomers to look Asian, black or Hispanic but to check their unique perspectives at the door or for women to wear makeup and skirts but be one of the guys in corporate policy.
>
> Diversity also needs allies to survive. Alliances must be forged with people in power circles.
>
> And everyone must drop the one-right-way, one-white-way mindset, incorporate diversity into their lives, and accept new ideas and perspectives, Linder said.
>
> "To get them hooked you've got to find something that they value more than their racism," Linder said.

It is difficult to imagine that some companies still don't realize that their policies and actions too often come from the "one-white-way mindset." Not being aware of issues that affect a diverse population can have a detrimental impact on business. As demonstrated above, diversity-sensitive advertising is especially important to a firm's good public relations and sales. It is a solution that can be forged only through inclusiveness.

<u>From "Remnants of rhyme still resonate with racism"</u>

> A friend pointed out an off-color billboard on top of a building at Westport Road and Southwest Trafficway in Kansas City, Mo.
>
> Apparently people hadn't learned from the bad publicity generated a few years ago from a lawsuit involving Southwest Airlines (see Chapter 3).
>
> The Boulevard Brewing Co. beer billboard uses the racist rhyme "Eenie, Meenie, Minie, Moe...." Each word is positioned with a period over one of four foam-filled glasses of Boulevard's popular Wheat, Pale Ale, Bully Porter and Dry Stout beer. The different beers also got darker as they went from "Eenie" to "Moe."
>
> I like Boulevard beer. It's home-grown. The company founded in 1989 on Southwest Boulevard by John McDonald is the largest spe-

cialty brewer in the Midwest. It's distributed in 11 states.

But the company's success doesn't excuse the use of the offensive rhyme to advertise the product.

Bob Sullivan, vice president and chief marketing officer with Boulevard Brewing, said no one had complained about the beer billboard. "It's a choice campaign," he said.

"It has nothing to do with race, color or creed," Sullivan said. "You would be the first person who's brought that to our attention."

The billboards started going up in different Kansas City locations in May. They will remain up until October, Sullivan said. The ads ran for two years in other media in 11 states.

They carry different messages of choice. One that had been up near 87th Street and U.S. 71 had used words positioned over the four different glasses of beer, saying, "Local pints of interest." A billboard with the same formation at 85th Street and Wornall Road says, "Collect the whole set." One at 75th Street and Wornall Road says, "To each their own." (Ouch on the grammar—but that change to keep from saying "To each *his* own" was meant to not exclude women beer drinkers.) One at 20th and Main streets said, "Which one are you?"

Those ads are eye-catching, cute and have no foul history attached. The "eenie, meenie, minie, moe" rhyme grabs people, but it has an awful history, which is far from cute.

Sullivan thinks that time and the wording change in the rhyme have been enough to disassociate it from its racist past. He said it would be "a huge stretch" now to make the connection.

I disagree. The history is too fresh. The rhyme still evokes the N-word, and no amount of beer will wash that down.

The feedback that this column generated was overwhelmingly foul. Hundreds of responses poured in from all over the country and the world after the column was posted on www.fark.com. What follows are a few examples.

E-mail: July 12, 2006

Get a life you RACIST idiot!

Why don't you, Jesse 'the corporate shake down Artist', and Al 'Twana Brawley' Sharpton, go and NIT PICK your own RACIST organization - the NAACP!!!

Otherwise if you don't like it, why don't you all go back to Africa if you think its so DAMN bad over here!!!

Once again, you must be the prized editor at your paper - The Kansas Shity Scar!

Adios Liberal LOSER!

E-mail: July 13, 2006

Hey, moron! you are so goddamned thin-skinned it's not funny!!! THAT is why I never read your so-called column. The only reason I read THIS one is because it had a photo of a billboard. You mentioned the case where those old bitches filed a lawsuit against an airline when a flight attendant used those words; WELL those thin-skinned bitches LOST the suit because the jury KNEW it was a joke!!! So wise up moron! If you think white folks are going to kiss your worthless ass every motherfucking time you holler RACISM, think again, stupid!! There are real men like me who would just as soon punch you in your big mouth than look at your sorry ass!! I hope the *STAR* pulls your so-called column! WILLIAM ROCKHILL NELSON would have fired your ass over this!!

E-mail: July 12, 2006

I read with interest your commentary this morning regarding Boulevard Brewing Company's billboard. I have driven past the billboard in question and it never dawned on me to make the connection you made. I believe it when Bob Sullivan says you are the first person to bring up this point.

I was raised by two loving parents who taught me to be colorblind and judge a person on what he/she does not what they look like. I hope I have raised my two daughters to reflect the same set of values. My question to you is, shouldn't we be past this type of discussion? Shouldn't we be concerned with the real issues of our time such as health care, jobs, terrorism and move past the politically correct discussions that amount to little more than window dressing? I guess this is easy for me to say, I am not black and I don't have your perspective on the issue. But having said that, I still think ALL of our time would be better spent caring about and working on issues that will improve the lives of all of our citizens instead of a beer company's billboard.

The Boulevard Beer Company changed the billboard caption to "Toasts of the Town" the morning the column came out. The brewery's reaction was swift and effective. Some changes, however, take much longer than logical or necessary and are "too slow for justice."

From "Promising plan for job parity"

African-Americans for decades have watched billions of dollars in residential and business construction reshape the metro area but haven't seen many black people included in jobs the booms created.

Tax giveaways encourage development. But they worsen conditions in the urban core, taking badly needed funds from the Kansas City School District whose students are mostly black.

The tax abatements also have hurt black breadwinners because African-Americans have received a disproportionately low share of the jobs from public and private construction. The black community's repeated cries for equal employment and economic opportunity have resulted in little action.

But it is important to celebrate a new development that could bring badly needed changes. MORE2, or the Metro Organization for Racial and Economic Equality, has brought construction companies, unions, city, community and faith-based officials together to create more construction jobs for African-Americans and women.

White churches and synagogues have joined with black churches in the long-standing struggle. "We're kind of the new kid on the block," Doug Smith, with Prairie Baptist Church, told about 300 people at a December meeting at the All Souls Unitarian Universalist Church.

In a follow-up meeting with *The Kansas City Star* Editorial Board, the Rev. Robert Hill, with the Community Christian Church, said "holy agitation" by the newcomers was needed. "We're not fatigued in the battle." There is no hesitancy, skepticism or cynicism.

I said, however, that what people of color have had to endure for decades before the current multibillion-dollar building boom was neither skepticism nor cynicism. It was a gut kick from steel-toed realism each time they sought employment parity from companies, unions and the city.

But the Jericho Table of the new metro group offers everyone a lot of badly needed hope. It is one of few times the white community has joined the black community to try to overcome the confounding, generational problems of racism and discrimination in this area. That's always encouraging.

The group formed the Jericho Table to push for the hiring and retention of more minority and women construction workers and contractors. J.E. Dunn Construction Co. and Turner Construction have made commitments. Other companies are being recruited to bring down the walls that divide the city over race and block people from employment.

At the December meeting, people sang "Joshua Fit the Battle of Jericho" and "We Shall Overcome." People mixed music from their faiths and the Civil Rights Movement with their resolve to economically improve the lives of urban residents.

"We're not done," said Teresa Guerra-York with Redemptorist Church. "For too long there has been a lot of talk about barriers and a lack of opportunities for minorities and women."

But she noted that the goals that have been developed need deadlines. Plans without time frames are wishes, Guerra-York said.

Clyde McQueen, with the Full Employment Council, added: "We have climbed the mountain, but we haven't reached the top yet."

Then-Kansas City Councilman Jim Glover told the Editorial Board that monitoring systems are needed with definitive goals. He said Emanuel Cleaver as mayor provided personal leadership, which helped create jobs and opportunities for minorities and women. The Jericho Table aims for structural change so that progress will remain ongoing.

Time is a factor. The construction boom won't last forever. Women and black workers and contractors need to be hired as soon as possible so they can benefit from the building boom. They also need to forge long-term bonds with general contractors, bankers and the insurance industry to be included in future projects.

Smith said the Jericho Table plans to hold people accountable. The few jobs and opportunities created need to be broadened.

"We see the accomplishments listed in the program as a beginning," he said. The Jericho Table hopes to get deadlines, specific hiring and training goals added to the commitments.

It is seeking incentives and legislative penalties. The group hopes to expand to include banks, bonding companies and developers. It also wants to reach beyond the city and into the suburbs.

The Kansas City area will benefit if all of these things take place. So will its long-neglected residents.

Although such efforts to right past wrongs are the correct actions to take, the feedback shows that a lot of people believe otherwise. Here are two examples.

E-mail: Feb. 1, 2006

Why is MORE singling out black people only? Just because there is 14 percent unemployment in the black community, means there is a huge racism problem toward black people getting jobs? A program that excludes all poor and disadvantaged people except black people is a fair solution? All people are on board with programs like MORE until you single out one race, which then turns into a racist program even though that's not the "intention". Racism is quickly shaping up to become a two way street in our society like never before in the last 70 years. Black people are not the only poor people in this country to get screwed and are no more special or deserving of this program than any other poor/disadvantaged person.

P.S. I am glad you mentioned JE Dunn, I drive by the IRS construction every morning and night and see quite the diverse group of workers.

E-mail: Feb. 1, 2006

I fail to see how another oversight group can produce more jobs for black people. The black people who have education, skills and motivation are already working.

What organizations like the Jericho Table and MORE2 are trying to accomplish can extend into the broader community. The "ripple effect" of businesses' embracing diversity is being felt in other sectors of society. The following segments will discuss solutions to discrimination in education and in the community.

Education

The wounds of discrimination leave scars. Some never heal. But there are programs and activities in education that allow everyone to learn from the trauma. The stories some tell must be recognized and accepted as part of national reconciliation process, so everyone can recover.

From "Mending lines of division"

> WARRENSBURG, Mo. - Stephen Ciafullo's letters compelled me to visit the world he keeps working to create.
>
> Ciafullo is an assistant professor at Central Missouri State University and director of the program and class called "Valuing Differences - Discovering Common Ground." The course began in the early 1990s after the initial not guilty verdicts of Los Angeles police officers in the beating of Rodney King sparked unrest nationwide and in Warrensburg.
>
> Since then, thousands of students have taken the eight-week, one-credit hour course to enable them to communicate across cultural lines, gain new perspectives, realize how much people have in common and learn from self-examination.
>
> Ciafullo helps give students a new-found ability to understand and not demonize others. The harmony they help create eliminates hurtful language and dispels misconceptions, assumptions and myths.
>
> Ciafullo and Eugene C. Stillman, campus advocate for students, took 13 women and six men in the class through a 40-step exercise on the day I visited. The desks were pushed aside, and a line split the room in half.
>
> Ciafullo asked the students to be silent but honest in stepping to the side of the room with windows if a question applied to their upbringing, heritage or actions. Ciafullo and Stillman also asked after each public disclosure for the men and women to look at those who crossed the line and at those who hadn't.
>
> "What are you thinking, what are you feeling and how has your situation influenced you?" the instructors asked. Initially the questions were easy. Students were asked whether they were raised Protestant. All but four crossed to the other side of the room.
>
> Questions on Muslim and Jewish faiths brought no movement. But one person crossed the line when Ciafullo asked whether anyone was raised in a nondenominational faith. Another crossed when quizzed on being Mormon or a member of the Reorganized Church of Jesus Christ of Latter Day Saints.
>
> Three crossed when Ciafullo asked whether anyone grew up in a

single-parent or divorced family.

Stillman said he noticed some shock and hesitancy when students were asked whether they were gay or knew someone who is. But the question produced a near universal response with all but three students crossing the line.

Four crossed when asked whether they'd been the victim of sexual orientation slurs. But 11 crossed admitting they had used such slurs on others.

"It forces us to think and to do some self-introspection and look and see how we operate in our own circles," said Ariane Fikki, a freshman anthropology major.

Fourteen students crossed when asked whether they'd been told they were stupid or dumb. Twelve moved when asked whether they'd been put down because of their ability.

A sign of our changing times was reflected in nine students revealing they'd dated interracially. A near universal response was in 16 crossing when asked whether they'd suffered discrimination because of their age.

Thirteen women crossed when asked whether they'd been victims of gender slurs. But two women and one man didn't move when students were asked whether they'd used such hateful words.

Eleven moved in the mostly white class when asked whether they'd been victims of racial or ethnic slurs. But 12 also crossed the line when quizzed on whether they had used racial or ethnic slurs on others.

Stillman and Ciafullo pointed out after the exercise that several persons had been both victims and perpetrators of slurs even though they knew the pain that such words cause. The instructors quoted Malcolm X who said, "Wrong is wrong no matter who says or does it."

I saw pain, sympathy and empathy in the faces of the students.

For victims, racism is perpetual and every instance represents "a death by a thousand cuts," Ciafullo said.

"How many of us have done something in life we're not proud of?" Ciafullo asked. The beauty of being human is we have the potential to learn from such mistakes.

"Nobody is perfect, but awareness, folks, is the first step to figure out where we need to go," he said. "The true test is living it every day."

Ryan Pettengill, a senior economics major, said because of the class he no longer tolerated putdowns. "Now I say something," he said.

That's the difference that all of us can exercise in helping to make our community better and America a more perfect union.

Students also can be enthralled with and moved by the stories that history shares. They listen intently and pick up the lessons that will help them fight the bigotry and prejudice they might encounter in the future. Both adults and young people benefit from the history-rich dialogue.

<u>From "Author's visit sparks next generation of readers"</u>

Sena Jeter Naslund sat on the edge of her seat in the library of Grandview High School in Grandview, Mo., and leaned forward, moving her still closer to the students.

The teens inhaled every word from the national best-selling author of *Four Spirits*. The students in Dana Dixon's creative writing class and Karyl Michel's junior English research and composition class had read Naslund's novel.

She spoke to them as part of the Pen/Faulkner Writers in Schools Program in which visiting authors discuss their books with students in schools in Washington, Chicago, Atlanta, Detroit and Kansas City.

Pat Wells, Kansas City coordinator of Pen/Faulkner, said the goal of the Ford Motor Co. funded project is to get teens excited about reading and writing. "It's to develop the next generation of readers and writers by getting students engaged in reading," she said.

The students see that the authors draw from events in their own lives and are motivated to write on the same world, national and local events that affect the students. Naslund explained in her Southern drawl that the "four spirits" in her book are the four black girls who died in the Sept. 15, 1963, bombing of the Sixteenth Street Baptist Church in Birmingham, Ala.

Naslund said she was a "nerdy, socially inept college student" then.

"I knew the world was changing around me," Naslund said. "But at the time life still seemed very ordinary."

She said her book attempts "to interweave the ordinary with the highly unusual." But Naslund, a Distinguished Teaching professor at the University of Louisville, said the book kicked around inside of her for years before she felt compelled to write it.

What motivated her was a front-page newspaper story she saw in the 1990s when she was in Sydney, Australia, on a tour for another book. The news story told of two men, Thomas Blanton Jr., 65, and Bobby Frank Cherry, 73, who were to be tried for the fatal church bombing.

Naslund said the past "reached half way around the world, reached back four decades and grabbed my heart and squeezed." She said for authors that feeling is irresistible. "This is the book that you always set out to write," Naslund said.

But she told the students that the success of earlier novels gave her the confidence to take on *Four Spirits*. "The book satisfied something that started in me a long time ago," Naslund said.

The book captures the faith and courage of the civil rights workers who met violence with nonviolent resistance. People changed.

"I think when things happen they do have repercussions for people spiritually," Naslund said. The lives of four girls - Addie Mae Collins, Carole Robertson, Cynthia Wesley, all 14, and Denise McNair, 11 - were taken by a senseless act of domestic terrorism in a city that many called "Bombingham."

"It was an unfair, unjust kind of system then," Naslund said of the 20th-century racism and discrimination against African-Americans. It projected an embarrassing image of America to the world as this country was pointing to the Soviets as the worst oppressors.

"It was a terrible image and terrible publicity during the Cold War," Naslund said. Students questioned her about why she wrote about that troubled period in American history.

Naslund said: "There was the element of guilt. When I look back at those times I wish I had done more."

She said the book is her response, blending fiction and fact to give people a new understanding of that difficult era in American history. The nation emerged better than it was before.

"This book is not just a description of a tragedy, this book is a description of triumph," she said. "Civil rights are not where they should be, but they are so much better than they were when I was your age."

A recurring theme in the book is violence doesn't work as a way to resolve conflicts.

Michel and Dixon said Naslund's visit made reading her book richer. The students said they enjoyed interacting with her.

"The author was wonderful," said Raisa Akram, a junior. "I loved her presence."

Chris Garcia, a junior, agreed: "It's not every day you get to meet one of your favorite authors."

"I want to read some more of her books," Justin Castro, a senior, said.

No one could ask for a better outcome from the Pen/Faulkner program.

The segregation of the 1960s has resurfaced as a horrifying element in schools today. But what's lost when the community surrenders to such oppression and no one speaks up with outrage?

From "Scrape away segregation to reveal diversity"

Winter always brings back some of my best childhood memories of long walks on frosty mornings to a storefront bakery in St. Louis.

The large, single-pane display window was always frosted, so no one could see the fresh cakes, pies, breads, doughnuts and other pastries. But people knew they were there, and many folks like me ventured inside.

I realize now the bakery was a lot like America. This country contains a delectable diversity in people and talent. However, segregation stands as the frosted glass, preventing us from seeing the goodness within.

That analogy could've been in the report by the Civil Rights Project at Harvard University. It released its study on the eve of the Rev. Martin Luther King Jr.'s 75th birthday and just months before the 50th anniversary of the Supreme Court's Brown v. Topeka Board of Education decision outlawing legal segregation.

The report titled "Brown at 50: King's Dream or the Plessy Nightmare" said gains were made. But in the last 10 years after court-ordered desegregation ended in many districts "there has been a major increase in segregation." Schools now are where they were about 1969.

That was the year I went from a mostly black grade school to an overwhelmingly white high school. But back then people wanted the great American experiment called integration to work.

They were chiseling away at segregation, giving people of color new opportunities in the great bakery called America. But efforts to end affirmative action and desegregation have chilled progress.

The effect has been the vast majority of African-American and Hispanic children are in intensely segregated schools and live in crushing poverty. Racial isolation condemns them to unequal education and diminished opportunities. "Students in segregated minority schools face conditions that students in segregated white schools seldom experience," the report said.

It cited the Kansas City desegregation case, saying between 1992 and 2001, black students' exposure to white classmates fell from 22 percent to 9 percent. In Kansas City, Kan., the drop was from 32.9 percent to 19.5 percent.

The nation is reverting back to the 1896 Plessy v. Ferguson Supreme Court ruling, which made segregation and separate but equal facilities the law of the land. But separate has never been equal for people of color.

Segregation remains the frosted glass keeping us from seeing the true goodness of America's diversity.

The report said, "Two of the clearest lessons of Brown and the entire civil rights experience are that segregation does not work and achieving desegregation requires explicit and enduring commitment." The study offered several solutions for a warmer, more progressive America, including:

Appointing judges and civil rights enforcement officials who know the Supreme Court was right in the Brown case "and that the job is far from over."

Naming a presidential commission to map steps to depolarize metro areas and build multiracial harmony.

Providing federal aid for multicultural curricula, multiracial schools and efforts to improve race relations.

Recruiting more students of color into the education profession.

Using housing subsidies more effectively to give low-income families access to middle-class schools.

Offering financial incentives and positive recognition to suburban schools that accept minority students from segregated schools.

Explaining to all Americans that white children also gain from integration.

Such things would clear away the bigotry, prejudices, discrimination and segregation in America. As the minority population grows, people must see that we live and work better together in multiracial schools and communities.

Like the bakery of my youth, the goodness is inside. But we have to let everyone see it so they'll step in and enjoy the richness of America's diversity.

Education offers people the opportunity to repair the damage of generations of bigotry. It is the best hope of stopping prejudice, racism and discrimination in their tracks. However, reversing racism won't be easy. John McKenzie set up a Web site for what he has called the Recovering Racist Network (www.rrnet.org). McKenzie believes that because we live in a country steeped in racism we can't help but be negatively affected by it. It is so pervasive in this country and so denied that it is like alcoholism or a drug addiction. We therefore need a program to recover from it. The first step toward recovery is to admit that you have a problem, and we have a problem in America. The teachings of the Baha'i Faith offer some solutions.

<u>From "A lasting challenge for us all"</u>

The Baha'i Faith is built on unity, equality, the elimination of prejudice and the end of extreme wealth and poverty.

The Baha'i sponsor a nine-week Institute for the Healing of Racism. One session happened to take place in a stone church built in the 1800s in the Rosedale area of Kansas City, Kan., a town where the underground railroad more than a century ago carried slaves to freedom.

Back then Kansas was a free territory and later a free state. It had been the home of some famous Abolitionists such as John Brown.

The free workshop, however, didn't attracted many people. Part of the problem involves getting people to give two hours per session of their free time.

But there's another catch. It amounts to a reality check for liberals.

You see, the Baha'i believe that everyone is born free of prejudice, but that we all eventually become infected with racism. It surfaces in racist jokes, negative feelings, being domineering, being fearful and preventing kids from playing with children of other races, said Vernon Pitchlyn of Kansas City, Kan., who led the workshop with Mark Zipf of Lenexa.

"We're all infected," said Barb McAtee of Overland Park, who attended the session with her son, Parviz Campbell.

Campbell said: 'But no one admits to themselves that they might be infected whether it's gross or subtle. Everyone wants to put on a banner that says I'm not a racist."

He laughed, saying, "This is hell on a liberal."

With videotapes, handouts and group rap sessions the workshop gave people the tools to cope with the infection.

In that way it helped people keep the disease in remission, and the number of racism survivors spreads. These are folks who don't want new flare-ups to occur and who want to unsaddle hate groups.

"We feel that dealing with racism is going to be an ongoing process," said Zipf. "We're going to have to deal with it our entire lifetime.

"We're doing this so future generations won't have to deal with racism."

Pitchlyn said everyone must work together to bandage racism's wounds and prevent new sores from developing.

"We also believe that racism is a spiritual disease, and that we must turn to a divine power to assist in the healing," Zipf said.

It helps to impress upon others how the stereotypes that underlie bigotry are untrue. One way stereotypes are being combated is by ridding standardized tests of biased material, images, and wording. As a solution, it seems so obvious, but for years it had been overlooked. In 1996 and again in 2005 I was part of a team of people from different professions and backgrounds who evaluated material destined for Missouri's standardized tests.

From "Bias in test is a) Unwanted, b) Ending, c) Both of the above"

COLUMBIA - The exhaustive process accompanies the Show-Me Standards exams. The tests gauge elementary, middle and high school students' knowledge and performance in math, science, communications arts, social studies, fine arts and health/physical education.

It's part of the Outstanding Schools Act of 1993, which sets high expectations for students' academic performance. Students will have to do more than answer multiple-choice questions. In some parts students will have to write how they got their answers.

"It's to determine what the students know and can do," said Jim Friedebach, director of assessment for the Missouri Department of

Elementary and Secondary Education.

But requiring more of students also has raised the bar for the state. Officials have worked with CTB/McGraw-Hill, a well-known test developer, and Missouri teachers to design the exams.

I joined business and community leaders, students and educators of different races and genders from cities and rural areas to test the test for biases and to determine whether the themes are "relevant to Missouri students."

It's like *The Kansas City Star's* mission of building diversity into the pages of the newspaper and keeping stereotypes and biases from getting in the way of the news.

The state wanted us to bleed the new exams of gender, racial, ethnic, religious, age, political and other biases so that they test students' abilities without hanging youngsters up on prejudices. It was the first time Missouri has done this, Friedebach said. But it followed new industry standards.

We split into elementary, middle and high school groups and spent the day studying stacks of really tough math problems.

"Every person's opinion in here counts and should be heard," said E. Lynn Holley-Green, CTB senior development manager.

No one held back in the middle school group I was in. We found that although math is about numbers, biases inadvertently factor their way into word problems.

One mentioned a "new housing project." Harold Player, St. Louis School District supervisor of personnel services, said that would have negative connotations for minorities. We suggested that "housing project" be changed to "housing construction."

Another problem had students delivering packages on bicycles. Marilyn Jones, a Boonville middle school math teacher, said children had such jobs where she lived. But urban folks like me said such tasks were rare in cities. Putting the character in a van solved our problem and made the scenario inclusive of people with disabilities.

David Lankford, Missouri Chamber of Commerce vice president, noticed boys seated at both heads of a table with six persons. We changed it so that a girl was at one end and a boy at the other.

Other revisions included making names gender-neutral. Streets and schools already included Truman and Ozarks as Missouri standards. But we added Martin Luther King Jr., Cesar Chavez and Ella Fitzgerald to build more diversity into the test.

"This is making me appreciate what the state has to do to make the tests fair," Jones said.

"It puts the real world in the exams," Player said.

> "I enjoyed it, and I learned a lot," said Steve Duncan, a Jefferson City banker.
>
> Missouri's diverse population is a natural resource for students.

It was good to see a few years later that the state had not abandoned its efforts to try to rid its standardized tests of bias and that it was relying on a diverse group of Missouri residents to help.

Certainly the three Rs are of utmost importance, and U.S. schools often do not make a good showing when compared with schools in other industrialized countries. But young people have been given a steady diet of monocultural information, which often kills their desire to learn, rather than stimulating their curiosity. Presenting a greater variety of cultures and viewpoints in textbooks and tests is one way to pull disinterested students back to learning. And when schools incorporate multicultural curricula to engage students, society benefits now and into the future. Active use of multicultural curricula also helps students discover and accept the Real America in spite of prevailing efforts to shut down that discussion. Teaching openness and going beyond tolerance are best.

People slowly and reluctantly are awakening to the fact that Muslims are part of America, too. Some Muslims were kidnapped and brought here from Africa as slaves. Others are immigrants or first- or second-generation Americans. It has taken a tragedy to get people to see that.

From "Fear keeps chipping away at freedoms in this country"

> A beautiful, 8-inch-wide collage of American flags flowed across each white table top at the Heartland Muslim Council dinner.
>
> The wide ribbons of love, respect and honest patriotism for this nation filled the program at the University of Missouri-Kansas City.
>
> Those wonderful feelings were built into the theme, "Getting Ready for the Muslim Vote in 2006." I expect them to play a winning role in elections.
>
> Ahmed Fannun Kanan, community bank director of Commerce Bank in Joplin and real estate developer, got the diverse audience to its feet when he cheered America and encouraged everyone to love this country. "Put both feet down in this country" not one in Palestine, India or Egypt and the other in America, said Kanan, who received the council's Community Leader Award.
>
> "You create your America," said Kanan, who helped build the Islamic Center of Greater Kansas City and a Muslim cemetery nearby. He served in the National Guard to "protect the United States. I love this country."
>
> He urged people to be proud of their religion and their heritage. Praying five times a day benefits him and other Muslims because they know they can't do wrong when they are facing God.

"You live in a free country," he said. "Don't worry about a thing."

Then-Jackson County Executive Katheryn J. Shields added to Kanan's rousing speech, saying we live in a time when elected officials and other leaders must show courage. "Our nation is being overwhelmed with fear," Shields said.

It is paralyzing the United States socially and economically and exceeds any rational elements of danger. Violent crime has declined steadily for 20 years, yet people feel petrified in their homes and neighborhoods, Shields said.

She blamed it on television and other media, which give people the sense that crime is at epidemic proportions. The "fantasy of fear" affects our society in real ways.

Muslims have felt the brunt of Americans' fear since the Sept. 11, 2001, terrorist attacks. Many have been looked upon and treated as if they are the enemy. They've lost civil liberties, and no doubt, many were the targets when President Bush allowed domestic eavesdropping without court approval.

Fear affects how Americans behave and how they allocate resources, Shields said. She talked about the proliferation of guns, which people carry, have in their homes and in their vehicles.

Guns give such folks a sense of safety even though firearms increase the likelihood that they will be used in suicides and to kill a family member or friend. "Fearful people demand more laws and harsher penalties regardless of the effectiveness or ineffectiveness of such efforts," Shields said.

Elected officials comply. In the 1990s, billions of dollars went into building new prisons instead of more schools, roads and factories.

Tuition and fees went up at state universities, putting education more out of reach of working families. Highways and other public structures keep deteriorating while our civil liberties are getting hacked up.

Metal detectors in schools and government buildings are monuments to lost liberties. More people are undergoing intrusive searches.

Shields said, "They do create an illusion of protection while generating an atmosphere of fear."

Shields said Benjamin Franklin warned that people who sacrifice liberties for safety deserve neither. "How much is fear costing us?" she asked. Is it a hidden tax of 2 percent or 5 percent adding no real value?

"How much does a fear tax act as a drag on our global competitiveness?" Shields asked. "What is the psychological impact of always being afraid? I suspect that the answer will not be good news."

It's why U.S. leaders need "to exercise some personal courage and not be panicked into seeing criminals or terrorists behind every bush.

They must vote their judgment," Shields said.

"Remember that the star-spangled banner can wave over the land of the free only so long as we remain the home of the brave," she said.

Mahnaz Shabbir, president of the council, told people that "on the other side of fear is hope." That spirit must prevail.

Denial, however, filled the feedback.

E-mail: Dec. 21, 2005

I must say I have been reading your columns for many years now and several questions come to my mind after finishing each and every one of them.

First, where do you find all these groups with the far out names? The Heartland Muslim Council? Lewis, I think I speak for 99% of your readers, nobody cares. Believe it or not, most folks see good in the world. Each day is not filled with fear, bigotry and hate. People live everyday trying to make it better than the day before. When is the last time you wrote a article that did not cover the plight of the Blackman, the Mexican, the Muslim or how whites are keeping them down and slowing their progression. I don't get it Lewis. What's your point?

As far as loss of civil liberties. You make a couple of interesting points. First, quoting Katheryn Shields as saying our country is overwhelmed with fear. Maybe not the country but certainly Kansas City. What's that murder count in KC this year? Maybe Katheryn should worry more about her county and it's biggest city and spend a little less time at dinners for the Heartland Muslim Council.

Finally, I know one of your pet peeves is the metal detectors at school, you have written several times about it. Instead of arguing the point, let me leave you one thought. I don't think public schools in Olathe or Blue Valley or DeSoto or Gardner or Spring Hill have them. No, they are mainly in inner cities, like Kansas City. Gee, that's the place with the record murder rate this year.

You tell me this is an assault on civil liberties. I tell you it is just another attempt to keep the Blackman down.

E-mail: Dec. 21, 2005

K. Shields needs therapy if she truly believes "our nation is being overwhelmed by fear". If the audience swallowed that line of reasoning they, too, need help.

Assistance in overcoming bigotry often comes from young people who are different. They are not as afraid of America's diversity. Their lack of inhibitions is part of the solution to overcoming the barriers.

From "A multitude of ways for diversity discussions"

Jeff Shehan said people should abandon their fears of others.

At Johnson County Community College in Johnson County, Kansas, a panel of young adults spoke of how much diversity is valued there and how to gain more from it. Students Jeremy Jones, Haydee Leon-Muñoz, Jeff Shehan and Natalia Garzon, an employee at the college, spoke during the "Breaking Down Stereotypes" program in March of 2002.

Jones is African-American. Muñoz is from Mexico. Garzon is from Peru. Shehan was with the Gay, Lesbian, Bisexual Student Union.

Society should be more open now than in the past and offer more opportunities for women, minorities and gays. But life isn't perfect.

Jones said black students often felt left out. Inclusion also is tied to one's socioeconomic status.

Shehan said gay, lesbian and bisexual students still detected some negative reactions toward them.

"There's too much fear for it to be perfect or near perfect," he said. "Everyone tries hard to make others feel comfortable, but at the same time, people are afraid, and that's where a lot of hurt comes in."

Jones said he sometimes contended with people who don't think he's black enough.

"Now I've gotten to the point where I just don't care," he said. "This is the way I am."

Henry Gueary III, then-president of the Olathe branch of the NAACP, made some good points. "We are all Americans. We all have to find ways to bridge our differences," said Gueary, who was on a second panel at Johnson County Community College called "Diversity Dialogue."

Others with him were Jessica Dumas, then a community builder with Kansas City Harmony; Robert K. Murphy, a counselor at the community college; Dick Vallandingham, director of student development; and Jeremy Jones, a student.

Dumas and Vallandingham agreed that progress occurs when people who are different share their stories and work together.

That doesn't come without risks, Murphy said. "But it's a risk that can enrich your life," he added.

Waking up to awareness

People won't see what individuals have to face until they have to walk a mile in others' moccasins as Harper Lee describes in her book, *To Kill a Mockingbird*. They must allow themselves to become able to empathize with others whose experiences are different in order to discover the Real America in others' tragedies and triumphs. Curiosity should drive the journey. Whenever I myself venture into parts of the undiscovered country that were unknown to me before—and of whose existence I was only vaguely aware—I am humbled by what I learn and experience.

From "A personal glimpse into the hardship of a disability"

The cries of an infant caught my ear as I boarded the packed Troost Avenue bus at 18th Street and with Yvonne Page and Lara Sander.

I know how that baby felt – helpless. Page and I were among the 150 persons, 23 of them students, who learned what it was like to live with a disability.

Page, with the Coalition for Independence, and I wore goggles that simulated a severe case of cataracts. We could only see blurred light and vague shadows.

"The goal is to increase the awareness of the general population to the contributions and skills of people with disabilities," said Janice Kelly, then-director of the Mayor's Office on Disabilities. The agency sponsored the seventh annual event with the Kansas City Area Transportation Authority's Share-A-Fare Program.

Sander, independent living counselor with the Coalition for Independence, guided Page and me from 1200 E. 18th St. to the Metro bus stop on Troost. She cautioned us about the uneven sidewalk and grass that protruded.

I never would have given that a second thought, but I quickly learned that without the benefit of sight, the bad sidewalk was an obstacle that could have sent me tumbling. I gripped Sander's right arm while Page clutched her left arm.

We rode the bus because many people with disabilities must depend on the Metro. "But transportation is the number one barrier to finding work in this area," Sander said.

"They just have no way to get from their home to their jobs. There is almost always a job that fits the person, but there's no way to get there. Or a lot of times you find a business, but there's no way to get to the person's house."

We got on the bus, but because it was full it could not accommodate some of the people in wheelchairs in our group.

"If a group of people in wheelchairs wanted to go somewhere together, it's difficult for them," Sander said.

Hearing voices of people talking without seeing faces was offputting. We also had to stand. Sander helped me find poles to grab as the moving bus lurched us about.

At 31st Street we transferred onto a second bus and rode it to Prospect Avenue, where we entered the Lucile Bluford Branch Library. Our simulation included getting a library card and a brochure of an upcoming event.

That meant I had to give my driver's license to the librarian and answer questions for the necessary paperwork. In the world without sight, trust is everything. But that blind trust is disconcerting, too.

Yet this is the way some people must live. I have a new respect for those sight-impaired individuals who get around in our community and are productive, even though our environment is less than accommodating for them.

At the library, someone offered to show me around the facility. I said that sounded like humor from the sighted world.

Page and I sat down at a table to talk. I managed to take notes despite the vision impairment. She said wearing the goggles helped her more clearly realize the difficulties of sight-impaired people.

"Our world is not open to people with disabilities," Page said. "I was having a difficult time just walking on the sidewalk.

"There was a sense of fear. If I was alone without sight, who would be sensitive enough to help?"

Even getting on the bus would have been nearly impossible if Sander had not been there to tell us when to step from the curb to the bus, where to hold on to the rail and when to hand our transfers to the driver. Sander helped us catch two buses back to where we started.

"There is a lot to be done to make this world disabled-accessible," Page said. "I feel that those who are visually impaired have the right to be as mobile as someone who is sighted."

It is important, because as the baby boom generation ages, cataracts will affect its vision. So will the growing incidence of diabetes. By aiding people with disabilities now, we're actually helping ourselves in the future.

Our words matter. They either build others up or tear them down. People with disabilities feel the sting. Individuals with mental illness are all too familiar with the explosive words that scream about society's stigma.

From "Tear down this wall of words" and "Kind words can douse fire of hate"

Fred Frese has gotten me to watch my language.

He did it in a speech at an Alliance for the Mentally Ill of Greater Kansas City banquet and again in Jefferson City on Mental Health Awareness Day.

The psychologist and second vice president of the National Alliance for the Mentally Ill said he's not at all fond of the way "chronically normal people" talk.

When horrible things happen, such as the bombings in Centennial Olympic Park, Atlanta, Ga., and on TWA Flight 800, people always label those responsible crazy, nuts, insane or wacko.

"If you fall into the category of 'crazy' you are immediately excluded from the entire operation of society," Frese said. "That which is 'insane' is removed from the community of us good people and put into the loony bin."

Frese and others say it's time to end such language.

The National Alliance for the Mentally Ill has started a campaign to sensitize people to mental illness. About 150 mental health consumers added to the effort at St. John's Conference Center at a self-help, anti-stigma forum called "Self-Advocacy: A Wide Spectrum."

"It's not acceptable to refer to us as wackos and in mean terms," said Frese, who has been hospitalized suffering mental illness. "We're going to change things so that mental illness will be considered like other chronic medical disorders like diabetes and heart disease."

The notion complements SuEllen Fried's Stop Violence Coalition efforts to "gentle-ize" the language. She and others advocate removing attack terms and violentspeak from the way we talk to each other.

"It's going to involve so much of a change in attitude, a change in the way we handle our rage, pain, anger and actions," she said. "It's such a significant way to start, because so much of the violence in arson, homicide or rape very frequently is tied into words."

People use mean and hateful words to belittle others and make them feel powerless. Retaliation often results in a one-upmanship of more vicious words until the flames of anger burn out of control.

Everyone must pledge to "gentle-ize" the language and search for substitute words to convey hurt or pain. Our conversations must put retaliation on ice and strive for solutions.

But making that happen will be like teaching people how to talk again.

That's because hatespeak is "in." Nasty one-liners and cutting remarks also fill the media.

Language instead should reflect the civility, restraint, manners and etiquette of humanity, Fried said. People should be very afraid that attack language will lead to more violence.

"It's in our own best interest to put peaceful, gentle language out there," Fried said. "The more we initialize it, the more we respond that way."

More people must become "weather changers," Fried said.

"Someone in an angry argument has the opportunity to change the atmosphere or to become the nonvolatile person," Fried said.

"Gentle-izing" the language would create a new and enduring energy of peace and safety for people everywhere.

Frese's push to change the language that uses words that are hateful to the mentally ill is equally important because some bills became law in Missouri making it harder for people who are criminally mentally ill to leave state care. But only a fraction of mental health consumers are criminal.

"We are not dangerous, killing, maiming maniacs that we are perceived as being in the media," Frese said. Thirty years ago, more than 500,000 people with mental illness were in state hospitals. Today there are fewer than 70,000.

Better medication, counseling and community treatment centers have enabled people like Frese to lead normal, productive lives.

"This is the best time in history to be a person with mental illness," Frese said. "We have much to contribute to society now that we have been freed from the asylums and institutions.

"The message is that treatment works! We consumers need to take the lead in speaking for ourselves and let the chronically normal establishment see us as fellow human beings."

Community Activities

The "chronically normal establishment" often forgets that people who represent the diversity in America also should receive all of the constitutional benefits and other privileges that come with living in this country. Reminding everyone of this has to be part of the solutions to making diversity work in our society.

From "A rare rewarding vacation"

People like me who have vacations take them for granted.

Nine adults with mental illnesses helped me see that. They traveled to St. Louis and stayed overnight.

It was their first vacation, and to them the experience was glorious.

Jerry Armstrong helped pilot the trip. At that time he was the consumer weekend drop-in center supervisor for Network Rehabilitation Services for People with Mental Illness. He also was vice president of the Ark of Friends of Greater Kansas City Inc., a mental health consumers advocacy group.

Armstrong explained that many "mental health consumers" never get a vacation. The brain diseases they suffer and poverty trap them in this town.

Many people like them don't have cars. They can't jet away on food stamps or do Section 8 time-sharing with people in other cities.

They just get by, said Sybil Noble, then-president and founder of the Ark.

The Network weekend drop-in center in Kansas City changed that by financing the out-of-town vacation for consumers.

I asked Armstrong to keep a travelogue. A lot of good things stood out.

The tour group steered around fast-food places, eating only at family restaurants in trendy parts of town. If only for the weekend, Armstrong vowed to free them of cheap burgers and fries.

But that created new challenges. Some of the travelers had never been to nice restaurants or ordered from menus.

Staying at a hotel also was new to many in the group. Lillie Belle Phillips and Vivion Johnson marveled at having cable TV in their room and stayed up all night sampling the cornucopia of channels and programs.

But before turning in for the night, the group had dinner at an Italian restaurant, walked through St. Louis' refurbished Union Station and enjoyed seeing workers there make fudge at one of the shops. They drove by the Arch and cruised through downtown and Laclede's Landing.

They also drove by St. Louis State Hospital to see what it looked like compared with mental hospitals on this side of the state, where some in the group had received treatment.

On the second day they checked out of the suburban hotel, had breakfast, visited Forest Park, the St. Louis Science Center and the St. Louis Zoo. They had lunch outdoors at a Central-West End cafe and dessert at a St. Charles ice cream parlor before heading back to Kansas City.

Service everywhere was great. Armstrong said one member of the group, who is homeless in Kansas City, said he wanted to stay in St. Louis to get away from the "panhandlers, street punks, hustlers, drug dealers and con artists."

"I'm scared of my own shadow here in Kansas City," said the man, who asked that his name not be used. "The trip to St. Louis was the best trip I've ever been on."

The travelers especially appreciated being treated like adults, which is something that Network Rehab does well.

"A lot of times they are treated like children," Noble said. "They don't need that."

Vacations enrich the lives of Rehab's consumers, leaving them feeling more confident, independent and connected with the community, said Jane Van Sant, then-executive director of Network Rehab. "It stretches them," she said.

I hope the trips continue so that more people with mental illness can enjoy the fruits of life that people like me regularly get to enjoy.

Housing also is a monumental problem for people with disabilities. Unless special design efforts are made, folks who become disabled find themselves locked out of their own homes.

From "Enabling homes and people"

A longtime friend whom I saw at the Rehabilitation Institute reinforced the importance of a meeting I attended there.

My friend had lost a leg to diabetes and was undergoing rehabilitation as many people have at the institute since it opened in 1947. The invaluable service returns people to the community at the highest level of function possible. But it sometimes opens huge doors of big problems for people like my friend.

Many of them leave the institute for homes that are no longer accessible to them. They find stairs they can't climb, bathrooms they can't use, bedrooms they can't enter and kitchens where items are out of reach.

That demand for more accessible homes triggered the startup of the Universal Design Housing Project. Paul H. Levy, coordinator of Independent Living Services and founder of Whole Person Inc., is the chairman of the housing project.

A project committee met for weeks ahead of the ground breaking. The first universal design home is a Habitat for Humanity house at 3520 Michigan Ave.

Mike Davenport, executive director of Kansas City Habitat for Humanity, said he welcomed the group and the concept for some of this area's Habitat homes. "I'm excited about them coming to work with us," he said.

Some officers in the Kansas City Police Department helped build the first house. The police officers also found the occupants of the 1,200-square-foot, one-story, three-bedroom home.

"I love the concept," Officer Jennifer Wolf said. "What we're hoping is that will become the standard so that anyone can live in a Habitat home."

A universal design home costs 2 percent to 5 percent more than a conventional house, said Kris Lancaster, regional affairs specialist with the U.S. Department of Health and Human Services and a member of the housing committee. This puts the total price at more than $50,000.

To rehabilitate an existing home to be accessible to a person with disabilities would run $15,000 to $20,000. Often, however, people who need to make the changes lack the resources.

Universal design housing eliminates the need to retrofit homes for the changing needs of people who have suffered illnesses, accidents or injuries or who, because of age, can't enjoy their residences anymore.

Some of the features of the houses include no-step entryways, front-loading washers and dryers, slip resistant flooring in the kitchen and baths, safer water controls on showers and tubs, a wide tub edge for safety, doorways that are a minimum of 36 inches wide and hallway widths of 48 inches. The emphasis is on safety, convenience and comfort.

Levy calls the changes he'd like for all new homes "revolutionary."

"People are fixed into the current housing designs," he said. "It's going to be difficult to sell.

"But it's the future. It's hard to sell the future to people unless you can relate it directly to them."

The committee plans to do that by showing people that as they age and change or because of unforeseen circumstances, the universal design home will accommodate their needs. "More people are catching on to the concept," Lancaster said.

Committee members are selling the concept to others. "If you're in this home, you'll never have to leave this home," said Larry R. Washington, neighborhood preservation initiative, then-director with Kansas City Neighborhood Alliance.

"It makes life itself a little richer," said DeBorah D. Williams, then-director of finance and development with the Kansas City Department of Housing and Community Development. As the population continues to age, universal design homes will grow in attractiveness and popularity. Young people will want them, too.

"I think it's an idea whose time has come," said Janice M. Kelly, then-director of the Mayor's Office on Disabilities. Such homes promote human interaction and productivity.

Kelly shared one other thought. She said people with disabilities, just like everyone else, want the opportunities to enjoy their share of the American dream, a home they can live in and savor.

Women play a big role in creating new trails to discovering the Real America. During Women's History Month in March 2002, former U.S. Rep. Patricia Schroeder of Colorado spoke at the University of Missouri Kansas City, where each year the Starr Symposium is held. Schroeder told her audience to delve into the diversity of history and not exclude women. Women represent a huge part of the diversity in America and have often struggled shoulder-to-shoulder with men. Schroeder learned from her 1988 presidential run that the media frequently don't report the stories of women's triumphs and challenges. And women's voices often go unheard.

For example, women have great urban design ideas for America's cities. People just have to listen. Special forums enable women's solutions to surface.

From "Shaping our neighborhoods humanely"

An old idea got a new life at the Starr Symposium on "Making a Woman-Friendly Kansas City." But the notion may seem way out of place in the south Kansas City area.

Several speakers told audiences at the University of Missouri-Kansas City of developments that feature "an urban village" style of living. The idea is to plan communities with ample parks, green space, community centers, public art, businesses, services and even farmers' markets.

Neighborhoods with sidewalks would interlock with well-lighted streets. All traffic patterns in the area would be safe for men, women and children without roads being too wide and heavily traveled or too narrow, deserted and intimidating.

Schools, churches and stores would be conveniently located so people could walk to them, and mass transit would be accessible. Public transportation also would accommodate women's needs to make multiple stops for trips to stores, day care and work instead of the traditional one-stop commutes to jobs.

That would connect neighborhoods and give people a greater sense of community, said Shelley R. Poticha, executive director of the Congress for the New Urbanism, based in San Francisco.

That's not what we have now in the south Kansas City area. Mass transit is almost non-existent.

A tangle of subdivision streets that aren't interconnected feed onto main arteries and then to highways. Traffic is congested, and the few main roads and highways are unsafe for bicycles and pedestrians.

Streets also are a twisted twilight zone of cul-de-sacs, dead ends and short drives. Hardly anyone at gas stations can give directions to every neighborhood.

The multitudinous subdivisions are too confusing for people to decipher. Because many streets are unsafe and there are few sidewalks, kids have to be bused to school or depend on "mom taxis" for rides everywhere.

People are at the mercy of their cars, and heaven help any of us if our vehicles break down. We'd be more panicked and stranded than a Florida driver in a Minnesota snowstorm.

"Many of our regions are in a state of crisis in terms of making them viable into the 21st century," Poticha said. "We haven't taken care of our environmental systems, land use and how they relate."

People at the Starr Symposium were asked to grade the areas in which they live, and the south Kansas City area received some of the lowest marks. Vicki L. Noteis, then-director of Kansas City's Planning and Development Department, explained why during a panel discussion at the symposium.

"I think when you look at south Kansas City it's probably the toughest challenge out of these areas defined because it's all built," she said. "But much of it was built on a pattern that we've found to be not that healthy – especially for women.

"It isolates women. It was built on a suburban pattern when many women were at home and not in the work force, and the transportation systems were designed for male heads of households as commuters.

"That's much harder to fix than open land that has an opportunity to do it right and Midtown, which does have an urban village concept –always did. It just has to be revitalized."

Construction in the south Kansas City area occurred in the post-World War II era when urban sprawl was the rage. "We sort of graze and move on and eat up land in our region," Poticha said.

That pattern continues today. "We're using up much more land than we are growing in population," Poticha said. "We're also beginning to drive much more."

The good news is that city planners now realize that such development trends can't continue. That's why they're advocating the creation of urban villages for new communities.

Noteis said such "women friendly" ideas were incorporated into Kansas City's FOCUS plan, the first comprehensive design for the city in 50 years.

But that doesn't mean that people living in traditional Southland subdivisions are left out of this new FOCUS loop. The key for them is to create a greater sense of community through more interaction, women at the Starr Symposium said.

By getting to know their neighbors, people can bridge the physical barriers that traditional suburban neighborhood designs created. It's how our area will survive and thrive well into the 21st century.

Women share the same diversity concerns worldwide. Too often, Americans think it's only something that affects our mothers, sisters, aunts, friends and grandmothers here at home.

From "Erasing barriers for women"

About 150 people struggled to midwife the birth of a better world for women.

The daylong event was the University of Missouri-Kansas City Starr Symposium 1999 titled "Gender Equity, Development and Peace for the 21st Century." It was the first of 10 regional conferences that built toward a United Nations special session in New York called Beijing Plus Five.

"I think we have the potential in the 21st Century where women and men are equal partners in the eyes of the world," Linda Tarr-Whelan, U.S. ambassador to the United Nations Commission on the Status of Women, told the audience.

That global event reviewed the progress nations have made since the 1995 Fourth World Conference on Women in Beijing. This was the inspiring event in which then-first lady Hillary Rodham Clinton pronounced that "human rights are women's rights, and women's rights are human rights."

The Beijing platform identified 12 concerns blocking women's advancement worldwide. They included poor or no education and training, poverty, bad health care, AIDS, violence and too-few leadership roles.

Not everyone has been as progressive. Materials handed out at the conference told how the United States since 1979 has resisted ratifying the U.N. Convention on the Elimination of all Forms of Discrimination Against Women. (That remains an impediment to progress.)

A problem facing woman is poverty. Speakers said women and children constitute most of the people in poverty. U.S. women hold most of the minimum-wage jobs and overall earn only 76 cents for every dollar men make.

That affects their diet and nutrition as well their quality of housing, child care, transportation, access to a good education, health care and the life they can provide for their children. Poverty, inequality, domestic violence and discrimination also strip women of power and render them politically and economically voiceless.

That's not good for families, the country or the world. But people at the Starr Symposium also shared solutions that have helped women in this area and in other countries.

They include Kansas City area groups making loans to women enabling individuals to successfully start their own businesses and raise their families out of poverty. Other efforts involve a more holistic approach to improving women's health.

Innovative groups in the Kansas City area such as Girls to Women push girls toward math and science so they'll enter higher paying nontraditional careers as women.

Lenexa Police Chief Ellen Hanson was among speakers who stressed that women become allies, role models and mentors to each other. Women must work for change, embrace diversity, promote better communications, level the playing field and champion the causes that are important to women.

The old monocultural ways have resulted in many diversity issues going unaddressed. But the problems haven't gone away. If anything, ignoring the problems only leads to more angst, anger and frustration for those who are different.

<u>From "Repairing America: Everyone - not just African-Americans - would benefit from reparations" and "Wanted: Truth, reconciliation"</u>

People pushing for reparations now might approach cities and corporations to search their archives for records showing they profited from slavery. It's the latest in the growing legal tangle surrounding this hot-button issue.

That R-word, reparations, causes many blacks and whites to split along racial lines. A lot of African-Americans favor reparations.

To them, reparations are back pay for nearly 400 years of government-enforced slavery, Black Codes, Jim Crow laws, segregation and discrimination, which continue to enrich whites at blacks' expense. The issue is as old as slavery in the United States. The topic picked up speed in 1988 when the U.S. government apologized and gave $1.2 billion, or $20,000 each, to about 60,000 Japanese-Americans who were held in internment camps during World War II.

The reparations movement also gained from Swiss banks, which in 1998 agreed to a $1.25 billion settlement with Holocaust survivors. It shifted into high gear when an alliance of civil-rights and class-action lawyers, called the Reparations Assessment Group, said in November of 2001 that it was preparing a lawsuit seeking reparations for the descendants of slaves. Compensation amounts range from $1.4 trillion to $10 trillion.

Randall Robinson, in his book, *The Debt: What America Owes to Blacks*, wrote, "America's contemporary racial problems cannot be solved, racism cannot be arrested, achievement gaps cannot be fully closed until Americans - all Americans - are repaired in their views of Africa's role in history."

Thandi Nhlengetwa from Soweto, South Africa, who spent two years studying at the Unity School of Christianity in Lee's Summit, Mo., offered a South African solution to our American problem. Apartheid was a system of oppression in her homeland that was as reprehensible as slavery was in America.

Apartheid's enforcers in the 1950s established "Bantu" or a system of inferior education for blacks to limit them to menial jobs. Nhlengetwa and I are the same age, but apartheid made her part of "the lost generation."

Children of the lost generation became the most militant and enlightened people, rebelling against propaganda and oppression. As a university economics student, Nhlengetwa recalls being swept into the Soweto uprising in 1976.

"One of the areas of oppression was language," she said. Afrikaans was to replace the Zulu language. "They wanted us to use the language of the oppressor. That's when we said, 'No! Enough is enough!'"

The end of apartheid in 1994 was accompanied by what Nhlengetwa called "swart gevaar," or black danger. White people feared a black revenge that never happened.

Instead, South Africa set up the Truth and Reconciliation Commission, which enabled perpetrators and victims to tell their stories on national TV. People confessed and showed remorse to get amnesty.

As people were telling their stories, a lot of wounds were opened up, Nhlengetwa said. "There were some people who did not want to bear the discomfort of that. But people need to tell their stories.

"The victims need to tell their stories, and the perpetrators need to hear the stories. I think in telling the stories, healing can take place.

"It was so powerful. People broke down, but they were heard and they were listened to."

Now the perpetrators who victimized South Africa's black communities have been welcomed back to help rebuild those areas and make amends. "For some it brought a sense of closure, and it brought a sense of forgiving," Nhlengetwa said.

That is unlike America, where people deny or suppress the truth of continuing oppression. Nhlengetwa said the reparations movement here should include the South African cathartic process.

Instead of this nation being divided about who might get thousands of dollars, it could become unified by rebuilding black communities damaged by slavery, discrimination, racism and bigotry. African-Americans could be restored to wholeness.

"I think it is a process of trying to make peace with our past," Nhlengetwa said. "Racism hurts everybody."

However, black Americans can't even get an apology for atrocities endured since 1619.

Yet, Nhlengetwa said the world is waiting for the reparations outcome in the United States because similar debts from colonial oppression are owed to African nations and Africans worldwide.

"The United States has an opportunity to set an example for the rest of the world," she said.

But we have to overcome our own centuries of denial first.

Many whites, however, disagreed vehemently. The following e-mail and voice messages capture some of their outrage over reparations as well as many racist expressions.

E-mail: Sept. 17, 2002

Instead of begging for reparations, you people should be on your knees giving thanks for your good fortune, all courtesy of white-regulated social engineering.

E-mail: June 27, 2003

All reparations have been paid long ago. There will be no additional reparations. Africans have already accepted all the reparations they will ever receive. Since 1963 large cities in America have doubled the numbers of police officers in every metro area police department in an attempt to protect peace-loving white and black people from young African males. The added expense has been part of your "reparations."

Get real, Lewis. White people think the worst of black people not because we missed the very tiny part of world history attributable to Africans but because of black crime, AIDS, habits of black males, and over 100 years of handouts, which continue today in every metro area of this country.

I wonder what will help Africans shed the chains of repression? Most every nation on the African continent has been an embarrassment to the rest of the planet.

Factoid: Black people owe white families reparations for the 780,000 white people they have murdered in the past 100 years!

E-mail: June 27, 2003

My family owes black Americans an equal chance, and that is it. This reparations stuff is either welfare by a different name or blackmail. There certainly is no justification for my family or others like us to have our tax money stolen.

Voice Mail: June 27, 2003

I read your article in the paper this morning, and I'm nauseous thereafter. Why don't people like you work to improve the image of your race rather than looking for a free handout? It's just disgusting, and I do not think you are bettering your cause. You make me extremely.... I have absolutely no prejudice until I start reading things like this. I think you are hurting yourself. Goodbye.

Voice Mail: June 27, 2003

There are no African Americans. There are no European Americans. We're all Americans. You're either an American or you're not an American. You're not an African American, you're not a European American. Stop promoting this crap, this garbage for people in your articles. It's divisive. Start preparing articles that have more to do with people getting on with their lives together making it a better America. This is what I would like to see as a reader in *The Star.*

Such negative feedback is why Maril Crabtree surprised me. After a Kansas City Harmony Community Conversations meeting at her home, she said she as a white person deserves reparations because of what was done to African-Americans.

"The wounds of our history are still there under the rug," said Crabtree, a lawyer who had practiced in Johnson County and now is a writer and editor.

Former slaves supposedly were promised reparations of 40 acres and a mule after the Civil War. That never happened. Only in 2007 are some states such as Virginia, North Carolina and Maryland apologizing for slavery.

"As a white person I have been deprived of the contributions that could have been made by generations of black people who have been kept from learning how to read and have been struggling to catch up," Crabtree said. "I don't see how we can deny that. But we seem to be going backward."

Crabtree used Robinson's book to explain her claim for reparations.

Robinson wrote that the United States must pay a massive restitution "to America's only involuntary members. It must help to rebuild the black esteem it destroyed, by democratizing access to a trove of histories, near and ancient, to which blacks contributed seminally and prominently.

"It must open wide a scholarly concourse to the African ancients to which its highly evolved culture owes much credit and gives none. It must rearrange the furniture of its national myths, monuments, lores, symbols, iconography, legends and arts to reflect the contributions and sensibilities of all Americans.

"It must set afoot new values. It must purify memory. It must recast its lying face."

Crabtree said that would help repair the social isolation keeping the races from coming together.

She's right. Those kinds of reparations are more valuable than money.

Bigotry and lies have masked the truth of black people's contributions to world history, leaving many whites to think the worst of minorities.

Crabtree agrees with Robinson: There needs to be a cleansing in America to accompany reparations akin to South Africa's Truth and Reconciliation Commission.

Such truth-telling would make life better by washing away people's anger, hurt, fear and shame.

"Life would be a lot richer in terms of the emotional type of freedom that everyone would have and the freedom to bring their own style into full bloom," Crabtree said. "It's the freedom to be who you are without living in fear of Jim Crow and without being picked up because you're the wrong color.

" ... I'd like to see us be able to dream a future together instead of separately. But we have to be able to get together to understand each other's realities in order to be able to dream a future that can be different."

CHAPTER 13
What's Missing—Social Bridging

The Long Search

So many puzzle pieces of beautiful shapes, cuts and colors
Each tells wonderful stories of America's many others
Often overlooked, discarded and dismissed
As something to do without, but when missed
In the mosaic it's clear
The piece that's gone is the one most dear
Finding it becomes a mandate
Though our painful history is to obfuscate.
But knowing the truth makes the search a calling
To fill the void without falling
For the lies
That tell us not to believe our eyes
The piece we seek is somewhere near
Never give up searching without favor or fear.

We don't have to all think alike and we'll never all look alike. But we need to work together for a better tomorrow. I feel it's important to understand how people of color–especially Asians–are woven into the cloth that is American society.

~Gil Asakawa

One way to dissolve the troubles that whiteness causes is for people who are different to spend time with each other—not fighting but talking and doing constructive things together. It helps to build what Robert Putnam in his book, *Bowling Alone,* calls social capital. It's the sense of trust, faith, hope and community that grows when people share ideas or details about their lives. There is a greater feeling of togetherness and shared purpose, too. New ideas are hatched when people talk. Those new ideas serve as the incubators for intellectual capital, which leads to new intellectual properties. But Putnam also writes in *Bowling Alone* that the richest social capital comes from sharing ideas and stories with people who are different. That creates what he calls a social bridging because we're actually bridging cultures to find better ways to get along and more innovations that lie outside our own villages of stagnation. Putnam writes:

> Some forms of social capital are, by choice or necessity, inward looking and tend to reinforce exclusive identities and homogeneous groups. Examples of bonding social capital include ethnic fraternal organizations, church-based women's reading groups, and fashionable country clubs. Other networks are outward looking and encompass people across diverse social cleavages. Examples of bridging social capital include the civil rights movement, many youth service groups, and ecumenical religious organizations.
>
> Bonding social capital is good for undergirding specific reciprocity and mobilizing solidarity. Dense networks in ethnic enclaves, for example, provide crucial social and psychological support for less fortunate members of the community, while furnishing start-up financing, markets, and reliable labor for local entrepreneurs. Bridging networks, by contrast, are better for linkages to external assets and for information diffusion.... Bonding social capital is as Xavier de Souza Briggs puts it, good for "getting by," but bridging social capital is crucial for "getting ahead." (22-23)

It is in communities of great need where innovation is constantly working. People have to be inventive to overcome hardships imposed by inequality. Such an enterprising spirit fully harnessed with equal opportunity and resources will enable everyone to benefit from new and progressive inventions that often-discounted people can provide. It is here, in this undiscovered America, that our future lies. Bridging social capital is the best way to expand our society's gene pool of ideas. The bottom line is that the richness of life lies in embracing diversity. The perpetuation of stereotypes and separateness shackles humanity as existential victims. There is no profit in it. There is a liberation and richness in learning from others who are different.

Racism's biggest price for people of color often doesn't get recorded. But it is in the time that it costs to be forced to struggle longer in school, missed earnings caused by delays in getting jobs or promotions directly linked to others' low expectations of people of color and because of racial profiling. Every traffic, airport or pedestrian stop steals time from the victims as well as the perpetrators and reduces America's competitive advantage. Putnam in his book, *Bowling Alone*, notes that this creates a deficit in social capital, which is historical and self-perpetuating. Putnam writes that it's all tied even to this day to slavery:

> Still more striking is the spatial correlation between low social capital at the end of the twentieth century and slavery in the first half of the nineteenth century. The more virulent the system of slavery then, the less civic the state today. Slavery was, in fact, a social system *designed* to destroy social capital among slaves and between slaves and freemen. Well-established networks of reciprocity among the oppressed would have raised the risk of rebellion, and egalitarian bonds of sympathy between slave and free would have undermined the very legitimacy of the system. After Emancipation the dominant classes in the South continued to have a strong interest in inhibiting horizontal social networks. It is not happenstance that the lowest levels of community-based social capital are found where a century of plantation slavery was followed by a century of Jim Crow politics. Inequality and social solidarity are deeply incompatible. (294)

It's not surprising, then, that social capital, which includes a sense of trust and reciprocity among individuals, runs higher in racially homogeneous northern states such as Minnesota, North Dakota, Vermont and Iowa than in racially diverse southern states such as Mississippi, Georgia, Louisiana, Texas, Kentucky and Missouri. In addition, because of oppression with roots in slavery, social capital tends to run higher for whites than for blacks. Call it part of white privilege. It gives the advantage to others with whom minorities must compete.

Overcoming racism takes the hard work of social bridging. It takes people who are willing to help others in the daunting task. Others teach us the best lessons imaginable when it's across the great racial divide.

From "Diversity and uniqueness" and "We need a hospitality lesson"

> Duane Feighner and I saw each other twice this month in places where good people care about unity and diversity.
>
> Our first encounter was at the General Services Administration's Unity Day program at 1500 E. Bannister Road. The second was at a monthly diversity coalition meeting that Minority Museum founder David Shapiro convened for a while at his home.
>
> Before we watched the movie "Bamboozled" at Shapiro's place, Feighner said he was impressed with the wisdom of the people who

shared the Unity Day panel with him and me. The diverse panelists' comments applied to all of America's minorities.

Feighner told the audience his American Indian name is Three Feathers. The World War II veteran explained how he grew up respecting the land, his elders, tradition and all living things.

Yolanda L. Arriaga, a staff scientist at Midwest Research Institute, told the audience of the surprise Hispanics have felt in being refused service because the color of their skin. But minorities must overcome and never internalize the rejection.

Part of that involves sharing their culture with others to create a new awareness. Others then must be willing to learn.

I told the audience that people of color face the uncomfortable paradox of wanting opportunities and equality just like anyone else while being appreciated for the difference they offer. Such diversity generates new ideas and raises standards.

But Reesha Kang Trznadel, an assistant regional counsel with Social Security, told the audience she often gets frustrated with people's perception of Asian-Americans like her. She cited polls that said a quarter of U.S. citizens harbor "strong negative attitudes toward Chinese-Americans."

There is the "perception that people of Asian decent are still not Americans, that we're perpetual foreigners," Trznadel said. Diversity programs help change that, but being involved in such initiatives is like having another full-time job "with little expectation for compensation for my time."

"If I am sharing my experiences with you in the context of promoting diversity, then I am in effect making my case to you to justify my American existence, for you to validate my experience," said Trznadel, who grew up in a small southeast Missouri town. "Very often, speaking about diversity means making mainstream Americans feel better about the fact that our country is diverse, saying, 'Hey, it's not so bad is it?'

"It means that there are people who believe that America is just for them, and people like me are being done a favor for being allowed to live here. This realization can make this full-time job of educating not a very fun one."

But the values, desires and expectations that people of color have for themselves and their children mirror those of the majority. People who are of different ethnic background feel a strong attachment to American icons and ideals.

One example was at the Opening Convocation Program of the 2003 Missouri Fine Arts Academy at Southwest Missouri State University in Springfield. Eva Peng of Maryville, Mo., a member of the faculty, walked confidently to the microphone and beautifully sang the national anthem. But Peng's rendition of "The Star-Spangled Banner" included her mainland China dialect, which flowed into the song, accentuating that aspect of this country's rich diversity.

Former Kansas City Mayor Emanuel Cleaver once pointed out that "diversity demands more skills, more commitment and more work than exclusion." But, said Trznadel, "the diversity challenge is worthwhile, in part, because it gives some people a voice, and it gives others an education."

"This knowledge will make them more intelligent, more purposeful and less afraid," Trznadel said. It also will make others more willing to know that "I am an American and whose American family history is Korean" who possesses "something unique to bring to the table, so don't discount me based on my race."

Tom McVeigh and Mark Ohrenberg, research associates with the University of Missouri-Kansas City Institute for Human Development, spoke to the audience about people with disabilities.

McVeigh said they represented the fastest growing minority in the country.

"It's one that any one of us could join at any time," he said. Yet, many employers won't hire them, causing too many people with disabilities to live in poverty.

"That's a national tragedy," he said. Historically many have been segregated from mainstream America.

People have to remember that "attitude affects outcome, and attitude determines accessibility," Ohrenberg said.

"If we open their minds, and they accept people for who they are then we will open our society," he said. "I think we need to start looking at people for who they are and not what they look like."

The points made at the Unity Day program were clear about the need to value what often-overlooked people contribute. However, the feedback showed that many whites view diversity differently.

E-mail: June 22, 2001

You missed a wonderful opportunity to promote diversity at the gathering you mentioned in your column.

You should have reminded those in attendance of the wonderful job the dedicated white doctors and nurses are doing for blacks in Africa.

You should have reminded them of the white couple in Overland Park, Kan., who brought to their home two or three young black girls from Africa. These girls had their arms cut, hacked and torched by black soldiers. The girls were patched up by those dedicated white doctors and nurses in Africa and later turned over to a white couple from Overland Park.

Now that they are in Overland Park, they will have more surgery

> performed, by whites, to correct the damage inflicted on them by out of control black troops. The white couple has two daughters of their own, and the new girls will attend school in Overland Park with them. The white couple will attend to all their needs. The needs being home, meals, clothing and education.
>
> And, maybe you could have mentioned the black male adult featured in *The Star* section of your employer's newspaper two weeks ago. He was taught to read by a white woman. She did such a good job, he has written and published a book for children. He's working on another at present with her help and guidance.
>
> Were any of those acts of kindness and concern mentioned? Probably not.

Too many people only see diversity from the perspective of what whites are doing for the world's "poor, unfortunate people of color." It's part of an age-old white man's burden that makes sharing a one-way activity. That tradition was best illustrated in Edgar Rice Burroughs' Tarzan books, which were made into movies shown repeatedly on television. The stories were popular because they glorified whites who were shown civilizing the savage blacks. People were never shown the richness of other cultures. Getting everyone to understand and appreciate the value that minorities provide remains the social bridge yet to be built to the Real America. Thank goodness some groups remain undeterred in their efforts toward that construction.

From "Racial harmony is getting a boost in Hickman Mills"

> Special training will help Harmony in Hickman Mills extend its multicultural teachings into the Hickman Mills School District and surrounding neighborhoods.
>
> About 30 people attended the Harmony in a World of Difference Workshop at the Johnson Educational Center, 10900 Marsh Ave.
>
> People trying to improve race and ethnic relations in the city are pioneers, laying a new foundation for the future, said Maggie Finefrock, then-director of Harmony.
>
> "The important thing is that we hold the vision," said Finefrock, who led the discussion. "It's got to be a sustained, courageous effort over a long period of time."
>
> Harmony in Hickman Mills developed as the black population of the school district and surrounding neighborhoods continued to increase in the mostly white south Kansas City suburb. The group's goal was to increase understanding among the races and reduce prejudice, said Wayne D. White, then-president of the organization.
>
> He said Harmony in Hickman Mills spent the previous year getting organized and becoming listed as a non-profit corporation. It now is inviting people to become members.

"Harmony in Hickman Mills has had an impact and is slowly growing," White said.

White and Donna Almai, then-vice president of the group, said people who went through the training will use it to help enlighten others.

"It's kind of breaking the ice," Almai said.

Finefrock had the Harmony in Hickman Mills members break into groups to discuss their differences and the things they had in common as human beings.

People should recognize diversity and celebrate their differences as one of this nation's strengths, she said.

Finefrock said that everyone must be aware of stereotypes.

"We have to be ever vigilant about the myths, lies and the stereotypes and discern them from the truth," Finefrock said.

The group watched a videotape about Harmony in a World of Difference and another tape called "Eye of the Beholder," which exposed white children and adults to the emotional trauma of discrimination and oppression. Finefrock said that one of the things "Eye of the Beholder" stressed was that people of different races must have empathy for each other.

"Prejudice is learned," she said. "We are socialized to believe it.

"The good news is it can be unlearned."

The more time we spend talking and listening to people who are different, the richer our lives become. But according to Jim Myers, in *Afraid of the Dark*, this isn't happening. In 1995, *USA Today* conducted a poll in which people were asked how often they had contact with others whose race was white (for blacks) or black (for whites). The results showed that

3 of 5 white Americans—or 96 million white adults—do not deal with black people every day. But in the same poll, 61 percent of black Americans—3 in 5—said they had contact with whites "every day." So there is a clear disparity here. Three in 5 black Americans *do* deal with whites every day, while 3 of 5 whites *don't* have daily contact with blacks.

Given such figures, it is enticing to imagine what an "average" encounter between black and white Americans would be like. The black individual will, on the average, have about seven times more experience along the color line than the white individual. So black Americans might even be more assured in dealings across the color line, while white Americans might find themselves less comfortable about what to say. (31)

Hispanics, Asian Americans and Native Americans also might be "more assured." As Myers notes, casual encounters across the racial divides don't often happen. Therefore, the shared discovery through social bridging must be purposeful.

It seems that young people often have a better understanding of how to make good race relations happen and why that is so important. The age diversity that they embody matters to the social bridging that must occur. Great organizations do outstanding work in pushing the boundaries of young people's acceptance of diversity. Young people then become the guides, showing everyone else the way.

From "Sowing seeds of tolerance"

> The large room at St. Mary College in Leavenworth looked like America.
>
> It was filled with white, black, Hispanic, American Indian and Asian-American students from high schools metrowide. They were teen-agers from different cities, socio-economic backgrounds and religions who openly expressed the joy of their friendship through diversity.
>
> Their goal was to get to know others who are different in the safe haven the college created before summer vacation ended and classes started at their schools.
>
> This was Anytown, a one-week residential program started in 1957 that helps teens see through others' eyes what the world would be like without oppression.
>
> The National Conference for Community and Justice, founded in 1927, is dedicated to fighting bias, bigotry and racism in America. Anytown and Unitown, a companion program in high schools, strive to dissolve the emotional, mental and physical violence that people who are different too often experience. The programs prepare young people to be leaders in making this nation extend its ideals of freedom, equality and opportunity to everyone.
>
> Juan M. Rangel Jr., then-executive director of the National Conference, invited me, Kansas City Police Officer John Lozano and former City Council member Alvin Brooks to talk with students about institutional racism and what youths can do to help eliminate it. From the letters and e-mail I regularly receive about columns I've written on race, I enabled the students to see that bigotry and prejudice remain a problem. I told the students of efforts to bring more people of color into the media, which improves news coverage.
>
> Lozano told them new Kansas City police recruits include more Hispanics, African-Americans and women, which helps build more diversity, understanding and trust in the force. "I'm wanting to do more and reach out," he said.

Brooks gave the students a U.S. history refresher course, telling them of the 1776 Declaration of Independence and the 1787 Constitution and how the high ideals of freedom, liberty and equality in each excluded women, people of color and the poor.

"There's something wrong with this kind of history," Brooks said.

He wrote the words money, politics and social stratification on a large piece of paper. Each has helped maintain systems of inequality. But money stood out for Brooks as a central culprit.

"This is what keeps this system in place," Brooks said. "He who pays the piper names the tune."

"We've got folks who are homeless," he said. "We've got people who need health care. This country was built on the backs of free labor."

Brooks urged the students who will be 18 before Nov. 7 to vote in the general election. He also said they should get involved in both major parties to help dismantle bigotry through political action and economic development.

Brooks told the students about the Statue of Liberty and recited the words it has projected for more than a century in this land of mostly immigrants. "Unfortunately some of those who left Europe to escape oppression became oppressors themselves in America," he said.

I added that research only now is uncovering what may be a hidden history of the statue: The original model was a black woman, and the monument was to honor freed slaves and the Union's Civil War victory. The gift from France was because America had taken a giant step with the abolition of slavery in fulfilling its revolutionary promise to make this country free for everyone.

I told the students who walked me to my van at the end of the session that they no doubt would face frustration in their post-Anytown efforts to continue to expand the promise of freedom and the elimination of oppression. But their involvement is essential to everyone's gains. They must keep trying just as Brooks and Lozano do.

"We're planting the seeds," Lozano said.

The students just happen to be America's newest gardeners for a better tomorrow.

From "Young enlistee in the war on injustice"

Lisa Ash is among those "gardener" teens working to end racism, bias and bigotry so that everyone has a place in the more perfect Union she envisions. The 17-year-old Liberty High School senior shared her winning smile and captivating words at a National Conference for Community and Justice's Distinguished Citizen Awards Dinner.

It was the second year I've heard a student who'd finished a conference diversity program boldly tell people how it had motivated her to do what she could "to be an ally, a bridge builder and a change agent." Ash was one of 65 students in area high schools who last year participated in Anytown.

"We spent the first several days identifying and examining our own personal prejudices and stereotypes," Ash told the audience. "We looked at how the media feed us these images, how stereotypes are developed, and did some pretty intense soul searching.

"I learned at Anytown that sometimes, all it really takes is one person to make a difference. One voice, if it is passionate enough, can be heard over the cacophony of violence and racism in our society.

"I have become aware of my obligation as a member of the sector of our society that has the power to work for social justice. To stand up for someone who can't stand up for themselves. To ask my friends not to use phrases like 'He's so gay,' and tell racist jokes. To give my time, my talents, my resources and my love to those who are yearning for acceptance.

"Anytown has inspired me to realize that I have the power and the opportunity to make a difference."

Juan M. Rangel Jr. said people needed to hear Ash's message.

"Here we have a young person in our community who is creating change," he said.

Ash said Anytown gave her the confidence to organize a food drive at her school, which collected 12,000 items to help fight poverty and hunger. It also motivated her to teach Sunday school at her church, the Community of Christ in Liberty.

Ash said doing such things offset any discouragement that might grow from knowing cycles of poverty and racism still existed. The nation has made great advances to bridge cultures.

"But I think about how far we have to go," she said.

Her parents, Jim and Pam Ash, said their daughter had always been thoughtful.

"The reason she was able to deliver (her speech) so powerfully is it came straight from her soul," Pam Ash said.

"She has always been one to be very perceptive of others' feelings, to see the need when other people don't, to see people hurting. Anytown was absolutely wonderful, because she was able to put flesh on many things she has believed all of her life."

Her passion also was in her winning entry last year in the Midwest Center for Holocaust Education's White Rose Essay Contest, which got her into Anytown. She noted how the Nazis used words to teach young people to hate Jews, people with disabilities, minorities, homosexuals and Gypsies.

"Language can create beautiful art or be a weapon of mass destruction," Ash wrote.

Isolation and propaganda feed people's hatred for those who are different.

"One must be exposed to the differences among those around him or her, and be allowed to experience the beauty of diversity," Ash wrote.

Rangel said: "We talk of youths being leaders of tomorrow. In reality, they are leaders of today.

"We shouldn't put it off until tomorrow."

People like Lisa Ash are working to make this world a better place, and the conference keeps enabling more young people to change the way things have always been.

From "One person makes world better place"

Rickeena J. Richards is another Kansas City teen-ager who has participated in the conference program. She has told local and national audiences that each of us has the power to "break down the barriers that prejudices build."

Her passion moved many people to tears because the racism that affected past generations now threatens young people. Richards' speech, "A Better Place - One Person at a Time," described her involvement in a two-day "Unitown" experience at her school, St. Teresa's Academy.

Richards explained how the "Privilege Exercise" works.

Participants join hands, standing shoulder-to-shoulder at half-court in the school gym. In response to questions, individuals either step forward for "yes" answers or backward for "no." Among the questions asked:

"Have either of your parents ever taken you to a museum?"

"Did your parents read to you when you were young?"

"I stepped forward to both of those questions because of my father's involvement and support in my childhood development," said Richards, a member of the Northeast Johnson County Branch of the NAACP Youth Council. "Yet, not everyone was as lucky as I was. There remained many behind me, however, even more stood in front of me."

Questions on race and gender forced Richards to take several steps back. As a black female, she'll likely earn less than white males doing the same job. The poor education many blacks receive also could saddle her with limited employment opportunities and impair her success.

As Richards found herself separated from her white and Hispanic classmates, she began to cry. Losing the hand of a Hispanic girl next to her hurt the most.

"Until that point, I felt that I shared something with her," Richards said. "I felt that even though we both stood so far behind everyone else we were not alone because we still held on to each other.

"When she let go of my hand, something in my heart moved, and I never felt so alone in my life."

She suddenly sensed that just by being born different, she had no control over many elements in her life. That left Richards feeling frustrated, sad and hopeless.

Richards realized how cruel and unfair the world is to people like her because of her gender and race. But she also felt relieved because her eyes had been opened.

Richards shared that story with people at an awards dinner of the National Conference for Community and Justice. The conference sponsors the "Unitown" workshops to help students shed prejudices. She also spoke in Houston at the National Association for the Advancement of Colored People's convention during the Afro-Academic, Cultural, Technological and Scientific Olympics.

The competition promotes academic excellence among young African-Americans with a wonderful theme: "Black is Brilliant."

Juan M. Rangel Jr. said: "For me, she's what we're trying to do, and that is assisting young people to recognize the power they have...being change agents and bridge builders. The excitement comes in the many lives she will affect and how she will ask other people to consider change around race."

Richards' parents, Gwen and Rich Richards, feel blessed by their daughter's new awareness and described what concerns many black parents.

"We always had the fear of this racism coming along and slapping her in the face," Gwen Richards said. "It hurts a lot more when you don't know it's coming, and you don't know why."

Often young people who haven't had to contend with racism are uninterested in finding out about it. It isn't part of their world and therefore isn't on their radar. Fortunately, many people and groups reach out to kids across social bridges to help them overcome the constraints of whiteness and racism. These people know it's the only way to overcome the barriers that separate us.

From "The kids can't be insulated"

Some suburban teens fidgeted in their chairs, giggled and enjoyed themselves until David Shapiro started to talk.

The Minority Museum founder and executive director gave a brief introduction and then showed videos of Holocaust atrocities that he saw in 1945 as an American GI at the Dachau concentration camp. Shapiro explained that the museum grew from that horror.

Shapiro pointed out his collection of articles and pictures of Jews, African-Americans, American Indians and Hispanics at what had been the museum's home at Boone Elementary School. They weren't fancy but each, clearly showed the groups' contributions, as well as the adversity each faced.

But the kicker came when Shapiro asked the kids for questions. The room, which had been alive with his passion and enthusiasm, suddenly became still except for a couple of easy queries.

"Come on, I've got a few more answers left," said Shapiro, a retired optometrist who started the museum in May 1991 from materials he had collected. But the young audience he wanted to shake the most sat as inanimate as the museum chairs.

Finally he surrendered.

The silence opened old wounds. "If we bury our heads in the sand, we, too, will be buried," Shapiro said.

I visited him later, and we talked about the teens. He said it was not uncommon for suburban kids to politely sit "unplugged" when he played the videos, exposed them to the museum and asked for questions.

It's different with urban kids, said Shapiro, who won a National Conference for Community and Justice award for his work. They're interested in his presentation, and it shows in their questions.

An example was a Kansas City alternative school he visited before the museum got its home in 1994. "They kept me mentally hopping with thought-provoking questions," Shapiro said.

They were sensitive, wise kids, able to comprehend with their heads and their hearts.

"Urban kids could identify with the atrocities," Shapiro said. "They know what prejudice is. They know what bigotry is.

"Suburban kids seem to me weren't affected directly. They weren't hit by bigotry and prejudice."

Their lives didn't include the more global experiences of people of color. They've never suffered discrimination.

To them, people who do are real only in a make-believe world of imagination, TV, videos, rap music and movies.

It's the story of indifference, said Leonard Zeskind, chairman of the Individual Liberties and Jewish Security Committee with the Jewish Community Relations Bureau.

"There's a huge social distance between the white kids and minori-

> ties," said Zeskind, who had tracked hate groups as research director for the Center for Democratic Research. "The white kids want to live and look into a white world.
>
> "They'd just as soon there wasn't anybody there to disturb the monochromatic nature of their existence. They're not the same as the Aryan Nation.
>
> "They just think the same."
>
> Shapiro wants to vanquish that hate and indifference.
>
> "Democracy and freedoms need to be fought for constantly," he said. "Bigotry doesn't take a vacation.
>
> "The bigots work 365 days a year, 24 hours a day, and we've got to be alert and fight them and fight them back nonviolently as the museum is doing."
>
> That's one way. Asking more questions is another.

Avoiding white privilege or racism in America isn't possible. Through social bridging each must be tackled head-on. Ronald Takaki in his book, *A Different Mirror*, quoted slave owner and President Thomas Jefferson, who worried about what he called a "race war":

> Deep-rooted prejudices entertained by the whites, 10,000 recollections, by the blacks, of the injuries they have sustained; new provocations; the real distinctions which nature has made and many other circumstances, will divide us into parties, and produce convulsions, which will probably never end but in the extermination of one or the other race. (75)

Efforts to build bridges by such groups as Project Equality, Harmony/NCCJ, and others have prevented Jefferson's worst fears from happening. In addition, communities are beginning dialogues to bring people together.

From "Everyone can afford diversity"

> Johnson County is just one of many places metrowide where people are gathering at diversity forums. Here's why: A Citistates report explained that race divides this community like a river.
>
> At a Harmony Week luncheon, John A. Powell, director of the Institute for Race and Poverty then at the University of Minnesota, said we are all linked together.
>
> He said our "common destiny" is that, regardless of other differences, we will grow old. More people are reaching retirement age and drawing Social Security with fewer workers to pay into the system to keep it afloat.
>
> But Powell said, "The Social Security crisis is a racial crisis." He said the white population, which has better schools, jobs and most of the wealth in America, is shrinking.

"The future workers of the world are people of color," he said. But if discrimination and racial inequities continue, minorities will be unable to keep Social Security alive.

Young people of color as the new majority need to be well-educated and have good paying jobs "so we can tax them," Powell said. "Our self-interest is part of our common destiny," he said.

Powell advocates regional solutions to racial problems. Common goals must include bridging racial divides, valuing others and sharing opportunities.

"We need to make injustice so costly in our society that no one could afford it and make justice so cheap that everyone could afford it," Powell said.

Diversity is our strength. The words almost sound trite because they are repeated so often by people who are the Sherpas guiding us away from bigotry to the beauty of diversity. Nevertheless we often find that there is no common language that would enable us to communicate our diversity.

Long before the Sept. 11, 2001, terrorist attacks there were Muslims in America. They are our neighbors, our friends, but our different faiths, habits, dress and customs may prevent us from seeing how much we have in common so social bridges across the differences can take shape.

From "Islamic school enriches discussion of diversity"

A video I had shown at the Minority Museum awhile ago and a discussion that followed prompted Ahmed El-Sherif to invite me to his daughter's school in south Kansas City.

I participated in a diversity discussion at The Islamic School of Kansas City. But the students, teachers and parents exposed me to a new vista of multiculturalism in America and south Kansas City.

Initially, I drove past the understated, recessed facility that houses the school. No big sign out front announces its presence.

After I had parked, a schoolgirl showed me inside. Classes had not yet started that morning. Well-disciplined boys and girls of different races and nationalities visited with each other and unflinchingly followed teachers' directions.

The girls wore hijab uniforms of a blue coat and white scarf. The boys' uniform consisted of dark pants and white or blue shirts.

Everyone in the 180-student school was dressed neatly. No one loitered in the halls, and no soda pop or junk-food machines were present. That was a refreshing sight.

I reported to the office and immediately was greeted by a school administrator. I extended my hand to her. She politely informed me that women there don't touch males.

I was in her world, and I knew enough to respect her wishes and her culture. The school was a safe place for me to learn.

El-Sherif was president of the area chapter of the American Muslim Council. His daughter, Fatimeh, attended the Islamic School. He invited me there after we had watched the video, "True Colors," at the Minority Museum.

El-Sherif wanted me to share the ABC-TV program with the students in the gymnasium. It shows how African-Americans often face "have-a-nice-day racism" in trying to find a place to live, work and get goods and services in America. They wouldn't know they were being discriminated against unless they could compare it with how a white person was treated and how the encounters of each person were captured on hidden camera.

The uniformed students assembled quietly in the gym. Another diversity lesson for me was seeing the boys sit in the front and the girls in the back. It was their culture, their way, and I was a student in their school.

But the boys and girls participated equally in the diversity discussions. I also played another video for the students that I had watched at the Minority Museum.

It's called "Faces of the Enemy." It shows how people throughout time have created enemies by dehumanizing and demonizing others in newspapers, films, television, cartoons and other media.

The media desensitize the public so that killing "the enemy" can be done with great ease. The video showed how the former Soviet Union pictured the United States as the enemy to its people and how we did the same thing to the former communist nation.

The videotape showed how Iran pictured America as the enemy, and how we used the same tactics on the Iranians. The program covered the dehumanization that took place in the media in Nazi Germany, enabling people of that nation to exterminate 6 million Jews.

In World War II, the Japanese depicted American and British leaders as beasts, and we did the same to the people of Japan. The video showed how similar patterns unfolded on both sides of the Vietnam War.

The program warned against people pulling away from one another and against isolation. That can escalate into negative images and then an all-too-real enemy is born.

The video talks about bridging gaps and discussing shared concerns. The students, adults and I did that at the Islamic School of Kansas City. We all left much richer from the experience of sharing.

People from other cultures and countries have the ability to see us as we are instead of how we prefer to see ourselves. But it can be difficult for them to understand racism in America. Its dimensions are both profane and fascinating. They limit the outcomes for people and, despite the segregation and all of the negative effects that racism spawns, some of its victims in a bizarre way nostalgically cling to bigotry as if that tradition represents the good old days.

From "We must all strive for unity"

> People must resist the temptation to react offensively to racism. Trigger words such as "boy," "nigger" and "coon" used to incite me to violence. The last time was when my brother, David, 16, and I, 15, had gone to a park with a white guy in our new neighborhood to play basketball when two white toughs spit racial slurs at us to force us to leave their turf. We fought instead, and I took on their best.
>
> Their words pumped up my rage. I beat the first guy. I then whipped the second who had jumped me in retaliation.
>
> But I didn't feel triumphant afterward. I felt awful. I had taken some hits and lumps, but that wasn't why I suffered.
>
> I hurt because I had hurt others whose words hurt me. It was as if the pain I had inflicted boomeranged and hit me with a force that was magnified many times.
>
> That's why that became my last fistfight and why I vowed to not let others' hatred and ignorance force me to resort to violence. Brutality makes us all victims and really big losers.
>
> The Rev. Martin Luther King Jr. taught that discussion directed toward new understandings provide better solutions. It goes beyond the '70s saying of "I'm not prejudiced."
>
> We're all prejudiced. That's part of being discerning human beings.
>
> But to relate to others better, we must confront our prejudices and then get them in check with the truth. Such actions also go beyond merely being tolerant of others.
>
> That's just putting up with something that you'd rather not. Instead we should value and embrace differences because it makes us more productive and enhances our communities.
>
> I have learned that actions toward harmony set off a powerful and opposite reaction toward discord by people who want hate to thrive. Rangel said as much in a diagram showing a tug of war between people who are racists and others who pull hard for unity.
>
> Caught in the middle is the bulk of the population. Rangel calls them "bystanders" who can be yanked either way.

People must get off the sidelines, see that there is a great nation to discover. They must form new social bridges with others who are different and these new adventurers in diversity must fearlessly start the journey.

CHAPTER 14
A Shameless Lack of Empathy

Homeless in America

Man, It's cold outside
Where's a homeless soul to eat?
The burden of poverty's heavy
Weighing hard on so many poor, tired feet.
Dodging cars 'cause nobody bothers to see
People on the street
Accept when glares burn
And contempt churns
Sending shame throughout poor homeless souls
The more fortunate hate the less fortunate,
Why? Only God knows.
Sleeping in shelters or under bridges
Ain't no way to live
But for the homeless, that's all "good" folks have to give.
Blamed for having no jobs, no health care, no
Home, no life like nobody knows
Society's not wanting, not feeling, not caring
Just hating for no good reason
Those who are homeless,
In these compassionless times – 'tis the season.

Ojos que no ven, corazon que no siente.
(Eyes that don't see, heart that doesn't feel.)
~Mexican-American Proverb

Clothes make or disable individuals. I first noticed this in 1993 when I took a break from doing particularly grimy house chores and went in my old work clothes to a fast-food restaurant. I was impressed with how surly the normally pleasant clerk was and how poor the service was that she provided. I wondered what had changed from previous times I'd been there. The answer lay in how I was dressed: the other times I had been in business attire. That incident was such a change from the '60s and '70s. I had worn those same clothes then, and never had a head turn or an attitude alter towards me. But that was a period of change in America—of Great Society programs, the Civil Rights Movement, the feminist revolution, the Chicano Movement, and the American Indian Movement. People tried more to accept others as they were or, at the very least, to quote the '60s phrase, to "live and let live." My fast-food experience made me wonder how widespread this new negative public feeling had become. That spurred me to take this question to the street: would everyday working people also be rude to folks who look impoverished? The answer unfortunately is, yes.

The hostility and incivility towards people who are less fortunate are surfacing as a larger issue in the Real America as taxes become more regressive, the wealth gap widens and equality becomes more elusive. So every year I put on those same old clothes that I have worn since I was in college in the early 1970s to gauge people's reactions to the increasing number of poor in our society. I walk the streets in those frayed and worn togs and go through public places to explore what it's like to be homeless. I then write columns about the experience to direct attention to the often-overlooked problems facing people who have low incomes or no incomes and those who are homeless. The ground-level view exposes a dire situation that exists throughout America.

From "The crisis cannot be contained"

> SEATTLE - This "Emerald City" wakes up ugly. At daybreak the homeless rise from concrete and grassy beds downtown in this city. I noticed them on an early morning walk during the Unity Convention for Journalists of Color.
>
> It was before traffic filled highways with commuters and workers lined up at the many coffee bars that keep this city percolating. The homeless rose from the feet of a statue of a long-dead chamber of commerce president.
>
> They rose from the recessed doorways of businesses. They stretched outside a hotel. They smoked cigarettes and awaited handouts near a food vendor.
>
> Seattle is just one of many cities that I've seen wake up ugly. Others are Kansas City; Atlanta; Tucson, Ariz.; Philadelphia; Washington; San Francisco; New York; Chicago; San Jose, Calif.; Phoenix; St.

> Petersburg and Orlando in Florida; St. Louis; and Los Angeles.
>
> Homelessness is a national crisis. The 1990 census recorded 228,621 homeless persons. But census officials acknowledge that the population is undercounted.

This great nation's homeless ranks in 2005 numbered about 750,000, according to a 2007 report providing the first national estimate in a decade. Forty-nine percent of the homeless are African-Americans, 35 percent are white; 13 percent, Hispanic; 2 percent, American Indian and 1 percent Asian. The causes of homelessness include low-paying jobs, unemployment, underemployment, domestic violence, poverty, prison release, substance abuse, a lack of affordable housing, a void in needed services and mental illness. U.S. Department of Justice data in 2007 show that 64 percent of the local jail prisoners, 56 percent of state inmates and 45 percent of federal inmates suffer serious mental illness, turning lockups into the primary mental care facilities of the 21st century. Yet these people are our neighbors and our family members.

From "The crisis cannot be contained"

> "We do such a good job that there are not a lot of homeless people visible," said the Rev. Stuart E. Whitney while executive director of re-Start Inc., which provides shelter for homeless men and families in the Kansas City area. "The more we serve, the better we do for the people, the more the general public thinks there's no problem.
>
> "We'd like to believe that every day it's getting better and better. For some folks, it's getting worse and worse."
>
> That means all of our emerald cities will continue to wake up ugly, and so will we.

It would be difficult to have lived in America and not seen the horrific pictures on television of the devastation that Hurricanes Katrina and Rita caused in 2005 in Mississippi, Texas, and Louisiana. Katrina especially blew away the veneer that covered poverty and racism in New Orleans and in America. We got to see that the poor people were the ones left behind in New Orleans when the "every person for himself" evacuation order was issued. We also got to see that poverty there, just as in the rest of America, disproportionately has the faces of persons of color. Yet a census study also found that in addition to the poverty rates rising nationwide, the median household income fell, declining from $44,514 to $44,436 based on two-year averaging. *The New York Times* reported that it was the first time on record that household incomes failed to increase in a five-year period (Leonhardt). The drop actually put incomes back at a 1997 level. The flip side is found in the 12th annual Executive Excess study by United for a Fair Economy and the Institute for Policy Studies. They reported in August of 2005 that the average chief executive compensation at 367 of the nation's largest companies was 431 times the average U.S. production worker's pay in 2004. In 2003 the CEO-to-worker pay ratio was 301-to-1 (Anderson et al. 13).

Contrary to popular belief in these conservative, compassionless times, no one wants to remain mired in a life of poverty. "It's too painful to stay" there, writes Ruby K. Payne in her book, *A Framework for Understanding Poverty* (11). Yet, while CEOs are being more than amply compensated, our country has not afforded all of its residents the opportunity to work in decent jobs, earn living wages that will support a family and be productive, taxpaying, civically engaged citizens in this community. It is a crime that this land has so much for those in the top income brackets but so little for the burgeoning bulk of the population at the bottom.

To add insult to injury, people who are better off make those who are less fortunate feel like pariahs. The folks on the street throughout America are degraded into thinking that the suffocating condition they are in is their own fault. That sense of feeling shunned and having to contend with it are among the "hidden rules" of poverty that Ruby K. Payne writes about (11).

But communicating across the class divide seems increasingly forbidden. It adds to the isolation and misery of being poor. Fear governs too many people. Those who meet the homeless on the street are afraid of them. Those who are working are terrorized over the possible loss of their jobs. Those who are homeless are afraid of what they will encounter on the streets in the brutality of the more fortunate or the assaults from other needy people. Fear is not a good motivator. Yet fear is what I encounter when I take my sojourns into poverty.

Good newspapers should hold up a mirror to society so that the words, pictures and artwork reflect back to the community what's going on. Newspapers also should democratize information, forcing it down to the person on the street so everyone gains from the complete view of the community. Journalism done that way enables the community to direct resources to things that need attention. That brings me back to my annual project of wearing my old clothes. I enjoy pulling them on when I have to work on my vehicles or do chores around the house. But in the last 10 years there's a growing level of discomfort, disassociation and fear that I have sensed from others every time I put my old clothes on and go out in public.

In 1995 I applied for welfare from the state and wrote about how degrading and depressing that experience was.

<u>From "Questions too private for many"</u>

The silence stood out the most.

It breathed as a quiet tension among parents and kids in the ground-floor waiting room of the State Office Building. I felt it when I sat down as just another soul applying for food stamps, Aid to Families with Dependent Children and Medicaid.

The hush of the families seeking assistance contrasts with the political noise in Congress over welfare reform.

But the W-word never crossed lips here. People sat in silence waiting for their number to be called partly out of embarrassment and partly because they didn't want to jeopardize their chance to get help.

Speaking out here is politically incorrect these days.

Waiting passed in slow somberness, frustration, anxiety and shame. Those feelings hit me when I filled out my applications, surrendering to the state details about myself, my family, job, finances and property.

Standing in poverty's long shadows would squelch the ignorant noise of most folks who've been duped into thinking deep welfare cuts would improve life for families in need.

Welfare is no chuck wagon. Many recipients subsist on less than a full-time minimum wage earner's $680 a month salary.

Few can take receiving so little when the ugly monster of welfare stigma is gnawing at them.

An Urban Institute study found that 64 percent of first-time recipients cycle off welfare within two years.

But more than three-quarters of those who leave welfare return to it. Low-paying jobs with no health care lack the booster rocket power to free families of poverty's gravitational pull.

Nationwide, most of the 14 million AFDC recipients and 27 million people on food stamps are children.

Peggy A. Torno, income maintenance director with the Missouri Division of Family Service, said that's true in Jackson County, too, where caseworkers in December took 1,465 AFDC applications and approved 1,107. They took 5,695 applications for food stamps and approved 5,048.

The demand is up and it's straining the state's ability to deliver. "I have about 54 percent of the staff that I need to do the work now," Torno said.

But silence prevails among workers, too. Speaking up for them also is politically incorrect.

Clients who spoke didn't want their names used. They just wanted the noise to end and for people to seek the truth.

"Life is so uncertain," one applicant said. "You might be up today, but you never know when you might need help."

Caseworkers try to be compassionate. "Our goal has always been to meet the needs of children and families, and that will continue to be the goal," Torno said.

> Holly Guinn was my income maintenance caseworker. She was efficient and friendly in asking questions and telling me I didn't qualify for welfare.
>
> Some of her clients break down in tears during interviews. For others, it's just another day.
>
> But she said she couldn't sit on the other side of the gray interview desk. People have to give up too much for too little.
>
> I shook Guinn's hand and left. A comfortable life waited for me outside this experience.
>
> But that's a luxury that a lot of people on the ground floor of hard times don't enjoy.

The Welfare Reform law passed in 1996 makes getting public aid even tougher. Efforts to reform the Reform law have failed.

In 1996, I wore my old clothes to try to get on at a midtown Kansas City labor pool. No one knew who I was. People who were dressed as I was were hospitable. Everyone else treated us badly. I was told to arrive at 5 a.m. on a Sunday if I wanted to get work. I got there at 4:45 a.m.

From "A shaky method of survival"

> I arrived 15 minutes early for the experience of being in a labor pool, but I was upstaged by about two dozen men and women whose hunger for work got them there sooner.
>
> We stood in line to sign our name. A man ahead of me looked at a board that told of available jobs.
>
> He counted down the list and then cursed. Unless someone ahead of us vanished, none of us in line would get picked for a $4.50-an-hour job that day.
>
> I signed the sheet anyway and waited. CNN news played on a TV, putting some people to sleep but keeping others awake.
>
> Hardly anyone talked as the room filled with 50 to 100 people for only 12 jobs. Cold days are slow like that, Jude Davila, Labor Ready branch manager, said later.
>
> The need for manual laborers picks up with warmer weather, ensuring that people who daily pool outside Labor Ready will find work. But the supply of people seeking jobs usually exceeds the demand.
>
> Downsizing and outsourcing trends have left many people without steady work.
>
> Some end up at labor pools, which offer a little hope for folks who'd otherwise have none.
>
> They're like Joe Wilder of South Dakota, who signed up recently because he had no job but needed money "real quick."
>
> Another was Rick Holder of Kansas City, who goes to Labor

> Ready from his restaurant job to earn badly needed extra money. "I've got a family to take care of," he said.
>
> "I think the people that come here, they need work," Doyle Torrence of Kansas City said while he waited for his name to be called. "They've got to eat and try to survive."
>
> The day I went, names were called and 12 were chosen for jobs. I left empty-handed, but I was thankful in a way that I didn't take work from someone who had to have it to just get by.

I went back to one of those labor pools a few years later and was surprised that I had to show proof of citizenship in order to get work. I think that is why many people seeking cheap labor now just pick men up in trucks in the Hispanic community of Kansas City. That is so much like the Great Depression of the 1930s, but no one in this country is screaming about this horrid condition. Where is the outrage? Places like those labor pools, along with payday loans businesses, title car companies and pawn shops are multiplying nationwide, which makes me doubt the prosperity that the people running our government keep telling us we are supposed to be enjoying.

In 1997 I wore my old clothes and walked into downtown shopping areas, department stores and the old Main Library. I was impressed with how badly people treated me, including some of my co-workers, who failed to recognize me. I did not hassle anyone, but the stares and body language really assaulted me. Afterward I went to the black community shopping districts and then to one in the Hispanic community. People in these places treated me really well. But when I went to four suburban shopping malls I again was surprised by the negative reactions I received.

From "Hard hearts cast a chill over the city"

> A toddler looked into my eyes and waved a friendly hello.
>
> I waved back before his mom picked him up and whisked him away from the Main Library downtown. The boy saw past my old Army coat, knit cap, frayed shirt, faded and stained pants, and ratty sneakers.
>
> His mother didn't. She was among hundreds of people who looked at me as if I were dirt on my walk through downtown, Westport, the West Side, the Plaza, Crown Center, the 18th and Vine Historic District, Linwood Shopping Center, The Landing, Ward Parkway Center, Bannister Mall, Town Center Plaza and Oak Park Mall.
>
> I got ugly stares at the Town Pavilion and City Center Square food courts, where people's body language said, "Don't sit by me." Well-suited folks see the homeless downtown every day. That's why it seemed so natural for many of them to ignore people like me.
>
> On this day only my GOP friend Gary Martinette saw past the

clothes and said, "Hi, Lewis." But he and his wife, Jan, have been former mayors of Grandview, an unusually racially and economically diverse near-suburban city.

Other exceptions were at Crown Center, 18th and Vine and the Linwood center, where strangers were friendly. In the 18th and Vine Historic Jazz District, one white woman stopped me to ask directions. She showed no fear or hesitation even though we were strangers.

But ill feelings toward me increased as I went south. One white woman at Ward Parkway Center clutched her purse in the parking lot and ran to the mall when she saw me.

Joe Colaizzi, Kansas City Rescue Mission executive director, and Stuart E. Whitney, then-reStart Inc. executive director, weren't surprised. Whitney said a Reagan-era cancer has been slowly eating away at the public's compassion toward low-income families.

People fear poverty and run from such unpleasant things. Or people ignore what they see, hoping it'll go away.

"There's kind of that elitist attitude that says anyone who's poor, black, Hispanic, not like us is somehow out to get us and take advantage of us," Whitney said. "It's now politically correct to be politically incorrect." Whitney described scenes of employers who pick up homeless whites before minorities. "The whole fabric of society is so immersed in racism, classism and sexism," he said.

That must change.

"Poverty is not good for a city," Whitney said. Neither is homelessness.

Ignoring people and problems just makes living here worse.

The column failed to change people's behavior. On the contrary, it may actually have hardened hearts more by pointing out the problems homeless people face.

From "Readers give second look at scorn"

A lot of readers didn't like seeing me in old clothes.

I had shed my suit for my old Army surplus coat, knit cap, frayed flannel shirt, faded and stained pants, and ratty sneakers to spend the day in 12 shopping areas to test people's reaction to my appearance of poverty. The results weren't pretty.

People looked at me as if I were invisible or filth. That hadn't happened before in my lifetime of wearing and feeling comfortable in old clothes.

I wrote about that ugly classism encounter in a March 22 column and followed it with a March 25 piece on how U.S. politics are hurting people who are poor at a time when the United Nations has designated 1997-2006 as the First World Decade for the Elimination of Poverty. I've gotten over the negative face-to-face reactions.

> But it'll take a while to make sense of the disheartening comments those columns generated from readers. If their 83 letters, faxes and e-mail and voice-mail messages were ballots, and the majority spoke for us all, then poor people would be voted out of their right to live in America.
>
> My test and readers' ugly comments tell me that today it's OK to show contempt for the less fortunate. What stood out most was that the longest and nastiest responses came from readers with computers.
>
> People with access to that expensive technology and the Internet generally aren't poor. But they don't like being reminded that they behave badly and that they're very afraid.
>
> Their e-mail told of how people dressed as I was trigger a fear of crime in them. They're afraid that people who looked like me will take things from them. But on the street, I begged for nothing, and no one else like me did either.
>
> Others thought the negative reactions were correct because no one wants the hassles or smells of the homeless. But my old clothes were clean in my walk through downtown.
>
> Also, I smiled often and treated people no differently than I would have if I'd been in a suit. Crime is a cop-out, and so is the public's now-turned-up nose to folks who are different.
>
> Other comments were stained with racism. They said no-goods like me must be avoided for not creating opportunities for self-improvement. Fingerprinting the poor isn't criminal. Welfare and raising the minimum wage just hurts society.
>
> Government intervention just makes things worse for people with money, they said. Let the churches eat the problem.
>
> But poverty and homelessness are too big for the faith community to swallow. Some callers and writers hung a "liberal" noose around my neck for mentioning Republicans and tracing the negative trend to the greed-is-good Reagan era.
>
> But I also said both parties today are responsible for pushing a cultlike worship of money and material things.
>
> I can only guess that people reacted so negatively because their greatest fear of poverty is that it could happen to any one of us. Most of us are just a paycheck away from the abyss.
>
> If that happened, everyone would see how unbearable the awful looks and nasty treatment are, which folks now sanction.

Keep in mind that readers nationwide who saw my column reprinted in their hometown newspapers also reacted badly in their letters, voice mail and e-mail, so this is not just a Kansas City phenomenon. It truly is an American sickness. I agree with Stuart Whitney that it can be traced directly to the presidency of Ronald Reagan and this country turning toward greed while it turned its back on the repairs offered by the Great Society programs of the 1960s and 1970s. They were labeled as failures by the right wing when nothing could be further from the truth. Talk radio, a fixture of those early years of conservative politics, trumpeted the "me"-ism. That media and societal punishment of the poor and people of color continues today, and those who are the most in need continue to pay the price.

In 2004, I spent three months in my old clothes visiting libraries because I was distressed that the opening of a new, ritzy library in downtown Kansas City, Mo., also was expected to include the exclusion of people who look homeless. The "compassion zone" that city officials wanted to create sounded good, but its purpose was to keep the poor and homeless out of Kansas City's gentrified downtown, and that's not right. What about the constitutional guarantees of freedom of movement, freedom of assembly and freedom of expression? What was being proposed was not what the Real America should be. Unfortunately, that is the America too many people confront.

In that 2004 sojourn into homelessness, I visited about 20 urban and suburban libraries in six different counties metrowide to check out whether people would be put off by individuals who looked homeless like me. Thankfully, no one seemed to care about folks who appeared to be homeless in the libraries. No one recognized me, either. I've had the same experience in libraries in Dallas, Orlando, Fla., and Tucson, where street people also go and cause no problems. So there is no need to ban them from the new Kansas City library or from libraries elsewhere nationwide, and thankfully no one so far has.

Public places need to be open to all people. Public accommodation laws are supposed to ensure that. Fortunately, they work at libraries, which welcome people who are homeless as much as those who are not.

From "Doors open to all; Libraries, as public treasures, should not exclude homeless"

> Three women and I arrived at the same time at the North Independence Branch of the Mid-Continent Public Library.
>
> One woman replied when I held the door open for them, "Chivalry is not dead." We laughed.
>
> It didn't matter that I wore my old Army coat, black knit cap, faded jeans and frayed shirt. I've dressed that way in January, February and March to gauge people's reaction to my appearance of homelessness.
>
> I wanted to see whether librarians and patrons felt wary or uncomfortable around me as some fear the homeless might make folks feel at the new downtown library. But people I encountered in the libraries were great.

I was just another patron, which is how homeless people should be seen at the new library.

It should be just as open and inviting to homeless people as the old downtown library was. People on the street had always sought shelter, read books and periodicals, used computers and napped at the old Kansas City Public Library until it closed in January for the opening of the new place.

The Main Branch was a midway stop for people walking from shelters east of downtown to the Grace and Holy Trinity Cathedral for a free midday meal. Now the city's neediest people may be "poverty profiled" and kept from the new library. Officials also are proposing a "compassion campus" near shelters to keep homeless people away from downtown's new library and upscale condominiums and loft apartments.

The compassion campus could include a homeless day center and soup kitchen. But people I talked with in January at a free blues concert by King Alex and the Untouchables for the homeless at the Grand Avenue Temple were outraged by plans to limit their freedom.

One homeless man said the irony is people like him would be excluded from the area they've helped rebuild. Homeless people often are picked up as day laborers rehabbing old buildings for new occupants.

I found people who appeared homeless at the Main, Westport, Northeast and Bluford branch libraries and the main library in Kansas City, Kan. But no one treated them differently from other patrons there or other libraries I visited.

At the libraries, teenagers arrived after classes. For younger children some branches seemed like after-school day care centers.

At a Lee's Summit branch young men sleeping at a table snored loudly. No one acted bothered. Libraries are public treasures with doors open to everyone.

I also found that the well-off downtown passers-by should be the occupants of a "compassion campus." For yet another year, they treated me badly because of how I was dressed. They need to see everyone, regardless of appearance, as a human being. What's happening now adds to the misery of the homeless.

"Anybody can become homeless," said Cindy Butler at the Grand Avenue Temple. "Everybody falls down sometimes."

She's right. Everyone needs kindness and warmth, especially at libraries.

I have found on these sojourns into homelessness that, because of the bad treatment I receive, I feel a natural tendency to start to look down and away from others as if I have suddenly taken on the heavy saddle of shame that they try to burden me with. Real homeless people naturally do that, and now I know why. Fortunately I shake out of it, understanding the emotional weight that people on the street must carry day after day.

A follow-up column in 2005 showed that the new Central Library downtown was not the problem. Again, as in my earlier examination, I found that people are the problem.

From "Compassion often evades the less fortunate among us"

The woman walking behind me froze when I turned to look at her after a stoplight flashed red.

That became her signal to hurriedly walk in another direction.

This is the 10th year that well-groomed people in the heartland have made me feel like garbage simply because of the clothes I had on.

The message is unspoken, yet unmistakable.

This year the exorbitant price of being poor went up. Missouri Gov. Matt Blunt plans to slash funds for social, mental health and health-care programs for the poor.

President Bush plans to do the same thing on a national level. Such acts will land more people in poverty and put those just getting by on the street.

Blunt and Bush fail to see what David K. Shipler notes in his book, *The Working Poor: Invisible in America*. The problems of poverty are "interlocking." Shipler wrote, "The first step is to see the problems, and the first problem is the failure to see the people."

Downtown on the street, people dressed in business clothes were going to lunch. Many stood outside smoking cigarettes. Others hurried to finish errands.

Nearly everyone looked at me and then quickly looked away. The red and white Salvation Army "HOPE" pin that I had on my coat was lost to passers-by.

A city that treats people as untouchables is a community that has lost its soul. People who also appeared to be homeless were friendly, telling me what the menu was at the Kansas City Community Kitchen at Grace and Holy Trinity Cathedral and offering a favorable critique of the free meal.

But I didn't stop to eat. I went to the Kansas City Central Library to see how people who look homeless were treated there.

Last year, plans surfaced of efforts to try to keep homeless people from the new library. Fortunately, that hasn't happened.

People who looked homeless were throughout the converted bank building. They mingled with others who were doing research or taking a break from work. An exhibit titled "The Art of Structural Design: A Swiss Legacy" attracted a mixed socio-economic crowd.

I went to the third floor, where I sometimes go to write columns for *The Kansas City Star.* When I'm in a suit and tie, people recognize me and stop to say hello.

In my old clothes, no one knew me. But one person, Betty Howard, who was on a break from her bank job, seemed to care. I sat at her table. When I asked, she didn't mind saying she was reading *The Laws of Spirit: Simple, Powerful Truths for Making Life Work* by Dan Millman.

She explained that it was about life, balance and compassion. I told her that I was surprised that she didn't mind talking with someone like me.

She asked, "What is someone like you?"

I said someone who looks penniless. She said the book from which she was taking notes helped her see the humanity in others.

"You can't judge people by their outside," Howard said. She explained that some people prejudged her. That never feels good.

Howard said she was not far removed from others who were less fortunate. She's from California and was raised by a single mother.

She, however, managed to go to college, get married and have three children. No one should be so quick to judge folks who are not as well off.

"I think sometimes you come to a point in your life where you've made mistakes, and a lot of people travel down the same road," Howard said.

If only her wisdom could infect others.

In 2005 I also noted on my walk into the world of homelessness that there are so many people on cell phones now walking the streets of downtown that they feel entitled to be disconnected from other people on the street. That is not good in a city that needs to have a sense of community for all of its residents.

In 1998 I went to Truman Medical Center, the hospital for the indigent in Kansas City, to see how I would be treated there. Health care professionals at Truman were great. The places that offer help and care to homeless people are a godsend.

From "Caring eyes see beyond the exterior"

When I return to Truman Medical Center on March 26 to see Mona Bahl and Gary Salzman, I'll wear a suit and tie.

I had shed those work clothes last week and gone to Truman Medical Center seeking a physical exam dressed in my old clothes. While health-care professionals at the city hospital were checking me out, I also was noting their reaction to my appearance of poverty.

I wanted to try to determine whether managed care and new Hospital Hill construction were squeezing out people in need. I wanted to see how our teaching hospital treated people seeking health care but who appeared to have no ability to pay. The hospital, which is part of Family Health Partners, swarms with 250,000 clinic and emergency-room visits a year.

That no doubt exceeds what other medical facilities handle. It'd be as if more than half of Kansas City's population annually went to Truman for health care. About 45 percent of the patients are Medicaid clients, 20 percent Medicare, and 30 percent are indigent or working poor, said John Miers, hospital finance director.

I was in the odd 5 percent with health insurance. I'd been here before as a patient in 1977 soon after I started at *The Kansas City Star*. I wanted to see and was impressed then with how people in need were treated. Marsha Landrum found that my name was still in her outpatient computer.

I also surprised her with the expired remnants of my TMC green clinic card. Landrum was efficient and caring before she knew who I was. Afterward she sent me down the hall to the green clinic, where I had been a patient 21 years ago.

I took my new book, *A Country of Strangers*, by David K. Shipler, to read. I waited to see a doctor with an array of older, younger, black, white and Hispanic people on March 4.

They got to stay. I had to leave. Hospital workers apologized, but rules didn't permit walk-in physicals. Calling the day before didn't count as an appointment.

A woman in the clinic scheduled me for the next day. I returned, seeing Bahl, a University of Missouri-Kansas City medical school student, and Salzman, a physician. To them I was just another guy in tattered clothes. But each treated me as if I were Bill Gates.

"You can be rich, but that can change overnight," Bahl said after the exam when I told her who I was. "God can take that away from you as soon as he gave it to you. The next day you could be homeless. That doesn't make a person untouchable."

Salzman agreed: "We try to do our best to treat everybody like we would want to be treated."

Bahl added: "If anything, you have to nurture them more. I absolutely adore my patients."

But poverty often leaves many with health problems. She said people my age walk in with high blood pressure, high cholesterol, enlarged livers, diabetes, obesity, heart problems, high stroke risks, prostate trouble and poor diets.

Salzman called Friday, saying tests showed I was boringly normal.

Bahl cheers such preventive health care. "If you can help one person get on track with health maintenance, you've accomplished a lot," she said.

I told Bahl that she accomplishes a lot more on a daily basis. That's exemplified by the care she and others provided to me, despite my shabby dress.

To better serve people who are homeless, students at the medical center decided to take their services to the street. They established the Sojourners Free Health Clinic in the Grand Avenue Temple in downtown Kansas City, Missouri. That church has a special outreach to homeless people, offering soulful healing, a soup kitchen and other services to people of many needs. Health care just happens to be one the programs. I visited the temple during a cold spell on my 2006 walkabout.

From "Health care for homeless"

The clinic opened in October 2004 and is staffed by University of Missouri-Kansas City School of Medicine students. The UMKC Center for the City helped them get connected to the temple at 205 E. Ninth St. as a community partner.

Seven young women and one man in medical school scrubs put up plastic pipes and shower curtains as makeshift examination rooms for patient privacy. People interrupted, asking for cough drops and Tylenol to ease their pain. Folks on the street hurt a lot.

Homelessness and the cold expose people to myriad health problems. They include back and knee pains, colds and flu, respiratory ailments, dental trouble, diabetes, asthma, skin infections and high blood pressure.

"We try to help the people as best we can," said Dan Purdom, a family practice physician and the faculty adviser for the clinic. "There are plenty of doctors to take care of people who have money. They're learning how difficult it is for people without resources to get the care they need."

Those without health coverage are among the sickest and neediest.

"I've learned how much we can do with few resources," said Lisa Roark, one of the clinic managers. "We all try to do as much as we can."

Brook Nelson, clinic executive director and a founder, said Sojourners had a budget of $3,500 a year and received about $20,000 in donated material. With more donated funds, it could expand its services to include additional medications and screenings for HIV and hepatitis.

"We're kind of limited now in certain things we can do," said Nelson.

Purdom said students created the clinic from nothing. They held fundraisers for it, decided what medicines to offer and what to put on patient charts.

"It's a great experience for them," he said.

They learn every week. At the end of each four-hour Sunday clinic, they have "learning circles" to review what they've picked up.

"I never would have known there are so many homeless people downtown," said Roark, who graduates in May 2007. "It says to me our system is broken."

Sarah Mackinson, who graduates in May 2008, took my blood pressure and checked my pulse. Another student checked my aching right knee. It's likely arthritis, he said. The care the students provided was excellent.

People with chronic conditions return to be examined and pick up prescriptions. Jerry said he got his blood pressure medication at Sojourners.

"It gives them the experience they need, too," he said.

David said he went to the free clinic because he trusted the people and the care he received. "They make it easy," he said.

"They don't question you," he added. "You're ill, and they take care of you. They don't judge you."

Chris, who was at the clinic for prenatal care, said many doctors were "holier than thou," which was a turnoff. The health-care providers at the clinic are different.

The church program borrows a passage from the Bible saying, "Love your neighbor as you love yourself." It also says, "What we do together makes a difference."

At Sojourners Free Health Clinic, there is no doubt.

What the press often project of homelessness is as ugly as the initial coverage and devastation left by Hurricane Katrina. Untouchable is the feeling that people pick up, and instead of doing something about homelessness, nothing is done at the very least, and bad behavior toward those most in need occurs at the very worst.

I see that when I dress in my old clothes. There are ugly words and stares full of hatred, but worst of all Kansas Citians just rush by and purposefully ignore the humanity of people who appear worse off than they are. A walkabout I took in 1999 with a companion was especially telling.

From "Icy stares into faces of poverty"

Jack Olsen, then-adjunct professor at Avila University teaching finance, was dressed in his old Army coat, faded jeans and a knit cap when he joined me on my annual trek to gauge people's reaction to the appearance of poverty.

We went to Hypermart, the Main Library, City Center Square, Town Pavilion, a downtown bank, City Hall, the Jackson County Courthouse, a thrift store, Blue Ridge Mall, Independence Center, Metro North, Station Casino, a barbecue joint and a department store.

Many people gave us cold stares. Others looked briefly and then averted their eyes.

Olsen, who retired in 1994 as a fund manager after 25 years with Waddell & Reed, was nearly hit by a car that was turning downtown. The driver on a cell phone didn't see us. "It's as if I didn't exist!" Olsen said.

We were invisible to a lot of people. Blue Ridge Mall surveyors ignored us. A woman shifted her purse to her other side and hurried into the Independence Center shopping center when she saw us in the parking lot.

"I'm only voyaging here," Olsen said. "This isn't my life."

The slights would be debilitating if they happened every day. A TV reporter who normally chats with me was unresponsive when I greeted him as Olsen and I passed the courthouse steps.

"He completely blew you off!" Olsen said.

Olsen and I noticed something else, too. African-Americans generally were more courteous, less fearful and more welcoming.

A white food court clerk at the Town Pavilion refused to acknowledge Olsen as he tried to ask where the restrooms were. Yet a black fast-food clerk at Hypermart greeted us with coffee, and another black man happily held a restroom door for Olsen, who is white.

Security guards noticed us, too, albeit warily at City Hall, the courthouse, the bank and the library.

"We value people based on their money all the way up the line," Olsen said. "I think it should be deeper than that.

"No matter what you wear, no matter what you look like, you are people."

And yet many define the trustworthiness of others by the clothes they wear. If that outside layer is deemed "unacceptable," then the person within becomes an outcast, something to be avoided. And people will squirm to get away from the socio-economic diversity that lives and breathes among us and that is manifested in our appearance. That came through loud and clear during the walkabout I took to the Kansas City International Airport and other metropolitan transportation hubs in 2002.

From "If clothes make the man, that's wrong"

The woman in the aluminum-colored coat didn't expect it, but I held her arm and guided her so she could safely exit the KCI Shuttle for the US Airways terminal.

Her arms were full of bags and books, and she couldn't see where she was stepping. "A gentleman! Thank you," she said.

I smiled, but I wanted to laugh out loud. She and I had sat together in the back of the packed van from a downtown hotel to Kansas City International Airport. She'd worked so hard to keep from touching me, as did the man who sat on my other side.

Other passengers were pressed shoulder-to-shoulder yet comfortably talked with others about their travels.

The man and woman beside me remained distant and silent.

When I'm in those old clothes they are clean; so am I.

My garments make me look penniless. That causes many passers-by in these compassion-challenged times to treat me as if I were diseased.

This strangeness is happening as the ranks of the homeless, jobless and low-income keep increasing. Poor treatment only makes these individuals feel worse.

That's especially deplorable now that the nation is at war and President Bush has urged Americans to aid others by volunteering their time to community service. No helping hand, sense of caring and trust should be color-coded or exclude people because they don't appear socially or economically acceptable.

That's why I enjoyed my hour-long stay at the Amtrak station in Kansas City. People left an arriving train and climbed a long escalator to Main Street.

Others came down the stairs and entered from a nearby garage to wait for passengers or catch the next train. Amtrak serves an ethnic, racial and economic mix of people. There was no indication that my being at the station, again dressed in my old clothes, had alarmed or bothered anyone.

The reaction was the same at the Greyhound bus terminal, which is downtown and near two shelters for homeless people.

A "No Loitering" sign was out front. The seats at the bus station are made of an uncomfortable wire mesh. I stayed there for an hour.

I bought a Coke at the snack bar. A friendly woman behind the counter handed me my receipt and pleasantly said, "Have a nice day."

That was so different from my experience at a KCI food court in Terminal B, where I got off the shuttle. The clerk operating the cash register at the crowded fast-food place gave a man in a business suit ahead of me a smile and a nice greeting. The businessman's change was put directly into his hand and he was given a receipt without asking.

The same clerk greeted me with a grimace. My change was placed on the counter, not in my hand. He gave me no receipt.

KCI is a place where I've always found people-watching to be fun. But I had never gone to the airport in these old clothes.

On this outing, folks stared disapprovingly at me or quickly looked away as I passed. People were mostly stalled in long lines at ticket counters or waited to clear tedious security checks at the gates.

The airport was patrolled by men and women in National Guard fatigues. I bothered no one and tried not to arouse suspicion.

I left after two hours and boarded the KCI Shuttle back to the downtown hotel.

The driver, who told me he had immigrated to America, was friendly. In this country, money and business interests matter the most, he said.

As we rode, a Marvin Gaye song played on the radio:

Woo ah, mercy mercy me

Ah, things ain't what they used to be, no no

Where did all the blue skies go?

Poison is the wind that blows from the north and south and east...

Things aren't what they should be. Somehow people must see the humanity in others regardless of appearances.

The person with the greatest need for kindness today could be any one of us tomorrow.

During my walk in 2000 I had company in homelessness, which helped soften the blow of my assumed state of poverty. We visited churches in the Kansas City area and found that not even these are sanctuaries against others' hated stares, which keep people in need in a constant state of oppression and rejection.

From "Humbled and homeless"

In a perfect world, the journey Janet Brown Moss and I took into area churches dressed as homeless people would've turned out differently.

"I would have liked for someone to come up to me and say, 'I'm so glad to see you here,'" said Moss, then-coordinator of the Congregational Partners Program with Kansas City Harmony. "People should have asked, 'Do you live nearby? How is it you happened to come to our church?' and be very genuine about it."

That would have embodied the "WWJD" on today's fashionable jewelry, meaning What Would Jesus Do?

Christianity is supposed to be like that—welcoming, loving and ministering without prejudice to all souls, especially the poor.

One pastor even said in his sermon, "We can't take a spiritual shortcut around civility."

But a lot of people did on the Sundays last month that Moss and I visited five churches.

Moss accompanied me in an orange knit cap, tattered purple coat, old flannel shirt and pink sweat pants. Unknown to others, her partner, Joel Wakham, joined us in casual church-going clothes to watch people watching us.

I've done this before at shopping malls and other places. Going to church grew from an e-mail message a woman sent me last year about a pastor who dressed as a homeless man and stood outside his church before entering, noting how people distanced themselves from him.

Moss and I followed that pattern. Wakham went in first.

Many well-dressed people passed Moss and me as we stood outside before entering a black midtown Kansas City church, a white mega-church in south Leawood, a white midsize church in Overland Park and a white Northland church.

Service had already started when we arrived at a black Kansas City, Kan., church.

The good news is no one turned us away or cursed us despite our appearance as an impoverished interracial couple. But at best people overall were only politely distant.

Our sojourn clearly showed that the twin social diseases of classism and indifference have infected our faiths.

At the midtown black church, people went out of their way to make Wakham, who's white, feel welcome. "I sat down, and people came to me," he said.

Moss, who assists congregations of different faiths develop trust and communication with each other, said, "I felt they were warm, but nobody came to us."

Wakham added, "It seemed to me people quit going down the row right after you sat there."

The Leawood church featured theatrical lighting, a fabulous sound system and video cameras that projected pulpit actions and the words to hymns on big-screen TVs. Moss noted that when we were separated in the lobby, people avoided her. "It was like there was almost this circular shield around me," she said.

Outside the churches where we stood, people who passed Moss and me either looked at us with disgust, avoided eye contact or were friendly.

Some people at the Overland Park church seemed distant.

"What I noticed was when people shook hands, there was just a little split-second hesitancy from everyone," Moss said. "For the most part it was like we weren't there."

At the Overland Park church, a woman in the pew where Moss and I sat moved her purse from between me and her and substituted it with her coat.

"It's kind of a different culture out here," Wakham said.

At the Northland church, which offers valet parking, attendants asked Moss and me if we wanted rides from where we'd left my van. Most of the people made us feel welcome.

The Kansas City, Kan., church was the same way. "I felt people were welcoming and inclusive," Moss said.

Children, however, gave all of us curious looks because we stood out. One girl used a compact mirror to stare at me.

At three of the churches, we saw people we knew. A half-dozen recognized us and spent time to hug, shake hands and chat. Others didn't bother to look past our clothes.

"I see so much potential if people would come together out of their faith or the faith they say they have," Moss said. "Faith that even though I'm afraid, even though this is uncomfortable, even though this is foreign, I'm going to take that risk to get to know people who are different and be purposeful and intentional in seeking out difference until the difference feels familiar."

I pray that one day it will happen before thy kingdom comes.

That day, unfortunately, still seems far off. Each time I do these kinds of columns I get blasted by folks who are greatly offended that I would have the brass to "out" people like them who openly exhibit bad behavior toward others who appear destitute. In the winter of 2001, I visited and wrote about Midtown banks that I used to frequent, which now house check-cashing services.

From "When 'haves' bully 'have-nots'"

The mercury topped 10 degrees when I stepped onto the street last Friday and into the world homeless people face every day.

On this outing, I parked at the new Costco store on Linwood Boulevard and walked to Broadway. People in warm cars pulling away from fast-food driveways hurriedly locked their doors as I walked past in the chilling cold.

Motorists at intersections angrily honked their horns and a few nearly ran me down when their culture of the car collided with the pedestrian nature of the homeless. Our humanity suffers when the "haves" bully the "have-nots."

People on the street in Kansas City's winter are true survivors. Their ranks may grow as energy prices climb, companies lay off more workers and families' emaciated savings run out.

In the 1970s I used to do my banking on Broadway and Main Street. I even dressed then in that same old Army coat in those more accepting days.

Times have changed, and so have three of my old banks. They're payday loan and check cashing joints now.

I went into six of those businesses. The employees - most behind bulletproof glass - were very friendly. All the people waiting in lines with me also were black.

I felt outraged. But customers at one place accepted the 16

percent charge for cashing personal checks and 6 percent fee for payroll checks. Payday loans of $50 came with a $12.50 charge, or 25 percent markup.

None of that surprised Gary Dymski, associate professor of economics at the University of California-Riverside. He was in Kansas City last fall speaking on racial inequities in credit.

"When you have no place else to turn, the monopolies can name their price," Dymski told me this week. He called the people in line with me "the unbanked."

Minimum deposit requirements, overdrawn accounts, bill juggling and sporadic work histories put them outside banks' doors. Dymski said they constitute 14 percent of all U.S. families.

He added that some researchers said nearly half of all African-American families were among the unbanked. That's a 21st century tragedy. But friendly fringe-banking services are happy to take them in.

Yet such services strip mine what little wealth is left among many people in the urban core. They become poorer while folks in the suburbs with greater access to banks and investment get richer.

"The inner city is running a trade deficit, so to speak, with the rest of the world," Dymski said. People are spending down, or "deaccumulating wealth," in pawn shops and fringe banks as inner cities nationwide continue to devolve to Third World status.

"Kansas City has classic American urban problems in very stark terms," Dymski said. Reversing them will take a united effort by banks, businesses and people reinvesting in America's urban cores.

Education and the housing stock must be renewed and the tax base resuscitated. An investment also needs to occur in the people so they can earn a living wage and not just get by or survive on the street.

No one should be left in the cold.

When I wrote that column, I got this from a reader:

Woe are the poor "unbanked" negroes. Perhaps if they saved the funds that they squander away on lottery tickets, gold teeth and malt liquor they could meet the minimum deposit requirements. Fat chance though, as that would require self-discipline, which is something that white-regulated social engineering has stripped from you brown people since birth.

People are never bashful about showing their true colors. It amazes me constantly that they are so certain and so smug in their hatred of others who are different. Some reactions I receive to the columns blame the victim:

E-mail: March 10, 2004

I was wondering when you were going to perform this stunt again!!

> You know libraries should not be shelters for the homeless! Should we give them soup and sandwiches there, too?? A little TV perhaps?? I doubt these folks are reading *The Wall Street Journal*. They are probably looking at porn and God knows what!
>
> The public has a right to go into a library and not have to see someone who has not bathed in a week and has urine running down his leg! I have an idea. Why don't you suggest to *The Kansas City Star* that they start a homeless shelter there! They could drink coffee and eat doughnuts with Jason Whitlock and keep warm and watch how the news is made! If they ever got up enough gumption, they might even ask for a job! That's a little extreme, I know!
>
> The folks down at *The Star* are a liberal bunch. I think this would be a good soup kitchen/job training center for the homeless. Instead of cursing the darkness, you could light a candle!
>
> You are a classic liberal. You always want to bring everyone down to their level. Why not ask them to come up in the world? Could you ask them to quit drinking or drugging and have some self-discipline?? Maybe you could ask why these folks can't stay in one place very long. That might prove to be very interesting.

This is an e-mail from one of my frequent detractors. Others attack the messenger. On my winter 2003 sojourn into homelessness, I actually visited the area's largest soup kitchen and wrote about how it daily serves hundreds of the community's less fortunate.

From "A hot meal in invisible suffering"

> The stranger in line with me shared his American dream.
>
> He wanted a good job that paid a livable wage. He said he was a fast learner and wouldn't shrink from hard work.
>
> He wanted money in his pockets, a home of his own and someone to love to share his dream.
>
> It didn't seem like too much to ask for a man turning 43 years old this month.
>
> But his dream seemed far-fetched from where we stood with hundreds of men and women waiting for a hot meal at the Kansas City Community Kitchen at Grace and Holy Trinity Cathedral downtown.
>
> Some of Kansas City's top citizens went into the church on other business. They glanced at the line but looked away.
>
> People I passed downtown did the same thing. Men and women who appear impoverished or homeless are invisible.
>
> It's as if they live and suffer in another dimension where no one sees them and few people care. I first noticed that about 10 years ago. It hasn't changed.
>
> A TV news van drove by the church. But it didn't stop at the

area's largest soup kitchen, where every weekday volunteers serve this community's longest lines of need.

Dave Nichols, the kitchen's culinary program director, said the basement facility seats 80. But from noon to 2 p.m. it serves about 600 people.

The numbers have mushroomed since the Sept. 11, 2001, terrorist attacks. Back then it served 325. The kitchen depends on 350 volunteers each month and gifts of food and cash from donors.

The man with the American dream explained how the soup kitchen works. He directed me to a woman who handed 2-inch square numbered cards to everyone.

"Without a number," the man said, "you don't eat." Other soup kitchens where I've volunteered aren't as regimented. But they aren't as large.

The woman gave me No. 58. All the number cards said "God Bless America." Indeed.

The woman was the gatekeeper. She called out numbers as space at tables opened in the serving area.

People of all ages, races, faiths and ethnicities streamed from the street into the line. Voices spoke different languages in the crowd.

"Food is kind of a common language," Nichols said. People keep coming as the bad times get worse.

The soup kitchen began in 1980 - then serving about 75-100 daily - just before the Reagan revolution began dismantling government safety nets. The numbers have increased sixfold and threaten to go higher as more social service programs collapse while President Bush pursues the war against terrorism, a war in Iraq and tax cuts for the wealthiest Americans.

"A lot of people come here because money is tighter now," Nichols said. They're the unemployed and the underemployed. "They come here so they can afford the other things in life."

The woman called my number and a half-dozen others. We moved quickly to the serving line, got a tray, either coffee, purple Kool-Aid or water and found a seat in the crowd.

Talking isn't encouraged; eating quickly is.

"They understand if they take a chair the persons outside don't get one," Nichols said.

I hurriedly ate two sausage patties, two slices of bread, some potato slices, a salad, two breakfast burritos topped with cheese, a cinnamon roll, the cup of purple yogurt and the Kool-Aid. That was a lot of food, but probably the only meal many would get. The man with the American dream got done fast and left.

He's a veteran of this place. But it shouldn't be that way in the

> greatest nation on the planet.
>
> I sent the kitchen $100. It was for the meal and to help feed others as they wait for the American dream.

The $100 was a donation from my own personal funds. Yet this is what I got from a regular "fan":

> Now Lewis, you were supposed to inform me prior to your next homeless negro vermin excursion so that I could urinate on you for better effect. You would have undoubtedly been more convincing had you been sporting the stench of urine. And how negro-ish of you to thieve a homeless person's grub. That's right, Lewis... Some homeless dude went hungry that day because you gobbled his grub. And how kind-hearted of you to donate $100 to the cause... Courtesy of your expense account, no doubt. Excellent entertainment, Lewis... A real rib-tickler.

Too many of us want to pay someone to sweep away the problem of homelessness. Move those people someplace else! Many in the majority say the same thing about minorities, and I hear a lot of that when I write about diversity, multicultural education and people of color. James Loewen's book *Sundown Towns* shows quite clearly that, from 1890 to 1930, this country did exactly that—violently evicting African Americans from towns throughout the United States. Laws were passed which formalized the prohibiting and boldly posted signs that read, "Don't Let the Sun Set on You, Nigger." African Americans who worked for whites in those towns had to be gone before sundown or face assaults or death. Suburbs with government-enforced racial covenants followed. The restrictions and some of the signs even remained in place until near the start of the 21st century. America is treating its homeless people in a similar way now in some cities. They are evicted from their longtime dwellings, violently beaten in some places and even murdered.

But we have to start treating others in all walks of life better because those whom we encounter now who have to live with being the less fortunate among us could easily be us some day. We must never forget what one reader from Freeman, Mo., wrote in reaction to one of my columns on homelessness: "There but for the grace of God go I."

CHAPTER 15

Solutions Behind Bars: The End and the Beginning of a Journey

Losses to A New Slavery

Metal dragging on concrete makes a rhythmic mournful cry.
It heaves with each man's shuffle and every family's sigh
Of losing a loved one to useless prisons, 2.3 million now,
And more than half of them black and Latino locked up with no hope—how foul—
Of being the breadwinner, husband, father, son, uncle or nephew, just despair
For the loss that started with inequitable prenatal care
And continued into the schools with foul marked-for-failure labels,
Unfair!
So the dragging cries of communities of color sing
The blues to music of shackles' chains
Slinking across smooth concrete and linoleum floors, keeping time,
People now find
Stolen lives from communities of color shifted to rural places for economic gains
Progress wanes
Lost independence, opportunity and freedoms escape
As our men march to these beefy rural guards' pace
Two communities trapped in corporate, bad government's and racism's grip
Of one impoverished group guarding another, and neither gaining from the script.
The heavy bars, the razor wire, the slamming doors,
The tortured souls
Fed into Americas gluttonous PIC, prison industrial complex,
Fattening the rich, further damaging the poor, left perplexed
Adding new generations to the miles of human cages
Of a new slavery that grips the nation
With gleaming Big Houses across the land, new plantations
Harvesting profit from misery's cruel plan
All to benefit what we call The Man.
There's no joy in such black pain
Only families' tears and continuing shame,
Dragging with each man's shackles, handcuffs and chains.

I believe that my redemption symbolizes the end of a bad beginning and a new start.
It goes beyond, in a sense of being liberated from one's sins or atonement in itself.
I feel that my redemption mostly or primarily encompasses the ability to reach out to others.
~Stanley Tookie Williams

The population in prison is growing and becoming more diverse. In America, nearly half of the people in prisons are African Americans. Add to that Hispanics who are incarcerated, and the ranks of people of color swell to more than 50 percent. That figure is grossly disproportionate to the 13 percent black and 14 percent Hispanic people in the general population. Social scientists have developed a way of measuring the cost on a mass scale in terms of years of life lost. It's a way of looking at potential harm to communities and specific populations after a disaster. For example, the Sept. 11, 2001, terrorist attack in New York City that brought down the World Trade Center and killed 2,900 people represented 90,000 years of life lost. That is the loss of productivity of human beings whose lives were tragically cut short, according to the Urban League *State of Black America 2003* book. People in prison have not lost their productivity through loss of life. Many are legitimately behind bars for crimes. But there are far too many held for convictions in narcotics cases. Their productivity stagnates because they are incarcerated. The book says that:

> In the United States now, there are more than 450,000 individuals incarcerated for non-violent drug offenses. This number alone equals the [years of life lost] that would be associated with 15,000 deaths of people in a similar age group. For the last thirty years of drug incarcerations, the total [years of life lost] is equivalent to more than 200,000 deaths—twice the number of U.S. soldiers killed in both the Korean and Vietnam wars. (158)

A comparison with another war has been made by Kathy Kelly. She draws important links between life for people in Iraq and life for 2.3 million individuals in America's many prisons.

<u>From "The crimes of war in Iraq, of prisons in U.S."</u>

> Kelly has been in both places. A teacher and founder of the Chicago-based Voices in the Wilderness, she has made many humanitarian trips to Iraq, before the current war, during its start and afterward.
>
> As a longtime peace activist, she has been arrested and incarcerated in several places, including the Cass County (Mo.) Jail and Pekin Federal Corrections Institution in Illinois.
>
> She wrote about the lockdown of war that everyday people in Iraq face and the prisons that Americans contend with at home.
>
> "Every time I left Iraq, during sanctions, war and occupation, I felt as if I were leaving one big prison," Kelly wrote in her book, *Other Lands Have Dreams: From Baghdad to Pekin Prison.* "How ironic that Voices in the Wilderness members were accused of being criminals, while we felt, every time, like we were leaving the scene of a vast crime.

"But whenever I have been released from U.S. prisons, into comfort and security, I have also felt like I was walking away from a vast crime. These crimes are connected. I see a war that is also going on here at home."

During that crime, the United States is spending billions of dollars fighting the war in Iraq, which President Bush started based on dubious intelligence. More than 2,500 U.S. troops have died, and more than 10,000 others have been wounded. Thousands of Iraqis have been killed and wounded since the invasion began in March 2003.

Prisons in the United States are wasteful places, too. State, local and federal governments spend billions of dollars to lock up people instead of providing education, rehabilitation and prevention. Prisons and jails pull fathers and mothers from their children and taxpayers from communities that need human, social and financial resources.

"When money, talent and resources are poured into military systems and prison systems, while health, education and welfare systems compete for inadequate budget allotments, we can expect constant warfare abroad and the quadrupling of prisoner populations at home, which has occurred in the U.S. over the last 25 years," Kelly wrote.

"Military and prison structures don't train recruits to view 'the enemy' or 'the inmate' as precious and valuable humans deserving forgiveness, mercy and respect even if they have trespassed against us. These systems don't foster the notion that we ourselves could be mistaken, that we might seek forgiveness, or that we might together with presumed outcasts create a better world.

"Look to Scriptures for such views – they're there – but don't expect love of enemy and the Golden Rule to guide military, prison or intelligence systems anywhere in the world."

Kelly worries about the children in Iraq and those of people in prisons in America. It's a growing concern now that women's incarceration rate is growing faster than men's. A recent Bureau of Justice Statistics report showed that the number of women behind bars in state and federal prisons in 2004 was up 4 percent compared with 2003 - double the 1.8 percent rise in male prisoners.

Kelly wrote, "The prison-industrial complex is a cruel extension of U.S. war-making against the poor in our country."

Relating Kelly's experiences was meant to expand people's thinking about losses in both war and prison, yet vociferous feedback showed a lack of empathy or compassion for the ex-offenders, their families or the communities to which they return. The messages express no concern for the cost of maintaining such an unsustainable, destructive penal code.

E-mail: April 12, 2006

I've always thought that you were one of the most misguided people on the planet but Kathy Kelly makes you appear almost reasonable.

News flash for Ms. Kelly...these people are in prison because they were convicted of a crime. They are separated from their families because they chose to either murder, molest, rape, rob, sell drugs or whatever and are now paying for that choice. Why should anyone excuse this behavior, as Ms. Kelly suggests we do? Whatever happened to personal responsibility and paying one's debt to society? Ms. Kelly is simply another clueless, hate-America leftist who thinks this country is the root of all evil.

E-mail: April 12, 2006

First of all you are talking apples and oranges. The war in Iraq may not be the best fought battle ever but it was justified. Not only that but if Iran keeps up its threat of nuclear ability, we should go blow there ass off the planet.

Secondly, prisons are not for rehabilitation. They are for punishment and retribution. In my opinion, prisoners have no rights; unlike the opinions of the despicable ACLU which should also be put to death. If the judicial system was competent, more criminals would be put to death and more criminals would have much longer sentences as they deserve.

But incarceration does no one any good. There must be a societal will to reduce the need for imprisonment and decriminalize the image of black people. That, however, is not how people in this country feel about ex-offenders.

E-mail: Nov. 8, 2002

Like a dog with a poor nose and eyesight, you continue to bark up the wrong tree. Prisons are built to house criminals regardless of the color of their skin. As it happens, more blacks commit crimes than whites with the result more are in jails. That is what the facts show; not that building prisons causes blacks to commit criminal offenses. Your continual search for excuses, other than culpability, remains counterproductive.

In his book, *Amazing Grace: The Lives of Children and the Conscience of a Nation,* Jonathan Kozol suggests a motive for incarcerating thousands of people of color: "If you want to get your outcasts out of sight, first you need a ghetto and then you need a prison to take pressure off the ghetto. The fact that it doesn't make financial sense is not the point. Short-term terror and revulsion are more powerful than long-term wisdom or self-interest" (142).

But James Loewen offers a different view in his book, *Sundown Towns.* Despite African Americans being welcomed in just about every county in America after the Civil War, thousands of towns and suburbs throughout the United States violently and by law evicted their black populations from after the end of Reconstruction well into the 20th century. Even though these communities in the North, East, Midwest and West became all white, they still depended on black labor. Loewen wrote:

> Sprinkled about the United States, often located at the edge of sundown towns or a few miles away, are other, smaller black communities, most of which never incorporated, many with dirt roads, off the beaten path. They are the flipside of sundown towns – places to which the excluded have retreated to live, yet close enough to nearby white towns to work. I call them "townships" because some of them resemble South Africa's black townships, those gatherings of shacks built by squatters that supply maids for Johannesburg's white households and janitors for its industries. Like Thokoza and Soweto, in America often these were haphazard gatherings of ramshackle houses, many of which were not, until recently, served by amenities such as city water. Some still are not.... To some degree, these communities resemble reservations – places to which whites restricted African Americans whose labor they desired but whose presence they did not want. (84-85)

But whites also historically frequented these places for illicit purposes including prostitution, gambling, alcohol during Prohibition and illegal drugs. Loewen writes

> White sheriffs and police chiefs often wink at deviant or illegal behavior in black townships, as it fulfills three functions at once in the white community. It relieves the demand for the deviance, which usually involves victimless "crimes" like drinking, gambling, buying drugs, and buying sex. It avoids arousing the forces of priggery because the behavior does not take place in neighborhoods they care about, hence is not salient. And it further stigmatizes both the black township and African Americans in general. (87)

That stigmatization continues as blacks bear the brunt of the punishment for drug crimes, for example. Some facts compiled by Douglas A. McVay on drug use and convictions show that in 1999,

> [a]ccording to the federal Household Survey, "most current illicit drug users [were] white. There were an estimated 9.9 million whites (72 percent of all users), 2.0 million blacks (15 percent), and 1.4 million Hispanics (10 percent) who were current illicit drug users in 1998." And yet, blacks constitute 36.8% of those arrested for drug violations and over 42% of those in federal prisons for drug violations. African-Americans comprise almost 57% of those in state prisons for drug felonies; Hispanics account for 17.2%.

McVay adds that [a]mong persons convicted of drug felonies in state courts, whites were less likely than African-Americans to be sent to prison. Thirty-three percent (33%) of convicted white defendants received a prison sentence, while 51% of African-American defendants received prison sentences. ("Drug War Facts")

In other words, most whites committing drug-related crimes *aren't* doing the time, making it look as if most of the criminals are black. This is not justice served; it is racism, plain and simple.

Prisons serve as a wedge, keeping African Americans separated from one another. Men in prison call it the 20th and 21st century forms of American slavery. There are many striking similarities. Each strips the black community of human capital, financial capital, intellectual capital and social capital. Once capital is taken away, it's hard to reclaim. For even when the men and women go back to the neighborhoods and families that gave birth to them, they often return to inequality and are confronted with the perpetual image of blacks as criminals. The situation is an ongoing American tragedy that starts with deficient schools offering a poor education that leads individuals to make bad choices that almost seem designed to feed the prison industrial complex in this country. It disproportionately targets people of color. And even though the cost of incarceration is enormous in lives squandered, there are those who profit from the prison-industrial complex now firmly established in this country.

From "Potential locked up in prisons"

> Angela Davis drew many parallels between slavery and today's growth of the prison industrial complex.
>
> Each is a profitable economic system, Davis told more than 500 people at the University of Missouri-Kansas City. Slavery boosted the economy of the South, where U.S. wealth until 1865 was concentrated.
>
> Prisons today are a boon to rural communities, creating jobs, new housing, restaurants and hotels. Inmate labor also generates capital.
>
> Like slavery, "we've reached the point where the prison economy is not marginal to the larger economy," said Davis, a 1960s radical, author and professor in the history and consciousness department at the University of California-Santa Cruz. But prison growth drains resources from health care, education and jobs. "It devours funds needed for institutions that let people lead decent lives," Davis said.
>
> Like slavery, prisons also are violent places where many black people suffer. Racial profiling, unfair drug laws and judicial inequities contribute to blacks heavily subsidizing the prison-industrial complex.
>
> Slaves had no rights and couldn't vote. Davis said prison has become "a major impediment to a democratic society," one that leaves

many African-Americans "civically dead."

Davis noted that the abolitionist movement helped end slavery in the 19th century.

"In the beginning of the 21st century, we should be talking about the abolition of the prison system," Davis said.

Randall G. Shelden, in his book *Controlling the Dangerous Classes*, argued that "imprisonment is one among many forms that have developed over the years to contain and house those individuals who are part of the dangerous class."

Prisons after the Civil War helped re-establish white supremacy. Through "convict leasing" prisons provided "an abundant source of cheap labor to help rebuild the war-torn South." Jim Crow laws helped change prisons from being mostly white to mostly black, Shelden wrote.

For example, in 1855, 66 percent of the 200 inmates at the state prison at Nashville, Tenn., were white. By 1879 the prison's population soared to 1,183, and 68 percent were black.

Shelden wrote the penal system now "is sort of a ghetto" reserved largely for "racial minorities, especially African-Americans - which is why this system is being called the new American apartheid."

The growth of prisons parallels the 20th century rise of the black middle class. According to the Census Bureau, the median household income for blacks in 1999 was the highest ever recorded. Also, 51 percent of black married-couple-families had incomes of $50,000 or more compared with 60 percent of whites. Incarceration slows the black community's economic progress.

Prison growth also mirrors hopeful periods for blacks. The first from 1790 to 1830 followed the American Revolution when slaves also fought for freedom against the British.

The second wave of prison growth from 1830 to 1870 paralleled the abolitionist movement, the Underground Railroad, the end of slavery and beginning of Reconstruction. Prison growth from 1870 to 1946 occurred during the end of Reconstruction, the migration of blacks from the South to jobs in the North and West.

"The last two eras (1946 to 1980 and 1980 to present) have seen the greatest growth in the prison system," Shelden wrote. That also parallels the integration of the military and the Civil Rights Movement.

Davis urged people to do more to create a better environment outside of prison to eliminate the need for incarceration. Society needs alternative sentencing, improvements in education and jobs.

We don't need more prisons.

But that's not how people who sent feedback felt. More prisons, not fewer, was favored. Getting tougher on crime, especially involving blacks, was their mandate to elected officials. Their denial of racism is overpowering.

E-mail: Nov. 8, 2002

"Close a prison; stop a crime" will never sell in a civilized society.

E-mail: Nov. 8, 2002

Today's opinion has got me going early this morning. Do you agree with Angela Davis' assertion that slavery and blacks in prison are similar conditions because of white supremacy?

Sometimes I wish I were black so I could prove to you that black people survive just fine in the current environment. I am of the opinion that blacks are in prison because they had the choice to commit a crime whereas with slavery blacks didn't have a choice.

Articles like the one this morning contribute to the reason I take high blood pressure medication. Once again, you have forced me to quit reading your articles for a while because they are absurd.

People lose so much in walled off, segregated communities and then in prisons where isolation continues the devastating effects. In an essay in the National Urban League's *State of Black America 2003,* "The Impact of Mass Incarceration on Public Health in Black Communities," Ernest M. Drucker says, "the massive scale of imprisonment and the long sentences are having disastrous effects of their own. This includes the creation of a large and embittered population of ex-offenders who return to their communities changed for the worse" (154).

Kansas has almost 16,000 people in prison. Missouri has more than 40,000. The inmates are made to feel as if they are outcasts, and most of these individuals are people of color. But I have learned from visiting prisons in Kansas and Missouri on the invitation of the men that the inmates are people, too. They are seeking a connection with and guidance from those on the outside. It's as if they metaphorically are trying to build a runway on which to land their limping airship for their return to society. When they've had me speak, I often talk about the need for them to use their time to study and rebuild themselves. In one speech I spoke about a new fist.

A fist symbolizes strength, power and a way to give us control over our life and destiny. This new FIST is an acronym and starts with F, for financial freedom. With each dollar saved, we grow wealth. Wealth is dependent on an old saying: It's not what you save that counts, but what you spend. Spending has to be only for what is needed and what will be assets now and in the future.

The "I" in the FIST stands for intellectual freedom. We all become more intellectually free with every book that we read and with every lesson that we learn. Each adds to our intellectual capital, which companies will pay for, so that our intellectual freedom helps to grow our financial freedom.

The "S" stands for spiritual freedom. There are so many different faiths in prison; each found in the United States can also be found behind bars. Through individuals' knowing their God, they can feel a sense of purpose. Faith will carry them through life's worst moments. It is enough to change their destiny.

The last letter in this new FIST is "T." It stands for togetherness. We must remember that, no matter how bad things may get, we are never alone. As people in any community, we need to turn *to* each other instead of *on* each other.

Despite many obstacles, the men I have gotten to know in prisons strive to climb out of the mental, emotional, physical and economic hole that a criminal record puts them in. Many use their time constructively. They want to be better for their families and their communities when they are released. Prison gives them time to think, time to read and time to rebuild.

From "Proverbs and penal codes"

Over time, I've collected ideas from new, old and emerging African-American communities.

The first comes from Kwanzaa celebrations sponsored by NAACP Branch 4071 at the Moberly Correctional Center in Missouri and the African Awareness Organization at the Lansing Correctional Facility in Kansas.

The men in each prison have taught me that they now constitute a new African-American community because nearly half of the 2.3 million people behind bars in this country are black.

Overlooking them is wrong. A book of African proverbs that I received at a celebration for the holiday honoring the Rev. Martin Luther King, Jr. adds wisdom here: *Not to know is bad; not to wish to know is worse.*

The men said they strove daily to live the seven principles of Kwanzaa, which are unity, self-determination, collective work and responsibility, cooperative economics, purpose, creativity and faith.

I told the men in each prison that living such ideals was important for their resurrection. All African-Americans must be as focused and as inventive to overcome the obstacles to equality in these conservative, zero-tolerance times.

The Rev. Delores Hill of Faith Walk Ministries in Paris, Mo., said at the Moberly gathering: "We've got to figure out a way to tear down those walls that separate us. We want unity instead of division.

"We want faith instead of hopelessness. Locking people up is not working."

I also liked what Leon Dixon, founder of the W.E.B. Du Bois

Learning Center, told the men in the Moberly prison branch of the National Association for the Advancement of Colored People: In the card game of life, we must play the hand we're dealt.

He encouraged African-Americans in prisons to use their sentences for myriad convictions as study time. Dixon urged the black men to turn the prison into a sanctuary for learning.

"You need to form a priesthood and band with one another with a sense of purpose," he said. The constructive wisdom should flow from prisons with the men's eventual release and become a 21st century renaissance for African-Americans.

The book of African proverbs adds to that idea stating, *Knowledge is like a garden; if it is not cultivated, it cannot be harvested.*

In the old African-American community at the King celebrations, the Rev. Joseph Lowery underscored the need for black people to wise up. Recently Lowery, who co-founded the Southern Christian Leadership Conference in 1957 with King, said there were "forces within this country seeking with titanic megabytes to redefine, remake and remold this nation in their own image."

It has resulted in a "prison crisis" for African-Americans because a disproportionate number of people behind bars are black. The majority profit from the growth of America's prison industrial complex. Like slavery of the last century, it is the ugly part of a new black history that African-Americans must end.

"We're carrying on an affair with the prostitutes of greed," said Lowery, who also called for affirmative action to be maintained. "America needs a spiritual revival."

The book of African proverbs offered, *The ruin of a nation begins in the homes of its people.*

In the emerging black community, the Rev. Saundra McFadden-Weaver said at a Johnson County King celebration that discrimination had left people of color trailing whites in college admissions, income, wealth, employment and home ownership.

"We need a new beginning with loving ideals of service to humanity," said McFadden-Weaver, pastor of the Community Fellowship Church of Jesus Christ. "We must make justice happen now.

"This is the year 2000, and we need to approach it with love in our heart and sharing in our commitment and service to humanity. Now is the time."

More hope emerged at another Johnson County King celebration.

"As we look to the next millennium, we can't be isolationist," Nathan Longhorn, an American Indian, said at the Northeast Johnson County NAACP program. "We've had similarities. We've all had struggles."

> Each minority group has a history of innovativeness and survival, which has greatly benefited this nation. Such triumphs will light the way from the twilight of this century into the promise of the next.
>
> To me that conviction will replace hate with education, unity and love. My bets are on this African proverb, *Hope is the pillar of the world.*

In the many instances that I've visited the inmates, I've seen them live the proverbs mentioned in the column above. The population of the United States is a blend of so many different cultures' and countries' wisdom, and people in prison are no exception. The rest of this chapter will highlight the proverbs from the above column and a few others to illustrate what people behind bars are doing to start new journeys in their lives. The inmates also give instruction on how individuals on the free side of the razor wire can improve ex-offenders' lives as well.

Proverb: Not to know is bad; not wishing to know is worse. (Nigeria)

The Million Man March did a lot to boost the spirits of men behind bars. It did not create any insurrections. It just let men know what they had to do to improve themselves for the benefit of the black community.

From "Marches inspire men in prison to step out of the shadows"

> Two invisible men in different states beckoned, and I answered their calls.
>
> One was Richard Jackson, executive director of the East Central Kansas Economic Opportunity Corp. and chairman of the Ottawa, Kan., Black Awareness Committee. The other was Eric L. Wesson, then-education chairman of NAACP Branch 4071.
>
> Both black men are invisible for different reasons. Jackson is just a hard-working citizen. Wesson was an inmate in the Moberly Correctional Center on Jackson County robbery convictions.
>
> Wesson got my attention first, saying imprisoned black men were as moved by the Million Man March in Washington and the 1,000 Man March in Kansas City as others were who participated or watched on TV. That's a new positive effect of the historic events.
>
> It adds to the marches' momentum in community and personal uplift, reconciliation and responsibility.
>
> Jackson asked me to speak at an Ottawa service commemorating the Rev. Martin Luther King Jr. Wesson invited me to an after-march program at the Moberly Correctional Center, which began housing inmates in 1963. Curious – that's the year King gave his "I Have a Dream" speech at the first historic March on Washington.
>
> I explained in Moberly and Ottawa why men like Jackson, Wes-

> son and me are invisible. I pulled the term from Ralph Ellison's 1952 novel, *Invisible Man*.
>
> Ellison, who died at age 80 in 1994, wrote that blacks are invisible in America because many whites don't see us as equals. But I told the curious and captive audiences that I had a '90s addendum to Ellison's enduring work.
>
> Black men like Jackson and me become visible when we fail in school or work, act like stereotypes or turn to crime because it matches the bad-to-the-bone image that white America has of us.
>
> Prison is a way of making such visible black people invisible again.
>
> But the majority of black men are invisible because we work, raise families, pay taxes and vote. We go unnoticed because we don't stoop to America's low expectations of us.
>
> The historic marches changed our invisible status. They made masses of everyday black men visible in a positive light. We shared wholesome ideas, peace and a love for humankind, and gave young African-Americans a new hope for what they can become.
>
> The work toward black community betterment continued with the Greater Kansas City African-American Leadership Summit. Such conferences help people realize that being black in America is not about the worst pathology in this nation.
>
> Instead it's a story about a race of people overcoming the hardships of slavery, legalized segregation and stereotypes. We've become noted inventors, scientists, doctors, lawyers, artists, athletes, soldiers, scholars and just good citizens. The marches and the continuing programs are large public displays showing that when we stand together, the sight is impossible to ignore.
>
> The black men behind bars said they've kept marching in spirit by educating themselves to prepare for their release. Wesson said the theme of the movement at Moberly is "If not now, then when? If not here, then where? And if not with me, then whom?
>
> "The march gave us the emotional high. This organization tries to keep the spirit alive."
>
> With help, these invisible men will retool and join people like Jackson and me as we strive to keep stepping from the shadows.

People need to get over the myths they have about prison and the individuals who live in them. Prisons should be places for rehabilitation. But with the loss of Pell Grants, which had ensured that ex-offenders could get a college education behind bars, prisons too often are just holding areas where a more negative education occurs. That could change if more people stepped out of the shadows and spoke the truth about prisons. One ex-offender, however, told me after a visit I made to the prison in Lansing, Kan., that when people leave and can keep from returning, they try to put the experience in their past. They never speak of the prisons. It's in that silence that the myths grow, and the media help perpetuate those myths.

From "Dispelling prison stereotypes"

In some speeches I've given and workshops I've conducted, I've talked about the men I've met at prisons in Missouri and Kansas.

They are not untouchable people. I enjoy talking, shaking hands, hugging and spending time with men striving to rehabilitate themselves.

I made the 340-mile, round-trip drive on consecutive Saturdays last month to deliver speeches at the Moberly Correctional Center. It was sunny but cold when I attended the Nation of Islam Saviors Day Celebration but warm with driving rain for the NAACP Branch 4071 Black History Month tribute to African-American women.

The men are avid readers of *The Star*. When they ask me to speak to them, I try to do what's possible because most of them will leave prison someday.

For their rehabilitation, they need to feel hope from the outside instead of harshness.

In speeches to Kansas City area audiences, I've said I'm always in awe of the men's abilities. Many are ravenous readers and great thinkers.

They just happen to be in prison for a range of offenses. I've called the men undiscovered intellectuals because of the talent in them that the free world never tapped.

I saw that in a young black man I met in January at the Lansing Correctional Facility in Kansas. He discovered in prison that people in our brutal world had unjustly said he was incapable of reading, writing and comprehending. Behind bars he's being taught now, and he's enthralled with learning.

My prison encounters aided me during a community diversity workshop in January. A man in the church audience said something that fed the stereotype of whether anyone could trust former inmates not to harm people.

I responded that my faith was that the men were raised in the same society as I was with the same core values. Each was better than his worst moment.

The inmates also have had to reach beyond their fear that people on the outside don't care about them and that journalists like me profit from their misery. Gambling on trust beats relying on satellite technology, which the Kansas Corrections Department was to start using to track the whereabouts of some offenders released from prisons.

We're all vulnerable when any of us can be stripped of our civil liberties.

One woman who had volunteered in prison affirmed what I said about the inmates and trust. Another woman shared a quote from Terence, a great thinker and playwright.

Terence was born in 190 B.C. in Carthage, which was a wealthy trading center in northern Africa. Just like about half of the 2.3 million people in America's prisons, Terence was black. He also was a slave.

Terence like many of them was brilliant. His Roman owner educated and then freed him, enabling his great intellect to soar.

The Terence quote that the woman in the church shared applies to people in prisons. Terence wrote, "I am a man, I count nothing human as foreign to me."

She said it meant that any good deeds people have done, she also is capable of doing because we're all human. She added that she has the capacity to do any wrongdoing that others might do, too.

I shared her words from Terence with the men at Moberly.

But I also let them know of a report that showed that during President Bill Clinton's eight years in office, 673,000 people were sent to state and federal prisons and jails compared with 343,000 in President George H.W. Bush's four years and 448,000 in President Ronald Reagan's two terms.

The Justice Policy Institute study showed that the incarceration rate at the end of the Clinton administration was 476 per 100,000 citizens vs. 332 per 100,000 at the end of Bush's term and 247 per 100,000 at the end of Reagan's administration.

But the Moberly inmates didn't need a study to know the trend. Instead of building or rehabilitating schools and teaching children, states are constructing multimillion-dollar prisons, said Byron X Britton, then-president of the National Association for the Advancement of Colored People prison branch.

Rural communities thrive on the revenue the prisons near them create in a perpetual and self-sustaining economy of misery.

In Moberly, I joined other speakers in motivating the men toward self-discipline, responsibility, personal achievement and growth. They'll have to take those qualities with them when they leave prison.

They must strive to dispel the stereotypes, work to never be locked up again and keep others from falling into the trap, too.

Proverb: Knowledge is like a garden; if it is not cultivated, it cannot be harvested. (*Guinea*)

The intelligence of men who are incarcerated is too often overlooked.

Like many people who have been oppressed, ex-offenders possess talents borne from being forced to experience prisons' depths of depravity. Life behind bars has helped them to develop a unique inventiveness and multi-faceted problem-solving skills. They have an almost organic ability to cope with and overcome the worst that life might throw at them. Many other diverse population groups that have been kept from the mainstream have that same ability. Our nation needs people like them with such special talents to be competitive in the global marketplace. The cunning and well-honed intellect can help them to become accomplished. Men and women in prison need to understand that they should be valued instead of treated like pariahs. Watching ex-offenders flower has been a joy. I tell them they are like arrows, which must be pulled back in order to fly forward.

The men in prison often seek the things they never had in their lives when they were on the free side of the razor wire—such as fathers. They know that good parenting isn't something that's readily taught, and access to caring parents is far from guaranteed. Telling my experiences of benefiting from good parents and striving to be a good parent were among the many things I share in my visits.

From "Fatherless men cherish dad's lessons"

> The unexpected happened after I had finished a speech and fielded a few questions from some men at the Lansing Correctional Facility.
>
> In addition to thank-yous and strong handshakes, the men in the African Awareness Organization surprised me with appreciative hugs. That made my drive to the Kansas prison and the hours away from home very worthwhile.
>
> I'll return tonight to celebrate with the African-American men at their annual banquet. It will be a time of hope and inspiration for better tomorrows.
>
> They said visits like mine from beyond the razor wire help their feast of positive feelings grow. One man said candidly that I had shared truths with them that their absentee dads never did and never could.
>
> That was quite a compliment and a change from the angry eyes of a young man I had encountered about two years ago when I spoke to a class of inmates at the same facility. I had upset him by talking about my dad.
>
> His anger opened old wounds for both of us. He said his father was never around to give him discipline, guidance, love, respect, responsibility and other lessons in blood and sweat I got from doing hard, honest work with my dad.
>
> The man missed those gritty, invaluable qualities that dads forge in unruly boys to help them become resilient men. I'd felt that wrath before as a kid in my poor St. Louis neighborhood, where few of my peers had

dads. They communicated their anger with taunts and fists.

The Lansing man and I talked through our differences to a new understanding. My recent meeting with the African Awareness Organization then added to my feelings about the men.

We talked about racism being in the bricks and mortar of America. Black men must share strategies for overcoming that trauma so we can help lead our families past it.

I told the men that bigotry today often is in code. To survive, we must know the code and not fall victim to anger.

I told the men that they had to build up their minds through the heavy lifting of reading and studying. That would make the time they're serving for their offenses work for them so they would emerge from prison as intellectually free men.

That freedom must include knowledge about the history of Africans in America, which schools seldom teach. I told the men they should follow the African-American tradition of sharing that intellectual capital so black youths will embrace education instead of shunning it, living down to the media stereotypes of us.

I told the men the new ideas and sweat equity they'd generate could enable them to become economically free men, too.

They could do it by avoiding fast lanes to easy street that lead to ruin. I told them, as my dad told me, that they should sidestep easy credit. Becoming overextended for pretty things is just a modern form of indentured servitude.

I told them that instead of creature comforts, they should spend money on investments that would add to their earning power. They should strive to live below their means and save at least $50 every two weeks from the jobs they get.

They then can watch the interest on that mounting sum grow as if they'd won the lottery. That economic freedom could allow them to invest more in new enterprises, citizenship and better ideas.

I also told the men to embrace a spiritual freedom by worshiping their God and sharing that love with others. No one had ever shared such man-to-man positive truths with them. They communicated their deepest gratitude with hugs.

Proverb: The ruin of a nation begins in the homes of its people. (*Ashanti*)

Women constitute one of the fastest growing segments of the people in prison. With the high number of black men in prison, families are torn apart. The effect on the community is devastating, as the Urban League

2003 book points out: "Each prisoner's family must carry its own burdens and find ways to compensate for the loss. When this phenomenon occurs on a large scale and for an extended period of time, it becomes a transformative force of its own" (159). The book continues:

> Beneath the collective damage are the individuals who are affected. More than half of incarcerated men have children of minor age, and more than half of them were living with their children at the time they were sent to jail or prison. For women, the percentage in both instances is 80 percent. . . . The incarceration of a parent disrupts children's social environments and the financial stability of their families—weakening parental bonds and placing severe stress on the caregivers left behind. This often leads to a loss of discipline in the household, and to feelings of shame and anger in children that manifests itself in . . . behavioral problems in and outside of school. . . .
>
> Mass incarceration systematically undermines black family life on a scale not seen since slavery, by destroying the very social capital needed to prevent crime in Americas [sic] black communities. And, because it affects a substantial segment of African-American families, mass incarceration may contribute to the persistent deficits in the physical and psychological health and well being of the entire black population. . . . From a public-health perspective, we must consider America's high rates of incarceration a negative measure of the society as a whole—akin to such other societal problems as AIDS, infant mortality, addiction, homicide, or school failure. (159-165)

This system of incarceration is part of the well-guarded, dangerous and damaging America that hurts those behind bars and their nuclear and extended families who are not. The Urban League 2003 book points out that "we must also reduce the collateral damage to the children, families, and communities most affected by enacting policies and establishing programs to help them when their family members are sent to prison and when they are discharged from prison" (165). Not having such things in my back yard, or NIMBY, is insufficient here. Just saying "hell no" to returning ex-offenders is unacceptable. We must think of better ways to help released inmates develop their social capital.

Such progressiveness, however, works against the economics of incarceration and recidivism. Prisons are moneymakers for companies in America. But there are better ways to put so much human capital to use.

From "Prisons as industries"

> MOBERLY, Mo. - Sgt. Frank Brown proudly detailed the accomplishments of NAACP Branch 4071 at its 26th Annual Freedom Fund Banquet.

It's remarkable because the branch consists of inmates in the Moberly Correctional Center. Brown, a corrections officer, told about 200 inmates and their guests that the men donated money for scholarships for students in St. Louis, Kansas City and mid-Missouri.

Brown said the men donated $1,300 to children of the war in Kosovo.

Then-NAACP Branch President Byron X Britton said the men planned to make contributions to children who were war refugees in Africa. "We're going to stop existing, and we're going to live," he said.

The men were incarcerated for offenses that include murder. Saturday donations included awards to Kansas City's W.E.B Du Bois Learning Center, which is named for a founder of the National Association for the Advancement of Colored People.

Du Bois predicted in 1900 that America's most vexing problem this century would be "the color line." It's fitting that the men set their Freedom Fund Banquet theme as "Our New Direction in the New Millennium."

They intend to better themselves through education and rehabilitation so they'll leave prison ready to be productive members of society. They also want to help remove the color barrier, which, like the razor wire around the prison, keeps too many black people from America's promise of equality.

But the men face a Goliath-like struggle.

A June 1999 *Atlantic Monthly* article titled "When They Get Out" said the men's release "is almost guaranteed to produce localized but considerable economic problems." Prison construction and inmate population growth in the '90s fed America's prison industrial complex.

Just as the military industrial complex built up the armed services during the Cold War, prisons now pump jobs, new businesses and money into communities. Inmates serve as a source of cheap labor for contract services.

The *Atlantic Monthly* said prisons in America have been like "an enormous public works program" for the 2.3 million people behind bars. Any mass release of inmates from such stealth jobs could cause unemployment numbers to soar.

But what's also bad is the disenfranchisement of people in prison. In most states a felony conviction results in the loss of voting rights. Because nearly half of the 2.3 million people behind bars are black, the toll is heaviest on African-American communities.

"The political implications for the next century are troubling," *Atlantic Monthly* reported. In some cities "the proportion of black men of all ages who lack the right to vote will rise to about one-third by 2020."

What's worse is this: "Mass incarceration followed by mass release into subcitizenship will undermine the great democratic achievements of the past half century." It would be similar to the post-Civil War South in "excluding huge numbers of African-Americans from the political process." They'll pay taxes but have no say on how the money's spent.

In my speech at the banquet, I told the men that when they're released, they must help keep others out of prison. I also asked them to get everyone who can vote to cast ballots in every election.

In addition, I urged them to help keep children in school. A Jan. 7, 1999, *Black Issues in Higher Education* article titled "The Fund-a-Mentality Difference Between Prisons and Schools" reported that state financing for prisons from 1977 to 1995 increased more than funding for public colleges.

Missouri and Kansas made that list. The Missouri Department of Corrections in 1999 had a $500.7 million budget for 25,540 inmates and 64,000 people on probation, parole or other supervision.

The budget had risen 162 percent from $191 million in 1990 when 14,946 inmates were behind bars and about 42,000 people were on probation, parole or other supervision. Financing for corrections grew twice as fast as the state foundation formula for more than 500 school districts.

About $1.88 billion went to Missouri school districts in fiscal year 1999, up 72 percent from the $1.09 billion given out in 1990.

This state and nation must shift priorities and money toward education to reduce prison population growth. Education is this country's greatest asset. Prison is society's Goliath-like liability.

But prison often is where people find new beginnings.

From "NAACP prison branches build leadership skills for inmates"

MOBERLY, Mo. - Many sidebar conversations occur at the NAACP Freedom Fund Banquets at the Moberly Correctional Center.

Prett Rollins III, then-first vice president of Branch 4071 of the National Association for the Advancement of Colored People, and I talked of our families. I had met his son years ago at an area elementary school. Rollins said his son is taller than he is now, and Rollins towers over me.

We talked of the NAACP, the nation's oldest and largest civil rights organization, celebrating nearly a century of ensuring that constitutional guarantees of freedom, equality and opportunity apply to everyone. That struggle is endless.

The National Urban League notes in its book, *The Complexity of Black Progress: The State of Black America 2004*, that prison remains one of the biggest concerns. More than 818,900 black males are in jails, state and federal prisons.

The Justice Department's Bureau of Justice Statistics notes that part of the increase in the inmate population over the previous year was because of "truth-in-sentencing" laws that limit early releases. Mandatory drug sentences, get tough anti-crime policies enacted in the 1980s and '90s and "three strikes and you're out" laws for repeat offenders also contributed to the higher numbers.

It's not that black Americans commit more crimes than other groups. The zero-tolerance punishment they get is just more severe. Families like Rollins' feel the effects.

The Urban League report notes: "This increasing imprisonment of African-American males - even as crime rates continue to decline - is one of the most astonishing dynamics in the world today. Although black males are only about 6 percent of the total U.S. population, they comprise slightly more than 44 percent of America's prison and jail inmates."

"Experts predict that if incarceration rates remain the same, 1 in 3 black males born in 2001 will be incarcerated at some time in their lives (compared to less than 6 percent of white males born that year)."

Rollins and I talked about that, too, because the goal of the NAACP's prison branches is to return ex-offenders to communities as assets rather than liabilities.

The NAACP gives them leadership skills that some ex-offenders I know have plugged into the community upon their release.

Getting out is a joy, but it also creates leadership vacuums for NAACP prison branches. I've spoken to men about that at prisons in Cameron, Jefferson City, Farmington, Tipton and Moberly.

NAACP prison branches need ongoing training, mentoring and succession plans. That includes rebuilding ex-offenders' confidence. Rollins said incarceration robs men like him of that self-reliance.

David K. Shipler, author of the book *Working Poor: Invisible in America*, told a University of Missouri-Kansas City audience that experiences of repeated failures in school, relationships, on the job and in the judicial system leave people with deep feelings of "incapacity." Men who've been in prison and in the worst scrapes often use words like "fear" and "afraid" to describe job searches.

They're afraid they'll be asked about their police records and afraid they'll fail if they're hired, Shipler said. People often feel alien in the corporate world. "This sense of incapacity can affect performance," he said.

But confidence is a teachable trait. I told Rollins my mom's story of learning confidence from her mother in how to handle my older brother, David, after his birth in 1954. David cried when Mom picked him up, making Mom less certain of being a new mother. But her mother demonstrated that the baby sensed her uncertainty and cried, fearing she might drop him. Grandma showed Mom how to firmly hold babies so they'll know they're in good hands.

Leadership is like that. People need to be assured that they're in firm, confident hands. It's encouraging that Rollins, now the NAACP branch president, and the other men continue to build their confidence and leadership skills. Their families and a grand canyon of needs in the black community await their release.

Kindness counts—especially in prison. But too few people in these times of hard-hearted politics understand that. Compassion from the outside is the cornerstone needed for people behind bars to rebuild their lives.

From "Hard time hardens inmates"

Michael A. Nelson said some things that many people wouldn't want to hear.

Nelson, who was the El Dorado, Kan., Correctional Facility warden, and I talked as we toured his prison. We went through a clean visiting area.

The family atmosphere made it look more like part of a day care than a prison. Nelson showed me the gym with basketball courts, weights and aerobic equipment.

Newer prisons such as El Dorado are less harsh-looking than older institutions. "We want to approximate outside living because one day they will be on the outside," he said.

"If you're real harsh and unnecessarily oppressive or cruel, that will manifest itself out in the free community when they are released," said Nelson, who stopped often to talk with inmates. "Prisons ought to teach people how to act in the free community."

Most people, however, think back-breaking labor and deplorable conditions will make inmates want to get out of prison and never return. Alabama grabbed headlines in 1995 when it resurrected chain gangs with felons breaking rocks.

I hope we don't follow that gravel trail south.

"The whole attitude has to change so we can begin to talk about what can we change in the basic environment in terms of opportunity, education and housing to help prevent criminal activity," said the Rev. Nelson Thompson, president of the Greater Kansas City chapter of the Southern Christian Leadership Conference. "We've got to have alternatives."

State and federal prisons now are overflowing nationwide with a record population.

Blame it on longer sentences and fewer paroles as society gets tough on crime. Of the prisons I've visited in the last year, the old lockup in Jefferson City was the most daunting. The men were agitated, and they cursed and catcalled visitors.

That didn't happen in Kansas.

"We try to stay away from that convict persona," Nelson said. "The inmates are polite, and that comes from the way we manage the place."

The yard and classrooms were civil at the Lansing Correctional Facility, too, where I spoke with a group of black inmates and ate at a banquet of the 7th Step Foundation, honoring men for changing their lives.

Lloyd Parkinson, a 70-year-old former inmate and 7th Step of Topeka vice president, told the men that prison was still "a school of misery" and lost freedoms just as it was when he left it years ago at age 32.

Inmates, he said, need to shake the prison peer pressure and train themselves for success in the real world.

Inmates must exercise, get high school equivalency degrees and college diplomas and acquire job skills behind bars.

"We do want them to occupy time constructively," Nelson said. "The majority of Kansas inmates are going to be released.

"We want to give them an opportunity to improve themselves while they are incarcerated."

It may be politically correct these days to be cold-hearted and tightfisted with convicts, but that shortsighted approach never pays in the long run.

Proverb: Hope is the pillar of the world. *(Kanuri)*

E-mail: Feb. 17, 2004

Sir, your article clearly shows what is wrong with black society. Blacks keep blaming everyone but themselves. There is no personal responsibility. It's their fault they don't stress education. Illegitimate children everywhere! Sports heroes who are street thugs. Rap, gang-banger culture. It's time some black leadership started discussing these issues instead of looking for a racist in Idaho. Why don't you lead instead of wasting your time whining! After you read this and start yelling racism, why don't you think about it for five minutes. Have a nice day.

Blaming the victim prevents people from understanding the social causes—racism and discrimination—that create poverty and cause prison time. The truth is that African Americans are confronted consistently with inequality, racism and discrimination, all of which affect their individual accomplishments and experiences. Struggling for equality under these two weights leads to hopelessness. Without hope, motivation for a better future is low. Finding hope, hope for a promising future, hope that racism and discrimination can end is essential to discovering the Real America.

From "Cloaked racism persists; Poverty and prejudice make equality unattainable"

Racism and ongoing disparities continue to challenge African-Americans.

The NAACP's *Crisis* magazine cover story, "Growing Up Black," says black children make up 15 percent of the nation's 70.4 million people younger than age 18.

The November/December 2003 article said about 48 percent of those black children live with single mothers, and 12 percent, or 1 million, are reared by a grandparent. Single parents and grandparents are exceptional people, but rearing children alone can be draining.

It's little wonder that 57 percent of African-American children live in low-income families, and 30 percent are in poverty. That's double the national average.

The effect is many black children grow up without proper housing, good nutrition, adequate health care, positive adult supervision and quality education. All parents want the best for their children. But for too many African-American parents, poverty and racism make the best unattainable.

The National Urban League's *State of Black America 2003* said black women who head families suffer discrimination because of their race and gender, making them "the major prototype for the 'feminization of poverty.'"

For generations, education has enabled people of all colors to rise from poverty into the middle and upper classes. But that's at risk for African-Americans, too.

The Dec. 15, 2003, issue of *The Nation* says schools' zero tolerance policies may be combining with the No Child Left Behind law to get rid of low-performing minority students, freeing schools of sanctions for failing to increase achievement.

"The school to prison pipeline often starts because teachers and principals are calling 911 and criminalizing student behaviors that in more tolerant times they would have handled themselves," *The Nation* said.

Closet prejudices and cloaked racism account for the full force of the law hitting minorities while many whites get second chances and leniency.

Crisis reports that black kids constitute 44 percent of all young people detained, 46 percent of youth sent to adult court and 58 percent of children sent to adult prisons.

Crisis also points out that the suicide rates for black youths have increased, narrowing the gap with whites.

Guns remain a problem for African-American youths, too. *Crisis* reported that in 2000, more than half of the children murdered with guns were black.

But here's the encouraging news: The 2003 Urban League report notes the unparalleled resilience of African-Americans. Black families have overcome horrors, ranging from slavery to domestic terrorism.

Hope persists. *Crisis* notes that African-Americans have a buying power of $688 billion, compared with the total American purchasing strength of $8.2 trillion. I used to think the black buying power was fantastic until I figured it was only 8.4% of the $8.2 trillion. It should be nearly double $688 billion to be at parity with blacks' representing 13% of the total U.S. population.

Crisis reports that the high school completion rate for African-Americans in 2001 was 87 percent, compared with 59 percent in 1971. The high school dropout rate has narrowed to 11 percent for blacks, compared with 7 percent for whites.

A lot of work remains to end racism and the disparities. Bringing the challenges to light is the only way to end them so everyone can progress in the 21st century.

The feedback shows, however, that people prefer the truth to remain in the dark and blacks to be behind bars. Such feelings fit a historical trend.

E-mail: Feb. 13, 2004

You take the cake!! Feminization of poverty, HUH? Only a lefty would come up with a term like that!! You libs have a term for everything!!

You should let your readers know that *The Nation* newspaper is a socialist, communist paper!! It makes the *Village Voice* look like the *National Review*.

You say black families have had to overcome domestic terrorism?? What's that?? If it's a black man beating his girlfriend then maybe!! I would say it's young black males that do the most terrorizing! But we can't mention that!

The cause of poverty isn't so much racism, it's the lack of a father in the home and the Great Society programs that go along with that! Studies show that blacks who stay married earn about as much as whites. Why don't you insist that blacks give that a try and stay in school instead of blaming whites and America and the schools?! That's what you're doing!! Maybe if there was a male around to give advice and guide black you they wouldn't end up in prison!!

How do Asians and others who come here do so well by in large, and they don't have a leader?? Don't wait around for someone to come along and make everything equal in life. Go out and obtain it. – like Oprah!!

E-mail: Feb. 13, 2004

I can't help myself. I have to respond to your editorial piece in today's *Star*.

Please consider this point of view: Stop the whining and finger-pointing. Although there is plenty to whine and finger point about, it just comes across as passive and powerless. Start taking at least some responsibility for the state of today's African American family.

Where are the fathers of the 48 percent of children living with a single mother?

By their absence are they not accountable for the "feminization of poverty?"

Are fatherless children not at greater risk for poverty, drugs, etc.?

Just maybe full equality would be attainable if we all first looked inward for strength and solutions. My hat's off to Spike Lee. No whining there. He just expects the best from our young people.

Despite what people think, despite the stereotypes they've consumed, despite what the media continue to project, prison can be a place where people are radically transformed into better individuals.

From "Healing even behind bars"

MOBERLY, Mo. - Prison changes people. It had that effect on the Rev. Larry Maddox of Springfield.

Maddox, pastor of New Growth Ministries and president of the Springfield branch of the NAACP, was a first-time, initially reluctant visitor to Moberly Correctional Center's NAACP branch.

Butch Babbs started things off, singing James Weldon Johnson's "Lift Every Voice and Sing." He was joined by three other men in prison gray clothing. They beautifully harmonized on the difficulties they had faced in life.

"Lied on, you know that I've been lied on, but I'm still here," the men sang as inmates, guests and Maddox in the prison chapel clapped and cheered. "Burdened, I've had my share of burdens, but I'm still here.

"Dark days, I've had my share of dark days, but I'm still here. Disappointment, I've had so many disappointments, but I'm still here. ... Through it all I've made it through another day's journey, God kept me here."

Maddox told the men he realized during the program that the letter inviting him to the prison was "more than an invitation."

"To me it feels more like a call," he said.

The inmates' singing brought tears to his eyes.

"They're in here singing about 'I made it,' and we're out there complaining that we can't make it.

"There is a struggle in here. There is a struggle out there. I learned today it's how we get through the struggle. God is on our side."

Maddox also revealed his own personal struggle with prison. A son is incarcerated in Atlanta, and Maddox has never visited him.

Going to the prison program at Moberly, he said, forced him to rethink his inflexible stand.

"You have changed my mind," Maddox said. "My heart goes out to all of you.

"Let me tell you, you can make a difference. I was not the daddy I ought to have been. As a father I tried to do right."

Other more tempting things drew his son, getting him in trouble with the law. It is not unusual for African-Americans like Maddox to turn away from their adult children who are incarcerated. Black people, like most others, believe in law and order, right and wrong, and feel righteous in their stand.

But Jesus walks in prisons, and miracles happen daily. Maddox said the men turned him around.

"The first thing on the agenda is setting some time to go see my son in Atlanta," he said.

The men cheered. An American Indian who has not seen his father in the decades he has been behind bars asked Maddox to be his spiritual father.

"That really touched me," Maddox said.

Other men let him know how he had moved them, too.

"God is doing things in here," Maddox said. "God loves us all."

People in prisons have fallen out of society. Because of the crimes they committed, they don't fit.

Maddox drew applause and smiles from the men, saying, "Jesus didn't fit either."

Joseph Jones, a big man who was the emcee of the program, cried as he shared that he had lost a parent while in prison and that his son was now in a foster home. Jones applauded Maddox for the change of heart about visiting his adult child.

Maddox, who gave the opening prayer at the program, asked to speak again toward the end. He said in a recent telephone interview that he told his congregation upon his return: "I thought I was going to say some things to them.

"What happened was, the message was to me from them. God had to get me there to say some things to me, which means I had to come back here to change some things."

The music sung by the men, he said, helped soften him on many hard personal matters confounding him. The resolve of the men to reshape themselves to be productive citizens with the help of one of the nation's oldest prison branches of the National Association for the Advancement of Colored People moved Maddox.

It was glorious to see. But such efforts get little attention compared to the headlines that Toby Young made after John Manard's escape from Lansing Correctional Facility through her Safe Harbor Prison Dogs program. The imbalance is a tragedy.

Maddox's transformation was phenomenal but not unusual in prisons, where Jesus walks and miracles happen.

Proverb: A single bracelet does not jingle. (*Congo*)

Visit any prison in your community and the chances are great if you are black that you will run into someone you went to school with, went to church with, sang in the choir with or just enjoyed talking to. The experience of being with others creates music, happiness and hope, and that is what the men and women in prison are striving to do.

From "Changing attitudes, faces"

JEFFERSON CITY - A man with braided salt-and-pepper hair walked up, held my hand for a long time after a speech I'd given at his NAACP branch banquet and asked in a soft voice, "Do you remember me?"

He was dressed in the uniform of inmates at Algoa Correctional Center, where the eighth annual National Association for the Advancement of Colored People banquet took place last month. Its theme on that stormy night was "Changing Faces."

I asked the man with melancholy eyes and a tentative grip to give me some clues. He said we had been students together at the University of Missouri-Columbia.

He remembered Keith Kunihiro, my best friend at MU and long after college. He and Keith had even gone fishing together, and the man vividly remembered the good time they'd had and even how big the fish was that they'd caught.

We had a mutual friend, Debby Brown, and we last saw each other at Debby's wedding more than 20 years ago.

Recalling names isn't one of my strengths, but I suddenly blurted out "Arnold!" We reminisced a bit longer while others were served dinner.

I asked how he landed in prison after graduating from college and starting a promising health-care career.

He replayed some of the words I'd shared in my speech. He was chasing fast money and got caught up in the criminal justice system.

Now Arnold and the other men at the banquet are dedicating themselves to making the "Changing Faces" theme their reality.

Nancy Van Zant, who at the time was Missouri Department of Corrections management training coordinator and volunteer coordinator of the 16 NAACP prison branches in Missouri, said the men were donating what little money they had to needy children and non-profit groups. They were providing scholarships at schools and supporting black community programs.

"I'm inspired by you," said Van Zant, who is now Region IV co-ordinator of NAACP prison branches. "What you're doing is getting ready for the day that you're released.

"You are changing faces."

"This is simply giving you an opportunity to serve others," Michael Murphy, superintendent of Algoa, said in his speech to the men at the banquet. "It's an opportunity for you to claim your citizenship by giving to others.

"Whether you like it or not, you're a role model. Others will be watching you.

"You are not just a role model for the inmate population, but you're a role model for the staff, and you're a role model for me. Your work makes for a safer, cleaner, more effective correctional center."

Van Zant said she was shocked when a young man at another correctional facility where she had spoken had asked her whether the NAACP was a new national basketball league. Schools and the NAACP need to better educate children and adults about the history of the nearly 100-year-old organization.

Terran Austin-El, an NAACP member at Algoa, described it in a way that most young people could appreciate: "The NAACP is the largest, oldest, baddest, boldest, most revered, most cussed and most discussed civil rights organization in America."

Van Zant told me during dinner that helping the inmates was her calling.

"I have a special sense of what God has called men to do - be leaders, good family men, providers and being able to take dominion over what God has given," Van Zant said. "I feel that the men who have fallen; they have strength, but they have exercised it in ways that have caused them to fall.

"They have served the wrong master with their gift. They really need redirection so that their godly gift will be used in a godly way. We have to direct them for good vs. evil."

Marvin Hayes, Algoa NAACP branch president, and David Morrow, branch vice president, said Van Zant had ripped out the negative in the men, replaced it with positives and helped them be gentlemen. They said she never steered them wrong.

Tyrone McQueen, NAACP branch treasurer and secretary, said in his benediction: "A motto people need to use in life is: 'We are here to change. We made mistakes. But don't condemn us for life.'"

That's how I feel about my college friend, Arnold, and about all of the men focused on "changing faces" in the state's NAACP prison branches.

One of the joys in answering invitations to speak to the men in prison is the audience hungers for an inspiring message. But they also share their own messages. These men show that they possess a great quality—they want to do everything they can to improve themselves. They are at a time in their lives when they soak up knowledge and instruction like great sponges.

From "Their shot at redemption"

JEFFERSON CITY - Letters from James Tyndal and Donald V. Cline brought me to the oldest prison west of the Mississippi River.

Tyndal was an inmate at the maximum-security Jefferson City Correctional Center. Cline then was associate superintendent at the then-65-year-old prison.

Each wanted to show how a unique in-house, inmate- and staff-run drug and alcohol rehabilitation program is changing men's lives. It's called the Intensive Therapeutic Community.

It started six years earlier after inmates asked the director of the Missouri Department of Corrections for a long-term drug treatment program. The director challenged them to create one.

The offenders and staff did, borrowing from such things as the 12 Steps in Alcoholics Anonymous and other successful programs that create a community around inmates changing their addictive and criminal behavior.

"The mainstay of the program is they take ownership," said Cline, who received an award for the program at the 101st Annual Conference of the Missouri Association for Social Welfare. "They realize they are their brother's keeper. They realize they have to work together."

That's important because drugs and alcohol are linked to up to 80 percent of all crimes, Cline said.

Jerry W. Ellison, substance abuse unit supervisor, walked me through the prison. Several people told me, "If you sober up a horse thief, you still have a horse thief."

The criminal behavior and the addiction must be confronted. The inmates are doing that, and it has made them better men.

"I have some solid footing now," said Tyndal, who started drinking beer and smoking marijuana and cigarettes at age 7. Feeding a methamphetamine habit landed him in prison. "I know that if I make the right choices today, it will help me out tomorrow."

For the six months to one year of the program the men in the Intensive Therapeutic Community are isolated from the rest of the population to keep them from reverting to the "con-mentality." Their quarters were spotless. They dressed neatly in gray slacks and program T-shirts, containing an eagle with a snake and chain in its talons.

Ellison said the snake symbolizes alcohol and drugs. The chain stands for the broken addiction, and the eagle embodies the men soaring free of their former lives.

The men stood at attention. In unison they greeted me as I entered their living quarters. Regime and discipline play big roles in their rehabilitation.

"Many of these guys never learned discipline," Cline said. "That's why they're here.

"What we're hoping for is right living. We don't tolerate excuses. You're responsible for what you do."

Inmate facilitators Darryl Burton and Richard Brown said the program worked through "spiritual confrontation, isolation and decontamination." Burton and Brown said they work to give the men a new commitment to life.

"I have an opportunity to be a role model for positive change," said Burton, who had been a drug dealer.

"It gives me a new way of living, a new way of thinking and a new way of problem-solving," Brown said. "What brought me to prison was mainly my drinking."

Nearly 250 men are in the program now, and there is a waiting list of about 500 people. About 150 have moved back into the general population of nearly 2,000 inmates.

Corrections officials said the program graduates were easier to manage. They could help change others in prisons.

Offenders in the program are between the ages 18 and 61. They've been convicted for driving while intoxicated, serving four years or less; some are serving life without parole on murder convictions. About 60 men have been paroled, although parole is never promised to those who complete the Intensive Therapeutic Community.

"Some of these people won't get out," Cline said. "The whole idea is they can live better lives."

Many people have noted the difference. "A mother wrote, 'You gave me back my son,'" Cline said.

I like what Kenneth Gilbert wrote in an essay for me: "I am truly sorry for being the person that I was. I will never be that person again."

Tuesday marked the 30th graduation. The program even compelled paroled offenders Craig Lancaster and Kenny Heistand to return to a summer graduation I attended to see others benefit as they had.

"I came back because it makes me feel good in my heart seeing those angels sitting in here," Heistand said. "It makes me feel good to still see that glow in them."

I know what he means. I could see it, too.

But that is not what the public wants to read. Prison progress and learning go against stereotypes, as the feedback shows.

E-mail: Nov. 7, 2001

Well, you did it again, bleeding hearts for criminals. No criminal should be given parole so they can continue to kill, rob, do drugs, rape, you name it. There should be no second chance after they have served their time if, or should I say when they break the law again.

E-mail: Nov. 7, 2001

You missed your inmate friends so much you had to rejoin them and extol on their social achievements. How moving! What would you do without immature children and incarcerated inmates? Do you ever read the daily paper besides pollute it?

Proverb: Wisdom does not live in only one house. *(Ashanti)*

Some of the men I have met in prisons sometimes call me at work. Others I see in stores or as they go about their daily normal lives in the city. It is wonderful to see them strive to become productive, taxpaying citizens. It is important to recognize the gold in that diversity in our population.

From "Building hope behind bars"

A man interrupted my holiday bell ringing downtown for the Salvation Army and said, "Remember me?"

How could I forget? Ben and I had met years ago at the Moberly Correctional Center, where I've been a guest speaker at inspirational programs that men like him had put together.

Ben and the others were serving time for myriad offenses. But they also were members of the National Association for the Advancement of Colored People Branch 4071 in the Moberly prison. In it they've worked to remake themselves from liabilities to society into assets for their eventual release.

Ben and I shook hands as we talked in the cold. He has a job now. He's paying taxes, and he's putting his life back together.

"Ninety-seven percent of the inmates we have incarcerated are someday coming out," said Tim Kniest, then-public information officer with the Missouri Department of Corrections.

"Any positive activities they can get themselves involved in that broaden their view of the world are worthwhile in helping offenders see there is something beyond themselves and that they are part of a community of people working together as a unit accepting responsibility."

The NAACP complements Department of Corrections programs that provide treatment, education and work for inmates. Such efforts have helped lower recidivism from 32 percent in 1993 to 19.2 percent.

I told the men at Moberly they should be proud because their efforts in the NAACP's oldest prison branch west of the Mississippi River had spread to other penal institutions. Missouri inmates in those other places have written to me about new prison NAACP branches, gifts they've given to the community, Kwanzaa programs and events surrounding Black History Month celebrations.

The men also needed to know they had helped Ben and others released from Missouri prisons make successful transitions into society.

Amos Pearcil, with the NAACP branch, added, "We need to think as much of our neighbors as ourselves."

The Rev. Willie Henderson, with Apostolic Church of Jesus Christ in Kansas City, told the men: "You cannot return to this prison. It's time to make that change and add some purpose to your life."

Byron X Britton, then with the NAACP branch, added, "If we continue to do this, there is no telling where we can go."

From "From prison, hope and promises for change"

The men at the Jefferson City Correctional Center drove a similar message home during their program on the Millions More Movement. Just because they are in prison doesn't mean they must accept being left out of the national effort to improve the black community.

I had read many stories on the Millions More Movement in several newspapers and on the Internet.

I watched a lot of the speeches given during the mid-October 2005 event on C-SPAN. The gathering partly was to commemorate the 10th anniversary of the Million Man March, which Nation of Islam Minister Louis Farrakhan called on Oct. 16, 1995, for African-American men to show reconciliation, responsibility and atonement.

Ten years ago, men at the Moberly Correctional Center helped me understand the scope of that national commitment for renewal. Last month, some men at the prison in Jefferson City helped explain the larger task that lies ahead.

"People ask, 'What was the need for another march?'" Bryan C. Muhammad said to about 100 men who gathered in the chapel of the new prison. "What we need as a people is a movement.

"A movement outlasts a march. We need something that will take us from this point into the future."

It's as important as the Civil Rights Movement.

"We want our sons and daughters to go further in life than we have gone," Muhammad said. "Surely we don't want them to end up in here. Our job is to study and learn in prison houses all over America."

He urged the men to not just lift weights but to build up their minds by reading books to advance "mentally and spiritually." That will enable them to help rehabilitate the black community in cities nationwide when they eventually are released from prison.

The movement calls for unity among African Americans and other people of color.

It demands a lasting atonement, reconciliation and responsibility. It calls for better education and an end to substandard schools and learning.

The movement calls for economic development in the black community - something that is desperately needed. It insists on political power through people voting. It seeks reparations for the descendants of slaves.

The movement demands an end to the prison industrial complex in America in which 2.3 million people are incarcerated. That's more than any other country in the world and more than at any other time in world history, Kathy Kelly, founder of Voices in the Wilderness, wrote in her book, *Other Lands Have Dreams.*

The movement insists on high quality health care for African Americans, artistic and cultural development and world peace to end "wars of foreign aggression waged by the United States government against other sovereign nations and peoples. We demand an end to senseless violence, and advocate peace amongst street organizations (gangs) and youth."

The men at the Jefferson City prison also insisted on an end to the violence among African Americans in this state and elsewhere. Fighting prevents people from focusing their energy on uniting to improve education, create new housing, businesses and jobs, and end the flood of black people into prisons.

"Some of us still have that sick mindset of hurting your brother," Muhammad said.

The Millions More Movement has prompted the men to start a "Bridge the Gap" program. In it the men will hold book drives to benefit children. They want to encourage young people to read and write book reports that will be submitted to the project.

Kids with winning essays will be awarded prizes, including bicycles, Playstations and iPods to encourage students to read more, Terrel Williams told the audience.

"It's not true what they say," Williams said. "We're not monsters in prison. It's time to work. Things that need to happen, we can make them happen ourselves."

Darryl Williams added: "From this day forward, let's move with action. It's time out for anything else. Let's stand up and be men. Let's stand up for one accord, one aim, one destiny."

Rahman Muhammad, who drove to the prison from the Nation of Islam Muhammad Mosque No. 30 in Kansas City, told the men, "This Millions More Movement, brothers, is millions more moving toward liberation."

Freedom is both the end and the beginning of their journey.

CHAPTER 16
Enabling the Journey

Bridge Building

Build me a bridge like a Noah's Ark
One for people to cross whether near or far
From ignorance about others of different faces
Where racism's not the boss, a bridge to places
Of hope and joy and fun that lifts us above poverty
Hopelessness and despair
To liberty and land of plenty and beauty, we share
Vanquishing hate,
Leaving only hope, caring and faith
Where people talk forging new understandings and ideas for cures
Shredding today's problems, to expose green pastures we're lured
To the land of glory where humanity can now thrive and endure.

...I have seen that in any great undertaking it is
not enough for a man to depend simply upon himself.
~Isna-la-wica (Lone Man)

One of the most difficult tasks people face is resisting the urge to embrace the prejudices and stereotypes that we all have about others. They are deeply embedded in everyone whether people recognize it or not. These many awful feelings burble forth with the least provocation. It happens when people see others who are "not like them." Scattered throughout the previous chapters are the voice mail, e-mail and regular mail I have received in which people freely express an array of the bigotry that fills the moat of America.

What must never be forgotten is that the socio-economic effluent does not flow in only one direction—from the majority to minorities. It instead slops around mightily, backwashing from the majority to minorities, from minorities to the majority and among all minority groups. Everyone ends up splashed with the smelly, hurtful prejudices, stereotypes, bigotry and discrimination, and we sling the slop on others as well.

Some young people through rap music try to charcoal filter some of the filthiest aspects of the mainstay hurtful words of America. They spell the barbs—such as the N-word—differently, and that is supposed to make them OK. They also repeat the racial slurs often enough and use them in a different context. They spray them with a perfume of everyday greetings and then think the historical stench of the slurs will fade. That's the premise; however, the historical power of the racial epithets remains just as toxic.

The toxicity of such rap media messages has a lasting effect on young people. White males are the nation's largest consumers of rap music, which carries a message of rebellion, irreverence, defiance, belligerence and independence. Generations of young people have embraced those qualities, as they should in a process that enables them to later define themselves apart from their parents. However, complications set in when race is aligned with the negative markers. White people grow out of their rap music and hip-hop artist collections, but the racial markers they may harbor from them will add to the polluted moat of bigotry, stereotypes, prejudices and discrimination. If a hard shell of conservatism then forms, as it often does when each new generation ages, then individuals will have a nearly impossible time crossing the moat of biases to discover the Real America on the other side.

Sadly, people of color inflict the hurtful words and acts on people who look like them and on individuals in other minority groups. Such behavior in the moat of discrimination, prejudice, stereotypes and hatred enables few to escape. People keep clawing at each other. Their lives are devalued, and so are their chances to work together, build a sense of community and progress to the other side to discover the beauty in the Real America right in front of them.

In addition, teachers, the overwhelming majority of whom are white, unwittingly trap children in the moat. White-focused college entrance exams add to the moat. People of color get caught in the moat when the person taking job applications is either of a different race or serves to maintain the "standards" of the majority at the company. If minorities do get hired, they will have to constantly swim the moat of biases in performance reviews, in winning pay raises, in interactions with co-workers and with the public, and in any promotion they may seek. The fact that they have to swim this moat puts them at a disadvantage with respect to their white co-workers who often are given a drawbridge to success via white privilege.

Yet the moat persists.

Understanding what lies on the other side of the moat of hatred and biases is important. People mired in the muck need to become aware of the Real America in which they can prosper. That would serve as motivation for folks to work together so everyone can escape the moat and cleanse himself and herself of the stench of stereotypes, prejudices and discrimination. We have to do as Ronald Takaki instructs in his book, *A Different Mirror*, and learn the travails of our own race, learn what other people have endured and overcome and then teach others these many lessons. It is imperative that people get past the mainstream bias that exists for groups that have been held apart for centuries.

From "It takes a village to put out some fires"

> In 2001, Harry Belafonte addressed the National Association of Black Journalists convention. Belafonte told of a conversation he'd had with the Rev. Martin Luther King Jr.
>
> King pondered the years of struggles for equality, freedom and civil rights. Belafonte, a human-rights advocate, said King also seemed troubled.
>
> King said, "I've come to think that perhaps we may have integrated into a burning house."
>
> "I asked, 'What does that mean?'" Belafonte recalled. King replied, "It means we may have to become firemen."
>
> That was in addition to King saying, at his Nobel Peace Prize acceptance speech in 1964, that African-Americans had to courageously and nonviolently force this nation to fulfill its constitutional promises to everyone.
>
> 'We feel that we are the conscience of America - we are its troubled souls - we will continue to insist that right be done because both God's will and the heritage of our nation speak through our echoing demands," he said.

The need for that conscience and those firefighters is as important today as it was in the '60s because the flames of violence, inequality and injustice continue to burn in America.

<u>From "We mustn't expect black heroes of the past to save us"</u>

It will take the whole village of socially conscious people to put out the inferno.

But don't expect the Buffalo Soldiers to gallop over the high hills of the past to douse the flames.

The heroic African-Americans can't save us from the assault on black people today.

Don't expect Charles Drew, the black physician who pioneered the modern-day blood bank, to step out of the past with a heaven-sent serum to wipe out the hate and prejudice we have for one another.

Don't expect inventor Garrett A. Morgan to arrive from the past with new versions of his traffic signal and gas mask to stop racism.

Don't expect famed abolitionists Harriet Tubman, Levi Coffin and Sojourner Truth to step from their ages-old graves to lead us beyond the fog to the promised land on an Underground Information Highway.

The future has to be radically different for everyone in this country and the world. So many challenges exist, and they can only be overcome with everyone's involvement in finding a solution.

In February of 1995, Discovery astronaut Bernard Harris Jr. became the first back person to walk in space. He dedicated the accomplishment during Black History Month to all African-American achievements.

To me he was saying don't expect someone to step out of the past to save us from today's problems. We all have to walk together on this long journey toward equality - one step at a time.

In order to overcome the trauma of this country's many persistent "isms" and discrimination that have debilitated so many in this country for so long, we must dredge and drain the pestilent moat together, put out the fires that King foresaw and walk with others across the vast, empty spaces to make it possible for all of us to discover and thrive in the Real America.

CHAPTER 17

The Unacknowledged, Forgotten, and Ignored: Destroying the Stereotypes

Brighter Tomorrows

Even the women on welfare got pride
It gleams in their beautiful brown eyes
Feeling some day they'll overcome
The hurt and pain that's been done
To them and their children, too.
Some ain't even got no shoes.
But the future gives these strong women hope
Beyond the rundown tenements, roaches, rats and the dope
Sold by peddlers of the pain
Bought for escape and short-term gain.
But like the mothers of slaves,
Freemen, domestics, housekeepers and maids
Today's hope wells and swells as it did for generations past
It endures the worst trauma and forever lasts
It's in these women of color's eyes
And no matter the hardships the gleam like their love will never die.

Although the world is full of suffering,
it is full also of the overcoming of it.
~Helen Keller

Truth is on the side of the oppressed.
~Malcolm X

Throughout this nation's history a resistance force of individuals has defied convention and overcome "the way things are." They have refused to accept the limitations of bigotry, stereotypes, prejudices and discrimination. They have held tightly to the ideals of the Declaration of Independence and the Constitution. They know from the world's most liberal documents heralding "a more perfect union" that America can be better. What follows are some stories about a few of these courageous people. As diversity multipliers they reach out to discover the Real America and capture great riches in return.

She opened minds and opened doors

Dorothy Lorentino got the long-deserved recognition as an inductee in the National Teachers Hall of Fame in Emporia, Kan.

Lorentino, then 88, of Lawton, Okla., has her nephew's research to thank for it.

Cornel Pewewardy, then a University of Kansas assistant professor of education, found that she opened public schools for American Indians. "I had the opportunity to attend public schools, but if it wasn't for people like my aunt, I wouldn't have had that privilege," said Pewewardy, who has a doctorate in educational administration.

"I would put her beside Rosa Parks, Jackie Robinson, Jim Thorpe and the Brown family (in the 1954 Brown vs. Board of Education of Topeka Supreme Court case, which made segregation illegal). She is a freedom fighter.

"This story is about the struggle for freedom, the struggle for justice and the struggle for equality in this country."

Lorentino, a Comanche, remembered that her father, Charlie Sunrise, in 1915 took her in a horse-drawn buggy to her first day at the Cache public schools near Lawton. She was 6 years old and the only American Indian enrolled there.

But she didn't stay long. The Cache public schools barred American Indians, saying they would infect white children with diseases and filth.

"The Bureau of Indian Affairs schools were so far away from their homeland that they were boarding schools," Pewewardy said. "So many thousands of miles from home, kids got lonesome, sick and died."

Those who survived suffered inhuman things.

"Early education for American Indians was designed to exterminate them," Pewewardy said.

"The curriculum had nothing to do with their culture, and they were prohibited from speaking their tribal language.

"They were forced to conform to be like the white man. It was an education for assimilation."

The bureau schools were unacceptable to Lorentino's parents. They sued on behalf of her and her younger sister, Winona, seeking admission to the public schools. The family won the case in 1918, opening the system of education to American Indians nationwide.

Lorentino and her sister, who died in the 1940s, received college degrees and became educators. "She was very forward-thinking," said Dave Eldridge, executive director of the National Teachers Hall of Fame, of Lorentino's 34-year career in special education.

Her work contributed to her being among the five educators of students in kindergarten through 12th grade inducted into the hall of fame. "She had quite a splendid history of teaching," Eldridge said.

That included using her multicultural heritage to develop ways to teach children whom other educators had written off. "I knew there were cultural and language differences at school, and I was willing to work through them, not around them," Lorentino said.

Her goal was to get children to love learning.

Lorentino, who is retired, said she had received a deluge of congratulatory calls and letters from people nationwide after the selection committee met in Kansas City and announced its picks. "Just the idea of an organization like that accepting me, I feel it's such an honor," she said.

Pewewardy said he thought his aunt's induction benefited all American Indians who, in public education, occupy "the rock bottom" spot in test scores, attendance and dropout rates.

Lorentino's victories in court and life shine with sunrays of hope for all people of color who thought none existed for them in America.

Dusting off history in KCK

Esperanza Amayo wants people to know what Saturnino Alvarado did for Hispanics in Kansas City, Kan.

But mostly, she wants everyone to know the history of Hispanics in this community. So little of their stories - tragedies and triumphs - has been chronicled. Stories like Alvarado's.

They need to know that Alvarado, a shoe repairman, did the unthinkable in the 1920s for Hispanics in Kansas City, Kan.

The school district then operated under what Robert M. Cleary called "a tri-racial system of education." The best schools were for white students. A second and unequal set of schools were for black students, and a third, the Clara Barton School, was for Hispanics.

Cleary wrote about the unusual system of public school segregation in his 168-page University of Missouri-Kansas City master of arts thesis titled "The Education of Mexican-Americans in Kansas City, Kan., 1916-1951."

The costly and inefficient school system was maintained for decades. Whites' widespread prejudice against African-Americans and Hispanics kept it alive.

But Hispanics, drawn from Mexico by area meat packing and railroad jobs, had no high school.

Alvarado in 1925 began what turned into an international campaign to open the all-white Argentine High School to his two children, Jesus and Luz Alvarado, as well as Marcos De Leon and Victoria Perez. He encountered strong resistance. But Alvarado persevered, appealing to the Mexican consulate.

The U.S. State Department got involved. Officials wrote on Oct. 30, 1925, that under the treaty with Mexico, Hispanics "must be regarded as friendly aliens and as such extended the same privileges as those enjoyed by American schoolchildren."

Officials on Nov. 9, 1925, also suggested that injunctions be issued against anyone who tries to hinder Mexican children from attending Kansas City, Kan., schools peacefully.

Two years after the struggle began, three of the Hispanic students enrolled at Argentine High School.

Among Amayo's memorabilia are pictures of them in the 1927, 1928, 1929 and 1930 high school yearbooks.

Amayo, 74, has become an amateur historian for the Hispanic community in Kansas City, Kan. Her studies have led her to seek public recognition for Alvarado.

She wants the new $7.2 million 12th Street bridge over the Kansas River to be named after him and have a plaque describing his deeds.

She successfully campaigned to get the auditorium at Argentine Middle School named after Alvarado. He was also inducted into the Mid-America Education Hall of Fame largely because of Amayo's tireless efforts.

A street, Alvarado Drive, is named in his honor. "But nobody knows where it is" or why it has that name, Amayo said.

Racism in education for Hispanics didn't end with the Alvarado struggle. Amayo recalls the rejection she experienced when she tried to enroll her younger brother, Joe Rangel, into a white grade school during World War II.

She said she told the principal that Hispanic men were fighting and dying in the war, but their children couldn't so much as attend a neighborhood school.

The principal later admitted her brother. Yet Amayo faced similar rejection with her own children.

"There are so many hurts in this world," Amayo said. "Why does this hurt so much?"

To understand the hurt, people need to know the history of Hispanics in Kansas City, Kan.

Stories like Alvarado's. Stories like Amayo's.

But Amayo fears the history of Hispanics' climb from segregation to success could die with her generation.

"Look at our age," Amayo said of herself and her 79-year-old brother, Solomon Rangel. "It's important because what library can you go into and read about our history?"

People need to know what Hispanics faced, the heroes who help them overcome and then never forget.

History, written in stone

Bruce Montgomery pointed to four sets of grooves in the marble floor at Union Station.

Most people overlook these historic marks. They're on the main floor near the elevators and restrooms. The deep grooves were made by the knees of black men who buffed out a living shining shoes.

The indentations are all that's left of that way of life. The heavy elevated chairs where customers sat - and the four pair of metal footrests - are gone.

So is the bootblacks' box of polishes and tools. But the holes through which the chairs were bolted to the marble are there.

An old Union Station bench sits where the shoe shine chairs once were. But people like Montgomery, a tax examiner for the Internal Revenue Service, remember what was there. He wants others to know that history, too.

These grooves tell of the job limitations African-Americans faced. Yet the marks also symbolize hard work, honor and dignity.

"Historically it speaks to the times," said Gwen Grant, president of the Urban League of Greater Kansas City. The grooves also echo the Urban League's early 20th century history of helping black people from the South find jobs in places like Kansas City.

"That is so powerful," Grant said after seeing the indentations. "How many hours? How many years? How does a man view himself when his whole life's work is on his knees?

"It speaks to the dedication and the character of these men."

Jobs like these and railroad pullman porter positions were among those the Urban League helped black men get. It's from such beginnings that African-Americans advanced.

"This is honorable work, and it still is," Grant said. She wants people to know about the grooves.

The indentations are as historically significant as the bullet holes from the infamous June 17, 1933, Union Station Massacre mostly because the bootblacks touched thousands of Kansas Citians like Montgomery.

His first shoe shine happened here. It was 1961. He had his oxblood wingtips shined on the way to sign up for the draft, when he was 19 or 20.

The men worked quietly but efficiently with muscles flexing and shine rags popping to a rhythm as they buffed his shoes.

"These guys were the best," Montgomery said. "They made you feel like you had a new pair of shoes."

Despite the shine, he was declared ineligible for military service. "Unfortunately, I had flat feet in those pretty shoes," he said.

He recalled that the stand was where businessmen, servicemen and other travelers ritually read newspapers, smoked and got their shoes shined.

Seeing the grooves puts people in touch with that past.

"I just felt it's kind of sad that it's not noticed," Montgomery said. But then again, the men who did this were not noticed.

"They probably were able to launch their children into a better way of life than they had. But their stories need to be told."

Turner White, chief executive of Union Station, said the grooves told a story of how African-Americans were restricted in what they could do and say.

"There are generations who remember this place far differently," White said. "There is another way of life. It was a city parallel to this one."

But shoe shining is a disappearing art, said Ace Carter, who for 15 years has shined shoes at the Hyatt Regency Crown Center hotel after he retired as a letter carrier. "The drawback to me is the casual way that people are dressing now," Carter said.

Many people wear athletic and canvas shoes instead of dress shoes and boots.

"There's no money in shoe shining anymore," Carter said. "It's just an art that's fading away."

That makes memorializing the grooves at Union Station more important so people won't forget.

A fine place to build our pinnacles

Every time I clean the house, wash dishes, cook or do other chores, I think of my dad's story about Thomas Fuller.

I heard it a thousand times as a kid when I worked at dad's chemical company in St. Louis. Dad still tells the tale, and I still listen.

The story is part of an African-American oral tradition.

You see, my grandfather, born in 1880, told my dad about Fuller. It has been a family story since the days of slavery.

Just like me, dad doubted the tale until he'd read of Fuller's fame in a book about the greatest scientists and mathematicians of all time.

Jeanette Smith, manager of the Julia Davis Branch of the St. Louis Public Library, verified the generations-old story for me with faxes from the book *Black Presence in the Era of the American Revolution 1770-1800,* the *Negro History Bulletin* and a 1959 issue of *Jet* magazine.

Enjoy the story: At age 14, Fuller was kidnapped from Africa and sold into slavery near Alexandria, Va. He couldn't read or write but became known as "the Virginia Calculator" for his ability to solve difficult math problems in his head.

His owner, Elizabeth Coxe, would lend Fuller to other white people who would do such things as have him walk the boundaries of their land to compute the acreage for government records. Fuller performed the complex calculations for plantation owners' bookkeeping and construction needs.

But his problem-solving often wasn't instantaneous. Whites would tell him their problems and give him the mathematical variables, and he would go about doing his normal chores. A day or so later he would give people the correct answer.

But William Harthorne and Samuel Coates of Pennsylvania doubted Fuller's ability.

They challenged him to calculate the seconds in 1 ½ years. He correctly said 47,304,000 seconds.

Then they asked for the number of seconds in the life of a man who had lived 70 years, 17 days and 12 hours. Fuller responded, 2,210,500,800.

But the men, who had done the problem on paper, yelled that the Virginia Calculator was wrong. Fuller, however, replied, "Massa, you forget de leap year."

Dad always laughed when telling that part. What I learned from Fuller was how to develop ideas and innovative solutions while doing rote chores.

At a fall multicultural education conference in Kansas City, Kan., Peggy McIntosh described it as the combined ability to work above and below life's "fault line." McIntosh, associate director of the Wellesley College Center for Research on Women, said our society defines success in pinnacles of preciseness which people achieve by breakthroughs in their professions.

That's the solo, lonely existence of a winner that leads to pay, prestige, promotions and power. Below the fault line is "the other world without verticals."

It's the world of washing dishes, doing laundry, cleaning house, cooking, mending, doing repairs, arranging car pools. ... "This is the repetitive upkeep of the world without which the pinnacles of the world couldn't be built," McIntosh said.

It's where there is a sustaining connectedness of friendship, community and love. Our success as human beings lies in both worlds, McIntosh said.

Thomas Fuller's story brings that truth to life. He died in 1790 at age 80, hailed by newspapers as one of the world's great men of math and science.

It's incredible that more than 200 years later he still has lessons to teach.

Improving the quality of life

A $5,100 scholarship opened up a new future for Sybil Noble at Avila University in Kansas City, Mo.

I've never seen her so excited. I met Noble and her husband, Jerry Armstrong, years ago.

Since then they've taught me a lot about people with mental illness. They've shown me that millions of people like them struggle to overcome the awful stigma of mental illness as much as the disease itself.

People with mental illness all hope someday to live productive, trouble-free lives. Hope for Noble flowered a year ago.

She and Armstrong called then, saying she'd applied for the 1998-99 Eli Lilly Schizophrenia Reintegration Scholarship. They were ecstatic when Noble got a letter last May saying she was one of 51 winners out of 1,800 applicants nationwide.

She called later to tell me her first-semester grades. We got together at Nichols Lunch to talk, eat and celebrate.

"All the classes really challenge me to think in new ways and learn all I can," Noble, 34, said. At Avila she stays focused on her studies and her teachers.

No one treats her differently, and she's made a lot of friends.

"I feel really lucky," Noble said. "The thing is it's like school and is therapeutic for me. It's keeping me out of the hospital."

Reoccurring mental illness from age 18 to 32 had caused Noble to annually spend three to four months in hospitals for treatment. That changed about two years ago when she started taking new medication.

"I think it's neat that Eli Lilly recognizes that schizophrenics could succeed and be integrated and go to school," said Noble, founder and then-president of the Ark of Friends of Greater Kansas City, a support group for consumers of mental health services. "It seems like everything is clicking. Everything is going the way it is supposed to."

One semester Noble received a C in two-dimensional design, a B in philosophy and an A in communications. Another semester she took world religion, American national government and the history of art therapy.

"She comes out of class with so much excitement," Armstrong, 54, said. "I never could have sent her to Avila College. There's no way on our income."

Noble plans to reapply for the scholarship in seeking a master's degree in art therapy.

"She's really admirable," said Susan Lawlor, coordinator of the art program, professor of graphic design and Noble's adviser at Avila. "Every student I have should be as optimistic and as excited to be here as Sybil is.

"I've found her whole optimism and her whole passion to be really kind of moving."

Mary Hynes, associate professor of theology who teaches world religion at Avila, said Noble is a noteworthy student. She asks to do extra work, stops by Hynes' office to ask questions and offers information that complements the course.

"That's why she stands out, which of course teachers love," Hynes said. "She's impressed me as someone who's serious about her studies."

Noble also worked in community relations at Western Missouri Mental Health Center, where Jan Mercer Donaldson considered her to be a role model. "Sybil challenges the stigma people might have of mental illness," said Donaldson, director of community relations at Western Missouri.

"Avila University is not an easy school," Donaldson said. "What Sybil has done is prove you can have a quality of life. School opens up a future for her that truly represents self-sufficiency. It's power and a gift."

Noble proudly graduated with a bachelor's degree from Avila University in May 2006.

Retirees relish rockers

Rock 'n' roll jams at John Knox Village.

America's most beloved pop music, however, seems out of place at one of the country's oldest and largest continuing-care retirement communities. But to quote 65-year-old rocker Bob Dylan: "Times, they are a-changing."

At the village in Lee's Summit. Mo., the average age is 83. The 2,100 residents range from 59- to 103-year-olds.

The low end is where older rockers of the world enter as the new kids in the village. It's not difficult to imagine rockers at the retirement community considering that books now trace the music's infancy to the 1940s and its explosion to 1956.

Face it. The darlings of rock 'n' roll aren't young anymore, and neither are their earliest fans.

I never thought Mick Jagger would be older than the president of the United States, but the lead singer for the Rolling Stones is at least three years older than Bill Clinton.

I never imagined Clinton's Mom as one of Elvis Presley's biggest fans. But Virginia Kelley, 69, was proud to say she worships The King.

Mary E. Rose likes him, too. She began jitterbugging in high school in the early '40s and then danced her way into rock 'n' roll.

The 1946 Kansas State University graduate and retired TWA technical accountant has lived at John Knox for four years, where Elvis keeps her company with such classics as "Love Me Tender," "I'm All Shook Up" and "Blue Suede Shoes."

Rose also watches his old movies on cable TV. "They're just good old-fashioned kind of movies: Boy meets girl and everything turns out neat," she said. "Of course he sings, and that is an attraction, too."

But she said she would rather listen to his music than watch him sing because she never liked the way he curled his lip and sort of sneered.

A crossover rock fan is Gerald Jones, 83, who plays Linda Ronstadt and Natalie Cole CDs on his "hi-fi."

Their easy rock shares playing time with Natalie's Dad, Nat King Cole, Louis Armstrong and, of course, Frank Sinatra.

Rock also rolls with the villagers, entertaining them on tour buses. Jean Harris makes sure of it.

She's the senior travel representative at the village and an incredible Elvis fan. At age 12, she watched him perform and screamed herself hoarse.

Harris danced to his music and saw him sing in concert before he died in 1977. She has all of his tapes, CDs and videos of many of his movies.

"I don't believe he's dead," Harris, 49, said half-joking. "I can still watch him; I can still enjoy him."

Villagers razz her in good fun when she plays Elvis instead of the older music. "But they all love it," said Harris, whose mom lives at John Knox.

They also like Bobby Darin's "Mack the Knife," the Lettermen and many country music singers. Those artists and Elvis have become big planks in the inevitable crossover from Benny Goodman and the Big Band era to rock.

Dance is another bridge. Ironically, more young people from the city than seniors enroll in ballroom dance classes at John Knox. But more village people sign up for pop-culture line dances.

"Music and dance can bring people of all ages together," said Maria Timberlake, then-assistant vice president of resident relations at the village. "I think that's a great thing."

Going undercover to expose the horror of hatred

EMPORIA, Kan. – Kaila Williams has felt the hatred and bigotry that Muslims have experienced since the Sept. 11, 2001, terrorist attacks.

That sentiment didn't receive much attention in the coverage since the national tragedy. But the hatred unleashed toward Muslims and Arab-Americans has been a national horror.

Kaila, 17, is the opinions editor for *The Echo*, the newspaper at Emporia High School in this city of 26,760 persons about 115 miles southwest of Kansas City. After Muslim students reported being harassed, Kaila decided to investigate.

She darkened her skin with Revlon makeup and put on an olive-colored jilbab. The robelike garment covered her so that only her eyes and part of her nose were visible.

Then the 5-foot 6-inch teen walked through the Wal-Mart Supercenter about a half-mile from her school. She described people's reactions in a Nov. 16, front-page, first-person story in *The Echo*.

The Emporia Gazette did a Nov. 21 front page article on Kaila's experience. It ran in other newspapers and generated letters to Kaila from as far away as England.

Many people were touched and said she bravely got folks to see how badly they were treating their neighbors. One Muslim girl said the story made her cry. She didn't think others could understand.

"It made me realize how much this does affect everyone," Kaila said. "I guess I know what they are going through.

"But I could take off the clothes, and I could take off the makeup. I just can't imagine living in a place where you are defined by where you come from and the actions of others."

Kaila got the idea from John Howard Griffin's 1961 book, *Black Like Me*. Her dad, Bary Williams, told her about the novel of a white man who colored his skin and went out to learn what it was like to be black.

"She was not afraid to go out and try something like this," said Keith Hughey, the school newspaper adviser.

Her mother, Nina Williams, and grandmother, Mary Russell, were apprehensive. Kaila's father went with her into the store. "My dad said, 'Just be careful,'" Kaila said.

Bary Williams said he was not surprised by what happened. He said it was an eye-opening experience for Kaila.

In the store a couple of persons were friendly. But "most either stared or backed away in fear," including people Kaila knew from Flint

Hills Christian Church, where she worships.

She wrote in her article that one woman said, "We don't need none of that here!" A man "glared at me as I passed. Fear knotted in my chest as I looked into his hard, cold eyes, for the first time seeing raw, undisguised hatred; it was directed at me."

Another woman said, "Damned foreigners!"

That offensive behavior is a national problem. Then-Attorney General John Ashcroft had been quoted saying things about Muslims that seemed disparaging to some. Television evangelist Pat Robertson's slurs also work against President Bush's best efforts to keep the public from turning against Muslims as people did against Asian-Americans during World War II.

Arab-Americans, Muslims and Sikhs have filed federal complaints, saying they've been attacked, illegally fired, harassed or victimized by workplace bias. Reports reveal discrimination in schools, racial profiling at airports and other incidents. This hatred must end.

Saeeda Safi, a 24-year-old student at the University of Missouri-Kansas City, said many Muslim women like her who wear jilbabs suffered because of their faith. "I feel like it's something that's going to be there," said Safi, who on Feb. 17 organized a benefit for Afghan war victims, which raised $50,000.

"There are some who say, 'Go home!'" she said. "Well, this is my home."

Safi praised Kaila for exposing the problem.

"Here is a person who stepped out of her comfort zone," Safi said. "She had no need to do that other than relate to another human being, which is an awesome thing to do."

Kaila learned that hatred and prejudice remain problems in America. "These are still things that we need to realize that we need to work on," she said.

"I hope it gets better for them," she added. "That's what I am trying to do is make it better. I hope people can accept them, that they are people, too. They're not Osama bin Laden. They're just like you and me."

Each of these students has a unique story of success

FAYETTEVILLE, Ark.- Quantrell Willis, a graduate student who wants to be a college administrator, tells a cotton-fields-to-college story.

He defies the media stereotypes showing young people of color as no-accounts who shun books and school. He has the drive, discipline and determination to make his dreams happen.

But more than that, he has the roots to grow to that lofty height. Willis, who's black, remembers a visit from his mother and father on campus. His dad was nearly in tears.

"I think it was him seeing me taking advantage of opportunities that he wishes he had had," Willis said.

His parents had picked cotton for a living. Yet they always encouraged him and helped him value education. His mother exposed him to culture to lift him beyond the fields from where they came.

"She would always give us the newspaper and buy books," Willis said. "Ever since I've been reading, my mother and father always pushed me to do well in school."

To round out Quantrell's education, his father taught him how to work on cars, till the soil, drive a tractor and cut down trees. There's great value in those things, too.

Willis was one of four students I shared lunch with during a speaking engagement at the University of Arkansas. These students value education and college. Getting to know these students was motivational and countered the stereotypes of young people of color.

Pamela Acosta, a journalism major, has parents who came from Mexico for opportunities in America. They do janitorial work at night so she and her sister can get a good education.

"By my parents working here, they could give us those material things they didn't have," said Acosta, who's Latina. "I am proud of them. Because of them, I am able to get an education."

The war in Iraq compelled her to choose journalism as a profession. She wants to be a foreign correspondent and travel the world.

"I want to make a difference," Acosta said. "That's what everybody says, but I really do believe I can make a difference, even if it's covering a small Hispanic event."

Nichelle Sullivan, who's seeking a master's in broadcast journalism, was born in Brooklyn and raised in North Carolina by her godmother. She developed a love for learning and pushed herself to take high school honors classes.

Sullivan, who's black, expected more from life after high school than the traditional factory work or military career. She knew college would give her the transferable skills to fly beyond jobs that might disappear and strand people without strong academic wings.

"I didn't want to be an average person," she said. Sullivan went to college, though some friends and family members thought it was a wasteful pursuit.

"I love going to school," she said. "I love learning new things. I wanted to be in an intellectual atmosphere."

She got her undergraduate degree in speech, theater and television at Fayetteville State University in North Carolina with a minor in English.

"I'd love to be a foreign correspondent," Sullivan said. "I'd love to work for CNN."

Some people where she's from can't visualize her dreams.

"They think that's crazy," Sullivan said. "To them, I'm the same old Shelly they knew. I don't know if they really care."

RaeGina Covington is a nontraditional graduate student. She had been a Spanish teacher in Columbus, Ohio, public schools and at a community college after getting her undergraduate degree in 1995 in foreign language education from Ohio State University.

Covington, who's black, credits her mother for helping her value education. Her mom supported her while she pursued her dream. Her mother, a small woman, was a giant in clearing obstacles for her. The barriers included some educators who thought Covington wasn't academically fit.

"I felt there was nothing I couldn't do as long as my mother was there to support me," Covington said. "There was nothing I couldn't achieve."

Covington has traveled to Japan to continue her educational enrichment. She's seeking a master's degree in journalism at the University of Arkansas with a focus on video documentary production.

These students' stories of academic determination are heartening. They counter the stereotypes of young people of color. They are just four among tens of thousands around the country whose successes often go untold.

He paints what he sees

Frank Parrino likes Roy Burgess' painting of a Russian woman who wore a red print dress and a scarf while she got dirty with farm work.

What also stood out was that the robust woman, who smiled and blushed a little, had on a string of pearls. She had dolled herself up with jewelry because she'd heard an American – Burgess – was visiting her community.

Parrino loves the contrast and the gritty realism in Burgess' photo-quality pastel paintings. Many of the artist's paintings were on display at Paradise Playhouse in Excelsior Springs, Mo., where Parrino is executive director.

"I feel like I am a curator of a museum when his work is hanging there," Parrino said. "To think we had a talent like that in our town and hardly anyone knew it."

Burgess said he had completed about 100 different paintings and had about 60 in his private collection.

They get people of different races, ages, religions, nationalities, ethnicities and socio-economic groups to talk. When that happens, age-old barriers fall.

"People ask us so many questions we can't even get our work done," Parrino said.

"People love to while away the time during intermission in there."

Burgess has captured America's true diversity, enabling people to see folks like those they encounter every day. Many have been pushed away by mainstream America and live outside the margins of today's good times.

But Burgess makes them glow with a beauty of real people who have a unique character and an earthy, embraceable essence.

Burgess, 53, painted the Russian woman while he was in that country exhibiting some of his work of people from this area. His paintings include homeless people, African-American and Hispanic graffiti artists, Paseo Academy teens hanging out in Kansas City, Mo., American Indians, Iowa farm folks with whom Burgess had grown up and Excelsior Springs residents.

The Russians loved Burgess' paintings of the Paseo Academy teens whom they saw as irreverent American youths. They liked the small-town scenes of people doing everyday things such as men shearing sheep.

The paintings of Kansas City's homeless men also moved them. Those were images many Russians didn't know existed in a land of such fabled wealth.

But Burgess also is like the people he paints. He's a self-taught artist whose work appeals to everyday folk. However, he lacks the credentials and network that people in the artistic community respect, which puts him in the margins, too.

But area offices, factories and corporations with wall space should exhibit Burgess' work so more people could talk and bridge the gaps that separate us.

"The work was so different," said Wilhelmina Stewart, then-program director of the Bruce R. Watkins Cultural Heritage Center, where Burgess' art had been displayed.

"It was very outstanding.

"He could feel the pain and passion of these people. His artwork seemed to be drawn from those people. It was very, very touching work."

I'll never forget his 4- by 6-foot portrait of Juan, a Hispanic teen with a Mohawk haircut who was pictured in front of mural art the youth had done on the West Side.

Then there was the painting of Larry in rural America. Larry sat in a blanket-covered, well-worn easy chair and had a beer in his lap.

Burgess showed me the 4- by 7-foot portrait of Jim with his black leather outfit, motorcycle and helmet.

Charles was a painting of a black man with dreadlocks pictured in soft colorful light with a cat and plants on a front porch in the Valentine area.

"So many people don't get to see the other side of these people," Burgess said as he showed me his work. "They don't get to know the other side."

I liked the beauty and simplicity in Burgess' pictures of American Indians in South Dakota.

The ones he did of homelessness and alcoholism in Kansas City also are striking.

"I've always been drawn to people on the fringes of society," Burgess said.

"I expect social justice and find very little of it," he said. "It just bums me when I find people who think they are superior."

I liked his street scene outside an Excelsior Springs diner. Male and female teens in the bed of a GMC pickup truck shoot the breeze with two guys in a red convertible that had pulled alongside them.

These are paintings more people should view, enjoy and discuss. The conversations always add to the value of the art. They bring down walls and build up our respect for America's diversity.

Re-creating flesh reveals its beauty

Dust and a lot of bodies fill Larry Kirkwood's home near Troost Avenue.

The two are part of the art Kirkwood began creating nine years ago to graphically illustrate the diversity and the beauty of the human body. One large body cast that he made with plaster forms taken from a real person sits nude and headless in a tan living room chair.

Others decorate the walls. A life-size torso lies on the table in his dining room.

"I'm trying to call attention to the aesthetics of the body," said Kirkwood, who has exhibited his work in galleries throughout Kansas City and at universities and studios nationwide.

He has made about 500 body casts from about 483 people who have let him spread petroleum jelly on their flesh and take plaster forms of their nude bodies. About 300 body casts populate his home. Many have large, fleshy arms, tummy rolls and beefy legs.

"Large people make the most beautiful pieces," Kirkwood said.

He helped me see that. Kirkwood has used many bronze, dark green, red, black, purple, gold and other colors to paint the resin-coated and hand-sanded sculptures. Each possesses a unique beauty that Kirkwood has isolated as art.

"I'm trying as much as possible to call attention to the sculpture of the body," he said. "If you just focus on one aspect, you leave out the other things the person is. We have to be able to see the other aspects of ourselves."

We walked upstairs where Kirkwood has dozens of body casts stored. Some are men; many are women.

Every race is represented.

"I say if you're racially prejudiced then show me which one is which," Kirkwood said. "As humans we come in a variety of colors."

And they're all beautiful. People need to learn to love that.

The alternative is discrimination, and that's something everyone pays for. Kirkwood points out a few of his more notable body casts.

One is of a woman before and after liposuction and breast implants. Another is what he calls a pregnancy series, showing body casts of a woman getting larger as her pregnancy progresses through the nine-month period.

One woman who had breast implants had to have them removed. "There are basically two big holes there," Kirkwood said.

That sent him into one of the many lectures he has made to Girl Scout counselors and university audiences on body image, media marketing and how people should be happy with who they are and the bodies they have. He has told this same thing in one-on-one conversations with teenage girls suffering eating disorders.

"There's somebody telling you who you are and how to live your life because they are trying to sell you something," Kirkwood said. He wants people to feel a new sense of self-confidence when they walk away from places where he exhibits his work.

"There's so much (junk) out there," Kirkwood said. "The beauty industry goes to great lengths to make you hate your body so you'll buy their products.

"They don't make money with people being satisfied about themselves."

But Kirkwood wants people to accept who they are and know that they and everyone else are beautiful.

Some places he exhibits have a hard time embracing that concept. They get uptight because the body casts he displays are nude.

They see his art and see only sexual content. But what he is trying to show is that the body is so much more. People are more than their sexuality.

"I want people to have to look at themselves in a different manner," said Kirkwood, who walked through his house in blue shorts, a T-shirt and flip-flops. "I want this to help in the change of attitudes."

"I'm dedicated to taking this around the country until it does make a difference. The reality is I've gotten the education of my life."

Kirkwood said the body casts will last a lot longer than the people who shared their images with him will.

Some of his models have already died.

That indicates that he has a lot beyond the flesh for people to see.

Miseducated teen gets lesson

ST. LOUIS – An awards ceremony at the St. Louis Science Center honoring my dad's lifelong contributions in chemistry brought our family together.

After a big plaque was presented by the American Chemical Society, we celebrated at a restaurant and then went to the family home to talk. The plaque and the center's exhibits to Dad's ongoing work help validate his contributions to research and the absolutes of science.

It's one of many awards he has received. They offset the discrimination he's faced as an African-American in the profession he loves and also honor his resistance to ever being a victim.

At home we laughed and talked. Somewhere in the stream of thoughts, my brother-in-law, Walt, shared an experience he had where he, my sister, Renee, and their three sons lived in Blue Springs. Walt was a longtime Federal Railway Administration employee, and he'd been a tireless volunteer in youth athletics.

His efforts helped young people in eastern Jackson County have creative outlets for their energy in football, basketball and baseball leagues. My dad used science to reach and teach kids. Walt used sports to develop such virtues as discipline, self-esteem, creativity and enterprise in young people.

Like Dad, Walt also insisted that young people show respect for him and others. That's why the story he shared of his encounter with a teen-age boy at a Blue Springs convenience store made everyone in our family gasp.

Walt said he was reading a newspaper in the store when he heard the loud, base, thumping vulgarity of hip-hop music on some young person's car radio. He looked up and noticed that the teen in the car playing gangsta rap music was white.

That's not unusual. I've been on Kansas City streets in similar situations. I've heard loud rap music coming from a car at a traffic light only to look and see that the driver and passengers were white.

Rap long ago hip-hopped over racial lines and today counts young white people among its main customers. It's bizarre, especially considering that in the 1950s and 1960s bigoted whites trashed First Amendment free-speech rights by trying to ban black rock 'n' roll music because of its "evil" influences on white children.

Thank goodness those days are gone. But what happened next to Walt was beyond bizarre. The white teen strolled into the store in the baggy, hip-hop clothing of today's youth.

Walt didn't know the kid, yet the youth felt compelled to say, "What's up, my nigger?" It's a stupid hip-hop phrase that no thinking person of any race would ever use. I was stunned when Walt recounted the episode, and so was everyone else.

We had shared a stellar moment of pride with Dad in which his accomplishments continually soar past the degradation of racism. But that hip-hop moment brought us back home, back to America's thorniest problem. Centuries have not erased the meaning and the power of the n-word to both hurt and enrage African-Americans.

Several of us repeatedly asked, "What was that kid thinking?" There also was the whole subscript of ownership embodied in what the teen said. "My" ties to white people owning African-Americans during slavery in this country's ignominious past.

No matter how much some people want to deny it, such racial concerns have stalked this country for generations. The teen whom Walt encountered didn't understand that. He'd never been taught.

Walt, however, with the emphasis and passion of a coach helped the teen realize how foolish he was to pick up that hip-hop phrase and use it on anyone. Walt told him of the historical holocaust of slavery chained to that word.

He educated the teen on the stereotypes, bigotry and discrimination that still drip like blood from that word. He said the youth may hear actors and rappers sling that word around in a foolish, ignorant and careless fashion. But neither the teen nor his friends of any color should ever make the mistake of following those stupid media examples.

The media constantly confuse young people into doing ill-advised, costly and often offensive things to try to act cool and impress others. Walt explained that the boy owed him the same respect that he'd give to an older white man as well as an apology.

The teen was beside himself with shame and profusely apologized to Walt. The hip-hop slang had disappeared from his voice.

He was just a kid again, although intensely aware now of America's past and how he should best conduct himself and greet others today.

Similar beyond a bloodline

WASHINGTON – We ate with our fingers from a common plate at Fasika's Ethiopian Cuisine and looked at each other with wonder.

He and I had been pen pals 18 years. Our odd relationship even merited mention in a history book: We're both journalists – he for *The Washington Post* and I for *The Kansas City Star*. But we'd never met until that summer day.

His long-distance call brought us together: "Lew Diuguid, this is Lew Diuguid!"

It had to happen. We have the same odd first name, and our Scottish surname (pronounced Du-gid) makes us palindromes because it spells forward and backward the same way.

The only difference is Lew's middle initial is H. Mine is W.

At the time of our meeting he was 60 and I was 40. He's also white; I'm black. Life is better than fiction.

Lew and I began corresponding when my byline appeared in May 1977 in *The Kansas City Times* and *The Star*. Some of his friends saw my name and wrote me, shocked that Lew Diuguid would leave *The Post!*

Some of my friends saw his byline in *The Post* and wrote him, stunned that I had landed such a great job right out of college! Lew and I exchanged those letters and have stayed in touch.

My mom even sent me a letter on the oddity, which I shared with Lew in 1978. Lew showed it to me at our lunch, saying he keeps the mail I send him.

Jeez, even my mom never did that! Shop talk would have been a natural for two newspapermen. Lew, an assistant foreign editor, has been with *The Post* 33 years, and I've been here 18.

But we talked about an old subject of our correspondence: Could we be kinsmen? Both of our roots trace to Lynchburg, Va. My dad is from there, and so are some of Lew's forefathers.

But Lew said his dad traced their roots to William Diuguid, who in the early 1700s came to this new world from Scotland. Lew, a graduate of Virginia Military Institute, was named after Revolutionary War Gen. Andrew Lewis.

My lineage gets fuzzy around the Civil War and slavery. Eleanor Harris Macrae mostly tells the white side of the family story in her book *William Diuguid of Buckingham County, Virginia.*

The black side stays in the shadows. It's not unlike other American literature and history.

Macrae quotes family Bibles and records. But they don't include the miscegenetic relations between married, white Diuguid slaveholders and the black women with whom they had slave children.

I do know that I was named after my grandfather, Lewis Walter Diuguid, who died the year I was born.

Our family surname should have been Thornhill, my dad says, because that's the name of the white man who had a child by a Diuguid slave.

But after the emancipation, that black woman on the Virginia plantation took the Diuguid name.

According to the Macrae book, the Thornhills and the Diuguids were kin.

That could make Lew and me distant cousins. We found that we share other things, too.

We're second in birth order, and our older brothers helped steer us into journalism. We both have daughters – him three; me two, although he has two grandchildren.

We both wear glasses, and our moms suffered Alzheimer's disease. We also own family vehicles of our different generations: Lew drives an old station wagon, and I have a van.

He likes an occasional cold beer and holding on to friendships. So do I.

Related or not, we found that we have enough in common to stay friends for a lifetime – the Lew who's white and I.

A starting point on the road to improvements

The often intense Friday morning discussions turn heads at the McDonald's restaurant off the Interstate 70 exit on Prospect Avenue.

The 2-year-old "Eggs & Enlightenment Forum" is open to the public. The attention it generates is encouraged. The African-Americans who participate pick the topics.

They research the subjects and share ideas. Others offer their viewpoints.

The 8:30 to 10 a.m. gatherings provide an opportunity for ideas to emerge to improve the black community. On the Friday I attended, Eggs & Enlightenment chairman Sonny Gibson talked about the downside of bank loans.

"People work hard and think, 'I can only make it if I go to the bank and borrow money,'" said Gibson, a retired federal housing director and black community historian. "But it is an illusion."

Khadijah Hardaway, a youth advocate, questioned that assumption.

Gibson said budding entrepreneurs don't take into account that they will have to repay those loans with interest and without excuses.

"That bank note that you sign when you go borrow a half-million dollars or even $200,000, you sign away everything," Gibson said. "It isn't empowerment. It's a burden."

Richard Tolbert, a trustee with the Metropolitan Community Colleges, talked about economic development.

"It may be true that industries are built on cheap, non-white labor. So what?" he said. "Other groups are running into the future, and they are not waiting for us."

Tolbert then talked about developing what he called "a black Wal-Mart" in the most depressed section of Prospect Avenue. He said such a store should include liquor sales. "Stores that get liquor licenses and sell liquor tend to last longer than those that do not," he said.

That ignited a debate over the black community having too many liquor stores and billboards for alcohol and cigarette products. "I don't drink, but we ought to make the trade-off," Tolbert said.

Archie Williams, an educator, countered: "I don't think we can use something that is part of our destruction to be part of our building."

Iman Murad Karriem, who's in advertising and promotions, added that leaders of a community have to inject morality and righteousness into their actions for the community.

"We couldn't kill the people we were trying to save," he said. "If all you want is money, you'll probably do anything."

Maurice Herron, a community development consultant, said he also was concerned about the proliferation of convenience stores in the black community charging high prices for goods. "It exploits whatever potential for wealth creation there is in any community," Herron added.

Karriem then said apartment tenants must accept communal rules for life to go smoothly for everyone.

"I'm lost," Gibson said to others' laughter. "What are you talking about?"

Tolbert said, "The apartment building is a metaphor."

Williams added that it's about people cooperating and working together.

The black community needs that and more.

Ambition, godliness has helped her abide

Addie T. Dumas switched on the lights when I entered her home.

"I only turn the lights on for company," Dumas said.

She added that she had no need for them. She has been blind since 1992.

Glaucoma is to blame. Yet Dumas, 91, remains positive, idealistic, insightful and an inspiration.

"She's a great person to be around," said Beatrice Jordan, Dumas' friend of 13 years.

But her life hasn't been easy.

Dumas was born Jan. 9, 1915, on a plantation where her grandparents lived and worked in Alabama. Her mother as a teenager was raped by two white men.

"The boys' mother told them that she did not want any half-white nigger baby on their plantation," Dumas said. The "night riders" then paid her family a visit. They "proceeded to shoot their guns into the house that my grandparents were living in on the white people's plantation," Dumas said. "The night riders thought they had destroyed the whole family."

But her grandparents had taken to the back roads, carrying Dumas in a flour sack. They were too familiar with white supremacist hate groups.

"We made it from the sticks in Alabama to some sticks farther away," Dumas said. "But their lives were saved as was mine."

However, a rough life of cotton sharecropping followed with her grandparents, whom she addressed as her mom and dad and her mother as her sister.

Dumas learned to value hard work and a good education. She graduated in 1931 from the eighth grade at Hopewell School. But that was as far as black schools went. She wanted to go away to high school and then to college, but her family had other plans.

"My grandfather said no," Dumas recalled. "He said, 'No daughter of mine would leave home unless she was married.' His emphasis was on marriage, and mine was on education. I couldn't stay on the farm picking cotton."

She vividly recalled her fear as a girl living in the South and the lynching of a black man accused of fondling and trying to rape a white woman. His mutilated body wasn't found for a week.

"When you grow up under such stress and trauma as that, you don't forget it, but you try not to let it bother your life," said Dumas, a member of St. Stephen Baptist Church for 70 years. "I don't have any bitterness or anger or anything. That's where the godliness comes into my life. I don't hate them – white people – who were so nasty and did such dirty and ugly things to my family and even to me.

"There are some decent white people, too. If there hadn't been them, we wouldn't have made it."

Dumas' train ticket out of the South and $4 cash came on Nov. 3, 1932, when she took a job as a cook for a Rolla, Mo., man. Dumas that year married James Frank Walker. He was a hotel porter and barber. They moved to Kansas City on April 16, 1934, where he worked in a barbershop and unloaded coal at a Missouri Pacific roundhouse. But he was killed in an accident in 1938.

She married twice more, outlived each husband and had no children. Dumas' work life mirrors America's black women's. She was a domestic, was employed in a bakery and was a riveter at the B-25 bomber plant in Kansas City, Kan., during World War II.

She also had dreams. One was to one day vote. It was something that poll taxes and literacy tests kept her grandparents from doing.

She cast her first ballot in 1936 for Franklin D. Roosevelt. She always votes and encourages young people to. People must be part of the decision-making in America.

Dumas favors Democrats.

"I have always received more in the way of my livelihood for my survival under Democrats," Dumas said. "When (Herbert) Hoover was in – I almost starved to death under that man."

Another goal Dumas had was learning to drive. She did that in 1933. Then she wanted her own car. In 1953 she got a Nash Rambler. At that time women couldn't buy cars or get credit without their husbands' involvement.

Dumas also had a dream of being a nurse. She accomplished that in 1950 when she got a job as a psychiatric nurse's aide at KU Med Center. She retired on April 1, 1977, as a psychiatric technician.

In her life she has traveled the world, singing with her church choir and taking others on her journeys. Plaques noting her good deeds hang above her fireplace.

Her goal now is to live past age 100. I said I'd return for an update interview with her when she's 101.

Helping people keep their toothy smiles

People without a lot of options packed waiting rooms at four dental clinics that Barry Daneman, Michael McCunniff and I visited.

Many of them bear the face of poverty. It's a mostly hidden condition of the working poor and people who are financially destitute or homeless. But look closely, and it will become obvious.

People's missing teeth are a painful barometer of the financial distress facing a growing number of individuals in our community. It's in the darkened spaces, vacuous smiles and sunken cheeks where teeth once existed.

I got a glimpse of how desperate things are from Daneman, clinical associate professor and director of advancement, and McCunniff, associate professor of dental public health and behavioral science, both at the University of Missouri-Kansas City School of Dentistry.

Often in pain, people begin arriving about 6:30 a.m. at the dental school, and by 8 a.m. the waiting area is full.

"It's a combination of poverty and putting things off until they can't stand it any longer," Daneman said of emergency visits.

Oral health care is like that. Often, dental insurance costs extra. People try to do without it.

Eventually, neglect and decay claim their due. Since July 2004, the dental clinic has extracted 20,201 teeth, Daneman said.

Every day 450 persons wait at the dental school for free or reduced-cost dental care of all sorts. The place operates at capacity yet manages to fit in emergencies. Oral X-rays are back-lighted near dental school students who work on patients with many needs and few resources.

A symphony of dental drills and suctions perform on patients in an almost auditorium-like dental chair area. Saving people's teeth and giving them healthier smiles is the mission of the dental school.

But Missouri lawmakers' Medicaid budget cuts dropped dental benefits for adults older than 20, those with developmental disabilities, mental illness, the elderly and those with medical conditions. The action worsened the problem of unattended dental care.

Daneman, McCunniff and I drove to Swope Health Services, the Cabot Clinic and the Seton Center, where the waiting rooms and parking lots were full. People on tight budgets are having to choose between paying the rent, making car notes, buying food or seeing a dentist.

"Dental is usually the last thing that is taken care of, and then usually it's for acute problems," said P.J. Young, dental director at Swope Health Services.

People put off dental care until they need a $200-to-$1,000 root canal or a $350 crown.

"They opt to get it pulled for $40," said Brenda Lasater, clinic manager at Seton Center Family and Health Services. "You can't continue to do that."

It adds up to more people with more teeth missing. Seton Center sees 8,000 people a year seeking dental care.

Lost teeth compound poverty's problems. People with missing teeth are self-conscious and often put their hands to their mouths to try to cover their appearance.

Their smile also disappears. People with missing teeth lose jobs and promotions. They aren't allowed to work the front counters of fast-food restaurants.

But even worse, lost teeth take individuals' health on a downward spiral. Without Medicaid assistance, people can't afford the $800 to $1,800 cost of dentures.

"They end up having to gum everything," McCunniff said.

That leads to an unhealthy diet. People with few or no teeth eat more processed foods instead of healthier fruits and vegetables.

That promotes obesity, diabetes and heart disease. Medication for those and other serious ailments also leave patients open to more tooth decay, bone loss and other oral damage.

McCunniff said a poster at the dental school advised that without teeth people can't enjoy good nutrition. Without good nutrition people can't have good health, and without good health then the question is, what is life?

"Oral health care is definitely a barometer of how fiscally stressed they are and how emotionally stressed they are," said Leonard Lausten, associate professor and director of special patient care at the dental school.

People also erroneously think tooth loss goes with aging. With proper care, tooth decay is preventable, Daneman said.

"You want to go out of this world with teeth," McCunniff said. "You don't want to go out the way you came in, gumming everything and eating baby food."

The joy in the job is giving people their smiles back. But that can only happen if health-care safety-net programs are fully restored.

It's time the United States puts an end to the Confederate States

Filmmaker Kevin Willmott asked a Donnelly College audience some provocative questions.

"Do we live in the USA or the CSA?" said the assistant professor at the University of Kansas School of Theater and Film, who is behind the movie "CSA: The Confederate States of America." "Our country started out the CSA. We've been trying to become the USA ever since."

Willmott's movie is a "what if" about the South winning the Civil War.

"Did the Confederates lose, or did they win?" he asked. "We did not teach them our way of life.

"We adopted their way of life. The South loses on the battlefield, but they win in their attempt to hold onto their way of life."

Willmott's film includes an advertisement for Sambo X-15, a fictitious invention for car performance. He said the ad was drawn from a real product, Sambo axle grease, which was made in this area.

He also noted that Kansas fought for the freedom of slaves. But afterward, segregation became the law of the land.

It's a sad commentary as the nation mourns the death last week of Coretta Scott King. Her passing follows Rosa Parks', who died in October at age 92. Parks' refusal in 1955 to give up her seat on a Montgomery, Ala., bus, launched a boycott led by King's husband, the Rev. Martin Luther King Jr. That started the Civil Rights Movement.

These great icons have died, Willmott said, but people of color remain in the back of America's bus in the CSA instead of the USA.

Consider that authorities are still investigating an incident that took place a few miles from Donnelly.

Kansas City, Kan., police on Nov. 18 allegedly used force, chemical spray, and racial and sexual slurs while breaking up a tame birthday party for about 30 teenagers.

Nationally, Hurricane Katrina ripped away the thin veneer covering racism in New Orleans, where black people had been stranded by poverty and discrimination decades before the storm.

It could have been any American city, where too many minorities live in poor housing, suffer high jobless rates, go to deficient schools, get bad health care and enjoy few opportunities.

A recent analysis by a Brown University sociologist shows that New Orleans could lose as much as 80 percent of its black population because the people whom the hurricane displaced may be unable to return.

They have been dispersed, or disappeared in America.

President Bush in his State of the Union address noted Coretta King's passing but didn't say enough about what was being done for Katrina's victims. Their needs won't go away. King would have been disappointed, and so would her husband, who worked tirelessly for minorities and the poor until he was assassinated in 1968.

But Willmott hasn't given up hope. This nation, he said, has actually been founded three times in its attempts to form a more perfect union. The first was after the Revolutionary War, then in the Civil War and finally after the Civil Rights Movement.

A fourth founding of America lies ahead as the demographics of the nation change and the percentage of minorities equals that of white people. The passings of America's civil rights icons creates opportunities for new leaders to emerge in the ongoing struggle.

Willmott pointed to the ethnically and racially diverse Donnelly crowd, saying: "Your generation is going to face: What is America going to be?

"What is America going to turn into – an America that looks like this room or one that keeps harking back to the America of the past that looks nothing like this room?"

He urged people to pull together to vanquish the CSA, or cowboy USA, which was never real.

"We can't kill everybody we have a disagreement with," Willmott said. That "gang mentality doesn't work."

He urged students to become filmmakers to challenge stereotypical media images of people of color with the truth.

Then the rebirth of America can happen with diversity and opportunity leading us to new centuries of hope, peace and prosperity.

Creativity and expression can replace culture of chaos

The past 20 years have salted Emanuel Cooper Jr.'s mustache and hair with a scholarly amount of gray and given his eyebrows an artistic bushiness.

Cooper is the owner of Euphrates Gallery Inc. We met when it opened at 31st and Main streets.

The gallery grew out of Cooper's frustration as a black, 1978 Kansas City Art Institute design graduate. "I couldn't find a job because I wasn't the right color," he said as we sat on his backyard swing.

But Cooper had a vision for Euphrates. It was to develop an audience for black art and connect artists with people who craved their work. But the audience was "invisible" and went unacknowledged.

Cooper is a visionary. Twenty years ago, there was no 18th and Vine District, no Bruce R. Watkins Cultural Heritage Center, no First Friday attracting thousands of people to the Crossroads District and no exploding interest in art and art galleries downtown.

"I think he hears the beat of a different drummer," said Diane E. Bratton, past president of the Association for the Study of African American Life and History Inc. of Greater Kansas City.

Cooper welded cross-cultural experiences in art and disciplines into Euphrates. He got that from his independent studies in Great Britain, where "everything in the world opened up," he said.

"I learned what was important to culture," said Cooper, who got a master's degree in art and design education in 1995 at the Rhode Island School of Design in Providence. "I learned about the importance of the institutions of the libraries and the institutions of the museums and how they are vital to culture. The libraries housed those documents that we hold dear to each culture. With the museums I learned that they really function as treasure chests. These are places where artifacts are collected and exhibited."

The Phillis Wheatley Elementary and Lincoln High School graduate fondly recalled the city bus trips when his mother took him and other kids to the Nelson-Atkins Museum of Art. "I remember those big wonderful columns and inside was this wonderful artwork – just beautiful colors, shapes, forms and how it was exhibited, giving importance to it," Cooper said as we sat in the backyard of the home where he grew up in the shadow of downtown.

To Cooper, art is a window helping people understand who they are and the journey that has advanced our civilization. Euphrates, which closed as a gallery in 1987, continues to help chronicle the black experience in that journey.

Cooper's education and travels in Europe, Asia and China enlarged his understanding of art to include math and science in a way not unlike the work of Leonardo DaVinci. "I would suggest that we should be teaching art differently in schools," he said.

If people saw it as a total package, no one would cut schools' art budgets. Others also need to view art as Cooper does: It brings out the creative talents in people.

"We are going to either create positive things that are beneficial to society and culture, or we are going to create chaos," he said. "It's natural to us. When you remove the opportunities of expression, you set it up for chaos."

Cooper sees that as a cause behind last year's rising homicides. The absence of jobs and other forms of creative expression put "chaos or the desire to be negative under pressure."

Bratton said: "I think he believes in what the Bible talks about: people perish for lack of art, culture, history and a lack of opportunity."

Our community can change that by giving people artistic ways to express themselves. Young people find that "they have less options to choose from so they are going to either hurt you or they are going to hurt themselves," Cooper said.

They need to see the joy in art and the joy in discovering that they can be lifelong learners.

"Once you find the joy in learning, you can't escape it," he said. "Nothing else is important. It gives you an insight that is not common."

Euphrates has gone from a being a place to a sponsor of special events including lectures by Harvard Professor Lani Guinier and University of Kansas Chancellor Robert Hemenway. Cooper plans in 2007 to have a special tribute to the work of Aaron Douglas.

Douglas was an art instructor at Lincoln High School in the 1920s who went on to become a giant in the art world during the Harlem Renaissance. "The irony is there has never been a major celebration of this guy's life anywhere," Cooper said.

It's fitting that it is to take place in Kansas City and even better for Euphrates to promote it.

Walking a mile in his shoes

When I drive the interstates and highways in the Southland I always look for Jim.

I had seen him off and on over the last nine years walking along the shoulders and in the medians on U.S. 71, Interstates 435, 470, and other major arteries and streets. At first I thought maybe he had an old vehicle like mine that kept breaking down despite the best efforts to keep it going.

But I never saw him walking from or to a car. Then I thought perhaps he just hitches rides wherever he needs to go and walks between the times he's picked up.

But I had never seen him giving traffic the thumb.

Then I thought that maybe he was just looking for aluminum

cans and that was how he supported himself. Callous motorists' litter stretched over enough road could have become Jim's gold. But I never saw him carrying trash bags clanking with empty cans.

Jim's longstanding habit of walking the highway defied my assumptions. Strangely enough, that made me think of Black History Month.

Many people either assign erroneous reasons to the month-long recognition or dismiss Black History Month altogether. They fail to understand that Negro History Week, started in 1926 by noted historian Carter G. Woodson, grew out of a desperate need of African Americans and others to fill in a missing segment of world history.

Black history – a vital element to our understanding of humankind- was deleted because of slavery and a centuries-long need of one race of Americans to profit from the struggles of another. But through self-determination and need, Negro History Week grew to become Black History Month.

But it's only through studying, asking questions and having a conversation with people who are different that we can learn from such diversity. That drove me to promise myself to one day stop and talk with Jim.

Rushed schedules and unyielding traffic kept that from happening until a year ago, when I saw Jim walking in the cold on U.S. 71. I pulled over just south of Red Bridge Road, but when I got out of my van Jim bolted down the north embankment onto Red Bridge Road.

But I had a promise to keep, so I ran down the south slope after him. We breathed heavily and stared at each other from opposite sides of Red Bridge Road.

I was black and dressed in a suit, tie and overcoat. Jim was white with long blond hair and beard. He wore an MU Tigers cap and layers of clothes with a jacket open in the front, giving air to a man hot from walking.

Traffic seemed to stand still, and in silence our gaze stayed locked for what felt like an hour. Then I crossed the street with pen and reporter's notebook and asked whether I could talk with the man who walked.

We did, but only briefly. Jim told of being harassed and hassled by motorists and police. That's why he ran from me.

No one ever tried to understand, and he tired of attempts to get them to see that he just liked to walk as people did before the land became crowded with roads and cars. He talked to me only because he liked to read and had followed columns I'd written like this in *The Star.*

So he had watched me as I had watched him. We shook hands and smiled – happy with the encounter that quenched our mutual curiosity.

But he made me promise not to pull over again when I see him. Just honk, wave, or both, he said, and "I'll know it's you."

I'll never forget that moment with the man content to go at his own pace, nor will I ever stop looking for Jim.

A Civil Rights Haunting
A Play

What About Us?

Tell me a story
Of great explorers
Of inventors and scientists, too
Make it my wish that somehow it were true
That these brave men and women would be people of color who look like me and you.
These people are largely not found in American literature or books of U.S. history
Missing are tales of their valiance and inventiveness to awe people like me.
Alas all we see on the news each night
Is filled with violence and strife
Of people of color cutting, shooting, robbing, raping and killing
Self-perpetuating, lateral violence without instilling
Hope and dreams of greatness today or to come
Because the real stories of the Real America don't include the people we've come from.

. . . the richness of human diversity cannot be abolished any more than
Mars or Jupiter. Difference is the nature of life,
it is part of our moral Universe.
Without difference, life would become lifeless.
~Adlai Stevenson

Note: This play is meant to be seen as a cross between Charles Dickens' *A Christmas Carol* and the hit holiday movie, *It's a Wonderful Life*. It can be read by one person as a monologue, which is how it is written, or divided into parts—the Angel, John, Mimi and the Narrator—so it can be performed by actors.

The play is in response to feedback I have received my entire newspaper career from people who have expressed hate and disdain toward African Americans when articles appear in the newspapers about conditions that blacks suffer or positive things that blacks have done. For example:

> Letter: May 2, 2001
>
> The black race has no culture, history or heritage before slavery times. Where are the great black explorers, composers, scientists, theologians, authors, etc.? There are none. Black Americans are only a few generations out of the Stone Age, and modern Africans are still Stone-Agers living in the most abject pathetic world-class poverty and disease ridden conditions. I suppose whites are discriminating against them and holding them back from their true potential. It's obvious, your race is not a civilization building one, and the cloths of civilization are ill-fitting and uncomfortable.

~~~~~~

"A Civil Rights Haunting"

John and Mimi never thought too much of people of color. Few if any live in their community. However, they get their negative impressions of African Americans from the ones who come into their home on television.

"Look at that," John said to Mimi. "They're on the news again doing everything that's bad."

On the news, the couple see black people being arrested for drugs, or caught on video cameras holding up stores, arrested for abusing and murdering their children and accused of misusing government or company funds. On entertainment programs, black men are skirt-chasing buffoons, and black women have ugly attitudes.

"Change the channel, John," Mimi said. "Oh no! There's reverend what's-his-name complaining again about racism. I don't get it. Didn't the Civil Rights Movement solve that? I wish there were no black people in this country. Then things would be heavenly."

That statement caused a light to flash in the couple's living room and an angel to suddenly appear. "Hello, John. Hi, Mimi. I am here to grant your wish."

"Who are you?" John asked.

"I am a civil rights angel. I was someone who was in the struggle on earth that didn't have a happy ending. So I've remained a soldier to the cause, meeting with people like you. I am here to help you see what this nation would be like without black people."
~~~~~~

John and Mimi were ecstatic and couldn't wait for the outcome of what they thought would be a better world. The angel waved his hand on that hot summer day in the couple's air-conditioned home and said your wish has been granted. Another light flashed, and the angel added:

"But you might want to rethink what you have wished for. I will stick around in case you want to change your minds."

The house suddenly became oppressively hot. Mimi asked, "What happened to the air conditioning? I can't live without air conditioning."

The angel responded, "But you wished for there to have never been any black people. You obviously weren't aware that modern air conditioning is an outgrowth of the work of Frederick Jones, who holds the July 12, 1940, patent for inventing the practical refrigeration system for trucks and railroad cars. Frederick Jones was a black man."

John went into the kitchen to get a beer from the refrigerator. But the refrigerator wasn't there. "Hey, who stole my refrigerator? I thought you said our wish was going to be granted?" John charged, assuming that someone black had taken his refrigerator.

The angel laughed and responded: "Your wish was granted. The refrigerator is gone because of the inventions patented on Nov. 4, 1879 by John Standard and Thomas Elkins, who were African Americans."

Mimi said: "This is too strange." She looked around and noticed that her house suddenly had become pretty dirty. "Why is this place so filthy?" she asked. "I always keep it well swept and mopped."

The angel said: "You didn't know? Lloyd P. Ray, a black man, got the patent on Aug. 3, 1897, for inventing the long-handled dust pan, and Thomas W. Stewart, a black man, on June 11, 1893, received the patent for the clamping mop. That thing, like your modern easy-to-use mop, could wring water out with the aid of a lever."

Mimi said to John, "I'll get a paper bag to collect some of this mess so our place won't look so bad."

The angel replied, "Don't bother, Mimi. Your wish took care of that convenience item. W.B. Purvis, a black man, received the first patent for a paper bag machine on Feb. 12, 1884."

John shouted: "We don't have to put up with this bull.... come on, honey. Let's leave this, whatever he is, here by himself."

Mimi said, "Wait, John. I have to go to the bathroom first." But when she pushed open the bathroom door she saw that the toilet was gone.

The angel said, "That's because Thomas Elkins, a black man, invented the forerunner to today's toilets called the chamber commode. He got the patent on it on Jan. 9, 1872."

John searched everywhere for his shoes, but never found them. "I know I left them right here in the living room by my chair," John said, scratching his head.

The angel replied: "I am sure you did, John. But your shoes are gone not because you misplaced them but because of your wish. You should know that Jan Matzeliger, another black man, developed the first shoe-lasting machine and holds the March 20, 1883, patent on it.

Mimi looked at John and exclaimed, "John, look at your clothes. They are wet and wrinkled."

The angel responded: "That's another drawback of there being no black people. You see, George T. Sampson, a black man, invented and holds the June 6, 1862, patent on the clothes dryer, and Sarah Boone, a black woman, has the 1892 patent on improvements to the ironing board."

The angel added: "Forget about getting back any dry cleaning that you may have had out. Thomas L. Jennings, a black man, not only got the patent on that process on March 3, 1821, but despite slavery being in full bloom at that time, Mr. Jennings also was the first African American to win a patent on an invention of any kind in the United States. Oh, by the way, the first black woman to get a patent in this country was Sarah Goode. That was on July 14, 1885, for a folding cabinet bed. If you lived in a one-room studio apartment, something like that would have been essential because of limited space!"

John pointed to Mimi's hair. "You look awful, too!" he said to her. "What happened?"

The angel responded: "You no longer have the grooming tools of everyday life. The hot comb or curling iron was patented on Dec. 21, 1920, by Walter Sammons, a black man. On top of that, the forerunner to today's hair brush was patented on Nov. 15, 1898, by a black woman, Lyda D. Newman. One other thing, that perm that you used to have, well it's gone, too. You see, the chemical process was developed by this country's first black millionaire, Madame C.J. Walker in 1900."

Mimi noticed that her nephew's Super Soaker® water gun that he had left from his visit was gone. "I put it by the door to the garage so I wouldn't forget to return it to Bobby. It's his favorite toy," Mimi said.

The civil rights angel explained what had happened. "Lonnie Johnson, a black man, invented and holds the Dec. 14, 1991, patent on all pneumatic water guns," the angel said. "More than 250 million of the flow actuated pulsator Super Soakers® have been sold because of the invention by the National Aeronautics and Space Administration engineer."

John said: "I've got to get out of here. This has to be a dream." He opened the door but noticed that the grass came up to his chest. "I just mowed that yesterday!" he said. "What happened?"

The angel responded, "You wished for no black people in this country. John Albert Burr, a black man, holds the May 9, 1899, patent on his innovations that revolutionized lawn mowers."

Mimi said, "John, it looks awfully dry, too. I thought you said that sprinkler system would keep it green?"

The angel responded: "That's not John's fault, Mimi. That's your wish. You see, the lawn sprinkler was invented by Joseph W. Smith and patented on May 4, 1897."

"Golly, John, I thought our house had become terribly dirty, but just look at the streets!" Mimi said.

The angel replied: "That's your wish again, Mimi. You see, Charles B. Brooks, a black man invented and holds the March 17, 1896, patent on improvements to the street sweeper."

John said: "Hey, where's the newspaper? It was supposed to have been delivered long before now?"

The angel sighed: "Forget about getting the news. They use computers and telephones. The forerunners of computers were typewriters. Typewriters were invented and patented on April 7, 1885, by Lee S. Burridge and Newman R. Marshman, black men. And both land lines and cell phones depend on the work of Granville Woods, a black man, to transmit voice and data. He holds the April 7, 1885, patent on the apparatus for the transmission of messages by electricity over the same line, and he has the Oct. 11, 1887, patent on the device that allows the transmission of speech over electrical wires."

"I definitely have to get out of here," John said. But when he got into his car it just wouldn't go.

The angel responded: "Oh, you are hard to convince. Your car won't start because it has no spark plugs. Edmond Berger, a black man, didn't get a patent on the spark plug, but he is credited with its invention in the1800s. Your sport utility vehicle, the car of choice in the suburbs, also is an automatic. Patented innovations by Richard Spikes on Dec. 6, 1932, made that automatic gear shift possible. By the way, another black man, Dr. Lincoln I. Diuguid, invented a gas saver patented on Sept. 3, 1985, which boosts the mileage of vehicles by increasing the burning efficiency. Benjamin F. Jackson, who also was black, holds the April 30, 1901, patent on improvements to the automobile, including vehicles having interchangeable motors and generators.

"Even if you could go you wouldn't get very far because there are no traffic lights anymore. Why? Because Garrett A. Morgan, a black man, invented and got a patent on the first three-way automatic traffic signal on Nov. 20, 1923. There are no more buses, either, because its precursor was the electric trolley, which another black man, Elbert R. Robinson, invented and got a patent for on Sept. 19, 1893. Those skyscrapers you see out there? They aren't safe at all. Why? Because Alexander Miles, a black man, created an automatic mechanism for closing off the elevator shaft to prevent people from falling to their deaths. He holds the Oct. 11, 1887, patent on the device. And heaven help you if you were to get into an accident because there would be no blood bank if you needed a transfusion. Why? Because Dr. Charles Drew, a black physician, developed those life-saving innovations in 1940. Also don't forget that Lloyd Hall, a black man, invented and got the May 31, 1960, patent for sterilizing hospital and physician supplies to eliminate bacteria, molds, yeast and spores. You know hospitals used to be considered places where people went to die because they weren't as clean as they are today thanks to a black man's invention."

It was getting dark outside so John and Mimi slunk back into their very hot house. But it was dark inside. "Turn on the lights, Mimi," John yelled.

"This is weird," Mimi said. "There aren't any."

The angel responded: "That's part of your wish, too. Lewis Latimer invented and patented the carbon filaments for electric light bulbs on Jan. 17, 1882."

John and Mimi had had enough. "OK," John said. "We understand. Give us back the black people of the world and all of the things inside and outside of our house that they were responsible for creating."

The civil rights angel laughed and waved his right arm overhead. That strange light flashed again, and the angel disappeared. One by one, everything in John and Mimi's home that had vanished with their first wish was restored. In addition, the couple now had a new appreciation of African Americans.

EPILOGUE

Diane M. Kappen, Ph.D.

My association with Lewis began in the early 1990s. We met at a diversity forum sponsored by *The Kansas City Star,* where Lewis mentioned a diversity video that addressed –isms of many kinds in a rather generic form to present the difficulties caused by prejudice. I was teaching introductory psychology as a graduate student at the University of Kansas (KU) at the time, and asked Lewis if I could borrow the tape for my classes. He said yes, but that he would come with the tape to facilitate a discussion about its content afterward (I guess he didn't trust a white woman to do the job!). Both classes were made up of white students with three or four students of color in each. After watching the video, Lewis' efforts to lead discussion led to nowhere. White students seemed to be unable to discuss racism and prejudice, homophobia, sexism and other –isms. Students of color were more willing to reveal their thoughts. The lack of response by the white students surprised me; I thought the clear message in the video would inspire them to think about the effects of prejudice and how to rethink their own prejudicial beliefs. Their lack of response also affected Lewis, who quickly wrote an opinion piece about the experience in *The Kansas City Star* that would appear in the next day's paper. That column appears in Chapter 1.

Students who read the column confronted me the next time our classes met with questions like: "How could you let him write that?" "We aren't prejudiced and privileged." Their responses made me wonder how they could resist the logic presented in the film, why they did not participate in the discussion, and why they were angry when their behavior was exposed. Those questions inspired my doctoral research on white privilege as well as a long cooperative effort with Lewis to try to overcome the prejudices and discrimination that occur because of white privilege.

White privilege is often confused with earned privilege. This privilege is not earned, however. It's like a ladder. In order to succeed in life, we all must climb a ladder with each rung representing a step toward success. White people start out on the first or second rung of that ladder because they enjoy some benefits based solely on the color of their skin. For example, I recently applied for a new job. I had no qualms that the color of my skin would affect the interviewer's opinion of my potential. I was able to start out from the interview with the expectation that I would perform well, learn well, and could be trusted. It never occurred to me that this experience might be different for other people who might be immediately viewed with suspicion because of their color. This is white privilege—the experience of advantages that are not earned and the assumption that every person's experience is the same so that the possibility that others' experiences might be different never enters the white person's mind.

As I began my new job, others helped me climb to the next rung. Training is part of everyone's ladder; we all have to learn new information and will be tested on it. If I miss information, or cannot solve a problem, or need more explanation because I don't understand something, someone will help me. There are others on white ladders who benefit from helping me succeed—the entire company will benefit if all of us on the ladders help one another become the best employees possible. I accept their help, indeed I expect their help. It's assumed, it's normal, it's the way it is. In an America where everyone on their way to success is white, this system would work very well.

But the Real America consists of many colors and cultures with a variety of religions, economic statuses, sexual orientation and two genders. Ladders of different others must be climbed to succeed also. People of color, however, don't get to start out on the first or second rung. They start out on the ground. Their evaluations are influenced by the biases attached to their color. They have to prove their trustworthiness and abilities before they are allowed to climb even to the first rung. They have to climb, learn and be tested without the advantage of having skin that is some shade of white. As they climb the rungs toward success and find they need help because they don't understand something, there are no ladders of color around them, only white ladders. Those on the white ladders are generally unaware that the differences in color have an effect on people's success, much as my psychology students. So people of color receive little help from people on the white ladders. Furthermore, if people have trouble climbing ladders of color, their requests for help might be perceived as inadequacies and inabilities that would preclude climbing to the next rung.

The assumption that white experiences are normal for everyone regardless of color creates a blindness in white people. They are unable to see that the experiences of other ladder climbers are different from theirs. Crossing the bridge to find the Real America is impossible if you don't know there is another side—you would not realize that there is anything to cross over to learn about.

This blindness was painfully evident at a college where I taught several classes each semester. Many faculty members were concerned that our students were not developing the ability to accept or even tolerate people who were different from them and that there were too few professors, staff, administrators and students of color. There was a diversity initiative in place where faculty and staff were encouraged to discuss differences. The program had three goals—one was to develop the ability to discuss differences, another was to accept diversity in others, and a third was to ultimately transfer that ability to students.

The results of the discussions were negligible. When meetings were held, few attended. Usually, white folks talked about -isms from white folks' perspective with little if any input from people of color. As I became more involved in the diversity effort, we asked community leaders to speak, held forums, invited students to participate, and tried to broaden the brave efforts of former diversity leaders. Although the discussions were generally valuable, few attended, and the result of those meetings was also negligible. Many of us who were doing our best to expand the diversity initiative asked if attending diversity programs could be a faculty requirement. The answer is that unlike businesses, colleges cannot force their workers—faculty, staff and students—to attend these programs. There is no requirement for those in charge of learning to incorporate diversity in classes or in relationships with fellow workers. The diversity initiative was a dream on paper.

And so much like the students so long ago in my psychology classes during graduate school, many of my fellow faculty members, staff, and the students who are our future, remain unaware of the differences among us.

It could be that those in charge at the college, or the students at KU ask themselves,"Why should we go to all the trouble to find out how others feel, how difficult or easy it is for them to succeed, what hurdles they face, and even such simple daily experiences as differences in hair and makeup and clothing styles?" One reason discussed in the formula chapters suggests that knowing others enhances us all. Crossing the bridge between color and cultures will let us learn about others so that we achieve greater productivity.

Another reason that might make strong business sense is that when we are climbing our ladders toward success, by helping others and accepting help we will all be able to climb more effectively. For example, if a group of ladders belong to a particular business, all climbers helping others climb will enhance the ultimate productivity of that business.

Yet another reason is that human beings are social beings. We thrive on interacting with others. When we exclude particular others, we might still fulfill our social needs, but we are missing a wealth of ideas, feelings, and warmth that those different from us can provide. The current fear and avoidance of homosexuals, for example, precludes enjoying the companionship of warm, caring people who have the same goals, feelings and expectations from life as heterosexuals.

Crossing the bridge to discover the Real America is even more important today than ever. The creation of this book comes at a time when our nation is slipping deep into the chasm of racism that we have never completely climbed out of. Even as this book is going through its final revisions, disturbing reports about isolating our nation's children in religion-based home schooling, about the degradation and deportation of Hispanic people, about the promotion of the Christian God as the only possible God, about major universities being accused of racial discrimination, about the dismissal of affirmative action programs in many institutions appear in the news. There is a wave of regressive actions that will only lead to increased divisiveness, distrust, and hatred.

On September 3, 2006, *The Kansas City Star* reported that "a movement is pushing parents to forsake public schools, viewed as hostile to their faith" (Crary). What harm can come from parents giving their own children an education in the comfortable, safe haven that home provides? What harm can come from children learning in an environment that promotes faith in God and incorporates that into every day's lessons? Most people would say no harm, sounds good. But here are a couple of things to think about.

Not long ago, the United States was involved in supporting the Taliban in Afghanistan in efforts to prevent Russian infiltration. We gave them weapons, we allowed the Taliban to grow, we encouraged their strength. The combat left many Afghan children parentless, and those starving children were provided food and clothing in schools called *Madrasas*. At school, these kids grew up with a narrow sense of the world; they learned that their religion was the only religion, that people who interfered with their pursuit of their religion were evil, were a source of social infection, were infidels. Many of those kids became terrorists, protecting their nation and religion by killing as many infidels as possible.

Michelle Goldberg discusses the religious fervor she found during the interviews she held when researching her book, *Kingdom Coming*. She found that the individuals in the Christian religions seem harmless, that they are friendly and warm. Yet, she notes:

> Sometimes it's hard to reconcile this benignancy with the violence of the movement's rhetoric. It's tempting to think that all the talk of war, of taking the land, subduing God's enemies and building the Christian nation, is just harmless hyperbole.
>
> Before I began this book, I did some reporting in the Middle East. There, too, I was usually received warmly and treated with humbling generosity. It would be a mistake to conclude from that, however, that the region's antipathy toward Jews and Americans is not real

> and dangerous. In my experience, people are often kinder than their ideologies, and always more complicated. Yet individual decency can dissolve when groups are mobilized against diabolized enemies, especially when they believe they're under attack.
>
> America is full of good people, but something dark is loose. There's a free-floating anxiety that easily metastasizes into paranoia and hatred for the same enemies always targeted by authoritarian populist movements—homosexuals, urbanites, foreigners, intellectuals, and religious minorities. Rationality is losing its hold; empirical evidence is discounted as the product of a secular worldview or a scheming liberal elite. (22)

People are afraid. They are afraid that their religious beliefs are being undermined by the secular educational system. They are afraid their children will be influenced away from family beliefs. The only way to be sure that doesn't happen is for parents to control education. These children will grow up strongly believing that homosexuals are evil, that intellectuals hate God and are trying to destroy faith through science. And those beliefs will persist, because these children, learning in an isolated environment, will meet no homosexuals, will meet no foreigners, will not be exposed to scientific methods and evaluation, will not learn about other religious beliefs. In short, they will not learn about the Real America—and, in fact, they will be trained to avoid it.

From the perspective taken by this book, the valuable contributions made by those home-schooled children may be lost to those who they are taught to disregard. Crossing the bridges between the future adults will become harder and harder as home schooling expands and our current educational system, which tosses all the kids into a common social environment where they are exposed to differences, is further destroyed.

Can this dismal future be avoided? From the perspective of this book, if we are able to cross bridges to discover and accept the valuable differences that others provide, we will all benefit. We will multiply our production and social capital exponentially. If we learn to lend a hand to those on ladders that are a different color from our own, or if we overcome the fear of asking for help from those who are climbing ladders of different colors from our own, we can enhance productivity to achieve a common cause. This sounds easy, but my experience says it is not. White privilege is a hard egg to crack. Fear is very difficult to "untrain." Racism and other –isms seem to underlie much social behavior. Yet influencing people to cross the bridge is possible.

Three incidents give me hope. One is a study that was performed by Stuart W. Cook in 1964, 1970, and 1971. The study appears in a *Social Problems in the Seventies*, by Lawrence Wrightsman, a professor at the University of Kansas whom I was fortunate to know and learn from. Cook wanted to find out what would happen to prejudiced attitudes when antiblack people (racists) interact with black people under conditions that require working together toward a common goal. His study was conducted in the South in the 1960s, a time when racism was overt, particularly in southern states. Twenty-three crews were formed and were told that they would learn to operate a railroad system together over the course of a month. Based on previous tests of racism and personality traits, each crew included one highly prejudiced female participant and two other women. On each crew, one of the other women was black, the other white, and both were confederates who behaved in prescribed ways to see how the prejudiced woman would respond. As the women operated the railroad system, the black confederate behaved as though she was equal to the white women and she revealed information about herself and about the injustices of experiencing discrimination. It was made clear to all participants that intolerance of blacks was not acceptable with the white confederate discussing her feelings that racism was wrong over the course of the study. There were many opportunities for the women to talk with each other. A bonus was promised if the women did a good job. After working together for about a month, the racial attitudes of the prejudiced white women were retested. Thirty-five percent of the women changed to less negative attitudes toward blacks after interacting on the railroad task. In a control group that did not interact in mixed groups, none showed attitude change. Observed behavior changes included the following:

> When the lunches arrived, the crew discovered that blackberry pie was being served—the subject's favorite. As the black confederate ate her pie, the subject kept turning her eyes to the pie as if hypnotized. Finally, after the black confederate cast aside her half-eaten slice of pie, the subject turned to her and said, "Betty Jean, would you mind if I ate the rest of your pie?" Surely, had the prejudiced white been told one month before that she would soon be eating a black person's leftovers, the suggestion would have been met with ridicule! (331)

This study suggests that under the right conditions, even the most prejudiced among us can be influenced to cross the bridge to the Real America. Another story comes to mind to show how people can be influenced to cross the bridge. I taught a class with the ambiguous title Psychology of Social Problems at the University of Kansas which left me free to teach what I wanted using textbooks of my choice, as long as we addressed possible psychological causes of social problems. I started from the assumption that most white students resist accepting the idea that racism and other –isms exist. I realized that their resistance could actually stem from a lack of knowledge about the history of racism and discrimination in the United States. To teach them about the roots of –isms, I chose James Loewen's *Lies My Teacher Told Me* for their semester text. These white students, unlike the students that Lewis found so challenging, eagerly discussed social problems like white privilege, racism, homophobia, and more. They expressed interest, and many said they learned more in that class—beyond psychology—than they had learned in all of their years at KU. Their comments suggested that a tactic to crack the hard egg of white privilege might be to shock people out of their long held and misinformed beliefs. The Loewen book is presented to do just that.

As Lewis mentioned early in this book, my dissertation studies show another factor that might make people more willing to cross the bridge. Those studies showed that when white men and women are told about white privilege, it matters who does the telling. White men more readily admit their privilege when a white male discusses it, suggesting that similar others are more influential to white men. Quite differently, however, white women more readily admit their privilege when a black male discusses it. This suggests that white women might be more influenced by those they feel have suffered similar –ism experiences. If we want people to be more willing to cross the bridge to discover the Real America, we might carefully consider who might be more influential in guiding people toward the bridge.

Even if we are on the bridge, it can be difficult to discover the differences in others who inhabit the Real America if we have no safe and noncompetitive environment to reveal our selves and our ideas to others. In that regard, it would be hard to close this discussion without mentioning the late Dr. David Shapiro, founder of the Minority Museum. David, who was an optometrist with the Army, spent many years of his life fighting hatred and bigotry after witnessing the horrifying remains of both live and dead people at Dachau after World War II. He built the museum collection around documents, photos and artifacts collected at Dachau and through donations from other U. S. Army soldiers who were assigned to the concentration camps at the end of the war. David initiated a monthly group meeting where people could safely and openly discuss diversity in order to understand each other. He felt that discussion led to learning, which led to reasonable evaluations of each other based on truths rather than on bias and bigotry. Most of those who participate in the discussions leave with a load of knowledge. The group has expanded from about fifteen to over forty. That's quite a few people trying to cross the bridge each month, but it leaves many stranded on one side. We need to reach those people and help them all cross the bridge to discovering the Real America.

WORKS CITED

Allen, James, Hilton Als, John Lewis, and Leon F. Litwack. *Without Sanctuary: Lynching Photography in America*. Santa Fe, N.M.: Twin Palms Publishers, 2004.

Anderson, Sarah, John Cavanagh, Scott Klinger, and Liz Stanton. *Executive Excess 2005: Defense Contractors Get More Bucks for the Bang. 12th Annual CEO Compensation Survey*. Institute for Policy Studies and United for a Fair Economy. 30 Aug. 2005.

Bavley, Alan and Lynn Franey. "More go without health coverage; The percentage of uninsured Americans is at the highest since 1998, with poverty rate steady." *The Kansas City Star* 30 Aug. 2006: A1.

Bezruchka, Stephen. "Health and Poverty in the US." *ZNet.org* 9 Dec. 2003. 9 June 2006. <http://www.zmag.org/content/showarticle.cfm?SectionID=10&ItemID=4647>.

"Black History Month - African American Inventors." *About.com*. 2006. 28 June 2006. <http://inventors.about.com/od/blackinventors/a/Black_History.htm>.

Brown, C. Stone. "A History of Resilience." *DiversityInc*. Apr. 2005: 54-60.

"Chicano Leader Rodolfo 'Corky' Gonzales 1929-2005: 'He Was the Fist. He Stood For Defiance, Resistance." *Democracy Now!* 15 April 2005. 15 April 2005. <http://www.democracynow.org/article.pl?sid=05/04/15/1337236>.

Chideya, Farai. *Don't Believe the Hype: Fighting Cultural Misinformation about African Americans*. New York: Penguin Books USA, 1995.

Clark, Christine and James O'Donnell, eds. *Becoming and Unbecoming White: Owning and Disowning a Racial Identity*. Westport: Bergin & Garvey,1999.

Cohn, D'Vera and Tara Bahrampour. "Minority population growth presages demographic shifts." *The Kansas City Star* 10 May 2006: A6.

Constantino, Renato Redentor. "The Colors of Memory." *CommonDreams*. 29 April 2005. 29 April 2005. <http://www.commondreams.org/views05/0429-32.htm>.

Crary, David. "Different dropouts." *The Kansas City Star* 3 Sept. 2006: A2.

Cropp, Fritz, Cynthia M. Frisby, and Dean Mills. *Journalism Across Cultures*. Ames: Iowa State Press, Iowa, 2003.

Davis, Stanford L. "Buffalo Soldiers & Indian Wars." 1999. 20 June 2006. <http://www.buffalosoldier.net>.

DiAngelo, Robin J. "My Class Didn't Trump My Race: Using Oppression to Face Privilege." *Multicultural Perspectives* 8.1 (2006): 51-56.

Eisler, Riane. The Chalice and the Blade: *Our History, Our Future*. San Francisco: HarperCollins, 1995.

Ellison, Ralph. *Invisible Man*. New York: Vintage International, 1947.

"2020 foresight: China, India are stars; U.S. won't be sole superpower, intelligence analysts say." *The Kansas City Star*. 14 Jan. 2005: A2.

"Fugitive Slave Law of 1850." *Wikipedia*. 20 May 2006. 28 June 2006. <http://en.wikipedia.org/wiki/Fugitive_Slave_Law_of_1850>.

Gabriel, Larry. "Watermelon Man." *Metro Times Detroit* 24 Oct. 2000. 22 Mar. 2005. <http://www.metrotimes.com/editorial/story.asp?id=793>.

George, Henry. "The Chinese in California." *New York Tribune*. 1869.

Goldberg, Michelle. Kingdom Coming: *The Rise of Christian Nationalism*. New York: W.W. Norton & Company, 2006.

Gordon, Jacob U., ed. *The Annals of the American Academy of Political and Social Science: The African American Male in American Life and Thought*. London: Sage Publications, 2000.

Gray, Steven F. "Recognizing Stereotypical Images of African Americans in Television and Movies." Yale-New Haven Teachers Institute. 2005. 22 Mar. 2005. <http://www.yale.edu/ynhti/curriculum/units/1996/3/96.03.05.x.html>.

Hankins, Gladys Gossett. *Diversity Blues: How to Shake 'em*. Cincinnati: Telvic Press, 2000.

Howard, Gary R. *We Can't Teach What We Don't Know: White Teachers, Multiracial Schools*. New York: Teachers College Press, 1999.

Jackson, Linda A. "Stereotypes, Emotions, Behavior, and Overall Attitudes Toward Hispanics by Anglos." Research Report # 10. Jan. 1995. 9 June 2006. <http://www.jsri.msu.edu/RandS/research/irr/rr10.pdf#search=%22%22Stereotypes%2C%20Emotions%2C%20Behavior%22%22>.

Jadakiss f and Anthony Hamilton. "Why." *Kiss of Death*. 1 Aug. 2004. 2 July 2006. <http://www.topdog08.com/2004/08/rap_lyrics_of_t_11.html>.

Kozol, Jonathan. *Amazing Grace: The Lives of Children and the Conscience of a Nation*. New York: HarperPerennial, 1995.

Lawrence, Keith, Stacey Sutton, Anne Kubisch, Gretchen Susi, and Karen Fulbright-Anderson. *The Aspen Institute Roundtable on Community Change: Structural Racism and Community Building June 2004*. The Aspen Institute, 2004.

Lee, Robert G. *Orientals: Asian Americans in Popular Culture*. Philadelphia: Temple University Press, 1999.

Lieb, David A. "Missouri police prone to pulling over black drivers." *The Kansas City Star* 26 May 2006: B4.

Leonhardt, David. "Poverty in U.S. Grew in 2004, While Income Failed to Rise for 5th Straight Year." *The New York Times* 31 Aug. 2005: A9.

Loewen, James W. *Lies My Teacher Told Me: Everything Your American History Textbook Got Wrong*. New York: Simon and Schuster, 1996.

---. *Sundown Towns: A Hidden Dimension of American Racism*. New York: The New Press, 2005.

Lucas, Bill. "The Cherry City." *Salem Online History*. 21 June 2006. <http://www.salemhistory.net/commerce/cherries.htm>.

McIntosh, Peggy. "White Privilege: Unpacking the Invisible Knapsack." *Peace and Freedom* July/August 1989: 10-12.

McVay, Douglas A., comp. "Drug War Facts." Oct. 2005. 10 Aug. 2006. <http://www.drugwarfacts.org/racepris.txt>.

Meadows, Angela Johnson. "To Be Asian in America." *DiversityInc*. April 2005: 28-47.

Meadows, Angela Johnson and Oriol R. Gutierrez Jr. "Finding Their Place." *DiversityInc*. Oct. 2005: 56+.

Minor, Robert N. *Scared Straight: Why It's So Hard to Accept Gay People And Why It's So Hard to Be Human.* St. Louis: HumanityWorks!, 2001.

Montuori, Alfonso and Isabella Conti. *From Power to Partnership: Creating the Future of Love, Work, and Community.* New York: HarperCollins, 1993.

Navy & Marine Corps WWII Commemorative Committee. "Navajo Code Talkers: World War II Fact Sheet." Department of the Navy, Naval Historical Center. 12 August 1997. 17 June 2006. <http://www.history.navy.mil/faqs/faq61-2.htm>.

Ogletree, Charles J., Jr. *All Deliberate Speed: Reflections on the First Half Century of Brown v. Board of Education.* New York: Norton, 2004.

Ortiz, Peter. "The Hidden Disability." *DiversityInc.* Oct. 2005: 69+.

Pewewardy, Cornel D. "Fluff and Feathers: Treatment of American Indians in the Literature and the Classroom." *Equity and Excellence in Education.* April 1998. 22 Mar. 2005. <http://www.hanksville.org/storytellers/pewe/writing/Fluff.html>.

---. "From La Belle Sauvage to the Noble Savage—The Deculturalization of Indian Mascots in American Culture." *Multicultural Education* 6.3 (1999): 6ff.

"Poll finds schools are more hostile for blacks, Hispanics." *The Kansas City Star* 31 May 2006: A5.

"Professor Preacher Michael Eric Dyson on the State of the Country: 'Some of Us are In First Class, But The Plane Is In Trouble.'" *Democracy Now!* 14 Oct. 2005. 15 Oct. 2005.<http://www.democracynow.org/article.pl?sid=05/10/14/1353201&mode=thread&tid=25>.

Putnam, Robert D. *Bowling Alone: The Collapse and Revival of American Community.* New York: Simon & Schuster, 2000.

Robinson, Randall. *The Debt: What America Owes to Blacks.* New York: Penguin Putnam, 2000.

Ross, Leon T. and Kenneth A. Mimms. *African American Almanac: Day-by-Day Black History.* Jefferson: McFarland & Co., 1997.

Russell, Katheryn K. *The Color of Crime: Racial Hoaxes, White Fear, Black Protectionism, Police Harassment and Other Macroaggressions.* New York: New York University Press, 1998.

Shipler, David K. *A Country of Strangers: Blacks and Whites in America.* New York: Vintage Books, 1998.

"SNCC Activist Ekwueme Michael Thelwell: 'People Fought, Died And Bled for the Right to Vote.'" *Democracy Now!* 8 Aug. 2005. 9 Aug. 2005. <http://www.democracynow.org/article.pl?sid=05/08/08/1420230>.

Smith, Jessie Carney. *Black Firsts: 4,000 Ground-Breaking and Pioneering Historical Events.* Detroit: Visible Ink Press, 2003.

Suarez, Ray. *The Old Neighborhood: What We Lost in the Great Suburban Migration: 1966-1999.* New York: The Free Press, 1999.

Summer 1994 Media Studies Journal: Race – America's Rawest Nerve. New York: Freedom Forum Media Studies Center at Columbia University, 1994.

Swedlund, Charles. *Photography: A Handbook of History, Materials, and Processes.* New York: Holt, Rinehart and Winston, 1974.

Takaki, Ronald. *A Different Mirror: A History of Multicultural America*. Boston: Little, Brown and Co., 1993.

---. *Strangers From a Different Shore: A History of Asian Americans*. Boston: Little, Brown and Company, 1989.

Thandeka. *Learning to Be White: Money, Race and God in America*. New York: Continuum, 1999.

The State of Black America 1999: The Impact of Color-Consciousness in the United States. New York: The National Urban League, 1999.

The State of Black America 2002: Opportunity and Equality = One America. New York: The National Urban League, 2002.

The State of Black America 2003. New York: The National Urban League. 2003.

The State of Black America 2004: The Complexity of Black Progress. New York: The National Urban League, 2004.

The State of Black America 2005: Prescriptions for Change. New York: The National Urban League, 2005.

The State of Black America 2006: The Opportunity Compact. New York: The National Urban League, 2006.

The State of Black America 2007: Portrait of the Black Male. New York: The National Urban League, 2007.

Thomas, R. Roosevelt, Jr. "From Affirmative Action to Affirming Diversity." *Harvard Business Review*. 68.2 (1990): 107-117.

Tucker, Maria Luisa. "Finding Words to Talk About Race" AlterNet.org. 16 Jan. 2006. 27 Jan. 2006. <http://www.alternet.org/story/30755/>.

Upton, Barbara and John Upton. *Photography*. Boston: Educational Associates, 1975.

Wilson II, Clint C. and Félix Gutiérrez. *Minorities and Media: Diversity and the End of Mass Communications*. Newbury Park: Sage Publications,1985.

---. *Race, Multiculturalism, and The Media: From Mass to Class Communication*. Thousand Oaks: Sage Publications LTD, 1995.

Woods, Gail Baker. *Advertising and Marketing to the New Majority*. Belmont: Wadsworth Publishing Co., 1995.

Wright, Kai. "Upward Mobility." *Mother Jones*. May/June 2006. 9 June 2006. <http://www.truthout.org/issues_06/052306HA.shtml>.

Wrightsman, Lawrence S. *Social Psychology in the Seventies*. Pacific Grove: Brooks/Cole Publishing Company, 1972.

Woodson, Carter G. *The Mis-Education of the Negro*. Trenton: African World Press Inc., 1993.

Wu, Frank H. *Yellow: Race in America Beyond Black and White*. New York: Basic Books, 2002.

Zinn, Howard. *A People's History of the United States: 1492-Present*. New York: HarperCollins, 2003.

APPENDIX A

List of Columns by Chapter

Introduction: What's diversity got to do with it?

As always, gifts flow both ways (June 14, 1997)
Slaying the beasts in us all (Nov. 18, 1993)

Section 1: The Cutting Winds of Discrimination: The Situation Now

Chapter 1—Whiteness in Charge

Privilege feeds a system of racial division (Feb. 26, 2003)
True colors of white privilege (Feb. 2, 1999)
Obstacles abound in starting honest talks (Mar. 1, 2006)
Diluting the power of privilege (Mar. 14, 2003)
Blind to 'white privilege' (Nov. 17, 1999)
Assessing white privilege (Oct. 4, 2000)
Heritage is not something to hide (Aug. 26, 2005)
Johnson County's race issue (Feb. 2, 2000)
A chance for understanding (Feb. 11, 2000)
Leaving a noose at work or school is no laughing matter (May 3, 2000)
Noose incidents reflect need for racial understanding in the Heartland (May 26, 2000)
Inaccurate portrayals, symbols insulting to American Indians (Jan. 25, 2006)
Billboard ignores history (Feb. 23, 1999)
Step 1 Admit to racism (April 6, 1996)

Chapter 2—Undeniable Discrimination

A sad case of hidden identity (July 29, 1997)
Racism taints some home sales (Oct. 18, 1997)
America's quickening pulse (July 5, 2000)
Paying a price for discrimination (Dec. 22, 1998)
A just reward for injustice (May 9, 2001)
Celebration muted in racial profiling decision (Mar. 1, 2002)
Laws address discrimination, but biases must change first (Nov. 25, 2005)
Pulled over unfairly (June 20, 2001)
American Indians face taunts (May 15, 2002)
Young people face harsh realities (Feb. 3, 2006)
Battling the cycle of hatred (May 27, 1993)
Bigotry raises its ugly head (Dec. 2, 1991)
Intolerance scars Muslims in U.S. (Dec. 8, 2004)
We must expose all racism (July 10, 1999)

Racism is no longer undercover (July 25, 1998)
New craters are blasted every day (June 27, 1998)
It's time to abolish the chop (Oct. 22, 1992)
Cruelty continues to fester (Nov. 19, 1992)
Unhealthy racism a la mode (Dec. 1, 2000)
A death sentence for blacks (Aug. 19, 2005)
Treatment in need of treatment (Mar. 4, 1995)
Painful venturing outside one's own culture (Jan. 6, 2006)
Sykes takes rights seriously (Nov. 30, 2001)
Tough times for black farmers (Aug. 28, 2002)

Chapter 3—Undercover: Jim Crow, Esq.

Marooned in KC by Subtle bias; Area needs equal accessibility to public transportation (Nov. 5, 2004)
Welcome mat is not in sight (April 30, 1992)
Ghosts of segregation; Decades after civil rights movement, businesses that discriminate deserve 21st century boycott (Feb. 25, 2005)
We need a hospitality lesson (Sept. 24, 2003)
Singing the Westport blues (June 21, 2000)
Racist arrows at Valentine's (Feb. 18, 2000)
Diversity embraced in Taiwan (Sept. 3, 1994)
The lesson of education inequality (Oct. 25, 2002)
Educators have much to learn (July 7, 2000)
A history ignored; American Indians deserve to be recognized (Jan. 13, 2006)
Book paints colorless picture of American fatherhood (Mar. 2, 2005)
Of women, silence and rage (Mar. 3, 1998)
What's in a name? Often, discrimination (Feb. 19, 2003)
It's all in how you say it (Mar. 2, 1999)
Nursery rhyme's racist roots; Airline case demonstrates why verse should become obsolete (Feb. 4, 2004)
History draws color line in U.S. (Feb. 18, 2004)
A linguistic weapon too risky for light banter (April 19, 2006)
Flaws were numerous in this dubious election (Jan. 27, 2006)
Politics with a conscience; Summon courage on gay marriage vote (June 11, 2004)

Chapter 4—Chained: Effects of Oppression

Browbeaten black and blue (Oct. 6, 2000)
Victims of racial stress (Feb. 23, 2000)
Rx: More blacks in health care (Dec. 6, 2000)
Embracing diversity means accepting others and yourself (Aug. 12, 2005)
Challenge can defeat stereotypes (Dec. 10, 1994)
Saturday's child works hard (Mar. 22, 2000)

Misconceptions, mistakes magnified a tragedy (Sept. 7, 2005)
Unfair gap found in home value (Feb. 12, 2003)
New center a chance for a new start (Feb. 22, 1997)
Planting seeds that end hate (Oct. 9, 2002)
Inject compassion into government (April 23, 2003)
All blood is the same color – red (Feb. 8, 1993)

Section 2: The History Leading to Today

Chapter 5—Removing the Whitewash
America's many faces tell its story (Nov. 25, 1997)
Teachable moments in history (April 3, 2002)
Educational expeditions advance black history (Feb. 8, 2002)
Matters we must talk about (Feb. 6, 1997)
Let's remember our heroes (June 17, 2005)
Two groups share entwined history (Oct. 10, 2003)
Culture must not be forgotten (Oct. 14, 1997)
Hispanics will help build future of U.S. (April 28, 2004)
California's Latino legacy (Aug. 30, 2000)
U.S. needs a uniting solution, not a dividing wall (May 24, 2006)

Chapter 6—The Media: Continuing the Indoctrination
Are "Homies" the right images of Hispanics? (Jan. 31, 2003)
Fog blocks the truth (Aug. 29, 2001)
Too many discount the minority vote (Aug. 11, 2004)
Gangsta rap feeds into the media's image of urban despair (Oct. 30, 1996)
Gangsta rap's sharp, deep wedge (May 28, 1994)
What kind of heroes are these? (April 2, 1992)
Young woman speaks out to change minority stereotypes (Nov. 16, 2005)
Reminders of battles fought for civil rights (Nov. 2, 2005)
The rising voice of Hispanics (May 4, 2001)
Media bear responsibility for dysfunctional views of women (Nov. 9, 2005)
Taunts can't mask lack of leadership (Sept. 29, 2004)
Harmful reflections; Some ads create pictures of perfection that are unattainable for women (Mar. 26, 2004)
Unmasking myths is taxing for Muslims (Sept. 5, 2003)

Chapter 7—Hate: The Worm in the Apple Pie of America

Section 3: Discovering the Real America

Chapter 8—The Undiscovered Country: Taking Arms Against a Sea of Troubles

Chapter 9—Diversity Formula I—Indestructible Talent

Schools add AIDS to curriculum (July 15, 1993)
Teacher's Specialty: Inspiration (May 22, 1997)
Barriers call them to action (Jan. 25, 1993)
Keep the 'able' in disabled (July 28, 2000)
Avenue of Hope: Alphapointe Association for the Blind fits into revitalization of Prospect (July 9, 2004)
Politics with a conscience; Summon courage on gay marriage vote (June 11, 2004)
Don't 'pass' on pride (Feb. 28, 1994)
Stories of gay community have found a voice (July 30, 2004)
'Until everyone has those rights' - New office welcomes students of all sexual orientations to UMKC (Aug. 22, 2003)
New ideas on illness are needed (June 3, 1993)
Prisoners get another turn at bat (June 23, 1998)
Dismas snub hurts ex-offenders (May 17, 2002)
A minority of minority businesses (May 24, 2000)

Chapter 10—Diversity Formula II—Talk is Priceless

Dance to the Music (Feb. 9, 2000)
Time to Relive the Experiment (July 7, 1998)
After years, friendship lingers on (Aug. 10, 1999)
Talking about race relations breaks the ice (Feb. 22, 2002)
Walking together is one step closer to racial understanding (Oct. 23, 1996)
Celebrating a culture step by step (Sept. 19, 1998)
Hispanics are on the move (Aug. 24, 2001)
Matters we must talk about (Feb. 6, 1997)
On permanent probation (Dec. 27, 2000)
Fear could stop the peace train (Oct. 1, 2004)
Filmmaker gives glimpse of the road from terrorism to peace (Oct. 1, 2003)
Absolutely nothing to be afraid of (Oct. 28, 1993)
Both sexes must resist the wreckage that dooms partnering (Dec. 7, 1994)
Teens are Friends, indeed (Dec. 17, 1992)
U.S.S.R. was never like this (May 14, 1994)
U.S. through another lens (Nov. 19, 1999)
A few things are worth taking home (Dec. 1, 1998)
Mother Newman's wit and words are always worth a smile (June 28, 1995)
A century of life has been filled with the spirit of Christmas (Dec. 20, 1989)
He's back on the road to freedom (Nov. 8, 1990)
Trusting union from days past (Dec. 8, 1998)
Our fates are linked together (Feb. 14, 2003)

Chapter 11—Diversity Formula III—Act for Change

A hard shell to crack (Mar. 14, 2001)
Hope springs eternal (Aug. 17, 2001)
All are diminished when one person is demeaned (Feb. 27, 2002)
From hope to growth and beyond (Oct. 28, 1995)
Marching in pursuit of happiness (Sept. 23, 1997)
The next positive step comes today (Oct. 25, 1997)
Economic freedom could end income inequity (Feb. 9, 2005)
Color this board game frustrating (June 12, 2002)
Time hasn't yet erased U.S. racism (April 1, 1997)
Becoming attuned to the sensitivities of Islam (Mar. 29, 2006)
An education for everyone: Schools need multicultural effort (Nov. 6, 1996)
From behind bars, men reach out to help Kansas City; charter school receives boost from inmates in NAACP branch (Mar. 5, 2003)
Living on generosity; Tough times are tightening the 'poverty belt' (Aug. 4, 2004)
Unlocking the voices of inmates (May 18, 1996)
Artists in residence (June 27, 2001)
Symposium helps better opportunities for women take flight (June 5, 1996)
To effect change, we must unite (Oct. 3, 2003)

Chapter 12—Community Solutions: Doing More

Protecting everyone's civil rights (Sept. 20, 2002)
Diversity is a wave of future (Dec. 31, 1992)
Remnants of rhyme resonate with racism (July 12, 2006)
Promising plan for job parity (Feb. 1, 2006)
Mending lines of division (Feb. 28, 2001)
Author's visit sparks next generation of readers (Feb. 23, 2005)
Scrape away segregation to reveal diversity (Mar. 5, 2004)
A lasting challenge for us all (May 6, 1993)
Bias in test is a) Unwanted, b) Ending, c) Both of the above (Aug. 7, 1996)
Fear keeps chipping away at freedoms in this country (Dec. 21, 2005)
A multitude of ways for diversity discussions (April 24, 2002)
A personal glimpse into the hardship of a disability (Nov. 13, 2002)
Tear down this wall of words (Sept. 7, 1996)
A rare rewarding vacation (Nov. 19, 1994)
Enabling homes and people (Feb. 4, 2000)
Shaping our neighborhoods humanely (Dec. 11, 1997)
Erasing Barriers for women (Oct. 15, 1999)
Repairing America: Everyone—not just African Americans—would benefit from Reparations (June 27, 2003)
Wanted: Truth, reconciliation (June 6, 2001)

Chapter 13—What's Missing—Social Bridging

Diversity and uniqueness (June 22, 2001)
We need a hospitality lesson (Sept. 24, 2003)
Racial harmony is getting a boost in Hickman Mills (Jan. 30, 1992)
Sowing seeds of tolerance (Sept. 1, 2000)
Young enlistee in the war on injustice (July 23, 2003)
One person makes world better place (July 19, 2002)
The kids can't be insulated (May 6, 1995)
Everyone can afford diversity (May 31, 2002)
Islamic school enriches discussion of diversity (May 27, 1999)
We must all strive for unity (Jan. 13, 1996)

Chapter 14—A Shameless Lack of Empathy

The crisis cannot be contained (July 17, 1999)
A shaky method of survival (Mar. 30, 1996)
Hard hearts cast a chill over the city (Mar. 22, 1997)
Readers give second look at scorn (April 5, 1997)
Doors open to all; Libraries, as public treasures, should not exclude homeless (Mar. 10, 2004)
Compassion often evades the less fortunate among us (Mar. 9, 2005)
Caring eyes see beyond the exterior (Mar. 14, 1998)
Health care for homeless (Mar. 3, 2006)
Icy stares into faces of poverty (Mar. 6, 1999)
If clothes make the man, that's wrong (Mar. 6, 2002)
Humbled and homeless (Mar. 10, 2000)
When 'haves' bully 'have-nots' (Feb. 9, 2001)
A hot meal in invisible suffering (Mar. 7, 2003)

Chapter 15—Solutions Behind Bars: The End and the Beginning of a Journey

The crimes of war in Iraq, of prisons in the U.S. (April 12, 2006)
Potential locked up in prisons (Nov. 8, 2002)
Proverbs and penal codes (Feb. 25, 2000)
Marches inspire men in prison to step out of the shadows (Feb. 7, 1996)
Dispelling prison stereotypes (Mar. 21, 2001)
Fatherless men cherish dad's lessons (June 13, 1998)
Prisons as industries (Sept. 3, 1999)
NAACP prison branches build leadership skills for inmates (Nov. 11, 2004)
Hard time hardens inmates (Dec. 16, 1995)
Cloaked racism persists; Poverty and prejudice make equality unattainable (Feb. 13, 2004)

Healing even behind bars (Mar. 17, 2006)
Changing attitudes, faces (July 27, 2001)
Their shot at redemption (Nov. 7, 2001)
Building hope behind bars (Jan. 5, 2001)
From prison, hope and promises for change (Dec. 2, 2005)

Chapter 16—Enabling the Journey

It takes a village to put out some fires (Jan. 11, 2002)
We mustn't expect black heroes of the past to save us (Feb. 15, 1995)

Chapter 17—The Unacknowledged, Forgotten, and Ignored: Destroying the Stereotypes

She opened minds and opened doors (June 21, 1997)
Dusting off history in KCK (June 28, 2002)
History, written in stone (July 31, 2002)
A fine place to build our pinnacles (Feb. 18, 1997)
Improving the quality of life (April 12, 1999)
Retirees relish rockers (Feb. 1, 1993)
Going undercover to expose the horror of hatred (Mar. 20, 2002)
Each of these students has a unique story of success (Feb. 15, 2006)
He paints what he sees (April 20, 2001)
Miseducated teen gets lesson (Dec. 13, 2000)
Similar beyond a bloodline (Sept. 16, 1995)
A starting point on the road to improvements (Aug. 2, 2006)
Ambition, godliness has helped her abide (April 26, 2006)
Helping people keep their toothy smiles (May 3, 2006)
It's time the United States puts an end to the Confederate States (Feb. 8, 2006)
Creativity and expression can replace culture of chaos (Jan. 20, 2006)
Walking a mile in his shoes (Feb. 29, 1996)

My thanks to The Kansas City Star *for allowing the use of the above columns. They can be found in their entirety* at **www.kansascity.com.**

APPENDIX B

WHITE PRIVILEGE: THE INVISIBLE KNAPSACK

The following privileges identified as being connected to "whiteness" were compiled by Dr. Peggy McIntosh, associate professor of the Wellesley College Center for Research on Women, and featured in "White Privilege, Color, and Crime: A Personal Account," which is excerpted from Images of Color, Images of Crime, *edited by Coramae Richey Mann and Marjorie S. Zatz, published in 1998 by Roxbury Publishing Company, Los Angeles, Calif. (See Chapter 1, "Whiteness in Charge.")*

1. I can, if I wish, arrange to be in the company of people of my race most of the time.
2. The day I move into new housing that I have chosen, I can be pretty sure that my new neighbors will be neutral or pleasant to me.
3. When I am told about our national heritage or about "civilization," I am shown that people of my color made it what it is.
4. I can be sure that my children will be given curricular materials that testify to the existence of their race in all classes, in all subjects, at all grade levels.
5. If I want to, I can be pretty sure of finding a publisher for this work on white privilege.
6. I can go into a supermarket and find the staple foods that fit with my cultural traditions, or into a hairdresser's shop and find someone who can cut my hair.
7. I can swear, or dress in second-hand clothes, or not answer letters without having people attribute these choices to the bad morals, the poverty, or the illiteracy of my race.
8. I can do well in a challenging situation without being called a credit to my race.
9. I am never asked to speak for all the people of my racial group.
10. I can remain oblivious of the language and customs of persons of color who constitute the world's majority without feeling in my culture any penalty for such oblivion.
11. I can criticize our government and talk about how much I fear its policies and behavior without being seen as a cultural outsider.
12. I can easily buy posters, postcards, picture books, greeting cards, dolls, toys, and children's magazines featuring people of my race.
13. I can go home from most meetings of organizations to which I belong feeling somewhat tied in, rather than isolated, out of place, outnumbered, unheard, held at a distance, or feared.
14. I can choose blemish cover or bandages in "flesh" color and have them more or less match my skin.

15. I can turn on the television or open to the front page of the newspaper and see people of my race widely and positively represented.
16. Whether I use checks, credit cards, or cash, I can count on my skin color not to work against the appearance of financial reliability.
17. I can arrange to protect my children most of the time from people who might not like them.
18. I can take a job with an affirmative action employer without having co-workers on the job suspect that I got it because of race.
19. I can choose public accommodation without fearing that people of my race cannot get in or will be mistreated in the places I have chosen.
20. I can be sure that if I need legal or medical help, my race will not work against me.
21. If my day, week, or year is going badly, I need not ask of each negative episode or situation whether it has racial overtones.
22. If a cop pulls me over, or if the IRS audits our tax return, I can be sure it is not because of my race.
23. If I get angry and ask to speak to "the person in charge," I can be fairly sure I will be talking to a person of my race.
24. I did not need to teach our children about systematic racism for their own daily physical protection.
25. I can go shopping alone in department stores near my house without being followed or harassed by store detectives on the grounds that I may be shoplifting or soliciting.
26. We were able to teach our children that the police were their allies, and they should dial 911 if they had an emergency.
27. In my neighborhood, I can be sure that the police will not harass me because of the color of my skin.
28. In my neighborhood, any police officer who might need to arrest people in my family is likely to be a person of my race.
29. Criminality is not imputed to me as a genetic component of racial character; I am not assumed to belong to a group of people predisposed to crime.
30. The word "criminal" in the dominant culture does not conjure up the faces of people whose skin color is like that of my father, mother, brother, sister, husband, nieces, or nephews.
31. I have never heard or read the suggestion that all the people of my color ought to be locked up or killed. Even Islamic fundamentalists do not call for the killing of all people of my color, only certain "morally corrupt" ones.
32. In World War II my grandparents, despite having German ancestors two generations ago, were not locked up by the U.S. government in internment camps on the suspicion or pretext that they might be traitors.
33. Nearly all of the lawyers and judges who study, write about, argue, debate, and practice law in the U.S. are people of my race.
34. Lawbreaking by the U.S. government with regard to treaties with Indian people was not taught to me as a criminal aspect of my racial heritage.

35. Deceiving Indians is not described as a genetic or inherited trait of Caucasians.
36. Refusing to honor Indian treaties today is not shown to me as lawbreaking by white people.
37. The U.S. government has never made it a crime for me to speak my native language or observe the religious ceremonies of my parents and grandparents.
38. The prison system is thoroughly controlled by people of my race.
39. The Constitution I am subject to was created by people of my ethnic heritage to apply to some people of my ethnic heritage and to not apply to people of other races.
40. I am assumed to be entitled to whatever legal defense I can afford even if it allows me to be acquitted of a crime I have committed.
41. If I am suspected of being guilty but am acquitted, I will be seen as someone who got through the cracks rather than as a person who especially deserved not to get through the cracks.
42. Those who have been able to afford the high cost of legal training have been, for the most part, people of my race.
43. Lawyers featured as experts by the media are overwhelmingly people of my race.
44. Those who have been able to pay lawyers' fees and legal costs have for the most part been people of my race.
45. A successful tax evader in my ethnic group is usually portrayed as a cheater or even a victor, but not as an inmate criminal or a representative of a whole race of people who drain society.
46. A deadbeat dad in my ethnic group is portrayed in the media as financially but not sexually irresponsible.
47. When I walk into the courthouses of my country, I can expect respectful treatment from the receptionists.
48. As a child, I heard jokes and the soundtracks that cast people of other races as habitually dumb and coarse, or else sneaky, shifty, sly, malicious, or underhanded, and left people of my race protected from such typecasting.
49. The voiceovers of criminals, shifty individuals, and villains in Disney films and in ads rarely sound like people of my racial/ethnic group.
50. If I stand in line at a bank teller's window, no one looks strangely at me as though they have a problem with my being there.
51. If I suffer damages and decide to take a case to court, the people I see in the legal system will probably be people who are trained to trust my kind and me.
52. I can stand behind another person at an ATM machine without being feared as a potential mugger.
53. If I am laughing with my friends on a street at night, it is not assumed that we are in a gang.
54. A realtor has never discriminated against me to "protect property values."

55. No one has ever suggested that I might have dealt drugs in order to afford a certain car or house.
56. The men of my race who took 400 billion dollars in the 1994 U.S. S & L (Savings and Loan) scandal are not branded as criminals or seen as enemies of the U.S. people even though the money has never been returned.
57. When I think of prisons, I do not have to think of people of my race as disproportionately serving time in them, having longer than average sentences, and being executed in greater numbers.
58. I am allowed to believe, and encouraged to believe, that people of my race are in general law-abiding rather than law-breaking.
59. TV shows and films show people of my color as the main defenders of law and order, cleverest detectives, best lawyers and judges, and wiliest outlaws.
60. Portrayals of white males on TV as criminals and violent individuals do not incriminate me as a Caucasian; these males, even the outlaws, are usually presented as strong men of a quintessentially American type.
61. Illegal acts by the U.S. government, in the present and in the past, around the world, are not attributed by whites to Caucasian immorality and illegality.
62. Bad race relations in the United States are not attributed by whites to criminal behavior, despite a history of race-related breaking of laws by whites over the entire span of Anglo-European life on this continent.

APPENDIX C

Brief Biographical Information on the Authors of the Chapter Quotes

Dedication

T.S. Eliot (1888-1965)
White
Eliot was a great American poet of the twentieth century who won the Nobel Prize for Literature in 1948.

Chapter 1:

Daniel J. Boorstin (1914-2004)
White, of Jewish descent
Boorstin was Librarian of Congress from 1975 to 1987. He was a writer and historian.

Chapter 2:

Polingaysi Qoyawayma (1892-1990)
Hopi
Polingaysi, or "Butterfly sitting among flowers in the breeze," was a teacher and writer who used traditional Hopi legends to help her students bridge the gap between the Hopi culture and language and the American culture and language.

Chapter 3:

Rev. Martin Luther King, Jr. (1929-1968)
African American
King was a Baptist minister, leader of the Civil Rights Movement, and winner of the 1964 Nobel Peace Prize.

Chapter 4:

Rodolfo "Corky" Gonzales (1928-2005)
Chicano
Gonzales was a boxer, political activist and poet. He was considered the "fist" of the Chicano Movement.

Chapter 5:

Rev. Martin Luther King, Jr. (1929-1968)
See above.

Chapter 6:

Maya Angelou (1928-)
African American
Angelou is an award-winning poet and actress who was very active in the Civil Rights Movement.

Chapter 7:

The Dixie Chicks (formed in 1989 in Dallas, Texas)
All-white female country music group: Emily Robison, Martie Maguire, and Natalie Maines
The quote from the Dixie Chicks' song refers to the strong, negative reactions they received after Natalie Maines criticized President George W. Bush.

Richard Rodgers (1902-1979) and Oscar Hammerstein II (1895-1960)
White
Rodgers and Hammerstein wrote Broadway musicals in the mid-twentieth century that were very popular.

Chapter 8:

Helen Keller (1880-1968)
White
Keller was a writer and lecturer as well as a socialist activist. She was deaf and blind.

Chapter 9:

Eleanor Roosevelt (1884-1962)
White
Roosevelt was a political leader, working tirelessly for African-American rights, civil rights and human rights. She is believed by some to have been bisexual.

Chapter 10:

Amy Tan (1952-)
Asian American
Born in California of Chinese immigrants, Tan became a fiction writer in 1985. One theme she writes about is mother-daughter cross-cultural relationships.

Chapter 11:

Susan B. Anthony (1820-1906)
White
Anthony was a leader for civil rights, against slavery, and for women's right to vote.

Chapter 12:

Pastor Martin Niemöller (1892-1984)
White, German
Niemöller was a Lutheran pastor who spent 8 years in Nazi concentration camps. He was an anti-Semite and conservative, but later became a pacifist with socialist leanings.

Chapter 13:
Gil Asakawa (1957-)
Asian American
Asakawa is a Japanese-American writer and editor, who has an online column called Nikkei View.

Chapter 14:
Mexican-American Proverb

Chapter 15:
Stanley Tookie Williams (1953-2005)
African American
Williams was a leader of the Crips street gang. He spent years on death row for murder but from 1993 to his execution in December of 2005 was an activist against gangs, writing several children's books denouncing violence.

Chapter 16:
Isna-la-wica (Lone Man)
Teton Sioux

Chapter 17:
Helen Keller
See above.

Malcolm X (1925-1965)
African American
Malcolm X was an American Muslim who fought for civil rights and advocated black pride. He was active in the Nation of Islam and as a Muslim minister.

Adlai Stevenson (1900-1965)
White
Stevenson was a journalist, lawyer, and well-known statesman. A statue of Stevenson with his famed "hole in the sole of his shoe" is located at Central Illinois Regional Airport.

(Footnotes)
[1] "Those Were The Days," by Lee Adams and Charles Strouse.

Printed in the United States
201932BV00003B/52-147/A

9 781599 424217